This book analyses the parallel, different and related aspects of the discovery of poverty in the late 1950s and early 1960s, and the role of education in the American 'war on poverty' from 1964, and in Britain from the appointment of the Plowden committee on primary schools. It examines changes in policy emphases, the relationship between research and policy, and the transatlantic interactions and silences involved. Based on archival and interview material the book offers new insights into the role of the Plowden committee in shifting attention from social class to poverty, and it discusses in both the American and British contexts the concepts and theories involved in the changing fortunes of the educational war on poverty in the 1960s and 1970s.

The book is the product of a ten-year study of the relevant British and American policies and, apart from its coverage of a substantial body of literature, draws on interviews with leading actors in the policy field, researchers and practitioners. The Silvers set the two national developments in their respective traditions of educational and social science research and their economic systems, and continue their analysis through to the changed economic, political and educational contexts of the 1980s. The central foci are the sources, contours and outcomes of policy-making in the field of poverty and disadvantage.

An educational war on poverty represents a major contribution to the study of the recent social and educational history of Britain and the United States, and the range and depth of research, reflected in two substantive national bibliographies, will make it an essential reference source for scholars and policy-makers on both sides of the Atlantic.

An educational war on poverty

An educational war on poverty

American and British policy-making
1960–1980

Harold Silver

and

Pamela Silver

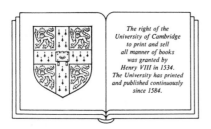

The right of the
University of Cambridge
to print and sell
all manner of books
was granted by
Henry VIII in 1534.
The University has printed
and published continuously
since 1584.

Cambridge University Press

Cambridge
New York   Port Chester
Melbourne   Sydney

Published by the Press Syndicate of the University of Cambridge
The Pitt Building, Trumpington Street, Cambridge CB2 1RP
40 West 20th Street, New York, NY 10011, USA
10 Stamford Road, Oakleigh, Melbourne 3166, Australia

First published 1991

Printed in Great Britain at the University Press, Cambridge

British Library cataloguing in publication data
Silver, Harold, 1928–
An educational war on poverty: American and British
policy-making 1960–1980.
1. Education related to social change
I. Title II. Silver, Pamela
370.19341

Library of Congress cataloguing in publication data
Silver, Harold.
An educational war on poverty: American and British
policy-making, 1960–1980/Harold Silver and Pamela Silver.
    p.   cm.
Includes bibliographical references (p.   ) and index.
ISBN 0 521 38149 5
1. Poor children–Education–United States–History–20th century.
2. Poor children–Education–Great Britain–History–20th century.
3. Education and state–United States–History–20th century.
4. Education and state–Great Britain–History–20th century.
5. United States–Social conditions–1960–1980. 6. Great Britain–
Social conditions–1945–7. United States–Social policy.
8. Great Britain–Social policy. I. Silver, Pamela. II. Title.
LC4091.S48 1991
379.41′0973–dc20   90-20583   CIP

ISBN 0 521 38149 5 hardback

UP

Contents

Acknowledgments

We have worked together on this book since, in 1980–3, we carried out a research project funded by the Social Science Research Council, entitled 'British and American educational strategies against poverty in the 1960s and 1970s'. That project and further work since 1983 form the basis of this book. The work has taken us, together and separately, to many parts of the United States and Britain, to large numbers of discussions and interviews, to libraries, archives, private collections, public offices, and elsewhere. Given the volume of material that we have processed, the number of visits we have made, the range of issues that have been involved, we are aware that neither of us could have completed the work without the other.

The debts we have incurred have been legion. The outstanding one was to the SSRC, which, by the time we reported, had become the Economic and Social Research Council, for funding the project and enabling Pam to work on it for a period full-time. The Lyndon Baines Johnson Foundation later provided a scholarship which made it possible to consult records at the Johnson Library at the University of Texas at Austin. We are profoundly grateful to those people listed in the appendix who were interviewed – in some cases more than once – or with whom we had invaluable discussions. For access to collections of documentation we are particularly indebted, in the UK, to A.H. Halsey and George Smith of Oxford University's Department of Social and Administrative Studies, and to Charles Betty, District Inspector in Nottinghamshire; and in the US to the late Francis Keppel at Harvard University, and John F. Jennings, Counsel for the House of Representatives Committee on Education and Labor. Librarians and archivists at too many institutions to name gave consistent help. We are especially indebted in this connection to Anne Newhall, archivist of the Ford Foundation in New York. Much of the research was accomplished while at Bulmershe College of Higher Education, Reading, and we are grateful to the librarians there and at the University of Reading Education Library. We would like to express our gratitude to our former colleagues at Bulmershe College, now amalgamated with the University of Reading, for their support.

In the years that we were engaged in the collection of material we did not meet with a single refusal in either country to be interviewed, to meet with us, to share information, or to help in the many ways that have been important to us. People have often been embarrassingly willing to give us their memories and the contents of their filing cabinets, and to be indiscreet. No one but us has any responsibility for what we have made of all of this.

Abbreviations

AFL-CIO	*American Federation of Labor and Congress of Industrial Organizations*
CAC	*Central Advisory Council for Education (England)*
CAC Wales	*Central Advisory Council for Education (Wales)*
CAP	*Community Action Program*
CDP	*Community Development Project*
CED	*Centre for Information and Advice on Educational Disadvantage (UK)*
	Committee for Economic Development (US)
CERI	*Centre for Educational Research and Innovation*
CRESAS	*Le Centre de Recherche de l'Education Specialisée et de l'Adaptation Scolaire*
DHEW	*Department of Health, Education and Welfare*
EEP	*Educational Enrichment Program*
EPA	*Educational Priority Area*
ERB	*Educational Research Board (of the Social Science Research Council)*
ESEA	*Elementary and Secondary Education Act*
ETP	*Early Training Project (Tennessee)*
ETS	*Educational Testing Service*
FF	*Ford Foundation (archives)*
FT	*Follow Through*
HEW	*(see DHEW)*
HMI	*Her Majesty's Inspector(ate)*
ILEA	*Inner London Education Authority*
IQ	*intelligence quotient*
JD	*juvenile delinquency*
LBJ Lib	*Lyndon Baines Johnson Library, Austin, Texas*
NCTE	*National Council of Teachers of English*
NDEA	*National Defense Education Act*
NEA	*National Education Association*
NEIA	*National Education Improvement Act*

NIE	*National Institute of Education*
OE	*Office of Education (of the Department of Health, Education and Welfare)*
OECD	*Organization for Economic Cooperation and Development*
OEO	*Office of Economic Opportunity*
OU	*Open University*
PLDK	*Peabody Language Development Kit*
SDC	*System Development Corporation*
SEO	*Scottish Education Office*
SES	*Sustaining Effects Study*
SSRC	*Social Science Research Council*
TES	The Times Education Supplement
WHCF	*White House Central Files*
ZEP	*Zone d'Education Prioritaire*

1 Introduction: A Proper Complexity

Poverty was 'rediscovered' and became a serious issue in public debate and policy in Britain in the late 1950s and in the United States in the early 1960s. In both countries after the Second World War there was a popular and strongly held view, by governments as well as by political and social scientists, that poverty had either disappeared or had survived in 'pockets' or in highly specific cases which would be eliminated either by an expansive, affluent society or, in the British case, by careful 'welfare state' planning. In the late 1950s, British social administration researchers, largely associated with Richard Titmuss, began to thrust their rediscovery of poverty into public consciousness, as did a number of American writers in the period of the Kennedy administration in 1961–3 on the basis of investigations mainly of Appalachia and the urban ghettos. Taking different forms and with different emphases, there was also mounting concern with the concept of inequality, related in the United States primarily to race and civil rights, and in Britain to social class, the latter increasingly centred from the 1950s on divisions and inequalities in secondary education.

Varying amounts of attention and different solutions were applied to poverty and inequality in the two countries, but both concepts re-entered public debate as signals that the optimistic economic and social forecasts of the late 1940s and 1950s had not yet been fulfilled. The criteria by which poverty had been measured, and had been assumed to have been severely diminished, began to be challenged. Strategies began to be evolved in the United States, especially from the end of the 1950s, for dealing with concentrations of poverty – often meaning, but not articulated as such, areas of racial tension – in the inner city, where the magnitude and intractability of the problems created by mass internal migration began to be realized. By the beginning of the 1960s the Ford Foundation was funding its 'Great Cities – Gray Areas' programme, to which the problems of 'in-migration' and 'in-migration transient pupils in depressed areas' of major cities were considered to be central and which appear regularly in the Foundation's records of the period.

The mechanization of American agriculture had impacts on population movement and distribution before, during and after the Second World War, in ways and to an extent which had no parallels in British concerns. Immigration in the late 1950s and 1960s was, however, to prove such a parallel, though without the same sense of urgency and permanence in its effects until the late 1960s and 1970s. From the early 1960s the American pressures for social and political change were responded to with experimental educational solutions. The Kennedy administration attempted unsuccessfully to promote comprehensive federal legislation for educational improvement, but poverty and disadvantage were not features of the legislative efforts and were only beginning to assume a central place in federal policy and planning when Kennedy was assassinated. The Johnson administration transformed federal involvement in education and social action in 1964 and 1965, under the slogans of a War on Poverty and the Great Society. The Economic Opportunity Act of 1964 produced Head Start, launched the following year. In 1965 the Elementary and Secondary Education Act secured the approval of Congress, and Title I of the Act was explicitly designed to combat poverty through the schools. An enormous range of developments, projects and programmes, followed under these and other auspices, including foundations, further legislation and state enactments. Follow Through, from 1967, was initially intended to sustain the Head Start, preschool momentum into the schools. Compensatory education entered the official vocabulary, with California in 1963 passing the first state law – the McAteer Act – 'specifically providing for compensatory education programs to aid culturally disadvantaged children' (A: McAteer, 1963, 48). Controversy appeared and intensified around concepts such as deprivation and disadvantage – cultural, linguistic, social, psychological, educational and economic.

The second half of the 1960s in the United States witnessed intense interest and investment in, hopes and campaigns for, evaluation of and disappointment in, mainly preschool and early childhood education and a variety of related measures designed to 'combat poverty'. From the creation of federal task forces and departments to local community action, the target and the processes closely linked education – especially early childhood education – to the war on poverty. Investigation and action were shaped accordingly and a formidable volume of experience and descriptive, analytical and campaigning literature was accumulated. The federal government was involved as never before, not only in funding, but in commissioning research, promoting discussion, disseminating material and issuing guidelines. The whole of this agenda of discussion was fundamentally different from the interests in education that had been dominant in the 1950s, when the focus had been on attempts to expand and modernize the system in response to demographic pressures, shortages and inadequacies, and international events. Education in the United States had become increasingly central to political and social policy, and its role in overcoming poverty and disadvantage a matter of increasing public interest and debate. What has been called 'the American public's love affair with education', by that point more than a century old (A: Aaron, 1978, 65), had become something quite different in its formulations from what it had been a decade earlier.

In Britain in the early 1960s no such link between education and poverty was established. The widespread preoccupation (rarely passionate enough to be called a love affair) with education was in terms of access to equitable secondary and higher education structures – notably the political battle over the comprehensive school. The sociologists' concern with poverty contained little or no important reference to education – their target was weaknesses in the welfare state, and the needs, for example, of the elderly. Educationists, on the other hand, were not explicitly concerned with poverty. Questions of poverty as a phenomenon and an issue surfaced to some minor degree in the work of inequality, more strongly in the Newsom committee's report on *Half Our Future* in 1963, and most significantly in the Plowden committee, which was appointed in that year and reported on *Children and their Primary Schools* in 1967, after the American poverty concerns had become international currency. The central Plowden recommendation for the creation of Educational Priority Areas was the first real parallel in Britain to the American research and policy emphases, and the EPA decisions and projects which followed drew at least partly (as did the Plowden committee itself) on American experience. Community action, inner-city and other projects in the late 1960s and 1970s, together with the various projects which also aimed at compensatory (or what the EPA national project preferred to call 'complementary') education, gave the appearance of formulating, after a time lag of half a decade or more, British versions of established American practices.

It is those sequences of events, or more particularly the assumptions and motivation which informed them, that form the basic structure of this book and of the questions embedded in it. One of its starting points was to try to understand the eruption of poverty as a major policy target in the United States around 1964, the flurry of new educational departures at its core, and the speed and scale at which academic, political and popular debate took shape – including bibliographies, readers and directories of projects (for example, A: Gordon and

Wilkerson, 1966). In the American case there was the excitement and its aftermath to be understood. In the British case there were important differences in the issues addressed in the early 1960s, but the echoes of the American experience in the Plowden report and the EPA and other policies and projects at the end of the 1960s raised interesting questions. It is important to emphasize, however, that this is neither two parallel and separate studies nor a comparative study. It is an exercise in recent history which attempts to trace and interpret a number of related events and similar purposes, and their connections. As a comparative study it would need to probe in far greater depth the structural, political, cultural and other respective, underlying explanations of the events, in an effort to establish comparative meanings of a strictly defined kind. It is comparative, in fact, only in that the parallel and sometimes related British and American concerns with education, poverty and dis-advantage address the same or similar issues, and illuminate each other. While the focus of the book moves at different points from country to country, it is hoped that the connectedness of the patterns of events remains, and becomes increasingly, clear. There are chapters in each of the sections of the book which are intended to reinforce these historical and analytical emphases.

What the sequences in both countries illustrate most directly are the problems of analysing the nature and purposes of educational and social reform. The processes of the 1960s raised questions about strategies and the motivations of participants, intentions and expectations, ideological positions and changing vocabularies, in ways similar to earlier developments around popular or radical educational movements, and other periods of pronounced social change and reform responses. The fact that the developments of the 1960s were recent, had left continuing structural, political and educational legacies, were controversial, and were in some respects being abandoned or superseded, made it all the more necessary to rescue them from the dogmatic myths already accumulating around them. These were complex developments and the purpose of the study was to try to restore to them some of their proper complexity.

The target of the research underlying this study was, therefore, the sources of intentions to use education in various ways to overcome poverty, to break the 'cycle of disadvantage', to compensate for environmental deficiencies, to discriminate positively in favour of those most in need. One important element in this analysis proved to be the range of formative participants – private foundation and government, psychologist and sociologist, politician, administrator and teacher, journalist and community activist. The study of sources of educational and social policy therefore included those aspects of the recent history of academic disciplines, their status and stage of development, research interests and directions, which fed into the debates, experiments and policy formulations, and were welcomed or met with resistance and challenge. Of importance was the adoption, rejection and evolution of changing interpretations of the timing, nature and effectiveness of compensatory intervention in early childhood, the role of preschool, school and parent, the focus on solutions through areas and community action, or through family and school and the identification of individual children in need or at risk. The research therefore led to an analysis of considerable documentation in both countries, but especially in the United States where the published and unpublished sources available were vast. The research also led to the widely diverse constituencies of participants implied by the outline of complex inputs and purposes. Some of the people interviewed ran the danger of defending past positions or present commitments, and discussions with many of the past participants often pointed to the need to disentangle meanings from different levels of operation and perception. The Americans interviewed, for example, ranged from a former Republican Senator and (at the time of interview) state governor, through lawyers and academics, to state and federal administrators and classroom teachers. The British included Her Majesty's Inspectors, project leaders, professors and adult educators.

The research therefore had to contend with problems associated with investigating recent events, with problems of oral history, with uncertainties about access to and the availability of documentary sources and about the use to which they might be put, the different British and American official approaches to confidentiality and the freedom of information, and the difficulties of entering a wide area of research, parts of which had been of considerable interest to sociologists, economists, political scientists and evaluators. Some of the American consultants and participants in the processes under investigation had been identified early in the work but for various reasons were no longer accessible by the time interviews were planned. In general, however, the problem with archival and documentary sources, as well as information from people, became one of coping with the volume of material. The research in Britain was on a narrower front, and given the constraints – though fortunately also the ambiguities – of the Official Secrets Act and the thirty year rule, there were possibly more obstacles than were met in the United States. In both countries, however, there was remarkable openness in response to enquiries and sustained questioning.

There was available, therefore, a considerable range of published material, readily accessible reports and records, less publicly accessible documentary material such as minutes, memoranda and correspondence, taped interviews, and the outcomes of postal enquiries and consultations. This evidence was rarely 'complete', in the sense that it did not satisfy the researchers' need for data, and it was not a 'sample' as understood by social scientists. Interviews were restricted by geographical and other constraints. It was rarely possible to be systematic in conducting what some sociologists and evaluators define as 'triangulation', but an effort was made to pursue further evidence to reinforce, test or balance opinions about specific events, especially where these related to important judgments that had to be made. For example, since much of the content of and commentary on the educational legislation of the War on Poverty might be described as 'liberal-democratic' or radical in tone, it was important to interview at least one of the key Republican actors in the events. A second and different example was the attempt to discuss the same questions about specific aspects of the British experience with researchers, academics, HMI and members of official committees. Kirst and Jung have suggested the importance of this approach in policy analysis, exploring 'congressional intent' not just via statutes but by triangulation with Senate and House hearings and special reports (A: Kirst and Jung, 1980, 25–6). In approaching, under the conditions of difficulty over British official records, an analysis of the Plowden committee, for example, the exploration of points of interest at the intersection of different perceptions is more elusive but if anything more important. The Plowden committee represented such a crucial juncture in the processes being studied that it was paid particular attention, and the narrative, analysis and judgments were built on published and unpublished commentaries, primary sources and interviews with people who were involved in or with the committee.

Not all the events and judgments in this project were put to such a test but, where possible, the accounts have been the product of detailed textual scrutiny of published, archival and privately held material, together with extensive interviews around the salient issues. There was no area of investigation where it was felt that the resources were inadequate for research purposes.

Particularly elusive in all of this investigation has been the changing, often rapidly changing, vocabulary, and much of the analysis in this book is concerned with the implications of the shifting emphasis on and versions of deprivation and disadvantage, and the variety of other terminologies that have come and gone across these decades. Of obvious interest was the concept of a 'war on poverty' itself. When President Johnson declared unconditional war on poverty in 1964 the theme became an immediate element of everyday political vocabulary. Sargent Shriver, at the time director of the Peace Corps and shortly to become director of the first outcome of the war on poverty – the Office of

Economic Opportunity – began his statement to the House Committee on the War on Poverty Program:

I might start off by saying the objective of this program is an all-out war on poverty. We believe that this is a program which, if effectively and intelligently carried forward, will eliminate grinding poverty in the United States.

America now had a greater understanding of 'the complex causes of poverty' and what was now needed was to put resources and knowledge to work 'in an all-out attack on poverty in which every sector of our society will join' (A: US Congress, House, OEA, Part 1, 20). The metaphor of war required the conviction of victory, and when the House Committee on Education and Labor reported in June of 1964 on its consideration of the Economic Opportunity Bill it began:

The United States is the first major nation in history which can look forward to victory over poverty. Our wealth, our income, our technical know-how, and our productive capacity put this goal within our grasp. (A: US Congress, House, Report, 1964, 1)

The scale of what was envisaged was perhaps new in 1964 but this was not the first announcement of a war on poverty. John F. Kennedy is described as having 'coined the phrase' when candidate for the presidency in August 1960, in a speech in New York marking the fifteenth anniversary of the signing of the Social Security Act. 'The opening battle, Kennedy had remarked, against suffering and deprivation had been won in the 1930's; but the war against poverty and degradation was not yet over' (A: LBJ Lib, OEO Admin History [1969], 8).

Francis Keppel, Commissioner of Education, and often central to the discussion in this book, in an address entitled 'Poverty – the only war we seek' in March 1965, drew his title from a book published in 1945 by Arthur Goodfriend, a book published, Keppel underlined, before America discovered Appalachia and automation (A: LBJ lib, Federal Records, Keppel addresses, 3 March 1965). The American war found earlier and earlier antecedents, in the pre-war policies of Hoover and Roosevelt for example. In Britain, Harold Wilson published an article in 1959 entitled 'The war on poverty'. Looking ahead to the election of a Labour government he responded to a challenge to commit the Labour Party to action against poverty and, although he did not use the term 'war' in the article itself, his analysis of the socialist approach to inequality spills over into the terminology of a 'fight against poverty' (B: Wilson, 1959, 413–15). There are other progenitors of the idea, if not the vocabulary, and British and American combatants in the war have referred back to the statements and policies of Lloyd George, Lord Beveridge and Richard Titmuss.

If the notion of victory in such a war subsequently seemed to have raised expectations too high, and to have been based on tenuous evidence, it is important to remember the various sources of confidence which underlay especially the American conviction. In exploring these sources it will also be important to remember the extent of the shock waves that rolled through the American investigations, the literature, the administration, the politicians and the public at large in the early 1960s at the discovery of the depth and persistence of poverty. The stakes were suddenly high, the resources apparently available, and the necessary strategies beginning to emerge. The British response to the evidence on poverty was less dramatic and less widely disseminated. How education came to be a central feature of the answer to poverty is therefore a major issue, part of the response to questions such as 'what war?', 'whose war?', 'why *war*?'. In policy terms the distance in the United States from Appalachian white poverty and the black ghettos and civil rights movement to education is a short step. Reform, response, renewal, modernization, change – whatever the vocabulary of explanation there were resemblances between the American preoccupations and those of the British also constantly establishing new fronts – at different levels of education, in school, preschool and post-secondary education, community development programmes, urban aid, inner city schemes of various kinds, an emphasis on expanded opportunities and new parameters of welfare and social policy. Reform of one kind or another returned to a central position in social science debates. With the discoveries and rediscoveries of poverty, class, educational and social disadvantage, powerlessness, and a range of conceptual machineries to explain and overcome them, reform – liberal or radical – was never far from the surface of public discussion. The easy assumptions of the post-war drift towards affluence and 'the end of ideology' having evaporated, the 1960s saw the emergence of a concern with strategies, relating to apparently old and intractable problems in a period of changing contexts and determinants – what to do about poverty and inequality in a landscape which now contained automation and the cold war, continued internal migration (in the United States) and immigration (in Britain), and the new political assertiveness of various constituencies. New strategies meant new conflicts, particularly over the boundaries of reform and revolution, of radical reform and social control, of change and of accommodation to the status quo.

Perspectives on the recent past change rapidly. The central analytical difficulty of approaching those interconnections has been the profound changes in public policy, popular attention and academic concern while the research has been taking place. The initial work on this study was done mainly in the period 1980–3 and, of course, the questions to which answers were necessary and important changed significantly across that period and in the following years when further work was done and the analysis was taking shape. What began as a history of a highly significant thread in twentieth-century educational and social policy internationally, seemed to some people to have become, by the second half of the 1980s, an obituary. It is true that there is scepticism at many levels about the processes and the purposes discussed here, although there has been a resurgence of American concern and policy-making for disadvantaged children in the late 1980s. It would be wrong, however, to pretend that all the questions asked, assumptions made, strategies adopted, policies recommended and directions in which they pointed need to be 'rescued' in the same forms, and will re-emerge in similar shapes. It would also be wrong and foolish, however, to imagine that the changed economic and political frameworks and priorities of the 1970s and 1980s have wiped clean the page earlier filled with so much animation. The issues and the targets have not gone away. Many of the activities, structures and dynamics generated still continue. The controversies still simmer. The roles of government, public agencies, private finance and people, in relation to education and participation in educational processes, while differently contoured, remain to be argued over. The relationship between education and other social and economic policies is still a subject for debate. There is no pendulum or cyclical theory of history to sustain this discussion, but issues as sharp and as persistent as these are bound to find their way to centre-stage. It is therefore important to remember, to reanalyse, to build on, more than a quarter of a century of intention and effort of very particular kinds.

One of the historical components of this study is therefore the unrelenting question of what governs historical attention. The emergence of historical interest in either long-term processes (what some historians have identified as the 'longue durée') or the specifics of major events or newly dominant ideologies or 'mentalities', is itself a matter for historical analysis. Poverty, reform, school and society, are not new phenomena or new to scholarship. The questions that surround and inhabit them are familiar to sociologists, other social scientists, policy analysts and political scientists. The direction of historical interest in these issues may relate both to their identification and definition by other social scientists and to the emphases of government or popular political or social processes. 'Before poverty became a public issue in the mid-1960s', it has been pointed out, 'American historians had almost totally ignored the subject' (A: Gelfand, 1981, 146). And although many of the ingredients of poverty and of policies related to it are encountered in previous historical work, it is true that the American historian had not accepted poverty as an organizing concept for research until its new political profile was established in the 1960s. In both Britain and the United States, for similar reasons, historical interest in women and racial and ethnic minorities was not widely visible until the same period. Aspects of the history of education can be identified in the same way. Historians have until recently been concerned with the history of institutions, of administrative structure, of legislation. It was pointed out in Britain in 1968 that 'so far, there does not seem to have been any major work of social history devoted to the historical aspects of home–school relations in this country' (B: Sharrock, 1968, 188), and again it is true that the home, the parent, the community, and to some considerable extent also the children, had until the 1960s been hidden from the history of educational processes. In the latter case, the lack of such a home–school history is considered 'unfortunate since the insights [such a history] could afford might aid a clearer view of the best way ahead'. It is not obvious that historical analysis offers such immediately useful illumination, but there is no reason why historical attention should not be devoted to recent as well as longer-term or longer-distance continuities and changes.

Many of the questions addressed here are in fact similar to those encountered in discussion and controversy around the creation of the Sunday schools in the late eighteenth century, the motivation of nineteenth-century reformers of various kinds, the contribution of a Horace Mann or a Kay-Shuttleworth to educational policy and philosophy, the creation of a child-centred psychology, a 'progressive' curriculum, or a 'ladder' to secondary education. The details of the relationship between individual action, mass movement or opinion, and total context, change considerably across these periods, but the problems of analysing the relationship remain. Who defines the issues and the policy answers is as much a concern of historical analysis of the anti-poverty pressures and intentions of the 1960s as it is of the establishment of compulsory education in both countries in the late nineteenth century or earlier approaches to mass schooling or factory legislation. Around issues as salient as those involved in poverty and its related dimensions of experience and action there can be no justification for historians *not* becoming involved.

Whatever the difficulties of recent perspectives, the difficulties of using oral evidence, the problem of the historian's own involvement as actor or spectator, the strategies of historical analysis are applicable to recent versions of change and reform and their attendant assumptions and vocabularies.

Part I
A pattern of events: United States

2 Poverty and education: changing concerns and concepts

Poverty and its related concerns and concepts leaped to the centre of the stage in American politics and educational and social policy in 1964–5, but the complex groundwork had been determined particularly in the previous decade. The key strands in the developments of the mid-1960s are visible in the late 1950s in terms of migration, slums and cities; civil rights and issues of race and desegregation; the interest of psychologists in early childhood and the effects of environment; the manpower concerns of cold war, Korean war and space race. By the early 1960s all of these were converging into a set of policy definitions given impetus and focus by the 'discovery of poverty'. It was around the concept of poverty and associated social and educational phenomena that the new configuration of analyses and purposes took shape.

Poverty was not new to America, nor was the search for educational and other social remedies. American discomfort became acute in the 1960s, however, given new awareness of the nature and extent of its own strata of poverty and world preoccupation with poverty and hunger. What Americans learned most clearly at this point was that post-war hopes that their own poor and 'pockets of poverty' would diminish and disappear through sustained affluence had proved to be unfulfilled by the early 1960s. The British were to find similarly in the late 1950s that their post-war welfare state had also failed to eliminate poverty.

Post-war America held strongly to the view that the economic base of continuing prosperity was unassailable. From the late 1940s began two decades of 'unprecedented prosperity', (A: Miller and Rein, 1965b, 276). Built in to the economic success story was a set of assumptions about the changed basis and nature of American society. Sustained prosperity would mean the end of poverty, class, conflict and the need for 'socialized' solutions to welfare and other problems. A cynical reflection on these underlying post-war assumptions came from one of the best-known American writers:

We have never had it so good. In the years after World War II, sociologists' tag phrases such as the 'affluent society,' the cant of politicians in slogans like 'Peace and Prosperity!', the constant flood of commercials on television proclaiming the bigger-and-betterness of everything, and the ever-soaring graph lines of well-being, of rising gross national product and Dow-Jones averages and rates of employment – all these hints and signs seemed to vaporize in a cloud of illusion around our heads: We were all rich. (A: Hersey, 1965, 67)

John Hersey's next sentence, from the vantage point of 1965, read: 'The only trouble was that a lot of us were poor.' The important point, however, is that the vocabularies and apparent realities of affluence and prosperity were believed, and that the expectation of an unendingly soaring graph of economic and social success was strong.

One of the mainsprings of the newly fashioned optimism was the sense that the battles over pre-war social issues were over. Prosperity 'encouraged the notion that America was a classless, consensual society' and promoted an 'optimistic sense of national well-being... suburbanization was fashioning a purely middle-class nation'. Class was obsolete (A: Patterson, 1981, 84–5). The problems of the 1930s and the New Deal solutions which had been sought amidst protracted controversy seemed no longer relevant to the post-war economy and society. The New Deal aspirations and the welfare policies of the Roosevelt era never disappeared from political view, and the war on poverty of the 1960s was frequently to have its origins traced back through the Truman period to the New Deal. One of the principal economic designers of the war on poverty called the Economic Opportunity Act of 1964 a 'logical extension of Franklin D. Roosevelt's Social Security Act and Harry S. Truman's Employment Act' (A: Lampman, 1974, 66–7). Elsewhere he traced the anti-poverty programme back to President Hoover in the 1920s and President Roosevelt in the 1930s (with a wide glance at Britain and Lloyd George's 1909 budget, which he announced as 'a war budget for raising money to wage implacable warfare against poverty and squalidness' (A: Lampman, 1965, 12–13). Although this tradition and these policies remained alive, the dominant approach to social issues at least until the late 1940s was shaped by the awareness of a general rise in incomes and the increasing potential for self-help.

It is important, in this as in other respects, to emphasize the role of amnesia in politics and popular opinion. Past crises and disappointments are easily forgotten in the United States, and the policy emphases of the post-war period and of the 1960s readily illustrate the process. Poverty was a crucial public issue at many points in nineteenth- and twentieth – century America, as it had been in earlier European and American experience. The reliance on successful, competitive economics to sustain social peace and progress had at different times arrived and departed in the United States. Programmes of aid and relief had alternated with punitive and more comprehensive policies. Public responses to poverty had been shaped by civil disorder and the threat of disorder, by campaigns for compassion or for equality and justice, by political disaffection and changing allegiances (A: Piven and Cloward, 1971, ch. 1). Lampman clusters the variety of efforts used in the United States 'to move people out of poverty, to prevent retreat into poverty, and to meet needs of those in poverty' into four basic strategies – to make the market system work and thereby maintain economic growth and high employment; to adapt the system to the needs of the poor; to change the poor and adapt them to the system; and to relieve distress (A: Lampman, 1965, 4–9). What Americans (and not only Americans) were easily able to forget was the brief and uncertain impact of the changing policy emphases based on such different approaches, and particularly past failures of reliance on the market system. American confidence in sustained market growth and effectiveness was boosted from the 1940s by its scale and continuity, and the record of past failures and disillusionments could easily be set aside.

One of the central difficulties in analysing these shifting policies and emphases and their relationship to education has been the consistent public opposition to the extension of the federal role. American interpretation of federal and state roles in education was to be an important element in explaining differing British and American approaches to educational policy in the 1960s, particularly the nervousness to be overcome in planning and adopting policy changes in many areas of American legislation up to and after 1964. The debates around federalism were another illustration of American reluctance to confront the nineteenth- and earlier twentieth-century experience, notably in education. Advocates of greater federal involvement in education in the 1960s had constantly to expose misconceptions by opponents of federal aid, based on what Wayne Morse, one of the key education spokesmen of the Democratic Party, considered to be a constricted conception of education. He pointed out in 1961 that federal aid had been given to education since the eighteenth century through the Northwest Territory Land Ordinance, for military education and research, for higher education and, more recently, through the GI Bill and the National Defense Education Act – what was lacking was general aid to improve the quality of schooling, and that he believed to be important enough to merit federal aid as a matter of urgency (A: Morse, 1961, 5–6). This kind of reminder of historical precedent and the definition of what constituted 'education' was to recur frequently in debates in Congress and elsewhere and was to figure prominently in reinterpreting for the 1960s and after the policy dimension of America's 'century old love affair'.

In the dominant assumptions and policy approaches of the 1940s and 1950s and those of the 1960s there is a constant tug-of-war between legislative action and public intervention on the one hand, and private and local initiative on the other hand. There were national and international political pressures of various kinds. War itself and its legacies constituted one element in the ways acceptable policy and action were defined. The roots of community action, to figure so prominently in the decisions of the mid-1960s, have been traced, for example, to the forms of community action developed in the United States in the First World War, including 'War Fund' campaigns, followed by the 'Community Chest' and 'Community Councils'. As a result, 'community service co-ordination was wedded to the voluntary social-service sector and to fund-raising' (A: Kravitz and Kolodner, 1969, 31). The New Deal programmes of the 1930s attempted to build on such bases, and were accentuated by the Second World War. The 'maximum feasible participation' of the poor, which proved one of the most controversial elements in the war on poverty, has in fact been described as originating both in the area projects of the 1930s and in the conception of 'community development' which emerged in and after the war. President Truman, in his 1949 inaugural address, proposed that the United States should

> sponsor and support community development programs in underdeveloped nations throughout the world. These programs rested on the canons that indigenous leadership and resources could be discovered and developed in each community, and that such leaders would be able to articulate the needs, desires and aspirations of the community. (A: Rubin, 1969, 17)

The implications of such public policies in one domain for future definitions in another are clear, even though the direct line of descent – notably through the civil rights movement – is not easy to distinguish. Models, precedents, targets and definitions had accumulated over the decades and were available when the direction of public attention began to change in the early 1960s.

It has been necessary to talk so far about dominant assumptions in the post-war period, but then as in any other period there is the danger of making exaggerated claims of a common ideology or a homogeneous public opinion. If that is one end of the spectrum of historical error, at the other end is the danger of searching for precursors and progenitors of later developments in linear descent. The related concepts of poverty and social class illustrate the point. Across the late 1940s and 1950s concerns about poverty, whilst not salient in public policy, remained alive in one form or another. While, similarly, the overriding assumption about class was that it was obsolete in the new affluence and consensus, class did not cease to be an issue. In 1948 Allison Davis published *Social-class Influences upon Learning*, a booklet which attacked the middle-class assumptions and narrow, traditional activities of the schools, and the blinkered middle-class cultural assumptions of teachers. The booklet was frequently re-issued, and Davis himself is described as having made 'a dramatic impact on the audience at the White House Conference on Education [in 1950] by declaring that 40 per cent of children go through school untouched by it, except for acquiring a meager literacy' (A: Taba, 1964, 149). An equally well-known analysis of the deficiencies of American education, or more specifically of access to schooling, was a book by Warner and colleagues in 1946, with a sub-title as important as the title – *Who Shall be Educated? The challenge of unequal opportunities*. The book examined class, caste and other hierarchies, resisted the notion that more room was being created at the top (it was too soon when the book was written to base an argument on economic expansion), saw economic mobility as decreasing, and proposed what later became known as meritocratic solutions to problems of educational inequality.

The language of social class was not common, however, even in the 1950s. Psychologists and sociologists often looked to analysis in terms of socio-economic status. One study published in 1957, for example, offered a characteristic approach to children's conceptual thinking, indicating differences between children from higher and lower social status backgrounds (A: Siller, 1957). By the beginning of the 1960s 'lower-class' was being used almost interchangeably with 'slum' as an epithet with child or school. Issues were emerging around the relationship between analyses in terms of class and of race, and in the emergent attention to a range of concepts – including inequality, poverty and disadvantage – social scientists began to confront the persistent evidence of class. Patricia Sexton, in a 1961 study of *Education and Income: inequalities of opportunity in our public schools*, found difficulty in using the concept of social class, but accepted it (A: Sexton, 1961, 10), and indeed even in the 1950s the 'incidence of low incomes' and the vocabulary of social 'stratification' and 'slum children' was often a euphemistic way of evading the use of social-class terminology (A: Witmer and Kotinsky, 1952). Sociologist S. M. Miller and socio-linguist Courtney Cazden recall the novelty of encountering and using the language of class in the late 1950s and early 1960s, Miller emphasizing the difficulty of using the concept and its attendant analyses in the 1950s, and Cazden meeting them in the early 1960s – in both cases at least in part through the strong British tradition of class analysis (Cazden, Miller interviews). In the 1940s and 1950s, however, the conflict-laden messages of class were submerged beneath the interpretations of a consensual society.

It is in those contexts that the educational concerns of the postwar period need to be viewed. The main policy emphases had to do with school provision and quality, with the role of the school in the consensual, but flawed, society, with the removal of inequalities and irrationalities, with the contribution of education to the maintenance and expansion of prosperity. *Who Shall be Educated?*, whilst out of the main stream in one sense, was inside it in its search for the elimination of status differences and the improvement of competitive educational chances. The improvement of the system itself was the target of those writers who sought, among other things, the 'equalizing of the quantity and quality of elementary and secondary education offered in all our states' (A: Tead, 1947, 49), and who were aware by and large of 'pockets' of educational and social problems. Given the later preoccupations attached to the concept of the community school, it is interesting to look at the annual yearbook of the National Society for the Study of Education for 1953, entitled *The Community School*. The volume of papers contains little or no sense of *urban* community or of major social problems to be solved other than by the better management of resources. The chairman of the Society's committee on the community school, introducing the volume, does indeed focus on the power of the community to contribute to social renewal – the main social problems being those of food, shelter, clothing and recreation. There is a discussion, here, as in other contributions, of the impact of machinery on rural conditions, but the school is seen essentially as a contributor to the creative use of leisure and to good citizenship (A: Seay, 1953, 2–8). Of particular interest is a contribution on 'The community school as a social instrument' by C.W. Hunnicutt, who was later to edit a book on urban poverty which contained a picture of acute social and educational problems. His emphasis in 1953 was on the school's increased roles in vocational education, in the prevention of juvenile delinquency and generally in solving what appeared to be residual problems. The tone is an important indicator of the time:

We are generally agreed that all people should have a chance at education, though only recently have we approached this ideal in practice. children geographically isolated now have school buses; financial-equalization schemes help impoverished communities; racial barriers, physical handicaps, or subnormal intellectual capacities no longer prevent adequate educational opportunity to the degree they once did; and most children now reach the secondary level before leaving school.

Schools were in a 'peculiarly advantageous position to play a leading role in community welfare programs' and could even stimulate 'a desirable dissatisfaction with the *status quo*'. Education had already helped to raise living standards, and in cooperation with other agencies could provide care for various material and emotional needs (A: Hunnicutt, 1953, 182–8).

The search was essentially for forms of modernization, and particularly for the buildings, the equipment, the new technologies of learning – foundations and public authorities were investing in language laboratories, programmed learning and other schemes. At the same time the search was for talent. Sizer suggests that if the poor child was the concern of the 1960s, the golden boy of the 1950s was the 'gifted child' (A: Sizer, 1970, 340). Of central concern were buildings and the best use of resources. In 1954 President Eisenhower launched a series of conferences, nationally and within states, on education, and six topics were proposed for discussion by the planning committee: What should schools accomplish? How to make schools more economic and efficient? What were school building needs? How to get and keep enough teachers? How to finance and build schools? How to obtain public interest in education? Embedded in their report to the President in 1956 was a concern for the gifted and the talented, without reference anywhere to poverty, the disadvantaged or any of the vocabularies and categories that were soon to come on to the agenda (A: Committee for the White House Conference, 1956, 1–12). The reasons for such preoccupations are not far to seek. Discontent with the schools in the 1950s was associated, as Stephen Bailey often emphasized, with 'the largest explosion of the school-age population in the nation's history', with what he and others referred to as the 'baby boom' (A: Bailey, 1981, 28; Bailey, interview). The 'ruthless pressure of numbers upon the American school system' arose from an increase both in the birth rate and in school attendance. From 1949–50 to 1965 numbers in grades 9–12 roughly doubled. Enrolments jumped from 2.2 million to 3.7 million in seven years from 1946 (A: Bailey and Mosher, 1968, 4–5). The increasing school population was taking place amidst a post-war shortage of school places, the deterioration of buildings and teacher shortages. Additionally, the demographic picture was one of a rapidly shifting population, under the impact above all of agricultural mechanization. It is estimated that the farm population in 1940 was some 31 million, and that by 1980 the figure was 6 million. The main exodus began in the mid-1930s. Between 1940 and 1964 a US census of agriculture showed a net transfer of some 17 million people from farm to non-farm residence, with a decline of 3.6 million in the years 1959–64 alone (A: Clark, D., 1984, 146; Smith, T., 1974, 11–34). The strains on the educational resources of the cities were, as we shall see, enormous, given the rapid and substantial levels of migration from the countryside to the towns, from South to North, from the Appalachians or Ozarks into the urban areas. The implications of all of these demographic factors for education were to be considerable, and they would dictate many of the preoccupations of the 1950s and the early 1960s.

The strains were on particular school systems in particular states and districts, and given the long history of opposition to general aid by the federal government resources were unequal and often pitifully lacking. Federal aid to education was widely seen as being unnecessary – as public assistance of all kinds had come to be viewed with suspicion – or dangerous, with an implicit threat of federal control or interference, and the undermining of local freedom and democracy. Movements and proposals for general aid – including by President Truman – collapsed in the 1950s at least partly for fear of federal control as creeping communism – one of a trio of obstacles described by Bailey as the 3 R's, 'reds, race and religion' (interview). Indeed there was educational legislation during this period but only abortive attempts at general aid. The urgency was reflected in a statement by Eisenhower in 1956: 'the need of American children for schools is right now, immediately, today!' (A: Committee for White House Conference, 75), but proposals by the President's committee in that year, and other similar proposals, for federal aid were surrounded by controversy. Pressures for expansion of higher education and of schooling at all levels met with solid opposition, schools were overcrowded, and in urban areas particularly systems creaked or neared breakdown. From the 1940s and 1950s, therefore, the Kennedy and Johnson administrations of the 1960s acquired a great deal of unfinished educational business.

Two landmarks of federal legislation in the post-war period need to be mentioned. The first, the GI Bill of Rights, was enacted in 1944 and proved to be a major development in federal funding of education. The financial support to veterans of the war (covering education costs of up to $500 a year for up to four years, plus subsistence allowances) turned out to be 'the most important program of massive federal aid to education enacted prior to 1965' (A: Tyler, 1974, 166) and was to be frequently quoted as a considerable precedent for federal action. Michael Harrington, whose 1962 book *The Other America* was one of the crucial texts of the war on poverty, argued in 1965 for the equivalent of a GI bill in the war against poverty (paying people to go to school, for their tuition, books and living allowances) and in the process described the GI bill as 'one of the most successful social experiments this society has ever had' (A: Harrington, 1965a, xii–xiii). Nearly 8 million veterans of the Second World War benefited from this scheme, as did nearly 2.5 million Korean war veterans.

The Soviet launching of Sputnik and its announcement of the space race produced the second landmark. Some commentators consider that the combination of the cold war, the Korean war and the Soviet space challenge were the overriding stimulus to increased federal involvement, and Keppel refers to Khrushchev as 'the best education commissioner America has ever had' (A: interview). The National Defense Education Act which followed Sputnik in 1958 was directed at improving access to and the performance of higher education. It brought the federal government further into the provision of financial aid to education, and established a model of federal–state partnership in the administration of such aid (A: Bartlett, 1961, 21). The historian of the Sputnik crisis and the NDEA suggests that they transformed the politics of federal aid, and provided the basis on which the argument of extended federal aid for the education of children could be conducted (A: Clowse, 1981). Commissioner of Education Sidney Marland was able to point out later that the NDEA was enacted in the context of the search for 'our best students', an emphasis that was later to widen into other concerns (A: in Tolo, 1973, 47).

One of the profoundest changes taking place in the United States amidst these various pressures was that related to segregation and the emergence of a new scale of civil rights activism. From the point of view of education the most important event of the 1950s in this regard was the outcome of the *Brown v. Board of Education* case before the Supreme Court in 1954. Rejecting the principle of 'separate but equal' and segregation as a basis for schooling, the Supreme Court made *Brown* a milestone in the civil rights movement and in educational history, altering the ground-rules of American politics, and pointing towards the limited Civil Rights Act of 1957 and the crucial Civil Rights Act of 1964, which made possible some of the educational legislation which followed. In 1954 Keppel, then Dean of the Graduate School of Education at Harvard, wrote in his annual report that the Supreme Court decision would probably be for historians the most important event of the year, and at the same time he offered what proved to be an accurate picture of what lay ahead:

Experience has shown that the American people cheerfully put tasks on the shoulders of the school systems with little realization of the difficulties involved. The national optimism about what education can accomplish is both a blessing and a danger. The vast majority of the teachers and administrators in the public schools have every intention of going forward to carry out the letter and the spirit of the law; there are many among them, however, who hope that the schools will not be expected to accomplish a social miracle in the face of the latent or active opposition in homes and communities in both North and South. (A: Harvard, 1954, 1)

Brown, for all the difficulties that were to follow (and Keppel was to meet them directly when Kennedy appointed him Commissioner of Education in 1962) had considerable long-term implications. It laid the basis for further federal involvement in educational legislation, support and intervention. Though concerned with desegregation as the immediate issue, it was the catalyst 'that set off the enormous political, social, and economic changes in race relations of the late fifties and the sixties' (A: Levin, 1979a, 108), and not least changes in public opinion. It is not possible to assess the importance of the civil rights movement in the war on poverty and the educational legislation of the mid-1960s without emphasizing the long impact of the movement in the 1950s and the *Brown* decision which it produced and which gave it impetus.

It is important to the link between education and poverty also to emphasize further the impact on education of the migration to which we have referred, and of the particular impact on the inner cities and the suburbs. In the middle years of the century, wrote one researcher, 'American population movements dwarf the tribal invasions of the early Middle Ages and the westward surge in American history': between 1940 and 1960 the population of the suburbs of the large cities grew by 26 million (A: Shaw, 1963, 91). The concern with rural migration and its implications for city schools was one that focused on both black and white migration, and initially registered if anything more surprise at the condition of the white migrants, particularly from the desperately poor Appalachian regions. The director of guidance services in the Cincinnati public schools, writing about 'Disadvantaged Newcomers to the City', talked of public indifference in the early 1960s to the rural migrants from the Southern Appalachians, with their traditional lack of respect for 'the value of formal education', their short-range goals and 'leisurely pace' (A: O'Hara, 1963, 25–6). Characteristic of city reports of this kind was once sponsored by the Baltimore section of the National Council of Jewish Women in 1961. The report, 'The Unaccepted Baltimoreans' had as its sub-title, 'A study of white Southern rural migrants (the "culturally different" urbanites)'. It proclaimed with a great sense of urgency that 'within recent years, and especially now, the minority of Southern Mountaineers, an increasing drain on the city's economy, is crying for citizen interest and action', and it examined the cultural characteristics of these and other Southern white rural migrants. The mountain migrants particularly needed 'acculturation' to the ways of the city, and to be persuaded to abandon their negative attitudes towards education:

'The academic progress of these culturally disadvantaged children in our schools *is the major educational problem confronting the Department of Education at this time*,' said Dr. George B. Brain, Superintendent of the Baltimore Public Schools. 'One of every 5 children attending the City Schools at the present time is retarded in his academic progress as a result of cultural deprivation'...A high rate of mobility and truancy...explains some of the handicaps in educating these youngsters...One principal referred to the teachers as missionaries and saints...one cannot consider schooling apart from such factors as health, welfare, housing and recreation. These needs must be met before basic knowledge and skills can be taught. (A: FF, Baltimore, Kolodner, 1961, 1–8)

The National Education Association and its *NEA Journal* expressed constant concern in the early 1960s about the state of the schools in the rural areas, and the problems of the city schools in attempting to cope with the influx. The secretary of the NEA department of rural education commented in 1963 that the rural disadvantaged continued to stream into the cities, but millions remained behind in areas where rural school systems had in general not taken direct steps 'to develop programs for their disadvantaged comparable to the experimental efforts under way in many cities'. Both the rural areas and the cities were faced with the problems of the rural disadvantaged, with 'a low level of aspiration, a tendency to set only short-term goals, values which differ somewhat from acceptable norms, and a general unfamiliarity with cultural activities which lead to enriched living' (A: Isenberg, 1963, 27).

The picture of rural migration is perhaps most clearly seen in a report on *Education and the Disadvantaged American* published in 1962 by a commission sponsored in part and published by the NEA. Progress towards equal opportunity had bypassed some Americans who were 'living in virtual isolation from the rest of society'. Large-scale migration had placed them at a severe disadvantage because their cultural patterns were not 'attuned to the spirit and practice of modern life'. They were not able to adapt to technological development, were less accustomed to change than other Americans, were emerging from ways of life being rendered impossible, were not able to find unskilled jobs and were less able than others to be trained. Poverty, disease and, in many cases, racial discrimination were continuing handicaps, alongside their mistrust of schooling and government, and inescapable, continuing geographical mobility (A: Educational Policies Commission, 1962, 1–5). The urban community was growing in scale, diversifying in social and racial composition, and encountering unprecedented problems. The US

Office of Education was at the beginning of the 1960s describing the urban context of school problems in the following terms:

As the result of a social and economic revolution leading to urbanization, almost two-thirds of the people of the United States are concentrated in 212 metropolitan areas. This upheaval of home and family and social organization has, of course, brought great problems to the cities. They are problems of education, health, and housing; of sanitation and transportation; of social adjustment and employment; of delinquency and crime.

As a result, the Office of Education was 'widening its field of vision to recognize more clearly the effects of social-demographic problems on education'. From an initiative in 1961 followed a Conference on the Impact of Urbanization on Education in May 1962 (A: US DHEW, 1962, 237). It is in this context that attention was directed to the education of the 'slum child', the desperate condition of education and the cities which Conant and others addressed, and the need for rapid, effective policy decisions. Even by 1960, it has rightly been emphasized, poverty and economic inequality had still not become accepted as a proper field for public policy (A: Aaron, 1978, 16). How important black migration and the condition of the black communities in the cities were to the mounting recognition and the direction of policy interests is a question to which the discussion will constantly return. This is a question not just of the numbers of migrants but also of the cultural characteristics of the new urbanites, the language and nature of the interpretation of the cultural and education problems facing analysts, campaigners and planners at every level of the educational system and of government.

Awareness of the existence of mass poverty and of the failure of economic growth seriously to diminish what had previously been seen as a temporary and receding problem made rapid strides across a very short period. The search of the Kennedy administration for anti-poverty solutions was hampered by the fact that 'economists and practitioners were only just beginning to discover poverty' (A: Davidson, 1969, 6), and that public opinion was only just being alerted to the extent of the problem and the dangers. By 1964 it was being pointed out that the focus on economic growth and the increase of wealth had been an evasion from issues of inequality (A: Miller and Rein, 1964, 12). Allison Davis, continuing the emphasis he had placed from the late 1940s, underlined in a 1962 paper that 'at least one-third of our total population consists of slum dwellers, tenant farmers, and farm laborers'. In the discussion following Davis's paper contributors focused on questions of 'ghetto and slum districts', 'slum children', deprived groups and areas, and districts 'declining into slumhood or having already reached it – not a section of a community but an entire community' (A: Davis, 1962, 9,

43–52). The directions from which the new awareness, emphases and sense of urgency appeared at the beginning of the 1960s were various, as data emerged and interpretations changed.

One of the sources of ambiguity in approaches to poverty in the late 1950s and early 1960s was the publication of Galbraith's *The Affluent Society* in 1958. Galbraith subsequently had cause to complain that more people had read the title than the book and even, in the mid-1960s, to defend himself against accusations 'that he had misled everybody by his writings about *The Affluent Society*. Galbraith argued that "one of my principal purposes was to urge that growing wealth will not, of itself, solve the problem of poverty"' (A: Cater, 1968, 103–4). It was not only those people who failed to read the small print of the book, however, who misconstrued the emphasis Galbraith may have intended. The central message about poverty is contained in two pages of the book, where he makes the unambiguous case for modern poverty being thought of ('usefully' thought of, for some perplexing reason in later editions) in two broad categories. 'Case' poverty relates to 'some characteristic of the individuals so afflicted', and 'insular' poverty describes those islands where everyone is poor. Buried in the argument of this section of the book is the firm belief that 'the most certain thing about modern poverty is that it is not efficiently remedied by a general and tolerably well-distributed advance in income'. Later revisions of this argument completely altered the tone and intent of that passage, to read:

The most certain thing about this poverty is that it is not remedied by a general advance in income.

The critical change is the omission of the word 'efficiently', and indeed the tone of the remainder of the chapter does suggest that Galbraith thought the remedies via growing national wealth to be difficult but not impossible (A: Galbraith, 1958, 253–5; edn of 1970, 260–2).

Obliquely and ambiguously, therefore, Galbraith drew attention in the late 1950s to the persistent problem of poverty in affluence, and there were others also who dissented in one way or another from the 'optimistic view', documenting rural poverty and alerting congressional bodies to the need for action on 'pockets' of poverty (A: Levitan, 1969, 12–13). During the Kennedy years there were key economists in influential places in the administration who were increasingly formulating the problems and possible answers relating to poverty, but the work was not to be visible until 1963 or later (A: Aaron, 1978, 16–19). The turning point was, in fact, to be 1961–3, when new public metaphors and images of poverty emerged, amongst them being a famous review by Dwight Macdonald in *The New Yorker* entitled 'Our

Invisible Poor', a review which opened with the following commentary on Galbraith:

In his significantly titled 'The Affluent Society' (1958) Professor J.K. Galbraith states that poverty in this country is no longer 'a massive affliction (but) more nearly an after-thought.' Dr. Galbraith is a humane critic of the American capitalist system, and he is generously indignant about the continued existence of even this nonmassive and afterthoughtish poverty. But the interesting thing about his pronouncement, aside from the fact that it is inaccurate, is that it was generally accepted as obvious. For a long time now, almost everybody has assumed that...mass poverty no longer exists in this country. (A: Macdonald, 1963, 84)

The book which began to reconstruct public opinion along different lines was James B. Conant's study of the American high school which bore the title *Slums and Suburbs*, and appeared in 1961.

One of a series of reports on American education produced by Conant, former president of Harvard and influential educational policy commentator, *Slums and Suburbs* offered the United States various kinds of data and proposals, but above all images which many have considered either influential or crucial (Keppel, interview; Bailey, interview). This was particularly true of the well-known summary on the second page of the book: 'I am convinced we are allowing social dynamite to accumulate in our large cities'. He believed that a continuation of the position was a 'menace to the social and political health of the large cities...the whole problem of financing public education in the large cities is a major national concern' (A: Conant, 1961, 2). The short fuse was attached especially to these city slums, and Conant's educational priorities were determined by that awareness. The book, without offering a detailed analysis of poverty, and approaching it overwhelmingly in terms of Negro ('black' did not begin to replace the term in popular usage until the end of the decade) conditions and education, struck a popular chord, given the source of the comments. Conant's anger caused one kind of ripple, his solutions caused others. One of his central proposals was to provide an improved secondary curriculum, which, by incorporating a strong strand of vocational education, would better enable disadvantaged youth to make a transition to employment. This approach to the problem had been controversial since the debates about vocational education in the early decades of the century, and among other things seemed to be attacking the schools for failing to provide appropriate curricula. Conant found himself attacked, therefore, from opposite directions – as an apologist for the capitalist order, and as a member of a group of mainly radical critics of the schools whose preconceived stereotypes of schools and teachers were unjust and 'academic'. One hostile commentator later portrayed him as a member of a mythical

'Society for Criticizing Urban School Teachers' – alongside, for example, Frank Riessman, Patricia Sexton and John Holt (A: Ornstein, 1971b, 361). Conant had changed the agenda of educational and social debate.

It is worth remembering that while Conant was writing the book, the Commissioner of Education, Sterling M. McMurrin, was responding to a request from a House of Representatives committee for comments on 'The Present Condition of American Education'. McMurrin emphasized a growing recognition of the importance of education, the urgent need for Congressional concern and action, and a wide-ranging list of candidates for federal support. Although there was reference, in 1961, to wasted talent and the wasted energies of countless people, and the nation's failure to establish an appropriate, high-quality system of education for the 'enrichment of the national culture', McMurrin makes no reference at all to the kind of issues addressed by Conant, and represents none of the sense of public urgency arising from the social condition of large sections of the American population. By 1962–3 the 'optimistic', bland and mildly concerned tones of the 1950s voice, still audible in McMurrin's 1961 survey, were being rendered obsolete from other sources. Two other books are credited, and rightly so, with having finally shifted the terms of the debate as begun by Conant, and doing so very shortly afterwards.

The voice of white poverty was heard most clearly from Harry Caudill's *Night Comes to the Cumberlands: a biography of a depressed area*. Appearing in 1962, Caudill's book described in vivid detail the decline and rape of the land in the Appalachian valleys, the total backwardness to which the populations had been confined, the low standards of living, the high rate of illiteracy, the incurable levels of unemployment, the overwhelming sense of social disaster in eastern Kentucky and similar areas of the Appalachians (A: Caudill, 1962). The fate of these areas, as we have seen in the case of the 'unaccepted Baltimoreans', was to be a strong element in the consciousness of many of the cities affected by in-migration. John F. Kennedy was troubled by his experience of West Virginian poverty in his presidential campaign and, in 1965, one of America's best-known investigative writers on education was reminding the United States that 'The Schools of Appalachia' were beset by antiquated equipment or the lack of it, irrelevant textbooks, obsolete materials, and – in spite of the state aid since Caudill wrote – schools and conditions still far behind those of the rest of the nation (A: Schrag, 1965). With the NEA and others adding their voices to the rising chorus, the context and content of educational discussion was changing rapidly.

The second and most famous of the books which transformed the discussion was Michael Harrington's *The Other America: poverty in the United States*, also published in 1962, and featured most prominently in Dwight Macdonald's *New Yorker* review. Kennedy possibly read Harrington's book and more certainly read Macdonald's article (A: Lemann, 1988, 43). Harrington's and other analyses of poverty were undoubtedly effective in reaching and influencing the Kennedy administration, and whether or not Kennedy read and was impressed by the book is itself of minor importance. Keppel's comment that the event must not be over-dramatized is the important interpretation: it must not be suggested 'that the President had read Harrington, and lo and behold!...He read a lot of things...certainly somewhere between 1960 and 1965–6 there was a substantial change of view as to what the important issues were' (Keppel, interview). Dwight Macdonald criticized Harrington for popularizing the treatment of the problem of poverty 'a bit too much. Not in the writing...but in a certain vagueness' (A: Maconald, 1963, 84), and America's small traditional left-wing criticized the liberalism of its portrait of poverty, and its failure to offer a socialist critique of class (Cohen, D.K., interview). What Harrington did, however, was make the issue of poverty finally accessible and urgent.

Harrington's argument, vividly presented, was that the poor were invisible in American society, and increasingly so. No one cared, no one treated poverty as a matter for public, Congressional, legislative action. The 'old' poverty of previous generations contained elements of hope and aspiration, but the 'new' poverty was impervious to hope, as the poor were imprisoned in their culture of poverty, inescapable conditions, and a society which demanded increasing credentials to which the poor had little access. Paying tribute to Galbraith's pioneering attempt to present the issues, Harrington underlined that his own calculation of 40–50 million Americans living in poverty disposed of arguments about 'case' or 'insular' poverty. The poor were white urban hillbillies and a variety of others: a quarter were black. It was a poverty of the old and the young – his review of the statistics and definitions led him to the conclusion that roughly a quarter of the American population was poor, and probably a third of those were under eighteen. Others proposed even higher figures – and Harrington himself was in 1965 calculating that between a quarter and a third of young people were poor (A: Harrington, 1962; Harrington, 1965b, 28–9). By 1965 he was also describing the new poor as 'internal aliens', displaced by automation, old, unemployed (A: Harrington, 1965a, vii). Harrington, and other early combatants in the war on poverty – Paul Jacobs and Kenneth Clark, for example – were invited to take part in some of the deliberations on anti-poverty policy and legislation, had radical reservations about the direction of the war on poverty, but were willing to go along with the new movement (A: Yarmolinsky, 1969, 38; Jacobs, 1965; Jacobs, 1967; Jacobs, 1968).

The impact of Harrington was not, however, as Yarmolinsky points out, at the operational level. It is clear from the currents of discussion after 1962 that the gathering impact of Harrington, the new pictures of poverty by Caudill and others, and the increasingly available economic analyses from the Institute of Social Research at the University of Michigan, from Gabriel Kolko and others, were reshaping public vocabulary, if not consciousness. Robert Lampman, whose own statistics Harrington rejected as too cautious, was, with other activists, reshaping the administration's agenda. A book published in 1964, under the title *War on Poverty*, began with a chapter on 'The paradox of poverty'. It opened:

This is the revealing and paradoxical story of today's America – a country of unprecedented wealth and prosperity that harbors in its midst 35 million people without sufficient food, shelter, and clothing. It is the story of one out of five Americans who live in poverty, shame, misery, and degradation. It is also the story of people who cannot be separated from statistics, and whose plight is never fully realized unless you see the hopelessness on their faces and the plea in their eyes. (A: Humphrey, [1964], 9).

The author was Senator Hubert Humphrey, and he – like Kennedy – had heard the messages whilst campaigning in West Virginia in 1960. The language and the conceptualization, however, are those of Harrington, whom, in a later chapter, he quotes. In 1966, as Vice-President, and with the war on poverty having been launched, Humphrey was talking about the social service system 'that has inadequacies – particularly for the poor in this affluent America', and about schools having the opportunity to 'strike at the roots of poverty' (A: Humphrey, 1966, 55–6). The language, the concepts, the awareness, the sense of paradox and guilt, had been fundamentally changed by Harrington and others in that very short space of time at the beginning of the decade. The movement from 1964 to ensure and to recruit the participation of the poor was to produce critiques of the Harrington style of portraiture. In 1964, S.M. Miller, one of the keenest and most perceptive of the critics, declared Harrington to have been wrong in presenting the poor as passive, inert and apathetic (A: Miller, 1964, 213).

The politics, the language, the opportunities, had changed by 1964. Similarly, it is important to indicate how far and how rapidly educational emphases and interpretations were changing.

3   Education: children and intervention

Just as policies relating to poverty have a long and elusive history, so do theories and innovations relating to early childhood education. The two histories have never converged as formidably as they did in the United States in the late 1950s and 1960s. Never has psychologist spoken so directly with politician, educator with policy maker. To attempt to explain this convergence is to face the historical problem of continuity and discontinuity, the relationship between the event and the long process. The nature of the relationships between research and experiment in the field of early childhood, the roles of researchers and funding agencies, the emergence of policy issues and political needs, the transition from private endeavour to public policy, are all basic to the exploration of the 1960s. This is especially true in the preliminary phases of the American developments here under discussion, but they are true also of Britain – with a different typology of participants. The main elements in the analysis for this chapter are threefold – the work on early childhood and related experiments, the involvement of the Ford Foundation, and the Kennedy administration. A further element, the educational components of the war on poverty from 1964, are the substance of the following chapter.

A European and American interest in the education of young children emerged in the nineteenth century, primarily in relation to various forms of 'rescue' – rescue from inappropriate formal schooling, rescue from the ignorance and dangers (to individuals and to the social order) of urban conditions, rescue from breakdowns of family, church and other forms of authority which accompanied the transition from a predominantly rural society. The emergent interest was expressed in the pursuit of new ideas and practices relating both to childhood and to education, associated with the impact of Rousseau or Pestalozzi in continental Europe, Blake or Robert Owen in England (B: Silver, 1965; McCann and Young, 1982; A: Shapiro, 1983). The infant school, Froebelian approaches to the kindergarten and child study were legacies of the nineteenth century in Europe and the United States. What the twentieth century, especially from the 1930s, was to emphasize and illuminate was the nature of child development, and the relationships between that process of development and the wider environment, the family, the social and economic structure.

By the 1920s in the United States psychologists had attached to the early years a new sense of significance, and coupled with the growing interest in the nursery school, the emphasis on early childhood as a crucially important period for future intellectual and emotional development was producing a search for wider understandings and newer forms of action. The work of Arnold Gesell at Yale was signalling the importance of the early years, and one historian of preschool education in 1927 summarized the view that was being established: 'poverty, ignorance and neglect press with exceptional weight upon children of preschool age'. Indicating also the international nature of the interest and the effort, she reported that 'England is seeking a remedy'. She was able by this point to refer to Gesell's work, to the Child Welfare Research Station and 'preschool laboratory' at the State University of Iowa, to other nursery school developments in the United States and Britain, and to the range of purposes being debated for the preschool movement (A: Forest, 1927, 294–334). Some of the research and experiment was directed towards mental hygiene, habit training, social consciousness and similar targets, using a range of techniques and philosophies from behaviour inventories to a variety of curriculum innovations (A: Almy, 1964, 12). The ways in which early childhood experience provided a basis for staged growth was to be a particular theme of research from the 1930s as the concept of stages of intellectual and emotional development emerged from the cruder, more hypothetical versions that had been current during the nineteenth century, and as Piaget and others began to indicate new directions for experimental research. Iowa established its first preschool group in 1921, having created the Research Station in 1917. Although its range of environmental and social concerns was wider than that of most previous early childhood research, it sustained a steady focus on the need for and impact of nursery education itself. Its explanations incorporated the importance of supplementing home care, extending young children's experience of community life, parent education, and the adoption of relevant new nursery school practices. These included, for example, not only the interest in independent activity and play developed by the progressive education movement, but also the deliberate fostering of social relationships, aspects of health and safety, and systematic enquiry into the links between children's physical and cognitive development (A: Iowa, 1934). The messages of success in accelerating children's development and overcoming social handicaps were received with some scepticism in the academic community. Iowa's pioneering work was to be rediscovered after the Second World War.

There are three points to make about this period in American work on early childhood. The first is that it meshed in with, but to some extent diverged from, the parallel British interest. A more sociologically oriented analysis was emerging in Britain, concerned with the wastage of human resources, differential access to schooling in Britain on the basis of social class, and the socially conditioned incidence of child disease, ill-health and lack of opportunity. Secondly the focus on early childhood was not new. What was new was the scale, range and academic basis of the work that was developing in relation to it. A visiting American professor from Teachers College, Columbia University, told a British audience in 1933 that the growing interest in preschool education of many kinds in many countries was

in itself no innovation; the advance which has taken place in the last few years lies rather in the incorporation of the pre-school as an essential element in the education, using that word in its broadest sense, of the individual... At present the purposes of the pre-school vary all the way from a simple demand that the young child be given the opportunity to live a healthy life in a healthy environment... to the claim that the first six years are the most critical of our allotted three score years and ten. (B: Kandel, 1933, 11)

A footnote to this passage when published expressed scepticism about 'critical periods', and drew attention to the adaptation of the British nursery school to provision for the American well-do-do, with the children becoming 'guinea-pigs of the inquiring psychologists and psychiatrists'. Thirdly, pre-war American interest in early childhood was predominantly concerned with children's emotional and social development, had few sociological dimensions, and dealt mainly with the children's 'inner feelings' (A: Spodek, 1979, 150). Very little of the literature, even that of Iowa, is directly and explicitly concerned with the analysis of education in a context of inequality, poverty or social class.

The directions in which the Iowa work had pointed were followed most significantly by Hebb, whose path-breaking *Organization of Behavior* was published in 1949. Hebb's argument, sustained through this 'neuropsychological theory', as his sub-title described it, was consistent and clear. A variety of research had now demonstrated that 'all learning tends to utilize and build on any earlier learning', so that 'much early learning tends to be permanent', involving a transfer from early to later learning. Learning capacity was therefore influenced by early experience and the nature of growth. In two or three crucial pages

Hebb rejected accepted views about intelligence, and the comparative use of IQ measurements. Social, environmental, cultural, educational contexts operated so differentially as to make these unacceptable:

Negroes living in the United States make lower average scores on intelligence tests than whites do, but we cannot concede that the Negro has a poorer brain than the white... Negro and white do not have the opportunity to learn to speak the language with equal range and accuracy, are not usually taught in equally good schools, and do not have equally good jobs... All this we can accept; but when we do so we must recognize that we have completely undermined the argument that differences of IQ among white, native Americans are determined by heredity... no two social backgrounds are identical and we do not know what the important environmental variables are in the development of intellectual functions. (A: Hebb, 1949, 109–10, 299–300)

Scanty but strong evidence demonstrated that 'environment has a major effect on the IQ', though 'the essentials of this environmental influence' could not be specified. Hebb underlined, however, the important contributions of 'wealth, prolonged schooling, or "intelligent" parents', and the need for psychology to explore the problems involved: 'the fact is... that we know almost nothing specific about the matter. The country may be full of potential geniuses, for all we know' (*ibid.,* 301–3).

Hebb was to serve as an important text for the developments of the 1950s and early 1960s. The extent of the changes in perspective even at the beginning of the 1950s can be judged from a major report which resulted from a 'midcentury White House conference on children and youth'. The report, *Personality in the Making*, appeared only three years after Hebb's book, and was the outcome of wide consultation. It addressed questions of environment and 'cultural considerations'. A chapter entitled 'Income Level and Health of Personality' discussed the range of effects of low income – biological, social, cultural. It pointed to the relationship between low income and amount of schooling, educational opportunity, and handicaps which led to a child often being 'accounted dull at school even though his intelligence is as good as that of the majority'. Tests were culturally slanted and operated against slum children. All of this was related to the incidence of low income – an emphasis that was not to achieve full recognition for another decade: estimates made for the conference indicated that in 1950 'only about half of the children who lived in cities belonged to families with an income that met the Bureau of Labor statistics standard'. In the country as a whole 27.8 per cent of children were in families with a cash income of less than $2,000, and about a half had under $3,000. Some studies suggested that a family income of at least $6,000 was necessary to meet health and educational needs comfortably – and under 10 per cent of children were in that category (A: Witmer and Kotinsky, 1952, 105–25).

Research and documents of this kind were new in the strength of their emphasis, and were signposts to changed operational and policy focuses rather than representative of extensive ground already won. The 1950s continued to produce a substantial literature of early childhood in terms of, for example, *The Magic Years* (A: Fraiberg, 1959), with a stress on psychoanalytic concerns relating to adjustment, health or imagination, and without reference to the questions of disadvantage, socio-environmental distinctions and schooling taking shape elsewhere. These included the important field of special education, which, in the United States as in Britain, was to be a direction from which interest in compensatory education and related questions was to come.

If the 1940s and 1950s was a period of 'conception' in the emergence of 'modern early childhood education', the period from 1958–64 has been suggested as one of 'construction', and that from 1965–71 as one of 'revolution', to be followed by periods of 'reflection' and 'reaffirmation' (A: Hodges and Smith, 1980). If Hebb is the key figure in the period of conception, McVicker Hunt is crucial for the period that followed. Hunt produced a series of texts in the 1960s, which, collected in *The Challenge of Incompetence and Poverty : papers on the role of early education* in 1969, were to be widely influential, in Britain too. Hunt's impact had begun to be felt, however, early in the 1960s. The message of his *Intelligence and Experience* in 1961 was particularly clear. In it he began a relentless attack on the concept of 'fixed intelligence', which had dominated the approach to the measurement of intelligence. It was this concept which had prevented investigation of the effects of early experience on later intellectual capacity, and from psychoanalysis and other sources Hunt took evidence of the role of experience in the development of intelligence. Hunt, in this book as elsewhere, rooted his approach in the history of analyses of intelligence, their conceptual and empirical bases, and against that background explained the derision with which the Iowa findings on environmental factors had been met. From Hebb and Piaget he drew support for a new conception of intelligence, a rejection of the concept of fixed intelligence, which had produced decades of false advice to parents and educators, and a declaration, which – more than anything that had gone before – indicated the change of mood and direction:

...the assumptions that intelligence is fixed and that its development is predetermined by the genes are no longer tenable...it is no longer unreasonable to consider that it might be feasible to discover ways to govern the encounters that children have with their environments, especially during the early years of their development, to achieve a substantially faster rate of intellectual development and a substantially higher adult level of intellectual capacity...

That was the central, sustained message that Hunt and others were now to deliver in many forms and arenas, and the constituency and target of Hunt's appeal were equally clear: 'the chances are fairly good that the behavioural sciences can make a contribution of great social, as well as theoretical, significance' (A: Hunt, 1961, 3–7, 28–33, 347–63).

The research–policy convergence of the mid-1960s was in part a response to such signals, though as we shall see it was also a response to the confidence generated by experiments of various kinds on the ground – a widely reported Demonstration Guidance Project was begun in new York in 1956, and from it came the much discussed Higher Horizons project in 1959; Samuel Shepard began his nationally known work in the Banneker district of St Louis, Missouri, in 1957; and, of central importance to our theme, an Institute for Developmental Studies was established under the direction of Martin Deutsch in New York in 1958. Underlying all of this work was an increasing conviction not only that intelligence was not fixed and predetermined, but also that the intellectual retardation which resulted from deprivation of various kinds could be reversed. The years 1963–4 saw the research and the theory gaining rapid public momentum. In 1963, for example, David P. Ausubel emphasized the importance of optimal learning environments as early as possible in order to reverse intellectual retardation in culturally deprived children, who needed teaching of above-average quality but normally received the opposite. Ausubel's central theme was that cumulative intellectual deficit reflects the cumulative impact of a deficient environment, resulting in inability to cope with the demands of the school curriculum, alienation and demoralization (A: Ausubel, 1963). The following year Ausubel was again emphasizing the cumulative nature of intellectual deficit, the effects of environmental deprivation, and the possibilities of enhancing children's IQ by early experience enrichment, overcoming the difficulties culturally deprived children found with abstract modes of thought and language (A: Ausubel, 1964).

Also in 1964 appeared Benjamin Bloom's influential *Stability and Change in Human Characteristics*. The central message of Bloom's analysis of the available research was that about 50 per cent of the intelligence that could be measured at age seventeen resulted from development that had taken place before the age of four, about 30 per cent between the ages of four and eight, and about 20 per cent between eight and seventeen. Bloom's environmental explanations were sharp and clear:

These results make it clear that a single early measure of general intelligence cannot be the basis for a long-term decision about an individual. These results also reveal the changing rate at which intelligence develops, since as much of the development takes place in the first 4 years of life as in the next 13 years...a conservative estimate of the effect of extreme environments on intelligence is about 20 I.Q. points. This could mean a difference between a life in an institution for the feeble-minded or a productive life in society. It could mean the difference between a professional career and an occupation which is at the semi-skilled or unskilled level.

Drawing on Hebb and others, Bloom began the process of identifying those environmental characteristics which could positively or negatively affect intelligence and school achievement: 'these include communi-cation and interaction with adults, motivation and incentives for achievement and understanding of the environment, and the availability of adult models and exemplars of language, communication, and reasoning' (A: Bloom, 1964b, 88–9, 188).

The final indication of the importance of these years was the publication in 1964 of an issue of the *Merrill-Palmer Quarterly of Behavior and Development* which contained papers delivered at a December 1962 Arden House Conference on Pre-School Enrichment of Socially Disadvantaged Children. Deutsch's Institute had been one of the sponsors – and Deutsch himself wrote the introduction to the issue of the *Quarterly*. The purpose of the conference, he wrote, had been to 'explore from various directions the possibilities for accelerating the cognitive development of young children', focusing particularly but not exclusively on children 'from disadvantaged circumstances'. The emphasis was on 'the empirical and theoretical rationale for early intervention', and on appropriate methods (A: Deutsch, 1964b). Deutsch contributed a paper on 'facilitating development in the pre-school child', writing cautiously about the present state of knowledge, but pointing to the role of the behavioural scientist as facilitator in preparing children 'for optimal social participation' (A: Deutsch, 1964a, 250). Other papers included one by two of Deutsch's associates on 'the social context of language acquisition' – one of the authors being Vera John, who was to be one of the American researchers working in a field parallel to that being developed in Britain by Basil Bernstein (A: John and Goldstein, 1964). McVicker Hunt's paper to the same conference, on 'the psychological basis for using pre-school enrichment as an antidote for cultural deprivation' was also to become the first chapter of his *The Challenge of Incompetence and Poverty*.

Here and elsewhere Deutsch and others were constantly to refer back to Hebb, to Hunt and to Iowa (A: Deutsch, 1965b; Gray, Klaus & Ramsey, 1981a). Dominant in the argument was the general issue of environmental deprivation and its effects, and the research was increasingly directed towards specifying the nature of the relationship between development and learning on the one hand, and particular environmental factors on the other hand. Galbraith had discussed education as an investment to enable people to cope with the environment, but researchers were now constantly emphasizing how the environment was responsible for success and failure in cognitive, developmental and education terms (A: Galbraith, 1958, 258–9; Cynthia Deutsch, 1965). The same sources of explanation were attracting further attention – including from sociologists. By 1963 Harry Passow, for example, was collecting together a substantial body of work on education in 'depressed areas', by authors drawing on Higher Horizons and similar evidence and on analyses of the learning process (about which Martin Deutsch contributed a paper) (A: Passow, 1963). Professional frontiers were being crossed in this way, but the psychologists can claim credit for the central impetus of the 1950s and this period of the early 1960s.

The concept of 'cultural deprivation', as some of this discussion indicates, had by this point penetrated the academic community and become one of the organizing concepts of the discussion. Ausubel, Deutsch and others used this and related vocabularies of disadvantage and deprivation, in most cases weaving together cultural and en-vironmental explanations of preschool conditioning, lack of motivation and preparedness for the demands of schooling. Their use of this conceptual framework closely paralleled that of the sociologists who, in addition to drawing data and support from some of the same sources, also referred back to the work of Warner, Davis and others for explanations of how children were disadvantaged by their class, environment and schooling (to which middle-class children could more easily adapt, and of which working-class parents and their children were said to have low expectations) (A: Clausen and Williams, 1963, 82). The psychologists were more and more pointing to the cumulative nature of the handicaps and failures, and Deutsch in particular was probing the responsibilities of the schools, including their failure to prepare personnel for the problems faced by disadvantaged children (A: Deutsch and Associates, 1967, 40–2). The schools, teachers and educators in general were being allocated blame for the failure of, particularly, Negro and slum children to benefit from schooling (A: Silberman, 1964, 251–2).

We shall return to a consideration of projects and programmes, their backgrounds and outcomes, but it is important here to emphasize the work of Deutsch's Institute for Developmental Studies, given its relationship to the Ford Foundation, and the role that Martin Deutsch,

Cynthia Deutsch, Vera John and others played in the whole thrust of the 1960s. The Institute, created in 1958, launched a 'program of educational intervention at the preschool level' in 1962, and extended the programme to the third grade in 1964, 'recognizing that continuous reinforcement is essential if early gains are to be maintained and elaborated'. The Institute therefore worked on curriculum development, in-service training for teachers, community and parent programmes, and a wide variety of research activities and studies aimed at overcoming learning disabilities – especially in the field of language:

Based on the assumption that the child's potential intelligence is not fixed at birth and that his development depends on the *quality* of his early interaction with the world around him, Institute scientists are actively investigating such variables as socioeconomic status, race, family composition and living arrangements, child rearing practices and language styles as they affect the child's cognitive development.

A survey had revealed that variations in verbal skills were directly attributable to socio-economic background rather than to race, and 'the findings of this study supplied further evidence of the damaging effects of social inequalities in our society' (A: Church and Eisman, 1968, i–ii). While later critiques of the analysis based on environment and early intervention focused on the ways these 'blamed' the child, it is important to remember that Deutsch in particular addressed the problems of the *school* as an agency of discrimination and perpetuation of the status quo. In a sense, he wrote in 1965, 'the institution of education – the school – *is* the *status quo*. It often operates through huge politically oriented bureaucracies that continually inhibit its potential for change and for developing strategies for meeting social crises such as those inherent in the new urban America' (A: Powledge, 1967, 7). The results of the early work were encouraging, the preschool enrichment programmes enhancing children's manipulative, social and cognitive skills: 'activities which increase auditory and visual perception and discrimination, concept development, and the meaningful use of language are stressed' (A: Olsen, 1965, 79). Vera John in 1963, emphasizing how little the development of the 'urban slum child' had been studied, herself pointed to social class as the main explanation of difference in language skills (A: John, 1963).

At the same time as encouraging results were beginning to emerge from New York, hopeful signals were beginning to come from the Early Training Project, associated primarily with Susan Gray and Rupert Klaus and the Peabody College in Tennessee. The project, directed towards 'culturally disadvantaged children' at Murfreesboro, began with a ten-week summer programme. When it began, the team later confessed, 'we thought naively that it was possible to design a program that would be strong enough to offset the early handicaps that these children experienced. Our naivete was short-lived' (A: Gray *et al.*, 1981b, 216). Here, as in other programmes, theories and practices based on the brief 'innoculation' of children were to the superseded by more systematic, longer-term programmes, taking account explicitly – as in this case – of the mediocrity or rigidity of the public schools. Susan Gray had, like Deutsch, begun the operation in the late 1950s, in her case initially as an exercise for students in the college, and this had grown into the Early Training Project, which began its data collection in 1961 and became involved with children and their parents the following year. The work is described as coming out of the problems of the public schools as seen in the light of the *Brown* decision, its repercussions in the South, the problems of migration, and the evidence emerging from the work of Piaget and Hunt, with particular reference to Hunt's 1961 *Intelligence and Experience* (A: Klaus and Gray, [1968]; Gray and Klaus, 1963). Some sixty children were involved, in experimental and control groups on classical lines, and additionally with what became known as a 'distal' group geographically far enough away to avoid 'contamination' by the two experimental groups concerned. Whatever the later disappointments, by 1963 and after two years of operation the project was reporting significant gains by the preschool children on the experimental programme, though adding that 'such findings must be taken cautiously' (A: Gray and Klaus, 1963, 10–11).

During the first three or four years of the 1960s, therefore, information from experimental projects was joining other psychological and sociological evidence of the handicaps encountered by children from lower-income groups, in some cases – as in the Tennessee project – relating to black children, in others more widely based, and often producing analyses in terms of socio-economic and class relationships. The pressures of urban, civil rights and demographic changes were contexts in which the new emphases were being made, and the elements of a new intellectual climate were clearly visible. The discovery of poverty was being accompanied by a movement in the behavioural and social sciences to confront questions of the relationship between disadvantage and education, and their complex connections with the processes of change taking place in the United States. Of paramount importance in this convergence of processes was the role of the Ford Foundation.

In the 1950s the Foundation was funding educational projects designed essentially to modernize the system – helping to develop library resources, medical education, teacher education and the like, and supporting work in such areas as educational television and film. The 'Public Affairs' work of the Foundation included from the mid-1950s an interest in 'metropolitan area studies' – essentially town planning. While the education work of the 1950s was aimed at raising standards and coping with the classroom problems of demographic and related change, the public affairs dimension was coming closer to the salient problems of the inner city. By the end of the 1950s the two were coming together in what became the Great Cities Schools Program – resulting in the launch, essentially from 1960, of an educational anti-poverty policy. The 'Great Cities – Gray Areas Program' brought together and transformed the two earlier thrusts of the Foundations's work (A: FF, Annual Reports 1955–60; Meade, [1979], 1–5).

It was Paul Ylvisaker more than anyone at Ford who, in the late 1950s (he joined the Foundation in 1955), took it 'to a different constituency', starting with the problems of migration and the city. He recalls how one of his colleagues, Alvin C. Eurich, 'began talking with school super-intendents of the major cities, and the Education Program…was *the* powerful Program at the time. And Al began to fool around with a league of fourteen superintendents headed by Ben Willis of Chicago'. They asked Ford, in effect, for some 'millions to throw at the problem'. Resisting a 'sloppy' approach to handing over large amounts of money, Ylvisaker promoted a 'field force' which went to fourteen cities, talked with the superintendents in the context of local power structures and the civil liberties movement, and got them to 'explain their intentions'. The records show, as Ylvisaker suggests they do, 'the amount of homework we did' (A: FF, Ylvisaker interview, 16–26). The work in the cities that were chosen (Detroit served as the pilot from August 1959) put the Foundation in the forefront of efforts to relate education to urban and social issues, and helped to mobilize the emergent intellectual and political energies which we have discussed. The aim in all cases was the 'improvement of education in depressed areas', the linking of concern for the situation in the 'gray areas' (a neutral vocabulary developed by Ford in the late 1950s) with the problems of school failure, dropout, attendance, low aspiration and achievement (A: FF, Annual Report, 1960, 27–8). Within this overall framework Ford was to support other efforts – including Mobilization for Youth in New York, also in the early 1960s – but the important first steps to the Foundation's new perspective were those related to school and preschool. It is important to remember, however, in the case of Ford as in that of the educational legislation of the mid-1960s, that the educational focus was part of a growing and explicit concern with community action on a broader front (A: Ylvisaker [1963]):

Seeking a bolder and more comprehensive approach, the Ford Foundation provided large developmental funds for coordinated programs in such areas as employment, education, and social services, under the auspices of a new community agency uncommitted to the existing service structure. (A: Kravitz, 1965, 1–2)

The policy, the scale of the effort, and the procedures and targets represented a set of responses to a newly perceived and differently interpreted situation.

The Foundation was at this stage seeking to promote forms of intervention which would, as Detroit reported at the end of the first year of its pilot scheme, provide educational programmes 'to achieve more optimum educational benefits for children with limited educational backgrounds' (A: FF, Detroit, 1960, 1). The target was described by the Detroit project in what it considered the helpful vocabulary of 'culturally deprived' and 'transitional neighbourhood' – helpful in that it was better than that of 'slum children' and 'slum neighbourhood' – even though, the project realized, the new vocabularies were also euphemisms and still ran the risk of becoming labels (A: FF, Detroit, 1962, 1–2). Detroit, as other projects, operated in many directions – including staff orientation, parent involvement, the redirection of the attention of public services, the adaptation of school curricula and organization, and the widespread use of outside specialists and increased numbers of community and school personnel. Among hypotheses to be tested were: that school staffs needed help in becoming more effective in meeting the needs of children whose backgrounds and value systems were different from those of the teachers and schools; that home and community needed to be involved constructively to improve attitudes and motivation; that school–home links needed to be strengthened; that small additions to school staff would greatly improve school effectiveness; and that closer study of the needs of the children concerned would result in more appropriate expenditure of funds, better preparation of teachers and improved curricula and organization (A: FF, Detroit, 1960, 2–3). Ten other cities were almost immediately to join the Great Cities programme, as proposals were negotiated and approved after 1960.

The strategies chosen in the different cities had important variations. Pittsburgh, for example, whose proposal was approved in May 1960, wished to develop 'the use of teaching teams to improve the education of in-migrant, transient pupils in depressed areas'. It intended

to reorganize completely the learning environment in a cluster of five elementary schools whose attendance areas constitute a semi-isolated, depressed community. By developing new patterns of organization and new techniques of teaching, we expect to neutralize educational handicaps... (A: FF, Pittsburgh, 1960)

The Milwaukee proposal, approved at the same time, was also aimed at in-migrant and transient children, but pointed to 'orientation centers' and remedial classes, in order better to prepare and place children in schools (an experiment had already been conducted in 1959). This scheme also involved meetings of school personnel, the use of consultants, parent education activities, and the elaboration of suitable, special curricula for in-migrant children in need of 'acculturation' and compensatory experience of various kinds (A: FF, Milwaukee, 1960a; 1960b; [1961]). Philadelphia, also approved in May 1960, proposed the establishment of a 'school–community coordinating team', in order to 'concentrate on the discovery and development of talent in the culturally different and in the reduction of juvenile delinquency among the culturally different'. A team approach would bring about 'realistic working relationships between the teacher, the child, and the parent' and result in appropriate elementary school programmes (A: FF, Philadelphia, 1960, 1). A year later Philadelphia was already reporting 'spectacular increases in the achievement of individual children', though emphasizing 'a normal rate of progress for all children' and an 'encouraging' first year (A: FF, Philadelphia, 1961, 59).

The St Louis project was for a 'school and community work-related education program' and aimed to involve the educational system, business, management and labour organizations in tackling widespread unemployment in the city, by upgrading 'the work potential of the culturally different'. (It is interesting to note the response of some of these proposals to current critiques of the concept of cultural *deprivation*, the phrase 'culturally different' being used in the Philadelphia proposal, and being substituted by hand for 'culturally deprived' wherever it occurs in the St Louis proposal.) The main feature of an accompanying 'summer remedial reading project' was the concentrated training of school teachers in remedial reading and spelling techniques. A year later the project reported that as a result of the summer programme 'and the application of their newly acquired reading skills to the work of the regular classroom, these pupils did achieve, during the semester following the remedial instruction, a gain equal to that expected of normally achieving pupils in the area of reading' (A: FF, St Louis, 1960a; 1960b; 1961, 30). Chicago's project was aimed at older children who had been held back and had not entered high school. Baltimore's project was for 'early school admission'.

Two projects merit particular mention, as the ones which most directly intersect with the interest in early childhood and preschool developing at the same time. The Baltimore project, negotiated with the Foundation in 1961 and 1962, was for a three-year programme of 'educational enrichment and training of pre-school children from deprived areas of the city'. A North Carolina project, negotiated in 1964 and 1965, was the only one in the overall programme not to be based on one of the 'great cities', and from an initial emphasis on older age groups was redirected as a preschool and early elementary school project.

In the decade after 1950 the Baltimore school population rose from over 120,000 to over 170,000. The hypothesis the project proposed to test was that

a program of special learning activities for 4 and 5 year old culturally deprived children focused on providing culturally enriched learning experiences will help overcome the academic handicaps which confront these children upon entering the regular elementary school programs. If mothers learn how to nurture and to guide their children, the mothers themselves will value and participate in activities which will contribute to the children's culturally significant experiences.

The programme was to be designed accordingly, establishing 'teacher –mother teams' to work with groups of thirty children (each team to contain one trained primary teacher, one occasional other teacher, and two volunteer mothers), focusing on language skills and communication experiences, and widening horizons. The children were to have 'a balance of action and quiet, stimulation and serenity', their health was to receive attention, and a wide variety of teaching techniques were to be employed, involving parents as much as possible. The Foundation used Martin Deutsch on this, as on other occasions, as a consultant, and his view of the draft proposal was that it relied too much for its intended success on teachers and administrators who had been 'trained in traditional methods largely based on the problems of the middle class child'. The experience of his Institute and elsewhere suggested that a new methodology was needed 'for teaching children coming from environments with the degree of impoverishment characteristic of the urban classes and particularly the minority group child' (A: FF, Baltimore, Deutsch memo 1961). The programme as finally approved laid considerable stress on research activities, the initial use of two pilot centres, later to be expanded, the teacher–mother team concept, and the focus on child growth and development studies.

A political development of considerable help in winning the Foundation's support for the Baltimore project was the adoption by the City Board of Education on 12 July 1962, of a formal resolution declaring 'its intent to offer educational services as a part of the program of general educational services to qualified culturally disadvantaged children who otherwise would be ineligible for enrollment because of chronological age, if the research findings of the project suggest the wisdom of so doing' (AA: FF, Baltimore, Brain, July 1962, annex; Public Affairs Department, 1962, 3–4). Henry Saltzman, who, at the Ford Foundation, was the person most concerned with many of these projects, wrote to Ylvisaker in August drawing attention to the resolution of the Board, and commenting, 'this could mark an historic point in American education's progress – or it may be only a "scrap of paper." In any case, it is the first such resolution that I know of in the post-war era' (A: FF, Baltimore, Saltzman, 1962). The recommendation from the Public Affairs Department to agree the project suggested that the Baltimore school system was in effect going to lower its entrance age to meet the needs of deprived children, and the Board's resolution on the subject 'may be a momentous one for public education in the United States – pointing the way for a major breakthrough in educational philosophy and practice' (A: FF, Baltimore, Public Affairs Department, [1962], 4).

The Foundation took an active interest in the project, receiving and commenting on reports, and visiting Project Help, as it became familiarly known. Saltzman took an interest in the research, the methodology, the problems (including initial resistance on the part of some white families to taking part in the project), the impact on the children and the community (A: FF, Baltimore, Saltzman, 1965). Catherine Brunner, the project coordinator, published accounts of the project and its emphases on children's communication skills, quantitative thinking, aesthetic values, health and self-concept, and on parent involvement (A: FF, Baltimore, Brunner, 1963; 1965). A member of the City Board and Dean of the University of Maryland School of Medicine told a conference in 1964:

What you probably want to know is why we're willing to spend a third of a million dollars on a few hundred culturally deprived children...our Early School Admissions Project is not just an affair of the heart. It's an experiment whose research findings have great implications not only for Baltimore City but also for other Great City school districts as well. (A: FF, Baltimore, Stone, 1964, 1)

Since the North Carolina project was not approved until 1965, it enters a later phase of our discussion. The launch of the project, however, forms part of the process begun by the Ford Foundation at the beginning of the decade. Terry Sanford was elected Governor of North Carolina in 1960. At a dinner in his honour on his retirement in December 1964 Commissioner Keppel talked of Sanford and North Carolina being 'ahead of the parade', and of Sanford as the 'Educational Governor', who had spent some four years dealing with foundations, recruiting financial aid and popular support, developing new approaches to education, and working to bring schools, welfare and civil organizations together to break the cycle of poverty. One of his successes had been to recruit the Ford Foundation in the endeavour (A: LBJ Lib, Keppel addresses, 4 December 1964). Sanford had, in fact, sought support of every kind to combat poverty and improve schooling, and was aware of the links between the two. The disadvantages of poverty 'were varied and many', he wrote in 1966, 'but all of the disadvantages led to one common difficulty. These children came into a school system not organized to treat with them...They were caught in a cycle of poverty, condemned to remain in poverty, and destined to raise their children in poverty'. One of the aims was to improve the schools, another was to put the children 'in a position to understand why learning was important'. He looked for ideas and money, persuaded the Assistant Superintendent of Public Instruction to prepare a proposal for a national foundation and, though they were not 'plagued with the gray areas problem' as were the selected large cities, they ended up talking to Ylvisaker and others at Ford, including the president of the Foundation: 'I had begun to realize that I had stumbled into the whole confusing pattern of poverty in America while trying to find better ways to educate the children of the disadvantaged'. The outcome was an extension of Ford's city programme to an experimental state-wide programme in 1963 (A: Sanford, 1966, 120–8).

The following year negotiations began around what was originally a proposal from Duke University, at Durham, for a Center to Improve Educational Opportunities for Underprivileged Youth, a proposal which had the 'whole-hearted support' of Duke, North Carolina College, the school system of Durham City and County, and a broad preparatory and advisory committee (A: FF, Durham, Connery, 1964). Edward Meade Jr and colleagues from the Foundation visited Durham in December, and Meade reported that they had had to undo some of the assumptions about what needed to be done. The universities and colleges were not enthusiastic about focusing on the elementary school, but before the meetings ended they had realized that the Foundation was interested in that level of education 'and more primarily at the lower end...We deliberately moved the focus of the projects from the colleges and universities to the schools' (A: FF, Durham, Meade memo, 1964). An initial 'academic' approach was therefore overcome, and a new proposal in January 1965 was more determined to accomplish an intensive educational programme which would 'alter the landscape of Poverty', making use of a 'longitudinal stimulation program', an 'infant evaluation project', a 'nursery school segment' and a process from preschool to ungraded primary school. Mario Fantini, one of the Foundation team who had visited the previous year, wrote to Meade immediately on receipt of the proposal to report that it was now 'a vast departure from the original', with an emphasis on early education, a definite research focus, and a clear intention to get institutions to work together (A: FF, Durham, proposal, January 1965; Fantini memo, January 1965). All was not to prove well at Duke, the collaboration was not as close as had been hoped, and the lack of experience and emphasis on early childhood education and city schools at Duke in particular meant that the project was not to have the impact originally hoped (A: FF, Durham, Report, [1972]). What the Foundation had attempted to achieve in this wider setting was, however, the same as in the city situations where its main support had been directed – a new impetus through the preschool and early grades of elementary schooling to deal more effectively with disadvantaged children and their needs, through a range of strategies bringing the system, the schools, teacher education, the communities, the parents, more effectively into action on behalf of the child (A: FF, Durham, 1971; Shenkman, 1968).

Ford was investing heavily in the programmes. By January 1963 it had put $3.5 million into the eleven Great Cities School Improvement Program projects alone, and was already committing or about to commit substantial sums to related projects – in Oakland, California, New Haven, Connecticut, Mobilization for Youth, North Carolina, and the research base it was helping to establish, notably through support for Martin Deutsch's Institute in New York. Although Deutsch had other sponsors, including Carnegie and federal government departments, Ford was originally the largest (Deutsch, interview). What the Foundation was also doing was producing a climate of opinion, a nation-wide interchange of information and a momentum of policy-related activity. Its projects were occasions for consultation and platforms for dialogue between researchers and politicians. Early in Milwaukee's project, for example, it held a workshop on the problems of in-migrant and transient pupils, and the speakers on 1 September 1960 included Philip Hauser, a sociologist from Chicago, Martin Deutsch, and members of the Ford staff, including Saltzman. St Louis held a meeting on 21 May 1960, at which Ylvisaker and Saltzman were both present – and here, as elsewhere, local educational and political activists were involved. The St Louis discussion embraced topics such as the problems of population growth and migrancy (with speakers from the National Conference of Christians and Jews and the University of Missouri, a former Mayor and a representative of the Department of Parks and Recreation). Population change was certainly seen as 'our most critical problem' – with in-migration largely by Eastern Ozark whites, Delta negroes and Delta poor whites – and much emphasis was given to attendant issues of housing and services, including education. The most important common denominator of the Great Cities projects was seen as the emphasis on reading as 'an absolute prerequisite skill for culturally different children', and success depended on 'the re-education of teachers', the involvement of the schools and other community agencies, and confident relationships between school and family (A: FF, St Louis, Report, 1960a). The network of consultants was widening, though at the beginning Ylvisaker relied heavily on Deutsch. Susan Gray, Ira Gordon, Harry Passow and others who were to become key figures in the mid-1960s were gradually brought into the picture, and the Foundation's own staff assumed increasingly active roles, with Henry Saltzman, the 'education person' on Ylvisaker's staff, being the key staff member in this field (Meade, interview).

The range of the Foundation's involvements widened, though with the same sustained commitment to work on behalf of the disadvantaged. By 1964, for example, it was supporting summer 'enrichment' programmes at Yale (a 'summer school for able high school students whose environment inhibits their full personal and intellectual development' began that year), and at a consortium of institutions belonging to the National Association of Independent Schools which, based at Boston, created an Educational Enrichment Program in 1964 to increase opportunities for children with 'shortcomings in their daily environment' (A: FF, Yale, Report, 1965; FF, National Association of Independent Schools, EEP, 1966, 3). Across the four or so years since the Great Cities School Improvement Program had been launched, Ford had established itself as the foundation with this central concern to confront the linked problems of education and poverty. A letter to the foundation from a professor at Duke University in November 1964 expressed the hope that 'your "revolution against poverty" proceeds as fast as you would like' (A: FF, Durham, Connery, 1964). Terry Sanford described the gray areas programmes as 'early skirmishes in the war on poverty' (A: Sanford, 1966, 125). The *New York Times*, in a January 1964 special education survey, contained an article presenting Ford's preschool projects particularly, citing Meade and Saltzman, emphasizing the contribution of Deutsch's work in Harlem and the Lower East Side, and the lowering of the school enrolment age in Baltimore (A: Terte, 1964). The projects, their hypotheses, the research and the experience were being publicized and generating other projects and activities. The number of locally sponsored, state-sponsored or foundation-sponsored projects was growing rapidly, though, as one commentator pointed out in late 1963, there were millions of newcomers in the big city slums, enormous problems of educating migrant and other disadvantaged children, but so far there was 'only a beachhead of knowledge' on how to teach them (A: Shaw, 1963, 97). In an analysis of race problems published the following year, Charles Silberman wrote of the large amount of experimentation going on in the large cities (with school superintendents collecting Ford Foundation grants 'much the way Indians used to collect scalps'), and commented approvingly that 'the projects usually succeed admirably; they demonstrate that whatever technique was being used can substantially improve the performance of Negro youngsters'. Despondently, and indicating that the question of outcomes was beginning to loom large in discussion of the projects, he added that 'for the most part, however, nothing much happens as a result; once the "demonstration project" ends, the schools involved slip back into the same old rut' (A: Silberman, 1964, 255–6). Attention was being directed not only to innovation, but to the ability of the schools to sustain change.

What we have now underlined is the variety of factors which explain the rapid acceleration of attention to education as a policy instrument from 1964 in particular, but it is important additionally to emphasize the crucial role of the developments which took place under the Kennedy administration, in terms of policy formulation and attempts at legislation. The sequence of bills presented to Congress from 1961 was a persistent attempt to enhance the federal role in the solution of educational and social problems. The problems Kennedy faced were, in his view, more technical than ideological (A: Aaron, 1978, 146, 167), but however the resistance to federal involvement and Congressional obstacles to solving the issue of segregation are described, they were two of the hurdles legislation failed to surmount. So, particularly, in the case of education, was the use, or non-use, of federal funds for de-nominational – particularly Catholic parochial – schools. 'The tailoring of a school aid program', wrote one trade union commentator in 1961, 'is now a matter of practicalities rather than principles. The argument on principle is worn out'. Attempts to promote educational legislation in 1961 led to what has been described as a 'debacle' (A: Graham, 1984, 18–21). A 1962 attempt at legislation was abortive, and it was with the specific assignment to prepare a comprehensive education bill for 1963 that Francis Keppel was appointed Commissioner at the end of 1962. He inherited a situation of frustration and bitterness, particularly since the opposition of the National Education Association to the 1962 bill had also meant the defeat of proposals it contained relating to higher education (A: LBJ Lib, Keppel interview, 1968, 5–7).

The 1963 'omnibus' bill that emerged faced the same obstacles, but it was hoped that they were, after the experience of the previous year particularly, now more easily surmountable. Kennedy's own commitment to educational measures was growing. In 1961 he had set up a White House Panel to advise on research and development – and Keppel had been a member of the panel whilst at Harvard (A: Bruner, 1966, iii). At the same time, using the expertise of Wilbur Cohen and others, he had highlighted a range of domestic targets, including both medicare and education (A: Cohen, W., 1977, 189). Sorensen, who was centrally involved in many of these policy discussions, suggests that education was the domestic issue that meant most to Kennedy, the one to which he devoted most time, and one which – in spite of the setbacks of 1961–2 – attracted his increasing attention (A: Sorensen, 1965, 358). Within his administration. A policy emphasis was emerging, then, within his administration, which attempted to define directions resulting from the awareness of poverty, including the role of education in federal legislation. In 1963 Congress, and the framing of an educational bill for it, therefore assumed particular importance. When the bill was introduced in the Senate and the House in January 1963 Kennedy delivered a Special Message, which began: 'Education is the keystone in the arch of freedom and progress'. He underlined that 'ignorance and illiteracy, unskilled workers and school dropouts – these and other failures of our educational system breed failures in our social and economic system...' The time for debate about federal aid was past: 'we can no longer afford the luxury of endless debate over all the complicated and sensitive questions raised by each new proposal on federal participation in education'. The bill before Congress was intended, among other things, to expand 'special educational services' and improve education in 'slum, distressed and rural areas'. He was banking, therefore, on Congress giving approval to the proposed 'single, comprehensive education bill, the National Education Improvement Act of 1963' (A: Kennedy, 1963, 7–8).

In June Kennedy invited 250 educators to meet with him to discuss segregation and lack of opportunities for minorities – at a time of racial disturbances, and with Kennedy showing increasing interest in specific schemes – notably to solve the drop-out problem (A: Morse, 1963, 13–14). After Kennedy's assassination, and after the comprehensive bill had seen only some of its component parts survive through to legislation, the Office of Education called 1963 a year of 'gathering momentum' a 'pivotal and promising year for education' (A: US, HEW, 1963, 217). The 1963 bill did not, in fact, directly address questions of poverty and disadvantage. It addressed the expansion of opportunities in schools and higher education, the improvement of quality – to include improvements in teacher education, salaries, buildings – vocational education, special education, continuing education and libraries. When the bill came before the house Committee on Education and Labor in February, its chairman, Adam C. Powell, whose insistence on the prior solution of issues relating to segregation had helped to defeat previous bills, described education as 'democracy's most important business'. The US was becoming a second-class educational power and he hoped that the problem of church and state would be solved 'once and for all'. Failure once again to achieve agreement on federal assistance would mean the decline of the United States and the West in general. When the main personnel responsible for the bill (Secretary of Health, Education, and Welfare Anthony Celebrezze, Assistant Secretary Wilbur Cohen, and Commissioner Francis Keppel) appeared before the committee, their emphasis was on the comprehensive nature of the bill, the overcoming of various kinds of educational handicap, and the provision of equal opportunities for all citizens (A: US Congress, House, NEIA Hearings, 1963, 1–2, 61–71). A proposal relating to deprivation was in fact dropped in Congress. Out of the whole range of proposals in this broad approach to federal involvement, only those elements dealing with vocational education and assistance to higher education became acts of Congress, which adopted both in December 1963, and the Higher Education Facilities Act particularly underlined the need for colleges and universities to 'accommodate rapidly growing numbers of youth who aspire to a higher education' (A: US Congress, Public Law, 88–204, 1). The core of the educational policies being constructed in Kennedy's last year was to continue to be part of the administration's repertoire after his death, and to re-emerge rapidly in new shapes.

If the metaphor of a changed agenda was ever justified it was in relation to education in these Kennedy years. It was changed from a variety of directions. Education had become, and was increasingly becoming, part of what Allison Davis in 1962 called the mobilization against Russia (A: Davis, 1962, 28), and part of a heightened consciousness of the need to modernize and to solve basic social problems. The Kennedy period was one of reassertion and redefinition of liberal positions, though Lander has shown convincingly how the political left, including the small active socialist movement, managed to project issues during this period into the debate (A: Lander, 1967, 1968, 1971). The war on poverty, in the analysis of Daniel Moynihan who himself entered the debate at many points and in many guises from the 1960s, began to be shaped by the liberal intellectual community after it attained a measure of power under Kennedy in the early 1960s (A:

Moynihan, 1968, 6). There can be no doubt that the commitment of Kennedy himself helped to dictate the agenda priorities, and even those on the political left who suspected the direction of both Kennedy's and Johnson's policies gave Kennedy credit for boosting the confidence of the mid-1960s in education and social change (A: Harrington, 1965b, 27). In all these respects, suggested a Johnson biographer, Kennedy set the agenda for his successor (A: Kearns, 1976, 179). It is important to underline some of the ways in which the Kennedy period shaped salient emphases, and was itself conditioned by some of them.

The appointment of Keppel as Commissioner points towards some of the emphases and explanations. Keppel, as Dean of the Graduate School of Education at Harvard, brought with him some of the concerns and styles of Democratic liberalism. One thread in his experience that is relevant to this analysis was his awareness of the importance of the early childhood movement. Keppel had brought to Harvard as early as 1949 one of the key researchers in the field of child development, Robert R. Sears. Sears was not in the tradition of Hebb and Hunt that was to prove so crucial, but his emphases in the field of child rearing, parent education, the dependence of the child on the family environment and its values, all pointed to explanations of achievement and failure not very distant from those that were to become prominent in the 1960s (A: Sears *et al.*, 1957). The emphasis was above all on the child's behaviour as a product of his immediate social experience (A: Maier, 1965, ch. 4) and it was therefore only a short step to a concern about the nature of that experience and its limitations in specific situations. With support from the Rockefeller Foundation, Sears became head of a laboratory of Human Development at Harvard in the academic year 1949–50, and in his report on the Graduate School of Education the following year Keppel incorporated a lengthy account by Sears of its purposes and activities, ending with the following paragraph:

These various research activities of the Laboratory belong in the category of basic research. This is a deliberate choice on the part of the staff. The solution of social problems on anything more than an exigency basis depends on the discovery of the basic laws of behavior, both individual and social. Our current research reflects the conviction that the most efficient attack on practical education problems is determining the conditions under which children's behavior is modified. Once the main outlines of these conditions emerge, our task will be to discover the most practical ways in which such knowledge can be utilized by the schools. (A: Harvard University, 1950–1, 6–10)

Although Keppel was himself no expert in this field, he reflects on the Laboratory of Human Development that he knew of the research, heard discussion about it, knew of the 'very considerable evidence' of the influence of the early years on children's moral, physical and other development:

There wasn't as much information then as I think there is now, but it was certainly starting... Frankly, I wasn't all that impressed with the quality of the management and the personnel in the schools, and damn few of them knew anything about little children.

What Keppel brought to Washington, therefore, was a sense of the need to support programmes reaching out to younger children and therefore his support, when the time came for Head Start, not under the school system, but through the Office of Economic Opportunity. Asked if he was making the connection between early childhood and disadvantage before going to Washington, Keppel was cautious:

I'm not sure that they were going through my mind at the same time, but they may have been, that is, the children from poverty homes, broken homes, or homes with bad diet and everything else... There probably was something of that... I just sort of got it by the osmosis of being around at Harvard where research was being done on children below the school age... It was through Robert Sears, who had a sense of the kind of research that was going on to try to understand the mixture of physical and emotional experience and supports... (Keppel, interview)

This sense of child development in context, which Keppel shared with an increasing academic and professional community, was to prove vital to the events of 1964 and after. It was present from his appointment as Commissioner in November 1962, as one thread in the administration's commitment to educational advance. Immediately after Kennedy's death Keppel wrote a guest editorial in the *Saturday Review* under the title 'Into the Century of the Educated Man', in which he described Kennedy's strong personal interest in the development of the proposed legislation for 1963, in a climate of receding anti-intellectualism. In the 'new frontier' of liberal educational policy 'the climate for intellect had manifestly improved', and Kennedy and Keppel had discussed programmes 'that would encourage young people to study and to put academic excellence at the top of their own list of priorities' (A: Keppel, 1963, 267). Emerging in the stresses and strains of racial and other politics were federal policies which located the problems of school achievement in contexts now being subjected to research and debate.

Early childhood and child development were one element in that process, but equally significant in the Kennedy years was the growing interest in the implications of school failure, the relationship between schooling and employment, the incidence of juvenile crime and the question of school dropout strategies to motivate adolescents. In both the United States and Britain after the Second World War there was (as in the period during and after the First World War) public concern about the 'youth problem', with a considerable literature analysing the patterns of young people's behaviour and activities. The emphasis began to shift in the late 1950s, however, from an interest in cinema attendance, youth clubs and other pursuits to the explanation of deviant behaviour. The education editor of the *New York Times*, for example, wrote a graphic survey of the issues under the title *1,000,000 Delinquents*, examining the components of the breakdown of family and public forms of authority, and looking at a range of child-rearing, school and family strategies against potential delinquency. He rejected the harsh-treatment 'woodshed' approach to delinquency in favour of environmental understanding and community measures such as good housing and recreational facilities. All states and communities needed what some had already established – 'Youth Commissions to co-ordinate all antidelinquency activities' (B: Fine, 1956, 353). Only four years later Cloward and Ohlin, following this path of concern, published the most influential of the explanations of delinquency, and of its likely scale and impact.

Delinquency and Opportunity – sub-titled 'a theory of delinquent gangs' – tackled the question of how delinquent sub-cultures arise, how to explain the delinquent act. It analysed different types of delinquent sub-culture – based on criminal values, violence ('warrior groups') and drugs. The authors ascribed class differentials in the value attached to education largely to the availability of educational opportunities and the pressures of slum communities. The answer to delinquency was community reorganization, functional substitutes for violence, drugs and anomie (A: Cloward and Ohlin, 1960). Crime, and particularly juvenile and youth crime, was beginning to be discussed in terms of crisis. In parallel with emergent school and early childhood strategies there appeared a variety of attempts, particularly in the early 1960s, to analyse the roots of delinquency, and to mount projects which would explore possible solutions. Throughout these wider ripples of activity ran the environmental emphasis dominant in the Cloward and Ohlin analysis, an emphasis which – as with early childhood concerns – pointed towards the possibilities of forms of institutional or community intervention. The most important of the projects to be mounted, on the Lower East Side of New York, was Mobilization for Youth, planned from 1958 and funded by the City of New York, the Ford Foundation and the National Institute of Mental Health from 1962. It was 'the first comprehensive attempt to combat delinquency through intervention involving an entire community', a first step towards the community action programmes that were to be the cornerstone of the Economic Opportunity Act, and just as controversial (A: Brager and Purcell, 1967,

17–26). In the same direction as the Mobilization project, however, went federal action and legislation. The signals from the Ford inner city projects and the youth delinquency concerns were being picked up clearly at federal level, and in May 1961 a President's Committee on Juvenile Deliquency and Youth Crime had been established under the chairmanship of Robert Kennedy. The committee was itself much influenced by the work of Cloward and Ohlin, and sponsored a variety of projects on the Mobilization pattern, sharing with the Ford Foundation an emphasis on changing institutions, encouraging local leadership and looking to such areas as education, vocational training and community service for possible solutions (A: Frieden and Kaplan, 1977, 27–8). The search was uniformly one for intervention strategies which would undermine the attitudes and structures of the delinquent sub-cultures to which their members conformed, and which themselves related to the environmental and educational conditions under scrutiny at the same time.

Mobilization for Youth was held by some to be dangerously radical, and by others to have rapidly lost its way among the competing models and forces of action (A: Riessman, 1965a, 407). The Juvenile Delinquency and Youth Offenses Control Act of 1961, which empowered the President's Committee to fund pilot projects (including the proposed Mobilization project), was deemed by others to have failed, and to be bound to fail, as part of what radical critics saw as the 'much larger failure on the part of the government to solve the basic problems of poverty, unemployment, and discrimination' (A: Arnold, 1964, 351–2). Youth employment was to become a major issue in the debates surrounding the legislation of 1964 and 1965, but under the Kennedy administration the issue – if not the range of attempted solutions – had already become one of central importance. All of these areas of concern found a particular focus in the dropout problem.

Keppel remembers President Kennedy taking a personal interest in the problem in the spring of 1963, saying 'Why the hell doesn't somebody do something?'. As a result:

we started doing something or other. We got conferences and all sorts of things going on...I asked for some money from...the emergency fund, and the President unloosed $250,000 and did some tapes and some TV things. It worked, by the way. He had a kind of instinct that you could make an issue out of this and get some of these kids back in school...what he was concerned about was that the unemployed youth was social dynamite in this society...he started that whole business going. (Keppel interview, 1964, 12–13)

On this basis a campaign was launched, and Keppel reported on it a year later. It had been launched on an emergency basis with presidential funds 'on the theory that the failure of so many Americans to gain a high school education was a sufficient national emergency to warrant some extraordinary step to call the Nation's attention to the problem'. The move was intended to encourage state and local school authorities to mount similar programs of their own:

By the large I believe last summer's program had the intended effect... A check of twenty-one of the larger cities that participated in the program last summer indicates that twelve of them... have succeeded in obtaining funds for some form of special summer dropout program this summer.

The intention was to collect data on the reasons for dropouts, attitudes towards school, and ways of motivating youngsters to remain in or return to school: 'The 1963 crash program had one decided effect: It stirred up the troops and brought some results' (A: LBJ Lib, Keppel memo to Lee C. White, 12 June 1964, Gen Ed). Correspondence from Keppel and White House aides confirms the confidence that this first year of the dropout programme generated. Cities, schools, community organizations, churches and others responded by mounting summer programmes for disadvantaged youngsters. Announcing the programme in August 1963 President Kennedy explained it in these terms: around a million youngsters would either not return to high school the following September, or would fail to complete the school year.

We're now talking about the lives of a million young American boys and girls who will fail to meet their educational requirements in the next few months unless we do something about it... I'm asking school principals, clergymen, trade union leaders, business leaders, everyone in this country to concern themselves.

The funds would be primarily to appoint guidance counsellors 'to see if we can get some of these boys and girls back to school. They will appreciate any effort we make for the rest of their lives' (A: LBJ Lib, *Philadelphia Inquirer*, 2 August 1963, WH Aides, Panzer). A press release by Lyndon Johnson in December 1963 suggested that the results had been far better than expected: 'we still have to learn our way in this type of activity... But one conclusion is justified. Any community in America that wants to lick the drop-out problem can do so if a real effort is made locally.' Examples were offered from a variety of cities suggesting that the different means employed had resulted in a fall in the numbers dropping out (A: Press release, 1 January 1964, WH Aides, Panzer).

Here, as in other areas of intervention in the early 1960s, short-term outcomes could easily generate such optimism. How incautious some of the conclusions drawn from these activities were, and how confused such activities might look from the social science base of some of the participants, can be deduced from a description of some of his involvements by sociologist S.M. Miller. In the late 1950s he increasingly addressed questions of poverty:

I moved to the Youth Development Center at Syracuse, which was in '61. I decided that I would work on dropout youth, and employment problems of young black males. That was really when my serious interest began. The first paper I did was for a conference in Washington on school dropouts, for Dan Schreiber... who had been a school superintendent in New York City and left for a couple of years to run a Project Dropout for the National Education Association... They held a conference in Washington with Paul Goodman, Edgar Friedenberg, Martin Mayer... this first paper I wrote was on types of dropouts, it was an influential paper because it tried to discriminate among different types of situations, and also emphasized the employment side rather than the psychological side of these issues... I did some empirical work in Syracuse on school dropouts, wrote some other things that were published in small circulation... I wrote an enormous number of short memos and papers, most of which I think weren't published, but which I sent around to people I knew who were growingly influential in foundations and in Washington. And I was close to some of the people on the staff of the President's Committee on JD... some of them went over to OEO...

Miller had no official position in these connections and became what he called 'more of a gadfly raising issues, and early on, I think in that very first types-of-dropout paper, I raised the issue of credentialism' (Miller, interview). At this level of activity, as with the work on early childhood, specialists were being attracted to analyse and conduct research, at the same time as major policy directions were being decided around them.

What we are witnessing in this period, therefore, is an accelerating process of research, policy-making and action, interwoven with a variety of attitudes, assumptions, concepts and theories which an increasing number of people, coming from many directions, were trying to make explicit, articulate or debate. Concern about poverty, its components and implications, had become public property. Kennedy, his administration, and the processes at work through the early 1960s, had made education an increasingly important domestic issue in the United States. Poverty analysis and proposed solutions were receiving increased publicity and public attention, particularly from 1962. The bibliography of work on poverty was expanding sharply from 1960 (A: Aaron, 1978, 17; Congress, House, Committee on Education and Labor, 1964, 224–7). By 1964 the House Committee reporting on *Poverty in The United States* was able to review and use that literature, as part of its analysis of the nature and extent of poverty, and its anticipation of Lyndon Johnson's forthcoming message that was to 'describe the new attack and propose specific programs' (*ibid.*, 18). The struggle was to translate the 'discovery' of poverty into interpretations and pro-grammes, and both proved more complex than the excitements of the early responses suggested.

Part of the problem was the depth of the shock felt by those encountering the situation and the problems for the first time. When, with government support, a doctoral fellow joined the Early Training Project at Nashville, Tennessee, she did her dissertation field work in Cahoma County, Mississippi, and what she found was

an extreme poverty area out in the country, and I personally had never seen poverty as I viewed it down there. I just didn't realize it existed. I think I was not unlike most people in our country from the middle class, who realized that there were people that were poorer than I, but we didn't realize that people were starving, literally, that babies were dying of starvation, that babies were dying of cold weather, because their homes were in such a horrible condition. It was really quite a shock for most of us. (Foster, interview)

In the search for explanations and solutions other problems, often grounded in inexplicit or ill-formulated attitudes and assumptions, quickly surfaced. How extensive was the problem? What counted as poverty? How might explanations reconcile problems that seemed psychological with those related to traditions, physical environment, opportunity, discrimination, employment...? Analyses based on theories of social class were, as we have seen, politically sensitive in the 1950s and, in fact, S.M. Miller and David Riessman wrote a study for which they were unable to find a publisher as a book but which became a series of influential articles, widely reprinted. By the early sixties class was becoming a more frequently used analytical instrument, though not without substantial opposition (Miller, interview). By 1963 the Year-book of the National Society for the Study of Education, on the theme of child psychology, could contain a paper on 'Achievement' devoted to reviewing social-class influences on children's development, and the relationships between social class and parental expectations and values (A: Crandall, 1963). Prominent in the controversies about the relationship between class and poverty, and the social and cultural manifestations of both, was the concept of the 'culture of poverty' which Oscar Lewis had projected into the discussion from the end of the 1950s:

the culture of poverty is both an adaptation and a reaction of the poor to their marginal position in a class-stratified, highly individuated, capitalistic society. It represents an effort to cope with feelings of hopelessness and despair that develop from the realization of the improbability of achieving success in terms of the values and goals of the larger society (A: Lewis, O. 1968, 188).

We shall return to the problems encountered in the early and mid-sixties in handling this and related concepts, but what they indicated was a continuing ambiguity about attitudes to the feelings and aspirations of the poor and to the values, goals and power structures of the larger society. Much of the controversy of the next few years was to revolve around that ambiguity.

There were other problems of interpretation and attitude. In the United States as in Britain discussion was taking shape around the question of the linguistic impoverishment of the poor, with attempts to understand the relationship between language and education and social structure often being reduced to simplistic terms, as in the case of one 1963 account by a reading specialist of the US Office of Education:

Hugh?...unh-hunh...nuttin...naw...wuh?...'cuz...unh-unh...sho! Is this a readiness-for-reading vocabulary? Definitely not! Yet, unfortunately, these 'words,' with variations for emphasis and inflection – plus a few other one-word sentences and a generous sprinkling of vulgarities – comprise the speaking vocabulary of many culturally disadvantaged first graders. These and other strange noises that take the place of standard American English reflect the impoverished language background of these children... The above is not to say that culturally disadvantaged children cannot communicate with each other. Some of them have developed 'scat' language to a high level of fluency... teachers need to approach English language instruction for these children as if they were teaching a foreign language. (A: Cutts, 1963, 23)

Crude and controversial though such portrayals were, they reflected the awareness that children were entering school without the linguistic and conceptual apparatus to handle the school's processes and debate was to intensify around the question of 'blame'. Accounts of the cultural disadvantages of the poor contained what some critics saw as blame levelled at the poor themselves, rather than at the system which failed them. Typical of the concerned analysis underlying policy moves in the early and mid-sixties was one by Wilbur Cohen, a key figure in the education and welfare policy process. Poverty, he emphasized, had been responsible for a high rejection rate for military service on grounds of low physical and mental ability. Those born into poverty were 'stunted in emotional, intellectual and social development', and a concentrated, simultaneous attack on the problems was needed on many fronts, continuing a range of policy directions begun in the 1930s. Stimulation, motivation, better housing, urban renewal...these were the ways to tackle the bleak world of poverty (A: Cohen, W., 1964, 3–9). As many were pointing out, however, such analyses, liberal and well-intentioned as they were, underestimated the failures and responsibilities of public institutions, and especially the schools. An example of the attempt to divert attention away from the family and child towards the school, written the same year, suggested that the competitive styles of the classroom were 'completely inconsistent with the facts of life on the street. It is not individual against individual; it is gang against gang'. Failure in school was public and omnipresent: 'everyone knows who flunked the test'. What the schools were in fact saying to children was – 'We don't like you and we don't like your families – and we suspect you don't have a decent family anyway' (A: Grambs, 1965, 38–41). The range of attitudes towards poverty and the poor was finding expression in a very extensive debate now taking place in a large number of educational journals, occasional publications, and the press widely. Some of it, particularly in the work of such writers as Frank Riessman and Kenneth B. Clark, was attempting to draw attention to the belittled strengths of the poor, and particularly of the black family and community, for whom 'poor' was often a euphemism. The Baltimore schools were being reminded in 1963 that 'the key issue in looking at the strengths of the inner city child is the importance of not confusing difference with defect', and that the family of the inner city child was marked by a high degree of cooperation and mutual aid. These group values had 'an extremely potent motivating force if you can tackle them and put them together', and the ways children had to negotiate life in the slums produced characteristics on which schools needed to learn how to build (A: Eisenberg, 1963–4). The distinction between difference and deficit, and the value to be placed on the cultural characteristics of the working-class or poor child, were to produce prolonged controversy from these early years of the 1960s.

It is important to emphasize that whilst much of this discussion of the poor related directly to the condition of black America, it was not exclusively so, particularly in the early stages of the growing public interest. Much of the discussion, and many of the projects, were directed at the disadvantage visible in the urban ghettos. Migration and related factors were not solely a black phenomenon, although the economic and social conditions and public voices of protest of black Americans inevitably identified them most with the salient problems here under discussion. Even when the civil rights and other movements of black and other minority populations were dormant their potential could have a basic political impact. Democratic liberalism particularly was conscious of both the principles that needed to be pursued, and the political price to be paid for not pursuing them – in terms particularly of loss of black support for the Democratic party. Cloward and Piven have analysed the eruption of legislation for the cities in the 1960s as an outcome of political realignments resulting from black migration, and pressures for change from blacks who now had votes. The volatile, crucial black vote was, in their view, at the heart of Kennedy's strong stand on civil rights, and the networks of new agencies that emerged in the early 1960s were 'merely structural reflections of political concessions' (A: Cloward and

Piven, 1975, 272–82). Whatever the motivations – and they were probably more complex than such an account suggests – it was most frequently against the backdrop of the politics of race that the concepts of cultural deprivation or compensatory education were seen.

The ambiguities inherent in the concepts and the attitudes they reveal were obvious from the outset, and became increasingly so by the middle of the decade. Kenneth B. Clark, a black psychologist and prominent contributor to the national debates, spoke in 1965 on 'The cult of cultural deprivation': 'Probably there is no issue in American education which is being discussed more today than the issue of the education of the culturally deprived'. The educational retardation of Negro children, he continued, was a well-known and documented fact in the public schools of Northern cities, and he traced – here as in other writings – the changing explanations for that retardation:

Historically, among the earliest explanations was that the poor performance of these youngsters was to be accounted for in terms of their inherent racial inferiority ... it is no longer fashionable for educators to talk about the academic performance of Negro youngsters in racial terms, or in terms of inherent racial differences.

Clark went on, however, to argue that the change in explanations had not removed from schools educational practices based on old assumptions, and to point to the weaknesses of the theory of cultural deprivation which had grown out of the liberal tradition. There had in the early 1960s been enough projects to demonstrate that 'if human beings are taught, by and large they learn. And if they are not taught they do not learn. When they do not learn we find all kinds of alibis to explain why they are not learning' (A: Clark, K.B., 1965). Clark's argument placed cultural deprivation as a phase in the undermining of traditional explanations and attitudes. The net was being cast more widely, however, to take in discussion about the structure and content of education itself. In doing so, educators were constantly reminded of white poverty and the diversity of the 'new poor' – Harrington's 'internal aliens', the old, the unemployed, those displaced by automation (A: Harrington, 1965a, vi–viii). The Appalachian rural poor continued to feature prominently in the discussion and, indeed, in a 1964 article on 'The politics of poverty', Douglas Cater rested his argument about categories of the poor and projections for an automated future on the Appalachian areas of eastern Kentucky, western Pennsylvania and western Tennessee, without mention of the deep South or the black areas of Northern cities (A: Cater, 1968; O'Hara, 1963). When the House Committee on Education and Labor conducted its detailed survey of *Poverty in the United States* in 1964, it in no way saw the 'poor' as a euphemism for 'black'. In the circumstances of the inner cities the euphemistic interchange of 'poor' and 'black' did indeed often occur. Ambiguities of attitude and interpretation were to be found in the projects and programmes that abounded in the early 1960s – ambiguities often concealed by the strength of the confidence and the earnestness of the endeavour. The problems related not only to definitions of the target population or assumptions about environmental or school inputs and intended outcomes. It was not only that it was difficult to present the grand design; it was difficult on the ground to interpret the impact of chosen strategies. New York City's Higher Horizons programme illustrates the position clearly.

Begun in 1956 as a Demonstration Guidance Project in a single junior high school, the project initially set out to institute a programme for the 'early identification and stimulation of able students who are not now identified...a program to overcome the stifling of education motivation in children from families struggling economically and without an educational tradition' (A: Schreiber, 1961, 3). It was a saturation programme, based primarily on ideas of cultural enrichment, and the success of the project led to its expansion to become Higher Horizons in 1959. The expanded programme covered thirteen junior high schools and services to thirty-one elementary schools which fed them. The programme was adapted to provide for all children, 'bright, average and slow, unlike the Demonstration Guidance Project which was concerned primarily with the academically talented'. The objectives for the new programme included the identification of children's abilities and interests, stimulus and support, the raising of children's cultural sights by experiences not otherwise available, appropriate teacher training, and the involvement of parents and community agencies (ibid., 4–5). The report at the end of the first year of operation was enthusiastic about what had been achieved in relation to children, parents and teachers, reporting substantial gains, for example in reading scores, by comparison with non-Higher Horizon schools (ibid., 15–18). Accounts of the project report enthusiasm and improved morale (A: Shaw, 1963; Wrightstone, 1964) but also difficulties arising from the wider and less intensive distribution of resources, and the failure to sustain the project beyond 1966. It was clearly seen at the time as an important breakthrough and influential project, a model adopted by other cities and pivotal in the developments associated with the Ford Foundation and what followed from them (A: Kaplan, 1963, 70; Ribich, 1968, 63–8). The outcomes of this pioneer scheme of compensatory education were, however, perceived in different ways. The programme coordinator and others saw the results in 1961 as encouraging (A: Schreiber, 1961; Krugman, 1961,

23–4); Riessman described them the following year as an outstanding success (A: Riessman, 1961, 99). Martin Mayer publicized the scheme in 1961 in his widely read book *The Schools*, seeing it as a fine achievement not unmixed with serious problems: he was impressed with the range of visits made by the pupils to colleges, hospitals, plays, the opera, the Roosevelt home, shops, parks and football games (and at some institutions 'saw Negroes and Puerto Ricans getting a higher education'). He was also clear about the failures involved in what the coordinator called 'trying to instil middle-class values into lower-class kids', with the inevitable impact on the homes, and the frustrations for many children in trying to cope with the programme, and the social adjustments implied (A: Mayer, 1961, 130–7). Some commentators saw the project as a model for elementary schools in the South (A: Brazziel, 1964) but others took up the theme of schools attempting to 'make the poor like us', or pointed to its expensive and limited nature, fine on paper but rarely, if ever, fully effective (A: Olsen, 1965, 83; Ornstein, 1965, 106–7). Judgment was coloured by the choice of criterion, and controversy surrounded the declared cultural and particularly scholastic objectives, and the problems involved in evaluating such a complex operation on the basis of tests (A: Wrightstone, 1960). Attendance, morale, aspiration, motivation, parental attitude, community support...none of these was easy to interpret, and the relationship between achievement and resources was assumed rather than explored. Fred Hechinger, writing in *The New York Times* on the demise of Higher Horizons, described the failure to estimate the real costs of expanding the initial project successfully, and the failure to support the attractive programme of visits with adequate means of sustaining 'everyday educational effort, with constant reinforcement by good teachers, in small classes or even in individual instruction' (A: Miller, H.L., 1967, 168–70). There was no difficulty in identifying worthy aims and positive outcomes but it was not easy to agree on the ultimate aims, and the means of achieving them.

The crucial feature of the projects taking place in the late 1950s and early 1960s was their cumulative impact. Efforts to link in practice, the aims of education and the elimination of disadvantage resulting from poverty or race, achieved considerable publicity. The range of projects was considerable. Some took, for example, the path of 'talent search'. The progenitor of much of this kind of policy and action was Project Talent, which began as a research project of the American Institute for Research and the University of Pittsburgh in 1958, sampling high school students to determine the factors which governed educational accomplishment. Initial findings indicated that 20 per cent of the high school students in the top quarter of attainment did not enter college, and 15 per cent or so of those with IQs of 120 or over did not continue their education for financial reasons (A: Flanagan, 1964; Keppel, 1966, 23). Initiatives were taken at many levels to identify talented students and to establish programmes which would encourage and help them to enter higher education – New York's Demonstration Guidance Project, and Kennedy's dropout programme being at least partly in this mould. Scholarships of various kinds were created, including a National Achievement Scholarship in 1964, funded by the Ford Foundation, to support black high school students wishing to enter college. Yale University, like many other institutions, established a summer programme:

In response to the call in 1963 by President Kennedy for institutions of higher education to bring their resources to bear in the attempt of the nation to solve the complex of problems arising from racial discrimination in the United States, Yale University, with the assistance of the National Science Foundation, the Ford Foundation, and several other philanthropies, and in conjunction with Hampton Institute, established in 1964 the Yale Summer High School...to provide to one hundred able boys who were being held back by the interwoven burdens of cultural deprivation, educational disadvantage, and economic hardship, an intensive educational experience...(A: FF, Yale, Report, 1965, i)

The Independent Schools Talent Search programme brought in colleges like Dartmouth and Amherst, running summer programmes and supporting talented boys and girls for a three or four year college preparatory programme at private preparatory schools, over 1,400 being so placed in the years 1964–9 (A: William Jewitt Tucker Foundation, n.d.). The legislative and other developments of the mid-1960s put these initiatives into perspective as limited contributions to the main policy thrust, and resting on increasingly questioned assumptions about the objectives of such selective strategies.

The impact of single projects could be far-reaching, and none more so than that in the Banneker district of St Louis, Missouri. Dr Samuel Shepard, Assistant Superintendent in charge of the schools in this black district of the city, began from 1957 to try to raise achievement generally in the schools. Shepard was black, a charismatic person, with very clear ideas about what he wished to achieve and how to set about it. He took personal charge of a district-wide project to improve reading scores, bring the schools into closer contact with the homes, and dramatically increase children's motivation by a variety of means (including a Mr Achiever programme by which children were introduced, in person or on the radio, to black adults describing their work). Although Shepard denied any 'wild claims' for the project (A: Shepard, 1964, 18) the message rapidly circulated that much was in fact being achieved. Children's attendance rate was apparently rising markedly, collaboration between teacher and parent was taking place in a number of new ways, and increased achievement by the children was being registered, particularly in reading (A: Asbell, 1966; Friggens, 1964; Shepard, 1964; Crow *et al.*, 1966). As the educational movement of the early 1960s took shape Shepard was invited to speak at meetings, and Banneker became a familiar point of reference in the developing literature. The evidence seemed to point, as Kenneth B. Clark saw it in 1965, to important changes by simple means: there had been in Banneker no major changes of curriculum, instructional techniques or the children's social background, but improvements were 'definitely evident'. He later underlined that there had been no evidence of change in the cultural background of the children, but in the classroom, with an 'intensive, yet inexpensive and relatively uncomplicated approach', the median in reading had risen. The children, although still 'culturally deprived', were now either up to or above grade levels. The basic change had been in the attitude of the teachers, and established explanations of retardation were thereby being overturned (A: Clark, K.B., 1965b, 143–4; 1969, 34–5).

Someone who participated in the Banneker project from the beginning describes what was happening on the ground. She was a teacher of reading, one of the additional resources provided for these schools by the city budget (though Shepard also raised outside funds, including funds from Rockefeller for an after-school programme). Shepard visited all the schools, explaining his aims to the teachers and administrators, emphasizing the need to improve children's achievement and producing charts to show the relative league tables of each school in comparison with others in the district and the city. He stressed the need for teachers to visit the homes in order to establish relationships within which parents would more comfortably be able to visit the schools. Many of the middle-class teachers were 'hesitant or fearful', but the visits took place, and meetings of parents were well attended. Shepard introduced a 'parents' pledge' by which they undertook, in public, to provide their children with dictionaries, space in the home, and various other kinds of support. Workshops for parents and training sessions for teachers were introduced. To reduce the social distance between teacher and home, Shepard urged the teachers not to come to school in large cars. Responsibility for administering and reporting on tests was at first given to individual schools, but the substantial gains claimed proved less impressive when a centralized system of testing was introduced. As districts were reorganized in response to desegregation requirements, the Banneker district as such no longer existed after 1965, and the introduction of Title I federal funding from the same period put the kind of work introduced by Shepard on to a new footing. Shepard himself moved to a post in Chicago.

The witness for the above details, herself at first a teacher of reading in the district, then a principal, and later a Title I administrator, was clear that there was no systematic evidence for any changes of attitude as a result of the project, but argued from her experience that teachers' attitudes to children and to parents did change. She was also aware of the considerable national attention being given to the project, and visitors to observe the schools were frequent during this period. The evidence ultimately of gains in children's reading and other scores proved flimsy or controversial, but judged in other terms the project was both exciting and influential (Langley, interview). As with other interventionist projects, the claims for its outcomes were seen both as evidence of a striking success, and as illusory: 'If you knew these schools, the Sam Shepard claims sound unreal' (Berlak, interview). Ambiguity and controversy were never far away from the enthusiasm of projects such as this. Characteristic of the situation was a joint effort by the St Louis Human Development Corporation and the Graduate Institute of Education at Washington University, St Louis, to report on the feasibility of an extended investigation of the Banneker schools and project in 1965. The feasibility report was in essence ambivalent. There were considerable obstacles – most of them attributable to pressures on schools and administrators – to investigating the schools, but it was not impossible to do so. The report outlined what was known about the schools and the particular role of Dr Shepard, but Arthur G. Wirth was unable to recommend a study of the history of the project itself. Three scheduled interviews had been cancelled by Shepard, and a fourth could not be arranged in the time scale available: 'Dr. Shepard's secretary indicated no written records existed other than a two-page mimeographed summary already on file at Washington University'. Although Wirth believed a study of the general background of the Banneker project was feasible, 'his conclusion regarding the narrower focus – the historical analysis of the Banneker educational program – was more pessimistic. He found no assurance that either the contacts or the data for a long-range study would be available' (A: Charters, 1965, 10–11). The lack of reliable data was to continue to be a salient feature of projects of all kinds throughout the 1960s.

By the time the war on poverty and the major educational legislation relating to its purposes were framed in 1964 and 1965, a plethora of local, city-wide and state-wide initiatives along these and other lines had been produced. From 1961 the Philadelphia public schools, for example, were testing the hypothesis that 'children of limited background could be helped to raise their academic achievement if they were provided with an educational program designed to reduce the effects of marginal living conditions and the lack of experiential supports to learning'. The programme emphasized language arts and the in-service training of teachers, innovations in teaching and materials, changes in the grouping of children and a variety of different kinds of evaluation (A: Wilkerson, 1965, 429). In 1961 the *NEA Journal* was reporting on the Ford-supported school-work project in St Louis, and evidence that fewer boys and girls were dropping out of the project group than out of a control group (A: Brotman, 1961). The following year, between January and March, it reported on a series of 'Stirrings in the Big Cities'. In Chicago it looked at a number of projects particularly at the elementary school level, involving parents in meetings and in classes, the expansion of teacher education placements in Chicago schools, and summer pro-grammes. From Detroit it reported on the Ford Great Cities project, and the local establishment of advisory committees for a high school World of Work programme, school-supervised work experience, and related job guidance and research projects. In Boston it found early support and bilingual programmes, an Operation Second Chance programme for boys identified as potential dropouts, a pre-appren-ticeship programme, and others (A: Siebert, 1962; Lee, 1962; Cunningham, 1962). Chicago was experimenting in 1962 with com-pulsion on able-bodied welfare recipients who were 'undereducated' to attend classes or forfeit their welfare payments. So popular was the scheme by 1963, apparently, that it had been considerably extended and the compulsory element withdrawn as unnecessary (A: Brooks, 1963). Chicago was reporting annually on its various strategies to respond to the needs of 'newcomer' populations, which included 'the Spanish-speaking people from Mexico and Puerto Rico and the Negro and white people from rural and urban sections of the South'. The basic philosophy so far as schools were concerned was that a classroom, 'in order to be democratically conducted, must involve pupils, teachers, and also parents' (A: Chicago Public Schools, 1964, 15, 130). Many such reports were of dedication and enthusiasm, none of them was able to report sustained analysis of the experience. Reporting on a research project in Quincy, Illinois, on the school experience of culturally handicapped children, a professor at the University of Chicago explained the purposes of a modification programme being implemented: to improve understanding of the child, to provide a richer background of intellectually stimulating experiences through the better use of community resources and school facilities, and to enlist parent support. The first year's results could already be reported, in terms of parent involvement and other outcomes, but a more structured approach to the project was becoming necessary across the four schools taking part. The project was described as an 'action programme', and the report explains:

In the scientific study of education there are times for rigorous controlled comparisons between two approaches, but we did not feel that we were at this point yet. Rather we felt that we would gain more if we ranged more widely in our explorations ... we are not carrying out a uniform program in each of the four schools, but rather are attempting to find success-producing techniques in a school, and then extend this technique to as many other schools as find it appropriate. (A: Liddle, 1963, 26)

This distinction between 'rigour' and 'exploration', between the action and the research components of action research, and the difficulty of establishing exactly what constituted 'success', were to reappear in many forms in both the United States and Britain.

As the scale of the projects and programmes, and then of legislation and federal involvement, grew, questions of evaluation and systematic report inevitably became more prominent. State initiatives were either based on federal developments, or, like the McAteer Act in California, meshed in with the federal decisions which followed swiftly on their heels (compensatory projects under the McAteer policies were under-way in 1963 and were drawing three-quarters of their funding from federal sources in 1965). However sporadic and unsatisfactory much of the early reporting and evaluation material proved to be – including, in the early stages, under federal enactment – the intentions of the educational campaigns and projects seemed both clear and productive. Children were apparently learning more effectively. The special treatment designed for the children and communities of the poor seemed to pay educational dividends. A range of experience and good practice was being built up. Schools and educators were being brought into closer touch with the realities and needs of the urban and rural poor, migrant populations, the aspirations of the racially and economically oppressed, the unrecognized or unfulfilled potential of the disadvantaged child.

Across this period of the late 1950s and early 1960s the underlying mood of the emergent pattern of educational action and policy was one of confidence. The central emphasis on environmental handicap and its attendant social, cultural and educational features produced a diversity of programmes and activities pointing in a similar direction, urging that demands for political rights, for civil rights, for economic and social measures, were inseparable from the proposed educational solutions. Robert Owen and the cooperators and early socialists in Britain, and their communitarian offspring and allies in the United States, had said something similar in the 1830s, for example. Political reform, the Owenite movement underscored, was irrelevant without social re-organization. The educational reformers and the support they rapidly gained in the 1960s were announcing that none of the other rights would be of real benefit if masses of people remained imprisoned in their environmental constraints. The tension was in part to be translated into terms of compensatory education and/or desegregation.

A major new basis for federal involvement in educational reform had been laid, founded on the confidence of the interventionist message. Children previously labelled as problem children, retarded, slow learners, underprivileged and under-achievers, wrote Hilda Taba in the important issue of the *Merrill-Palmer Quarterly* in April 1964, were now more usefully being described as culturally deprived. She hoped this would not prove just another euphemism, but that it indicated 'a new statement of the problem we are facing and a new approach to it. The previous designations described only the difficulties of such a group in school. "Cultural deprivation" points to a possible cause of the phenomenon' (A: Taba, 1964, 147). The explanations and experience seemed to offer a basis for more sustained and more widespread action. Not everyone, of course, was convinced, and the interpretations did not necessarily converge. A review of a decade of commentaries on education published in 1966 showed an immense range of responses to the new programmes and policies – from the most positive to the most cynical (A: Smith [1966]). Congressmen Quie was engaged in promoting the concept of *educational* disadvantage in the mid-1960s in opposition to what he considered the unpersuasive arguments deriving from *poverty* criteria: 'poverty was a fad at that time' (Quie, interview).

In the two or three years before the declaration of the war on poverty, however, there were enough confident messages being received to provide starting points for the policies being formulated in the last days of the Kennedy administration and the early Johnson years. Two examples will illustrate sources of confidence and energy available to those who orchestrated the next phase of development. In 1961, an associate superintendent of schools in New York City wrote about the Demonstration Guidance Project and Higher Horizons that 'the results are heartening'. Could schools compensate for 'the meager backgrounds that children from deprived social and economic homes bring into the classroom? The answer must be a clear "yes"' (A: Krugman, 1961). The coordinator of New York State's Project ABLE, on leave to help with the NEA Project on School Dropouts, wrote two years later of the value of what came to be called reverse discrimination (or positive discrimination in Britain following the Plowden report of 1967): for disadvantaged youngsters it could be argued that '*equal* educational opportunity... does not necessarily mean the same *kind* of education; in most cases, it means equal *plus* more of the same in greater depth, quality, and appropriateness'. Those reluctant to commit resources in that way could now be reassured that 'almost without fail, these programs bring sparkling dividends which benefit the rest of the school program and the wider community' – and this was true of programmes at pre-kindergarten, pre-college and every other level. He cited in support evidence from a considerable range of cities and states of the Union (A: Kaplan, 1963). Practitioners and administrators were relaying the message as well as academics and researchers. The educational and social science agenda had been profoundly changed since the mid-1950s, and the conflicts and aspirations of the Kennedy years had set the scene for a new federal politics and wider policy concerns.

4   Learning their way out of poverty?

President Johnson is reported to have described the educational programme of his War on Poverty, at a planning meeting, in the following terms:

This is going to be an education program. We are going to eliminate poverty with education ... This is not going to be a handout, this is going to be something where people are going to *learn* their way out of poverty. (A: Ashline *et al.* 1976, xvii)

Accurate or not, the reported comment encapsulates the mood that Johnson inherited and to which he gave his authority. In his Message on Poverty to Congress on 16 March 1964 he announced the goal. There were immense opportunities, there was unfinished work to be accomplished: 'To finish that work I have called for a national war on poverty. Our objective: total victory' (A: Ferman, 1965, 426). In his Message on Education to Congress the following year, Johnson announced the forthcoming education bill as having 'a national goal of full educational opportunity', targeted particularly at the children of low-income families: 'poverty has many roots but the taproot is ignorance'. He told America again in January 1965: 'we must start where men who would improve their society have always known they must begin – with an educational system restudied, reinforced, and revitalized' (A: US Congress, House, Committee on Education and Labor, 1965, 2–10). The aims and means for conducting the war were quickly adopted and made explicit by Johnson and his administration. His Vice-President, Hubert Humphrey, summarized the theme in 1964, with metaphors and concepts embodying assumptions that now had common currency in policy-making circles:

... increased investments in education are the key to the door through which the poor can escape from poverty. Education enriches the entire community, the whole nation. It enables us to lift the economic and cultural floor of our nation – so that even the relatively poor may not be as poor as their forefathers. (A: Humphrey, 1964, 141)

We have considered some of the sources of such assumptions and destinations and means of arrival. Within the federal machine the signals we have indicated in the last chapter were running strong. Although the 1964 Economic Opportunity Act ('to eliminate the paradox of poverty in the midst of plenty') did not include the preschool explicitly among its targets, the Office of Economic Opportunity it created under Kennedy's brother-in-law, Sargent Shriver, rapidly went in that direction and produced the Head Start programme. Johnson's 1965 Message, outlining what was to become the Elementary and Secondary Education Act, referred to the 'marked success' demonstrated by preschool programmes in New York City and Baltimore. We are not concerned in detail with why these signals proved so irresistible to Johnson and his advisers, but it is important to identify some of the components involved. Why a war, and why this war?

We have traced elements in the pressures for social and political change. In the background were the implications of the growing civil rights movement, in the early 1960s, population growth and re-distribution, unemployment and juvenile delinquency, the inadequacies of school facilities and provision, and the variety of interpretations of poverty and its relationship to economic and social issues. There was also, as we have seen, the surprise and disappointment at the discovery of the extent of poverty, and the alarm at the mounting paradox of poverty amidst plenty. Kennedy had looked for expanded educational effort knowing that there were federal resources that could be devoted to the effort if the political and religious obstacles to federal involvement could be overcome. Productivity was rising, but its benefits were being unequally distributed. The Council of Economic Advisers considered in January 1964 that 'the fruits of general economic growth have been widely shared', but poverty remained a 'bitter reality for too many Americans' and a major effort was needed to make progress against the remaining level of poverty (A: US Congress, House, Committee on Education and Labor, 1964, 33). Johnson and his administration were well aware that in significant ways poverty was different in the 1960s from what it had been in the Depression years of the 1930s. Johnson's own account of this difference pointed to the Depression years as having been concerned 'mainly with educated and trained people who had been temporarily dislocated by the sickness of the economy' whereas

the poverty of the 1960s, the paradoxical poverty in the midst of plenty, was of another breed. The economy was booming. Jobs were plentiful, but the unemployed were incapable of filling them. The most significant aspects of this new poverty, once the spotlight of attention was thrown on it, were the dismaying nature of its stubborn entrenchment and the total entrapment of its victims from one generation to the next.

A man was poor if he had too little money, but he also had inadequate education, medical care and nutrition, and had no real chance to train for a job – a cycle which he handed on to his children (A: Johnson, 1972, 72–3). The focus on educational weaknesses and potentials in a period of apparently unending economic growth is therefore easy to detect and to understand.

Also clear is the constant reference back from issues such as income, unemployment and education to the race issue. Poverty, argued sociologist Nathan Glazer in 1965, was an issue in America – unlike in Britain at that time, with which he was drawing comparisons and contrasts – precisely because it was a race issue, because the civil rights movement had made it one, and because the United States did not have federal, government and bureaucratic structures within which to formulate responses and solutions of the kind possible in Britain and other countries (A: Glazer, 1965a, 77–9). Two strategies available in the accepted traditions of American social reform were to legislate for civil rights – and this was to be a major policy direction of 1964 – and to promote sustained economic growth. The combination of these and related measures was to promote both the war on poverty and the outcome which Johnson postulated – the Great Society. Education was a key element in promoting growth and solving social problems. There was a cost to be paid in economic and human terms for failure to act – and the relationship between the educational and social strategies chosen and the computable costs of success and failure was never far distant from the policy arguments. It seemed possible to make the necessary investment in the context of economic growth – which was therefore to benefit education and to benefit from it. A participant observer in the White House processes described Johnson as 'retaining to the end a belief that so long as the Gross National Product continued to rise, all conflict could be contained' (A: Kearns, 1976, 189). Education was in some respects, therefore, one of the coins with which consensus might be bought.

It was other things, however. It was also part of the liberal tradition, and the whole war on poverty can be interpreted as a liberal reform programme whose time had come. The 'war', and Johnson's anxiety to be seen as the 'education president' (A: Kearns, 1976, 230), were the expression of his understanding that Kennedy's assassination, coupled with the political and economic conditions he inherited and could now shape, were the opportunity for major reforms in that liberal tradition. In education alone (including such areas as health and nurse training) Johnson was to leave office with 'under his belt some sixty education bills' (A: LBJ Lib. Halperin interview, 1969, 3). As one observer of the scene from an administrative position in Congress put it, Johnson, immediately on taking office, took up the civil rights and economic opportunity issues and, certainly in the latter case, 'I think the feeling was that he was picking up a Kennedy ball here and running with it' (A: LBJ Lib, Perrin, interview, 1969, 21). While putting his own stamp on the events and policies of 1964–5, Johnson was indeed taking over intentions, personnel and vocabularies from the Kennedy years. On one aspect of this the records are in agreement. Walter Heller, chairman of the Council of Economic Advisers under Kennedy, went to see Johnson the day after the assassination and took up with him the poverty programme that Kennedy had approved before his death: 'His immediate response was, "That's my kind of program...I want you to move full speed ahead"' (A: *Newsweek*, 13 September 1965, 22; Blumenthal, 1969, 149). Johnson's own account is only marginally different: 'I'm sympathetic. Go ahead. Give it the highest priority. Push ahead full tilt' (A: Johnson, 1972, 71). Johnson was willing and able to move in this way, rapidly, because he had a sense of a changed constituency following the assassination, and then his landslide confirmation in office as President in the election almost a year later, an election which gave him a Democratic majority through which he knew measures could be passed in a way that had not been available to his predecessor.

Having announced the 'war' in January 1964 in his first State of the Union message to Congress, he outlined his vision of the Great Society to the University of Michigan in May. The resonance is slightly messianic, certainly that of a crusade both political and moral:

...in our time we have the opportunity to move not only toward the rich society and the powerful society, but upward to the Great Society. The Great Society rests on abundance and liberty for all. It demands an end to poverty and racial injustice, to which we are totally committed in our time. But that is just the beginning. The Great Society is a place where every child can find knowledge to enrich his mind and to enlarge his talents...(A: *New Republic*, 1964, 41)

To dismiss this as mere rhetoric would be as historically misconceived as to dismiss the utopianism or millennialism of late eighteenth-century or early nineteenth-century reformers as mere rhetoric. In both cases the time seemed propitious for rapid, positive change, and in Johnson's case the means appeared to be at hand to make the vision real. The Great Society was already being embodied in legislation to guarantee civil rights and promote community action. The culture of poverty, the unemployment brought about by automation and modernization, the barriers to knowledge and full citizenship, all seemed amenable to the new policies.

One of the many problems to emerge from this momentum, especially in education, was to know exactly how rapidly and fully legislation and action were expected seriously to influence the problems being addressed. It was soon to become clear that the ambiguities in evidence in previous years were not only disposed of, but were perhaps even magnified, in the new crusading atmosphere. This was to be one of the judgments that could be made after the event:

It is instructive to read the actual texts of the laws of the Great Society. What is amazing is not how much but how little they say. They are vague, empty formulas...The Economic Opportunity Act (EOA) was slapped together in a tremendous hurry...Vagueness and the grant of enormous discretion provide a way in which the real decisions, the tough decisions could be delayed. (A: Friedman, 1977, 38–9)

One hesitation about this judgment must be that in this case as in others, vagueness and discretion imply not only the possibility of delay, but the possibility of continued dialogue around ways and means, alternatives and flexibilities for action. The Great Society formulas need not be interpreted in conspiratorial terms. They can, however, be considered alongside expressed intentions and commonly understood anxieties. We shall return to this area of judgment in relation to the Elementary and Secondary Education Act, but here it is worth taking as a touchstone the early commentary of John Hersey. Hersey, novelist and active in support of the public schools, wrote a piece on 'Our Romance with Poverty' in 1964 outlining the transition taking place from the private anti-poverty efforts of earlier years to the new federal policies 'the trailbreakers for the public spenders in this particular wilderness have been, of course, the foundations' (and he focuses on two such efforts, in Virginia and New Haven, Connecticut). His argument is directed to the necessity of a principled approach particularly to the shaping of 'the educational aspects of the nation's "war on poverty"', as without such principles the exercise could degenerate into hypocrisy and chaos. Although school-centred approaches might be the most effective, 'education in isolation cannot wipe out poverty...Education is, alas, not the panacea many wish it were.' In the search for workable and comprehensive community programmes the sums so far committed were 'absurdly inadequate' – a more massive attack was needed. With great percipience Hersey relates his concerns about the present with his fears for the future:

The first battles in the war on poverty will not bring the sudden end of dropouts, delinquency, narcotics addiction, unemployment...To continue the war will be to fly in the face of *apparent* failure for years, perhaps decades, perhaps generations. Yet still, bearing in mind the alternatives, it must be fought.

He concluded that 'as far as possible, the poor themselves should be involved in the planning and execution of these programmes' – a demand already being embodied in the legislation, and about to become one of its most controversial features. He was aware that 'the places where it will be hardest to mount programs will be precisely the places where they are needed most'. Finally, with all his reservations about the war and its likely features, he sees the opportunities. Even the 'tentative explorations' of the first anti-poverty bill 'may prove to have been a good thing': permitting flexibility in the early stages and opening up the possibility of larger programmes. Democrats and Republicans alike need to face up to the conflict ahead: 'This is one war that had better be wisely fought' (A: Hersey, 1964, 525–36). To these conclusions, in a later version of the article, he adds: 'Finally, this will be a long war' (A: Hersey, 1965, 71).

For these reasons, and against this background of expectation and haste, 1964 saw the emergence of poverty not as something new in the political process but as a major – and to large numbers of people unexpected – public issue (A: Lander, 1967, 1968, 1971). It was accompanied by an interest in schools and education unprecedented in this century, and for Johnson himself, a former school teacher, to use education 'to break barriers built by poverty and fear and racial injustice – this is the most exciting task of our times' (A: Johnson [1966], 65).

The precise political and administrative mechanisms by which the signals of the earlier 1960s were received and translated into programmes and planning would need to look in detail at how opinion, research and political aspiration were interpreted and channelled into action. The 1960s American relationship between education, public policy and public opinion and action would need to be pinned down in the networks and machineries through which messages passed and became part of the policy process. Some of the components of these networks have already been identified – the Ford Foundation and the local projects whose agendas Ford helped to establish, and which in turn reformulated Ford's own agendas; Kennedy's staff, some connected with or involved in the Ford or the Juvenile Delinquency work; researchers and programme promotors who gave advice to Ford or testimony to congressional committees. What the networks provided rapidly in the Johnson period was a core of experienced professionals, coming from a variety of directions, to begin to fill the leadership roles in the policy, administrative and research and dissemination processes gathering momentum. Critical at the level of federal policy making was the operation of the 'task force' system, to a degree under Kennedy, but crucially under Johnson.

Kennedy's task force on education, which reported in 1961, indicates one of the ways in which the components began to form into a significant network. Its chairman was from a university – Frederick L. Hovde, President of Purdue University – but more important for this discussion was the presence of Alvin Eurich, a Ford Foundation vice-president, Benjamin Willis, superintendent of Chicago's public schools (and one of the key figures in the 'great cities' negotiations with the Ford Foundation), and Francis Keppel, who was before long to become Kennedy's Commissioner of Education. Johnson's all-important 1964 task force was under the chairmanship of John W. Gardner, President of the Carnegie Foundation (who had been a member of the 1961 task force). It included James E. Allen, Jr, Commissioner of Education for the State of New York, and Sidney P. Marland, Jr, Superintendent of Pittsburgh schools (both familiar with important Ford and other poverty-area educational projects), the Mayor of St Louis, Missouri, and the President of St Louis University, as well as David Riesman from Harvard – and Francis Keppel, *ex officio* as Commissioner. Between 1961 and 1964 the channels of bureaucratic, political and academic communication had run together and the task forces were just one of the levels at which the messages were relayed and debated (A: Hawkinson, 1977; Kearney, 1967). At other levels the experience and policies of city-wide or state-wide systems, such as Chicago and California, were circulating and penetrating the federal processes, and the 'demonstration' outcomes of Higher Horizons or the newer projects in New York or Tennessee were being echoed.

Although those networks and levels of communication were vital elements in producing the Elementary and Secondary Act in 1965, two prior political decisions enabled it to emerge as the main instrument linking schools with the war on poverty. First was the critically important Civil Rights Act of 1964. All the attempts at educational legislation in the Kennedy period had faced congressional difficulties stemming from race and desegregation issues. Representative Adam Clayton Powell invariably introduced amendments linking proposed measures to desegregation, requiring implementation of the 1954 Supreme Court decision. 'Powell amendments', faced with conservative opposition, threatened to destroy any educational proposal. The 1964 Civil Rights bill benefited from Johnson's commitment and previous experience as Majority Leader in the Senate, where more than anyone, he had steered through a Civil Rights Act in 1957. The new Act, outlawing discrimination in all federally aided programs, 'had very special educational consequences... the race issue was removed from the political calculus of those supporting or attacking increased Federal aid to education' (A: Bailey and Mosher, 1968, 30–1).

In 1963–4 the Johnson administration faced the problem of legislative response to the need 'to keep in step with the Negro revolution' (A: Littlewood, 1966, 41). Kennedy had begun the process of trying to keep in step. Keppel's view of 'dramatic' versions of Kennedy's response to the Harrington revelations was that it was not

dramatic at all. I would tend to put the dramatic side of it on the black and white, and the very rapidly increased sensitivity to minority black problems... Martin Luther King led a parade down in Washington in the summer of 1963... and it was a dignified enterprise... and I think that made the President of the United States, Mr Kennedy, pretty sensitive. (Keppel, interview)

In May 1964, before the Act was passed, Keppel was speaking at a meeting of the National Association for the Advancement of Colored People on the subject of 'Civil Rights and Education Now', and he described the forces of civil rights as 'undergoing their most critical period of struggle. Protest and reactions to protest are intensifying...' (A: LBJ Lib Federal Records, Keppel addresses, 28 May 1964, 2). A month later addressing the National Association for the Advancement of Colored People, Keppel commented that 'segregation... by law or by custom, by edict or tradition, by patterns of employment or patterns of housing... hurts our children, Negro and white alike. And nowhere is the damage more devastating than in education for democracy'. This was a time of 'high expectation', long-awaited legislation was nearing its final passage, and it was going to need implementing in practice (A: LBJ Lib Federal Records, Keppel addresses, 26 June 1964, 1). The passage of the Act, he later reflected, 'cleared away one of the fundamental obstacles with regard to any administration's program in education' (A: LBJ, Lib, Keppel interview, 1968, 8). The passage and implementation of the Civil Rights Act had direct consequences for Keppel's Office of Education.

When appointed US Commissioner of Education, he had brought to Washington one of his students, David S. Seeley, a lawyer turned educationist. As assistant to Keppel, Seeley suddenly found himself in 1964 (at the age of 33) operating the machinery set up to implement the 1964 Act:

I came as an Assistant to Mr. Keppel in the summer of 1963 and the Civil Rights actually passed in the summer of '64 and – I won't say quite unexpectedly, but in any case without anything like the required amount of planning it dumped on the Office of Education enormous responsibility for carrying out what basically was a social revolution in at least one part of the country.

With the meagrest of resources Seeley now found himself, with Keppel and a few others, having to frame guidelines for the schools:

I'd say it took us at least six months from the time the bill passed in early July of '64 until the first instructions were issued at the end of December – it took us all that time to even begin to get oriented to what the policies would be. (A: LBJ Lib, Seeley interview, 1968, 2–5)

Keppel's memory of the same period was a vivid one. The Act – and particularly its Title 6, which involved the federal executive in breaking up separate black and white schools systems in the South – was important, and

The President was all for it. And he damned near drove me crazy...We had 5,000, I think it was, school districts in the South that were in effect black and white schools. And we went through all sorts of difficulties, the President played no part in this personally, in trying to get the damned executive branch to agree on how to proceed. I finally helped to jam through some that were called guidelines on desegregation...because the fellows down South were saying, 'Well, for God's sake, if you're telling us to do something, tell us what it is.' You can't just sit there in Washington saying, 'Reform, reform, reform.' (A: LBJ Lib, Keppel interview, 1969, 18–19)

The civil rights movement had in 1964 reached an important moment of influence with government policy, not least in the field of education.

Also in 1964 came the Economic Opportunity Act, addressing problems of employment, education and training, and promoting policies which included community action. The President of Ohio University and former planning director of the Job Corps, related it specifically to the youth drop-outs whose condition had attracted so much attention under the Kennedy administration, and whose plight appeared to be insoluble without a revolution: 'The Economic Opportunity Act may be the beginning of such a revolution. The major attack in this war on poverty is on the problems of an alienated youth' (A: Alden, 1965, 69).

The Act (Public Law 88–452) was passed in August 1964. It recognized the progress made in 'economic well-being and prosperity', but also the continued poverty of substantial numbers of people. The United States could achieve its potential

only if every individual has the opportunity to contribute to the full extent of his capabilities and to participate in the workings of our society. It is, therefore, the policy of the United States to eliminate the paradox of poverty in the midst of plenty...by opening to everyone the opportunity for education and training, the opportunity to work, and the opportunity to live in decency and dignity. (A: US Congress, House, 1964, 1)

Title I of the Act was concerned with youth programmes (Job Corps, work-training programmes, work study programmes), Title II with urban and rural 'community action programmes', and Title III with the specific problems of poverty in rural areas. The community action programmes under Title II were intended to mobilize resources, to provide services and activities 'of sufficient scope and size to give promise of progress toward elimination of poverty or a cause or causes of poverty', and – the most important and best-remembered phrase of the Act – to do so 'with the maximum feasible participation of residents of the areas and members of the groups served'. One process by which the aims were to be achieved was that of 'bettering the conditions under which people live, learn, and work' (*ibid.*, 9). A transition had been made in the Act from concepts of education and training as technical procedures for economic growth or for job preparation, to a more complex approach to the interacting causes of poverty, and the wider strategies necessary to confront it. Some of the proposals related back to former policies and experiments with vocational preparation: 'conceptually, however, the Act leapt beyond the goals of vocational education' (A: Bailey and Mosher, 1968, 32).

The Act was planned in a political whirlwind. Competing emphases on employment and incomes and on education and training, competing channels for the distribution of federal grants, competing mechanisms for planning and then implementing the Act, needed to be confronted. In 1963–4 active anti-poverty planners in the Bureau of the Budget and the Council of Economic Advisers had developed proposals which combined community action programmes and education grants for the poor (A: Jeffrey, 1978, 28). The dynamic and direction of a new task force under Sargent Shriver, proved to be different, however. Although the proposals that were 'educational' or potentially so are visible in the final Act, they became almost inexplicit. Youth and adult training became central, and definitions of community action became broad enough for educational implications to be read into them. The report on the proposed Act submitted to the House of Representatives by its Committee on Education and Labor in June made it clear that 'general aid to elementary and secondary schools is not within the contemplation of this part [of the Act], and is specifically barred' (A: US Congress, 1964, 11).

The task force, Shriver and his deputy, Adam Yarmolinsky, drew on recent experience in various ways. Their own members, associates and advisers included Harrington and Paul Jacobs, early radical poverty 'war veterans', and Paul Ylvisaker of the Ford Foundation, the main designer of the Foundation's 'gray areas' policy. Yarmolinsky came to economic opportunity planning from defence, but had previously, among other things, been a consultant to foundations, including the Ford Foundation's gray areas programme, and came with what he calls 'a continuing interest in problems of poverty, urban affairs, civil rights – that whole constellation of problems'. When Shriver was given the assignment by President Johnson to put together an anti-poverty programme

I was one of the few people he called to help him, and I for a while spent evenings after a twelve-hour day at the Pentagon working with him, planning, and he asked me to become his deputy, and take leave from the Pentagon, which I did.

He had become involved with the Ford Foundation because he knew Paul Ylvisaker: 'these things don't happen in a very organized or systematic fashion'. He had become involved with the Fund for the Republic, an offshoot of the Ford Foundation, had contact with Foundation people – contact maintained in a subsequent period in publishing and as a consultant to Foundations (in 1960 he had conducted a modest evaluation of a Carnegie-supported schools project in Arizona). Together with other leading participants in the early planning – James Sundquist, Patrick Moynihan and Wilbur Cohen, assistant secretary in the Department of Health, Education, and Welfare and an expert in social security since his New Deal days – Yarmolinsky became involved in balancing the claims of 'finding jobs for people and preparing people for jobs'. The initial decision was preparing for jobs, for two reasons:

First, because we thought it would take longer, and second because we had perhaps naive faith in the consequences of the President's tax program to increase the number of available jobs ... obviously if you're preparing people for jobs that could be called education. I think we had deep scepticism about the ability of the American education system, education establishment, to do very much for the population that we were concerned about.

Political opposition to Yarmolinsky, because of his past radical stance on civil rights in particular, prevented him from becoming deputy director of the new Office of Economic Opportunity. When he was no longer involved, the question became

whether the Head Start program should be run by the education bureaucracy or by the poverty bureaucracy which was beginning to develop, and I think it was clear to all disinterested observers that you did a lot better with the poverty bureaucracy because they paid attention to the poor people. (A: Yarmolinsky, interview)

The attention paid to poverty by social scientists and journalists, the projects associated with the Juvenile Delinquency committee, the Ford Foundation and other concerns with urban issues, had come together at an auspicious political moment, and produced a burst of federal activity impossible in the Kennedy period. Another member of the task force which planned the anti-poverty programme wrote in 1965 that the experience of the Ford and Juvenile Delinquency projects had been mixed, but the fact that they had taken place at all and had been debated 'escalated long-festering problems into wide public view, so that discussion of them as critical national issues could no longer be evaded' (A: Kravitz, 1965, 2). The OEO's own 'Narrative History' of the period describes the zest which went into the enterprise, and the speed with which it had to be and was accomplished. The task force on poverty was apparently labelled in Washington the 'Poor Corps', and the time was one 'of chaos and exhaustion when energies were fueled by excitement and exhilaration – itself, at times, the product of…"the beautiful hysteria of it all," as one participant put it' (A: US OEO, [1969], vol. 1, pt. 1, 28). The outcome was the bill 'to mobilize the human and financial resources of the nation to combat poverty in the United States', processed by Congress between March and August 1964.

The networks had produced for the 'poverty war' a core of liberal intellectuals familiar with the recent ideological currents and experiments. Daniel Moynihan saw the launch of the war and of the Economic Opportunity Act as its cornerstone as basically that of an intellectual community (A: Moynihan, 1968). Johnson was later to wonder how Shriver had managed to get himself surrounded with so many 'kooks and sociologists' – though one history suggests that Johnson may have used some of his sexually vivid vocabulary in the comment (A: Patterson, 1981, 147, 247). Behind the language of 'mobilization', 'powerlessness' and 'participation' lay what one commentator called an 'experiment in federalism' (A: Davidson, 1969), with new vocabularies, new aims, the extension of some older ones and 'deep scepticism', in Yarmolinsky's phrase, about a variety of entrenched bureaucracies. One reflection on the changed agenda of American public discourse – following years of conservatism and McCarthyism – was that of Mayor Walsh of Syracuse in a statement to the House Subcommittee on the War on Poverty Program, during its hearings in April 1964: poverty and dependency were not inevitable, and 'perhaps the first step in the cure of poverty today is to spread the idea, once regarded as Marxian, that society is responsible for much of our poverty' (A: US Congress, House, Hearings, pt. 2, 1964, 801). Conservative opponents of the bill were to focus less on the 'Marxian' implications, than on the powers given to the OEO and Sargent Shriver as its director.

Johnson's Message on Poverty to Congress in March 1964 recommended the proposed act because, together with a group of other opportunities it would 'give every American community the opportunity to develop a comprehensive plan to fight its own poverty – and help them to carry out their plans' (A: Johnson, 1964, 423). It is clear that this intention was not based on any organized pressure from constituencies of the poor, but it contributed to the further mobilization of the poor, particularly the black, urban population. The impetus and resources made available by the Act raised acute questions of power and leadership, the nature of and responsibility for welfare and social services, including education. Once the Office of Economic Opportunity was operational some commentators were quick to point out that the effort to bring communities into action against their own poverty might have questionable economic outcomes but distinct political ones. For the first time in many communities 'Negroes are represented on official boards...The War on Poverty is helping to change the political structure of cities.' The Act, despite the 'ballyhoo' of the War on Poverty, produced changes (A: Miller and Roby, 1966, 76–7). The launch of local community action projects in many parts of the United States produced pressures for participation, difficult attempts to turn the much-publicized rhetoric of the Act into political reality on the ground.

In many places, local groups soon found themselves in conflict with those traditionally responsible for community and services administration. A staff assistant to Daniel Moynihan described what happened from 1964 as the federal government financing a revolution 'against local governments and against itself' (A: Blumenthal, 1969, 132) until, in 1967, local agencies financed by the OEO were brought under local government control. Yarmolinsky was to reflect that in the planning of the poverty programme 'the power potential...of the poor themselves was largely overlooked' (A: Yarmolinsky, 1969, 50). By the time the ESEA became a focus of public attention, new currents of political debate and action were beginning to flow.

Miller and Rein pointed out in 1965 that it was a weakness of the anti-poverty campaign that it was being attempted without the support of strong interest groups (A: Miller and Rein, 1965b, 276). The economic and social implications of the civil rights movement were clear enough, but the anti-poverty legislation and action were addressing either different issues or the same issues from a different direction. The majority of America's poor were white, and what the OEO was asked to respond to were the needs, not the politically expressed demands, of the poor, a need perceived through the statistics of unemployment, the national distribution of wealth and the socially visible by-products of poverty. The House hearings on the Economic Opportunity Act received messages of support from labour unions for the Act and for the President's 'desire to eradicate poverty and misery from this land'. The Air Transport Division of the Transport Workers Union of America, for example, told the Subcommittee on the War on Poverty Program:

There is no justification for poverty and misery in a country as abundantly endowed with human and natural resources as the United States. The existence of belts of misery in our cities and in that part of the Nation called Appalachia is a blot on our national honor ... The members of the air transport division stand solidly behind the President in this great crusade ... (A: US Congress, House, Hearings 1964, pt. 3, 1626)

Miller and Rein were correct in underlining that there was support for community action but no strong constituency organized and active around the planning and the implementation of the Act. It was therefore simpler for opposition to the Act to take shape in localities and states and to begin to influence the operation of the OEO and its aims and procedures.

The mayor of Syracuse was in favour of federal grants under the poverty programme being made direct to the community, to be directed at the problems of the community and for action to be directed by the community (A: *ibid.*, pt. 2, 798), but most mayors and many other representative leaders reacted with various degrees of hostility to processes which bypassed or undermined their authority. The Republican minority on the House Committee on Education and Labor, in its objections to the proposed Act, quoted the US Conference of Mayors, which had stated that legislation to involve 'local citizen action in a war on poverty must clearly place the responsibility for program development and execution with responsible local government' (A: US Congress, House, Committee 1964, 74). Once the Act was passed the mayors and others resisted the policies of the OEO and its director, Sargent Shriver (whose nickname of the 'antipoverty czar' was widely used by Republicans in Congress and amongst mayoral and other opponents of the new federal-community axis). State governors also exercised their right of veto over projects, with Governor Reagan of California being one of the 'champion vetoers' (A: Davidson, 1969, 3). In some cases the community action programmes were resisted by professional welfare workers and administrators, and hostilities deepened in many cities between newly emerging community leaderships and established city hall and welfare machineries.

A final point to emphasize about the poverty programme in general and the Economic Opportunity Act in particular is the range of implications for education that became explicit around the Act. Throughout the hearings prior to the passing of the Act there was constant discussion of the twin themes of the relationship between poverty and ignorance, and the need for a war on poverty to be an educational war. The director of Cook County Department of Public Aid (a county which includes Chicago) told the Subcommittee on the

War on Poverty that 'any meaningful attack upon poverty must have education as a first and indispensable priority. A massive attack on illiteracy and a correction of educational deficiencies must come first...' Under questioning he described the Chicago anti-illiteracy campaign and re-emphasized the centrality of education (A: US Congress, House, Subcommittee, 1964, pt. 3, 1491–5). A representative of the National Education Association told the Subcommittee that 'the most effective war on poverty, in the long run, is a war on ignorance' (A: *ibid.*, pt. 2, 1101). This thread was never far from the concerns of the committees and Congress, and from public debate.

Of particular interest for future developments was the interpretation of the poverty programme in terms of the preschool emphases that had emerged strongly in the early 1960s. There are some revealing signposts in the discussions. One of the Subcommittee's earliest discussions was with Secretary of Health, Education and Welfare, Celebrezze, accompanied by Assistant Secretary Cohen and Commissioner of Education Keppel. Edith Green, one of the most pugnacious of the House Democrats, secured from Celebrezze the assurance that although the Title II community action proposals relating to education were 'patterned after the juvenile delinquency legislation', they were not intended as a juvenile delinquency programme: the similarity lay in the 'coordinated attack'. She pressed Keppel directly on the apparent absence in the bill of anything relating to education below the age of sixteen, except possibly in Title II. Was it really educationally sound to focus purely on age sixteen and after? Keppel's answer was that one should never give up, there were useful things to be done between ages sixteen and twenty-one, but the community action programme, nevertheless

would be educational and would, I hope, be proposed by the communities. Community proposals would include work beginning even in the preschools where, I am sure you are right, one has to go, particularly for the children who come from tragically poor and often broken homes... I would hope that the programs in education that are presented by the community would start at the early ages. (A: *ibid.*, pt. 1, 146–7)

When the Committee on Education and Labor itself reported to the House over two months later, it indicated, as we have seen, that the bill did not propose to give 'general aid' to elementary or secondary schools, but that community action could involve multiple use of institutions – including school playgrounds after school hours, and premises of various kinds to 'provide day care for preschool-age children' (A: US Congress, House, Committee, 1964, 11).

The Act itself made no specific reference to preschooling, but the implications were clear enough. Educators were quick to respond. Two articles in the educational press in January 1965 indicate the firmness of the response. In *Childhood Education* the head of the Bureau of Elementary Education of the California State Department of Education outlined the proposals contained in the Economic Opportunity Act and underlined the 'possibility of using these funds for the establishment of nursery schools with appropriate child development classes for parents'. The Act debarred grants for general aid to elementary and secondary schools but not nursery schools: 'rarely in the lives of any of us are we confronted with such an opportunity... Plan your role now!' *Phi Delta Kappan* summarized some recent commentaries on the educational opportunities provided by the Act, under the title 'Administrators: Seize the Initiative Now!' One commentator had seen the Act as offering 'the necessary support for many programs and particularly to develop pre-school demonstrations with culturally disadvantaged children' (A: Heffernan, 1965; *Phi Delta Kappan*, 1965). The Economic Opportunity Act illustrates how education in general, and preschooling in particular, engaged various levels of local and federal opinion. The poverty programme covered a wide area, taking in the root causes of poverty as well as the minutiae of local action – including, either directly or by extension from other priorities, education. The responses were to be formulated and given shape at different levels and in many forms.

The metaphor of 'shape' in one sense fits Head Start, which grew directly out of the Economic Opportunity Act, and rapidly took a place in public consciousness. In another sense it is inappropriate, since the definitions, interpretations and strategies of Head Start, and within a short space of time the judgments made about it, were disparate and often inchoate. In retrospective view, Head Start in the mid-1970s was described as 'combining the newest findings in educational psychology with the then current community action philosophy of political liberals' (A: Steiner, 1974, 61). A preschool policy in which a number of salient social and economic problems were competing for solution, Head Start proved to be OEO's most exciting and popular programme, and one in which so much hope and confidence were invested that all kinds of confusions and disappointments were rapidly produced.

Sargent Shriver convened the first planning committee for Head Start in January 1965. People involved in early discussions, either as planners, consultants or advisers of one kind or another included a range of psychologists and early childhood specialists such as Jerome Bruner and Urie Bronfenbrenner. One member of the planning committee disclosed later in the year that in the early planning stages the project was referred to as the 'Kiddie Corps' and Harold Howe II, who followed Keppel as

Commissioner of Education, told a story that was around at the time 'that Johnson wanted to call Head Start the Baby Corps' (A: Osborn, 1965, 98; Howe, interview). The project brought together ideas about community action and preschooling, day care and parent education or parent support. Yarmolinsky and others saw it as a deliberate bypassing of the 'education bureaucracy' in its location with OEO, and the pioneering nature of the policy and the specific strategies was often an explicit criticism of the established school system. Given the political environment in which Head Start was born, however, it aroused hesitations rather than resistance, and was in general welcomed enthusiastically – some of the difficulties stemmed in fact from its optimistic and over-enthusiastic planning and reception. A *Wall Street Journal* reporter, with the first summer programme about to be launched, described the atmosphere surrounding it:

In typical Texas style, President Johnson's Project Head Start to prepare 500,000 underprivileged children to begin public school next fall comes on big and loud. The program is 'crash' all the way. The plans have multiplied five-fold in about as many months and will grow more, leaving even dedicated fans a bit breathless...A corps of publicists heralds the program's every move. A crescendo of sorts come with 'Head Start Day' ceremonies today at the White House...Mrs. Johnson will receive the project's symbolic flag from antipoverty director Sargent Shriver...Danny Kaye will entertain. (A: Karmin, 1965, 1)

The 1965 summer programmes (the transition to full-year programmes began the following year) were indeed produced breathlessly, nationally and locally. The first local projects were rushed together mainly under the auspices of school systems, with community action programmes beginning to take over mainly in 1966. There was controversy, over aims and strategies and expectations. Martin Deutsch, as a member of a national advisory commission for the project was suspicious of intentions to train teachers for two to four weeks, and to achieve literacy for Head Start children in a crash summer programme:

All over the country newspapers had headlines on a 'new miracle program' to change our school system. I gave interviews at the time, I wrote articles... and said this is simply not possible – this is nothing but a political game. So when I said this at the first advisory committee meeting I was asked to resign. They wanted to allow the public image that a miracle cure was possible... I said it just won't work, and what is going to happen is – your traditional racists are going to say...it's impossible to teach these children... Shriver wanted 100 per cent consensus...two of us walked out at the time, one was Ted Sizer, who was a Dean at Harvard, and myself...(Deutsch, interview)

A description of the launch of Head Start in Chicago in 1965 suggests how the scramble to begin looked on the ground. Critics remembered 'the frantic haste with which this program had to be put into operation from scratch'. Staff were new, job descriptions non-existent, channels of communication had to be created 'on an hour by hour basis'. Of the 23,000 children enrolled for this first programme, 20,000 were enrolled by the Chicago public schools and the remainder by the Catholic Archdiocese and a couple of dozen smaller agencies. Volunteer assistance came from many sources: parents, the medical profession, upper-middle-class ladies. There was an unexpected amount of paper work. There were doubts by the end of the first summer session about the constituencies of children they had reached:

Physicians who examined the children remarked how well-dressed and healthy they appeared to be. There was evidence that some of the centers, possibly in eagerness to fill their rooms, solicited the enrollment of children from small families with substantial incomes. The children observed by the author in nearly two dozen centers seemed not to fit the pattern of cultural deprivation described in current sociological studies...(A: Gaebler, 1966)

These difficulties and pitfalls do not conceal the surprising fact that the project had erupted rapidly, out of various antecedents, including the attack on fixed intelligence, the campaign for civil rights, the social reform targets of political liberalism and foundations, and the confidence basic to the Economic Opportunity Act. Given those complexities of origin, it is understandable that the hastily defined aims and hurriedly adopted strategies were often unclear or unstable. Whatever its educational intensions it was conceived not as an educational programme but as 'a local community action effort – not a kindergarten, but a "communigarten" program', one which mobilized doctors, lawyers, mothers, social workers, psychologists, clergymen, public officials – and teachers (A: US, OEO, 1967, 4). Although it was a 'preschool' programme, in its planning and operation it never focused exclusively on 'academic preparation', firmly embodying elements of social work and welfare, medicine and nutrition, family intervention and the values of citizenship. Local aims, often ill-defined, have to be deduced from the operational forms of the projects. Balanced against the ideological niceties of the national discussion and perception is the experience. For some, increasingly a majority, of the children involved as Head Start reached its targeted constituencies, the project provided an experience of regular meals, a first encounter with the zoo or an elevator, the first medical or dental examination (A: Wolfbein, 1967, 212–14). For many parents it was their first experience of public decision-making, or their first adult contact with teachers or social workers or doctors (A: Zigler and Valentine, 1979, 291; US, OEO, 1967, 31). The parent and community involvement intended, and often achieved, was different from anything previously associated with the public school system. The use made of community resources was different. The difficulties were to lie in the inherent combination of enthusiastic practical efforts and the expectations of, if not a miracle cure, at least significant, rapid progress in harnessing education to the job of raising the poor out of poverty.

Eligibility for the Head Start or other poverty programmes was determined by criteria for identifying children from 'culturally disadvantaged' backgrounds: the measures used from 1965 were those of family income and eligibility for other forms of welfare. Initially, the Head Start project used available, often extremely vague, vocabularies. Massachusetts summarized its implementation of the project in the following terms:

Programs were established in communities where previous studies had identified either a high unemployment rate, high poverty level of income, or deteriorated and dilapidated housing. Other communities, not so readily identified as needy, established programs to serve their local pockets of poverty... The primary object of Head Start was to effect a change in the life chances of the preschool age child ready to enter kindergarten or first grade in the fall, if he came from a culturally disadvantaged family or lived in a culturally disadvantaged area. (A: Curwood et al., [1966], 44)

Aims expressed in this form gave rise to objections and reservations, much as discussion of the 'culture of poverty' or 'cultural disadvantage' was giving rise to such reservations. Sympathetic critics pointed out from the first that Head Start was failing adequately to define such concepts as deprivation, disadvantage and even poverty (A: Egland, 1966, 295). These reservations sat alongside those of experts like Martin Deutsch, when reported in places like the *Wall Street Journal*: much of Head Start, wrote the reporter, was 'shrouded in the vagueness of experimentation' and was therefore 'roundly criticized by Dr. Deutsch and others'. Deutsch, 'very much in sympathy with Head Start's objectives, remains apprehensive. "There is some evidence," he says, "that children who do get a 'head start' which has no follow-up momentum will return to their original failure levels... we are spreading too little money too thin over too many communities, at too rapid a rate' (A: Karmin, 1965, 10).

The aims of the Head Start programme were therefore bound up with the political drive to have it established and operational rapidly, picking up the thrust of the educational and social science research and overruling its hesitations. Beneath the surface of the commonsense and attractive approach to this preschool programme lay a good deal of confusion and controversy. One witness of the beginnings of Head Start in Mississippi reflected on what she felt as she worked with teachers engaged in the Head Start programme in 1965–6:

In many ways I thought the Head Start program was a monster by the tail because it got very politically involved very soon... all of our Congressmen very much wanted to bring a Head Start program to their district and there were a lot of issues. Should this program be primarily a means of supplying manpower for the adults so that they could better support their children?... more community oriented, so that it could bring the resources of the community itself to bear on the poverty situation as it existed?... should the program be primarily educational or developmental for the children? I don't think that issue was really ever resolved.

The Follow Through programme was soon to learn from Head Start the need for greater clarification of goals so that real experimentation could occur: Head Start was, in that sense, not an experimental programme (Foster, interview).

Head Start was 'political' in another sense, especially in Mississippi, where funding was at one stage to be discontinued amidst raging controversy about the subversive nature of the programme in that state. The politics of introducing Head Start everywhere and obtaining a slice of the federal funding available strengthened the image of a self-contained initiative that would propel children into the school system better prepared to succeed there and in the competition for life chances. At the outset there were assumptions about the ability of children to cope with schools as they were, assumptions that Deutsch and others failed to dispose of, but which very soon afterwards had to be abandoned. The process was preparing children to succeed in school conditions that failed to sustain the momentum and, in fact, militated against success. At its simplest, as Keppel pointed out in 1966, programmes such as Head Start 'will falter – and may even cause greater disillusionment – if they are not followed by "quality education" in the schools themselves'. Slum schools had the least experienced teachers, and others were scarcely attracted to teach in such schools 'where walls are cracked and dirty, where windows are broken, where libraries are poorly equipped or nonexistent, where classes are crowded...' It was not surprising, in those conditions, that children failed to learn (A: Keppel, 1966, 44–5). The 'educational' issue of Head Start had rapidly led to sharp questions about the schools.

Like the rest of the community action programme, Head Start faced the problems of community involvement – in this case primarily parent involvement. Like the rest of the programme, however, its conception of involvement or participation was not without contradictions. For many advocates – including Frank Riessman – one of the key interpretations was that of the recruitment of parents as paid auxiliaries, in order to provide parent employment and experience. For others the conception was one of parent education or voluntary support by parents, active political involvement by parents or the influencing of parents. Parents needed to be 'involved' in one way or another, and the intention was explicitly part of local statements of aims, and of planning. Administrators, participants and researchers recorded widespread parent enthusiasm. One account describes the awakening of 'community interest in the preschool child' in Chattanooga, Tennessee. By participating in the

discoveries with their young children, the first Head Starters, parents have deepened their interest in the knowledge of the kinds of activities which develop young children. Parents' interest spread into the neighbourhood: moreover, Parent Advisory Committee reports and parent interviews indicated the variety of needs that the program had met and the depth of appreciation individuals felt... the community, or many in the community, were drawn sympathetically into the validity of this new program. (A: Broman, 1966, 483).

This account by the local supervisor of the 1965 Head Start program quotes statements by parents enthusiastic about perceived changes in their children's behaviour and progress, and the Head Start projects reported in the early days the perceptions of 'success' reflected in such comments. Here again, however, alongside the dominant voice of enthusiasm was the growing voice of criticism: the Parent Advisory Committees required by OEO were weak or functioning poorly; parents were being bypassed; they were not being involved *enough*; parents were being given misleading information (A: Curwood et al., [1966], 45; Meier, 1966, 126).

There were other negative features of the early days of Head Start, some resulting, for example, from the difficulties of teachers recruited for the project in adjusting to either ebullient children or involved parents (A: Levens, 1966; Omwake, 1966). The initial messages from the Head Start centres, however, were mainly positive. Some of those who attempted systematic observation in the summer of 1965 (it was too early a date to interpret the process as 'evaluation') produced strongly favourable reports. The Educational Testing Service, for instance, using regional teams of 'distinguished professional people', observed 1,300 classes at 335 centres across the country. They reported, among other things: the certainty of the teachers that with their classroom aides they had made far more rapid progress than they would have expected in the normal kindergarten; the value of the range of outdoor activities and the involvement of other adults; the emergence of new reinforcement techniques in learning, lively forms of instruction, and the importance of purposeful experience. Learning by doing was a reality, seen by observers as they moved about the project centres:

Without exception, these observers noted that in centers where children were active and involved and doing things that were of interest to them, they were learning at least some of the skills and knowledge established by the Office of Economic Opportunity as desirable goals...

Where Head Start classes were teacher-centred or subject-centred, on the other hand, the children sat uninvolved in rows in 'the autocratic classroom' (A: Dobbin, 1966). The Head Start experience rapidly generated amongst participants and observers the conviction that it was working and having impact. The confusion in ideology was also a confusion in practice, over play and 'real' learning. Meier reports the issuing of contradictory instructions, teachers' bafflement and lapse into orthodox ways, and the superficial impression of success as teachers reported virtually a 100 per cent success rate in the improvement' of children's learning. Nevertheless, there was a public demand, and preschooling was seen to have an important contribution to make to solving war on poverty issues (A: Meier, 1966). Superficial or not, the early reports were of such eagerly described phenomena as the children being more 'exploratory', the impact on children and parents being one of enthusiasm and willingness to participate, and in general of high expectations. It was much of this record expressed in terms of attitude, motivation and activity that convinced many researchers that the programme was not 'experimental', in the sense that these did not represent measurable outcomes, were short-term and impressionistic and did not – as Deutsch had pointed out – necessarily imply later learning success in the conditions of the kindergarten and early elementary school grades.

We shall return, in relation to Head Start and to the Elementary and Secondary Education Act, to some of the conceptual problems inherent in the programme and their implications. It is important at this point merely to underline that Head Start was, as the National Education Association described it, a 'popular anti-poverty program under the Economic Opportunity Act', even, in grander terms, 'OEO's most spectacular venture' (A: NEA, 1968, 7; Seligman, 1968, 90). The preschool focus won considerable public support – an achievement not without the criticism that in doing so the community action programme was turning 'to safe, popular "national-emphasis" programs' (A: Davidson, 1969, 11). Head Start was preparation for school, but at the same time an implied critique of school; its Child Development Centers and range of services and intentions pointed towards possible new understandings of the factors affecting children's learning and achievement, and of the concept of education itself. There were to be considerable difficulties raised by the transition of Head Start children to the regular schools, and by the next phase of evaluations of the programme. In the first three years of the programme, in its initial summer form and then as a year-long programme, some two million children had experience of it. The close involvement of psychologists and teachers, national policy-makers and local politicians, social scientists and parents, meant that the threads of interest in the preschool, early childhood and action against poverty had been drawn together within the operational development of the Economic Opportunity Act. Title I of the Elementary and Secondary Education Act which followed in 1965 shared many of the origins and contexts, as well as the dynamic, of Head Start, with many of the same and related intentions, strengths and weaknesses in policy and practice.

5   Education and the prime target

In many respects Title I of the Elementary and Secondary Education Act was the climacteric. John W. Gardner's Task Force on Education, which reported in November 1964, was one of the agents which was pulling the threads together, weighing the precise role and potential of education in achieving the Johnson programme. Its summary begins: 'This is a fateful moment in the history of American education...To imagine that we can build the Great Society in a few years would be a mistake...education will be at the heart of the Great Society'. There were long processes at work, and Sputnik did not deserve the credit 'for sounding the alarm...Sputnik was no more responsible for the general ferment that ensued than for the sunshine of 1957 – Sputnik was just there when it happened' (A: LBJ Lib, WHCF Box 37, pp i, A-II-1). Francis Keppel was fond of describing Khrushchev as America's 'best education Commissioner', the space panic as the trigger for the educational developments which followed. Whatever weight is given to that event it is a combination of processes that accounts for the 1965 concentration of the educational attack on poverty. As one analysis of the politics of this educational 'victory' concluded: 'the final passage of the school-aid bill cannot be explained by a single major change at the exclusion of others...victory must be viewed in the context of several inextricably interrelated factors' (A: Meranto, 1967, 131).

After hearings in sub-committees of the House and Senate, the bill was enacted with extraordinary rapidity in April 1965 clearing the Senate on 9 April by 73 votes to 18. Adam Powell had reported to the House on 8 March from the Committee on Education and Labor, and Wayne Morse to the Senate from the Committee on Labor and Public Welfare on 6 April, in almost identical terms. The bill was, as many commentators have underlined, initiated by the Executive, kept intact by the Committee on Education and Labor, with Keppel orchestrating support at many levels. From beginning to end there were almost no changes in the draft, and opponents of the bill in the Senate had to battle against a 'no amendments' decision (A: Eidenberg and

Morey, 1969, chs. 4–6; Bailey and Mosher, 1968, 45; Hawkinson, 1977, 107–11).

Title I of the bill addressed directly the issue of education's contribution to the war on poverty. The Gardner Task Force had been adamant that if general aid to education was not possible (and it favoured such aid) because of religious and other difficulties, then other means of supporting the schools must be found. It underlined the by now familiar message of the environmental handicaps encountered by children in low-income families and, in a section entitled 'Education of the Poor', it urged that resources should be directed more intensively to areas where the urban and rural slums were located. Title I, as presented to Congress and as adopted, started from the same point – the need for high quality educational programmes 'because of the strong correlation between educational under-achievement and poverty'. Maximum resources, the best available personnel and modern techniques, needed to be provided in elementary and secondary school systems 'where there are concentrations of America's children of poverty'. Selective military service rejection rates as based on mental tests were known to correlate with states with the lowest per capita income. Dropout rates were in inverse ratio to income levels. The committees had received convincing evidence that children were performing inadequately not for lack of mental aptitude but because 'environmental conditions and inadequate educational programs...carry the major responsibility'. The central intention of Title I legislation, therefore, was to provide $1.06 billion to local school districts, with the purpose of 'broadening and strengthening public school programs...where there are concentrations of education-ally disadvantaged children'. The money would hire additional and special staff, provide facilities and equipment, and meet any costs designed 'to accomplish the objectives of the title'. A formula was presented based on the number of children from families with annual incomes of less than $2,000 – the formula to be subject to review and modification. The funds would be made available to State educational agencies, which in turn would finance the programmes and projects of local school districts approved under Title I. Local districts would determine their particular educational needs, and though no funds could be authorized 'for providing any service to a private institution', elementary and secondary school pupils not enrolled in public schools could participate in some of the services to be provided (there was provision for dual enrolment, educational media centres, mobile services and other services in which non-public school pupils could take part) (A: US Congress, Senate, Committee on Labor and Public Welfare, 1965, 4–12).

The other titles of the Act, involving such developments as educational research, the strengthening of state administration of education and related provisions, are not our concern here. Title I was part of a comprehensive Act of a kind not previously possible in the United States, and the Act itself was part of a comprehensive attack – if not an entirely cohesive policy. Keppel told a House sub-committee that Title I was 'the heart of the President's program' to secure a proper federal role in education. Describing himself as on this issue being 'a little more emotional than I usually am' Keppel also alluded to preschool programmes as 'a new field in the United States but, of course, in Europe people have been engaged in it for a century' – and he drew also on the Baltimore experience (A: US Congress, House, Committee on Education and Labor, General Subcommittee, Part 1, 1965, 84, 114, 142). The Act, the discussions in committee and the House and Senate, and in the wider constituencies involved, reached out in all the political, research, experimental and other directions we have traced, and at the centre of discussion was invariably the dual concept of what the reports to Congress described as 'concentrations of America's children of poverty' and 'concentrations of educationally disadvantaged children'. Not all participants agreed that there was a job to be done. The debate in the House produced defences of the existing situation, or defences of the ability of the existing machineries of school district and state to handle problems. Republican Charles Goodell, while in favour of action which did not involve federal 'interference', regretted that in the committee hearings and House debate 'almost nothing has been said about the extraordinary progress we have made in this Nation in providing education. The mistaken impression is left that our educational system is in dire condition'. Many poor children 'do attend some of the finest schools in the entire world'. All American children had the advantage of free public education, the private and parochial schools made a major contribution to broadening educational opportunities, and 'the progress of American education in the past 10 and 20 years is a near miracle' (A: US *Congressional Record*, vol. 111, no. 53, 1965, 5592, 5798).

The proponents of the bill were convinced that it was a major landmark in American educational history. In the House Carl Perkins called it the 'greatest legislative challenge ever faced by any Congress', and John Brademas, aware of the religious issues that surrounded the bill, began his speech:

I am the Methodist nephew of a hard-shell Baptist preacher. My mother belongs to the Disciples of Christ Church. My father is Greek Orthodox, and before coming to the Congress of the United States I taught at a Roman Catholic college. If I can find myself a Jewish bride I would represent the finest example of the ecumenical movement in the 20th century.

He described the bill as 'historic' (A: *ibid.*, 5559, 5573–4), and in the Senate Mike Mansfield considered it to be 'alive with promise and hope' as well as practical, and through it Congress had the opportunity 'to write its name large and indelibly as the creator of a new day in American education' (A: LBJ Lib, WHCF Box 37). Many of the protagonists in these debates had been involved in the hearings in the committees, for example, Perkins, Brademas and Goodell were all members of the General Subcommittee on Education of the Committee on Education and Labor.

The debates revealed all the aspirations and limitations contained in the analyses and experiments of previous years. Education was to contribute to the Great Society by strengthening the preschool measures already in force, by improving the quality of classrooms, by targeting those most in need, by developing motivation, by the expectations of improved job opportunities and changed life styles that resulted from education and expertise. The billion dollar injection proposed in order to achieve some of these things also raised the spectres of federal control and the first steps towards the public funding of parochial education. The legislators could hear mounting public debate around these issues. With the civil rights legislation of the previous year the obstacle of a possible 'Powell amendment' had been overcome. Negotiations with the Catholic church were diminishing its resistance to federal support for public schools which could undermine the parochial schools. The ability of disadvantaged children in all schools to benefit from the funds being made available, not to the parochial schools, but to public agencies, won over key Catholic opinion. An article in *The Catholic Educational Review* later in the year gave credit for the Act to Cardinal Spellman, describing it as a totally new concept in American education, an important attack on educational deprivation, and a step towards 'genuine and continuous working relationships between public and nonpublic administrators' (A: McCarren, 1965, 505–22). Within all the religious bodies, however, there was controversy over the implications of the bill and its proposals. In late 1963 and early 1964 correspondents were urging the President to give aid to the parochial schools, and demanding that he should not do so (A: LBJ Lib, WHCF Box 41). The editor of *The Baptist Standard* in Dallas sent the President a telegram in January 1964 in response to a press report

that you favor limited aid to parochial schools in poverty stricken areas. We have been proclaiming that you would defend church state separation and we regard this as a breakthrough in the wall that will become a precedent for government support for all parochial schools. I implore you to immediately make a public statement that you do not now and will not in the future consent to federal aid to parochial schools under any circumstances. I doubt that you could realize how disturbed millions of Americans are...

A reply from the President eleven days later indicated that the report was wrong, and there were no such plans (A: LBJ Lib, WHCF Box 37, 24 January and 4 February 1964). What this and the flow of messages from other quarters indicate is the contentious nature of the area, the legacy of hostilities and suspicions, and the difficulties of marrying recognition of the problems of poverty with educational action at federal level. The American Farm Bureau sent a telegram during the House debate urging opposition to the bill, because of the tremendous progress already being made in public education, and because the bill was a 'first step toward eventual Federal control of public education' (A: US *Congressional Record*, vol. 111, no. 53, 24 March 1965, 5554). The Chamber of Commerce produced an antagonistic 'Commentary on ESEA', giving rise to a nine-page White House point-by-point rebuttal (A: LBJ Lib, WH Aides, Moyers, Box 1). The Jewish community was deeply divided on the issue, and some bodies expressed strong hostility to the bill in 1965. A White House memorandum described the B'Nai Brith and the American Jewish Congress as 'all laboring mightily to defeat the Education bill' (A: LBJ Lib, Wilson to White, 11 March 1965, WHCF Box 38).

A speech by Keppel entitled 'Poverty – The Only War We Seek' was made to a Conference of the Union of American Hebrew Congregations on 3 March, as part of his attempt to win over Jewish support. A White House memorandum (undated, but presumably referring to this occasion) records that

Commissioner Keppel... encountered substantial opposition from the group's leadership on church–State grounds... The Union endorses Federal aid to education but for public schools and students only. Other Jewish groups which have entered reservations against the bill or portions of it on church–State grounds are:
American Jewish Congress
Jewish War Veterans
Jewish Labor Committee
American Association for Jewish Education
National Council of Jewish Women.
Jewish community split. Orthodox community strongly in favor. (A: LBJ Lib, HEW Subject Files, Reel 47; LBJ Lib, Records of Executive Departments, HEW, Addresses etc. by Francis Keppel)

A telegram from the American Federation of Teachers summarized the general view amongst professional educators. It commended the

President for championing the fight for better schools, described the programme recommended to Congress as 'an auspicious step toward victory in the long struggle to induce the Federal Government to assume its proper responsibility for the support of education', but asked for an increase in the proposed budget and safeguards for the public schools (A: LBJ Lib, WHCF Box 37, 5 January 1965).

Although there were controversies in Congress around the formulas on which funding to the states was to be based, tension between definitions based on low income and those based on educational disadvantage or backwardness did not surface significantly at this point. The main controversial issues were those associated with federal and local responsibilities and with the public/non-public schools dilemmas. Inherent in the debates were ambiguities about general and targeted aid, and the bill itself defined targeted areas and children and the operation of funding loosely enough for those who had hoped for general aid to interpret Title I as such, or at least as a step in that direction. From the early days of its implementation the flaws were to be detected and misuse of funds for 'general' purposes was to come under attack. The prevailing mood that surrounded ESEA, however, was one of confidence and enthusiasm, and no one projected the mood more clearly than Commissioner Keppel. In his many speeches in 1964 and 1965 he talked of the bill as a chance in a lifetime, its prime purpose of alleviating poverty, poverty as America's 'nearest foreign country', the importance of the civil rights movement in shaping change, the need for educational and other forms of action, and consigning myths about poor children being 'of a lower order', 'unteachable' and with no hope of academic achievement, to 'the ashcan of history' (A: LBJ Lib, Federal Records, Keppel addresses, *passim*). In *The Journal of Negro Education* he wrote that the ESEA might well demonstrate 'that our slums have been the Nation's greatest reservoir of untapped talent', using imagery not very different from that used by the Robbins committee on higher education in Britain two years earlier. The Act would help to remove expectations of failure. Teachers and others needed to understand the sources and importance of protest. He offered the equation – protest plus civil rights plus education meant the Great Society (A: Keppel, 1965d, 205–8). The ESEA treated poverty 'as a prime target for education', he told the American Association of School Administrators (A: Keppel, 1964d, 6). America had twice in a decade been taken by surprise, he told the Council for Basic Education: first by Sputnik and then by the discovery of underprivilege in a highly privileged society, the latter dramatized in Appalachia and by the civil rights movement (A: Keppel *et al.*, 1965, 3). It was Keppel who introduced into the bill a title which would seek to strengthen state administration of education, and he worked to allay the fears of those who saw the bill as a threat either to secular schooling or to the democratic tradition of state and local control. It was, in fact, a myth – he told the American Association of University Women – that federal aid meant federal control (A: Keppel, 1965b, 111). Keppel's role and reputation are confirmed from many directions. Albert Quie, who played the most influential critical role in the House Committee on Education and Labor (together with fellow Republican Charles Goodell and Democrat Edith Green), talks of Keppel as 'one of the few Commissioners of Education that had much to do with education policy' (Quie, interview). Samuel Halperin, legislative specialist on the staff of the Office of Education and from 1963 Director of the Office of Legislation and Congressional Relations, worked closely with Keppel and included him (together with Wilbur Cohen, Gardner and Harold Howe, Keppel's successor) in the category of 'rather phenomenal men'. Keppel was 'the politician par excellence... the great political broker'. He had

a very keen sense of why Federal education legislation had failed in the past. He took it upon himself... to bring some order out of chaos in the education community... [He] spent a lot of his time talking not with persons in the Office of Education but with education association leaders and influential members of the church groups, individual higher education authorities, and the like... he did try to reach a set of principles on which men could agree... (A: LBJ Lib, Halperin, Oral History Collection, Halperin, 1969, 2–9; Appendix, interview, n.d., 18–21)

In 1964, over the proposed Economic Opportunity Act, Yarmolinsky worked with Keppel on political issues and problems – 'ways of getting people to support the program, ways of keeping the program relatively intelligent and yet getting it through the Congress' (Yarmolinsky, interview). The Title I Manager of Minnesota described Keppel as 'well respected' in the education community (Hanson, interview). Keppel was obviously uniquely placed to bring together the pieces at hand to shape a basis for policy and legislation. He helped to impose on events a sense of strategic advance, turning the ESEA in general and Title I in particular into a negotiable attack on poverty and disadvantage. He was able to reassure the House General Subcommittee on Education in detail about the supply of teachers and about curriculum development, about the definition of poverty and about the deficiencies of school libraries, about the needs of preschool children and the in-service needs of teachers. On the need for reform in in-service and pre-service teacher education he added: 'as a former dean of a school of education – I am perhaps so far away from it now I no longer qualify as a witness – but in the older days it was clear to me...'. These moments when educational experience and political action came together demonstrated clearly what kind of a climacteric it was that had been reached through the ESEA in 1965 (A: US Congress, General Subcommittee, 1965, 82–140).

Even against the background of long pressures for educational improvement, and the build-up of interest in new educational directions, the rapidity of the adoption of the ESEA is remarkable. It shared with other elements in the anti-poverty programme the mounting awareness of the national emergency implied by such events as the burning of Watts in Los Angeles in the summer of 1965, the increasing visibility of black activism, and reminders of poverty-stricken Appalachia and its poverty-stricken schools (A: Schrag, 1965). The speed of the policy changes, in education too, can be judged by the fact that in 1963 and 1964 federal involvement to this extent could not be foreseen. Even as late as January 1964 *The New York Times* was reporting that President Johnson's plea for prompt action was 'unlikely to be heeded':

The consensus in the Capitol is that such a program (to aid elementary and secondary education) cannot win Congressional approval this year or in the foreseeable future unless some near-miraculous new formula for skirting the church–state issue can be devised. So far, no solution is in sight...(A: Morris, 1964, 78)

Although poverty and the educational imperative were not to reach the dimensions of political action and the 'new formula' needed for legislation until 1965, expectations were crowding into the national consciousness even as near-miracles were being discounted. In the same edition of *The New York Times* Fred Hechinger, one of the nation's foremost interpreters of prevailing moods in education, began his analysis:

Restlessness is the word that best describes American education's mood at the beginning of 1964. Everywhere change is in the air – some violent, some orderly, none of it clearly understood. Those in positions of power...are in the main educational conservatives; yet they sense that changes are essential and inevitable. (A: Hechinger, 1964, 73)

If the change in the air was not a response to precise pressures from precise constituencies, the expectation of demand and pressure has to be seen as part of the change not yet clearly understood.

The expectations which surrounded ESEA and the anti-poverty programmes in general were being embodied in new action processes, what Hersey described in connection with the example of New Haven, Connecticut, as the achievement of 'a never-seen-before coalition' of School Board, community social welfare agencies, business and union communities, churches, civil rights leaders and state and federal agencies

(A: Hersey, 1964, 531). Part of the confidence that quickly underpinned the ESEA in 1965 was a sense of wider national processes, the potential for new forms of action at other levels. If the Act signalled, for example, that the distance between educational action on behalf of public schools and private education could usefully be bridged – as one Catholic commentator put it, 'separate elements of our pluralism can meet' (A: Davignon, 1966, 9) – it was because talk of 'near-miraculous' solutions reflected movement within the pluralism. By the spring of 1965, Edmund W. Gordon, who chaired the Department of Educational Psychology and Guidance at New York's Yeshiva University, could write an editorial in the *American Journal of Orthopsychiatry* congratulating it and its parent Association on having lost their former isolation over problems of the disadvantaged. They now had 'many companions', and 'isolated and pilot programs which for years have struggled to stay alive suddenly now face the prospects of abundant support and massive replication', though he went on to draw attention to 'the pitifully small though growing body of knowledge available as a guide to work in this area' (A: Gordon, E.W., 1965a, 445).

Once the Act was in place, therefore, expectations were high, even if, as one of those deeply involved with it was to point out, what the Act said and set out to do was a good deal less grandiose than the expectations that in many cases were placed upon it (A: Halperin and Wayson, 1975, 147). We have seen the basis for and nature of the high hopes associated with the war on poverty overall, and obviously – given the centrality of education to the thinking about the whole strategy – much of the flamboyant language that went into its promotion followed it into the domain of public action in 1965 and 1966 particularly. For Johnson himself in 1966 education would be, he insisted, as long as he held office, 'the first work of our time' (A: Johnson [1966], 65). For Vice-President Hubert Humphrey, speaking at the same conference on the education of the disadvantaged, the ten-month old programme had already had 'a tremendous impact': the ESEA was the climax of the sixties programmes (A: Humphrey, 1966, 55–6). A new wave of interest in education had gathered momentum, and if an educational 'revolution' was not taking place, to many of the planners and the participants, and to the public at large it was beginning to look like one. Title I and its concern with the children of the poor were widely interpreted as a political godsend, though the specifics and the mechanics of the Act and the processes by which the educational attack on poverty was to take place were only hazily perceived. The optimism and good intentions that had come together gave the ESEA its aura not only in Washington speeches but also in the thinking of those now involved in state and local planning and implementation, in advising on the work for which Gordon and others saw such 'pitifully small' guidance in the knowledge and experience available. What little there was, therefore, became of supreme importance, and those involved in experimentation in relevant fields of education and applied social science entered the spotlight centre-stage. How much so, and in what frame of mind, can be clearly seen from the national conference on education and the disadvantaged at which Johnson and Humphrey spoke, held in connection with Title I of the ESEA in July 1966.

The discussions at the conference broadly accepted two frameworks, two sets of assumptions – the first, that Title I offered serious opportunities for change in schools and in society, the second that the obstacles were enormous, that advance under Title I was limited, and that the poor 'still have little reason to believe they matter as human beings. The disadvantaged, adults and children, are failing in the educational system, and the educational system is failing them.' Mario Fantini, from the Ford Foundation, emphasized that to succeed, educational reform had to address questions of power, to become a change agent, to create 'a subsystem for change'. Many participants, from all levels of the educational system, emphasized the conservatism with which Title I was faced, the attitudes to be overcome. One delegate described how in his area teachers were using Title I remedial classes as 'a dumping ground for their problem students, just as they had used vocational classes'. A New Jersey superintendent of schools, on the other hand, pointed to the change already resulting from Title I, prior to which

there was little action in the classroom. Teachers had been conditioned to expect failure, and had little outside contact with the problems of the disadvantaged. Title I provided health care and food service; it lengthened the schoolday and decreased class size. Title I gave us money to shake up the programs and gave status to teaching the disadvantaged.

Such positive images were echoed from Georgia and elsewhere. Confusion and ambiguity ran deep in the conference, however: the schools were succeeding, they were failing; new ways were being found, they were not being found; poverty was being addressed, poverty was being misunderstood.

A harbinger of the 'positive discrimination' or 'reverse discrimination' concepts that were to become important in Britain as well as the United States was to be found in a contribution by Edmund Gordon, emphasizing the equalization process that was taking place through Head Start and more widely. It was a process which might result in a reduced gap between the advantaged and the disadvantaged but that was insufficient: 'equalizing the opportunities ... will not compensate for the differences. We should go beyond equal opportunity to specialized opportunity.' The report from one panel discussion indicated agreement 'that not enough is being done, yet views ranged from "We've done nothing" to "We are doing *something* right".' Some contributors to the conference, particularly in discussion of the theme of 'The school views the child – and vice versa', underlined how little school principals, teachers and other educationists had been equipped by their previous training to confront the situations now being addressed. Edward Zigler of Yale University, who had been a member of the Head Start national planning committee, and already with a year's experience of guiding and administering the programme, attacked middle-class assumptions and attitudes (now beginning to come under attack from various quarters) as a failure to understand the very people the War on Poverty programmes were supposed to help: 'We need a cadre of experts who understand the poor. I have been struck by the numbers of people who think they *own* the poor, not just understand them'. There were also reminders of the relationship between the ESEA and the other urgencies facing the United States. In the words of the Title I coordinator for the Berkeley School District:

Whatever goals we have set for disadvantaged kids, they have not reached them…Educationally, we do have a bomb under us, under our whole educational system. (A: National Conference on Education of the Disadvantaged, 1966, 5–15)

ESEA had promoted action and raised expectations; the means and aims of delivery, however, and an acceptable rate of progress, had rapidly become crucial features of attitudes to the Act and to education in general.

In the implementation of the Act the ambiguities became obvious, including, for example, the application of formulas to identify districts and schools in relation to poverty, and children in relation to educational disadvantage. There was a tension between the precise targets and requirements of the Act and attempts to broaden the interpretation, to see Title I aid as a breakthrough towards general aid (A: Guthrie, 1968, 304). In addition, there were uncertainties about the level of aid – was it a major investment, or inadequate support for what had been heralded as a national crusade, what one commentator on the War on Poverty describes as 'a classic instance of the American habit of substituting good intentions for cold, hard cash' (A: Gelfand, 1981, 145)? And then, mixed in with the good intentions, the growing anxiety that the whole operation could turn out to be an unsuccessful exercise:

Can a program of compensatory education for the disadvantaged even at its best be salutary in any ultimate way without altering the disadvantaged environment giving rise to the disadvantaged child? Will the ravages of poverty and discrimination on the child's conception of life and of himself disappear if Appalachia and Harlem are permitted to remain as they are? (A: Getsels, 1966, 226)

Interpretations of the ESEA ranged from its being merely a step in the 'modernization' of the educational system, to a response – not to educational failure as such – but to its 'maldistribution among social, economic and racial groups' (A: Gordon and Wilkerson, 1966, 170; Cohen, D.K. and Van Geel, 1970, 224). The early difficulties of implementation often related to such ambiguities and uncertainties, but were also compounded by other problems.

The speed with which the legislation had been prepared inevitably meant a lack of preparedness in the states. There was most obviously a major problem in recruiting and training personnel of various kinds, notably teachers who could relate to the particular problems of disadvantaged children (A: Miller, J.O., 1969, 5; Neale, 1966, 8). Title I administrators had to be found, and the vague and often non-existent guidelines from Washington had to be interpreted. Many of those responsible for the implementation in the early days had, in fact, little contact with Washington, and although workshops and conferences were organized in many of the states these were, in the view of those who attended, often of little practical help. The number of officials administering the Act from Washington was extremely small: when Murphy looked at problems of implementation at the end of the 1960s he found that the Division of Compensatory Education, which was responsible in the bureau of Elementary and Secondary Education of the Office of Education, had three desk officers to monitor implementation throughout the United States (A: Murphy [1970], 10–11; 1973, 173). The often very small local offices had to relate to large numbers of schools and newly appointed project teachers, as well as help in designing grant applications and advise on priorities and procedures.

The greatest confusion concerned what was legitimate expenditure under the Act, and the most difficult area to monitor was the possible use of the 'targeted' funds for 'general' purposes. With an eye to which schools, which children, what equipment, what resources and what processes, came under Title I, the organizers in the districts often had an unenviable task – organizers who in some cases came from the classroom, in others from administration, and in some cases from working with existing federally funded programmes. At St Paul, Minnesota, for example, the first Title I coordinator had experience of administering federally funded vocational education programmes, and since the first year's funds came late in the year a lot of it was spent on equipment, 'like everyone did'. She was responsible for a large summer programme and (under Title II of ESEA) a large library programme, as well as 'keeping an eye' on a Neighborhood Youth Corps programme, Head Start and other programmes. When her successor took over in 1967

we were the contact person with the state as well as with Washington, D.C., the contact for the school district and anything to do with federal programs. We brought the information back and relayed it to the superintendents...We actually sat down and wrote up the projects at that point in time – other people might assist us...We did all the interpretation of the laws.

If some of this process seemed ambiguous, the coordinator (or 'consultant-in-charge') admitted 'it seemed so to us too'. They did work closely with the state offices, comparing their interpretations, talking with Washington, administering tests to determine low-achieving children, identifying a target population by test scores and not by poverty criteria (Pinkerton and Johnson, interview). The Title I administrator for the State of Minnesota (a former school super-intendent) was working in the context of eligible areas as determined by federal census data, though with the same emphasis on eligible children being determined by – at the beginning at least – elusive criteria of 'educational disadvantagement':

In general the early programs sort of shotgunned the problem and school districts that said 'we don't have a school nurse, therefore our children are disadvantaged'...'we don't have a psychologist, therefore our children are disadvantaged'...'we don't have this, we don't have that, therefore let's use some of that money for those things' – and for the first year we did allow that, but we decided early on that educational disadvantagement was tied to the 3 R's...so we said that Title I in Minnesota will be for basic skills...mathematics and reading...

When he first became Title I administrator he was 'just about going crazy, because no one really knew what the programme was supposed to be'. Title I was not something that most people concerned with schools had entertained as an idea 'in the realm of the possible':

There have been moves...to attempt to get federal dollars into local school districts, for much more than a hundred years...In that first year I read 1,440 proposals from school districts in Minnesota...sent back to the school districts – 'if you really want the money these are some things you have to do'...the program had to be educationally defensible, and had to be reasonably achievable, and it had to be logically measurable...It wasn't as tough getting people to administer it as it was finding staff, because...we had...a serious shortage...The next toughest obstacle was working *with*...those people – some of them were teachers, some of them were para-professional non-teaching staff...to get them into a mode of working with children in a way that was different...(Hanson, interview)

With different levels of available experience and expertise different states and school districts worked with different degrees of effectiveness and understanding. The problems of Minnesota, however, were in most respects shared elsewhere. In the early days of Title I in West Virginia, for example, the emphasis was on materials and equipment which had little or no relationship with the needs of the target population. Teacher aides were often used as 'general dogsbodies' rather than to provide the specialist help needed. An underlying problem was ignorance of the intent of the legislation, combined with a sense of need that was so great and widespread that it was easy to couch applications in 'compensatory' terms. Help from Washington review teams was not available until the early 1970s, the state was unprepared to implement the legislation, and there was a serious shortage of experienced staff (Taylor in Purdy *et al.*, interview).

In the first few years implementation meant complex and serious obstacles to be overcome, the identification of priorities, including an emphasis on language arts and remedial teaching, a relationship to other aspects of community development, and the redirecting of teachers, administrators and others towards new modes of working towards new objectives. Children were beginning to receive either individual attention for remedial purposes, or were taking part in enrichment programmes of various kinds. Training programmes, testing, target setting and evaluation, had been placed on the agenda, and federal policy-making was being translated into ambitious and often extremely difficult state and local procedures. The unaccustomed activities of writing proposals, interpreting and administering federal requirements, and reporting, were closely bound up with questions of experience, shortages, perceptions, and wide disparities in all of these amongst the states and regions. Such technical and human difficulties of formulas and staffing did not, however, detract from the sense of innovation, potential and promise that was shared by the Commissioner and legislators in Washington and those carrying the policies into the schools. Across the country there were widely different bases on which to build. What the Ford projects had attempted in some places was now to be attempted in areas where no such experience had been gained. There were vastly different judgments to be made about the quality of the schools and the teachers, and often suspicion or hostility on the part of teachers and administrators as to the explicit or implied critique in the legislation, alongside enthusiasm for taking advantage of the new opportunities. When the 'slum child' was put in any equation with the schools, many underlined the distance between the two, seeing the schools as 'factories of failure', prisons with 'benign warders' (A: Asbell, 1966, 26, 36). The issues that now began to surface most clearly arose out of these divergences. What, for example, was the most appropriate teaching style in the language intervention at the heart of the Title I schemes (summarized in one version as a tension between 'creativists' and 'correctionists' – and arguing that both were necessary) (Bailey, 1966, pp. 1–2)? The implementation process brought out any questions of children's health and welfare in ways that suggested reinterpretations of the schools' roles – bringing them closer to people's needs and lives (A: Coles, 1965). The school–home relationships became more sharply focused; ethnic, race and class issues were translated into the precise terms of project applications and classroom activity; the complexities of language were already exercising the researchers and educational strategists and Title I thrust the debates more deeply into the system. In this last context there were references back to Hebb and Hunt, consideration of the theories of class-based language 'codes' being developed in the United States, and in Britain particularly by Basil Bernstein (A: John and Goldstein, 1964; John 1965). Since reading and 'language arts' were crucial elements in implementation strategies, theories of language 'difference' and 'deficit' were at this point growing in importance. Researchers were beginning to emphasize 'how little we know' about the relationship between social status and language production, the potential uses of 'substandard English', and differences in language function: 'at the present time, we cannot completely resolve the difference–deficiency issue' (A: Gussow, 1965; John, 1965; Cazden, 1961, 248).

Involved in the implementation processes, therefore, were questions relating to the nature of compensatory education itself, and the assumptions on which Title I and its detailed projects were based. Did intervention and compensation 'blame' the child and the family? At a White House conference on education in 1965, for example, J.W. Getzels confronted some of the main issues in preschool education. It aimed at transforming the preschool lower-class child 'in accordance with the requirements of the prevailing school', but there were problems about imposing cultural values on the 'culturally deprived child' as if the child did not already have 'other values and experiences that are *assets*'. Could, secondly, 'the standards of today's school be taken safely as the model … Is this what we want for our children, or should not some thought be given … to the transformation of the school itself?' Behind such reservations reverberated his question: would the ravages of poverty and discrimination on the child disappear 'if Appalachia and Harlem are permitted to remain as they are?' (Getzels, 1966, 226–7).

Although Title I picked up on the momentum of earlier projects and programmes, it did not replace them. At local or state level other projects continued, in many forms, on different scales, with similar purposes. In 1965 Catherine Brunner was outlining the effects of the continuing Early School Admissions Project in Baltimore; the National Council of Teachers of English was reporting on a Task Force on Teaching English to the Disadvantaged; a special issue of *Educational Leadership* was devoted to 'Poverty and the School', including an article on a pilot project on 'An experimental curriculum for culturally deprived kindergarten children' in Racine, Wisconsin; Ferkauf Graduate School of Education at Yeshiva University, New York, was describing its Project Beacon, to train a corps of specialists for the public schools, rigorously prepared to meet the educational needs of socially disadvantaged children and their parents; California was continuing with its programme of legislation, including the Unruh Preschool Act, designed to 'provide equal educational opportunity to children of low income or disadvantaged families... improve their performance and increase their motivation and productivity when they enter school' (A: Brunner, 1965; NCTE, 1965; Olson and Larson, 1965; Project Beacon, 1965; Anderson, 1965, 9). Cataloguing and categorizing were accelerating, the most notable example being Gordon and Wilkerson's 1966 *Compensatory Education for the Disadvantaged. Programs and practices: preschool through college*, describing and analysing an enormous number of projects nation-wide. From 1965 Ford was funding a five-year 'language program for culturally disadvantaged children' at Durham, North Carolina (A: Shenkman, 1968), and both within and outside the Title I programmes research and experiment were continuing. Existing programmes were being adapted to meet the new demands, including the training and retraining of teachers. Under the National Defense Education Act, for example, a four-state project was initiated in 1965 to train teachers of disadvantaged youth (including in California), and from the previous year in fact NDEA funding had been used for summer and in-service programmes (Stone, 1969). Throughout the late 1960s reports were being published of projects of this kind being initiated – many of them carrying the title of action research (A: Rosenberg and Adkins, 1967), many of them with dramatic or optimistic titles or acronyms – Project Breakthrough (Cook County, Illinois), Project Mobilization (New Jersey), Operation Fair Chance (California) (Cook County, 1969; Carl, 1970; Lohman and Talagi, 1967).

At the end of the first year of operation of Title I a state like New York could already publish an account of *100 Selected Projects* (New York State, 1966) – at the same time, it should be noted, that the Higher Horizons project was collapsing in New York City. Older traditions were being harnessed to the new effort, and Maria Montessori in particular was being widely rediscovered: a 1967 book on *Montessori for the Disadvantaged* had as its sub-title 'An Application of Montessori Educational Principles to the War on Poverty' (Orem, 1967). A comment on a 1967 community schools programme in Boston captures much of the feeling attached both to Title I and to the multi-pronged educational efforts of similar kinds at this period of the mid-1960s: '... in the midst of collapsing social structures all across the nation, new cornerstones were being fashioned for the neighborhood of Boston' (Boston Community Schools, n.d.).

Given subsequent judgments made of the over-optimism, rhetoric, blindness to social and political realities prevalent in these developments, it is important to emphasize the climate of change in which they took shape. While education was central to the aspirations of the Great Society, the new world was not to be won by education alone. The education programmes stimulated, were accompanied and sustained by programmes in social welfare, and by other forms of legislation and action that make the optimism underlying Title I and its progenitors easier to understand. The war on poverty was also to be a revolution in social welfare, and from 1964 there was indeed a growth in social welfare programmes that was 'staggering' (A: Patterson, 1981, 164). Within education there was an awareness of the breadth of the social policies intended or being implemented under the Economic Opportunity Act, in health and social security, in urban and regional planning. An Appalachian Regional Development Act in 1964 was one such measure. Medicare – a Health Insurance for the Aged Act – became law in 1965. At the same time Medicaid – a programme of medical aid for those in need – brought the federal government into the financing (between 50 and 80 per cent) of medical costs. In 1965 Congress approved the establishment of a Department of Housing and Urban Development, and a task force related to that departure proposed a Model Cities Program which was implemented in 1966 through grants and technical assistance to carry out demonstration programmes. From the outset the programme was seen to have implications for urban education and led to a national conference on the Educational Dimension of the Model Cities Program (A: Campbell *et al.*, 1969). Behind this, as other such developments, lay what was described as reliance on 'a sustained White House commitment to social reform' and faith in 'the ability of rational planning to find solutions to the problems of the cities':

The stubborn facts of interest group politics, limited budgets, bureaucratic resistance to change, and the extreme pluralism of American society faded away before the image of a well-conceived federal blueprint for the slums, backed by a President with enormous power. (A: Frieden and Kaplan, 1977, 36)

The range of developments was not only widening to take in federal initiatives of many kinds, it was also addressing issues to which there were different kinds of possible solutions, including an emphasis on *area* strategies, for Appalachia or for the inner city. Education itself was being related not only to the 'cycle of poverty' but to comprehensive measures emerging from other directions in the war on poverty. A joint publication of the Office of Education and the Office of Economic Opportunity in 1966 underlined that the school official knew that 'no matter how dedicated, industrious and compassionate...his school cannot do the job alone'. It discussed hunger, clothing, nursing and other aspects of the world inhabited by the children and the school (A: US, Miscellaneous, OE and OEO, 1966). When Sargent Shriver appeared before the House Committee on the War on Poverty in 1964, he had emphasized how all-embracing was the proposed attack, how much greater was the understanding of the complex causes of poverty, and he related the proposed Economic Opportunity legislation to 'other programs of the Federal Government...concerned with education, health, employment, agriculture, economic climate, and so on' (A: US Congress, House Hearings, Part 1, 1964, 20). Some features of the new programmes and legislation straddled education and these other developments. The Economic Opportunity Act, for example, legislated as one of its youth programmes for a Job Corps, providing young men and women between 16 and 21 with residential opportunities for 'education, vocational training, useful work experience...' and other opportunities for education and training provided 'where practicable...through local public educational agencies or by private vocational educational institutions or technical institutes' (A: US Congress, House, 1964, pp. 1–2). Here, as with the Neighborhood Youth Corps, VISTA and other schemes, the principles involved and the variety of implementation strategies on the ground meant that many boundaries were crossed. VISTA – Volunteers in Service to America – was intended as a kind of domestic 'Peace Corps' and from 1965 volunteers were trained at universities, social action agencies and elsewhere to work in rural areas, city slums, among migrant farm workers, on Indian reservations and in other locations (A: Rees, 1968, 176). A *Vista Fact Book* in 1967 describes local projects involved with remedial education, home visiting, child development, parents in community action programmes, adult literacy, recreation, craft, self-help schemes, youth group work, home management, recruiting local talent to expand cultural and educational programmes, educating citizens in the government of cities, state policies...(A: US OEO, 1967).

Under the Higher Education Act of 1965, a Teacher Corps was also created, with the aim of improving the education and welfare of children from low-income families. The 'teacher interns' engaged in the programme were invited to consider a range of social and educational realities, to reflect on their own experience, and to provide 'better education for children who are turned away from the mainstream of American life' (A: Corwin, 1973; van Doren, 1967; US HEW, *Futures in Education*, n.d.). Whether at the level of official provision or of enabling legislation, Head Start or the regular classroom, planning for education or planning for welfare or urban renewal, the links between school and community were in some way constantly being underlined, and confidence in education being related to the world outside the classroom.

Any one of these mid-1960s policies, taken in isolation, is open to the charge of excessive idealism, rhetoric or diversion from the major social concerns of unemployment, racial discrimination, inequalities and poverty itself. The educational war, however, is a crucial feature of a comprehensive campaign which cannot be understood without the civil rights movement and legislation, the emergence of economic, urban, rural, welfare and other strategies. Of particular significance is the parallel development of an educational and a community action momentum. The immediate impact of the community action component of the Economic Opportunity Act was in terms of commitment to the creation of new organizational bases and a popular constituency. There are divergent views as to the degree of clarity involved in the aim of the 'maximum feasible participation' of the poor. These ranged from Daniel Moynihan's view of it as 'maximum feasible misunderstanding' on the part of a government with a set of theories and little idea of what it was doing, to a belief that the Act and its philosophy were designed to stimulate poor people's organizations, or perhaps even a deliberate ambiguity leaving the door open for a new conception of service for the poor and a contribution by the poor themselves in the shape of 'non-professional manpower' (A: Moynihan, 1969, 168–70; Brecher, 1973, 37–8; Riessman, 1966, 110–13). The fact that by 1966 the mayors who had felt their authority undermined were regaining control does not alter the fact that the war on poverty had provided a popular as well as a legislative stimulus to action for change, though not without resistance, conflict and failure. If, as one analyst put it, the policy was 'innovative but ambiguous' (A: Kramer, 1969, 1), it could as easily be described as ambiguous but innovative, and as a result, in the eyes of many, America would never be the same again – particularly given the priority to children and childhood education (A: Bookbinder, 1966, 476–7). There were difficulties and hostilities in the implementation of Title I as with other programmes, everywhere from the floor of Congress to the classroom, but for a period the intentions and the optimism represented the dominant environment in which the programmes operated. It would be wrong, however, to disregard the warnings given from many quarters from the outset that the war on poverty would require sustained commitment, effort and resources.

A final emphasis regarding the climate in which Title I operated and to which it contributed is the degree of acceptance of federal involvement, following the controversies of the Kennedy period and the (particularly Republican) opposition to the degree of federal intervention in education represented by many measures, but outstandingly by the ESEA. Opposition to a strengthened federal role in education certainly became muted in this period, and support for targeted federal funding was widely recruited. Opposition was dispersed if not dispelled, directed in many cases at new targets, often at the operational niceties of the new programmes rather that at the underlying principles.

No one doubted that the legislative programme of 1964–5 in particular meant that the United States had embarked on a new dimension and interpretation of federal responsibilities. Many of the new programmes were seen as innovations in 'federalism'. Job Corps, for example, was seen as signalling 'a new era in the relationship of the federal government with universities' (A: Alden, 1965, 85). The Economic Opportunity Act was 'an experimental approach to American federalism' (A: Davidson, 1969, 2). Peter Muirhead, Associate Commissioner for Higher Education under Keppel, expressed the view in 1968 that 'the most significant development in higher education in the last five years has been the awakened interest of the Federal Government in the support of higher education', though he added the emphasis that this support had been 'directed toward the mission of higher education, rather than directed toward the mission of the Federal Government' (A: LBJ Lib, Muirhead, oral interview, 1968, 3). The ESEA and all the poverty programmes had such a public resonance. It pointed towards historical associations, notably comparisons with the New Deal period and the relationship between the Civilian Conservation Corps of the 1930s and education – a relationship which raised similar questions about alternatives to the existing schools and the possibility of federal control (A: Gower, 1967). Keppel points to the previous tradition of twentieth-century effort, rarely successful, to bring the government more firmly into legislation on education – Truman and Roosevelt had both declared a commitment – though the difficulties were always greater than any experienced in the British parliament! (Keppel, interview). Keppel's view of the new federal presence was most clearly expressed in an address he gave in February 1965 to a Brookings conference of business executives. His title was 'Education: Issues and Trends in the Federal Role', and his message (here, as in almost all his addresses at the time) was of the sea-change that had required a shift in perspective and policy:

> There was a time when education was considered the private preserve of parents, teachers, school boards – and possibly students. Now education concerns the whole nation.

Government was now involved more than ever before – not 'from an appetite to create little or great bureaucracies, but because the needs of our times have called for action'. The federal involvement in the educational partnership had received an important stimulus from the GI Bill of Rights after the Second World War. No one doubted that Title I in particular also pointed into the future and towards continued and perhaps greater federal involvement; the problem lay in whether that implied a greater degree of *control*.

It is difficult to gauge the extent of local uncertainty about the new federal role, though those who participated in Title I at the local level were certainly aware of ambiguous responses to federal funding and what it implied. In Boston, for example, the Title I director, who worked in the Title I office from the day it opened, recalls that

> ...we were told from the beginning we were a part of the Boston school system. The check that we were issued and still are doesn't anywhere say Title I. It's a City of Boston check...from my experience, the concern of a lot of people was – if the federal government gets into education, they're ultimately going to try to take over. That was one suspicion they might have had. The other was...there were very conservative people...We had in this office eight consecutive years of federal reviews where a team of anything from four to eight people came up – and we were not at the beginning used to outsiders coming and right away we felt we were on the defensive...(Coughlin, interview)

In the Boston office they finally got on to first name terms with the federal 'outsiders'. Policy-making has to do with theories of intervention and control. It also has to do with who signs the cheque, the mix of conservative people and others, and the retention or rejection of images of the past – and ambiguous messages about the future.

Evaluation had made a grand entry into the vocabulary of social science and social action. An evaluation movement, especially in education, had been created, though it became most visible with the publication in 1966 of the Coleman report on *Equality of Educational Opportunity*, a report on segregation and education that had been commissioned by Congress under the Civil Rights Act. The Coleman report was the outcome of a major national survey, and it brought large-scale research into the service of policy-related evaluation. Between 1964 and 1966, however, the programmes we have been considering developed their own evaluation momentums of different kinds. Consideration of judgments that were emerging with regard to the educational war on poverty is a question of reviewing not just formal evaluations but also opinion more widely. It means considering the components and vocabularies of programmes and processes, the theories and ideologies they represented, the nature of the applause and the critiques becoming as important as the programmes themselves. Within their brief to report on the lack of educational opportunities 'by reason of race, color, religion, or national origin', the Coleman team underlined the process of which it formed one part:

The survey is, of course, only one small part of extensive and varied activities which numerous institutions and persons are pursuing in an effort to understand the critical factors relating to the education of minority children...(A: Coleman, 1966, 1)

It is with this 'effort to understand' the processes affecting not only minority children but also the 'children of the poor' as addressed by Title I and other measures, that we are concerned in this chapter.

Henry Aaron's analysis of 'the Great Society in perspective' is a good starting point. In *Politics and the Professors* he reflects (from the vantage of the late 1970s) on the war on poverty and 'the prevailing ambiguity about the nature of the problem (poverty or inequality; lack of income or lack of status or lack of power; unequal opportunity or unequal results)'. He shares with Moynihan the view of multiple and often contradictory objectives in individual programmes, and underlines the fact that the emergence of programme evaluation (using the tools of economics) was only just gaining currency as the war on poverty was declared. Evaluation of these programmes, 'and indeed of all government programmes affecting human resources, has proven extremely difficult. In some cases the benefits from the program cannot be measured with any precision' (A: Aaron, 1978, 28–31). With such programmes as Head Start and Title I, the ambiguities in intention and in the strategy are not difficult to detect, though in some cases we have seen a relationship between ambiguity and opportunity. Historians still argue over the multiple and contradictory objectives contained in almost every event, decision, policy and process. As the programmes we have considered were enacted and implemented it was not clearly understood how difficult would be the processes of evaluation and judgment.

As policies and resources for action unfolded, and as the concept of action research gained ground, there was an underlying need for experiment and development that was too urgent to wait for meticulous research and evaluation guidelines and procedures. Judgments about the success and failure of projects were often mixed, and where they were clear-cut, either positive or negative, they were inevitably based on hunch or the reading of incomplete, hastily compiled or anecdotal accounts. By 1966 – *one year* after the first Head Start summer programmes and the enactment of ESEA – Havighurst believed it was 'becoming clear that... The Head Start and Remedial Instruction programs of the Elementary and Secondary Education Act were not solving the problem of low school achievement by children of low-income families' (A: Havighurst, 1979, 25). Such after-the-event judgments are matched by equally firm judgments being made at the time, and in many respects a race was developing between efforts to develop acceptable forms of evaluation, and efforts to make whatever public and political capital possible out of summary judgments one way or the other. Within the projects themselves there were anxieties about the reliability of research findings – Henry Saltzman at the Ford Foundation, for example, reported in 1965 that findings in the Baltimore project were being distorted as between the 'experimental' and the 'control' children, with the latter being 'contaminated' by enthusiastic parents (A: FF, Baltimore, Saltzman, 8 March 1965). In 1966 the Educational Testing Service held a workshop on evaluating Title I programmes (involving discussions of the role of evaluation, selecting and developing evaluation instruments, and designing and interpreting the results of evaluation studies) (A: ETS, 1966). Within or alongside Title I or Compensatory Education offices, states were establishing evaluation units.

In the educational programmes developed in the early and mid-1960s evaluation at the operational level was generally taken to mean 'report', and amidst the enthusiasm that underpinned the majority of projects the reporting was most frequently on a range between mildly positive and – though occasionally with misgivings – enthusiastic. There is a mass of documentation, local and state-wide, produced by the Ford, Head Start, Title I and other projects in the mid-1960s, and even through to the beginning of the 1970s, which suggests positive outcomes as judged by test scores, teacher or parent observation, teacher involvement, child behaviour or intelligence measures. For example, an evaluation of the third experimental year of the Boston Educational Enrichment Program (six-week summer sessions, partly funded by Ford, for 'underprivileged' elementary and junior-high school pupils in the Boston area, run by six independent schools), produced the following reported results. The programme had had effects on the children who participated that were not evident in a chosen control group. The effects included:

Increased awareness of and interest in intellectual matters and a more positive attitude toward school... Greater awareness of and concern with middle class values. At the end of the summer, EEP children cared more about such things as neatness, cleanliness, punctuality, and honesty. Tolerance of others and willingness to cooperate... Creativity and imagination. Probably the most dramatic change observed was an increase in creative thinking on the Torrance Tests for most of the EEP children... (A: Vreeland, 1967, 55–6)

On a wider scale, California's 1965–6 description of research and teacher education projects for disadvantaged children are presented as a 'report', largely of the work done, while the following year it becomes an 'annual evaluation report' on compensatory education in the state. The conclusion by this stage, on the basis of standardized achievement tests, was that the achievement rate of pupils on Title I programmes had, in 'practically all cases', increased:

The range of gains was substantial. Relatively few districts reported average gains of less than a month for every month of instruction, while in some districts the average was almost three years' gain during the year.

The important conclusion was that 'the achievement gap that has traditionally existed between the disadvantaged student and the middle class student appears to be gradually closing' (A: California State Department of Education, Office of Compensatory Education, 1967, S-7-10). In following years the Title I evaluations point to differential pupil achievement related to large city, suburban, rural, resource and other criteria, with findings often less confident than in earlier reports, but in general – taking urban districts as an example – those sampled 'showed, almost without exception, that the students continue to make progress above that which is normally expected without Title I services' (A: California State Department of Education, 1968a, 42).

Such evaluations were repeated across the country. A report on the operation of Title I in St Paul, Minnesota, in 1966–7 is representative of the kind of focus widely adopted. Where teacher aides were being appointed, the teachers and principals reported on the success of the scheme (often judging the improved appearance or personality character-istics of those employed). The report contains evaluations by teachers, parents and pupils, and the generally positive statements reflect the enthusiasm for the methods adopted (field trips, library usage, resource deployment...) to achieve the aim of 'total educative effectiveness'. The evaluation data derive from questionnaires, interviews, observation and objective methods (A: Minnesota, St Paul Public Schools, 1968). The evaluations are obviously unsystematic, using instruments and pro-cedures which are crude and producing data on the basis of which it is difficult to make judgments, but which reflect the state of the programmes and of the art of evaluation at the time. The local evaluations are reflected in the considerable journal and other literature offering early views of the success of the programmes. Head Start and other preschool programmes attracted particular attention. One look at Head Start described the success as due to the pupil–adult ratio, when 'everyone in the program was important', including the disabled volunteer who delivered the juice and crackers:

Teachers noted improvement in the children's ability to communicate with others, to be part of a group, to listen and follow oral directions and to respond eagerly to new experiences. Certain negative and fearful attitudes towards policemen, firemen, nurses and doctors changed after children had an opportunity to get acquainted with these people. (A: Levens, 1966, 482)

Impressionistic evidence was widely offered to demonstrate that 'action programs transcend maxims and exhortations to provide concrete examples of the salvaging of human potentialities' (A: Goff, 1968). On many counts 'even the sceptics and others who refrain from committing themselves to an opinion until "all the data" are in' were persuaded by the increased friendliness and 'healthy familiarity' with school of Head Start children (A: Omwake, 1966, 479). Head Start, it must be remembered, was politically and for other reasons a popular programme, and even where teachers were suspicious of the new relationships with parents and community, the parents were generally reported as enthusiastic about the changed behaviour they perceived in their children, and were themselves often eager to take advantage of the opportunity to participate.

All of this was increasingly accompanied by criticism of the nature and reliability of the evaluative evidence. The techniques were seen as deficient, the assessment of outcomes as premature, the research and evaluation as adding little to what was already known (A: Herman, 1965; Passow, 1970, 46–9). The use of IQ tests was seen as inappropriate and measuring the wrong effects (A: Brazziel, 1967). The data available began to be subject to different interpretations. The positive evaluations of Higher Horizons, for example, as viewed by teachers and administrators were paralleled by disputes about the relationship of success to the extent of resources, and the gains made were seen as either marginal, non-existent or insufficient to justify the expenditure (A: Wrightstone *et al.*, 1964; Wolfbein, 1967; Ribich, 1968). A far from isolated account of 'Head Start or Dead End' in 1966 saw the programme as a 'hodge-podge of conflicting ideologies and interests', resulting in a superficial impression of success: 'one type of "research" consisted of requiring every teacher to list one way in which each of her students had improved under her care in the course of one year. This study indicated that 99.99 per cent of the students 'improved'''. Without a proper evaluation 'one is forced to conclude that almost everything is occurring somewhere and sometimes' (A: Meier, 1966, 124–9). What was happening was clearly the production at local level and for accountability purposes of largely positive reports, not untruthful but often superficial, and the emergence nationally of a call for more stringent evaluation, though with little clarity as to the kinds of measures to be used, or the effects to be measured.

At an early point many of the states understood the difficulty of achieving acceptable evaluations. California, for example, commissioned a report on the education of disadvantaged children, which proved to be a wide-ranging analysis not only of California data but also of what national evidence was becoming available. It confronted the problems of defining disadvantage and cultural deprivation, the main areas of pupil deficiency, the Coleman evidence, the variety of available school and preschool programmes, and the directions most likely to produce results (it also decided that where change was most needed was in the teacher) (A: Wilson *et al.*, 1966). Between the uncritical enthusiasms and the rejections were attempts to arrive at balanced verdicts about the achievements, failures and potential of the initiatives that had begun to be taken in the early 1960s and had culminated particularly in Title I. The problem for most participants had become not whether educational programmes could reverse the environmental effects that constituted the core issue in disadvantage, but what kind of programme, what kind of strategy, would be most effective.

Out of these explorations of ambiguity came, in 1967, the first piece of research to disturb the more sanguine expectations of Head Start – an evaluation of the effects of Head Start six months after the experience, by Wolff and Stein. Their study of the Head Start centres themselves indicated that parents of Head Start children were uniformly enthusiastic, that the children enjoyed the experience and then adjusted better to kindergarten and rated higher on teachers' rankings. Six to eight months after Head Start, however, the research suggested that there was no significant difference in the scores of Head Start and other children. The gains had been lost (A: Wolff and Stein, 1967). The argument from 1967 was to be less about the effectiveness of special preschool and school programmes, and more about whether the effects could be sustained. The Wolff and Stein research, and later analyses of long-term benefits from educational programmes against under-achievement and poverty, were to suggest the need for more stringent evaluation of Title I, and the need for a school strategy that would sustain the gains obtained at the preschool stage. The important direct outcome, to which we shall return in a later discussion, was project Follow Through in 1967.

In terms of evaluation, the Coleman report of 1966 was the watershed. It was a national report on national issues. It broke important ground in focusing not so much on equality of provision as on outcomes, achievement measures, the ability to compete equally beyond school. It examined questions of racial segregation and integration in schools and their effects on different racial groups, concluding that the gap between the attainment of white and minority pupils widened during the school years. The major differential, the report concluded, was less the result of differences in schools than in differences of home and economic condition (A: Coleman, 1965; Coleman et al., 1966). Detailed critiques of the methodology and findings of the Coleman report followed, concerned, for example, with the poor sample response, the number of large cities not included, an over-representation of suburban schools, and other defects in the research design. The important fact about the Coleman report, as we have suggested, was not its detailed findings, its strengths and weaknesses, but its contribution to a climate of opinion in which 'scientific' evaluation was coming to be expected. Ralph Tyler headed a Carnegie–Ford 'Exploratory Committee on Assessing the Progress of Education' (A: Bailey and Mosher, 1968, 177), and the question of measuring outputs was now coming more firmly on to the agenda (A: Kent, 1969). The assertive policies of 1964–5 were now raising questions that at the beginning had either not been asked or had been submerged in the rush to act.

This was largely true of the war on poverty in general, and the range of opinions about the effectiveness of the poverty programme (the vocabulary rapidly shifted from a war to a programme) was equally wide. It retained the optimistic support it had had at many levels. Wilbur Cohen was to reflect in 1973 that 'the Johnson legislative record is unequalled and probably will remain unequalled' (A: Cohen, W., 1973) and until the Vietnam war undercut the funding and the momentum – significantly from 1967, the enthusiasm was not seriously dissipated. There were those who knew that they were settling in for a long war, and those who, while voicing criticisms, considered the poverty programme to justify neither claims of its being a disaster, nor excessive optimism – with all its faults the thing was on the road: 'we would have liked another beginning, but this is it', commented Miller and Rein in 1965 (A: Shaplin, 1966; Miller and Rein, 1965a, 18). At the opposite end of the spectrum of opinion from those who underlined the good intentions and the possibilities of reform were vociferous critics who found the whole war on poverty misconceived. From the beginning there were arguments that the programmes were a substitute for spending real money on worthwhile economic objectives. *Newsweek* summarized these views:

that the war on poverty is not against poverty... but against the poor, that the government is trying to change them rather than change the institutional flaws (a weak educational system, for instance) that allow them to exist. What good is Head Start, it is asked, if Head Starters end up in dilapidated, understaffed slum schools?... the Job Corps does not create jobs (A: *Newsweek*, 1965, 29)

Evaluations of the war on poverty were inevitably therefore controversies over purposes, with the radical critics seeing the policy as a distraction from the 'institutional flaws', and worse, needing to be tackled. Of the critical voices being heard in 1965 and 1966, the most powerful was that of Saul Alinsky, who was particularly resistant to the timorous notion of 'community action' propounded under the Economic Opportunity Act. Alinsky kept up a barrage of attacks on the use of anti-poverty funds as 'a form of political patronage'. A genuine attempt to remove poverty was 'not a program for a silky-smooth Madison Avenue approach with a talent for avoiding controversy'. The people without power were not being involved in any shift of power, in fact the poverty funds were being used 'to suffocate militant independent leadership and action organizations seeking to arm the poor with their share of power to take their legitimate place in the American scene'. The anti-poverty programme could prove to be a massive relief programme, not for the poor, but for the 'welfare industry', for staff salaries and operating costs, simply putting poverty labels on 'old devices'. The war had become big business. A meaningful programme was dependent on the organized poor possessing sufficient power to win it, and that meant 'militant independent organization'. One of the bitterest conclusions reached about the nature of the war on poverty, and one which therefore coloured any assessment of its outcomes, was in Alinsky's verdict:

... as it stands today, the poverty program is a macabre masquerade, and the mask is growing to fit the face, and the face is one of political pornography. (A: Alinsky, 1965)

We are not here concerned with the totality of the poverty programme, but it is clear that judgments about the implementation and effectiveness of the prominent educational components relate to the degree of hope or scepticism engendered with the programmes themselves, and enter increasingly controversial territory as the political context changed, and as the data and reports were scrutinized and interpreted.

One important if elusive feature of these developments that we have identified was the new relationship between politics and social science constructed in the early 1960s, and the ways in which that relationship was translated into action and – of particular relevance here – into educational programmes. Part of the hesitation about the new directions derived from existing or developing doubts about the limits of rationality in the social sciences, particularly when analysing the *causes* of poverty (A: Rein and Miller, 1966), and planning appropriate strategies. The difficulty in this period is that it is not always easy to detect when the commitment to social science preceded policies and when they were adduced as substantiation. Moynihan's recantation of faith in social science was only a more dramatic version of the warnings issued at an early stage by, say, S.M. Miller within sociology or Martin Deutsch within education. Haveman talks retrospectively of one of the bases of the war on poverty being 'faith in the efficacy of social planning stimulated by social scientists and other academics whose public respect and influence was at its zenith' (A: Haveman, 1977, 3), and we have seen some of the ways in which that faith became operational.

The researchers, specifically, had been plunged into ambiguous and often difficult roles, their work being used as justification for, and they themselves being used as leading figures in, the new organizations and major projects. The 'President's task force' operations continued, and one which was chaired by McVicker Hunt, for example, reported in January 1967 on 'Early Childhood Development: a Bill of Rights for Children', and the references in the report were overwhelmingly to such work as that of Bloom, Cynthia Deutsch, Vera John and Bereiter and Engelmann, as well as that of Basil Bernstein and the pre-war American work of Skeels and Dye (A: LBJ Lib, Task Force Reports Box 4). The early childhood literature is particularly studded with reference to what 'the research shows'. When Senator Yarborough rose to speak in the debate on the ESEA, he began his discussion of the possibilities:

One of the programs which can be instituted under title I is preschool education for deprived children. Certainly if psychiatry and psychology have taught us anything, it is that the early years are of enormous importance in determining an individual's personality traits. The preschool programs are one of the most promising that could be carried out under title I. (A: US, *Congressional Record*, April 9, 1965, 7351)

To set alongside that degree of confidence it is interesting to take an example of the self-conscious position of those who, like the psychiatrists and psychologists referred to, were seen as justifying the confidence. Two psychiatrists, in a volume on the *Disadvantaged Child* in 1967, concluded a paper on child-rearing patterns with the following summary that is germane to the whole of our discussion:

Behavioral scientists in the United States are currently being pressed, more than ever before, into social action roles. There exists now an unprecedented demand for their services for the immediate development of new kinds of remedial and preventive programs for a large segment of the population, the lowest socio-economic group. But the scientists are not being allowed the luxury of conducting carefully controlled small-scale studies. They cannot await the long-range results of such studies but recently initiated by others. The critical need for large-scale corrective programs *now* is being made dramatically apparent and the opportunities for actions are being made more readily available. While obviously advantageous in many respects, this situation is not without serious dangers. (A: Marans and Lourie, 1967, 38)

This encapsulates the ambiguous climate in which the researchers worked and offered opinion and advice. There are difficulties constantly expressed relating to their research design and tasks, alongside the problems of defining, for example, the 'culturally deprived' populations with whom they were working (A: Bloom, 1964a), or the lack of understanding and proper attention being received by the concept of poverty which their work was to address (A: Miller, 1964). Keppel and others, as we have seen, were underlining the past neglect and present importance of research, but where the luxury of longer-term and carefully planned research was being enjoyed, it was in danger of contributing to action in only ritualistic or symbolic ways.

The work of Susan Gray, Rupert Klaus and colleagues on the Early Training Project was continuing across this period to refine instruments to carry their long-term programme beyond the 'innoculation' approach from which they had begun. They were planning learning experiences in environments which were 'predictable, organized, and rich enough in objects and situations that it was possible for the child to learn to order his world', working with parents in ways intended to be relevant to children's attitudes and aptitudes. They were exploring their work in relation to others – for example, that of David Weikart at Ypsilanti – in examining the kind of programme that would have lasting effects. They were critical of the schools' inability to maintain children's preschool gains, and concluded that a 'carefully planned developmental program can offset significantly some of the cumulative effects of cultural deprivation on a child's later school performance' (A: Gray *et al.*, 1966, 26, 102; Gray, 1966, 21–5; Klaus and Gray, 1965, 95). To the question of whether such a project could 'offset retardation' they were coming, after five years, to what they described as a qualified 'yes' (A: Klaus and Gray, 1968, 61).

Across the research and analyses that emerged from Martin Deutsch and his colleagues at the Institute for Developmental Studies there is a thread of both self-awareness and contextual awareness. In 1964 Deutsch was looking at how 'socio-educational engineering might provide the most facilitating architecture for maximizing human achievement'. In doing so he was aware of the extent of impoverishment, but also the 'still quite limited' extent of knowledge in the human sciences. Whether 'Negro, Puerto Rican, or Mexican-American, or poor mountain white', children from poor backgrounds were less prepared for school than their middle-class counterparts, but 'the school has failed to prepare to meet their needs' resulting in children's alienation and failure: 'while the school does not contribute to the initial problem (except through its effects on the previous generation), neither does it contribute to the overcoming of the initial handicaps'. Inadequately prepared children were interacting with 'inadequate schools and insufficient curricula'. In search of compensatory action based on empirical evidence, Deutsch was again the following year questioning the 'adequacy of the school environment', using Bernstein's British work on class and language and applying it to the condition of white Appalachian populations (A: Deutsch, 1964a, 1965a). Deutsch continued to express anxiety about the role of the social and behavioural sciences and to couple his analysis of environmental causes with critical evaluation of the schools. Using a broad definition of the skills needing to be acquired at preschool and early school levels, he explained – with an emphasis not always heard by critics of these early childhood theories and projects – that it was

not a matter of inculcating middle-class values but, rather, of reinforcing the development of those underlying skills that are operationally appropriate and necessary for both successful and psychologically pleasant school learning experiences...there is nothing fundamentally culturally loaded in a good or poor memory...(A: Deutsch and Associates, 1967, 140)

In 1967, Cynthia and Martin Deutsch, reviewing early childhood programmes, concluded firmly that the first generation of research had shown the *possibility* of arresting or retarding the 'accumulation of deficit', but that, contrary to statements in the popular press and views held by some government agencies, 'work in early childhood stimulation is far from done: it is in fact just beginning to develop the necessary prototypical models'. A report on the work of the Institute in 1967 warned the schools that they needed to be patient and courageous in the face of pressures from the sources of funds:

whether they be the Office of Education, the Office of Economic Opportunity, City Hall, a private foundation, a Congressman who measures the success of such programs in the number of riots that don't erupt, or a disgruntled taxpayer who wonders quite legitimately if his money is being wasted in a program that cannot possibly demonstrate its success next week, next month, next summer, or even in the next several years. (A: Deutsch and Associates, 1967, 386–7; Powledge, 1967, 26–7)

Within the academic community there were, together with such emphases, a variety of claims for cautious progress, as attitudes – if not conditions – were changing, as the range of programmes, from the most structured to the most open, began to estimate their impact and as the social science disciplines more directly addressed the issues of the classroom, the home and the community that had been part of the daily lives of practitioners. Research into language, motivation and learning difficulties was feeding messages of potential success into the system, just as evaluation messages and other critiques were raising doubts about the effectiveness of what had been undertaken. What the analyses were bringing clearly to the surface was uncertainty about where the 'blame' for children's failure lay. Were schools structured, as Hubert Humphrey asked, to suit the teacher or the child? Schools, he answered, had become too aloof from the community (A: Humphrey, [1966], 57–8). There were, as the conference which Humphrey addressed recognized, basic disagreements about the past record of the schools. One contributor referred to the 'rigor mortis' of the educational establishment, and the fact that schools were not even preparing children for the world of thirty years ago (A: National Conference on Education of the Disadvantaged, [1966], 10–11). Were teachers to blame? That, Ornstein suggested, was a 'fashionable target'. Teachers were described as desperate, without adequate support, or – in less generous terms – as paying a 'daily visit to a foreign country'. They had been prepared for their task by 'warmed-over versions of Sociology, Psychology, and Child Development I and II' (A: Ornstein, 1971b; Rioux, 1967, 84–5). It is important for any discussion of what came to be called the 'deficit' theory of disadvantaged children, that blame was being widely distributed in the mid-1960s, and schools and teachers were under severe attack for their past failures. Francis Keppel wrote in the *New York Times* early in 1964 that the *schools* were failing to teach the children most in need (A: Keppel, 1964a, 73).

Part of the difficulty – of the 1960s and now – in making the effort to understand the processes at work is the presence of vocabularies which had changing and often emotive overtones, vocabularies which could conceal intentions and purposes, or which could be submerged in a deluge of rival interpretations or controversy. The most prominent of such vocabularies, which reached into theories and ideologies of social reality, of racial and class discrimination and power, and of the possibilities and directions of social change, were those of cultural deprivation, compensatory education and deficit. All three were closely related, all were surrounded by alternatives, all were accused of being euphemisms for more sinister meanings. All proved to be conceptual staging posts towards other attempts to erect social interpretations and strategies. Cultural deprivation, for example, closely related in its origins to Oscar Lewis's 'culture of poverty', gained rapid currency from 1961–3, was welcomed as a replacement for biological theories of racial inferiority, but itself lost ground as more radical approaches to questions of race and racism exposed weaknesses in the conceptions underlying early theories of cultural deprivation.

'Cultural deprivation' formally entered the educational lexicon in 1961–3, when it was added as a category to the *Educational Index*. The volume covering that period contained twenty-one entries. The 1964–5 volume contained 122 entries, and by 1968–9 the number had increased to 370, with a variety of similar and branch headings (A: Ornstein, 1971a, 380; 1974, 5). The book that did most to trigger interest, debate and repetition was Frank Riessman's *The Culturally Deprived Child*. In 1962 (acknowledging the work and help of Martin Deutsch, S.M. Miller, Allison Davis and others), Riessman, at the time Professor of Educational Psychology at New York University, launched his discussion with the statement that one child out of every ten in the fourteen largest US cities was 'culturally deprived' in 1950, and ten years later '*this figure had risen to one in three*'. A note to this first sentence read:

The terms 'culturally deprived,' 'educationally deprived,' 'deprived,' 'underprivileged,' 'disadvantaged,' 'lower class,' 'lower socio-economic group,' are used interchangeably throughout this book.

The argument explored why such children did poorly in school, and the reasons often adduced for their doing so (lack of home tradition, inadequate language and reading skills and motivation...) but underlined instead the 'scant attention...given to the faults of the school'. 'What has happened', he asked, 'to the old idea that held if the children aren't learning, look to the teacher?' The complex of essential problems Riessman identified included discrimination, the reasons for children's ambivalence towards education, the 'culture of the school' and deficits in children's background. Culture itself he defined as 'an effort to cope with the surrounding environment', and the problems were those of the school's conflict of values with those of a group attempting to cope in particular ways. Riessman identified, partly on the basis of his own PhD work in the early 1950s, pro-education attitudes on the part of under-privileged groups, and reasons for the transformation of these attitudes into hesitation and resistance. He strongly rejected any interpretation of 'culturally deprived' as an inert or negative category – a criticism he made of the Higher Horizons project, which for other reasons he applauded. Higher Horizons suggested that for children in culturally and economically depressed areas 'school is their only positive experience of life', and this Riessman denied:

This viewpoint overlooks the many cooperative characteristics of family life and child rearing, the enjoyment of music, humor, the down-to-earth, informal, human relationships. It overlooks the angry protest that has begun to reap rewards in the South as well as gain national recognition. We cannot believe that school is the only worthwhile experience of these groups.

Riessman was rejecting a view that he regarded as ethnocentric, inaccurate and an underestimation of the deprived child – all of which made 'the educator's work that much more difficult' (A: Riessman, 1962, 1–15, 106).

Riessman and others were attempting to present the case for understanding 'cultural deprivation' in terms which took account of the strengths of the children and their backgrounds (A: Riessman, 1963; McCreary, 1965) but the concept was also being differently and often more narrowly interpreted. One reviewer of Riessman's book warned against the oversimplification of its message – largely by putting too much faith in what the schools can do: 'the schools did not cause "cultural deprivation," and, alone, they will not be able to solve it' (A: Schottland, 1963, 401). Benjamin Bloom warned that 'there is no simple means of classifying children as "culturally deprived"' (A: Bloom, 1964a, 4). The warnings, however, often went unheeded, and a simple logic from cultural deprivation to intervention was often constructed. Even while realizing the 'denigrating effects' of the concept, and using

Riessman's book as a starting point, the coordinator of New York's Project ABLE was able to present without reservations two character-istics of culturally deprived pupils: they were from the lower socio-economic groups in the community, and they were 'notably deficient in cultural and academic strengths'. The parents had 'simply been unable to provide the quality of background, outlook, initial grounding, and readiness for formal learning that middle- and upper-class parents provide as a matter of course' (A: Kaplan, 1963, 71). Other versions of the concept underlined the perceptual, linguistic, motivational and other characteristics of the children, often simply indicating what they did not know and could not do, without reference to the contexts in which these might be understood (A: Utter, 1963). At worst, the urgent and well-intentioned attempts to solve the problem of the culturally dis-advantaged or deprived produced a confused anthology of authors and ideas in the field. One Pennsylvania version told of the problem resulting from 'the educational neglect of that segment of the school's population which comes from the low socio-economic environment'. They were 'educationally retarded' when they arrived at school. Many 'potential dropouts come from culturally deprived environments'. The 'wise teacher' and welcoming preschool would assist in the transition for those 'children entering school from these neighborhoods (who) have had little experience in social living' (A: Stine, 1964, 1–4). 'Cultural deprivation' had become an important conceptual battlefield in the attack on America's 'No. 1 problem'.

Underlying the range of interpretations was the question beginning to emerge more and more explicitly in the middle of the decade: was cultural deprivation theory a euphemism intended to conceal deeper conflicts of class, race and inequality? Weighing attempts to understand the concept, Hilda Taba pointed to the way the concept moved on from older concepts of 'problem children, retarded, slow learners, under-privileged, and under-achievers' to a new term which was not just another euphemism, but pointed to causes (A: Taba, 1964, 147). Keppel, however, in a chapter on 'Inequality based on race and class' in a book in 1966, considered that labels like 'culturally deprived' or 'disadvantaged' were indeed descriptive of the children's backgrounds, but 'far too often...became alibis for failure to find effective ways to educate these children', a view which he later expressed as using the labels as euphemisms 'for the results of racial prejudice' (A: Keppel, 1966, 39; interview). From 1965 through to the early 1970s Kenneth B. Clark produced the most sustained analysis of the implications of the theory of cultural deprivation and its usages. He saw it as emerging from a liberal tradition to replace – following 1930s research – assumptions

about the inherent inferiority of the Negro. That much was positive, and
the theory of inferiority had now been buried. The new theory, with its
emphasis on stimulus deprivation, the power of the environment,
obstacles to learning, etc. did not, however, end the debate. Although
the theory of inferiority had gone, educational practice was still rooted
in its assumptions. A theory of cultures now simply brought racial and
class conflict more firmly into the school:

'The clash of cultures in the classroom' is essentially a class war, a socio-
economic and racial warfare being waged on the battleground of our schools,
with middle-class and middle-class-aspiring teachers provided with a powerful
arsenal of half-truths, prejudices, and rationalizations, arrayed against hopelessly
outclassed working class youngsters. This is an uneven balance, particularly
since, like most battles, it comes under the guise of righteousness.

Despite the strength of such statements, Clark's continuing analysis
remained bifocal. He could see, as well as the limitations of the theory,
the value of the direction in which it had pointed. What was now
necessary was to substitute a theory of 'educational deprivation', as
more specific and relevant, for the theory of cultural deprivation which
in the end was an argument for maintaining the status quo (A: Clark,
1965a, 30–3; 1965b, 129, 147; 1969, 27–30; Clark et al., 1972).

Mounting pressures to identify operational strategies, particularly
once the opportunities of the war on poverty had been opened up, meant
that key theories and concepts were as hastily adopted as the strategies
themselves. There was little enough time or motive to debate the
warnings or clarify the ideas, and social and political movements quickly
pressed ideas into service as steps towards fuller ideals.

The concept of compensatory education was a natural extension of
that of cultural deprivation, and was a response both to the implications
of environmental and cognitive deprivation, and to perceptions
associated with the early projects on language and learning. If, in
Deutsch's terminology, there were cumulative deficits, and in Ausubel's
retardation that was reversible, then some form of remedial or
compensatory education was the necessary response. New York's
Higher Horizons experience was widely viewed as the first effort at
compensatory education, and it ensured that the debate which followed
was conducted in terms of compensatory and not remedial education,
since there were pronounced 'enrichment' and developmental elements
in this project and others which influenced the direction of the war on
poverty. 'Enrichment' was designed to provide cultural experiences not
otherwise accessible to the children concerned. In 1963 Robert
Havighurst, for example, was urging enrichment programmes at the
kindergarten level, to give children 'a better start in school and thus a

better start in life'; in the elementary school and nursery programs for maladjusted youth at the junior high school level' (A: in Passow, 1963, 37–8). Could the schools compensate in these ways 'for the meager backgrounds that children from deprived social and economic homes bring into the classroom'? The answer, with an eye to Higher Horizons, 'must be a clear "yes"' (A: Krugman, 1961, 24). Another answer, however, was 'no' – enrichment for the sake of it missed the point. What was needed was not a new vocabulary, but relationships, experience with sequential meanings (A: Hess and Shipman, 1966, 285).

Discussion of compensatory education took place in the mid-1960s, therefore, at two levels: that of strategy, and that of theory or principle. At the strategic or operational level the concern was with focus and types of programme. In addition to the early focus on 'cultural experience', the centre of attention rapidly came to be supplementary programmes which would provide language enrichment, improve concept formation, facilitate abstract thinking and, through the improvement of reading skills in particular, prevent school failure. If Higher Horizons was the most common point of reference for the strategies, Deutsch's preschool programme was by 1964 the most common point of reference for the principle (B: Feldmann, 1964). One comment from 1972 (which might easily have been made at any time since the mid-1960s) was that 'early education has become such a badge of the war on poverty that in some circles it is considered almost undemocratic to raise the issue of the appropriate age to begin. "The earlier, the better" is the cry' (A: Anderson, 1972). Somewhere in the enormous range of compensatory education projects for the disadvantaged every element in the diagram of compensation was confronted, every partner was given priority, every element in the curriculum was highlighted, every researchable or addressable feature of cognition or motivation or self-image or difficulty was turned into a project, a programme, an approach. As one Title I administrator put it, talking of the early days of its implementation:

You really could write almost anything and couch it in such terms that it appeared to be compensatory... The need was just so great for anything that you could do in West Virginia that anything was compensatory. (Taylor, interview)

The concept, as distinct from the vagaries of its implementation, however, was widely perceived in relation to preschool programmes and Title I as *the* means of combating the educational and social effects of poverty. It was also widely perceived as standing alongside (though often in competition with) the desegregation of schooling, in making education responsive to the social goals of the civil rights movement. California's McAteer Act of 1965 specifically laid down that its provision for compensatory education 'shall not sanction, perpetuate or promote the racial or ethnic segregation of pupils in the public schools', and was intended to ensure compensatory services for disadvantaged children in integrated settings (A: California State Department, 1968b, 14). It was pointed out, also in 1965, that 'the impetus for a large number of compensatory education programs has emanated from demands presented by civil rights organizations representative of ethnic and lower socioeconomic groups. One needs only to attend school board meetings or public budget hearings in large city school districts to gain proof of this point' (A: Guthrie and Kelly, 1965, 71). The defence, sometimes flimsy or over-ambitious, of the concept was in terms either of more of the same education, or of a curriculum or learning process more in tune with the children's realities. Many of the defences were in terms not of equality but of equality *plus*, of compensation through more and better teachers, improved conditions of schooling and greater community involvement. The range of understandings of the concept matched the range of strategies adopted.

That there were reservations about compensatory education is only to be expected, given emergent attitudes to cultural deprivation, and to the war on poverty policies themselves. Getzels, as we have seen, asked the crucial question: 'Can a program of compensatory education for the disadvantaged even at its best be salutary in any ultimate way without altering the disadvantaged environment giving rise to the disadvantaged child?' (A: Getzels, 1966, 226).

Phi Delta Kappan was moved in 1965 to promote a debate under the general title: 'Is compensatory education only palliative?' The real barrage of opposition to compensatory education as such did not emerge, however, until the 1970s, when it was to be attacked as a form of 'progressive statusquoism', as naively optimistic, as attempting to shape children on the model of those who were 'successful' in traditional (increasingly held to mean 'middle-class') ways, as a fraud and a hoax and dangerous by raising false hopes (A: Farber and Lewis, 1972, 20; Levitan and Taggart, 1976, 119; Durham, 1969, 21; Winschel, 1970, 3). As with all educational and other reform strategies, it was to be accused of racism, and of simply representing more subtle procedures for socially controlling working-class and black children than under the impact of older theories of biological or class inferiority.

Interwoven with the concepts of deprivation and compensation was the growing confusion about deficit and difference, a confusion that was to be addressed without too much success in the 1970s. In linguistics particularly research was to be bedevilled by disputes over the descriptive and judgmental aspects of accounts of language differences between classes, races, ethnic groups or sub-cultures. The main thrust of this debate was not to take place until the end of the 1960s and into the 1970s, and was to focus – on both sides of the Atlantic – in part on the work of Basil Bernstein in Britain, and related to developments particularly in socio-linguistics and the sociology of knowledge. The debate was to revolve around the linguistic experience of working-class or black children, their verbal deprivation or otherwise, the stimuli of their culture, the relationship between their 'standard' or 'non-standard' English and their capacity for abstract thought, and other aspects of language which were located directly in the conceptual confusions of 'cultural deprivation' (B: Keddie, 1973). In the mid-1960s, however, this argument had barely begun in the United States, and an influential article by Courtney Cazden in 1966 was one of the first American attempts to place in perspective what she called 'Subcultural differences in child language: an inter-disciplinary view'. The central question was: 'in what ways is the language used by children in various subcultural groups simply different, and to what extent can the language of any group be considered deficient by some criteria?' She weighed the evidence on 'standard' and 'nonstandard' English, 'class dialects', vocabularies, and various forms of language 'impoverishment' that had been identified. She concluded that there was no evidence that nonstandard English was a 'cognitive liability', explored the massive evidence that children of 'upper socio-economic status' were 'more advanced than those of lower socio-economic status', agreed that much was being learned about language development, but concluded that little was known about differences in language function. She decided, as we have seen, that 'at the present time, we cannot completely resolve the difference–deficiency issue' (A: Cazden, 1968).

Behind such analysis lay the substantial interest in the class and ethnic distribution of reading disability, functional literacy and school attainment. The interest was developing by the mid-1970s both in the ways social institutions sustained such differences or deficits, and in the specifically linguistic, cognitive and educational mechanisms involved. Considerable numbers of the compensatory projects by now in place rested on assumptions about language, cognition and learning that had as yet barely begun to be tested. Although much of the activity and the reporting pointed to deficiencies in both the school and the environment, little was known about the specific processes which linked the child to the language stimuli of multiple environments – although the work of Bernstein and colleagues on differential language codes in Britain had already become a focus of major interest amongst researchers in the United States. What educational policy making and programme designing had as yet not fully recognized were the implications of a more complex understanding of the concepts which governed their approaches and their likelihood of achieving some measure of success.

One of the features of these mid-1960s developments was the diversity and interchangeability of the terminology through which the issues were addressed. The synonyms seemed endless, and were constantly catalogued with approval or exasperation. An article from the Educational Research Service, for example, submitted to the House hearings on the war on poverty programme in 1964, discussed the 'blighted areas', itself one of a range of synonyms, which produce children who are 'insecure, emotionally unstable, undernourished, socially maladjusted, and often potentially delinquent. "Disadvantaged," "alienated," "disinherited" – whatever term is used to describe these children, it oversimplifies a very complex problem' (A: US, House, Hearings, 1964, Part 3, 1627). The following year Kenneth Clark listed the most common synonyms in use for 'cultural deprivation': 'culturally disadvantaged, the disadvantaged, minority groups, socially neglected, socially deprived, school retarded, educationally disadvantaged, lower socio-economic groups, socio-economically deprived, culturally impoverished, culturally different, rural disadvantaged, the deprived slum child' (A: Clark, K.B., 1965b, 130). To this list Edmund Gordon added 'chronically poor', 'poverty stricken' and 'culturally alienated' (A: Gordon, E.W., 1965b, 641). In the second half of the 1960s the catalogue of 'synonyms' became 'euphemisms', with various attempts to escape from them – 'limited experience' was one suggestion to replace 'cultural deprivation' (A: Seligman, 1968, 85). To some commentators the 'euphemization' was necessary, in order to avoid pejorative labelling (A: Brazziel, 1966–7, 44); to others it was an inevitably pejorative exercise, and an evasion of class and racial realities; for most it was simply a convenient range of descriptors involving mild degrees of fashion and confusion.

The educational focus or underpinning of the war on poverty clearly involved elusive concepts, ambitious aspirations, the long gap between intention and implementation, diversity of perceptions and priorities, and problems in identifying targets for policy and action. A perspective on the educational complexities we have traced from the beginning of the 1960s to approximately 1966 requires three main emphases: the central process and accomplishment; the weaknesses; and the location of the educational endeavour in wider contexts of social critiques, theory and debate.

There is no doubt that the central educational process of the war on poverty was that of bringing childhood to centre stage, what might be termed the rediscovery of infancy, or at least its rediscovery amidst the potentials and urgencies of policy-making. If the war on poverty represented an alliance between government and social science, it was constructed in educational terms specifically on a relationship between economic and social policy on the one hand and theories of child development, the reversibility of early characteristics and the power of preschool and early education on the other hand. Head Start and Title I, the Ford and other projects, were built on that alliance and relationship. Preschool and compensatory education were recognized to be – alone – not enough, almost as soon as the concepts and emphases concerned entered the market place (A: Shaffer, 1968), but this did not lessen the newly found commitment to the disadvantaged child, and to strategies of educational intervention to achieve the development or the reversibility sought. Whatever the origins or meanings of the theories or ideologies involved, the elements we have considered came together in a new public awareness of the importance of the child.

By 1965 interests in childhood, child development, and educational and political attention to particular constituencies of children – in areas of black or Appalachian poverty or the children of migrants – had coalesced. There had been a build-up of research by those who were publishing widely on children's intellectual and language development (A: John, 1963; 1965). In 1964 Patricia Sexton, like many others, was commenting that 'recent months have seen a spectacular burst of citizen interest in the schools, perhaps unparalleled by anything in the history of public education' (A: Sexton, 1965, 248). The new programmes were directed at children, through them at their families, and beyond into the social issues with which the war on poverty was concerned. In a well-known book on early childhood, published in 1966, Maya Pines summarized, in relation to Head Start, many of these elements:

Head Start is a desperate last-minute attempt to make up for deficiencies not in the child, but in the educational system…Head Start actually offers a combination of social work, preventive medicine, and indoctrination in the virtues of school. Since poor families lack all three, Head Start often comes as a breath of fresh air…All these things are gains – and in particular cases, they may be enormous gains.

She pointed out, however, that this does not produce any real change in the children's 'understanding, language skill or ability to learn', so long as the focus is merely on the improvement of behaviour and enrichment. Head Start had not begun to provide a systematic approach to learning needed for success in school (A: Pines, 1966, 9–10). While the messages from educational and social science were often mis-heard or mistranslated, running through much of the 'indoctrination' was a sense of the positive characteristics of disadvantaged children. As one educationist put it, in 1966, in an article entitled 'Some positive characteristics of disadvantaged learners and their implications for education': 'The socially disadvantaged are not lacking in knowledge, culture, and skills, but possess somewhat different understandings and abilities because of the circumstances of their lives' (A: McCreary, 1966, 47).

While much of the literature of these early years of Head Start, Title I and other programmes contains oversimplified versions of the research on children's learning or the effects of environment, there is also in the growing literature on the teaching of the disadvantaged child an attempt to come to grips with the messages from Hunt or Bruner, Deutsch or Susan Gray, the experience of projects in Harlem or Milwaukee, distant echoes of Montessori or Iowa. The implications were as clear for schools as they were for children, and in policy terms Francis Keppel saw this very clearly. There were those, he commented in February 1964, who did not want the schools to be attacked, but 'the essential step to progress is to face up squarely to our shortcomings...we are simply not teaching hundreds of thousands who are now in our schools'. Descriptions of children as of 'a lower order', or as culturally deprived, were alibis for the failure of the education system itself. There was a need to recognize that

the substandard school is precisely the wrong school for the children of poverty...(they need) the most skilled teachers, not the least skilled: the least crowded classrooms, not the most crowded: the best of educational opportunity, not the least of educational opportunity. (A: LBJ Lib, Federal Records, Keppel addresses, 15 February 1964, 5–9)

Not for the first time, the range of public attitudes to children and their schooling included narrowness and generosity, cautious research and high idealism.

While the focus was often children and childhood, it was also, of course, kinds of children – black children, ghetto children, slum children, and the children of other realities and euphemisms. Increasing attention was beginning to be paid to the characteristics of the most deprived children, including prominently disadvantaged, urban – and most frequently black – children. The researchers, commentators and planners focused on language and other cultural characteristics, ranging from the most superficial to the most determined attempts to uncover the relationships between learning and the processes of racial discrimination. At one end of the spectrum were the simplifications or half-messages that became – to take an example from 1966 – pictures of children from depressed neighbourhoods, and 'homes where communication is customarily restricted to gestures and monosyllabic commands, many have little verbal language with which to clarify thought or to communicate with the teacher and other children' (A: Mackintosh *et al.*, 1966, 3–4). At the other end were attempts to understand specific behaviours, as in an article on the slum child's 'other world', showing that when asked to draw a child, black children most commonly drew a *white* child, because they had never seen a black child in a book, and suggesting that inattention and 'acting dumb' were deliberate and skilled responses, a form of survival technique (A: Asbell, 1966, 30–1). While there was much emphasis on the 'Negro condition' or the pathology of the individual child, there was also serious attention to the relationship between the child's different worlds, emphasis on the need to 'expand our middle class view of life' in order to understand more clearly the strengths and resilience of the disadvantaged child (A: Hamlin *et al.*, 1967). It was argued that improved learning would come via improved social conditions, school improvements and better understanding of the 'operational linguistic wealth' of the 'substandard speaker' (A: John, 1965, 3; John and Goldstein, 1964; Ornstein, 1965, 107). If children were a product of their environment, if schools damaged the children they set out to help, if discrimination and false assumptions stood between children and effective learning, and if the educational response to disadvantage and poverty was restricted by inadequate understanding, then it is not surprising that approaches to specific categories of children should come from a variety of directions, and point to a variety of policies and practices.

In the case of black – and particularly urban black – children in this period, the poverty relationship cannot be underestimated. The backgrounds of these children reflected, among other things, the growth of unemployment – from approximately 3 per cent of the work force in 1949 to 7 per cent in 1961 (as against a British figure which in the early 1960s was worryingly reaching 2 per cent) (A: Macdonald, 1963, 116). There was persistent evidence in the research, public debate and civil rights action that 'Negroes are poor because they are Negroes'. There were, researchers were discovering, major differences in children's learning and attainment between socio-economic groups *within* racial and ethnic sub-cultures, reflecting the uneven impact of economic improvements and racial discrimination. Surrounding the specific educational content of the war on poverty is the complex relationship between anti-poverty policies and the economics and politics of race. One of the participants talked in 1966 of 'the President's continuing problem of trying to keep in step with the Negro revolution' (A: Littlewood, 1966, 41). 'Keeping in step' related to the economic and social conditions out of which the revolution emerged, and visions of the removal of barriers to learning and to attainment had constantly to encounter the hard unemployment, discrimination and other realities of the children's worlds. Arising out of the explorations of juvenile delinquency, urban conditions, migration and other aspects of the social and political condition, were local and federal, public and private, attempts to find solutions – including those based on policies for geographical areas – policies in which education was, especially in the later 1960s, linked with 'model city' and other urban policies. The concept of 'compensatory education' was to some extent accompanied by less explicit but similar approaches to what in Britain came to be called 'positive discrimination'. Targeting specific localities as well as specific problems underpinned much of the 1960s and later policy discussion. An educational version of this discussion in 1971 quoted an American comment on the schooling of immigrants half a century earlier:

We cannot ignore the arguments for some sort of special educational provision for immigrant children...We wish in the schools to furnish an equality of educational opportunity; but we can no longer deny the fact of individual variation of powers and abilities, and the schools cannot bestow an equality of benefit through the same ministrations to all children; children equipped with lesser gifts by nature must be given more by nurture (A: Fein, 1971, 99, quoting Frank V. Thompson, *Schooling of the Immigrant*, 1920).

Half a century later this approach to positively unequal 'ministrations', took broader and more comprehensive shape. The focus on children was important in that wider frame of reference, but its weaknesses continued to derive from the failures of social policy to make significant inroads into the solution of major and refractory poverty-related problems. The search for area-related strategies as well as concern for individuals at risk was a range, and a tension, within the policy process, that was also to be present in the British developments of the later 1960s.

    The first important point of emphasis in this analysis, therefore, has to be the reformulation of public policy agendas to set disadvantaged children, their social and educational contexts firmly in the centre of public attention. Given the weak basis on which American social policy had rested, and the 'moral crusade' component of any reform process, the importance attached to early childhood and to the different constituencies in need of change represented a vital moment of opportunity that was being taken. The second emphasis, however, has to be the weaknesses and their origins. These have been located principally in the over-confidence generated by the combination of circumstances surrounding the launch of the war on poverty. The war itself, as we have seen, was not the product of public political pressures, but, having taken shape, it rapidly recruited substantial and optimistic support. Its relationship to the movement for civil rights was quickly perceived and, in this as in other ways, the enormous hopes pinned upon it at an early stage were expressed in vivid terms. A national trade union view was embodied in a statement issued by the AFL–CIO in February 1964, welcoming President Johnson's reversal of a decade of stagnation, pressing for bold measures and substantial funds to 'achieve meaningful progress in this worthy national crusade' and pointing to its implications for the race issue:

Successful war against poverty will automatically do more for American Negroes than for the population as a whole because they are such a disproportionately large part of our families still in want. But more than that, by taking the measures necessary to end poverty, we will create the conditions and climate that will enable us to end more quickly the ugly fact of discrimination in American life. (A: AFL–CIO, 1964, 433)

This optimism, as we have also seen, had roots in the educational and related efforts of the Ford and similar initiatives, in the early schooling projects, and in theories of learning and the environment. Despite warnings, reservations and criticism, excessive confidence was generated in rapid impacts on delinquency, unemployment, social conditions and the economy. The moment was widely seen as an educational turning point, even the most crucial one in America's educational history. The weaknesses inevitably therefore included a search for panaceas and quick-fix solutions. Simple curricular or pedagogical changes, support for or by the family and community, could quickly take on the character of major departures, only to find that longer-term processes of sustaining change and evaluating its origins and extent were more difficult, more consuming of effort and resources, and less conducive to public optimism. The very confidence in education as central to the drive against poverty inevitably invited disappointment, although most of the educational developments concerned did, in fact, assume parallel and related efforts in other fields of social policy. Nevertheless, the quick-fix solution almost inevitably detracted from the underlying effort once the enthusiasm for rapid success had been dented, particularly by the apparently negative findings of the crude but much publicized evaluations of the second half of the 1960s.

The educational crusade did, indeed, produce structures which were to last – including the Head Start structures and the state-wide Title I or compensatory education administration – but there was often an uncritical sense of inevitable continuity in some of the early attitudes to the war on poverty and its policies. Moments of ambitious change, when the nature and permanence of the conditions cannot be clearly understood, are not conducive to historical reflection, and in American conditions this is more true than anywhere else. Echoes of dim pasts did not trouble the new confidence. Awareness of the limited energies of moral fervour and public crusades was not part of the agenda of people eager to take advantage of a sudden withdrawal of previously insurmountable obstacles. In these ahistorical conditions it is possible clearly to see sources of weakness, though less easy to make accusations of malicious intent, to lay blame. In the policies and their origins, in the practices and their purposes, there were elements that can be discussed in terms of racism or social control, but in the historical circumstances of the early and mid-1960s such conceptual machinery is unhelpful. The underlying motivation, even where those elements are present, has to be seen predominantly in terms of the interpretation of the opportunities offered, the educational, political and social strategies already taking shape, and the confusions and naivetés possible in those conditions.

The third and final emphasis to be placed, therefore, is the way in which educational strategies related to social critiques and theories more widely. The educational policies under discussion were in many ways tied in with broader views of social change, social reform and social stability. The strength of the ties is visible, for instance, in the advocacy of area policies, and in the area basis of the formulas used for funding. The kind of emphasis that Galbraith placed in 1964 was repeated in some form in the ideas and proposals of most of those associated with the anti-poverty movement: 'let us... select... the hundred lowest-income counties (or, in the case of urban slums, more limited areas of substantial population and special need) and designate them as special districts'. In such districts the school buildings would be improved, an 'elite body of teachers would be assembled', grants would be provided for families to feed and clothe children and compensate for loss of earnings. For Galbraith this was not federal aid but simply the most effective means of attacking poverty (A: Galbraith, 1964, 26). In the Ford 'gray area' projects, the juvenile delinquency and other urban projects, and under the ESEA and other legislation, action was focused in areas of need – in ESEA terms, 'areas with concentrations of children from low-income families'. The general thrust of these developments was away from conceptions of individual pathology and towards the total environmental condition which underlay the research associated with early childhood or juvenile delinquency.

This approach to the environment, the issues and the possibilities of action, was shaped particularly by the Ford Foundation at the beginning of the 1960s. Sanford Kravitz, involved in the early anti-poverty programmes, refers to preceding emphases on the provision of services, and talks of the Ford Foundation's seeking 'a bolder and more comprehensive approach', funding 'coordinated programs in such areas as employment, education, and social services, under the auspices of a new community agency uncommitted to the existing service structure' (A: Kravitz, 1965, 1–2). Ed Meade, from within the Foundation, recalls the parameters of 'our quest to improve urban life':

You couldn't just deal with job training or neighborhood revitalization or housing without taking into account the education. That was a piece of that fabric...in the early 1960s we were overwhelmed with the growth of public education in this country, and the baby boom and all that – so we were engaged in a more general way – how do we get enough teachers, how do we get enough school buildings, how do we enrich the quality of the curriculum?...You could really improve the general fabric of the school by focusing on the disadvantaged group – who really are the people who, because they have fewer opportunities elsewhere, need school more than anybody else...(Meade, interview)

The intended interlock of action and targeted population did not prevent the emergence of new, competing bureaucracies and defensive attitudes in the provision of services. Finding the path to targeted or to comprehensive action was a problem deeply rooted in the conditions of American politics and administrative structures.

Poverty, as an explicit target of federal policy, did not – as we have seen – exist in the 1950s, and it was almost two decades after the end of the Second World War before policy came to be posited on something other than inevitable solutions through affluence. The poor became visible and Harrington talks of the 'invisibility to which the seventies once again tried to consign them' (A: Harrington, 1980, 244–5). This does not imply that there was clear understanding of what was meant by 'the poor' or 'poverty', or that there were not great distances between policy and intention on the one hand, and implementation and action on the other hand. Walter Miller has underlined the difficulty in American conditions of identifying vocabularies which adequately represent 'low-status populations', and suggests that the term 'the poor' was unfortunate, since its definitions caught up 'in the same net millions of people whose "problems" are very different from those of the population at issue'. S.M. Miller pointed to the difficulties of perception raised by the fact that the bulk of the poor were white, while a higher proportion of blacks than whites were poor (A: Miller W., 1968, 269–72; Miller S.M., 1964, 211; Miller S.M. and Rein, 1965b, 276). What is certain is that the movement to eliminate or to alleviate poverty (it is never entirely clear who was in pursuit of which target) had only the flimsiest basis in analysis of the causes of poverty, and of the diversities of poverty conditions. Breaking the poverty cycle, for example, became a catch phrase, often detached from the realities to which it was meant to apply. The Council of Economic Advisers, in its report on *The Problem of Poverty in America* in January 1964, offered the view:

If children of poor families can be given skills and motivation, they will not become poor adults. Too many young people are today condemned to grossly inadequate schools and instruction...Effective education for children of poor families must be tailored to their special needs...The school must play a larger role in the development of poor youngsters if they are to have, in fact, 'equal opportunity'. (A: US, House of Representatives, Economic Opportunity Act, Hearings, Committee on the War on Poverty, Part 1, 1964, 52)

The school is here seen, as it was widely, as the most effective means of breaking this economic cycle of poverty (A: Rogin, 1965; Kravitz, 1965), though the same role was also ascribed to the Community Action Programs.

Miller and Rein, in 1966, teased out the dilemmas inherent in such overarching approaches to poverty, and in the policy implications of different classification schemes relating to poverty. If 'children in poverty' suggested training and rehabilitation programmes, 'families with children in poverty' pointed to family planning. Policy decisions had no firm basis in the analysis of 'the characteristics of the poor and the causes of poverty', and Miller and Rein themselves outlined not only a typology of possible intervention strategies, but also six possible goals of attempts to reduce poverty: social decency; equality; mobility; social stability; social inclusion; economic stability and growth. Their underlying approach rested on the hazards of 'presumed causality': 'when we examine the causes of poverty, we begin to confront the limits of rationality in the social sciences' (A: Miller and Rein, 1966, 22, 25–38). The enormous literature of the mid-1960s which linked educational strategies with the reduction of poverty had little concern to explore those causes and therefore to consider how the educational strategies would actually *work*. There is often a kind of incantatory quality about the assertion that, given skills and motivation (or some other variant of the formula) 'children of poor families...will not become poor adults'. Miller, together with Rein and other collaborators, offered some of the strongest and earliest analyses of the conceptual weaknesses of the war on poverty.

Concepts such as compensatory education, deficit, difference and cultural enrichment suggest some of the same problems as the discussion of poverty itself. Education for which, or for which combination of, Rein and Miller's six possible goals? How to judge (and who to judge?) the 'success' of Head Start, perhaps at some point in time and place important as welfare or political education for the community, but less so in terms of children's 'academic' learning? Answers to those kinds of question go outside the specific poverty relationship which was being established in the early and mid-1960s and into discussions of alternative criteria of judgment. Alongside the poverty connection, for example, has to be considered the concept of inequality. Inequality was a fundamental concept in the civil rights movement, and assumed importance with the consideration of comparative educational and social outcomes of the early 1970s, particularly following the publication of Jencks's *Inequality* in 1972. Although the war on poverty did not dispose of the comparative issues involved in the concept of inequality, it set out – at least in the political rhetoric and the legislative intentions – to deal in the greater absolutes apparent in the 'elimination of poverty'. Defining poverty by income levels, selecting areas for additional funding on the basis of explicit criteria, setting targets which would 'break the cycle'... these and others suggested more attainable and tangible aims than those associated with the fight against racial, rural, employment or other inequalities. Inequality of wealth, declared Dwight Macdonald in 1963, 'is not necessarily a major social problem per se. Poverty is' (A: Macdonald, 1963, 88). The most common emphasis in any relationship between education and inequality is likely to be on changing social attitudes and equalizing access to the stages of education. The most common emphasis in the relationship with poverty has to do with improving specific social and economic conditions.

It is this latter hallmark of the attack on poverty that made it so rapidly vulnerable. Critics began to ponder the seriousness of a policy for the attainment of which the resources seemed inadequate, or which had so little short-term impact on the conditions it addressed. Critics from the left commented on the futility of a strategy designed to substitute slogans such as 'slums and suburbs', 'inequalities' or 'problems of the disadvantaged' for the realities of class struggle, or rejected the CAPs or other ingredients of the war on poverty in favour of rival political and community strategies (A: Sexton, 1965, 234–5; Riessman, 1965b). There were increasing doubts as to the ability of the federal government to effect change, or the wisdom of its attempting to do so.

Between 1960 and 1965, therefore, through a variety of channels, new concepts and vocabularies had entered the parlance of policy and popular discourse – talent, head start, maximum feasible participation, environment, early childhood, intervention, urban renewal, neighbourhood revitalization, etc. Through its early linking of urban and educational programmes the Ford Foundation had in some ways been responsible, in Meade's view, for the creation of the vocabulary of disadvantage, compensation and cultural deprivation in an educational context (A: Meade, interview). It has been possible for one critical review of the Ford Foundation's activities in education to ignore its role in these and related respects because its author looked solely at a narrow view of 'public education' policy, without reference to the urban momentum of the first half of the 1960s in particular (A: Buss, 1980). New processes also took shape, not least in the gathering emphasis on evaluation. The ESEA drove especially in that direction but it was not until the second half of the 1960s that this movement joined other factors in converting the early enthusiasms of the educational war into sustained uncertainty and disappointment.

The whole of this development, and most prominently its educational component, has echoes of past moments in American and European history when it seemed possible to its partisans to break through obstacles or structures and effect major change by similar means. The educational utopianism of some late eighteenth-century French revolutionists, or of Robert Owen and many early nineteenth-century British radicals, would be examples. A brief snatch of autobiography, only some five years after the launching of the war on poverty, suggests a state of mind and a set of circumstances not unlike some of those earlier examples. The writer comments on the 'instant status' of Head Start and the exaggerated claims that were made on the basis of early 1960s experimental programmes:

That such boasts were made – and possibly even believed – is now a matter of history. They characterized the mood of the period – one of *enthusiasm* and *optimism*. So excited were many of us by the possibilities of the program that we did not go on record to protest that a six-week summer program could not hope to develop a positive self concept, produce new levels of language competence, discover and correct an accumulation of five years worth of medical and nutritional problems, and convince parents that education was the solution to all their problems. Plus many other miracles... So we all surfed on the excitement and hoped we would not drown in our own foamy rhetoric. But many of us were uneasy. In an address given in the fall of 1965, by which time the enthusiasm had not diminished to any significant extent... this author warned that the inevitable sequel to over-sell was over-kill. (A: Caldewell, 1970, vi)

The transition was to widespread scepticism, and then disillusion. One of the difficulties from the outset had been the curious combination of circumstances, the curious alliances and searches for goals and constituencies, and above all the need to snatch at a unique moment. There were built-in uncertainties and hazards that participants failed to see, and in many respects could not have been expected to see. The downward spiral of the later 1960s was to be easier to understand than the high point from which it began. As Miller and Rein understood in early in 1965: 'We would have liked another beginning, but this is it' (A: Miller and Rein, 1965a, 18).

Part II
A pattern of events: Britain

7　Advancing from poverty?

The American developments we have traced in the 1960s did not have straightforward echoes in Britain, and were listened to and interpreted in ways it is important to explore. Also related to that process are the ways in which British and European messages were received in the reverse direction, and in general the kind of professional and political networks, and the publicity machine, which conveyed or failed to convey these messages. The analysis here is about silences as well as echoes and dialogue, and we shall return to some crucial aspects of these processes.

A connection between poverty and educational policy was not established in Britain in any sustained public and explicit form until the late 1960s and, specifically, following the publication of the Plowden report on *Children and their Primary Schools* in 1967, though there were important, parallel and in some ways connected issues and processes in previous decades. The sequence of public events which in any way matches or relates to that in the United States begins, however, in 1967 following crucial investigations and discussions – some significant ones of which were not publicized – in the Plowden committee. It continues through the designation of Educational Priority Areas and EPA projects from 1968, the use of Urban Aid funds and various urban and social policy initiatives of the late 1960s and early 1970s. There were, during this period, responses to the American experience from the early 1960s, but the British literature linking education, poverty and disadvantage becomes significant only at the beginning of the 1970s. The processes leading up to these events in Britain came from a number of directions, including the internal workings of the Plowden committee, the roles of Her Majesty's Inspectors of schools, the shaping of the 'welfare state' and the concern of sociologists and educationists with social class. The British vocabularies of discourse in the late 1950s and 1960s contain similar or in some cases the same elements as in the United States, but rooted and deployed differently. The constituencies of poverty were differently identified and often with different policy implications, and the attention of educationists in particular was differently engaged.

In Dwight Macdonald's famous *New Yorker* article in 1963, underlining the difficulties experienced by Americans in recognizing the newly revealed extent of poverty, he comments that 'the same thing has happened in England, where working-class gains as a result of the Labour Party's post-1945 welfare state blinded almost everybody to the continued existence of mass poverty'. He points to a series of articles by Richard Titmuss (based on a new book, *Income Distribution and Social Change*) as alerting the 'liberal public' to the fact that 'the problem still persists on a scale that is "statistically significant," as the economists put it' (A: Macdonald, 1963, 91). Macdonald – like other Americans by this stage interested in the work of Titmuss and other British sociologists on the working of the welfare state – pinpoints the elements, but mistakes the precise point at which poverty began to assume significance in liberal and socialist consciousness.

The rediscovery of poverty in Britain (following earlier nineteenth- and twentieth-century 'discoveries') took place from the second half of the 1950s, although the dominant mood of the 1950s – in spite of Britain's post-war economic difficulties – was one of underlying political confidence that poverty was being slowly eradicated. As in the United States, though for different reasons, the assumption was that poverty as it had been known in pre-war Britain was being defeated partly by growing affluence and partly by the redistribution of the nation's resources through the mechanisms of the welfare state. The famous Rowntree and Lavers study of *Poverty and the Welfare State* published in 1951 (as a third survey of social conditions in York, following previous studies in 1900 and 1936) concluded that the proportion of the working-class population 'living in poverty' had been reduced since 1936 from 31.1 per cent to 2.77 per cent, but that the reduction would have been only to 22.18 per cent 'if welfare legislation had remained unaltered' (B: Rowntree and Lavers, 1951, 40). Such analysis of the reduction in poverty, and of the trend that it seemed to indicate, did not go unchallenged – neither did the measures used, the existing possibility of accurate calculations of the numbers in poverty and the adequacy of welfare benefits. A report in 1952 which pointed out all of these shortcomings underlined that

The results of this survey have been widely quoted as proof that poverty has been largely eliminated in Britain, an interpretation not wholly intended by the authors. But there is reason to doubt both the results of this survey and the interpretations placed upon them. (B: *Planning*, 1952, 21 and *passim*)

In the conditions that prevailed in post-war Britain the message that was most loudly received and retransmitted in political terms was that of poverty being organized out of existence.

We shall return to some of the underlying features of this post-war situation as governed by the experience of war, planning for recovery and the Labour government's post-1945 construction of the 'welfare state', but it is important to note how strongly, between the war and the beginning of the 1960s, the combination of economic growth and welfare planning was seen as putting an end to poverty. The vision associated with Labour's legislation was expressed by left-wing Member of Parliament Ian Mikardo in 1948, in an election programme for Labour's second term of office. Discussing education policy, Mikardo looks ahead to the 'establishment of complete equality of educational opportunity', though 'even the total abolition of fee-paying will, by itself, be insufficient... Up to 1955, and perhaps beyond, there will still be disparities in income between different families, and there will still be some families which will find it a strain, even with increased family allowances... to maintain children at school beyond fifteen' (B: Mikardo, 1948, 5). Even allowing for unguarded formulations, the reference to continuing 'disparities in income' up to 1955 'and perhaps beyond' represents a considerable confidence in the direction of social change. It was Anthony Crosland, however, who most influentially argued the case in the mid-1950s for the erosion of poverty under the period of Labour government in 1945–51. He accepted the York findings and emphasized the importance of Labour policies in accelerating the diminution of poverty. He argued that average working-class personal consumption had risen between 1938 and 1950, whereas average national per capita consumption had not, and that in the same period wages had increased their share of total personal incomes. Post-war real wages had risen more sharply than other earnings and profits:

... when every allowance is made, the essential fact remains – that the rich are distinctly less rich, and the poor are much less poor. The levelling process is a reality even in terms of consumption standards; and Britain has an appreciably more equal society after six years of Labour rule either than it had before the war, or than it would otherwise have had. (B: Crosland, 1956, 43–53)

Even without reference to welfare provision or planning there was, by the end of the 1950s, a sense that poverty was ultimately to disappear in the course of general economic growth. The Crowther committee, reporting on education *15 to 18* in 1959, contained a section entitled 'The advance from poverty', in which it stressed that unlike its predecessor – the Spens committee reporting on secondary education in 1938 – the new report reflected a 'great increase in wealth-producing capacity... we are prescribing for a community that is one-third richer in material wealth'. The basis of the improvement had been full employment, inflation, progressive taxation and the social security schemes of the welfare state, the cumulative impact of which had been 'to divert the larger part of the rise in the national standard of consumption to the lower income groups. They have, therefore, gained proportionately even more than the population as a whole' (B: Ministry of Education, 1959a, vol. 1, 45–7). Although, as *The Times* complained in 1961, there were still deep social divisions, this was 'in spite of the virtual abolition of poverty' (B: quoted in Pedley, 1963, 1). Stephen Wiseman, in his 1964 *Education and the Environment*, made a similar point: 'the elimination of poverty is not yet complete, but the incidence is now only a fraction of what it was in the hungry 30's. And yet this great social amelioration has not produced any sensible levelling-out in other indices of social differentiation' (B: Wiseman, 1964, 177). Behind such comments stands a long and absorbing discussion of social class and inequality, both directly related to education. What they illustrate, however, is the continuing belief that *poverty*, as distinct from other relative conditions, was either virtually abolished or awaiting its imminent annihilation.

By the late 1950s the underlying assumption of an inevitable demise of poverty in expansionist conditions was beginning to be strongly challenged. In a lecture delivered in 1955, published as an essay in 1956 and in his 1958 *Essays on ' The Welfare State '*, Titmuss challenged some of the assumptions of social policy thinking, including:

that the intended or declared aims of social policy since the Beveridge Report of 1942 have been wholly or largely achieved in the translation of legislation into action… that the aggregate redistributive effects of social service activity since 1948 have wholly or largely represented a transfer of resources from rich to poor. (B: Titmuss, 1958, 38)

This essay, which Brian Abel-Smith described as 'the most influential essay Titmuss ever wrote' (B: *ibid.*, Introduction, n.p.), established a crucial pattern of analysis in British social administration. Peter Townsend challenged the Labour Party in September 1959, in the *New Statesman*, to base its policies on more systematic data regarding poverty and living standards, and Harold Wilson replied the following week that it was a mistake to 'draw too sharp a distinction between the objectives of greater equality and economic expansion', but denied that any Labour leader had ever accepted the view 'that an increase in national production automatically raises the poorest section of the community to a more tolerable position' (B: Wilson, Harold, 1959, 413). Titmuss and the emergent group of sociologists concerned with welfare state and poverty issues pin-pointed and with increasing sharpness attacked the 'myths' (as Titmuss regularly referred to them) surrounding the

economy and the welfare state in the 1950s. In a characteristic passage
in a lecture delivered in 1959, he vividly portrayed the 1950s as a decade
which had

> witnessed a demonstration of the effectiveness of the myth as a motive force in
> British political beliefs and behaviour. Chief amongst these has been the myth
> of the 'Welfare State for the Working Classes'. This has had a number of
> consequences. Reinforced by the ideologies of enterprise and opportunity it has
> led to the assumption that most – if not all – of our social problems have been
> – or soon will be – solved. Those few that remain will, it is thought, be
> automatically remedied by rising incomes and minor adjustments of one kind or
> another...it is coming to be assumed that there is little to divide the nation on
> home affairs except the dreary *minutiae* of social reform, the patronage of the
> arts, the parking of cars and the effectiveness of corporal punishment. (B:
> Titmuss, 1960, 3)

In 1962 he was castigating the failure to distinguish between the promise
of social legislation and its performance: 'the present generation has
been mesmerised by the language of "The Welfare State". It was
assumed too readily after 1948 that all the answers had been found to the
problems, of health, education, social welfare and housing, and that
what was little more than an administrative tidying-up of social security
provisions represented a social revolution' (B: Titmuss, 1962, 188).
Brian Abel-Smith and Peter Townsend wrote in 1965 that 'two
assumptions have governed much economic thinking in Britain since the
war. The first is that we have "abolished" poverty. The second is that
we are a much more equal society: that the differences between the
living standards of rich and poor are much smaller than they used to be'
(B: Abel-Smith and Townsend, 1965, 9). The following year Townsend
pointed to new forms of poverty which began to be recognized only in
the mid-1950s. The labour movement and the general public had
assumed that 'we had witnessed the "virtual elimination" of poverty'
(B: Townsend, 1967, 9). Between the concepts of poverty and inequality
there was confusion and uncertainty, and the sociologists of the late
1950s and early 1960s had to work hard to bring the issue of poverty on
to the public agenda, and to present a detailed analysis of the prevailing
'myths'.

The rediscovery and its projection into public consciousness, as in the
United States two or three years later, came from a small number of
investigators, though in the British case they were sociologists focusing
on social security, national assistance, housing and especially the elderly.
Education played no part in the analysis. The tradition out of which
the analysis grew was that of socialist, radical and liberal approaches to
public benefit. It was a sociology shaped in the London School of

Economics more than anywhere else. Its public impact was through the Fabian socialist lecture and pamphlet, the *New Statesman* article, the journals of social administration and centre-left politics, the conference and the edited collections of essays. Dorothy Wedderburn, working on the economic and social circumstances of old people in the late 1950s, and beginning to publish before the end of the decade, did not feel the 'rediscovery' as a dramatic event:

...partly because I'd never really thought that poverty had disappeared, so it really seemed like establishing something that you knew to be there... I think I saw it as not so much rediscovering poverty with surprise as simply being aware of the inadequacies of the so-called 'welfare state' (Wedderburn, interview).

In 1960 Audrey Harvey, a practitioner working in the field of welfare rights, produced an influential Fabian pamphlet entitled *Casualties of the Welfare State*. In it she pointed to the rise in post-war living standards, but nevertheless to the existence of a minority of the population still suffering great privation – a minority 'certainly to be counted in millions'. She began: 'That we have a divided society, which is rapidly becoming more sharply so, is painfully obvious.' Free medical services and improved pensions had mainly benefited the middle classes. The National Assistance Board had in 1958 given allowances to supplement 'inadequate pensions and benefit rates' to over a million people: over a million people, therefore, were living 'below subsistence level' for this reason alone. Two million people were on national assistance. It was not generally realized that there were children, mainly in large families, having to be treated for nutritional deficiencies. There was 'considerable medical evidence of semi-starvation among old people'. The sickness benefit rate was worth less than it had been in 1911. She drew attention vividly to poor housing, overcrowding and homelessness, as she was to do again two years later, in an article underlining the housing plight of the homeless, the sick, the disabled: 'it is much too commonly assumed by people who are comfortably housed themselves, that archaic living conditions now exist only in slum areas scheduled for clearance' (B: Harvey, 1960–, 7, 31–2; 1962, 81).

Sociologists were now, therefore drawing attention to the increasing numbers of people below or at the line drawn for national assistance and the ineffectiveness of national assistance (B: Abel-Smith and Townsend, 1965). Titmuss and his students (including Abel-Smith and Townsend) have been described as aiming, 'through the study of poverty, to offer a moral critique of and new public standards for British society' (B: MacGregor, 1981, 73), but the critique of existing practice and its deficiencies, and the programmes of improvement, were not a 'crusade' in the American sense. They were aimed at existing welfare structures, not at recruiting support for the kind of start represented by the war on poverty programmes. The critique was intended to destroy myths not by rhetoric and political appeal, but by sustained social research. Titmuss was pointing not only to naive beliefs in the impact of economic growth, but also to the increasing concentration of wealth (in the United States as well as in Britain) and to the bluntness of the instruments that had been used in trying to measure the nature and extent of poverty (A: Titmuss, 1965, 130–2; 1962, 188). Titmuss and his student-colleagues initiated what might be described as a professional campaign to influence public opinion and politics. Although the Labour Party has been said to have had a coherent strategy against poverty in the late 1950s (B: Townsend, 1967, 20), its 1961 policy statement *Signposts for the Sixties* is where the campaign might be said to have borne most fruit, with a critique of 'Tory affluent society' as containing 7–8 million people close to the margin of poverty, including the aged, the chronic sick, widowed mothers with young children and the handicapped (B: Labour Party, 1961, 24). Poverty had entered the British political agenda tentatively in the late 1950s, and decisively by the early 1960s. If the Titmuss group was most responsible for this penetration of public consciousness, there were other contributors. There was, for example, sociological interest in urban conditions, though not with the same impact as in the United States. J.B. Mays, writing in 1964 about juvenile delinquency in *Growing up in the City*, was exploring the effects of urban poverty and behaviour patterns in conditions of urban poverty as were his American counterparts, but much more as a lone voice, without the receptive political context to absorb and act on the message. Wiseman's *Education and Environment*, also in 1964, included juvenile delinquency, family background, neighbourhood and much else in his survey of the existing literature and research, but again, without the same direct impact on thinking about *poverty* (though the influence on thinking about *education* was more important). The most significant other contribution was that concerned with social class, with educational, social and other inequalities, the fact that 'we don't all live in the same society' (B: Abrams, 1963, 67) or – as the Newsom committee reporting in 1963 on *Half Our Children* was to emphasize – in homes, schools and districts which offered anything like similar opportunities. In these latter cases, however, the concept of poverty was associated with other inequalities and injustices, and contributed more to a climate of opinion than to the making of a specific policy agenda.

The critique of the welfare state was from the starting point of its inadequacy – either in conception or in practice – not of first principles. The components of the welfare state (around which term Titmuss placed inverted commas) confirmed the principle of collective responsibility which had found affirmation in wartime social policy planning – focusing largely on the work of Sir William Beveridge on *Social Insurance and Allied Services* in 1942 and on *Full Employment in a Free Society* in 1944, and on the legislative programme of the Labour government from 1945. The roots of the critique of the welfare state in the late 1950s were diverse – conceptual inadequacy, operational inefficiency, insufficient funding, lack of direction and data, optimistic reliance on the working of 'affluence' and economic growth, confusion between intention and practice. The roots of the welfare state itself were also diverse.

The concepts of collective responsibility and individual welfare were embodied in the flurry of legislation that followed the election of the Labour government in 1945. Its National Insurance Act, for example, proclaimed in 1946 that

Subject to the provisions of this Act, every person who on or after the appointed day, being over school leaving age and under pensionable age, is in Great Britain, and fulfils such conditions as may be prescribed as to residence in Great Britain, shall become insured under this Act and thereafter continue throughout his life to be so insured. (B: *National Insurance Act*, 1946, 1)

The National Health Service Act of the same year placed the duty on the Minister of Health 'to promote the establishment in England and Wales of a comprehensive health service designed to secure improvement in the physical and mental health of the people of England and Wales' (B: *National Health Service Act*, 1946, 1). In moving his Bill, James Griffiths, Minister of National Insurance, traced the legislative and political history of the various insurance schemes that were being consolidated, paying a socialist's tribute to his Liberal predecessor, Lloyd George, and particularly the Old Age Pensions Act of 1908, as well as to Beveridge. The Prime Minister, Clement Attlee, also drew attention to the broad origins of the bill:

This Bill is founded on the Beveridge Report. I would like here to pay a tribute to ... Sir William Beveridge himself, and ... to members of all parties who worked on it. The White Paper produced by the wartime Coalition Government, accepted by all parties, and by the country, is different in kind from all its predecessors.

R.A. Butler, for the Conservative opposition, emphasized that his colleagues had contributed their share 'to the making of this plan, and we wish to see it through'. He went on to underline that

We regard this plan as part of the mosaic or the pattern of the new society ... The whole philosophy lying behind these Measures, in which, I must make it quite plain, we have played our part and shall play our part, is that the good things of life shall be more widely shared; we look forward to a society of which the more unfortunate members are free from the direst dread of penury and want. (B: House of Commons Parliamentary Debates, 1946, 1741–5, 1766–8, 1906)

Whatever socialist ideals and energies were embodied in such plans and legislation, they were not unaccompanied by other elements and wider support. The aspect of the long and complex history of British attempts to provide specific and comprehensive welfare and social security arrangements that concerns us here is the strong (by comparison with the United States) pressure in the nineteenth and twentieth centuries towards state involvement, never easy, always controversial. Regularly on the national agenda was one attempt or another to reveal 'social evils' and remedy them, thereby, as Lloyd George put it, forcing 'the State, as a State, to pay attention to them' (B: Lloyd George, 1912, 31).

It is important to recognize how deeply the experience of the Second World War, following the social and economic traumas of the period between the wars, reinforced the sense of state responsibility for planning and provision. The war, for Britain, meant an enormous degree of national planning and control, out of which experience there also emerged a strengthened commitment to planning for what Butler was not alone in considering 'the new society'. For those concerned with anticipating and preparing for the needs of the peace, the war seemed not only to offer opportunities of building on earlier piecemeal efforts, but also to provide a revolutionary moment in which to make fundamental changes. On one wing of the Labour Party, Stafford Cripps was writing in 1943 about the failure of radical forces after previous wars to prevent a return to reaction and a 'relapse from idealism'. In 1918 attempts at reform had come too late, and there was a need to plan early, to take advantage of the revolutionary character of war (B: Cripps, 1943, 3–14). Aneurin Bevan, from another wing of the party, also described it as 'not so much a war as a revolution...the nature and structure of the post-war world is being determined by what we are doing whilst the war is on'. Beveridge's report on social security would, he forecast, prove to be the focus of 'one of the greatest battles of the twentieth century, and I think it will have to be fought fairly soon' (B: Bevan, n.d., 34, 43–4). Beveridge himself, using similar vocabulary, wrote in 1942 that 'a revolutionary moment in the world's history is a time for revolution, not for patching'. The war was abolishing landmarks of every kind, and it was time to prepare to defeat the five giants he identified as being on the road to successfully accomplishing the necessary revolution – Want, Disease, Ignorance, Squalor and Idleness. Two years later, he related the experience of war to the specific problem of full employment (against 'idleness') in a free society: 'The experience of war is relevant to peace: that unemployment disappears and that all men have value when the State sets up unlimited demand for a compelling common purpose' (B: Beveridge, 1942, 6; 1944, 29). The experience of war, in British conditions, was in fact one of deep acceptance of the supreme role of the state in enabling the pursuit of a 'compelling common purpose' to take place, and that understanding was transferred into the planning not only for post-war recovery but for basic social changes. The welfare state and its provisions were posited to a considerable extent on the role of the state in promoting what Harold Laski called 'positive freedom', a condition marked 'not by the absence of interference from the State-power but by the creation of opportunities it is right that it should organise. Absence of interference means freedom for the few; creation of opportunities means freedom for the many' (B: Laski, n.d., 115).

By the late 1950s the categories of poverty being rediscovered indicated both the failure of the state to understand and to tackle poverty and the increasing poverty arising from the depressed level of benefits, the erosion of free services and the value of pensions, and other policies and market forces. The welfare structures were being seen less as a combination of individualist and collectivist responsibilities, and the rediscovery of poverty was being paralleled by demands for greater means testing and a 'reversal' of post-War egalitarian policies (B: Titmuss, 1958, 34–5). In 1964 Titmuss reviewed the nature, working and limits of the welfare state, and in doing so set out the main contextual features for a discussion of poverty. The concept of the welfare state had entered political thought in the 1940s, and had become generally accepted

...as a wider definition of the role of the State in the field of social and economic policy, embracing more than the provision of social services. Most writers on the subject, whether on the right or left politically, take it to mean a more positive and purposeful commitment by government to concern itself with the general welfare of the whole community.

In the 1950s there had been general consensus about government ownership and planning, while poverty, social deprivation and exploitation had not been abolished. What had come to predominate was the view that 'by a natural process of market levitation all classes and groups will stand expectantly on the political right as the escalator of growth moves them up. Automatism thus substitutes for social protest'. From the standpoint of the 1960s those propositions looked dubious and unhistorical: workers had not achieved 'identical citizenship', and the problems of income and wealth distribution had not been solved (B: Titmuss, 1964, 29–31).

War, Labour commitment to forms of planning and control, bipartisan support for the broad directions of much wartime and post-war welfare planning, deep anxiety not to return to pre-war levels of unemployment and poverty, an existing – if erratic – structure of state involvement in aspects of welfare and social security ... all of these and other factors bear on the popular confidence in the ability of the welfare state apparatus set in place after 1945 to prevent the reappearance of poverty. The end of the Labour Party's first term of office marks the end of the period of serious government commitment to a nation planning these kinds of economic and social futures. Conservative policies from 1951 were in no sense designed to dismantle the apparatus, but central control ceded important economic ground to the competitive market, and the distance between the post-war planning intention and the operation of the welfare state began to grow. Disappointment on the political left was to be expressed from the late 1950s in terms of public processes in which public participation had not been effected or encouraged. The rediscovery of poverty, with its emphases on such areas as pensions and housing, sickness and child benefits, has to be seen in these contexts. The shape of the welfare state dictated the direction of the critiques. Both the context and the critique contained substantial differences from the American discovery of poverty which surfaced in the early 1960s. The 'welfare state', and the underlying direction of the anti-poverty campaign towards more effective collective responsibility, prevented any US-style 'moral crusade'. Beveridge was concerned with the economic causes of unemployment, not with a moral issue (A: Kett, 1982, 95–7). What in American terms was a level of shock and outrage (A: Glazer, 1965a, 71) was in Britain a professional and political response to the decline of an optimistic machine that had already been in place for a decade or more. If the underlying characteristic of the war on poverty was its fervour as a 'cause', in the dominant framework of the market economy, the characteristic of the British discovery of poverty and what followed from it was their expression within the political contexts of the welfare state.

8   Opportunity, equality and social class

A cluster of inter-related themes dominated discussion of education in the late 1950s and 1960s, focusing on comprehensive secondary education, educational opportunity and social class, and involving sustained political controversy and a growing impact by the sociology of education. None of these themes relate directly – until the later 1960s – to a discussion of the concept of poverty, but they are essential to understanding both the later British developments and the absence – until after the publication of the Plowden report on primary education in 1967 – of any emphasis on relationships amongst pre-schooling, disadvantage, the environment and poverty. There was during this period virtually no significant public discussion of the primary or nursery school, except in terms of numbers.

The discussion of education and social class has been the most prolonged educational issue of twentieth-century Britain. In its early phases, particularly in the 1930s and 1940s, it related to psychological views of intelligence. From the 1950s it was the central concern of the newly developing sociology of education. Philosophers have engaged in the discussion of the concepts, and the arguments in favour of wider opportunity have often been conducted in economic terms. Given the political repercussions of the discussion, important contributions to the literature were made, particularly in the 1960s, by political scientists. The discussions of the 1950s and 1960s built on decades of growing concern around such concepts as 'equality', 'equality of opportunity', 'democracy' and 'social justice', focusing on the structure of the educational system and on access by children from different social groups to its component parts. As early as the 1890s, in the context of two distinct educational systems – elementary for working-class and secondary for middle-class children – there were pressures within the labour movement for the adoption of the principle of equality of opportunity in education. At the 1896 Trades Union Congress, for example, a motion was put forward urging 'that our education system should be completely remodelled on such a basis as to secure the democratic principle of equality of opportunity'. Although this was amended to read that the system 'should be reorganized upon a broader and more democratic basis', the concept of equality of opportunity continued to be present in resolutions to future congresses (B: Schofield, 1964, vol. 1, 58–9). It was not until after the First World War, however, that concern for social justice found major expression in educational terms, coupled with programmes for educational action and structural reforms to secure 'secondary education for all'.

The effective starting point for this movement is the beginning of the 1920s. The crucial figure in establishing and sustaining a new consciousness of the relationship between social injustice and the existing educational system was R.H. Tawney. Tawney wrote *Secondary Education for All* for the Labour Party in 1922, served on the epoch-making Hadow committee which produced *The Education of the Adolescent* in 1926, and published his famous *Equality* in 1931. The discussion of equal opportunity in education began not in research but in socialist politics, in demands for an end to nineteenth-century class assumptions. 'The hereditary curse upon English education is its organization upon lines of social class', wrote Tawney in one of the angriest passages of *Equality*. Public opinion, he continued, was 'saturated with the influence of a long tradition of educational inequality'. The individual needs of children were not met because of 'the barbarous association of differences of educational opportunity with distinctions of wealth and social position' (B: Tawney, 1931, 142–4). By this stage Tawney and others were underlining the centrality of education to the concepts of equality and equal opportunity, exposing social injustice and social waste, and attempting to demonstrate the relationship between educational and social underprivilege. The aims pursued were, in general, wider access for working-class children to grammar schools, and the creation of a new kind of secondary school (called senior or modern schools) for those who did not go to grammar schools. Under the Hadow scheme of 'secondary education for all', which aimed at a break in schooling for all children at the age of eleven, these aims were beginning to be implemented in some areas of the country in the years up to the Second World War. What Tawney and the Labour Party were mainly anxious to achieve was 'the improvement of primary education and the development of public secondary education to such a point that all normal children, irrespective of income, class, or occupation of their parents may be transferred at the age of eleven from the primary or preparatory school to one type or another of secondary school, and remain in the latter till sixteen' (B: Tawney, 1922, 7).

Also in the 1920s and 1930s there were important elements of an emergent sociology of education, directly related to the interest in social class and educational opportunity, and representing what Hogben in 1938 described as *Political Arithmetic*. The contributors to this development were concerned with the combination of factors which contributed to unequal access to and achievement in education, and the implications for the economy and 'social progress'. The tone was set by Kenneth Lindsay in 1926, with an analysis of *Social Progress and Educational Waste*, in which he explored the factors influencing children's chances of obtaining a 'free place' or scholarship to grammar school. On the basis of a detailed account of the working of the system in a number of towns and counties Lindsay found it 'conclusively proved that success in winning scholarships varies with almost monotonous regularity according to the quality of the social and economic environment...One school in Lewisham wins as many scholarships as the whole of Bermondsey put together, seven poor London boroughs have an average of 1.3 scholars per 1,000 children in average attendance, as against 5.3 in seven better-placed London boroughs.' The conclusion was that alternative forms of secondary education needed to be available, and 'selection by differentiation must replace selection by elimination...proved ability to the extent of at least 40 per cent of the nation's children is at present being denied expression' (B: Lindsay, 1926, 8, 15, 23). The barrier to the grammar school was, as Lindsay underlined in the title of one his chapters, 'The barrier of poverty'.

One of the most careful, and most influential, attempts to analyse the intricacies of 'ability and opportunity in English education' was an essay under that title contributed by J.L. Gray and Pearl Moshinsky to Hogben's *Political Arithmetic*. Gray had two years earlier published a book in which, as a social psychologist, he had looked at *The Nation's Intelligence*. This was an outspoken expression of his view that whatever levels or measures of intelligence were used, the conclusion was inescapable: 'social inequality in the distribution of educational opportunities exists on a scale exceeding the wildest guesses of irresponsible agitators'. There was 'a vast reservoir of unutilized talent' and attempts to attribute differences in intelligence between social groups to genetic differences had no basis in 'reliable independent evidence'. The notion of fixed intelligence levels was in error 'when it denies that environmental agencies may affect ability...sufficient evidence exists to show that some part at least of the observed superiority of average children of prosperous parents can be attributed to the economic and cultural advantages they enjoy' (B: Gray, J.L., 1936, 3, 99–101, 134). The 1938 paper with Moshinsky was a more analytical, research-based statement, acknowledging the British and American literature which considered 'the relative ability of different social groups within a community', and immediately referring to the 'dubious nature of the evidence adduced to support the general inference that any observed differences are exclusively or even predominantly genetic in origin'. Data, resulting from the testing of 9,000 individuals between the ages of nine and 12 years 6 months in all types of school, led them to conclude:

The major part of these inequalities in educational opportunity remains after account has been taken of the relative ability of each social class. We are therefore dealing with disparities due to differences in social institutions, rather than to genetic inequalities.

Their figures showed 'nurtural as contrasted with natural differences in an important domain of social organization', though the authors were aware that the figures probably under-estimated the social origins of differences in opportunity, 'since the inferior mean ability of the less prosperous social classes may itself arise partly from their environmental disadvantages' (B: Gray and Moshinsky, 1938, 334, 415).

By the outbreak of war the climate of opinion had significantly changed. Local authorities implementing the Hadow proposals for reorganization were doing so in the full realization that they were pursuing a measure of policy dictated by conceptions of more equal opportunities, greater social justice and the need to diminish social inequalities represented in the educational system above all by lack of access for working-class children to post-elementary education. One of the most potent expressions of the parallel emphasis on the environmental and social constraints within which many children worked came from Sir Cyril Burt in *The Backward Child*, published in 1937. Burt denied strongly that 'backwardness' or 'stupidity' were an inevitable result of poverty. He explored in some detail how poverty impaired health and general knowledge, the impact of monotonous neighbourhoods, the nature of the home conditions in which children's language and intellect developed. The causes of educational backwardness, he stressed, lay outside the school: 'backwardness and poverty...go largely hand in hand', and educational backwardness related to high birth and death rates, overcrowding and the other features of poverty (B: Burt, 1937, 95–6, 102, 105, 118–33). The extent and range of the debate had grown considerably since the early 1920s. By the time Tawney wrote the introduction to a book on *Education and the Birth-Rate* in 1940, he saw the authors' further analysis of educational inequalities as witnessing 'the nemesis of a plutocratic educational system'. The authors' proposals in the book for a radical reconstruction of post-primary education, treating the different types of school as 'different species of one genus', were already 'old friends' (B: Leybourne and White, 1940, 12–13).

What was emerging, and was to replace the division between elementary and grammar schooling, was a pattern of secondary education in which selection was to be by 'differentiation'. Working-class and educational bodies had on the whole accepted the need for different kinds of secondary school, and the process of selecting children for grammar school places had become increasingly important. The distinctions between types of secondary school were reinforced by psychologists who, from the beginning of the century, had been asserting with growing confidence that it was possible to measure intelligence scientifically, and therefore to allocate children to the right kind of secondary school. In the 1930s intelligence testing gradually became accepted as a key element in the selection process. The Spens report on *Secondary Education* in 1938 based its analysis of secondary education on the view that 'intellectual development during childhood appears to progress as if it were governed by a single central factor, usually known as "general intelligence", which may be broadly described as innate all-round intellectual ability... Our psychological witnesses assured us that it can be measured approximately by means of intelligence tests' (B: Board of Education, 1938, 123). Since more specific, environmentally influenced aptitudes – the psychologists affirmed – became prominent after the age of eleven, transfer at eleven was obviously justified. The Norwood report on *Curriculum and Examinations in Secondary Schools* in 1943 distinguished unhesitatingly between different 'varieties of capacity' in children: there were pupils who were 'interested in learning for its own sake', those 'whose interests and abilities lie markedly in the field of applied science or applied art' and those who deal 'more easily with concrete things than with ideas'. It therefore strongly supported the division of secondary schools into grammar, technical and modern schools (B: Board of Education, 1943, 2–4, 139).

From a number of quarters, however, doubts about the division of secondary education, processes of selection, and the justice of the new organizational basis were beginning to be expressed. Within the labour movement reservations were being voiced as to the adequacy of the demand simply for 'secondary education for all', and the fairness of selection at eleven. Leah Manning, a Labour MP, said in the House of Commons in 1931 that 'there are no means of telling at that early and tender age what a child is going to be'. In 1937 another Labour MP,

Lees-Smith, pointed out that 'we talk of class distinctions and how to get rid of them, but a new class distinction is arising, namely, the distinction between those who pass an academic examination at the age of eleven and those who do not pass it' (B: Dean, 1968, 139). Support for the idea of 'common' secondary schooling increased during the war.

The 1944 Education Act enshrined the doctrine of phases of education, with secondary education for all according to age, aptitude and ability. Most local education authorities interpreted this to mean the tripartite system of different types of school, and the post-war Labour Ministers of Education did the same. Ellen Wilkinson, for example, defended the publication by the Ministry of Education in 1945 of *The Nation's Schools*, which justified the tripartite system; a revised version, *The New Secondary Education*, did the same in 1947. The whole subject was now a source of controversy within the Labour Party. Moves away from the assumption that secondary education for all necessarily meant different schools were being made in other quarters. The London County Council, under its Labour majority, in 1947 issued its plans for the reorganization of London schools, starting from the concept of equal opportunity:

...it is evident that it is now the duty of authorities to establish equality of opportunity for all children...Mere equality of opportunity, however, will not meet the case unless that opportunity is at the appropriate high level, and the requirement therefore involves the setting up of a standard not only of equality but of quality.

The LCC had decided in 1944 that the tripartite system did not match up to this philosophy, and that the plan should aim at establishing a system of 'comprehensive high schools' (B: London County Council, 1947, 7, 230). Some other areas adopted the comprehensive school principle, and the certainties about 'secondary education for all' voiced in the 1920s were now being disturbed by the view that a divided secondary school system was not adequate to the ideals that had sustained it. H.C. Dent, in 1949, wrote that 'hardly anyone appears to be prepared to face...the hard fact that to provide suitable secondary education for all children is so utterly different a problem from providing a special kind of secondary education for a few selected children as to constitute an entirely new problem'. What was now entailed was 'the most superhuman feat of thinking outside the categories of thought in which practically all our educational thinking has hitherto been done' (B: Dent, 1949, 114).

The focus in all of this accelerating debate was secondary education, with the 'utterly different' problem presenting a variety of solutions which might contribute to the promotion of the democracy and welfare at the heart of wartime expectations, and to the ideal of social justice that underlay the concept of the welfare state. The 1944 Act itself was in part a product of this social consciousness, but by the end of the 1940s there was a growing sense in radical political and educational circles that educational advance had been too limited. Still coupled with discussions of opportunity were questions of waste and rights. T.H. Marshall pointed out in 1949 that 'recent studies of educational opportunity in the pre-war years have been concerned to reveal the magnitude of social waste quite as much as to protest against the frustration of natural human rights'. The post-war situation was not yet solving either problem, as Marshall's discussion of the 1944 Act went on to show. Quoting the provision in the Act for education according to age, aptitude and ability, he commented: 'Respect for individual rights could hardly be more strongly expressed. Yet I wonder whether it will work out like that in practice' (B: Marshall, 1963, 111–12). For a quarter of a century from the outbreak of the Second World War the contributors to the discussion wrestled with the dual question of waste and rights, the relationship between education and both the economy and social justice.

What began to emerge in the 1950s was a detailed analysis of the inequalities of which the pre-war investigators had been aware, and of the failure of British society to confront those inequalities, in spite of the reorganization that followed the 1944 Act. We shall return to the impact of the sociology of education in this respect, but it is important to underline here the increasing attention being paid to social bias in selection for education. It was not only sociologists who became engaged in a critique of selection and its instruments – there was in parallel an attack by radical educationists on the process of selection, a landmark in this attack being Brian Simon's *Intelligence Testing and the Comprehensive School* in 1953. The most influential of the sociological analyses of the continued class differential in access to grammar schools was Floud, Halsey and Martin's *Social Class and Educational Opportunity* in 1956, a study of working-class and middle-class children in south-west Hertfordshire and Middlesborough. Basil Bernstein was in the late 1950s and 1960s also providing an influential theory of working-class and middle-class language codes, to explain the poor performance of working-class children within the terms of reference laid down by the schools. The socially conditioned educational disabilities of working-class children became dominant features of educational debate and radical programmes. In a pioneer book which argued the case for comprehensive (or 'omnibus') schools Lady Simon of Wythenshawe asked, in 1948:

How can we best carry out the new duty to provide secondary education for *all* children over 12... How can we combine this with ensuring real equality of educational opportunity? There are also some of us who are wondering how to organize the schools so as to bring about a more democratic state of society than now exists. (B: Lady Simon of Wythenshawe, 1948, 7)

To all of these analyses the concept of social class was central.

An important aspect of the concept of class in its British context has been the availability of the terminology in nineteenth- and twentieth-century social analysis from a variety of standpoints, though with varied interpretations and implications. Class as a concept was integral to the politics of nineteenth-century radicalism and the conservatism of Disraeli, and in the twentieth century has been the language of both description and conflict. From the late nineteenth century it was part of the vocabulary of Fabian socialism and of Marxism. Whereas the language of class was a late import into the American discussion with which we have been concerned, in Britain it was there at the starting line. In some versions, including that of Tawney, it might be confrontational. In some of the early sociology, including that of David Glass and colleagues at the London School of Economics, from which the pioneering work of the late 1950s and 1960s sprang, it could be more concerned with social status rather than class. In many cases it was simply a convenient language of social differentiation. The work with which we are concerned here was rarely concerned to explore the historical and political meanings of class in ways which were becoming more important to Marxist historians.

The educational critique in terms of social class, reached an important climax in the first half of the 1960s. In 1963 Philip Abrams pointed out that children know about social class even if they do not know the term (B: Abrams, 1963, 68), and some of the sociologists in the late 1950s and early 1960s were going beyond the statistics of access to different kinds of secondary education to the study of attitudes and consciousness, to the assumptions about schooling shared by – especially – working-class parents and their children. The emerging focus was the relationship between educational structures and processes on the one hand, and the class experience of children on the other hand, how children carried their experience of social class into the school. Studies such as Young and Willmott's *Family and Kinship in East London* and then more directly Jackson and Marsden's *Education and the Working Class*, examined attitudes to the grammar school, sources of resistance, understandings of schooling in the context of working-class culture (B: Young and Willmott, 1957; Jackson and Marsden, 1962), an interest which runs in parallel from Richard Hoggart's exploration of working-class life in *The Uses of Literacy* in 1957 to the growing interest in class and culture in the 1960s. J.W.B. Douglas's *The Home and the School* in 1964, as well as a variety of publications by A.H. Halsey, D.F. Swift and others looked directly at social class differences in secondary selection. The impact of the environment, commonly expressed in terms of class or socio-economic status, was, as we have seen, the focus, in the mid-1960s, of work by Wiseman (1964) and Mays (1962a and b). The attack on the class bias of intelligence testing became more widespread. The relationship between class and mobility remained an important framework for analysis, with Halsey pointing out in 1964, for example, that social class was no longer the 'implacable determinant of a man's life chances it once was', at the same time as calling for more investigation of barriers of class and culture in education (B: Halsey, 1964, 6–11). Two major reports were published in 1963 – the Newsom report on the education of pupils aged 13 to 16 of average and less than average ability, *Half Our Future*, and the Robbins report on *Higher Education*. Neither specifically used the language of class. The Newsom report, however, was concerned centrally with 'problem areas', 'education in the slums' and the social problems related to environmental, population and other factors, using J.B. Mays's identification of the relationship amongst delinquency rates, ill health and local conditions as one of its reference points (B: Ministry of Education, 1963, 17 and *passim*). The Robbins report used sociologists' data concerning the relationship between economic circumstances, measured ability and access to higher education, and, in a key appendix to the report, it presented the evidence in these terms:

The proportion of middle class children who reach degree level courses is eight times as high as the proportion from working class homes, and even in grammar schools it is twice as high. As has been shown, the difference in grammar schools is not chiefly due to lower intelligence, but rather to early leaving. However, it is not only in these schools that the wastage of ability is higher among manual working class children. There is much evidence to show that, both before the age of 11 and in later years, the influence of environment is such that the differences in measured ability between social classes progressively widens as children grow up. (B: Committee on Higher Education, *Higher Education* Appendix One, 1964, 46 and Part II, Section 2, passim)

In relatively strong or weak forms the relationship between educational opportunity and social stratification was being widely explored in the early and mid-1960s. The ways in which education was weighted against working-class children were on the agendas of sociologists and educationists, official committees and politicians, and in the forums of public debate.

The focus on social class and opportunity that emerged in post-war

Britain became a controversy about the comprehensive secondary school. A discussion of the directions of educational policy-making from the 1960s and beyond has to establish the reasons for this overwhelming educational agenda. Some historical threads have to be brought together at this point.

The outstanding feature of nineteenth-century educational history in Britain was the conscious establishment of two separate educational systems. The creation of an elementary school system for the children of the poor was an attempt to meet a new situation brought about by industrialization and the rapid growth of towns – the disruption of a traditional, rural-based social order. Cheap mass schooling was designed to provide basic literacy and to inculcate 'necessary' social and moral virtues. The 1870 Elementary Education Act, which supplemented the existing voluntary schools with rate-supported board schools, did not alter the elementary system's explicit identification with the children of the poor or with 'the working classes'. In this situation those old endowed grammar schools which had provided some 'elementary' schooling for local children began to shed this lower-level work and to aim at the higher standards of the more successful, more completely classical schools. The grammar schools were reformed, notably by the Endowed Schools Act of 1869, in such a way as to ensure their efficiency as *secondary* schools – providing for the middle and upper echelons of the community. Gradations of quality and social composition in these and most of the 'public' schools did not alter the fact of their identification with the children of the middle class. Victorian England knew that elementary education was for working-class children, and that the grammar schools were for middle-class children. This was as salient a fact of nineteenth-century England and Wales (the same would not be as true for Scotland) as the fact of class consciousness itself. Throughout the nineteenth century there were radical and working-class movements which saw education as part of a popular struggle to replace the existing social and political structure – often developing their own educational activities as part of their vision of an 'alternative' society. By 1870, universal, free and compulsory elementary education had become the main working-class demand, with little discussion of reforms which would enable poor children in large numbers to gain access to grammar school and university education. The concept of secondary education as a *stage* beyond elementary education was only beginning to take shape in the last quarter of the century.

The expansion of educational opportunity became a new aspiration in the context of the school boards created under the 1870 Act. Some of the boards began to confront the problem of the needs of older and abler elementary school children, and evolved *within the elementary system* forms of para-secondary education – senior classes, senior tops, higher-grade schools and evening classes. Although these still confirmed the separateness of working-class education, they presented a challenge to the grammar schools, and were seen as undermining the traditional classical and academic emphases of 'genuine' secondary education. Industrial competition from countries such as Germany, whose progress was demonstrably based on a better system of elementary and technical education, led to public finance becoming available in Britain and the development of a scholarship system for poor, able children from the elementary schools. The scholarship 'ladder' was erected, and the 'free place' system of 1907 followed. The 1902 Education Act had given responsibility for both elementary and secondary education to local councils and, under the 1907 arrangements, secondary schools in receipt of public funds had to provide not less than a quarter of their places free of charge to children from elementary schools.

The equality of opportunity that the Trades Union Congress had discussed in the 1890s could now be, and was, discussed in a different setting. A small fraction of working-class children was now reaching the grammar school, and manifestly *unequal* opportunity was being clearly demonstrated. The existence of a scholarship ladder also began to attract more middle-class children into the elementary schools, resulting in a problem of greater class differentiation within the contingent of children going from elementary to grammar schools. The Board of Education estimated in 1907 that children from public elementary schools constituted 'rather more than half the pupils in the (grammar) schools, those of them who paid fees and those who did not being about equal in number. But while some schools consisted almost entirely of such children, others had few or none of them, and their incursion on a large scale was dreaded.' In 1930 a committee reviewing the position set alongside the estimate the fact that in 1927–8

nearly 72 per cent of the pupils admitted had been in public elementary schools, and the great majority of them took up free places. No less than 42 per cent of all the places in recognized secondary schools were free of fees...To-day about 64,000 pupils proceed annually from elementary to secondary schools, about 38,000 of them as the result of competitive examination.

The committee quoted the Manchester education officer who had pointed out 'that at no period since 1902 had provision kept pace with demand: at the present time, in spite of the greatly increased provision of the last ten years, there are probably more suitable pupils demanding further education and failing to get it than at any time since the State assumed responsibility for education' (B: Joint Advisory Committee of the Association of Education Committees and the National Union of

Teachers [1930], 22–3, quoting Board of Education, *Recent Development of Secondary Schools in England and Wales,* and Spurley Hey, *Central Schools*). It is against this background of gradually increasing opportunity for elementary school children to obtain a grammar school education (or 'secondary', 'further' or 'higher' education – the vocabulary was interchangeable) that the discussion of opportunity, and ultimately of the comprehensive school, took shape. The numbers of working-class children reaching the grammar school in the 1930s remained modest. The two nineteenth-century systems were no longer totally separate, but the 'ladder' between them had not altered their basic configuration. For Tawney the situation was 'educationally unsound and socially obnoxious' (B: Tawney, 1922, 11).

In that historical framework appeared the movements to counter educational 'waste' and inefficiency, to restructure the system along Hadow lines and in response to radical demands for secondary education for all. The difficulty, as Dent rightly emphasized, of finding appropriate new forms of secondary schooling, was considerable, and led only to the tripartite (or bipartite, since secondary technical schools were relatively few in number) local schemes, but also to experiments along comprehensive or other lines. When, in 1961, the *Times Educational Supplement* conducted a survey of 'bilateral schools', for example, there was a substantial number of such schools, admitting 'academic' and other children to a 'two-sided' school (grammar and commercial, grammar and technical, etc.) within which there was an attempt to remove clear-cut boundaries (B: *Times Educational Supplement,* 1961, 1179–84). Most local authorities, as we have seen, opted for different types of school, and only slowly were the difficulties of achieving parallel status for grammar and secondary modern schools, and social inequalities inherent in selection for 'appropriate' schools, widely seen to be weaknesses in this interpretation of equal opportunity. For reluctant egalitarians, unwilling to accept a complete system of comprehensive schools in the public sector, a midway position seemed tenable with a mixture of selective grammar schools alongside non-selective comprehensive schools, a situation which became increasingly common in the 1960s. In both the Labour and Conservative Parties it was an effort at compromise, in the latter an attempt to balance the principle of equal opportunity against the concepts of 'freedom' and 'democracy'. Those who held the 'mixed' view were willing, in the final analysis, to abandon the concept of equal opportunity as being incompatible with British education traditions. The upholders of the 'comprehensive' view of equal opportunity – and this became true of the Labour government in office from 1964 to 1970 – considered that a full system of comprehensive schools, with the abolition of the grammar schools and of selection, matched in practice the principle of equal opportunity.

Pressure for comprehensive schools drew on the experience of the completely comprehensive post-war systems established in the Isle of Man and Anglesey, and of the early London comprehensive schools. Robin Pedley, one of the leading advocates of such schools, began a survey of this experience in 1954 with the statement that 'the field of debate on comprehensive schools is shifting from theory to practice'. He described the existing schools as 'middle of the road', organizing themselves with caution, reproducing (in streaming particularly) some of the features of the tripartite system – a source of some of the criticism levelled at the comprehensive schools in the mid- and late 1960s. The pressure to complete the reorganization, however, remained strong in the period leading up to the election of a Labour government in 1964, and in 1965 the Department of Education and Science issued its circular 10/65 on *The Organisation of Secondary Education*. The Labour Party Leadership, some of them reversing long-held principles, decided to move towards a fully comprehensive secondary school system, not by parliamentary legislation, but by persuasion, and the circular 're-quested' local education authorities to submit plans for reorganization if they had not already done so. In some areas much controversy and resistance was organized (and by the end of Labour's period in office in 1970 the circular had been only partially effective, and its withdrawal was one of the first acts of the new Conservative government).

The ancestry of the comprehensive school and the pressures from the early 1920s in particular explain the centrality of the comprehensive issue in the 1960s, and the agenda against which all other issues had to compete. Lady Simon established the perspective clearly in 1962: 'the most controversial issue that has arisen in educational thought and practice since the denominational battles of the nineteenth century is that of comprehensive schools' (B: Lady Simon of Wythenshaw, 1962, 72). By the mid-1960s, as many commentators were aware, the comprehensive school had become the principal *political* issue in domestic affairs (B: Wallace, 1965, 3). The *Times Educational Supplement* and the press generally contained extensive and angry correspondence in defence of the comprehensive school and in defence of the grammar school and selection. Local controversy was heated and protracted, often resulting in extensive reporting of the plans and their implementation. A report on Liverpool in 1964 may have been somewhat unusual, but was indicative of the depth of feelings:

This week the city council approved an 'all-through' system of comprehensive education for pupils aged from 11 to 18 or 19. On Monday, the day the council met, police dispersed a crowd of 400 grammar school children who planned to march...to the town hall in protest. The children, who had not given police the statutory 48 hours' advance notice of a procession, dispersed quietly...The Conservative and Liberal parties in the council put forward amendments...to allow more time to investigate the scheme but these were heavily defeated. (B: *Times Educational Supplement*, 1964b, 707)

The most sustained and scholarly attack on the principle of the comprehensive school was that of G.H. Bantock, the focus of whose opposition was the intention to use the comprehensive school as 'the instrument of a common culture', failing to understand basic social and cultural differences, 'fighting the wrong cultural battle with many of its pupils'. It was the place where 'our social consciences have been, in part, institutionalized'. It represented a tendency 'to think of our children as socio-political abstractions, simply as means to a more equal society'. Schools ought to be, not instruments of social and political revolution, but 'cultural agencies for the performance of certain specific and limited tasks' (B: Bantock, 1965, 108). Bantock emphasized in 1977 that for nearly twenty years he had been arguing that 'the crisis in our secondary education is cultural and cannot be met by the organisational device of the comprehensive school' (B: Bantock, 1977, 78). Most of the opposition, whether expressed in cultural, administrative or ideological terms, focused on the perceived threat to the values and high standards of the selective grammar school (and discussions in the 1960s of the expansion of higher education similarly reflected anxieties about the traditional roles and values of the university).

It is important not to underestimate the dominance of the comprehensive issue in educational debate, to the almost total exclusion of other educational developments from central positions in the thinking of the left. An article on 'Labour's educational policy' in the left-wing *New Reasoner* in 1958, for example, focused almost totally on types of secondary school, the independent schools, the ladder from primary to secondary schools, the educational case for the comprehensive school, the 'incubus of selection' (B: Ibbotson, 1958). The Labour Party's election policy statement the following year, reflecting a similar range of emphases, focused on the abolition of 'slum schools' and of the eleven plus examination, the question of grants for secondary and higher education, and education as a national investment. The only reference to primary education was in a comment on the size of classes in primary and secondary education (B: Labour Party, 1959, 2). *Forum*, a journal 'for the discussion of new trends in education', was throughout the 1960s the most consistent advocate of the comprehensive school and the ending of selection and streaming, and made those three issues in fact the overwhelmingly dominant content of its issues. Articles on the primary school often tended to be by-products of arguments for the comprehensive school, freeing the primary school from pressures to prepare children for the selection process (B: Freeland, 1962). In submitting evidence to the Plowden committee on primary education in 1964, the *Forum* editorial board called for primary education to be seen as 'of equal importance to secondary education', but focused on the question of school organization, with no direct reference to questions of disadvantage, inequality or social class, all of which were seen in the journal as critical to discussions of secondary education. A commentary on the primary school issues facing the Plowden committee, written by three junior school headteachers on the *Forum* editorial board, also focused on buildings, organization, curriculum, teachers and the transition to secondary education (B: *Forum* Editorial Board, 1964; Freeland *et al.*, 1964).

Neither in *Forum* nor elsewhere, in the period up to the publication of the Plowden report in 1967, was the primary school an 'issue' in the sense that the secondary school was. The primary school was 'there', surrounded by a certain image of success, and attracting a good deal of international attention. John Vaizey, in 1962, while underlining the chronic shortage of primary school teachers and the need for a restructuring of nursery and primary education (for example, to provide more half-time places), nevertheless introduced his discussion of the primary school: 'The primary schools are one of the good things in English education. The children are happy, the teachers are relaxed and efficient, and some of the new buildings are very beautiful' (B: Vaizey, 1962, 35).

The primary school did not attract serious discussion of the social, political and cultural values under sustained debate in the secondary field. It might be under-staffed, often in old and poor buildings or in other ways under-resourced, but it was basically unproblematic, except in the specific attention given to streaming and the impact of selection at eleven. In *Forum*, in the literature generally, and in the schools, there was, of course, awareness of these issues, and naturally it was the comprehensive school that was seen as the key to unlock these concerns. A sharp picture of that totality was painted in 1961 by Brian Jackson, describing his experience of ten-year-old boys in a streamed (A, B, C) school. The more he had got to know these boys ('of the C type', 'of the grammar school type', etc.) the more he was convinced that they had not been '"given" to us in these neat categories'; *we had manufactured them*. They were the product of the educational society that we had established ... Society demanded that they be selected and rejected at 11, therefore we pre-selected at 10, 9, 8, 7, 6' (B: Jackson, 1961, 6–7; also Jackson, 1964).

The issue of streaming, therefore, was a by-product of the campaign for the comprehensive school, and the primary school was not scrutinized with the same vigour as was the secondary school. Neither was nursery provision, discussion of which took place in terms of numbers, availability and resources. When the Department of Education and Science, in 1965, published extracts from letters it had received in response to a report on *Education under Social Handicap*, it quoted from a headteacher who believed that the remedy to problems caused by disadvantage 'should commence in the tadpole stage... The 15 year old problem child is a problem child at 5 (B: DES, 1965, first part, 4). Debate among educationists rarely confronted the implications of such a view.

Psychologists concerned with poverty in Britain did not, in the 1950s and 1960s, concern themselves directly with education, given that early childhood, early education and schooling in general were outside their focus on welfare state inadequacies and remedies. Educationists concerned with the comprehensive school and equality did not, in the 1950s and 1960s, concern themselves directly with the sociology of poverty and the welfare state, given that these did not impinge on the areas of principal educational attention that surrounded selection and the comprehensive school. The 1960s did, however, see the rapid development of a sociology of education.

We have seen the emergence in pre-war Britain of an interest in those aspects of the social condition which related to the sorting process in education. The British sociology of education brought to educational theory and practice an inherited empirical approach to exploring the relationship, a focus on the social and educational structures within which children succeeded and failed, and initially a massive concern with social class and selection. The problems at the heart of sociological investigation were not unique to sociology. Post-war sociology of education, while deriving energies from sociological theory and other sources, drew on British traditions of social investigation which themselves often had political, psychological, anthropological, economic and other origins. One of the characteristics – some would say weaknesses – of the sociology of education in the 1960s was that it embraced a broad range not only of specifically 'sociological' enquiries and theories, but also of contributions from social analysts who explored the same problems, often used the same data, and pointed towards at least similar conclusions, while entering the territory with other credentials. One of the most used texts in the field in the 1960s was Halsey, Floud and Anderson's *Education, Economy, and Society*, which relegated a reference to sociology to its sub-title, 'A reader in the sociology of education', and the contributions to which came from a variety of directions, including specialists in educational administration, economics and psychology. Vaizey's *Education for Tomorrow*, while not specifically labelled as 'sociology' (Vaizey was a professor of educational economics and administration), was popularly used as such, containing as it did chapters on topics such as 'equality and ability' and 'differentiation and selection'. Official reports such as *Early Leaving* (1954), *15 to 18* (1959) and *Higher Education* drew on data and conducted analyses widely perceived as 'sociological'. One of the most widely read books in the field in the 1960s, J.W.B. Douglas's *The Home and the School* (1964) was the product of someone with a medical background, who had worked on a casualty study in the war, had developed an interest in social problems, and was conducting a project sponsored by the Medical Research Council. Not being a sociologist he did not expect that his work would be taken seriously (B: Douglas, interview). What was happening was that to a degree discussions of, and research in, education, were becoming 'sociologized'. Jack Wrigley, for example, recalls of the work initiated by Stephen Wiseman with other psychology colleagues in Manchester in the 1950s that

the intention was to look at achievement from the point of view of socio-economic background...(Wiseman) had a very clear view, even when he began it, of a map of the Manchester area, of the scores in the various wards...I think he knew what was going to happen with the socio-economic data. As a psychologist he didn't neglect that side.

Wrigley, as a young research assistant, was required to produce narrow tests, Wiseman's intention being to produce meaningful results, while maintaining a broad view (B: Wrigley, interview).

A sociology of education developed, in any strict sense, in the period from the mid-1950s to the mid-1960s. It was heralded as much as anywhere in *Social Mobility in Britain*, edited by David Glass (including in Glass's own contributions to that volume), published in 1954. The subject had arrived when the first master's degree in the sociology of education was established at London University's Institute of Education in 1964. From the late 1950s the impact of the new sociology was becoming rapidly felt. One of the sociologists involved commented in 1969 that

during the last decade in Britain the sociologist had begun to play a part in the statutory administrative system as consultant, administrator and researcher. At the same time the findings of research are being assimilated into the folklore of teaching at what, given the small amount of research, may even be thought to be a dangerous speed. (B: Swift, 1969, 2)

As the development took place, there was a sympathetic response from some academics in adjacent fields, including psychology, where some like W.D. Wall 'tried to bridge hardline psychology and the outside world' (Sheridan, interview), while others would – like Wiseman – feel themselves in a state of 'tension' with the emergent sociology (Wrigley, interview), and areas of controversy or disagreement opened up between fields like social psychology and the new sociology (B: Swift, 1965). Work on the margins began to be absorbed into the mainstream. A study of children's health and illness in Newcastle upon Tyne, begun in 1931, began to produce results of importance to the new work by Douglas and others (B: Spence et al., 1954; Miller, F.J.W. et al., 1960). A study in Kent produced research data on 'the close relationship between reading and home background' (B: Standish, 1959, 32). Halsey, Floud and Anderson reproduced in their 1961 volume the early 1950s findings of a psychologist on the negative correlation between intelligence test scores and family size, and the implications for verbal and general mental development (A: Nisbet, 1953). A Welsh professor of education summarized the position in an inaugural lecture in 1957, commenting on the disillusionment which had followed the post-war promise of a new world:

Other factors in this broad and comprehensive term 'environment' began to fix themselves upon our attention. We became much more aware than ever before of the presence of large unseen influences whose power had been underestimated, forces to which we commonly apply the label 'sociological'. (B: Gittins, 1957, 186)

Social Mobility in Britain announced the mainstream thrust of a British sociology of education. In it appeared some of the outcomes of a programme of research directed by David Glass at the Department of Sociological and Demographic research of the London School of Economics. The programme as a whole was 'concerned with the processes of social selection and differentiation which are at work in Britain, with the formation of social strata, and with the nature, composition and functions of those strata'. Unlike the pre-war studies, this focused essentially on the 'middle classes', their occupations, social mobility, educational preferences and experience. Jean Floud analysed the educational experience of the adult population of England and Wales in 1949, F.M. Martin reported on an inquiry into parents' preferences in secondary education, and Hilda Himmelweit looked at the London data on social status and secondary education since the 1944 Act. Glass and J.R. Hall wrote on education and social mobility, concluding that 'parental social status and child's education tend to reinforce each other in determining filial social status ... Education as such appears to modify, but not to destroy, the characteristic association between the social status of fathers and sons.' It was, however, Glass's introduction that set out the framework within which the sociology of the following decade or more was to be most visible. This introduction differed from what was to follow in its emphasis not on class and class relations, but on the structure of social status, based on the assumption that there was a 'hierarchy of social status – that society is arranged in a series of layers – and that there are criteria which may be used to indicate the status level, or position in the hierarchy'. Before the 1944 Act was implemented, a child's level of education 'depended closely upon the social status of his (or her) father; social status being measured in terms of the father's occupation'. Differences in measured intelligence, could not themselves in 1949 account for educational differences: 'crude economic, together with more subtle social and cultural, factors account for the major differences'. Neither increased opportunities between the wars, nor the new 'secondary education for all' had eliminated educational inequalities, though the more obvious ones had been removed by the abolition of fees in secondary schools: even in the state system 'parental attitudes and aspirations, clearly related to social status and perhaps heavily conditioned by the education of the parents themselves, affect a child's chances of entering a grammar school, and further influence his level of achievement within that school' (B: Glass, 1954, 307, 3–16). Within this framework, and extending into the landscape of social class, a sociology of education was to take shape.

In 1958 Jean Floud and A.H. Halsey published an internationally oriented survey of the literature of the sociology of education, in which – alongside the high proportion of American publications in the accompanying 762-item bibliography – the British record looked extremely meagre. In a 1962 paper on the same theme, drawing on the earlier work, but with a new British emphasis, Jean Floud made her main focus the 'social distribution of educational opportunity', relating it to influences on selection and performance, testing, intelligence, the school as a system, manpower and the labour market (B: Floud and Halsey, 1958; Floud, 1962). This focus, and the related issues of educational opportunity and the operation of the economy, were to remain Jean Floud's personal emphases in her influential work in the early 1960s (B: Floud, 1961b), and formed the structure of the 1961 reader by Floud, Halsey and Anderson. In 1956 Floud, Halsey and Martin had mapped, for the two chosen areas, the incomplete revolution of the 1944 Act, and such detailed investigation of the relationships between educational experience and family and wider social considerations was to be the dominant feature of the 1960s sociology. *Social Class and Educational Opportunity* was, like much of the research that followed it, a study in social structure and mobility, broadening the discussion of opportunity in various directions: 'the conditions affecting equality of educational opportunity are now to be thought about in terms much wider than those of the material environment' (B: Morris, 1957, 46). Floud's summary of the position in 1961 for an OECD conference on ability and educational opportunity was that within wide limits 'the educability of children is determined by the subtle interaction of the social influences of homes and schools'. On the former

we are beginning to understand the influences of social background – the powerful influence of imponderables, such as the parents' ambitions for the family, the standard of living aimed at, and their conception of their responsibility towards their children – which form fairly clear patterns centred in the socio-economic status of the home.

On the latter, schools, and the conditions of success in them, 'we know very much less, so that we remain ignorant of many hidden characteristics of the learning situation' (B: Floud, 1961b, 108). She reminded her audience that a modern economy depended on 'maximising the educational output of every individual'. Educability came close to concepts of both social justice and economic efficiency. In a review of Pedley's *The Comprehensive Schools* in 1963, Halsey saw what was taking place as a process of expansion, not of equalization ('I used to think that the comprehensive school was a major instrument of egalitarian reform in education'). He saw very few of the secondary schools as being 'comprehensive on any definition', but accepted them as providing a 'human and efficient' educational environment: they provided a 'more efficient engine than does unreformed tripartism for the production of qualified young people' (B: Halsey, 1963). The dual target meant that there were two ways of looking at the outcomes of educational and sociological research. Halsey's own interpretation of possible directions for research and action was to prove centrally important when, four years later, the Plowden committee reported and he became pivotal to the development of work in educational priority areas.

Of critical importance to the development and direction of a sociology of education was the impact, from 1958, of the work of Basil Bernstein. From the outset Bernstein was concerned with the relationship between language and experience of the social structure, differences in the language uses of social classes. In his early papers he propounded a theory of language codes which was to have major impacts both on British sociology of education and internationally, and particularly in the United States. He explored the differences between what he began by calling a 'public' language (largely associated with lower working-class usage) and a 'formal' language, associated with the greater complexity of middle-class speech (B: 1971, reprinting 1958 and 1959 papers). He was later to develop the codes theory in terms of formal and concrete, elaborate and restricted language usages. Although his work related to the educational and sociological concerns we have discussed, it was distanced from them by the intentions of the theory he was seeking to develop. His reflection on the period emphasizes the connection but also the distance:

There was one group concerned with the pedagogizing of the working class...They were concerned with selection...with the institutional constraints in the schools. Then they were concerned with the knowledge constraints within the schools...basically it was a question of the working-class and pedagogy...It was optimistic...some kind of pedagogic transformation was possible...let's change the organizational structure of the school and everything'll be fine...It's a much more complex problem.

The sociology of education had itself also made 'a first move...concerned with the investigation of the quality of the population – this is the question of social mobility...It raised fundamental problems' (Bernstein, interview). In the early 1960s, therefore, what Bernstein was attempting was a theory that would link psychological and sociological explanations through a focus on linguistic forms (A: Bernstein, 1964, 251), and a research programme that would illuminate the processes by which class differences were manifested in linguistic experience and educational performance. By 1961 he had reached, with a paper reprinted in Halsey, Floud and Anderson, what he later described as 'the end of the beginning stage'. In the same year he was spelling out some of the implications of his approach to the analysis of class and language, and its relevance for understanding the difficulties experienced particularly by lower working-class pupils in school:

This will not hold in precise detail for every pupil, but we can say that the probability of finding such a pattern is greater if the pupil's origin is lower working-class. Such children will experience difficulty in learning to read, in extending their vocabulary, and in learning to use a wide range of formal possibilities for the organisation of verbal meaning; their reading and writing will be slow and will tend to be associated with a concrete, activity-dominated content; their powers of verbal comprehension will be limited; grammar and syntax will pass them by; the propositions they use will suffer from a large measure of dislocation; their verbal planning function will be restricted; their thinking will tend to be rigid – the number of new relationships available to them will be very limited.

There would be problems with certain aspects of arithmetic, with their attention span and with concepts. Contrasted with the implications of that 'public' usage, the middle-class 'formal' language had 'possibilities for sentence organisation...used to clarify meaning and make it explicit'

(B: Bernstein, 1961, 1964–5). Whereas middle-class children had access to both language forms, other children might be restricted to the public language.

Bernstein remained within the framework of social-class explanation. He wrote in 1963 of 'the vulgarity of social class', which still 'deeply penetrates the educational system at all levels'. Social class factors affected 'who is selected, when, where, how many, and for what'. They affected 'not only the level of educational attainment, but also the very structure of ability itself'. His programme for the research needed contained six points, relating both to the underlying theory and to the practical measures that were necessary:

1. The social process underlying educability;
2. The processes underlying cultural discontinuity induced by education, and the response of the teacher and the school to this relationship;
3. The processes which ensure that some training colleges impart to their students trained incapacity;
4. Changes in the social context of the teaching relation produced by the new technology...
5. The social processes underlying the image of the teacher;
6. A study of the major gelding devices which are built into educational institutions. (B: Bernstein, 1963, 92–4)

Within the overall messages of social class Bernstein was to develop an increasingly close-knit analysis not only of language but also of the curriculum and wider questions of cultural transmission. At a conference on 'obstacles to opportunity' in 1965 he challengingly began his statement by pointing to the social and educational questions central to the theories and research he – and by now his research unit at the Institute of Education – were developing:

I think I ought to explain that I am a sociologist and also an educationist and, perhaps for that reason I'm less concerned with jacking up a child's I.Q. by half a dozen points or seeing the school as a launching pad for educational sputniks. The concern of our research unit is the children who are the bottom 40 per cent in secondary modern schools, and in comprehensive schools. These children often travel so far down in the school that they may as well have gone by submarine. It seems to me that these children are deprived of a fundamental educational right, the right to a curriculum, and by this I mean a coherent, systematic, educational environment which is meaningful to families, teachers and pupils. (B: Council for Educational Advance, 1965, 23)

In this lie the roots of many of Bernstein's later explorations of compensatory education, the curriculum and other issues.

Although versions, often massively over-simplified, of Bernstein's language codes rapidly became a prominent part of what Swift called the 'folklore of teaching' (and of teacher education), the underlying importance of Bernstein's work in the early and mid-1960s was its direction of attention towards the question, no longer whether class was important, but how it worked. The question was not merely whether the reorganization of secondary education was necessary, but what schools did to pupils, especially those whose cultural conditions made access to the school's processes and meanings particularly difficult. If children's learning was through language, and if language was a complex product of school and home and wider environment, what would explain the derivation and operation of the child's linguistic apparatus? Halliday's summary of Bernstein's work denied that it was 'a theory of educational failure'. His theory was in fact 'a theory about society, how a society persists and how it changes: it is a theory of the nature and processes of cultural transmission, and of the essential part that is played by language therein. Education is one of the forms taken by the transmission process...' (B: Halliday, foreword to Bernstein, 1973, ix). How widely Bernstein's work has been misinterpreted or misused is not of direct concern here, but it is important to note that in the considerable attention given to his work in the 1960s and 1970s there was a tendency to interpret it as a 'panacea explanation' (B: Byrne and Williamson, n.d., 4) and for Bernstein's own cautions and reservations to be ignored (B: Barratt, 1974, chs. 3 and 4; Derrick, 1976, 28). Commentaries on and critiques of his work in the late 1960s and early 1970s (notably by Denis Lawton and Harold Rosen) confirmed the central importance of the directions in which Bernstein's questions and research pointed. The fact that Bernstein was consulted by HMIs (Burrows, interview) and was one of the three sociologists called as witnesses by the Newsom committee (there were only six witnesses altogether) indicates how centrally, within a very short space of time, Bernstein had placed his definitions of the relationship between class and language on the educational agenda.

Bernstein had in this way turned attention to the linguistic, educational and social development of the child, and the impact of social class in all of the child's environments, and the role of those environments in the child's learning experience. More than other educational and sociological preoccupations in the first half of the 1960s, therefore, his work looked for explanations of children's journeys through the whole educational process, and not simply at the pupil at specific periods of selection and rejection. He was, of course, not alone in directing attention to the whole of, or stages in, that journey. In 1963, for example, John and Elizabeth Newson published the first results of their study of children in Nottingham, this being an investigation of childbirth, babies and parenting in the first year of the babies' lives. The investigation was firmly placed in class and environmental structures of analysis, with chapters for example, on 'The class factor', 'Class trends in infant feeding' and 'Mothers, fathers and social class' (B: Newson, 1963). This and later products from the Child Development Research Unit (which began life in the psychology department at Nottingham University), continued the tradition of early childhood investigation and concern with child care that had existed since the end of the nineteenth century, and most recently in such forms as the Newcastle study and the work of John Bowlby, most popularly known through his *Child Care and the Growth of Love* (1953). In the 1960s, from Liverpool University's Department of Social Science, J.B. Mays published a series of studies with titles like *Education and the Urban Child* (1962a), *Growing up in the City* (1964) and *The School in its Social Setting* (1967), in which he emphasized the roles of home and mother, the poor relationships between school and family and neighbourhood, the controlling influence of social class, and the need for greater attention by schools to relevance and to links with the home. Prior to the establishment of the educational priority area projects (one of which was to be in Liverpool) Mays's work represents one of the most consistent attempts to portray schools at all levels, not just secondary, in their complex social settings, though his constant, strenuous indictment of the schools and the teachers, their failures of attitude and practice, was to be an obstacle to his playing an active role in the developments of the later 1960s.

In a critical review of Douglas's *The Home and the School*, Dennis Marsden commented on the research base of the book in tests administered to children at the ages of 8 years 3 months and just before their eleventh birthday, and continued: 'This is the first thing to note about this book: it is a very thorough study of a limited area of the education system, primary education, but in that system's own value terms and measurements' (B: Marsden, 1964, 81–2). Marsden himself, co-authoring the well-known *Education and the Working Class* two years earlier, would scarcely have referred to the secondary education which was the theme of the book that it was about 'a limited area of the education system'. Primary education was still a research Cinderella, and Marsden's apologetic tone confirms the fact. What *The Home and the School* did, whether because of its public health and medical context or in spite of it, was provide a further strengthening of the relatively submerged interest in the younger child and in the primary school. It followed an earlier report on *Children under Five* (1958) from the continuing study being carried out by the Population Investigation Committee, and carried 'A study of ability and attainment in the primary school' as its sub-title. It dealt with the same inequalities commonly discussed elsewhere, but was able to draw attention to such questions as the reasons for the deterioration in test performance, between the ages of eight and eleven, by 'children whose home circumstances are bad'. It examined this phenomenon in relation to social class and parental interest. It pushed the explanations further back into the earlier, including the pre-school, years. The book ended:

...it is likely that in the pre-school years the mental development of many children is stunted by the intellectual poverty of their surroundings. Here is a wide field for study. Perhaps we should think in terms of nursery schools which aim to give small children the stimulus that is so often lacking in their homes. But the first need is to measure more fully the impact of the family on the early processes of learning and on the acquisition of incentives before children reach school. (B: Douglas, 1964, xiv, xix, 37, 47, 57, 128)

In an article in the same year, Douglas and Ross reported on their findings that children in nursery school were more emotionally and educationally vulnerable than others, because of their home situation, including the larger percentage of mothers at work. At eight, children who had been to nursery school had higher test scores, but had lost the advantage by eleven, and by fifteen had fallen slightly behind. A larger percentage of children at nursery school were probably there *because* they had behaviour problems (A: Douglas and Ross, 1964, 75–80).

Cyril Burt commented, in a review of Douglas's book, that in view of the many studies that had now been carried out 'we no longer need any further attempts to demonstrate that the *general* environmental conditions associated with differences in social class influence children's *general* educational progress. What is now required are more specialized inquiries to show what particular elements in the environment influence what particular aspects of development in which particular types of child' (B: Burt, 1965, 263). Some of this 'more specialized' inquiry was in fact coming from such directions as Mia Kellmer Pringle's investigation of the nature and sources of emotional deprivation as derived from different social settings (B: Pringle, 1965b), from the very directions signalled by Douglas and his colleagues, and by Bernstein and his research unit. From a variety of angles there were to be other responses in the later 1960s and the 1970s.

The battle for and over the comprehensive school also continued unabated. Jackson and Marsden, in 1962, were portraying – in the traditions of Richard Hoggart and the work of the Institute for Community Studies – the working-class conditions in which attitudes were formed, and the selective secondary situation in which working-class talents were wasted. Crosland, in a speech on comprehensive education in 1966, drew on the whole range of research and inquiry –

from *Early Leaving* to Floud and Halsey, from Philip Vernon on selection to Douglas and others on environmental handicap, in order to place the comprehensive school in a context of 'social and even political values'. The old social and intellectual stratification, he declared, was no longer acceptable to democratic opinion in the 1960s (B: Crosland, 1974, 193–6, 210). The internal workings of the comprehensive school were coming more sharply into focus. Vernon, Simon and others were sealing the fate of intelligence testing as a means of selection. Little and Westergaard and others were mapping the broad territory of class differences in education. In the mid-1960s Swift was reporting in detail on research into such areas as 'Social class and achievement motivation', 'Meritocratic and social class selection at age eleven' and 'Social class, mobility-ideology and 11+ success' (B: Swift, 1965–6a, 1965–6b, 1967). The Newsom committee in 1963 was describing and discussing 'education in the slums', pointing to conclusions about 'area' problems and possible solutions similar to some being formulated in the United States. From the mid-1960s in particular the sociology of education was represented by a growing number of textbooks, reflecting the research, debate and emphases we have outlined. William Taylor, in 1966, described the sociology of education in the context of 'the immanence of social change', within which sociology in general had found itself less concerned with the 'grand sweep of history' than with the detailed analysis of social structure and process. The focus of the sociology of education was 'the way in which schools, colleges and universities are related to other institutions and structural features of the societies in which they exist'. At the broadest level this involved asking questions about the link between industrialization, technological change and educational provision, and inevitably about the role of the schools

as agents of social mobility, the extent to which children of varying social origins are provided with opportunities to find the place in society for which their 'abilities and aptitudes' fit them, and the degree to which the generally accepted principle of 'equality of opportunity' has meaning within a system that differentiates as well as selects and deals with pupils whose performances are not determined wholly by heredity.

The study was essentially one of the dynamic relationship between school and society (B: Taylor, 1966, 183–4).

This, broadly speaking was the basis of the texts produced from the mid-1960s. Whether the focus, as in Olive Banks's text in 1968, was the broad sweep of the economy, social mobility, the family, the schools and social change, or, as in Swift's 1969 text, the theoretical bases on which sociological approaches to education and culture, or the social functions and environments of the school, rested, at the heart of the questions posed was the social class system, selection and inequality of opportunity (B: Banks, 1968; Swift, 1969). In Ottaway's *Education and Society*, sub-titled 'An introduction to the sociology of education', the focus is culture, change, a historical picture of the social determinants of education, social structure, social policy, opportunity and the school. There is only passing reference to primary schools (B: Ottaway, 1953, edition of 1968). In Banks's *The Sociology of Education*, primary schools do not feature in the text or the index (comprehensive, grammar and secondary schools do). Nursery education is totally absent from all of these textbooks. The one substantial exception to all of the literature of the sociology of the school, where primary education does not appear to any extent if at all, was Blyth's two-volume study in 1965 of *English Primary Education* (part one of which was about the schools, and part two about their background). The study presented the schools as social institutions, examined their traditions, structures and processes, related them to their local environments, and discussed social class, religious, political, economic, cultural and comparative aspects of the schools. The analysis was conducted in terms of social class impact at various levels, and in various ways. It postulated in broad terms how children learn not merely the culture and roles of the family, but also the place of their family in the social order. It looked more specifically at particular types of pupil behaviour as it related to their socio-economic circumstances. The schools themselves no longer fitted into an old stratification model, and 'the melting-pot metaphor looks too far into the future'. What Blyth sought were ways of further breaking down the effects of the rigidities of social class (B: Blyth, 1965, vol. 2, 50, 113).

What the 1960s texts intended, and largely succeeded in accomplishing, was a new consciousness that 'education is mainly a social business'. The phrase is from *An Introduction to the Sociology of Education*, produced in 1962 by W.A.C. Stewart on the basis of the posthumous papers of Karl Mannheim. The emphasis throughout is on the crucial role of the teacher and the school, which can only be adequately filled if they regard their work 'as a serious attempt to understand and to contribute to the life of the community...No educational activity or research is adequate in the present stage of consciousness unless it is conceived in terms of a sociology of education.' As old social structures crumbled, and avoiding the pitfalls of fascism at one extreme and 'the complete anarchy of a deteriorated *laisser-faire* policy' at the other extreme, the aim had to be the practical one of a 'sociological diagnosis able to explain the main educational problems in terms of more fundamental structural changes operating in our society' (B: Mannheim and Stewart, 1962, 10, 155–9, 165).

British educational analysis from the mid-1950s to the mid-1960s was therefore in terms of class and inequality, the structure of the system, the differential acquisition of linguistic and other cultural characteristics. It was not, as in the United States, in terms of poverty and compensation. Embedded, and occasionally surfacing, in the decade or so that we have considered was a vocabulary of compensation, though unlike the American version it was not rooted in a conception of culture and social impoverishment as firmly articulated as in the United States. Researchers might comment on the difficulties of compensating for early experience or wonder what the school could do to compensate for deficiencies in the child's home environment made manifest in the school (B: Fraser, 1959; Barr, 1959). The nursery school might compensate for deficiencies in the home, or caring schools in general might be unable, alone to 'fully compensate' for bad home conditions and an unsatisfactory environment (B: Mays, 1962a; Winnicott, 1964; Wall, 1965). In some practical ways the nursery school might compensate by providing clothing, training, speech, etc., (B: Wilson, Harriett, 1966) bringing the child care tradition more firmly into the educational picture. Conceptually, however, none of these references represent the kind of sustained attack familiar in the United States in the early and mid-1960s. When *Trends in Education* (an HMI publication) talked in a 1966 article on 'Schools and social welfare' of children who fail 'through cultural malnutrition to reach their intellectual potential' (B: *Trends in Education*, 1966, 5), it did not derive from the same concepts and controversies as in the United States. These and related vocabularies were weaker than their American equivalents. British schools talked of 'remedial' work, a more technical approach to pupil failure. Sir Edward Boyle, in 1965, was incorporating the language of compensation into a wider phraseology, expressing an interest in 'the part that school can play as a countervailing force in compensating for differences in opportunity in the home, and … in helping boys and girls to a higher intelligence' (B: Council for Educational Advance, 1965, 13–14). In some of the discussion were hints of the later 'positive discrimination' of the Plowden committee, with demands for smaller classes or greater resources in schools in the poorest districts (B: North-Eastern Junior Schools Association, 1949, edition of 1960).

None of the literature to which we have referred was concerned with questions of immigration or race. By the mid-1960s the question of 'immigrant schools' and policy issues regarding the education of immigrants had established themselves as political and educational concerns, but not yet as issues for sociological analysis. The question of the educational distribution of the recent immigrant population, and questions of the teaching of English and other problems for the schools were, in the early 1960s, concerning particular local education authorities, the inspectorate and political debate (B: Boyle, 1963; Fabian Group, 1964). They were not yet in the indexes of the textbooks of the sociology of education.

What we have been witnessing, therefore, is the appearance in Britain of separate and unrelated interests in poverty and in the relationships between social class and – mainly secondary – education. There are clearly parallels with the United States, but also considerable differences. It is important to consider, before we turn to the Plowden committee and American and British developments of the late 1960s and 1970s, to what extent the American war on poverty and its educational components had echoes in Britain.

Primary education was effectively rediscovered in Britain in 1967. The American education programmes of the 1960s began to be discovered in Britain in 1967–9. In the latter case there was a time lag of almost a decade, but the concept of 'time lag' explains nothing. Some ideas travel fast. The educational content of the war on poverty, and of its antecedents might have been expected to do so. In the next chapter we shall focus on the Plowden committee, including its attitudes, vocal and non-vocal, to the American experience it investigated. Here we shall by-pass Plowden and look at how the British saw the American developments in the period from 1964 to the early 1970s. 1964 is important in this context as the point at which American anti-poverty policies and programmes began to have weak echoes in British publications. The British press and specialist educational publications were virtually silent on the formative years of the Ford Foundation's and other initiatives of the early 1960s. Not until 1967 and after did the work of the Foundation, Martin Deutsch, Susan Gray, Frank Riessman or Head Start, for example, receive public mention. From 1964 to 1967 there was a trickle of public comment on the American policies, though mainly on the war on poverty in general, not on education specifically. Only from 1971 did the education policies and projects seriously become public property in Britain. The analysis has to be of silences as well as sounds.

It is important first to recognize the 'private' networks in which information did circulate – though probably even here to a severely restricted extent. Bernstein, before his first visit to the United States in 1964, knew nothing of the American education projects before his visit (though he had connections in the American linguistics and anthropology fields, including through American visitors to London) (Bernstein, interview). David Donnison, professor of social administration at the London School of Economics when he served on the Plowden committee, was what he calls 'not very well informed' about the United States when he visited for the first time in the mid-1950s. He did not in fact visit the US in any 'systematic' sense until he went with the committee, though once Plowden was under way in late 1963 he began to read more and meet more Americans 'it was...very much part of the community we were working in' (Donnison, interview). Donnison attributes the Plowden committee's links mainly to its secretary, Maurice Kogan, who had been a Harkness fellow at Harvard and other centres of educational studies in 1960-1. There, Kogan was in touch with the Ford Foundation in connection with the teacher education issues which they were investigating at the time. He picked up little information at that time about anti-poverty issues, but did do so on the racial integration issue. By the time he and Donnison visited in 1965, however, poverty had become a leading theme (Kogan, interview). The sociologists of poverty and the welfare state had more sustained contacts with the United States. Dorothy Wedderburn did not visit the US until 1965, but by that time some of the others we have discussed had been on visits, and had lectured or conducted seminars in Washington, where they had 'very strong linkage with Health, Education and Welfare', particularly the members of the statistics group.

An important point underlined by Wedderburn in this latter connection was the basic reason for the contact: the Americans concerned were interested in, and were writing in their house journal about, what was happening in Britain. 'They were', she comments, 'very much influenced, in terms of their thinking about policies, I believe, by the British welfare state, and Titmuss was a very frequent visitor there.' She recalls her own first visit to Washington, going to lecture on poverty:

and their asking me what I'd like to do in Washington...and I said, 'see some poverty' – and this rather threw them actually...They had a Jesuit priest working with them in a black area behind the Capitol. I spent a day with him, and it was just unbelievable, to me, anyway...I had never in my life seen people queuing up for food, which they were doing early in the morning at the church door...I would still maintain that we didn't have poverty like that. (Wedderburn, interview)

For these sociologists, in these contacts – and we shall return to the particular point about Titmuss – the Americans were the learners at the policy level. The British were learning not so much about American policies and strategies as about the realities of American poverty. In the late 1950s and early 1960s the position was somewhat similar with regard to interest in American sociology and education by A.H. Halsey.

Halsey's first visit to the US was in 1956-7, when he was interested in and in touch with the 'remnants of American socialism'. He lectured on Crosland's recently published *The Future of Socialism*, the educational content of which, Halsey emphasizes, was its most radical feature. At Palo Alto he was aware of the Ford Foundation's roles, and his own interests in education while in the US focused on 'what you might call progressive education movements that were in any way sociological'. He was in the late 1950s, however, 'billed' in the US as someone who knew about the 'pool of ability'. What he represented in terms of European traditions was translated into different American terms:

European notions which were rooted very strongly in...social justice and allowing the working class to join the highest standards of cultivation that had already been available to the more privileged strata – in the American scene was heard as...an ineffective machine not producing the maximum national manpower and all of that kind of thing. A subtle change. But the message was going that way rather than the other way at that point, I think in the 1950s...I had no feeling that I was receiving education from them – rather a missionary in the opposite direction, at that stage.

After completing the survey of literature on the sociology of education with Jean Floud, he decided, while in Chicago in 1958–9, to produce the book which became *Education, Economy, and Society*. He worked with Jean Floud on it, and the publishers recommended the addition of an American to the team, though C. Arnold Anderson, who joined them, was not in the tradition of interests that was to point to the Great Society. That book, therefore, appearing in 1961, represented an interest in the international picture of sociology of education, and also Halsey's own firm foothold in the American debates. The point, however, is that apart from this edited textbook Halsey *wrote* nothing about what was happening in the United States of the late 1950s and early 1960s. Like Dorothy Wedderburn, he recalls little in the way of messages for formal relay to a British public: 'My memory of it...is that it was all word of mouth.' He knew a number of Americans who were very much involved in the American 'politics of education' or in welfare issues, including Daniel Moynihan, Seymour Martin Lipset and Harold Wilensky: 'I was learning about things from them all the time.' He picked up from them information about welfare policies, what was in party political platforms...'I would gossip that around the sociological fraternity'. Halsey also had conversations with Crosland, who was himself in touch with American social scientists like Lipset and Daniel Bell (Halsey, interview). In the early 1960s many of the signals collected in this way were either relayed 'around the fraternity' or submerged in the flow of information travelling in the opposite direction.

What specifically was known in Britain by the mid-1960s about the projects of the Ford Foundation and others is difficult to estimate, though it is unlikely that there were many people familiar with those activities – since nothing was being written about them. The beginnings of interest in the American scene coincided with the emergence of the war on poverty in 1964, when four articles appeared in the British press, mainly about the war on poverty, only one of them with education as the main focus, and three of them by Americans. In January, in *The Spectator*, an article contemplated the recent history of American economic expansion, the impetus given by Harrington to making poverty 'a fashionable *cri de coeur*', the impact of technological unemployment, and the particularly shocking revelation at the extent not only of poverty but also of illiteracy. A second article in *The Spectator* just over two months later began by announcing that 'President Johnson has declared a war on domestic poverty limited in scope, restrained in budget and yet with a surprising claim on the attention of his countrymen'. Amidst an American national sense of weariness and failure 'the deprived and the outcast are almost fashionable'. The poverty experts, few in number, had come to the problem out of exasperation with an America that was supposed to have abolished deprivation, critical of the values of capitalism. The article quoted from Christopher Jencks, viewing Johnson's approach as conservative, as a criticism of the poor, not of the mismanaged economy. It was not, in Jencks's view, 'just a war on poverty but a war on the poor'. A British readership was meeting the war and its critics simultaneously without too much in the way of hard information (B: Beichman, 1964; Kempton, 1964). *New Society* entered the field in July, with an article by a British observer of 'America's war on poverty', tracing the origins of the war to juvenile unemployment. Poverty had become 'a safe bet to be against... The enemy is well documented, if hidden to the casual observer.' The programmes outlined included youth programmes and community action programmes, education was mentioned more or less in passing, and the controversial features of the war on poverty were underlined (including potential conflict between 'experts and amateurs') (B: Angus, 1964). *New Era* in March published an account from Martin Deutsch's Institute for Developmental Studies of its 'preschool enrichment programme', a detailed commentary on its aims for children and for teachers, its stress on language, concept formation and perceptual discrimination, its development of self-image through the use of black as well as white dolls, and parent participation. The programme was too recent for there to be any tested results, but teachers were seeing evidence of improvement in interest and achievement by the children, and parents were showing increased involvement and enthusiasm (B: Feldmann, 1964). This meagre crop of publications can scarcely be said to indicate that all eyes were across the Atlantic, and at this stage there were no DES, research or other reports making public reference to the United States.

The position was little different in 1965. The *Times Educational Supplement* in January and *New Society* in September published reports, the former commenting briefly on the Great Society and on Head Start (describing Johnson as planning 'to creep up on this explosive issue'), devoting some of its fifteen sentences to Walter Lippmann's suggestion that Johnson's programme was to be 'founded on socialist and communist ideas'. The *New Society* report, entitled 'Helping poor children catch up', discussed – for the first time in these articles – the Ford Foundation's Great Cities School Improvement Programme, described a visit to Deutsch's pre-kindergarten experiment, and summarized the programme's assumptions, including the assumption that children from lower socio-economic groups do not lack experiences but do not get help in integrating them. The aim of teachers and psychologists working together was eventually to integrate 'disadvantaged children into the larger life of the nation' (B: *TES*, 1965; Mosher, 1965). Two books appearing in that year contained references to recent American experience. Mia Kellmer Pringle referred to an Early School Admissions Project in New York, and a variety of 'educational and community programmes designed for the culturally deprived child in the United States'. Dorothy Gardner, in a reference to 'good teachers', mentioned Marie Hughes of the University of Utah (who a couple of years later would be leading the Tucson Early Education Model of the Follow Through programme) (B:Pringle, 1965a, 138; Gardner and Cass, 1965, 19). Abel-Smith and Townsend also published in 1965 *The Poor and the Poorest*, one of the key texts of the sustained British 'discovery' of poverty, containing an indictment of both political parties for their 'vested interest in making the creation of a "Welfare State" seem a greater change than it actually was' (B: Abel-Smith and Townsend, 1965, 60). On the basis of this second crop of publications it cannot yet be said that the 'time lag' was being seriously overcome. A reminder of the lack of information yet available in Britain came in 1965 during a discussion following Basil Bernstein's paper at the conference on educational opportunity organized by the Council for Educational Advance. In the discussion, J. McNally from the National Foundation for Educational Research (and three years later the author of an article on 'Social deprivation and educational compensation') referred to American programmes 'for the educationally disadvantaged', and particularly Project Able at 'a school in Greenborough, somewhere in

Syracuse'. It is not clear where the information on this concentrated programme for the first year of schooling came from, but McNally concluded: 'I'm trying to find out what's going on in Greenborough' (B: Council for Educational Advance, 1965, 26). The game of finding out was being played surprisingly late.

In 1966–7 the pace began slightly to quicken. Under an extremely misleading title *New Society* in March 1966 published an article on 'The War on Poverty: what went wrong?' by the American sociologist Nathan Glazer. Outlining the work of the new agency – the Office of Economic Opportunity – and the community action programmes, Glazer's main message was of the difficulties and even dangers involved in promoting a set of programmes which, while 'giving a new voice to the poor', also reflected the American 'genius for setting up complex administrative forms'. Out of the positive ferment of organization, argument, conflict and discussion there was the danger that 'the degree of order that any social system needs will be undermined. The hope is that a creative disorder will ensue.' Glazer summed up the position by this stage of the war on poverty:

the performance is better than we had a right to expect. But I think we still have to take on the jobs which the anti-poverty programme... did not address itself to – reducing the unemployment rate, increasing the number of jobs, expanding and revising the social security and social welfare systems, improving the systems of job training, job counselling and job placement, attacking the failures of school systems and police systems.

In the end, Glazer added, 'a democratic policy cannot take the position that the major way to improve its institutions of government and welfare is to finance guerrilla warfare against them. It must take up the job of directly improving and transforming them' (B: Glazer, 1966). Glazer's question, sharply focused for a British audience familiar with the problems of improving and transforming its institutions, was in fact relaying back to Britain a message influenced by British experience. In the first issue of a new journal, *The Public Interest*, Glazer had only several months previously incorporated into an article on American poverty his reflections on 'leafing through' the previous six or seven months of *New Society*, and his article reflected discussions about Britain's focus on the allocation of resources, and on repairs and adjustments to its 'floor of services' (A: Glazer, 1965a, 73–4).

A small number of contributions focused on education. A *New Society* piece on 'How to help deprived children', four weeks after Glazer's article, briefly summarized a 1965 report by Gray and Klaus on their Early Training Project in Tennessee. *New Era*, later in the year, published an account of the Banneker project (B: *New Society*, 1966;

Baum, 1966b). A breakthrough at the scholarly level was a survey article in *Educational Research*, again under a bizarre title: 'Coloured Immigrant Children...their educational problems and potential – in the U.S.A.', which looked at American literature on 'compensatory programmes and remedial techniques for disadvantaged children', including the Great Cities programme, Higher Horizons and Banneker. It discussed the American work on cultural deprivation, and compared the two countries in terms of multi-racial societies and parallel need for attention to linguistics, sensory stimulation and so on (B: Goldman and Taylor, 1966). Ronald Goldman, co-author of this article, was to launch one of the earliest 'educational priority' projects after the Plowden report. In 1966 the focus on American developments was, however, still weak and unclear. Two articles in *The Teacher*, on 'Can the American teachers teach us anything?' and 'A way to stop the waste of talent' (B: Kenn, 1966a, 1966b) did not interpret the recent American developments. Elspeth Howe, writing for the Conservative Political Centre, and making the case for pre-school provision, referred to American research showing that children from under-privileged homes do better if given sound nursery education, but the research she mentioned was the pre-war Iowa research that was common currency in the Nursery School Association which she cited as the source (B: Howe, 1966, 8–9).

A straw in the wind at the beginning of 1966 was a report in *New Society* of a lecture given at the London School of Economics by S.M. Miller, an active figure, as we have seen, in the American situation and part of the 'word of mouth' network amongst sociologists concerned with poverty. The report indicated what Miller saw as the positive and the critical aspects of the war on poverty, and ended: 'Miller gives the impression that Britain is better prepared intellectually for a frontal attack on poverty than the United States' (B: *New Society*, 1966a, p. 4).

In 1967, the small number of journal articles were almost entirely concerned with education. One article in the *Times Educational Supplement* in April followed the common trend of misleading titles, this one being on 'Pointers for Britain in America's Headstart'– containing no discussion of pointers for Britain, but explaining the purposes and procedures of Head Start (some two years, it should be underlined, after the programme was first announced). A second article in September commented on the Follow Through programme then being launched as a 'Follow-up to Head Start'. In November the journal reported on a speech at a colloquium held at the American embassy in London. Hyman Bookbinder, assistant director of the OEO had flown in specially to tell the audience that 400 federal programmes were in operation, 'aimed at eliminating poverty, or at least the feeling of it, for in the kind of country that we have, poverty is more a psychological factor than an economic one' (B: Raynor, 1967, 1213; Ogletree, 1967, 537; *Times Educational Supplement*, 1967, 993). Who attended the colloquium and how this message was received, are not known. The range of journals showing an interest in things American began to widen. *Teacher in Wales* published an article on 'The American scene' by Meredydd Hughes, who had, whilst in the United States, heard Harold Howe II defend federal aid and the implementation of the ESEA, and also the President of the Chicago American National Bank predict that federal money would bring federal control and socialism. *Where* published an article tracing the origins and impacts of Head Start, commenting on 'the American school system proper' that: 'there is no doubt about the effectiveness of Head Start in either scientific or human terms' (B: Hughes, 1967, 15; Pollard, 1967, 6–7). Arthur Jensen wrote in *Educational Research* of the more meagre evidence available of the effectiveness of programmes for the culturally disadvantaged, and supporting the most structured programmes, those of Bereiter and Engelmann, and to some extent Deutsch and Susan Gray (B: Jensen, 1967, 17–18).

Two of the most indicative events of 1967, however, were a book and a typewritten report. The book, Marris and Rein's *Dilemmas of Social Reform: poverty and community action in the United States*, written with support from the Ford Foundation and the President's Committee on Juvenile Delinquency, made available in Britain, through publication by Routledge and Kegan Paul, the first coherent account of the origins of the poverty programmes, their content and ambitions, the opportunities and limitations of reform, and conflicts of interest from which they sprang and the difficulties of anticipating and controlling outcomes. Marris had spent a year as an independent observer of Ford's 'gray area' projects, and Rein had been invited at the same time to study the Juvenile Delinquency projects. Although their book did not focus on education, it placed it in appropriate contexts in the development of community action and poverty strategies in general (B: Marris and Rein, 1967). Important in a different way was a visit specifically to look at Head Start made in May 1967 by Elma McDougall HMI (again, nearly two years after the programme was first implemented). She visited HEW in Washington, the universities of Michigan and Stanford, and talked to administrators, school principals and superintendents and other specialists, and visited a number of Head Start centres and primary and nursery schools. She wrote a report for internal circulation in the inspectorate, in which she offered, in the words of a memorandum accompanying its circulation, 'a tentative assessment of its effectiveness and some conclusions as to its possible applications in this country'. The report itself explained that Head Start was designed to break the cycle of poverty. The need for such community action was apparent in the centres she had visited in Washington, Ann Arbor and San Francisco. The vitality and enthusiasm of the 'teachers' (her inverted commas) were outstanding. There were limitations:

With such a vast undertaking it is inevitable that some aspects of the programme are criticised. It is easy to criticise as impossible how any severe developmental deficiency can be made up in six weeks – but that valiant people of many races and creeds should be trying is a wonderful example to those countries who do so little for young children.

Whether this last category included Britain the report went to discuss. In the United States 'the spotlight has been directed to operation Head-Start to relieve real poverty, poverty which in this country is now comparatively rare owing to the social and health services. But poverty exists here.' While applauding what was taking place in the US, Elma McDougall considered that more training was needed for the teachers unaccustomed to working with young children. Head Start had opened up new ideas for the early care of children, including: schools open most of the summer; fifteen children to a group; three adults working in a single room; the centre providing health, welfare and psychological help; parents as an integral part of the staff; and a programme based on community action. The result had been a considerable impact on American preschool education. Could it have the same impact in Britain? The possible lessons were:

1. The need for a continuous programme of education for all from nursery through to the middle school years within the education system.
2. The definite need for trained adults to look after young children.
3. The beneficial educational results accruing from small groups.
4. The value of involving parents in the schools and in interesting them in the principles of child care and home economics.
5. The value of services, health and welfare, being centred on the nursery centre.

Her conclusions were that 'any future developments in nursery work shall be in the hands of the teachers, supported by research but not directed by it', and that 'any extension of provision for under-privileged children in priority areas shall be within the normal nursery educational practice and not a plan laid on for "these children"' (B: McDougall, 1967, 1–4). This was the first real attempt to consider the implications of a major American educational programme for the British scene and, coming as it did after the Plowden committee had reported and as the 'educational priority area' discussion was taking shape in Britain, it indicates that the American policy directions (Elma McDougall also reported briefly on the new Follow Through programme) were beginning to command serious and potentially influential attention.

By the following year interest in the American programmes was being heightened by the move towards educational priority areas, the launch of the 'EPA projects', and discussion surrounding the issues involved – including through the Labour government's Urban Aid programme begun in 1968. How markedly the climate was changing is clear from a second HMI visit to the United States, that of John Burrows HMI in May, though his report was not circulated to the inspectorate until December (and published, with the only change being the deletion of some case study material) in the HMIs' *Trends in Education* in April 1969. The internal memorandum circulating the report on Burrows' survey of 'The education of disadvantaged children: compensatory education in the United States', took a crucial leap beyond Elma McDougall's cautions into a more direct link between American and British policy. In Britain now:

All inspectors are concerned...with the educational problems of children suffering from social handicap and in particular with those of the immigrant children. Some of these problems, especially those which arise from differences of racial background, have existed for a longer time and have assumed a more acute form in the United States than they have, as yet, in this country.

The prophetic 'as yet' was echoed in Burrows's own report, and the memo quotes the report's statement that 'we have too many of the ingredients of the American social powder keg to be complacent about our EPAs. The parallels between the American inner city areas and some of our own are clear enough.' The memo concluded, therefore, with an emphasis that was new in British attitudes towards the American educational programmes: 'there is a great deal that we can learn from American experience, from American thinking, and perhaps most of all from that American determination which is willing to make big sacrifices to try to solve the problems'. Burrows visited Pittsburgh, Washington and New York, and related the compensatory education efforts to racial and other urban tensions. Like Elma McDougall he saw a safeguard in the British central control of education which had ensured 'certain national minima of staffing, training, building, equipment and educational performance', and in Britain's lead in teacher training. Burrows also dismissed the 'experimental kindergarten programmes' as of less interest than other aspects of what he saw (teacher aides, team teaching, etc.) 'since they resembled good (but not outstanding) reception classes in English primary schools. The interesting features were their apparently fairly rapid evolution towards the English model', with emphasis on pupil individuality, organizational flexibility and parental contact. The key feature of the report, however, was its realistic assessment of the present and potential features of the British situation, and the roots of the anti-poverty programmes as they related to British conditions:

The steady increase in the proportion of coloured immigrants, and the accelerating exodus of white families to the suburbs, presents an uncomfortable parallel to the American situation, and one which could similarly become menacing if unemployment developed and our immigrant pupils left school inadequately qualified. (B: Burrows, 1968, 1–3, 6)

Reflecting on one feature of the American scene, Burrows recalls that Elma McDougall and he saw the tendency to focus on projects as doomed to be unproductive 'until they related the programmes more to the whole mainstream of education'. He met Harold Howe, who told him that 'you have got ten years to avoid the blunders that we have made'. He visited the Ford Foundation: 'Ford started it really... Obviously they were doing a lot that was worth doing', though there was a feeling that they were pouring money somewhat indiscriminately into some of the projects (Burrows, interview).

At the level of the inspectorate and the DES, in the context of recent immigration, economic warning signals, and the attention being given to urban and 'educational priority' areas and problems, the American messages were now of more direct interest. The connection between decaying city centres and nursery schools and playgroups, between the American poverty programmes and British social conditions was becoming easier to establish. The literature reflected the fact. The magazine *Where* published a supplement in January 1968 under the general title of 'How much do we know about education in America?' It contained an article by the American Doxey A. Wilkerson on 'Helping poor children', outlining the compensatory education movement in the context of the cycle of poverty. It discussed 'cultural deprivation' and 'social disadvantage' and the emergence of such euphemisms for poverty, underlined the transition from the early uncritical enthusiasm to a more cautious mood and the negative, ambiguous or contradictory findings of the recent research. It located the failure of the movement to achieve its promise in conceptual difficulties, under-estimation of the abilities of poor children, the school itself as a 'cause of retardation', and obstacles to compensatory education raised by segregation. A second article in the same issue discussed the political and social issues raised by Head Start in Mississippi and made the point that in a Head Start centre in such a location 'by English standards of nursery education the day's programme of activities is unremarkable...An unflattering description of the National Health Service is greeted with unbelieving admiration' (B: Wilkerson, 1968, 22–4; Richards, 1968, 25–6). At the same time as drawing attention to the American experience, *Where* was also in 1968 indicating the rapidly growing awareness of the educational implications of immigration, with articles on 'Immigrant children in school' and on the work of the Association of Multi-Racial Playgroups (B: Preston, 1968; Jackson, 1968), an association that had recently been set up by the Advisory Centre for Education, the Indian Workers' Association and the Race Relations Committee of the Society of Friends to organize such groups in educational priority areas.

Confirmation of the fact that by 1968 the American work had begun to 'arrive' in Britain was provided also by a research review by Stephen Wiseman of 'Educational deprivation and disadvantage', in which he surveyed the recent American work by researchers like Passow, Bloom and Deutsch, stressed that the United States had acted on it in extending its nursery provision through Head Start, and suggested that this was a programme 'that we should immediately copy in this country'. In the same year, *Education of the Disadvantaged*, edited by Passow and others, received a welcoming review in the *British Journal of Educational Psychology* (B: Wiseman, 1968, 280; Bloom, 1968). Articles were appearing more widely, on Head Start in *The Teacher*, on American compensatory programmes in general and their relevance to Britain in the journal of the Association of Educational Psychologists and on the teaching of disadvantaged children in the preschool and the structured programmes of Bereiter and Engelmann in *New Era* (B: Fisher, 1968; McNally, 1968; Fulton, 1968). The Fabian Society published in its research series a particularly well-informed pamphlet on the American anti-poverty programme, suggesting that some of the American programmes were more socialist than the British ones after four years of a Labour administration (B: Whitaker, 1968, 20). The *Times Educational Supplement* reported on an article in the newsletter of the Confederation for the Advancement of State Education, in which the author described finding in Head Start centres the same professional standards as in British nursery schools and the same parental participation as in good British playgroups (B: Higgin, 1968; *TES*, 1968b, 28). The interest in poverty issues generated by Richard Titmuss and his associates was similarly being maintained. In 1968 Adrian Sinfield published in *Race* an article on 'Poverty rediscovered' in which he commented that some of the strategies emerging in Britain in educational and social development areas were 'coming more and more to resemble the community action programmes in the American War on Poverty'. Titmuss himself reprinted in that year an article on 'Social policy and economic progress' that had previously appeared in the United States, and indeed throughout the previous years Titmuss had kept up a stream of publications in Britain and the US in which he examined the implications of the rediscovery of poverty for policy in the two countries (B: Sinfield, 1968, 205; Titmuss, 1968, 1967a, 1968. A: Titmuss, 1965).

The traffic was intensifying in other ways. Professor Jack Tizard of London University's Institute of Education visited Tennessee early in the year, and looked at Susan Gray's Early Training Project. In June he wrote in a letter that it was 'quite the best thing of its kind I have seen anywhere'. This message was passed on to A.H. Halsey, who wrote to Susan Gray asking for a paper and to be put on her mailing list (B: EPA corres, 21.6.1968, 16.7.1968). The EPA project, beginning in the autumn of 1968, had an interest from the outset in the American research and activities. George Smith, appointed to the project, began to scan the literature for information, and in July 1968 met with Harry Passow to plan places to visit in the United States (Smith, interview). American experience was present in other projects – including a compensatory education project based at University College, Swansea – planning for which began in 1965, reached submission stage the following year and was approved in 1967. A compensatory education project based at Didsbury College of Education, Manchester, was launched in 1968 by Ronald Goldman, who had co-authored the 1966 survey of American compensatory programmes, and the project recruited an American to the team. Peter Mittler, at the time a lecturer in developmental psychology at Birkbeck College, London, also attended a conference on the socio-cultural aspects of mental retardation at George Peabody College, Tennessee, and like Tizard became acquainted with the work of Susan Gray and others (Mittler, interview).

In the literature of 1969, with Britain's own poverty programme taking shape through the EPAs, the Urban Programme and the Community Development Projects launched at the beginning of 1969, reference to the United States was direct but more dispersed. *New Society*'s main contributions that year, for example, included not only an article on Head Start (sub-titled 'LBJ's one success?') but also items on Britain's poverty programme which contained significant references to the strategies, difficulties and controversies of the American experience (B: Adam, 1969; *New Society*, 1969; Holman, 1969). It also contained a review of Moynihan's *Maximum Feasible Misunderstanding* (B: Marris,

1969). In June of that year, an article in the *Times Educational Supplement* began with the words:

Compensatory education is a term which has blown across the Atlantic. The Plowden emphasis on home backgrounds, the idea of educational priority areas and increasing interest in the pre-school years have helped it to gain currency here. (B: Trauttmansdorff, 1969, 1861)

By the end of the 1960s the winds were blowing more strongly in both directions. Americans like Maya Pines and Joseph Featherstone were relaying the messages of British primary education to the United States (as indeed was the Plowden report). The conference network had developed from the mid-1960s, when (in 1965) Halsey had been one of only three non-Americans at a conference on 'Poverty in America' held at Berkeley (the others were Gunnar Myrdal from Sweden, and the director for manpower and social affairs of the OECD in Paris). Halsey's paper on 'Youth and employment in comparative perspective' at that conference accompanied papers by Harrington and Glazer, Moynihan and Keppel, Riessman and many others (A: Gordon, Margaret S., 1965, v–xi). Five years later Halsey was one of the British participants at a conference at Ditchley Park, near Oxford, alongside a dozen representatives from British education (including the EPA project, the Didsbury project and other research projects), and a similar number from the United States, to discuss 'Education for the Less Privileged'. The conference concluded that it was important to have 'a continued exchange of information and ideas between Britain and the United States', which had their own particular problems, but whose 'basic aims were the same' (B: Ditchley Foundation, 1970, 29). Passow was one of the participants at a conference on 'Social deprivation and change in education' held at the University of York in the spring of 1972. Under Ford, OECD and other auspices other connections were being made, and other outcomes were to surface in the early 1970s. Passow's *Deprivation and Disadvantage* – containing a chapter by Wiseman and Goldman – was published in 1970 under UNESCO auspices in Hamburg.

What we have seen in this narrative of the 1960s, therefore, is a lack of initial interest in, or at least a silence about, the American involvement with educational policies and strategies against disadvantage and poverty. Even at the level of information little penetrated to the educational and social science press until 1967–8, and the discovery of any relevance in the American experience for British education did not take place until the end of the decade. The Ford Foundation and similar projects in the first half of the 1960s was of so little interest that even those British visitors to the United States who were aware of them (and there were probably very few of those) relayed nothing to a British audience, except through informal networks. Even after the flurry of American policy activity from 1964 the amount of public (including official) interest was minute. In addition to the public attention we have suggested, there were other, limited channels through which information and discussion probably took place, for example, in the planning of the Swansea, Didsbury and EPA projects, and above all in the work of the Plowden committee in 1963–6. We shall return in the next chapter to the Plowden investigations and to the relationship between the American experience and the gathering momentum of British anti-poverty policy. In bypassing Plowden, however, we have not distorted the *public* record of concern with the American educational war on poverty. For a substantial part of the 1960s there is a pattern of at first total and then relative silence that it is important to explain.

The first element in the explanation is the dominant position of secondary school reorganization. Since the American emphasis was on reversing the effects of disadvantage at an early age, the consequent projects and policies relating to early childhood, preschooling and the early years of elementary education did not match the dominant British concern. There were basic structural and conceptual differences between the two positions, and even the work of Bernstein, Douglas and – somewhat differently – the British educationists concerned with nursery education and early childhood, did not fundamentally alter the picture of massive concern with selection at eleven and the inequities of a divided secondary education system. The education journals most noticeably either did not receive or failed to respond to signals of the new thrusts of American educational policy. Not until Head Start was well established was there HMI interest. Attention was concentrated on issues of or relating to secondary education.

A second element is one of the variants of 1960s British complacency, relating to both nursery and primary education. Although, in the case of the former, the 1950s and 1960s saw constant reference to under-provision and demands for the easing of restrictions on the expansion of local authority nursery education, the essential philosophy of nursery education seemed settled. British nursery education, it was felt, was the product of a long and proud tradition, and what was needed was basically more of the same. One feature of this self-satisfaction was the sense that a relationship between nursery and infant education on the one hand and social disadvantage on the other hand was a thing of the past:

...the first schools for very young children to be set up in this country were in the sort of districts where parents were unable to give their children adequate care; physical and mental development became stunted during the all-important years of early childhood... the results of the early nursery schools showed a benefit to children and parents so great that a desire arose to provide nursery schools for the children of more favourable homes, and we now recognise that the nursery school has a valuable part to play in the development of all children... (B: Gardner, 1949, 5)

This particularly bland picture did acknowledge that the nursery school catered for the children of parents whose lives left them with little leisure to study the needs of their children, but post-war optimism had removed some of the pre-war emphasis on the role of early education in combating poverty and disadvantage. The 1937 version of the Board of Education's *Handbook of Suggestions* for teachers talked of such education as having been established 'as much for social as for educational reasons'. There were still homes

in which the children are not under good influence, and indeed whole areas where, owing to bad housing conditions, a low standard of living, the fact that the mothers are employed, or other causes, they do not develop as they should.

The role of the nursery school in those conditions included preventive medical activity, one of its main aims being 'the nurture of debilitated children' (B: Board of Education, 1937, 68, 72–3).

The development of the infant school in Britain in the early decades of the nineteenth century had indeed been grounded in the condition of the poor, and with mixed motivations as to the 'rescue' of the 'infant poor', and the nature of the educational policies and practices best suited to the endeavour (B: Silver, 1965; McCann and Young, 1982). The development of the nursery school in the early twentieth century had related to the same constituency of poverty. Like Robert Owen a century earlier, Rachel and Margaret McMillan saw a broad interpretation of early education as an essential ingredient in equitable social progress. In 1919, Margaret McMillan commented that there had been creches, baby-welfare centres, baby clinics and infant schools before, but 'the nursery School is... distinct in aim and method from all that went before'. The distinctiveness lay in the combination of creative imagination and play with all-round attention to children's health, including the concept of the open-air school. Her educational vision was a political vision – 'the History of Education is really the History of Democracy, and as the people advanced slowly in social hope and faith the level of their demands in education and nurture rose with the tide'. Former revolutions had meant the uprising of a people, merely changing masters, whereas

The aim of the open-air Nursery-School is the salvation, physical, mental and spiritual of the children of this country or of any other country form their cradles and up to the end of the first seven years. That is a pretty bold aim. It means revolution, but such a revolution as will make all the others that came before it appear poor and timid things by comparison' (B: McMillan, 1919, 12, 21, 317)

The nursery school movement as a whole was not committed to this 'revolutionary' fervour, but the work of Susan Isaacs and others can be considered as the process of idealism-into-practice. The British nursery school movement saw itself as having pioneered something of international importance, with the United States in the 1920s drawing inspiration from visits to Margaret McMillan, British visitors to the United States, and the importation of British nursery school teachers (A: Eliot, 1972; B: de Lissa, 1939, 251). There was a general view that the British infant school as it had finally developed as a stage of schooling for the over-fives was either uniquely British or at least a British invention (B: Board of Education, 1937, 68; Gardner, 1949, 7). The nursery school movement similarly saw itself as having established a tradition of child-centred, and in the 1950s increasingly family-focused, 'education', a concept seen as having embraced in recent decades the promotion of good health (including mental health), the encouragement of curiosity, constructive skills and creative abilities, and the socialization of children (B: Nursery School Association [1954]; Webb, 1974, 4–5).

Britain was, in fact, one of the few countries to develop compulsory school attendance from the age of five, and this combination of 'progressive' (or 'open', as it came to be termed) nursery and infant education, and the drive to expand rather than to rethink its purposes, raised obstacles to the reception of messages from the United States. If Baltimore was about early access, what did it have to tell the British? Visitors to the US, as we have seen, might question whether Head Start simply represented a process of America's catching up with the British nursery school. Was America merely carrying out Margaret McMillan's long-accomplished revolution? Were the related research into and projects involving early childhood really of interest to British academics and educationists whose main interest lay elsewhere? Were British sociologists, for example interested in early childhood? Clearly not, as A.H. Halsey agrees: 'Looking back to that I don't believe that it was part of anybody's consciousness', even though someone like Halsey would have in theory seen the importance of early childhood (Halsey, interview). There was no *need* for British education to listen in to the American dialogue, particularly when some of it increasingly contained messages about structured programmes by Bereiter and Engelmann and others, inimical to the dominant nursery and infant traditions.

What applied to nursery education and the infant years applied to the primary school in general. In 1972, introducing a book on the twentieth-century history of English primary schools and the progressives, Brian Simon began: 'The English primary school – or at least its most advanced section – is probably unique in the world, and is certainly arousing widespread interest, perhaps particularly in the United States' (B: Selleck, 1972, v). This had been true in the post-war period, and increasingly so in the 1960s. Vaizey's comment that 'the primary schools are one of the good things in English education', ten years before Simon's, reflected the sense of pride in a segment of the system that had in its post-war architecture as well as its pedagogy attempted to enact its progressive past in modern dress. If American visitors were coming to see this phenomenon, what did the British have to learn from the ESEA? What the Plowden committee produced in 1967 was confirmation of the uniqueness (though not without attention to the weaknesses) of the British primary school, and books like John Blackie's *Inside the Primary School* (which appeared under DES auspices in the same year as Plowden) might occasionally refer to but could largely ignore experience in other countries, including the United States. In an introduction to a series of booklets on British primary schools Joseph Featherstone, an American who played a key role in publicizing post-war British primary education in the United States, drew attention not only to the curricular, environmental and other aspects of the schools, but also discussed their relevance to the United States. The essential theme was of the confusion and faddishness of the American scene (B: Featherstone, 1971). Featherstone in a sense, therefore, merely confirmed at the beginning of the 1970s what the British had felt for a long time – that in this as in other contexts they had little or nothing to learn from the United States.

Another and related variant of the British attitude to the United States concerned the divide between the British (or more precisely Scottish on the one hand and the rest of the United Kingdom on the other) system of education, and the American lack of national system. The British had been educational system-building in the nineteenth century, and specifically through acts of parliament and official investigations in the second half of the century. For the British in the 1950s and 1960s, the 1944 Education Act represented – in spite of the weaknesses in practice and the dilemmas we have discussed – a triumph of comprehensive system structuring, bringing into partnership the central state, local government, the schools and the children and their parents. The post-war secondary school movement was aimed, in the vocabulary of the time, at 'reorganization'. Deficient though it may have been, the system was accepted fact. Corrections were to be to the system, either though such reorganization or by expansion, as in the case of nursery provision.

It would have been difficult, therefore for a British audience readily to understand and adopt or adapt the configuration of activities associated with the Ford and similar initiatives, the mode of operation of the committee on juvenile delinquency, and the emphasis on local projects either unrelated to or even in open conflict with the local school authorities. While it was possible by the end of the 1960s to extend the conception of educational action, the style of activity developing in the United States in the early 1960s did not fit an educational system still trying to implement a wartime act of parliament that only slowly became thoroughly operational. Involved in funding the research and development projects of the late 1960s in Britain were the Department of Education and Science, the Schools Council and the Social Science Research Council, all public bodies. While the Nuffield Foundation entered project development in the curriculum field, in the ones with which we are concerned here the funding agencies were primarily government departments or government-funded agencies. Bernstein had secured Ford funding but, in general, the British had not yet understood how such bodies operated, and saw little to parallel the British situation in the projects funded in American cities (or in the tensions that often surrounded those projects). What American legislation could be seen as doing was attempting also to bring into tentative federal planning the kind of national commitment to education that Britain had enshrined in legislation from the 1870s. Here again, if the Americans were trying to catch up with a long-established British national model, what was there for the British to learn?

This was true, of course, not only of education but of the whole political and social context. We have considered some of the background to the legislative and related activity that developed in the Kennedy years and burst into the metaphor of the war on poverty from 1964. The important contrast is with the British conception of a welfare state, and the importance of the divide cannot be over-stated. In 1965, as we have seen, Glazer used the British and other European cases to identify by contrast what was happening in the United States. He described as a paradox the sudden rise of public concern and political action with regard to the large numbers (exactly how many million did not materially affect the argument) of American poor. He estimated that the percentage on National Assistance in England was higher than that on public assistance in the US, and yet, he asked: 'why is there no outcry in England over the problem of poverty when three million people a year are dependent on weekly grants for direct need from the National Assistance Board?' The answer lay in the British social security system, where the question was one of 'tinkering with benefits and eligibilities', whereas in the US 'radicals, liberals and even some conservatives call for a social and psychological revolution' (A: Glazer, 1965a, 72–3). We have also seen the awe that the British National Health Service could generate amongst the Mississippi poor. If Titmuss and the British poverty specialists were so welcome in the US, and if the economic opportunity, education and welfare legislation of the mid-1960s pointed towards an American version of the welfare state, then again – what did the British need to listen to and learn from in the American experience?

The answers might seem to lie in two areas of major importance to British receptivity to American developments – poverty and its causes, and questions of race. Both of these could also be discussed as variants of British complacency in the 1960s. Of particular importance in the first connection was growing unemployment in the United States, the 'steady rain of unemployment statistics which we receive in our daily news reports', as one American put it (A: Brazziel, 1964, 382). Glazer commented that the British were ahead of the Americans in many spheres, but that American work training and retraining programmes were far in advance of anything to be found in England – the reason for which was obvious: 'our unemployment rates in general are higher, our youth unemployment is much higher, our fear of job loss through technological change considerably greater' (A: Glazer, 1965a, 75). From the British vantage point in the 1950s and early 1960s it was clear that the United States was facing unemployment on a scale and of a kind unknown in Britain after the war, and it appeared to be an American problem. Automation and technical change were not happening as rapidly in Britain, and there was little sense of a threat of serious unemployment as a result of them. We have seen some reflection of the American experience of technological unemployment in surveying British interest in the United States in the 1960s. In *The Spectator* in 1964 there was a grim picture of economic growth having no impact on the American unemployment figures, and a forecast of 11 per cent unemployment by 1970, resulting in part from 'the loss of at least 2,000,000 jobs annually due to technological advance' (B: Beichman, 1964, 135). John Burrows HMI, as we have seen, returned from the US in 1968 describing British cities as amenable to the same 'menacing' problems as American cities 'if unemployment developed' (B: Burrows, 1968, 31). An English commentary in 1970 talked of there being 'plenty of loose money in England and precious little unemployment. This may be the consequence of technological backwardness for automation is not yet destroying jobs in England as fast as it is in the United States' (B: Jones, 1970). The contribution of technological unemployment to poverty in the United States was a very different phenomenon from the kind of poverty that was attracting British attention in the early 1960s. Although parallels can be, and were, drawn between the processes of discovery in the two countries, as Dorothy Wedderburn suggested, Britain did not have the same extremes. On both counts, that of unemployment and that of the extremes of poverty, the American dilemmas seemed to be specifically American, and all of the 1960s US policies could be seen as addressing problems not, or not yet, relating to Britain. The overall view of American society, economics and politics helped to colour how the British saw American education also. David Hopkinson, an English HMI in rural East Anglia until 1964 and from that date HMI in adult and further education in the London area, reflected on the 1960s:

> I had no experience at all of the Americans. I never really read anything about Head Start and all this stuff, and I was never a viewer of Sesame Street... I saw this as a political issue in America, not a serious educational one, and in that I was probably wrong, because no doubt very interesting things and very useful things were learned about the actual educational process (Hopkinson, interview)

This was probably a representative view of the political framework within which the American policies and strategies for education as for other social processes were seen to develop. If the Americans were failing to cope with their market economy and their confrontational politics, then there could be little of importance in their policies for a Britain which had developed a basically consensual approach to the role of government, national planning and the welfare state!

A somewhat similar argument applies to questions relating to race or, in the British situation of the late 1950s and early 1960s, immigration. The American contexts of social and educational policy, of urban conflict and unemployment, poverty and inequality, contained significant, and often dominant, elements of race. The American preoccupations with desegregation and civil rights seemed, again, to be specifically American problems. If poverty was, or became translated into, a racial issue, then the British were – at least until the late 1960s – unprepared to see the equation as relating to the British situation. We have seen how little emphasis on the racial aspects of immigration was apparent in the official approach to education in the late 1950s and much of the 1960s. The question was seen as one of immigration, not one of race, and although the concentration of immigrants in particular cities and districts was seen as creating some difficulties for the schools, they were issues largely of assimilation and language. The British ultimately would know how to handle such problems, which would be solved more by underplaying them and handling them within universal policies than by addressing them too overtly. The Americans, it would seem, were paying the price for their history of slavery, racial discrimination and bigotry, and the educational and other solutions appropriate to that situation seemed not only inappropriate but possibly even dangerous for the British dealing with educational inequities relating to social class, on to which the problems of immigration were superimposed. Policy directions associated with race in the United States were therefore as unattractive to the Britain of the early and mid-1960s as were those associated with American unemployment and levels of poverty.

The 'time lag' in the British interest in American educational policies relating to poverty was therefore in fact a complex statement of British preoccupations and complacency, and of British conceptualization of American realities. By the end of the 1960s the relationship between education and poverty was being established in Britain, and race had become a policy issue. The imagery of America no longer prevented the United States from being seen and heard.

To these contributory explanations others may need to be added. One crucial one had to do with the accumulation of evidence in the second half of the 1960s (though most dramatically not until the Westinghouse–Ohio evaluation of Head Start published in 1969) of the apparent failure of the educational war on poverty programmes. Britain learned about the programmes more or less at the same time as learning of their difficulties. From 1966 Coleman was transmitting messages of the relatively small differences in achievement attributable to schools (though with achievement by black children more dependent on the quality of schooling than was that of white children). The immediate success, but lack of sustained impact in the early grades of elementary school by the Head Start experience, was a signal received simultaneously with news of the launch of Head Start itself. The credibility of these signals seemed to relate to processes which were themselves unfamiliar to the British. Given the forms of funding and the nature of the initiatives involved in the American developments, it is easy to see why the new process of 'evaluation' appeared. Presidential committees, Congress, federal and statewide agencies, wanted to know with some degree of certainty what were the outcomes of their policies, decisions and budgets. The sophistications of evaluation did not begin to be established until the 1970s, but the outcomes of rudimentary and either negative or conflicting forms of evaluation began to be heard in Britain almost as soon as the activities themselves were decided upon.

If evaluation and its outcomes sent transatlantic messages difficult to receive, so did the processes of research, for the precise reason that the research-policy relationship that had taken shape in the United States did not have a clear parallel in Britain. Policy-making in Britain, it is true, had behind it a long tradition of investigation, conducted mainly through national, official committees and commissions of one sort or another, but the sources of evidence used in Britain by the *Early Leaving* or Crowther committees in the 1950s, or even by the Robbins and Newsom committees in the 1960s, did not involve the same sponsor–research relationship involved in a Congressionally mandated project or an independent evaluation of a process-in-action. Not only was the content of the American messages unfamiliar or confusing to a British audience at this time, but so also seemed the whole context from which they emerged.

The result in Britain, until the end of the 1960s, was a complex mixture of disdain and neglect, incomprehension and rejection. There is no easy way to interpret silence. Many a crucially important nineteenth-century reformer vanished from the pages of the history books, for a variety of reasons for which it is not always easy historically to account (B: Silver, 1983, ch. 1). Interpreting silence has become a key process in feminist history. In the present case we have been concerned with a relatively brief period of time, but one for which the mechanical concept of a 'time lag' is not adequate. What we have traced is the slow build-up of an interest. It is not possible in parallel to catalogue the machineries of silence, because there is no way of knowing whether in specific instances the silence was that of ignorance or of the judgment that information was irrelevant or unimportant. What in general is clear is that for most of the 1960s British social and educational problems, while apparently similar in many respects to those of the United States, were differently defined and related to contexts which American experience appeared unable to illuminate. Nothing showed this more clearly than the Plowden committee's report on *Children and their Primary Schools*.

10   Plowden: direction finding

Primary education, wrote Lord Butler in 1968, was a new priority: 'the interest in primary education has come almost entirely from the Plowden Report' (B: Butler, 1968, 14). Interest in the Plowden report, which was submitted to the Secretary of State in October 1966, and published the following year, focused on two aspects: its endorsement of 'progressive' approaches to the primary school, and its clear recommendations for 'positive discrimination' and 'educational priority areas' as responses to economic, social, environmental and educational disadvantage. Against the background of existing priority for secondary education, and with a Labour government from 1964 moving towards more determined promotion of a comprehensive secondary school system, the Plowden committee had to determine not only what was distinctive and needed in British primary education, but also the strategies for establishing and communicating the priorities that emerged from its research, evidence and debate. We are concerned here only incidentally with the committee's explorations of and conclusions concerning the aims and practices of primary education, its staffing or management, though its attention to the stages of education, and particularly questions of transfer, is a link between established and new policy commitments. How the committee arrived at its analysis and recommendations with regard to children and their environment, parents and the community, educational priority areas and positive discrimination, the children of immigrants, health and welfare services, and nursery education, is the direct concern here, since at stake is not only a new public awareness of the realities of primary education, but also the committee's translation of its evidence and analysis in a set of perceptions of the relationship between education and disadvantage. The outcomes proved both influential and controversial.

The committee drew energies from two important sources: previous understandings of this relationship by its predecessor, the Hadow committee which reported in 1931 on *The Primary School*, and other analyses of and policies relating to disadvantage since the 1930s, and secondly the recent British and international focus on poverty. The importance of the Plowden report, and of the internal workings of the committee, therefore lies in its presentation of the issues relating to what the schools themselves had felt to be a 'forgotten sector of education' (B: Plowden, 1987, 120), and in the way it saw itself in traditions of approaches to educational and social problems.*

From the outset the committee used the 1931 Hadow report on *The Primary School* as a touchstone. The committee's working party which was discussing the relationship between the primary school and home and community recognized, in drafting its first interim report at the end of a year, that the Hadow committee had emphasized the fact that poverty affected children physically and emotionally. The Plowden committee had to establish what had changed, what use it could make of the tradition of analysis and policy that Hadow represented, and how much further it needed to go down a path of concern that had been a relatively minor Hadow emphasis: 'Despite this acceptance of the importance of the home, the Hadow Report did not give any prominence to it. The main reference occurs in a sub-section on environment which was tacked on to a chapter on mental development' (B: CAC, 1967, 29).

What the Hadow committee in fact recognized – with considerable help from Cyril Burt's evidence on the mental characteristics of children between the ages of seven and eleven – was the relationship between a poor environment and educational performance. The surprising point is not that the Hadow committee 'tacked on' a section on environment, but that it had managed to emphasize the environmental issue, proposing a restructuring of British primary education and its curriculum on the basis of what was known about the intellectual, emotional and physical development of children. In the introduction to its report, the Hadow committee drew attention to Burt's evidence that a 'squalid environment' had deleterious effects on physical and mental vitality. It drew attention to 'a marked correspondence between the distribution of

---

* The papers of the Plowden committee are still inaccessible under the official thirty-year rule. It has been possible for the purposes of this chapter to piece together a reliable picture of the work of the committee. Some members of the committee subsequently published commentaries or reflections. The secretary of the committee, Maurice Kogan, has published a number of accounts of aspects of the committee's work. It has been possible also to see some seminar or other unpublished papers by people who were members of or in some way associated with the committee. A number of these have also been interviewed. Other relevant documentation has been located, including some internal papers of the committee and its working parties. Where this material is publicly accessible it is referenced in the normal way. Where sources are not indicated, the substantiating information is in the possession of the authors. It should be pointed out that one other researcher has previously indicated that he had access to some agendas and other information about the internal working of the committee (B: Acland, 1980).

poverty and the distribution of educational retardation', the past underestimation of the effects of the environment, and the fact that a poor home ('poor' in the sense of being in poverty, as defined by Charles Booth) did not give the young child the same educational start as did homes with more adequate means, where children were encouraged to read and write, acquired greater general knowledge and 'the foundations of education':

For many young children from the poorest home all this is reversed. Their parents know very little of any life except their own, and have neither the time nor the leisure to impart what little they know. The vocabulary that the child picks up is restricted... There is no literature that deserves the title... His universe is closed in and circumscribed by walls of brick and a pall of smoke... (B: Board of Education, 1931, xix, 54–8)

Under the heading 'The main causes of educational retardation' the report also included a variety of factors which emanated from the poverty situation – absence from school, illness, insufficient or un-suitable food, and 'lack of culture in the home'. The Hadow committee also put educational failure down to deficiencies in the school system, to 'inappropriate teaching', including 'mechanical or ill-devised methods of instruction'. It pointed out that several witnesses had suggested that much backwardness was 'school made': schools adopted procedures which induced failure, one of them being to tell children 'directly or indirectly... that they are stupid' (*ibid.*, 85–7).

When, two years later, the Hadow committee reported on *Infant and Nursery Schools*, a similar undercurrent of reference to poor housing and other environmental handicaps was present, indicating their responsi-bility for a lack of stimulus, and arguing the case for more nursery provision under the age of five, notably in those areas where unsatisfactory housing affected the health and growth of the child. Support for the nursery school tradition which stemmed from the work of Rachel and Margaret McMillan in Deptford from 1911, was buttressed by evidence in a memorandum to the committee from Cyril Burt and Susan Isaacs (B: Board of Education, 1933, xxv, 37, 76–7, 101, 116–17). Timothy Raison, later to become a Conservative government minister, was editor of *New Society* and a member of the Plowden committee and, after its work was over, wrote that it had drawn on two familiar themes in British education, the 'belief in learning rather than teaching that characterised the great Hadow report of 1931 and the whole progressive movement', and the 'growing concern at the wastage of talent and injustices' that derived from the operational inequality of the system. Although Raison divides those two themes and ascribes the first to Hadow, the report was in fact informed by both (B: Raison, 1967, 46).

Another member of the Plowden committee, Eric Hawkins, director of a university language teaching centre, also, after the committee had reported, traced the similarities and differences between Hadow and Plowden. He pointed out that Hadow foreshadowed the discussions of the 1950s and 1960s on 'linguistic environmental factors', including the work of Bernstein, but also underlined the importance of the contribution of Cyril Burt to the committee, with his insistence on the effects of the environment. Following the publication of the Hadow report, its 'humane discussion, and Professor Burt's researches supporting it, of the effects of environment were forgotten and for the next twenty years such research as was conducted in the field of primary schooling in the U.K. was largely preoccupied with techniques for *measuring* mental endowment in children' (B: Hawkins, 1968, 20–1). We have seen the pre-war tradition of research into the social and economic context of educational opportunity and success, but in the present it is important to emphasize the prominent role played by Burt in identifying environmental constraints on children's ability to benefit from education – a role which has been lost in the considerable attention given to other aspects of Burt's research and publications. The work Burt did for these two Hadow exercises was amplified in the crucial chapter on the 'Causes of educational backwardness' in his *The Backward Child*. Here and in other parts of the book he analyzed the geographical distribution of educational backwardness, focusing on both the weaknesses of 'school conditions' (including inefficient teaching) and 'home conditions'. His argument was that both social and school conditions contribute to backwardness, and that backward children are the most numerous in the poorest and most overcrowded districts: 'backwardness and poverty...go largely hand in hand'. That partnership was visible in poor and insanitary households, high birth and death rates and other characteristics of such districts. Burt pointed out, however, that generalizations about poverty and backwardness could not be translated into judgments on specific individuals:

to include off-hand that in each individual case poverty is the main cause of dullness or incompetence would be neither just nor logical...The poorest tenements of London contain youthful geniuses, some of whom win – more of whom merit but fail to win – a free place or scholarship at a secondary school or college. Stupidity, therefore, is not the inevitable result of poverty, though poverty seems its commonest concomitant...

He suggested that the *main* causes of educational backwardness lay outside the school, and based his discussion on Seebohm Rowntree's definition of poverty. He suggested percentages of backward children in different categories of poverty, and discussed how poverty impaired health, limited knowledge and communication and worked in other ways to the disadvantage of children from homes with poor material conditions (B: Burt, 1937, 95–133). Burt's authority in bringing the issues of environment and poverty into the same arena of debate as did the work of Kenneth Lindsay, Gray and Moshinsky and others, must not be underestimated. In a paper on pupils and their families circulated to the Plowden working party on school and community, one of its members wrote:

One outstanding series of investigations, over the last half century, has been on the 'wastage' of ability amongst the children of manual workers. Sir Cyril Burt and the other pioneers of mental testing were able to show in the 1920s how large were the numbers of such able children deprived of education by the poverty of their parents.

When, in the changed circumstances of post-war Britain, attention turned again to questions of deprivation and the environment, there was a pre-war tradition on which to build.

The attention paid in the post-war years to early childhood, child care, environmental influences on young children, the effects of various kinds of deprivation, and the relation of all of these to education at the nursery and primary stages has been overshadowed by the questions of testing and selection for secondary education, and the comprehensive school. 'Education' has in this respect been narrowly interpreted, and concerns about aspects of children's lives and education up to the age of eleven have commonly been excluded from accounts of British education in the two decades following the Second World War. There were, however, scattered developments in the 1950s and early 1960s which speak to the issues addressed by the Plowden committee.

Much of the post-war concern was, of course, with the expansion or the improvement of facilities, to overcome the legacies of pre-war neglect and wartime destruction, to meet the new demands of the 1944 Education Act and the aspirations of optimistic parents. The Nursery School Association, for example, directed its energies to a campaign for wider provision, following a wartime moratorium and given the difficulties of establishing any priority for preschool education in the face of other priorities (B: Blackstone, 1971, ch. 4). From various directions, however, questions of school, home and community were raised. The North-Eastern Junior Schools Association emphasized that one of the 'basic requirements' of the junior school was that more attention needed to be paid to the home and neighbourhood conditions of children as 'the background for the children's school life'. Its recommendation was that 'the poorer the district in which a junior school is situated, the greater the need for speedy reduction in the size of classes' (B: North-Eastern Junior Schools Association, 1949, 13–15).

The out-of-school conditions of greatest concern were those which affected children's health, and against the background of the creation of a national health service, the first post-war investigation of children's health began in Newcastle upon Tyne in 1947, publishing as the first fruits of the research in 1954 *A Thousand Families in Newcastle upon Tyne*. The first question to which the project sought an answer was: 'What are the types and what is the incidence of the infective illnesses of infancy and early childhood in Newcastle upon Tyne?' (B: Spence et al., 1954). This investigation and its publications are important not least as related to other projects, including the one which resulted in Douglas's *The Home and the School*, which in turn was to have major importance for the Plowden committee.

By the late 1950s, as a result of the concern with social class, the findings of the *Early Leaving* report, and dissatisfactions with the implementation of the 1944 Act, an interest in the handicaps continuing to be suffered by children in poor environments was beginning to take clearer shape. The ultimately influential work of Bernstein began in the late 1950s. In 1959 *Educational Research* published an account of the relationship between children's reading readiness and ability and other experience. It faced the problem of providing different kinds of learning experience for children from different backgrounds, where primary schools drew on homogeneous or disparate home backgrounds:

The close relationship between reading and home background is not a recent discovery, but the Kent study does enable one to realise that different kinds of education may be needed in infant schools in different areas. This is probably possible where the social background is homogeneous but becomes much more difficult where the school draws its pupils from widely different social backgrounds. (B: Standish, 1959, 32)

The same publication, in 1961, contained two articles of related interest, and important as an indicator of the kind of research being reported on in the period immediately before the establishment of the Plowden committee. One article looked at teachers' attitudes, their definition of 'good' and 'poor' pupils' backgrounds, and the relevance for teachers' behaviour. The second article traced the growth of an interest in factors affecting children's school success in the inter-war period and after the war, and concluded that there was as yet no sociology of the school which took serious account of children's home backgrounds (B: Goodacre, 1961; Floud and Halsey, 1961). Also in *Educational Research*, in 1959, a discussion of 'Environmental conditions affecting intelligence', underlined the evidence that showed a positive association between intelligence test scores and 'the intellectual and socio-economic quality' of the home. It accepted that environmental factors played some part, but did not go down the path that was attracting most sociological attention. It argued, as others were to do in both Britain and the United States, that the correlation could be explained 'by inheritance of ability'. The evidence did not 'show unequivocally that the intellectual quality of the home is an environmental variable affecting the child's intelligence' (B: Lynn, 1959, 50–1, 59). Questions of intelligence and environment, school and home, were moving into more direct concern with the younger child. In a professorial inaugural lecture in 1957, the man who was to chair the committee on primary schools in Wales, paralleling the Plowden committee, talked of the disillusionment that had followed the post-war educational strategies to provide all children with a suitable educational environment. Professor Gittins emphasized that 'there was more to environment than mere schooling', including health and nutrition, clothing and money, but the post-war endeavours had pointed towards bringing the environment 'under control'. Between the war years and the late 1950s 'other factors in this broad and comprehensive term 'environment' began to fix themselves upon our attention. We became much more aware than ever before of the presence of large unseen influences whose power had been under-estimated, forces to which we commonly apply the label "sociological"'. He recalled a grammar school headmistress in 1942 stating that the type of home from which pupils came was

every bit as important for academic success as the quality of their intelligence. There were few in that conference at that time who would have been found ready to agree with her. She was regarded as unsympathetic and a snob, but far more educators would be found today ready to endorse her opinion, and they would be astonished indeed if they were charged either with lack of sympathy or snobbery. (B: Gittins, 1957, p. 186)

This was a not unimportant set of perceptions for someone who was to chair the committee for Wales, and at the same time be a member of the Plowden committee.

The implications of such views were also beginning to be formulated. W.D. Wall, as we have seen, was attempting to reach out from psychology to new socially oriented interpretations of schooling. In 1959 he published an analysis of what he described as 'cultural change and the challenge to healthy mental growth', in which he saw the changing relationship between family and the general culture as requiring greater understanding by educationists of the role of the environment. Nursery schools and other institutions were substituting for the family in many ways. Teachers needed to recognize that schools had to adapt to the often inadequate environment from which children were drawn: 'we must look carefully to see what is lacking and go as far as we can to supply it' (B: Wall, 1959, 87–92). From other directions – in the context of the welfare and health structures that had come into place since the war – the concept of 'deprivation' was securing increased attention. Mia Kellmer Pringle had from the mid-1950s been researching, publishing and encouraging other work on backwardness, maladjustment and a range of questions to do with deprivation. While the Plowden committee was at work she edited an influential book on *Deprivation and Education*, in which she identified three types of deprivation – that relating to children in residential care, that relating to children who were unloved or rejected by their parents, and that which resulted from growing up in a home 'which is culturally and educationally extremely unstimulating'. The child in the third category would be 'handicapped by environmental deprivation'. At the same time she published the papers of a symposium on *Investment in Children*, in which she and others – including Wall and J.B. Mays – discussed educational, social work and other strategies for dealing with the prevalent forms of child deprivation, including those resulting from 'environmental deprivation' (B: Pringle, 1965a, 1–2; Pringle, 1965b).

Much of the attention being given to issues of deprivation focused in Britain on questions of 'maternal deprivation' and the emotional life of the child in the family. The paramount influence in the 1950s in this concern with child care was John Bowlby, and specifically his book *Child Care and the Growth of Love*, in which he looked at the 'natural home group', how it operated and failed, how disruption of the family caused, in particular maternal deprivation when children were especially dependent and vulnerable between the ages of three and five. He saw family allowances and other public provision as important contributions to family stability, though he was at pains to point out that poverty itself was not generally or directly responsible for parental neglect (which might result from the ill health of parents, death, divorce, etc.). Here, in a subsequent lecture on 'The rediscovery of the family' and elsewhere, Bowlby established for a generation the centrality of continued maternal care for the child, and all the policy implications that flowed from that emphasis (B: Bowlby, 1953, *passim* and 104–5; 1954, 1–2). Other child care analysts and a later decade were anxious to replace Bowlby's emphasis on the inescapable and lasting effects of such deprivation with a greater sense of the reversibility of the effects of deprivation. Implied or explicit in discussions of the family and child care were the role of the school, how schools might support the child from an unhappy or unsupportive home, how proper diagnosis and response might be achieved (B: Winnicott, 1964, 205–10).

Some of these developments regarding the child, the family and the school were rooted in or promoted research, others – such as the work that stemmed from the nursery school tradition – were not, and attempted to relate traditions of work with disadvantaged children, families or districts to contemporary circumstances. As dissatisfaction with the post-war position in secondary education grew, so – if to a less publicized extent – did anxieties about the scale and nature of nursery provision. The child-centred tradition of the primary school appeared to protect it from the worst effects of social deprivation and streaming in preparation for selection to secondary schools appeared to be the main, often the sole, enemy of the adequate development of primary school pupils. The Plowden committee were aware, as the report shows, that the *Early Leaving* report of 1954 and the Crowther report of 1959 had turned class differences into policy issues. An early draft of the section of the Plowden report (paras 82–3) which discusses those earlier reports explained that 'in recent years, the effects of social factors in education have become a common place even to the point, perhaps, of being seriously overstated. The previous reports of the Central Advisory Council for Education – from "Early Leaving" onwards – have played a leading part in arousing attention to the role of environment in educational attainment.' We have stressed the vital role of the Plowden committee in placing primary education on the national agenda, but signals emanating from various directions and levels of education, including research, and steadily growing interest in children and their environment were available to the Plowden committee from the outset. Even the Plowden emphasis on 'positive discrimination' can be seen to have roots in some of the work we have discussed. A Ministry of Education volume of suggestions for primary teachers, published in 1959, contained a section on 'Special educational treatment', which contained the following passage:

There are…children who require special help because they have been severely deprived in their upbringing. If these do not respond to even a generous share of the teacher's attention it is clear that something more must be done for them. (B: Ministry of Education, 1959, 107)

Such a formulation points towards both specific forms of remedial education and wider concern with compensatory education (though that phrase had not yet entered the British vocabulary). What the Ministry was alluding to was not just a learning deficiency, but one which was related to upbringing and deprivation. The point is not that the Plowden committee had ready-made concepts and strategies which it could articulate, but that such ideas were available as sources of energy and impetus. The question is whether or how they entered the work of the committee.

There is, as Maurice Kogan has underlined, 'no easy explanation of the decision to appoint the Plowden Committee... It followed a long period of discussion within the Ministry and consultation with the Treasury about its scope. The then Prime Minister, Mr Harold Macmillan, was also consulted about the chairmanship' (B: Kogan, 1973b, 82). Following reports on higher and secondary education, the logic may simply have been that it was time for the Central Advisory Council to look at primary education, and it was given the remit in 1963 'to consider primary education in all its aspects, and the transition to secondary education'. The committee – as it became more familiarly known than under its Council title – was set up by the Conservative Minister of Education, Sir Edward Boyle, and it reported just over three years later to his successor, Anthony Crosland, the Labour government's Secretary of State for Education and Science (the post having been redesignated after the Robbins report in 1963). Whatever the reasons for the decision to investigate primary education, the decision was taken against the advice of the Chief HMI responsible for primary education, John Blackie. Plowden was set up

against my advice... The then Under-Secretary in charge of primary education said: 'And now, I think we must look into primary education... I propose to set up a new consultative committee'... I said, 'I don't think this is a good plan, because I think the thing is too tender a growth at the moment. A lot of very interesting changes are taking place. I don't believe the growth is strong enough...' I was quite wrong, by the way. I was very doubtful about the advisability of this enormous enquiry by a lot of people from outside who didn't know the background... I was overruled.

One or two people were approached to chair the committee, including Lord Amery, but it was Boyle who found Lady Plowden (Blackie, interview).

The choice of members for the Plowden committee was significant, and it is likely that Derek Morrell, a much-admired senior civil servant, played an important part in the selection. The members included two people described in the report as 'housewives and parents', one of whom was active in the Confederation for the Advancement of State Education; the philosopher A.J. Ayer; Sir John Newsom, who had chaired the previous committee which reported on *15 to 18*; five head teachers or deputy heads; a number of local authority administrators or school inspectors; and academics in fields of child health, language and education. Amongst these were a number of specialists in early childhood and primary education, including Molly Brearley, Principal of the Froebel Institute College of Education and Professor J.M. Tanner. Additionally, however, and crucial to our concerns here, was a group of members who came from sociology and social administration back-grounds. David Donnison was Professor of Social Administration at the London School of Economics, Timothy Raison was editor of *New Society*, and Michael Young was chairman at the time of the Social Science Research Council, and director of the Institute of Community Studies. A preparatory school headmaster who joined the committee in 1964 (reflecting on his 'Three years' hard labour') described the committee as 'constituted by a Conservative minister and reported to a Socialist... all shades from extreme left to fairly extreme right were represented, but politics were never once mentioned in our delibera-tions' (B: White, 1967, 14). Broadly based though the committee was, it contained strong enough representation from the social sciences for some of the signals of earlier and recent research to be carried into the committee, and with sufficient educational representation to overcome the fears that John Blackie had entertained. Stella Duncan, HMI, was seconded to the committee to work jointly with Maurice Kogan, its DES-seconded secretary, and the 'assessors' working with the com-mittee included Blackie himself.

The composition of the committee explains one of its first decisions taken when it met in October 1963 – to establish two working parties (the number was subsequently increased to six), one to consider children's growth and development, and the second 'to study the relationship of school, home and community', originally chaired by one of the headteachers, and then by David Donnison. Working Party 2 is the main focus of our interest in the internal working of the committee, since it was to be responsible for Part Three of the final report, which contained chapters on 'The children and their environment', 'Par-ticipation by parents', 'Educational priority areas', 'Children of immigrants' and 'The health and social services and the school child'. Why the committee took this particular decision at its first meeting is explained by Lady Plowden:

> ... if you look at the composition of the committee, certainly the second (working party) was envisaged in the people who were on it... We had David Donnison on it, who was very much concerned with social problems, we had Tim Raison... we had a couple of parents... The powers that be who chose the committee put those people on, and they made their voices heard. We were a fairly receptive body to that kind of thinking... David Donnison... and Michael Young – there we had the people who were all involved... This was part of primary education, the well-being of pupils, where they came from, what effect that had on it... This came from that group.

Lady Plowden's own work as a magistrate and in other respects had brought her into contact with 'the way people lived'. She took part herself in Working Party 2, as something interesting, and 'what I wanted' (Plowden, interview; Donnison, interview). To explain the choice of direction of the committee in this regard would require an analysis of the educational and social views of Sir Edward Boyle, Derek Morrell and others concerned as 'powers that be' in selecting the committee, as well as a more detailed account of how the processes of research and 'social opinion' related to the political configurations of the period. The important element here is the confidence displayed in social science and educational opinion when shaping the committee, and its receptivity to the emphases that resulted. The first two meetings of the committee were much involved with decisions regarding survey research to be conducted, information about existing research to be made available to the committee, and the priority to be given to the effects of selection on the primary school. By the time of the second meeting in December 1963 members of the committee had already visited seventy-five schools in Bristol, Manchester, Oldham, Salford, Rochdale, Nottingham and County Durham.

A significant feature of the Plowden committee was the fact that it was fed by and itself contributed to confidence in social science research in the service of policy making. In 1973, in a changed climate, Kogan reflected on the once prevalent 'optimism generated by the social scientists in the 1950's and 1960's... 10 or 20 years ago we were all certain that more education, better housing, good town planning would make us richer, happier, better balanced people able to relate more usefully and charitably to our fellows' (B: Kogan, 1973a, 1). The processes involved in the 1950s and 1960s in Britain were different from those we have examined in the United States, but similar bridges were being constructed between social science research and educational policy-making. There is a complex diagram that can be drawn of relationships between the social science and research developments of the 1950s and 1960s, their antecedents in the 1920s and 1930s, the assumptions reflected in the establishment and composition of the Plowden committee, its mode of operation, the research it commissioned, the evidence it considered important, and its final report. The Gittins report on *Primary Education in Wales*, also published in 1967, illustrates the same processes, pointing to one of the connections in the diagram when it considered that research shows that children are affected by the 'social and emotional environment as early as eighteen months and that a deprived or unstimulating environment can exert a lasting effect on the young child', and referring to the work of Kellmer Pringle in conducting the argument (B: CAC Wales, 1967, 57–8).

The Plowden 'comprehensive school', as one of the members termed it (B: Kogan, 1987, 13), set up working parties, in addition to the ones on child development and what they came to call 'social aspects', on structure (ages, stages, nursery), the curriculum, teacher training and financial and economic issues. It also had groups working on buildings and handicapped children. The membership overlapped, as in many instances did the subject matter (Working Party 3, for example, was as interested in the evidence or other material from Bernstein, Douglas and Martin Deutsch as was Working Party 2). Most members of the main committee served on at least two working parties, and there was most competition to serve on those concerned with structure and the curriculum. Working Party 2 produced its first reports on topics relating to the social services, as it was in that field that research reports first became available. It turned its attention later to what became known ultimately as educational priority areas and other matters. This working party was the 'heaviest research spender'. Donnison describes the directions in which it began its work:

Working Party 2 began by discussing plans for research with their departmental advisers and staff of the Government Social Survey – in particular the plans for surveys of children and parents...They also planned studies of social services and the schools...and discussed these with university research workers who carried them out. Later they devoted a lot of time to the studies which appear as Appendices 9 (the Manchester Survey), 12 (Gypsies and Education) and 14 (Variation in L.E.A. Provision)...Thus although all the research carried out in association with the Council's work was done for, and considered by, the whole Council, this working party was centrally concerned with most of these studies and initiated several of them. (B: Donnison, 1967, 3)

The lengthy terms of reference given to this working party are not generally known and are worth quoting in full:

(a) to prepare a statement for the Council on the interaction between primary schools and the communities of which they form part, taking into account (i) the effect on the schools and on individual pupils of consciously held parental attitudes to education (ii) the extent to which in a broader sense adult attitudes, behaviour and material setting, including socio-economic, neighbourhood and regional setting, affect the work of the schools and the performance of pupils (iii) the influence exercised by the schools through formal and informal association with parents;

(b) to advise the Council on the circumstances and ways in which effective collaboration can be established between primary schools and their local communities;

(c) to advise the Council on the means by which children can be compensated for an impoverished or otherwise inadequate social and cultural background;

(d) to advise the Council on all other matters concerning the relationship of school, home and community as are relevant to the Council's terms of reference.

The Council itself aimed to meet at more or less monthly intervals, met (often in sub-groups) with individuals or groups in whose evidence it was interested, received and discussed interim reports from the working parties, planned overseas visits – outstandingly to the United States, itself called for data and undertook policy explorations. On the former, for example, it asked the DES to supply information on the way it had dispensed its research fund since the creation of the fund in 1962 (and discovered that the total had risen from some £20,000 in 1963/4 to an estimated £357,000 in 1966/7). On the latter, the committee was aware, for example, that the new Secretary of State was planning a major development of the secondary comprehensive school, and that its own discussions of primary schools and transfer would be influenced by such a development. There was a case for the government waiting until Plowden had reported before deciding on its policy initiative, and Lady Plowden went to Crosland, who told her that comprehensive education would be national policy, that the committee did not need to produce an interim report on transition to secondary education, and that the government and the committee would no doubt keep each other informed of their progress. The committee, he suggested, could on that basis go ahead with their task of thinking for the long term. In December 1964, when she reported back on this visit, and on future occasions, the committee discussed the implications of government policy for its own thinking on transfer and other issues. The committee had, after all, agreed at its first meeting that it should make specific reference to the impact of selection on the primary schools. Crosland was later to comment to Kogan that there was a danger that such committees and their reports 'can slow up action, as Plowden would have done on comprehensive reorganization if I hadn't been very firm' (B: Kogan, 1971).

From the start the committee was therefore deeply involved with policy issues which had bases in the research and debates of the 1950s and early 1960s on selection and related questions, and at the same time it addressed the range of social and environmental questions encapsulated in the terms of reference it gave its Working Party 2. This working party was the main filter through which messages relating to poverty and disadvantage, and the social conditions which related to school processes and children's performance, were received by the committee.

The research conducted for the committee that was best known and occasioned the most controversy was a national survey of 'parental attitudes and circumstances related to school and pupil characteristics'. The report of this survey pointed out that previous Central Advisory Council evidence had been concerned with linking home circumstances and parental occupation with pupils' educational progress, but it was clear that the latter arose at least in part 'from the association between occupations and attitudes', and the committee decided therefore to 'estimate the influence of occupation, irrespective of attitudes, and of attitudes, irrespective of occupation' (B: CAC, vol. 2, 1967, 91). It was at the second meeting of the committee that Working Party 2 asked for approval for two research projects to be started quickly, one of which was this 'survey of parental attitudes to education'. Some concerns were expressed, but approval was given, and the DES was asked to commission the work to be done by the Social Survey Division of the Central Office of Information. In fact, preparatory work for this survey had been carried out by the secretariat before the committee ever met. Three members of a Ministry of Education Curriculum Study Group were part of the committee's secretariat – Maurice Kogan, Stella Duncan, HMI, and Miss Norah Goddard, an Inspector of Schools for the Inner London Education Authority. At the first meeting of the committee the chairman thanked these three for their preparatory work, and it is clear from a later commentary by Kogan that preparations for the survey were a key part of it. The survey and other possible research had been prepared so that the committee and its expert working party 'could rapidly decide whether to ask the Social Survey, HMIs, and others to make the necessary starts', with much of the initial survey design being undertaken by 'the remarkably able HMI who worked full-time with the Committee – Stella Duncan' (B: Kogan, 1973b, 93).

Another one of these starts – the second of those for which approval was sought at the second meeting of the committee – was a 'Manchester survey', which was conducted by Professor Stephen Wiseman and colleagues, and was concerned with ten-year-olds – an investigation of 'the relationship between the educational attainment of primary school children and environmental factors, with particular reference to the environment within the school' (B: CAC vol. 2, 1967, 349). An interim report submitted to the committee in October 1965 was effectively the report that was finally published in the second, *Research and Surveys* volume of the Plowden report. A third piece of work commissioned by Working Party 2 was a study of social services and their relationship to the schools, a study of three local authority areas named in the report as Smallham, Largeborough and Exshire, which were, in fact, Oxford, Birmingham and West Suffolk. The National Child Development Study was commissioned to produce a report on the cohort of children born in 1958, and starting from scratch they had eighteen months in which to do a 'mammoth job' – a study of 11,000 children (Davie, interview). By October 1964 Working Party 2 could report that the Social Survey had completed the interviewing of over 3,000 parents of primary school children in 187 schools, and that the schools and the HMIs were providing information on children's performance and school characteristics.

The working party received and solicited data from a variety of other sources, on questions of disadvantage, immigration and related social issues. John Burrows, HMI, for example, in October 1964 contributed to and discussed with the working party a paper on 'The state of primary education in a socially deprived urban area'. The paper was based on an HMI survey the previous year in nine boroughs of North and East London, aimed at studying conditions 'in the socially difficult and deprived areas'. It was not, Burrows's document explained, 'controlled research', but it drew on the 'experience, knowledge and judgement not only of the seven Inspectors concerned but of heads of schools, teachers, administrators, care committee workers, and in some boroughs of such diverse observers as the clergy and the police'. It described changing population and social patterns, the extent and effects of immigration, the tasks and problems of the schools. The work in some schools, it pointed out, was of high quality, but in junior schools particularly there was 'much stopgap and makeshift teaching', and a lack of leadership, staffing and 'reasonable facilities' meant that the area was 'educationally deprived'. Burrows also submitted a digest of available information on 'immigrants and the schools in the Metropolitan District' (of London), and with one of his colleagues discussed both submissions with the working party (Burrows, 14.10.64, 16.10.64). Later, in early 1966, when the working party was debating criteria for distinguishing 'social handicap' schools, it asked Michael Young to explore the working of a scheme for extra help to such schools (what became the 'educational priority area' schools) with Burrows and Her Majesty's Inspectors in the London area, and he talked several times with this group of HMIs. Burrows reported to Young enthusiastic support from the ten colleagues he questioned and summarized the criteria they proposed. Young circulated Burrows's account to the working party and described the response as 'rather heartening' (Burrows to Young, 3.5.66; Young to working party, n.d.). Although all such work by the inspectorate was not a formal part of the Plowden research, it reinforced the conviction of the working party and ultimately of the committee itself that their prime task lay in the deprived areas. Burrows's report on the primary schools in the nine London boroughs was 'a very key document ... It was on that kind of statement that the Education Priority Area policy was developed' (Kogan, interview).

The work of three researchers was of particular interest to the working party. The first was J.W.B. Douglas. Douglas's *The Home and the School* was published in 1964, and he supplied galley proofs to the

Plowden committee and met with it (Douglas, interview). Many members of the working party and the committee itself clearly saw Douglas's findings as among the most important early starting points for their work. Donnison, for example, considered him to be an important witness to the committee, as one of the most important people 'writing about educational attainment'. Kogan describes the committee as relying extensively on the work (Donnison, interview; Kogan, 1973b, 94). A summary of the book prepared for the working party by Michael Young placed it in a sociological tradition and pointed out how heavily the Robbins report on higher education had drawn on that tradition, showing as it did 'more fully than anyone has done before that "intelligence" responds to environment'. The summary emphasized Douglas's main finding as being that 'working-class children were doubly handicapped': they did less well in the selection process at 11 +, and then they 'deteriorated' further educationally after the age of 11 (Young, review note, n.d.). When the working party met with Douglas in June 1964 it had already collected from its members a comprehensive list of questions for discussion, about his findings, their implications, and the desirability of further research on the relationship between homes and primary schools.

The work of J.B. Mays was less salient in the working party than that of Douglas, but since the most relevant of Mays's work had appeared before the Plowden committee was appointed it was available as an early influence. Mays did not give oral evidence, but the committee was aware of his work in Liverpool as reflected in *Education and the Urban Child*, which was referred to in the final report, but also in 'Social disadvantage and education', which was published in *Educational Research* in 1962 and was circulated to Working Party 2. The interest of the article lay not only in its emphasis on social class differences as revealed in the study of secondary modern and primary schools in central Liverpool, but also in the conflict between the 'archaic curriculum' and the real lives of the children, and the need for action on several fronts – to reshape the teacher's traditional role, provide more adequate and better deployment of resources, and see the school as part of a programme of social welfare. Mays proposed that schools 'should strive to make themselves the focal point of local community effort, welfare and education', a message that was to find a ready response in the working party (B: Mays, 1962b).

The relationship with and response to Basil Bernstein was somewhat different. His work was recognized as important and Working Party 2 was particularly eager to meet him, though Working Party 4, concerned with the curriculum, was also interested. The meeting with Working Party 2 did not take place until January 1966, and at it there was discussion of Bernstein's research in the schools of West Ham, his understanding of the meaning and implications of 'deprivation' (a term he resisted) and 'social class', the relations between teacher and parent, and suggestions for the improvement of the schooling of children from 'restricted code' backgrounds. Some members of the working party thought the meeting productive, but Bernstein himself thought it an unhappy occasion (Bernstein, interview). It was clear to some of those present that Bernstein's hesitations about 'activity methods' meant that he was not in tune with the emphasis on 'progressive education' that was important to the committee in general. The working party responded with some ambivalence to his view of how schools should deal with social differences amongst children, and looked to further material for clarification of the issues. His further papers did not arrive until after the final draft of the Plowden report had been prepared (interviews, Duncan, Kogan), and in this as in some other cases the committee was unable to assimilate all the research and other evidence it had to process. What the working party and the committee had from Bernstein was further confirmation of their emphasis on the effects of poverty and disadvantage. They felt a vague sympathy with his analysis of language and social class, but felt that his conclusions probably pointed in directions other than ones that had already taken shape in their deliberations.

Working Party 2 was therefore the main vehicle through which the committee processed established and emerging views about the relationships between primary schools and social deprivation or disadvantage. The working party was searching for any kind of research-based or other evidence that could illuminate those relationships and suggest ways forward. It was not, therefore, from educationists alone that messages were received and considered. The working party was interested, for example, in the work of the Sparkbrook Association in Birmingham and its attempts to establish a 'family centre' in this 'twilight area' of the city. The Association was created in 1960, and in 1962 the city seconded a social worker to work full-time as organizer. It worked closely with statutory and voluntary agencies, and the centre it was planning aimed to 'promote the mental, physical and emotional development of the child'. It was to coordinate 'social, educational and medical work with families in the area', promoting group activities and research, and providing opportunities for the development of children 'affected by an unfavourable environment' (B: Sparkbrook Association, [1964]). The working party considered copies of the annual report and other published material, including a report in *The Times Educational Supplement* in April 1964, and members visited the Association. When

A.T. Collis of Birmingham University wrote a report on 'Social work and the schools' in Birmingham (the basis of the material on 'Largeborough' in one of the appendices to the Plowden report), he included a section on the Sparkbrook Association emphasizing the relevance of the principles involved. He drew particular attention to its efforts to develop cooperation amongst the various social services, teachers, employers, landlords, shopkeepers and others, and the proposed family centre was to be the first part of a social welfare complex in a redeveloped Sparkbrook (B: Collis, 1965).

The Sparkbrook experience was just one aspect of the working party's interest in 'social work and the schools'. It considered a substantial amount of evidence from various British organizations of social workers, education welfare officers and bodies such as the London County Council, as well as information and publications from the National Association of Social Workers in the United States. The committee itself considered making reference to the work of Edge Hill College of Education, where a social work course aimed to equip teachers to cooperate better with the social services. What the working party and the committee were taking into account, therefore, was a range of data taken from research projects, findings solicited and volunteered, descriptive and analytical material, relating to one of the key areas of investigation the committee had decided for itself at its first meeting – the relationship of school, home and community. Apart from this flow of information, the sociologists in Working Party 2 both interpreted and used it and also brought their own information to the working party. Michael Young for example, published an article in *New Society* in September 1964, entitled 'How can parent and teacher work together?' (B: Young, 1964), taking account of the lack of encouragement many children received from working-class parents. His article, drawing in part from Mays's work in Liverpool, and in part from his own growing interest in parent involvement in schools (B: Young and McGeeney, 1968a, 1968b), was part of the evidence considered in the discussion of 'social work'. Young also informed the working party about research conducted by Peter Willmott in Bethnal Green on antipathy towards teachers, who lived not in the area but out in the suburbs. Donnison was at the time working on housing and brought his expertise to the committee to the point at which members suggested that 'this committee knows too much about housing, we'd better keep down the amount we'll be writing about housing' (Donnison, interview). What is best known – and proved most controversial – of the research commissioned or used by the Plowden committee is the 'national survey of parental attitudes and circumstances related to school and pupil characteristics' completed for the committee in 1966 (B: CAC, vol. 2, 1967). The build-up of interest in social and educational deprivation, against the background of the sociological tradition we have discussed, and in the light of the flow of data into Working Party 2 in particular, is an important feature of the role of the committee. Donnison has summarized the position:

...although all the research carried out in association with the (Plowden) Council's work was done for, and considered by, the whole Council, this working party was centrally concerned with most of these studies and initiated several of them. It was the heaviest research spender of the Council's six working parties. The first reports it prepared for the Council dealt with the social services, because these were based on the first research and evidence to be completed. The working party next considered the needs of immigrant children, the creation of closer links between parents and teachers, and several other questions. Attention then turned, rather late in the day, to the priority areas. (B: Donnison, 1967, 3)

The concept of 'priority areas' emerged in the committee to incorporate these concerns with social disadvantage and educational need, housing and social work, immigration and school–home relationships. Available to the committee and its working parties was advice, experience and what Maurice Kogan calls 'disciplined observation' (B: Kogan, OU, n.d., interview), and elsewhere 'the recruitment of social science thinking' (B: Kogan, 1987, 19). Issues of social class and unequal opportunity were already of major academic and public concern, and in the pattern of discussion in Working Party 2 lies an interest which builds on such concern but addresses the salient issues of primary education in the particular context of social disadvantage.

The extent to which in their work the Plowden committee drew on American experience is interesting and significant in this connection, given the difficulties we have already discussed in interpreting British views of American policies and programmes in the 1960s. The Plowden committee visited a number of countries, including the United States for two weeks in May 1965. The committee was from an early stage familiar with some of the American developments, though in a very selective and unsystematic way. Some of the early evidence, including from the Nursery School Association, had referred briefly to the Ford-funded projects. Witnesses in discussion with Working Party 2 and others drew attention to recent American experience of cultural differences and their effect on children's performance in school. Bernstein underlined the difficulty of transferring American experience to British conditions. Young, Donnison and others had some knowledge and contacts, but most were established after the committee was formed. Papers by Deutsch and Riessman were circulated in the committee. Working Party

3, for example, concerned with the stages of education – including preschool – considered in some detail the implications of the work of Deutsch and Bernstein for an understanding of the lower school achievement of working-class children, had a number of Deutsch's papers copied and made available on loan to members of the working party. Donnison, who had visited the United States and had worked in Canada, had in fact had little academic experience of the US (and had no special interest in education) before the committee met:

I got to know more as time went by… There was a good deal of material I am sure a lot of us were reading at that time coming from the States… [The people we met in the US] were not people I already knew – one or two of them I had heard of, or read something of their work… (Donnison, interview)

Twelve members of the committee, together with members of the Secretariat and members of the Gittins committee on primary education in Wales, went to the United States, in Kogan's words, 'reasonably hopeful that the horrors of Harlem or Chicago's south side schools, or deep racial division, let alone a steep increase in the levels of unemployment among school leavers, could be avoided here' (B: Kogan, 1987, 14). Part of the time they stayed together, but for most of it they split into two groups with different itineraries. The New York visits included the Ford Foundation, Bank Street College and Deutsch's Institute of Developmental Studies. There was a meeting with Francis Keppel in Washington, and they visited schools, nurseries, universities, social work centres and others in Syracuse, Atlanta, Los Angeles, San Francisco, Chicago and elsewhere. Visits included a community school in New Haven, Connecticut, and a meeting with faculty and graduate students at Harvard's Graduate School of Education. The visitors therefore had contact with 'pre-school education for deprived children', projects on 'reversing social deprivation', programmes for 'culturally deprived' children, the training of 'teachers of the socially deprived', an internship programme for 'elementary teachers in disadvantaged areas', and other programmes and activities relating to school–community relations, programmes for 'slow learners' and a variety of teaching strategies that had become important in the American development of such programmes – including team teaching, programmed instruction, flexible scheduling, and parent participation. The visitors were clearly not unduly impressed by what they saw in most of the elementary schools. John Blackie thought 'we got awfully little from it' – Blackie having being particularly disappointed in the vaunted team teaching: it was 'no more new than anything we were doing in England' (Blackie, interview), and members of Working Party 4 on the curriculum seemed to share the disappointment in that and other aspects of the operation of the schools. Blackie thought that questions of disadvantaged children might have been of some concern to the visitors, but their principal interest in his view was 'how they ran primary education'.

Those members who were more interested in the questions of social disadvantage had mixed responses. At one level Donnison and Lady Plowden, for example, were unimpressed, again particularly by what they saw in classrooms (Donnison thought the examples of 'good practice' they saw were in a way 'behind Oxfordshire or similar places in Britain'), but the poverty-related experience was more important. Lady Plowden discovered that the parental involvement 'didn't seem to threaten the schools as people said it would'. In New York she felt that there were similar problems to the British ones and felt reassurance in the way people were handling them. Donnison, similarly, thought that they did not come back with a lot of 'directly applicable ideas or devices or procedures', but of real importance was the fact that some of the ideas being talked about in the Plowden committee were actually being implemented in the United States: 'it gave one courage to pursue proposals which we might have been more cautious about' (Interviews, Plowden, Donnison). Michael Young saw the roots of Plowden's emphasis on positive discrimination in the United States:

Influenced by what had been done before in the United States, the plea of the Report was for such 'positive discrimination' in favour of the underprivileged as would make the schools they attended first equal to those elsewhere and then better. (B: Young and McGeeney, 1968a, 5)

An enormously positive report to Working Party 2 on a day's visit to a community school in New Haven was echoed in the final Plowden report (B: CAC, vol. 1, 45–6). The two-page report on New Haven, as other written reports on specific topics relating to the visit, was circulated, discussed and considered in the drafting of the Plowden report. Nevertheless, as we shall see, very little of the American experience did appear in the final report, even though it was considered relevant at earlier stages. There was little or no attempt to recommend the importation of the kind of 'special programmes' that had emerged in the United States, and there was a recognition that the differences between the two countries were considerable in terms of the organization and operation of schools, differences between American perceptions of issues connected with race and those in Britain connected with immigration, and the general structure, financing and functioning of services related to education. 'Courage to pursue proposals' related more than anything else to the committee's elaboration of concepts of positive discrimination and educational priority areas.

Six working parties contributed to the production of the Plowden report, and each member of the committee took part in the work of at least two working parties. Working Parties 3 and 4, with their interests in preschool provision and the curriculum respectively, had overlapping membership and concerns with Working Party 2 for most of its life under the chairmanship of David Donnison. It was Working Party 2 that set the committee's main agenda in relation to 'social aspects' of primary education. Setting that agenda meant coming to grips with the meanings of deprivation in terms of individuals and families, cities and areas. The working party proposed to include in the final report a discussion of deprivation, explaining American programmes to 'reverse discrimination', underlining the different scale of social poverty and inequality in the United States, describing British situations where poor conditions had an impact on the level of educability and families were at severe risk. The working party, as we have seen, received evidence of these conditions and their relationship to schooling from various parts of the country, though in the documentation and in discussions with such bodies as the Fabian Society there was generally a lack of focus with regard to appropriate policies. The major survey research inevitably produced results after the working party had begun to formulate possible policy directions, though a report of the 1964 National Child Development Study, for example, was completed for the Plowden committee by April 1966. An interim report by Stephen Wiseman on research into the relationship between children's attainment in primary schools and environmental factors, was submitted in October 1965 (emphasizing the preponderant influence of 'home' over 'neighbourhood' and 'school' variables taken together). Young's research on parents and schools was begun with the Plowden committee specifically in mind, and a book of his suggesting some of the lines of interest that were to be crucial for the working party appeared in 1965 (B: Young, 1965). Although recent research on social class and education had been considerable, the working party and the committee knew that research relating directly to conditions in and affecting primary and preschool education was less so, for reasons we have previously discussed. The DES's own research fund had been established only a year before the Plowden committee was appointed (totalling £20,019 in the first year, but roughly six times that amount two years later), and an HMI Research and Publications Committee was not set up until after the end of the decade (Hopkinson, interview). In many respects, particularly in bringing data and analyses together from different disciplines and perspectives, the working party was in little explored and difficult territory. It was considering questions of race and immigration, for instance, knowing that in educational terms there was little systematic research or discussion, and gradually realizing – with help recruited from the Inspectorate and elsewhere – that the issues involved were more difficult than was generally understood. Discussions in the working party pointed both towards and away from treating the problems of immigrant children as special, or different from those of underprivileged children in general. Some of the evidence received by the committee focused entirely on resources and the availability of teachers. Race, in John Blackie's view, was not one of the things the committee was especially concerned with, because the problems in Britain were not as acute as they later became (Blackie, interview).

Working Party 2 began from the outset to disaggregate the problems relating to the analysis of primary schools in their communities, addressing questions of parent involvement, 'run down' schools, housing, delinquency, relationships between schools and the social services, school–community liaison and – particularly after the visit to the United States – the 'community school', seeing the primary school as a centre for community activity. Its members, particularly Michael Young, translated some of these concerns into discussion of and proposals for preschool provision for Working Party 3, where there was much discussion of whether the argument for the expansion of provision should be presented in connection with social deprivation or as important for all children. Underlying all of the investigations and discussion of Working Party 2 was a growing attempt to confront more systematically than had previously been the case in Britain the contexts of many primary schools, differently described in terms of deprivation, disadvantage – and poverty.

Much of the previous sociology of education had been within an analytical framework of social class, and by and large the working party members took that analysis and its implications for granted, and focused attention on the particular effects of poverty, poor environments, poor homes, the detailed conditions and outcomes of poverty. An early working party proposal – not included in the final draft – was to discuss the general evidence that educational attainment is associated with social class, a separate question, as the working party saw it, from whether poor home backgrounds affect educational performance. When the drafting of a chapter on children, their homes, schools and community, began at the beginning of 1966, the working party was anxious to indicate that the 'sharpest edge' of poverty had disappeared, but that 'real' poverty still existed. Data on food, health and housing were drawn from such sociologists as Abel-Smith and Townsend, Dorothy Wedderburn, Government Social Survey and other sources, though much of what the working party intended in this respect did not reach the final report. The emphasis in the working party was on unacceptably poor conditions, poor quality of life, and poor school buildings and classrooms. Parental attitudes, which figured large in the work of the Plowden committee and the survey research findings it received, were clearly seen in the working party as themselves related to social background and the parents' own education. In considering the impact of the environment on children's attainment the working party produced a number of draft formulations which indicated how far it had moved from by now familiar accounts of the operation of social class to the effects of poverty:

The fact is that, with primary as with secondary, the social changes of the last quarter of a century for all their pace and scope have passed some children by almost as if they had not happened, leaving the children marooned in the age of Hadow... in one way the absence of change has been as striking as its presence. People have been reshuffled in space against a backdrop which has remained obstinately the same. Divisions in society still exist. The poor are still poor. The children of the poor are still the children of the poor. (Working Party 2, March 1966)

Although formulations of this kind were not included in the final report, the intent and the concern were.

They remained principally through the adoption by the working party and the committee of the linked concepts and strategies of 'positive discrimination' and 'educational priority areas'. Members with different political outlooks recognized the appeal of the concept of positive discrimination. In the United States they had seen in operation the principle if not the exact vocabulary. As a Baltimore delegate to a National School Board Association meeting in April 1963 commented when reporting on their debates about improving education for 'non-whites': 'we must be prepared NOW to *discriminate* in their favor in the allocation of educational resources. To compensate means to do more which means to spend more' (A: FF, Baltimore, Phillips, 1963). At a late stage in the working party's procedings, with a terminology suggested by a DES official (B: Kogan and Packwood, 1974, 70), the concept became pivotal to the development of a strategy to deal with the effects of social, environmental and educational poverty. It meshed in with the search for criteria by which to decide on the distribution and concentration of resources, with the picture of areas of social deprivation offered by HMI Burrows and his London colleagues, and accounts of other areas. It was not until 1965 that the working party began seriously to elaborate an analysis of and policy for the 'socially deprived urban areas' addressed in Burrows's paper for the working party in October

1964. It pieced together the components of a picture of areas of concentrated disadvantage. In a subsequent discussion of the origins of the Plowden EPA scheme Donnison described it as encountering no opposition and there being no point at which anyone suddenly 'hit upon' it: 'it seemed the logical outcome of many years of social research', and of the Newsom committee's report *Half Our Future* in 1963 (B: Donnison, 1967, 3). The consensus is that Michael Young was the main architect of the proposals. He formulated ideas and drafted documents relating to them for working Parties 2 and 4, and introduced a discussion of their relevance to the expansion of nursery education at the committee. His, and the working party's, nomenclature for the scheme was not settled until almost the final stage of drafting, having ranged across 'development districts', 'educationally deprived areas', 'educational development areas' and other possibilities. Even early drafts of the Plowden report contained a chapter heading 'Educational Development Districts' or 'Areas of Special Difficulty'. The final title – chosen by either Michael Young or J.M. Tanner (Donnison, interview) – was only the final step in the piecing together of a picture, an approach and a set of principles on which to construct proposals.

In early 1966, as we have seen, Michael Young consulted Burrows and the London HMIs, who offered criteria on the selection of areas for the concentration of additional resources. The working party discussed possible formulas that could be used across the country without risk of distortion, including parents' occupation, assistance with school meals, national assistance, housing, educational standards, and particularly following Michael Young's lead, family size. In the spring of 1966, still using the language of 'areas of special difficulty', the working party was proposing to the committee that the report should emphasize the need for special 'discriminatory measures' in those neighbourhoods where a 'substantial minority' of children in need of them were concentrated. These were areas with a high proportion of low income groups, poor maternal care, large families, poor and overcrowded housing and other disadvantages, with educational and social results affecting secondary and higher as well as primary education.

Although the working party and the committee were conscious, and reminded themselves, that they were an 'education' commission, the direction they had set themselves at the outset had led to a concern with the effects of poverty and an analysis and proposals different from those conducted in the previous decade in approaches to education.

11   Plowden: making choices

The important aspects of the Plowden committee for us are the emphases we have seen emerging in the last chapter – contact with American ideas and practice in the war on poverty, and the elaboration of a strategy to combat the effects of poverty on education, not, as in the earlier concern with secondary education, to combat the injustices of social class with structural change. This approach to family and environmental poverty, 'area' solutions, preschool provision and the schools was to be carried into a variety of arenas not only as a direct result of the Plowden report, but also through the diverse agendas of debate and action it established. It would no longer be possible – as had been the case – for textbooks of the sociology of education to omit primary education, and discussion of educational priority areas in the report was to take educational research, policy and controversy in new directions.

The preoccupations of Working Party 2 and their drafting intentions became less sharp and explicit in the final report, though the basic intentions and proposals remained intact. Criticism of the report was to include a failure to take sufficient account of sociological factors, including particularly social class (B: Bernstein and Davies, 1969), and the over-reliance of the report and its commissioned research on the concept of 'parental attitude'. What has not been fully understood, however, is that the working party and committee deliberately chose poverty and related concepts as a more immediate and policy-productive context for the discussion of primary schools in deprived areas. The important weakness of the final report was not the absence of class but the absence of the sustained analysis of poverty, its realities, workings and implications, on which key sections of the report had been built. The report faithfully represented the outcomes of that preoccupation, but muted the preoccupation itself. This was not because those who did the drafting, including Lady Plowden herself who kept a critical editorial eye on all aspects of the final drafting, undervalued the attention to poverty and the social context of primary schools. Since

236

David Donnison, Timothy Raison and Michael Young had been placed on the committee, they made their priorities known and, in Lady Plowden's words, 'their voices heard' from the outset and the committee was a 'receptive body'. Lady Plowden's own background as a magistrate and her interest in the problems of families and the environments in which they lived, meant that their emphasis 'suited me very well' (Plowden, interview). There was no difficulty, therefore, in the EPA and other proposals reaching the final report, but they did so with the minimum of background explanation, in order to ensure that the focus of the report was perceived as being concerned with priorities for schools.

Five of the report's thirty-two chapters (including three concerned with future research, costs and a summary of recommendations) arose mainly out of the deliberations of Working Party 2, clustered in a section of the report entitled 'The home, school and neighbourhood'. A chapter on 'The Children and their Environment' focused on the 'power of the environment', including primarily the home. Post-war progress in material standards suggested that the grosser effects of poverty could continue to be removed, but social handicap among the children of semi-skilled and unskilled workers remained a reality, and educational equality could not be achieved by the schools alone. Starting from what earlier reports (*Early Leaving*, Crowther, Robbins) and the work of Douglas and others had demonstrated, the main question facing the committee was – what was it about home situations that mattered in relation to educational achievement? Floud, Halsey and Martin and others had helped towards an understanding of the influence of the home, including parental attitudes, and the latter had become a focus and finding of the National Child Development Study and Wiseman's work on Manchester. As a basis for the discussion and policy recommendations that followed this was a weak, even a peremptory, chapter, and reflected very little of the discussion of poverty, deprivation and disadvantage that had been at the heart of the working party's concerns and early drafting proposals. A second chapter, on 'Participation by parents', reflected both the work Michael Young had organized on behalf of the committee and the interest in the 'community school' that had been at least strengthened by the visit to the United States, and the chapter included, in its description of the New Haven community school visited, the only detailed account in the report of any of the American experience.

The third, and most crucial, chapter was entitled 'Educational priority areas', in a real sense the most substantial part of the working party's efforts that reached the final report. It explained past priority to new towns, and the prevalence in older cities of grim buildings and environments, with migratory populations and unappealing schools which failed to attract teachers and motivate pupils. These areas were in need of 'perfectly normal, good primary schools alive with experience from which children of all kinds can benefit'. Children in such areas were often educationally backward and teachers were often inexperienced. The educational aspirations of working-class families were rising, and an appropriate policy for the schools in their neighbourhoods was needed. The proposed nation-wide scheme was to help 'those schools and neighbourhoods in which children are most severely handicapped. This policy... colours all the subsequent recommendations in our Report'. Economic growth of itself did not solve problems. The principle already in operation by which government allowed supplementary grants to local authorities for particular purposes was a precedent for its extension to education: 'equality is not enough'. Districts where children and schools were 'most severely handicapped... need more spending on them':

We ask for 'positive discrimination' in favour of such schools and the children in them, going well beyond an attempt to equalise resources. Schools in deprived areas should be given priority in many respects... The schools must apply a compensating environment.

This last proposition, the report pointed out, was far from new and accorded with thinking and experience 'in many countries' (which in fact meant mainly the United States). Opportunity for children in such areas would only be the same 'if they have unequally generous treatment'. All local authorities where deprivation existed should be asked to adopt positive discrimination and regularly report on progress. The criteria for identifying educational priority areas and schools were outlined, though it was accepted that further study would need to be done before any formula was produced. They were: occupation; size of families; state supplements in cash or kind; overcrowding and sharing of houses; poor school attendance and truancy; proportion of retarded, disturbed or handicapped pupils; incomplete families, and children unable to speak English. The report also gave special attention to canal boat and gypsy families – probably among 'the most severely deprived children in the country' – but unlikely to be encompassed by such criteria.

A chapter on 'Children of immigrants' related to the increased numbers of immigrants in the previous decade, often concentrated in 'crumbling' urban areas, handicapped by 'unfamiliarity with the English way of living, by their language and too often by poverty and cramped living conditions'. It echoed current discussions about the possible need to disperse immigrant children where the concentration of non-English-speaking children operated adversely on the operation of a school. The report itself did no more than underline that if such dispersal took place it should do so 'with great care and sensitivity'. The chapter on 'The health and social services and the school child' elaborated the committee's call for social work to be developed in conjunction with schools and for relations between the schools and social services to be improved in various ways, in order to help families 'with difficulties that lead to poor performance and behaviour of their children in school'. Enmeshed in all of this were detailed recommendations which flowed ultimately from a concern with poverty in families, districts and schools, a concern that was more articulated in the originating working party than in the report itself.

Other chapters reflected related concerns that had been pursued in other working parties. The first chapter of the report, for example, on 'The children: their growth and development' included discussion of deprivation in relation to environmental factors, early adversity and the operation of social class and heredity. It considered children presented with the difficulty of transition to school from a social situation which did not prepare them for it, and included a brief discussion of the concept of cultural deprivation. A chapter on 'Providing for children before compulsory education' described the wide agreement among 'informed observers' that nursery provision was desirable 'on a substantial scale'. It concluded that a phased expansion of nursery education should begin with the proposed educational priority areas, and those neighbourhoods where general social conditions (such as high rise flats or lack of recreational space) made nursery education essential (B: CAC, 1967, vol. 1, chs. 3–7, 1, 9).

The Plowden committee was appointed shortly before the corresponding committee under Professor Charles Gittins which produced the report on *Primary Education in Wales* in 1968. In addition to the specific questions of the structure of schooling in Wales, bilingualism and rural schools, the Gittins report shared many of the preoccupations of the Plowden report, used many of the same research and other sources and produced many similar emphases. In one important respect, however, its emphasis was different. It indicated that research had shown that children were affected by their 'social and emotional environment as early as eighteen months and that a deprived or unstimulating environment can exert a lasting effect on the young child'. Nursery education played an 'alleviating or compensating' role in combating the effects of deprivation. Cultural deprivation might be the result of families unable to cope, but there was now more hope of preventing or reversing effects of deprivation if the process was begun early. Slow learners tended to come from families with low socio-economic status and poor educational backgrounds (B: CAC Wales, 1968, 67–8, 170, 428–9). This emphasis on early diagnosis and remediation pointed to somewhat different conclusions from those of the Plowden report which was ultimately more concerned with solutions based on areas. The Gittins report was less enthusiastic about educational priority areas, therefore, and Kogan felt that its reservations were based on a misunderstanding of the Plowden connection between social and educational conditions (B: Kogan, 1968, 127). There were to be different outcomes to the two emphases, on identifying children 'at risk', and on supporting deprived areas.

We have, of course, examined a particular focus in the work of the Plowden committee and in the report, but other working parties, the committee and the report had other aspects of primary education to consider. The underlying 'philosophy of primary education' of the report was variously described by critics and supporters alike as a statement of a liberal, progressive, child-centred or activity-centred approach to primary education. This philosophy was expressed most strongly in two chapters entitled 'The aims of primary education' and 'children learning in school', emphasizing 'individual discovery', 'activity and experience', 'personal discovery', 'opportunities for creative work', the complementary nature of work and play...as a basis – with equalized opportunities and compensation for handicaps – at all stages of education for the development of 'a balanced and mature adult', able to contribute to and look critically at society. Not all primary schools corresponded to such a picture, but it was 'a general and quickening trend' (B: CAC, 1967, vol. 1, chs. 15–16). The juxtaposition in the report of such a view of primary education and the strong emphasis on educational priority areas and related policies explains much of what was not included in the report, among other things any substantial reference to Bernstein, whose work on language had been of interest to the committee, but whose suspicion of 'discovery learning' conflicted with its basic philosophy.

The report was drafted by the Secretariat on the basis of the reports produced by the working parties as they went along. Members considered, approved or rewrote drafts, and Lady Plowden herself had a good deal of influence on its final shape (Plowden, interview; B: Kogan, 1973b, 92). While it reflected the research findings of the National Survey and other contributions we have discussed, it did not intend to be an 'academic exercise'. The report had behind it some three years of strong working party focus on social and educational factors

relating to poverty and disadvantage, and strong policies and recommendations to urge. This did not mean, in Donnison's words, that it
therefore 'disregarded evidence' or treated it in 'a biased way'. The
working party had to mobilize opinion inside the committee for a broad
concern with positive discrimination:

> We knew social class was very important, but we were not running an academic
> discourse about social class and education. There were a lot of books already
> available to do that. We were trying to present policy proposals and
> recommendations... I think we got more serious attention for social aspects of
> education than really any previous education report... it was very important to
> get the professional interests... in agreement and prepared to work together.
> (Donnison, interview).

Maurice Kogan and Stella Duncan, in drafting the report, and the
committee in giving it its final shape, had in mind not only the policies
that had emerged, and the bases on which they had done so, but also the
constituencies to be persuaded. The report left open some of the final
ambiguities to be solved regarding the precise definition and targeting of
areas, schools and children, as those concerned with any kind of
implementation were soon to discover. It reflected arguments from social
justice and efficiency, muted some of the earlier emphases of Working
Party 2 which had, for example, castigated many housing estates as
being 'cultural slums' and a system of schooling which produced 'half
educated children'. As Donnison and others suggest, coming close to
these realities and policies distanced the report to some extent from
wider arguments and, as we have seen, from some of its own mainsprings
of analysis. The massive emphasis on educational priority areas and such
related issues as parent–teacher cooperation, the coordination of
services, and the physical environment, sprang from the central drive to
bring past failures, the real condition of the schools and their contexts,
and new policies into the areas of government and public.

This also helps to explain why the American poverty programmes
faded almost completely from the final report. What remained were
desultory and mainly laconic references to Deutsch and other
sources, the preschool experiments to counter deprivation, and a few
euphemistic references to 'other countries', which sometimes meant
exclusively the United States. There are understandably only passing
references to team teaching and teacher education, and although the
New Haven community school survived into the text, almost nothing
else did. There is one reference to the American War on Poverty (B:
CAC, 1967, vol. 1, 60), which failed to get into the index. The ten direct
references to the United States in the report do not reflect the
committee's encounters with American evidence, projects, people and

ideas. One explanation lies, as we have suggested, in the disappointment with some of what committee members saw in American schools. This does not account, however, for the relative silence on federal, Ford and other area programmes and the American concern with the nature and implications of deprivation, and strategies to combat it, of which key members of the committee were keenly aware, and which all those who visited the United States or sat on Working Parties 2 and 4 in particular had addressed. The explanations are those discussed above in chapter 9. Early reports from and drafting in Working Party 2 did contain discussion of the American experience and this was dropped. Consideration of questions of deprivation and squalor amidst American affluence, and of how these issues were being tackled, were ultimately judged not to sit easily in the policy context being established by the committee. Pointing up the British education and social condition might be made more difficult by direct reference to American conditions and policies, which could be seen as deriving from different situations. Whatever strength the Plowden committee drew from the American experience was better silenced, given British interpretations of American differences based on extremes of poverty, race, juvenile delinquency, lack of central planning and funding machinery, and a weaker tradition of nursery and infant education. The consensus in the committee itself was not built on commitment to American analyses or solutions, many of which (for preschool or elementary school curricula, for example) were inimical to committee members emphasizing different traditions of early childhood education.

Timothy Raison, member of Working Party 2 and a future member of Margaret Thatcher's government, reflected when the report was published on the particular attention it drew to deprived schools in deprived sections of the country:

Their schools are old, the population – especially the abler part of it – is moving out, housing is lamentable, immigration presents acute problems, the social services are inferior, the atmosphere is one of demoralisation and teacher mobility is inevitably high.

Part Three of the report, on 'The home, school and neighbourhood', (containing the five chapters we have outlined) was, he considered, arguably 'the report's principal single contribution', with its proposal for the designation of EPAs and positive discrimination in their favour (B: Raison, 1967, 46). This picture and its attendant analysis and proposals marks the moment of transition from the British preoccupation with the effects of social class in relation to the secondary school, to a policy-focused concern with the effects of poverty. With weaknesses that were soon to be pointed out, the Plowden committee had sought not to debate social class but to interpret its workings in terms of the factors in the family and the environment that affected children's performance in the primary school, with parental attitude emerging as a suggested key factor. The committee had picked up the Newsom committee's important discussion – in *Half Our Children* in 1963 – of schools in 'slum' or 'problem' areas, of overcrowding and a drab environment, and turned it into a focused approach to the policy implications of poverty in schools and society. The report was called a 'climacteric as a statement of belief in social engineering', given the strength and extent of its proposals for action (B: Kogan and Packwood, 1974, 75). It had certainly altered the agenda of discussion about society and its schools. It had not declared war on poverty, but it had translated several strands of concern and analysis into the most important policy commitment yet formulated to tackling aspects of education in an explicit context of continuing poverty.

In the wide enthusiasm with which the report was greeted, the EPA proposals were received with especial warmth, in both main political parties, the trade unions, the educational organizations and the teaching profession. The press generally, with the exception of *The Daily Telegraph* (B: 16 May 1967), was supportive. From some quarters difficulties were voiced with regard to the designation of priority areas, including the danger of central government doing the designating. The Inner London Education Authority, endorsing particularly the EPA proposals, considering that these reflected existing ILEA policy, warmly endorsed the principle of positive discrimination and increased parent participation, but was reluctant to see the DES formally designating areas (and thought the labelling of schools would be harmful) (B: ILEA, Education Committee, 1 February 1967; Schools Sub-Committee, 29 June and 12 July 1967; *New Society*, 6 July 1967, 19). The National Union of Teachers thought the EPA concept matched its own view of the need for education to 'make good the deprivations suffered by some children', broadly accepted the criteria for designating the areas, but believed it would be necessary to designate some priority schools outside the priority areas (B: NUT, n.d., 2). *Education* thought the immediate impact of the report was greater than that of such previous reports as Newsom and Crowther (*15 to 18*) and reported a speech in which Michael Young had described the EPA proposal as the most important one in the report: 'The Plowden Committee is demanding that children in run-down schools in Britain's towns should at least be given justice. They have not had it since the war'. It reported meetings all over the country to discuss the report including one of over a thousand to listen to Lady Plowden, and a 'teach-in' – at which Michael Young gave his speech – at the London Institute of Education, which overflowed and had closed circuit TV in another hall (B: *Education*, 27 January 1967, 172, 176). The argument from the basis of poverty, disadvantage and the opportunity for a new policy direction had been broadly endorsed.

Debate in Parliament took place in March 1967. In the House of Lords, which was the first to debate the report, the EPA and related proposals attracted remarkably little attention. Lord Eccles (as David Eccles, a former Conservative Minister of Education) thought the idea of giving above-average resources to schools in deprived areas was 'really an extension of slum clearance, and in my view is wholly admirable in principle', though he foresaw great difficulty in choosing the criteria (B: House of Lords, 14 March 1967, 214). The most unambiguous support for the EPA proposals came from Lord James, Vice-Chancellor of the new University of York, a commitment which was to have an important later outcome. Support for deprived areas might have been an old idea, but what the report now proposed was 'genuinely radical':

Of course, we have long been aware of the way in which home and environmental circumstances ... affect a child's development and, in spite of the efforts of the school, make much of our talk about equality of opportunity sound like a joke in rather bad taste.

Newsom had provided the examples, Plowden had made 'hard suggestions'. Schools were only one agency for creating a better society, but these indicated means of helping to mitigate 'the effects of bad material and cultural background'. He strongly supported the committee's proposals for increased finance for the staffing and maintenance of priority area schools, and other proposals on the social services and the pointers towards criteria for the selection of the EPAs (B: House of Lords, 14 March 1967, 231). In winding up for the Labour government, Lady Phillips described the 'recognition of the deprived areas' as one of the most important recommendations in the report, but in the six sentences she devoted to it simply suggested that the Secretary of State would be looking into what could be done to find resources to 'give this some priority' (B: House of Lords, 14 March 1967, 264–5).

The House of Commons debated the report two days later, on the initiative of the Conservative opposition. Crosland, as Secretary of State, had a group in the DES working on the report and had not yet committed himself to supporting its recommendations. The debate was opened by Sir Edward Boyle, who had set up the Plowden committee, and on behalf of the Conservative opposition he now welcomed the report, its 'triumphant vindication' of the views of the pioneers of progressive education, and the emphasis on positive discrimination for EPAs. He used almost identical words to those of Lord James (in some places they were in fact identical) in his judgment of the importance of the proposals. He was looking to the Secretary of State to commit himself to financing at least the main recommendations in the report (B: House of Commons, 16 March 1967, 734–42). Crosland gave what he later described as an 'anodyne' speech (B: Kogan, 1971, 197), and was in general lukewarm and disappointing to many people. Although he had known the contents of the report for some six months, he was still unable to make a commitment to implementing recommendations, 'many (in Hansard he changed this to 'some') controversial, many fundamental, and many looking ahead to the late 1970s'. He thought the report's claim that primary education seemed always to get the worst treatment in class sizes, buildings and conditions and prospects for teachers was 'a little strongly worded' and blamed the Conservatives for having done nothing to remedy the situation in their thirteen years in power – a passage omitted in the Hansard version of the speech. On positive discrimination for EPAs, he thought it

a most radical recommendation, utterly convincing and a very striking illustration of what Professor Titmuss and others have recently been saying – that we cannot rely on economic growth alone to even out gross social inequalities.

He particularly welcomed the emphasis on partnership between parents and schools, but in focusing on some other detailed aspects of the report he was in general more concerned with criticizing his Conservative predecessors, pointing up the financial difficulties, and making a wait-and-see speech than in following through the spirit of his references to Titmuss and social inequalities (B: House of Commons, 16 March 1967, 750–63; Crosland, 1967). There is no doubt that the Departmental working group had succeeded in persuading Crosland not to commit himself too soon, and had catalogued for him the difficulties ahead in designating and financing EPAs.

Other Members of Parliament, particularly on the Labour benches, gave more determined support to the report, including its analysis of 'this rather long-suffering and neglected section of education' (B: John Forrester in House of Commons, 16 March 1967, 805). On both sides of the House, however, the EPA proposals were the leading priorities in speeches. Stan Newens, for example, believed the concept should apply to schools as well as areas – 'many slum schools still exist in good areas' (B: *ibid.*, 829). Shirley Williams, winding up the debate for the government, gave the most vigorous support to the EPA idea, which

goes far beyond the bounds of education alone. It is the concept that environmental poverty, poverty in terms of schools, in terms of turnover of teachers, in terms of housing, in terms of amenities – in terms of the total environment in which children live – can deeply affect educational achievement, and much of the most exciting research of recent years has pointed to this conclusion.

Children who 'failed' in that situation represented 'the failure of the system, not of themselves, and we need to put that right' (B: House of Commons, 16 March 1967, 843). There is a thread of analysis from that of poverty in the late 1950s through to Plowden's Working Party 2 and this kind of statement in 1967.

Immediate critical commentaries on the poverty focus, research data and interpretations of the Plowden committee were few in number, but built up mainly between 1969 and the mid-1970s. The most widely known became a chapter by Bernstein and Davies in a symposium entitled *Perspectives on Plowden* in 1969. This chapter, 'Some sociological comments on Plowden', was not so much an attack on Plowden as an attempt to suggest what sociological extensions to its arguments were needed. It did, however, point to the particular view of child nature and development (a 'horticultural' view) underlying the report and coming very close to being 'the semi-official ideology of primary education in this country'. It thought the report had omitted to consider the inter-relationships between 'the biological and cultural components of childhood', and an available perspective of social, economic and demographic changes. Although there was some recognition of social class, it seemed systematically to play down the importance of social class in education. The interpretation of the survey data in terms of parental attitudes as a major factor 'leaves open...speculation about the origins of the attitudes which parents exhibit' (B: Bernstein and Davies, 1969, 56–64). This last emphasis was to arise in other critiques, and had in fact already done so in a review in the spring of 1968 by American David K. Cohen of the second, *Research and Surveys*, volume of the Plowden report. Cohen thought that the focus on parental attitudes was important, but was surprised at the analysis diminishing the 'explanatory power of the traditional education-occupation measures':

It is curious that such an effort was made to focus attention on the importance of attitudes, and to reduce the importance of the social- and economic-class variables. It is tempting to speculate that this is related to the fact that attitudes might be changed by 'persuasion,' while the class variables would lead in the direction of structural social and economic change. Programmes of 'persuasion' are cheap, and disturb no one; structural change costs dearly, and even its prospect typically stirs great anxiety. (A: Cohen, D.K., 1968, 333–5)

Cohen's comments address both the choice of variables in the research, and the use made of the data. His statement of policy alternatives misses the historical dimension in the difference between the Plowden policy direction and the 'structural' implications of previous secondary-related analysis.

Glennester, in 1969, also followed the path of criticizing the analysis of 'attitude', but applauded the committee's work in extending what was known about the relationship between environment and attainment at school: 'in particular they have taken us beyond the unhelpful categories of social class and have established the main causal link to be that of parental attitudes'. It was the precise nature of the relationship between those attitudes and children's attainment that remained unexplained. The committee's time-scale, he suggested, had prevented it from making effective use of research to reinforce policy recommendations. There was, for example, no sustained survey of the 'slum areas' which were a focus of the committee's report, but 'if the Plowden Committee decided well on in its discussions to advocate priority areas there would be no possibility of initiating a major study of areas of the kind they were contemplating' (B: Glennester, 1969, 197–203). As we have seen, that was exactly the case. From 1971 Acland mounted an attack on the Committee's data and their interpretation of them. He believed that the evidence did not support confidence in EPA-type programmes effecting any significant change. Only a small percentage of lowest achieving pupils were in 'EPA' schools, the EPA aims were too diffuse, and the need was to concentrate resources not on areas but on underachieving children (B: Acland, 1971a, 450–3). Reworking the data Acland concluded that the variable of parent involvement was less important than those of class and income. Schools as at present constituted could not improve the position of the disadvantaged child (B: Acland, 1971b, 507–10). As American research was also suggesting, in Acland's view schooling played a smaller part in effecting change than was once thought, and on this and other issues he believed that the Plowden committee's thinking had been mainly done before any of their research became available; that parental attitude in fact equated social class, culture and income in determining academic attainment, and the committee's research did not in fact, support its findings and policies (B: Acland, 1973, v, 4, 234; 1980, 34–44, 48–50). Working on a 'Compensatory Education Project' in Manchester, Morton in 1969 described the preschool and positive discrimination proposals as 'liberal recommendations...intended to help a large group of children to 'adjust' to the alien (to them) culture of the schools and thereby to 'succeed' in later life. They were a 'minimal alternative' to doing nothing or pursuing a more radical policy of 'transforming the institutions of education and all other functionally-interrelated elements of the social structure' (B: Morton, 1969, 3). Other critiques in the early 1970s continued to stress that attitude could not be separated from variables related to the social situation of families (B: Bynner, 1972, 1975; Batten, 1975). Others probed the 'area' concept, suggesting that Plowden had based its analysis on the inadequacies of children, not of existing resource distribution, and had misunderstood social class, treating it as a form of 'behaviour' and not of 'relationship' (B: Byrne and Williamson, n.d., 21; Byrne et al., 1975, 7). Plowden's methodology relating to EPAs was described as misguided methodology, based on a fallacy that occurs 'when ecological methods of analysis are used: when aggregated or averaged data are used to characterize areas or institutions'. The fallacy had led the Plowden committee to a basic mistake: 'most poor families do not live in poor areas... it seems likely that the majority of disadvantaged children are not in disadvantaged areas, and the majority of children in disadvantaged areas are not disadvantaged'. Concepts like 'disadvantage' and 'deprivation' were a 'convenient shorthand' for many different social situations (B: Barnes and Lucas, 1974, 50–1, 56, 65). Most of these critiques were in terms of the shortcomings of the Plowden research, or the use made – or not made – of it. What systematic research the committee did in fact commission came after some of its main policy directions were undoubtedly well established. Once established there was, as Glennester – without knowing the specific circumstances – suggests, no possibility of initiating research in the time-scale available. The committee and its working parties looked, as they went along, primarily to other kinds of evidence.

The members of the committee were not unduly concerned to defend the research basis of their exercise, though on various occasions the secretary to the committee, Maurice Kogan, discussed the criticisms. His reflections have explicitly adopted a stance that Lindblom and Cohen most directly elaborated in the United States – 'research' is only one of the contributors to policy formulation, common sense or 'ordinary' knowledge being another (A: Lindblom and Cohen, 1979). Much of the writing with which Plowden was concerned was 'informed impressionistic writing', based on information from knowledgeable people familiar with the field, 'not research but disciplined observation'. Michael Young, for example, had brought into the committee the outcomes of 'exceptional work in East London', ethnographic work which anticipated methods that might have been used widely if Plowden had taken place ten years later (B: Kogan, n.d., OU interview). Although this was Kogan's response to critiques such as those of Acland, he felt that the Plowden approach did reflect some of the 'social science optimism' of the 1950s and 1960s (B: Kogan, 1973a, 1). David

Donnison held to the view that a crucial part of the Plowden argument was the existence of multiply deprived people in multiply deprived areas, though he recognized the need to bring clarity into the arguments for priority areas policies. While sharpening analysis of such questions as scale of the area in which to concentrate resources and policies for the services which so far failed to reach the poorest population, he continued to believe it essential to ensure that more and more services were designed 'to concentrate the richest mix of resources on people and areas with the greatest need'. The Plowden recommendations had been intended not merely

to identify a few schools in special need of help but to persuade education authorities to adopt a general policy of positive discrimination through their schools of the sort which housing and personal social services have long tried to follow (inadequate though their performance may too often be). (B: Donnison, 1974, 130–3)

F.M. White, head of a preparatory school (and one of four head teachers or deputy heads on the committee), reflected that the committee had differed from Hadow in that 'our predecessors had under-estimated rather than exaggerated the differences between children and of the homes from which they come'. The effect of parental attitudes had not been previously fully understood, nor had 'the cultural bleakness of many of the homes; particularly the absence of books: 'Hence our recommendations for the Educational Priority Areas' (B: White, 1967, 15). Eric Hawkins, Director of a Language Teaching Centre at the University of York, who had been particularly active on the committee on questions of education and immigration, reflected that Plowden had attached a new importance to 'nurture' or 'environment' as opposed to 'nature' or 'mental endowment' in determining a child's success in school. The 'silent revolution' of the 1944 Education Act had been an illusion, and the committee's emphasis on home environment and parental involvement in children's education was vital:

The hazard that poverty once represented may have been removed. The schooling is free, right up to university degree level. But if the home environment is 'discouraging' and if the teachers have not learned and practised techniques for 'persuading' or 'teaching' parents to encourage their children the damage to the child's educational prospects may be just as final and as predictable as ever was caused by poverty or malnutrition. (B: Hawkins, 1968, 19, 28)

Interpretations in the Plowden committee of the nature, extent and implications of poverty and disadvantage had clearly not been uniform, and the validity of some of its conclusions needed to be tested. What is clear from the report's immediate reception, the research-related commentaries, and the reflections of members of the committee and others associated with it, is the strength with which the educational priority area concept, and the social realities from which it sprang, had been projected into public consciousness. The Seebohm committee, reporting in 1968 on the social services, indicated the growing attention to the relationship between a child's environment and educational development. It quoted the Plowden committee's views on parental encouragement, and commented that it had received much evidence to show that there was 'grave concern among teachers, educational administrators and others over children who may be educationally crippled by a variety of social handicaps', and a desire for 'a more concerted attack upon the problem than the present services have been able to provide' (B: Committee on... Social Services, 1968, 63). Members of the Plowden committee met informally in December 1968, some two years after the report was published, to consider progress in its implementation. Government finance had included a £16 million building programme over two successive years announced in 1967, a major research project on educational priority areas, other research activities, and other allocations made under a new Urban Development Programme (commonly called Urban Aid) announced in 1968. The group issued a statement in January 1969 indicating that 95,000 copies of the report had by now been sold, with important international resonance. It regretted that the DES had 'formulated no systematic policy in response to this Report', but welcomed the piece-meal progress that had been made, including the recognition of EPAs by the Department of Education and Science, 'as defined by criteria very much in line with those suggested in the Report'. It indicated some of the local decisions that had been taken, with regard to special allowances for schools, 'teachers' aides', welfare assistants, help for immigrant children, and other developments. By this stage also the Council for Educational Advance was collecting detailed information on what was happening in the local education authorities, and it published its forty-nine local reports in May 1969, with a foreword by Lady Plowden. Of the four main fields in which there had been advances, she believed the evidence indicated, one was a greater emphasis on the child learning as an individual, and the other three related to EPA or EPA-related concerns: a greater emphasis on preschool provision, the need for greater partnership between home and school, and recognition of the EPAs – 'and the beginning of the giving to them of extra help – in teachers, in ancillary help, in building, in nursery provision' (B: CEA, 1969, 2). The Burnham committee responsible for teachers' pay had by this stage also agreed on bonus payments to teachers in priority areas.

Both the emphases and the outcomes of the Plowden report were greatly different from those of other reports which had addressed educational priorities in the previous two decades.

By the end of 1967 the American war on poverty was three years old, had been launched in a glare of optimistic publicity, and was struggling to fulfil its educational and political promise. In Britain poverty had been brought into focus, and the Plowden committee had transformed the policy agenda of education, but there was no declared war. The problems addressed were recognizably similar, but with major differences that provoked British resistance to or silence about the prior American experience. The end of the 1960s in the United States was to see conflict between, on the one hand, confidence in the existing ESEA, Head Start and other programmes, and their extension into the Follow Through programme from 1967, and on the other hand, strong and sombre evaluation messages of the effectiveness of such programmes. Other programmes, directed at cities and their ghettoes, at urban and social renewal, with an educational component, also waxed and waned. The conflict was to continue to be fought out in the 1970s in ways which, while 'war' was no longer a credible image for what was happening or intended to happen, might be said to constitute a serious campaign. In Britain, the work of the EPAs, Urban Aid, a generation of Community Development Projects and other policies directed at the renewal of run-down areas of cities, also took shape. A continuing 'campaign' in various forms was also a suitable image for British policy making.

The Plowden committee had, in altering the policy agenda, given weight, if not necessarily firm direction, to a number of the agenda items, apart from what it proposed about primary education in general, its organization, curricula, principles and practices. By and large both the committee and its commentators considered the EPA proposals to be its main contribution and we have seen how this represented a shift of emphasis for educational discussion and policy. Locating deprived children and schools in their 'ecology' in the ways the committee did was a considerable advance on a discussion of 'slum schools' in, for example, the Labour Party's 1959 manifesto, or the 'slum areas' or 'problem areas' of the Newsom report (B: Labour Party, 1959, 2; Ministry of Education, 1963, chs. 2 and 3). The focus on areas pointed the committee towards the function of schools – including their function as 'community schools' and in their relationships with parents – and towards seeing schools in their necessary relationships with other social services. The EPA recommendations saw the school as a mechanism for 'funneling resources to disadvantaged areas to compensate for these disadvantages' (B: Little and Mabey, 1972, 93), and situated schools and children firmly in the contexts of the social needs and services that influenced the condition of the family and the attainment of children. It is at this point that the Plowden report turned aside from direct treatment of social class, and where – as in the United States – the explicit starting points of poverty and class could be seen to point to different policy outcomes.

The report brought together, in fact, the preoccupation with class that had been concerned, within education, overwhelmingly with secondary reorganization from the mid-1950s, and the concern of some sociologists with the growth of specific forms of poverty, the distribution of social resources and the role of the social services – a philosophy of comprehensive social action (B: Townsend, 1966, 11; 1967, 1–3). The Americans Miller and Roby, in a book edited in Britain by Peter Townsend on *The Concept of Poverty*, suggested as an aim 'to recast approaches to poverty in terms of stratification', and to show that stratification theory 'can be refined and modernized through understanding of poverty action'. Casting the issue of poverty in terms of stratification led to 'regarding poverty as an issue of inequality'. A new focus for theory arose from an awareness of the realities of people's lives and of the available forms of action (B: Miller and Roby, 1970, 124–7, 143–5). In this case, as in others in the British experience, class theory was being not overturned or bypassed but made to consider the ways in which poverty was being experienced, conceptualized and addressed. Inequality had not, before 1967, been cast in terms of primary education, with the principal exception of the work of Basil Bernstein. Titmuss and colleagues had shown in fields other than education that economic power and social inequality had to be analyzed not only in terms of grand theory, but also in terms of the realities of the welfare state, its poverty and inequalities – with the attainment of greater equality becoming harder as cruder injustices were blurred and new forms of injustice and inequality developed and needed to be understood and confronted (B: Titmuss, 1960, 17–30). The EPA and related proposals were in a sense the translation of such messages into educational terms.

This was a social landscape of complex changes, one that the politics of race, for example, was only just beginning to enter, and into which the politics of gender had not yet significantly entered at all. A suggestion that Plowden underestimated race (B: Winkley, 1987, 45) does not take account of the fact that Britain in general 'underestimated race', and that Plowden was the first educational report to give prominence to issues of race in education. It gave prominence to all situations where the disadvantaged might benefit from 'positive discrimination' or 'compensation', and the fact that 'compensatory education' became a 'vogue' expression (B: Chazan, 1973a, 1), does not weaken the Plowden commitment to redressing inequality and disadvantage by a variety of education-related means, even if, as Cohen suggests, they were not to be structural or expensive. Plowden gave prominence to social science explanation, even if – in the spirit of the times – there was as much over-optimism in doing so as was present in the American policies of previous years. It gave prominence to a different approach to policy formulation from the approaches of its predecessors. If it is difficult to define the approach and the policies as liberal or radical or conservative (or some mixture of these) or some other vocabulary, it is because there is a permanent tension between grand ideological schemes and a concern with people in contexts. This makes the use of such vocabularies itself a complex act of ideological commitment.

Part III
Following through

12 United States: planned and unplanned variation

From 1967 and through the 1970s the American war on poverty subsided, fluctuated, but continued, in some of its original forms, in new forms, with the same or different emphases, and new efforts to understand and evaluate the educational strategies by which the campaigns were or could be conducted. Head Start and Title I of the ESEA remained central policy pivots, joined particularly by Follow Through, new local and state-wide projects, new sponsors, new figures in the landscape. There were other continuities, however, in the shadow of the doubts cast by the Coleman report in 1966 on the effectiveness of schooling, and from 1969 by a dispiriting report on Head Start from the Westinghouse Learning Corporation and Ohio University. Evaluation was to be the watchword of 1970s policy-making and funding, and in relation to all the major programmes it was to become increasingly – and contentiously – part of an attempt more reliably and publicly to judge their principles, procedures and outcomes. Head Start, Title I and Follow Through looked to new and diverse models of educational practice and in doing so spawned questions of comparative 'effectiveness', giving rise to a generation of academic consultants and commentators, and professionals sited in project or state-wide or district education offices. Evaluators helped to plan campaigns, and walked with the troops, judged their successes and failures, and established evaluation as a branch of educational campaign management, as of other types of legislative and executive warfare.

The interests of some of the pioneering projects remained essentially the same: to experiment, particularly at preschool level, with intervention approaches that would equip children from disadvantaged environments with the skills, confidence or motivation to overcome the effects of disadvantage, to succeed – on some measure or combination of measures – in and after school. As the children in these experimental groups moved into school and beyond, the interest was also, therefore, in follow-up studies to try to analyse the effects of preschool participation over time. Such long-term analyses on a broad basis were to prove

257

important in the 1980s, but throughout the 1970s projects such as those of Deutsch's Institute and the Early Training Project of Susan Gray and colleagues at the Peabody College, Tennessee, maintained a momentum of research. The Early Training Project, for example, had begun in 1959 (six years before Head Start), with a focus on a combination of different kinds of skills (sensory, 'abstracting', 'mediating', etc.) and attitude development. Having begun by thinking 'naively that it was possible to design a program that would be strong enough to offset the early handicaps that these children experienced', the naiveté proved short-lived (A: Gray, Klaus & Ramsey, 1981, 216). The confidence of the early reports on the project was not dispelled, but attention had to be paid to the way an initial rise in ETP children's measured intelligence was eroded in the early grades of schooling, that is, after the end of the intervention (A: Gray and Klaus, 1970, 918). Studies were to show that by the end of full-time schooling there were no traces of the early intervention in the 'intellective performance' of former ETP participants, but that there were enduring effects of a more general nature, including successful passage through grades (particularly in the case of young women). The loss of effect in terms of 'intellective performance' was explained by the small amount of input from the intervention programme by comparison with the massive effects over the years of the children's surroundings (A: Gray et al., 1981, 254). Poverty and its effects were resistant over time to preschool intervention as measured solely by intelligence or narrowly specific academic outcomes.

Federally planned programmes which came out of the Economic Opportunity Act or other legislation in the early war on poverty continued and – in some cases – were enhanced. The Teacher Corps, for example, was a feature of the 1965 Higher Education Act, intended to attract and prepare people to become teachers in areas with concentrations of low-income families. It did this by giving liberal arts graduates a brief (possibly eight-week) training period at a college or university, followed by an 'internship' in a group working with a professional teacher as team leader. Between 1966, when the programme began, and 1973 when an account and evaluation was published, several thousand such students and experienced teachers had been through the programmes. This, like other American programmes, and the EPA projects in Britain, was an 'action programme', and one of the interesting products of this and other programmes was to be a recognition not only of the differences between an 'action programme' and 'action research' on the one hand, and other kinds of research, but also of the tensions these differences aroused within the programmes themselves. Something like the Teacher Corps might need to be flexible and loose in design and objectives, but to be clear and precise for researchers following and evaluating the action. Between action personnel and researchers, therefore, in the United States as in Britain, there was room for conflict both in planning and in judging outcomes. The results of the Teacher Corps were by 1973 being judged to be disappointing, in part as a result of under-funding and conflict over the respective positions of the federal government and the teaching profession (A: Corwin, 1973, 1–5, 31). A more optimistic account of the Teacher Corps, prepared by the US Department of Education at the end of the decade, was based on a series of changes in the programme. From the initial focus on training new teachers to work in low-income population schools it had moved from 1974 towards a focus on the retraining of teachers, and then from 1978 to projects which demonstrated 'institutional change in colleges and universities and school systems'. The aims remained the same, the strategies tested and adopted changed (A: OECD, 1980, 237–53). In the case of the Teacher Corps, as with pre-school programmes, there had been increasing difficulty in identifying the relationship between intentions and outcomes, given the diffuse nature of both, and concern about how to judge those activities which had outcomes not easily, if at all, amenable to measurement. By the end of the 1970s, Teacher Corps was requiring detailed objectives addressing 'the diversity of needs represented by a multi-cultural school population', looking forward to further evaluation, reporting that children in areas with concentrations of low-income families benefited from 'more services, more individual attention and some innovative techniques', but the hoped-for impact of the programme on teacher education remained 'an open question' (A: ibid., 238–9, 252).

Upward Bound, supported by the Office of Economic Opportunity from 1966, as a 'precollege preparatory program designed to generate the skills and motivation necessary for success in education beyond high school among young people from low-income backgrounds and inadequate secondary school preparation', could (like the Teacher Corps to some extent) be judged by the number of students it supported. Within two years, for example, some 26,000 students a year were taking part in summer programmes run jointly by school teachers and college faculty, and receiving additional tutorial and other support during the pre-college and college year. On and off college and university campuses permanent services for Upward Bound students were being established (and administration of the programme was transferred in 1969 to the Office of Education) (A: US, DHEW, OE, 1969, 1–2; Greenleigh, 1969). Upward Bound, like the preschool programmes, involved both the targeting of a constituency but also the search for appropriate skills, delivery and learning methods. Here, as in most of the war on poverty programmes, there was not only continuing but also increasing interest in questions of language. Books on teaching disadvantaged children invariably focused on language, 'language arts', communication, reading and the findings – which did not cease to be controversial – of psychology, socio-linguistics and other academic fields relating to language. American interest in Bernstein's work continued, with his articles being frequently quoted, discussed and reprinted (A: e.g. Keach *et al.*, 1967). Continuing discussion of 'cultural deprivation' or the 'culture of the poor', regularly pointed to the analysis of language issues (A: Persell, 1977). Expanding interest in what a 1982 book titled *The Language of Children Reared in Poverty : Implications for Evaluation and Intervention* included detailed attention to mother–child linguistic interaction, suggesting, for example, the language skills that children from poverty backgrounds did possess, the differences in speech between these and middle-class children, and the frequency of certain kinds of language function in school settings (A: Farran, in Feagans and Farran, 1982). Bernstein's work continued to have an impact on all of this, surrounded by controversy, rival theories and misunderstandings, but never far from the argument.

One of the significant features of the late 1960s and the 1970s was the extent to which states and districts took the lead in developing programmes modelled on those of the mid-1960s or trying out new ground. A typical account of the many listings of one kind or another that became common in the 1970s is an account of the operational details of *Educational Programs that Work* by the Far West Laboratory for Educational Research, reaching its seventh edition by 1980. Apart from the local versions of national programs, it described such new ventures as an Early Prevention of School Failures in Illinois (an early screening programme); MECCA (Making Every Child Capable of Achieving) in Connecticut; Project Real in New Hampshire (providing comprehensive services for low-income children and their families), Project STAY (School to Aid Youth, mainly early identification of social, emotional and academic needs, in order to prevent school dropout), and a host of others. Acronyms were the order of the day. New Jersey had a programme to motivate alienated and apathetic disadvantaged youth in middle-class suburbs (Project Mobilization) (A: Carl, 1970). California and other states had summer institutes to train teachers of disadvantaged youth (A: Stone, 1969). Medford, Massachusetts, had an Operation RISE (Recreation–Instruction–Service–Enrichment), involving a range of summer field strips, medical screening, nutritional and other objectives (A: Medford, 1969). A three-year project begun by Marie

Hughes in Tucson in 1965 was concerned with the intellectual development of Mexican-American children, and blossomed into the Arizona Center for Early Childhood Research, became a Research and Development Center in 1972 and one of the Follow Through programme sponsors from 1968 (A: Hughes *et al.*, 1973; Tucson, 1975). Many of the projects were either directly or indirectly concerned with child health and welfare, counselling, delinquency, dropout, or following up the effects of 'summer learning and the effects of schooling' (A: Heynes, 1978), or of precollege programmes for minority and other disadvantaged youth (A: Yinger *et al.*, 1977). Some programmes were innovative, some were deliberately traditional. A Motivation Program by the Philadelphia school district, for example, from 1965 and throughout the 1970s, operated a highly structured, academic model directed at curriculum and cultural enrichment, counselling, parent and community involvement. By 1978–9 over 12,000 students had graduated from the programme, and 81 per cent of these had completed college. In 1979 3,200 students at nine high schools were taking part in the programme, there was an associated staff development programme, and the goals were declared as maximizing student potential, motivation and staying power, self-awareness, and desegregation (A: Philadelphia School District, n.d., 1978–9, 1979).

In considering the extent to which education had become a key element in social policy making in this period, it is important to underline the ways in which education was incorporated into nation-wide policies whose purpose was not primarily education. The Job Corps, for example, was concerned with basic education and skills training at residential centres for 16–21-year-old people living in poverty. The Corps was in fact instructed by the Economic Opportunity Act to develop and disseminate new techniques for educating disadvantaged youth (A: Levitan and Johnston, 1975, 1–2, 65). The Model Cities Program grew out of a task force report in 1965, and represented – as did many other of the mid-1960s programmes – a faith in rational planning, in this case to solve recalcitrant urban problems. Amidst all the attention given to the coordination and improvement of services, renewal, and coalitions to drive urban policy in new directions, education appeared as an important element. Education, it was made clear, could not solve the problems of the cities, but they could not be solved without education (A: Briggs, 1969, 30). The city schools had their own problems at the same time as being called upon to do more and better, and doubts were being expressed about the ability of schools in a programme like Model Cities to contribute effectively to special efforts directed at poor housing, poor amenities and disadvantaged conditions in general (A: Campbell *et al.*, 1969, 1–12; Taylor, 1969, 15–18). Since the Model Cities Program had the same requirement for community participation as other Economic Opportunity legislation, expectations were raised that the poor could strengthen their educational involvement under the programme. A study of attempts at community participation in a St Louis Model City Community School Project, in 1968–70, indicates how difficult, frustrating and abortive such an attempt could be, given hostility to popular involvement from mayoral, bureaucratic and established service directions, including education departments (A: Smith, C., 1977). The Model Cities blueprint and its educational components faded against the opposition of entrenched positions, limited budgets and bureaucratic resistance to change (A: Frieden and Kaplan, 1977).

Despite the difficulties, and the political and economic changes of the late 1960s and 1970s in the United States, a significant momentum of activity against poverty and disadvantage therefore continued. The district and state, public and private, efforts signal how successfully the policy intentions of the mid-1960s had been disseminated, and their pursuit through the 1970s can already be seen in the kind of project and programme we have, however fragmentarily, begun to indicate. In addition to such activities, however, there were three clusters of nation-wide efforts that are most central to a discussion of the anti-poverty efforts that survived in educational forms into the 1980s: Head Start and related preschool and early childhood programmes, including growing interest in the role and involvement of parents; attempts, notably but not exclusively under Follow Through, to prevent gains made under Head Start from being lost in schools, experimenting with special programmes operated in the schools; Title I of ESEA and related activities. In all three cases there were contingent and contextual questions, notably regarding poverty, and its relationship to issues concerning minorities; the evaluation of policies and their effects; the meaning and significance of compensatory education; the roles and effectiveness of schools; whether or not the war on poverty had been lost, could be won, or had ever been really started.

Head Start was from the outset a mixture of high ideals and confused – some called them chaotic – applications on the ground, enthusiastic reports and doubts about the lasting effects. It made a rapid transition from being a summer programme to a year-long programme, and by the beginning of the 1970s had developed a major interest in curriculum development, which continued throughout the 1970s with a greater concern with the quality of delivery. An expansion took place in 1978–82, and Head Start began to form part of the new long-term analysis of programme effects (A: Hubbell, 1983, 1–2). Head Start had not only survived, but the Economic Opportunity Amendments of 1978 increased the budget and strengthened local determination of eligibility criteria (A: US Congress, House of Representatives, 1978, 24–5). At several points the future of Head Start had looked uncertain, particularly once negative evaluations of the long-term effects of a Head Start experience had begun to appear. In 1969, a presidential message to Congress by Richard Nixon proposed to change and limit the role of the Office of Economic Opportunity, and in doing so he directed that Head Start be transferred to the Department of Health, Education and Welfare. He took the opportunity to indicate the disappointment there had been that its long-term effects appeared to be weak. However:

This must not discourage us...it only demonstrates the immense contribution the Head Start program has made simply by having raised to prominence on the national agenda – known for some time, but never widely recognized – that the children of the poor mostly arrive at school age seriously deficient in the ability to profit from formal education, and already significantly behind their contemporaries.

It was also clear that the schools 'as they now exist are unable to overcome this deficiency'. What was needed was a *greater* focus on 'those few years which may determine how far, throughout his later life, the child can reach' (A: Nixon, 1969, 1823–5). Head Start continued, but the primary concern remained the 'wash out' effect that took place when the child transferred to the regular school. From 1967 there were attacks on the use of IQ as a suitable measure of Head Start outcomes, on its aim to prepare for formal schooling, and on the goal conflict between Head Start and the schools, which stressed curriculum, following instructions, teacher leadership, etc., reversing the participatory direction taken by Head Start (A: Brazziel, 1968, 297; Greenberg, 1967, 315). As other evaluators were to continue to indicate, the difficulty lay not with Head Start's ability to enable children to make significant cognitive, motivational and other progress but with the schools, which were unable to sustain that progress (A: Datta, 1971, 66). Critiques of Head Start itself ranged from the lack of adequate training for and skills of the teachers, the conservative attitudes of organizers or teachers, unclear objectives and, in general, the gaps between intentions and practice (A: e.g. Bissell, 1973).

One attempt to overcome some of the weaknesses was the development in the late 1960s of 'planned variation' in which different models of programme and child development were deliberately brought into play on an experimental basis. Although this approach was more consistently adopted in the planning of Follow Through, Head Start went in this direction, only to discover the difficulty of making any reliable judgment about the relative success of different programmes, more or less structured, more or less cognitively oriented, or with other variations of emphasis. Eight models were introduced, and some claims for success were made where the teachers felt that the model 'sponsors' (the psychologists and others who designed the models) had something important to offer, and where there were adequate facilities and support available. Whether differences between the models were large or small children in these 'planned' programmes made greater gains on some measures than other children (A: Bissel, 1973, 79–80, 104). Others found that there were in fact no differences between children on planned variation programmes and other children, that there were few differences in terms of effectiveness amongst the models, and that planned variation had been introduced with insufficient preparation, time and resources, with weak experimental design and unclear objectives. There was a need nevertheless to carry on with careful planning (A: Smith, M., 1975, 107–8; Rivlin and Timpane, 1975, 14–21). In many respects Head Start continued to be at the heart of debate about community action, and therefore to be subject to conflict over policy relating to the involvement of the poor, or as some saw it, imposition on the poor (A: Levin, T., 1967a, 1967b; Levitan, 1969a). Head Start tended to be less vulnerable to such criticism since it had involved parents and the community in its activities to a large extent from the beginning.

In a number of ways Head Start moved increasingly from a child-centred to a family-centred process. The original intention to involve parents in the running of local Head Start programmes was strengthened in the mid-1970s by the adoption of 'performance standards' which encouraged parent participation, as well as providing services aimed at raising the educational awareness and support of the home. Some efforts to involve whole families were short-lived for lack of support from the Office of Economic Opportunity, but continued nevertheless (A: Charms et al., 1971). There was increasing recognition from the end of the 1960s, however, that parent involvement in the programme was the most important factor in lasting achievement – alongside the education and re-education of the professionals involved (A: Mendelsohn, 1970, 451–2). Head Start parents were therefore engaged as far as possible in the education of their own children, but were also engaged as volunteers or as paid employees in the programme – as well as often playing an active role in the control of the programme or as advocates or protagonists in relation to it, and to issues connected with it. Parents were also involved in other ways, for example through related programmes, including Home Start, which combined home-based and centre-based activities, a Child and Family Resource Program, which made 'family-oriented, comprehensive child development services available to children from the prenatal period through age eight', and Parent and Child Centers, providing 'health and developmental services to low-income families with children under age three' (A: OECD, 1980, 197). Various attempts were made during the 1970s to combine Head Start and other day care and child development services more systematically. A bill to provide additional and comprehensive help for children and expectant or nursing mothers had been vetoed by President Nixon in 1969, but from 1971 more successful congressional action produced support for more coordinated child development programmes linked with day care services and other family support. Research also began to focus on the impact of Head Start on families and communities as well as on children (A: Kirschner, 1970).

A review of research on Head Start from 1969 to 1978 analyzed fifty-nine research reports. Seven years later an 'analysis and synthesis' of all Head Start research to date covered 210 project reports (A: Mann et al., 1978; McKey et al., 1985). Head Start, like all the war on poverty legislation and programmes, including ESEA, superimposed a requirement for evaluation on the underlying intentions and optimism, with an increasing demand for reliable investigation, and an unbroken difficulty in reconciling the measures and instruments of evaluation with the elusive processes of action and response. Evaluations of Head Start and its impacts fall roughly into four periods. First, as we have seen, there were the immediate and continuing positive reports from the localities, troubled but not basically affected by early adverse judgments on the failure of gains to survive the initially brief summer programmes. Parents particularly were reported as enthusiastic about the Head Start effects, including changes in the children's behaviour at home, their health and learning improvements carried into the first grade (A: Broman, 1966; Brazziel, 1966–7). In general, researchers, commentators and the US Office of Education were satisfied that there were immediate effects, possibly short-term but potentially longer-term, as well as positive outcomes for teachers, parents and communities (A: Gotts and Pierce-Jones, 1968; Brazziel, 1968; US, HEW, Office of Education, 1968). One left-wing view from 1966 pointed to the 'hodge-podge of conflicting ideologies and interests', confusion, ambiguities, lack of purpose and leadership, inexperienced and useless evaluation, dreadful locations, lack of equipment, and contradictory instructions, all helping to explain both the early negative outcomes and superficial impression of success. Even this account, however, thought that education need not be a 'dead end' in the war on poverty if it took place 'with an emphasis on democratic purpose and respect for children's integrity' (A: Meier, 1966, 24–36).

The second phase began with the publication of the Westinghouse report of the 'evaluation of the effects of Head Start on children's cognitive and affective development', in 1969. From this point Head Start can be seen to be emerging from its impressionistic phase into one of attempts to base judgments on more sustained research, as well as critical evaluation of what had been produced so far. Westinghouse emphasized that, quoting the Office of Economic Opportunity, previous evaluation had been 'limited in scope and weak in design'. It had been voluminous but, the researchers concluded, 'scattered and inconclusive', repetitive, and merely a point of departure. It had not compared randomly drawn 'treatment' and 'control' groups, or in other ways followed necessary 'truly experimental' procedures. Such research had therefore not offered any clear evidence that 'compensatory efforts had produced meaningful differences on any significant scale or over an extended period of time'. The study's own findings included such positive data as success in encouraging parent participation, and parent approval of the programme and its influence on their children. The central conclusions, however, were that summer programmes had been ineffective in producing any persistent cognitive gains or affective development, and that full-year programmes were 'marginally effective in terms of producing noticeable gains in cognitive development that can be detected by the measures used in grades 1, 2, and 3, but are ineffective in promoting detectable, durable gains in affective development'. The summary conclusion of the whole study was that 'summer programs are ineffective and that full-year programs appear to be marginally effective' (A: Westinghouse, 1969, 15–16, 20–6, 243–5).

The report was quickly attacked as attempting to measure a 'total effort' in narrow cognitive terms, and as using sampling and evaluation methods which failed to understand the educational significance of Head Start and the ability of Head Start children to carry their gains through into the first grade, and in the case of urban black children, longer' (A: Smith and Bissell, 1970). Cicirelli, who had directed the Westinghouse study, defended its methodology and data against vigorous attack, expressing the disappointment of the researchers at not having been able to announce positive findings (A: Cicirelli et al., 1970). What followed was partly a battle over the data and interpretation, partly an acceptance of the underlying message and a search for explanations. Given the lack of staff training the findings were 'no great shock' (A: Miller, J.O., 1969, 14). A summary of research on the effects of Head Start from 1966 to 1969, including Westinghouse, looked for the factors which influenced child development, curricular differences, the balance of intention towards cognitive or social and emotional growth, and the potential of alternative strategies for family intervention (A: Datta, n.d.). The same analyst emphasized that negative evaluations reflected funding delays, the difficulty of training thousands of community people, and the fact that the field of education for preschool disadvantaged children had been created over a five-year period 'from the ground up' (A: Datta, 1971, 58–9). *Whose* failure, it was asked, was really under discussion – that of Head Start, the schools, the home environment, the lack of coordination among them...? (A: Stearns, 1971, 171).

Until the mid-1970s, a third phase was one of continuing puzzlement not only about Head Start's 'failures' in practical terms, but also about the conceptual and theoretical basis of compensatory education, cultural deprivation, the culture of poverty, the purposes and instructional assumptions of the programmes. Head Start at the same time continued and expanded, with an annual average enrolment of nearly half a million. There were those who reported discontent among staff at the centres (A: Payne *et al.*, 1973), others who reported increased competence among community participants (A: Shipman, 1973). Attempts were being made to sharpen the Head Start goals and incorporate the latest research on language or parents or the curriculum. Edward Zigler, Director of the newly created Office of Child Development, was dismissing the Westinghouse study as 'a rather shallow and poorly done evaluation' and, with some decline in the popularity of the programme, taking on 'the honest battle of trying to convince the decision makers that Head Start is a successful program' (A: Zigler, 1971, 142–3). From the mid-1970s and into the 1980s, the fourth phase saw increasing confidence in Head Start's ability to survive the complexities of changes in policy, funding, research and evaluation findings and conflicts of ideology. Evidence was accumulating of the conditions in which Head Start and preschool programmes in general could be most successful (A: Datta, 1975; Grotberg, 1977). Positive outcomes for children, families and communities were being identified over a longer time-span, and as reliance on standardized testing procedures as a basis for judgment of Head Start declined. Zigler and Valentine, in a major retrospective survey in 1979 treated Westinghouse as an indictment of the schools, underlined the need to move away from 1960s fallacies which included brief tokenistic programmes and naive environmentalism, and attacked the dominance of IQ in the making of judgments, something which should never have been allowed. Head Start was a success if not judged by that measure (A: Zigler and Valentine, 1979, 148, 368–9, 495–6). A range of analysts commented on lasting effects of various kinds, for various groups of children, in particular conditions (A: e.g. Takanishi, 1977; Seitz et al., 1981; Hodges and Cooper, 1981; McKey et al., 1985). Much of what was now being indicated was part of wider research and judgments about preschool education. Some of the judgments being made in the early 1980s arose out of consideration of more sophisticated research or more critical reflection. In some respects Head Start was seen to be more successful because of the impact of research, but in other respects policy was seen as still being too out of touch with research (A: Caruso and Detterman, 1981, 184–6). It had revealed throughout its career how little was known about childhood learning and development in the family. It had surpassed the early naive expectations, accomplishing 'everything but what it was originally supposed to accomplish: equal educational opportunity' (A: Slaughter, 1982, 3).

The 'revolution' in preschool and early childhood education of the mid-1960s was one that encompassed Head Start and the forms of experimentation and development that we have discussed, and the evaluation process was directed primarily at increasingly detailed understanding of their effects on their prime target – children from poverty backgrounds. The range of preschool programs directed to this end rapidly widened from the late 1960s. Sesame Street, for example, was not designed specifically as children's television for the disadvantaged, but the process of evaluation and the uses made of the programme soon established that it had a major presence in the compensatory education field (A: Sprigle, 1971; Ball and Bogatz, 1973). A more intensive focus on methods (including Montessori) and curriculum was accompanied by widening research on the respective impacts of different types of programme, often in the language of 'traditional' and 'structured', with an increasing accent on the effectiveness of the more structured preschool programmes (A: Weikart, 1967, 1972, 1981).

Concern was frequently expressed in the 1970s at the weaknesses involved in the conflict of underlying principles in the preschool field, or the failure to develop an adequate theory of preschool education, incorporating understandings of 'learning deficits', enrichment, the nature of language development, and elements other than the 'shaky' theory based on individualistic psychology (A: Blank, 1970; de Lone, 1979, 139). What was a theory and what was a strategy was not always clear, and in the development of new models there was indeed a mix of the pragmatic and the analytical. The Tucson Early Education Model was designed to build on children's own language usage, to develop motivation through play, and to incorporate British 'open education' methods (A: Tucson, 1975; Fillerup et al., 1976). The Ypsilanti Early

Education Program – which, in Britain too became one of the most influential – aimed to apply Piagetian principles to the preschool (A: Kamii, 1973). The Karnes preschool programme for the children of low-income families was a structured, cognitively based programme, as was the much publicized preschool work of Bereiter and Engelmann (A: Karnes *et al.*, 1974; *Report on Education of the Disadvantaged*, 1971). Public school systems established their own preschool programmes under the auspices of Title I. Working with children in special programmes was increasingly understood to be insufficient, and the relationship between preschool and school, preschool and home and community, was coming under greater scrutiny. One year of a self-contained programme was not enough of an answer. Questions of language, invariably at the head of the agenda, pointed beyond the preschool in all directions. A review of the position in debates about language deficit in 1977 reviewed the work of Cazden, Bernstein and others (including Bereiter and Engelmann, whose highly structured programmes treated children as if they had 'no language at all'). In summary the report found that invalid criteria were being used to evaluate minority students' oral performance; there was a failure adequately to investigate the repertoire of verbal skills; there was a widespread assumption that the use of non-standard language implied a cognitive deficit; and the properties of language were still insufficiently explored (A: Hill, C.A., 1977, 1–12). From 1972 the federal Office of Child Development funded the 'Home Start' programme to involve parents more in the educational development of their children, to support them in various ways in doing so, to supplement centre-based programmes, to explore the range of options in early childhood education. In the 1970s, issues of psychology and theory, language and curriculum, increasingly underlined the need to establish Head Start and other preschool programmes firmly in the context of family and community, and the development of work with parents was a central outcome.

Across the United States programmes were explicitly seeking to bring preschool teachers and mothers closer together, and increasingly to make the mother the primary agent in infant education. Federal programmes regularly legislated for parental involvement in planning and control. 'Parent programmes' became part of early childhood education. Colorado had an Added Dimensions to Parent and Preschool Education project. Washington state had Project Home Base, 'helping parents to teach their own'. New York had a Mother–Child Home Program of the Verbal Interaction Project to increase mothers' interactive behaviour. Missouri had a Parent–Child Early Education

Program, incorporating a Saturday school (A: Far West Laboratory, 1980, 3, 23, 26, 30). 'Home visitation' became a widespread feature of preschool activities, often explicitly aimed at parent education. Research was focusing on parental, especially maternal, attitudes, verbal interaction with children, or use of toys and play. As with early preschool developments expectations were often high and indeed impressive outcomes were being recorded – for the parent, the child directly concerned, and siblings (A: Powell, 1982; Slaughter, 1983). The most promising programmes were being identified as those using 'mothers as teachers', and the most lasting effects were being associated with the strength of family interest (A: US, Senate Select Committee, 1972; Bronfenbrenner, 1974).

Controversy in this connection centred on the meaning of involvement, and further 'blaming of the victims'. In the former case, Head Start, Title I and other programmes looked for a variety of ways in which parents could be involved in the educational process, when some were reluctant or intimidated, others were active and responsive. In some cases token efforts were made to involve parents, in others strong parent organisations evolved to ensure that they were 'participants' not 'recipients' (A: McLaughlin, n.d., 65). Centres and schools were in some cases ready for the partnership, in other cases they had to be pressured to accept it. Some influential mother–child home programmes developed, and under Head Start and other auspices Parent Child Development Centres or similar institutions were established. 'Involvement' therefore came more and more to mean 'education', and evaluators turned attention to the elements, styles, intentions and outcomes of specific parent education programmes (A: Clarke-Stewart, 1981; Goodson and Hess, 1978). The accusation of 'blaming the victims' was articulated particularly by Schlossman in 1978, describing parent education as the panacea of the 1970s, and another way of labelling the family as deficient: if parent education failed then the blame would be on the parents. Education was directed against maternal neglect and legitimated a 'new domesticity'. Blame attached not to a lack of economic resources, but to 'differential child rearing knowledge'. The home-based approach 'symbolizes on a small scale the conservative social philosophy that has triumphed...in the 1970s' (A. Schlossman, 1978, 788–808). Harmon and Zigler responded: Schlossman had misrepresented the policy-makers' perceptions of the role of parent education, ascribing to them 'self-serving, cynical, or naive motives', and arguing alongside other critics that parent education was 'a tool of repression of the poor'. Schlossman had decried the shift away from centre-based programmes, but 'no such shift ever took place'. He had used the Westinghouse report as part of his argument, but that had been 'fairly quickly discredited'. Schlossman's analysis lacked 'evidence from the real world', and what little he had was chosen to fit his assumptions, which added nothing to 'the debate over the appropriate role of parent education in a total strategy to help contemporary parents achieve their goals for their children' (A: Harmon and Zigler, 1980, 439–51). Preschool education and its location among interventionist strategies against disadvantage was operating differently, in a different environment and on a different scale from that of the mid-1960s, but was no less open to political controversy.

Follow Through was born in 1967 out of the first critical evaluation of the inability of Head Start to maintain gains once children were in school. Robert Egbert, the first director of the programme, described it to a committee of Congress in 1974 as 'a programmatic and legislative afterthought'. After the Wolff and Stein evaluation of Head Start Sargent Shriver proposed a follow-up for Head Start children, President Johnson requested $120 million for a programme for up to 200,000 children, and the programme was authorized in December 1967. It was therefore intended to be a service programme, but an almost immediate reduction in the funds allocated – to $15 million – produced a dramatic change in the design of the programme, and it shifted from a primary commitment to 'service to children' to 'finding out what works'. Follow Through 'now focused its attention on developing, examining, and refining alternative approaches to the education and development of young, disadvantaged children'. It became an experiment, not in 'the traditional, laboratory sense', but as a design for 'a bold assault on the institutional inadequacies that penalize children of poverty and ethnic minority groups'. This tension between its conception as social action and an experimental programme was to be central to Follow Through's development (A: Egbert, 1974, 121–3, 126–8).

The intention to build on Head Start remained. The document which set up the administrative framework for Follow Through laid down that in the school year 1968–9 it would serve 'children who were involved in Head Start or other quality preschool programs for disadvantaged children during the school year 1967–68 and/or the summer of 1968'. A statement in June 1967 had already announced the launch of thirty pilot projects 'to reinforce the gains that children make in the War on Poverty's Head Start program', quoting Commissioner of Education Harold Howe II:

Follow Through is an exciting new development in elementary education that will offer the disadvantaged child a very real chance to meet, on a competitive basis, the challenge and opportunity of education...The central concept of

Follow Through is to bring together the resources of school, community and family to help the child.

It offered individual diagnosis and prescription, using specialists and new teaching techniques, teacher aides, psychologists, social workers, doctors and others. Parents would be involved in planning and operating Follow Through programmes (A: FT, Memo [1967]; FT, Fact Sheet, 1967). It settled down to work within the broad but ambiguous and potentially difficult definition that this implied:

> Follow Through is a research, development, and evaluation program designed to identify, develop and validate approaches to the education of low-income children in the early elementary grades. Follow Through is the largest educational research and development program ever undertaken. (A: Cherian, 1973, 3)

Beginning amidst the 'clouds of doubt' (A: Cohen, D.K., 1975, 148–9) that already surrounded the preschool programmes and the ability of schools to sustain the effort, and tailoring itself to the budget drastically reduced from the initial expectations, Follow Through quickly turned 'approaches' to the education of disadvantaged children into alternative 'models'. A series of meetings in 1967 and 1968 brought together Head Start, Title I and other activists, specialists in early childhood education, and the programme developers, people who had some standing in the field of new programmes for 'young, poor children' (A: FT, Meeting, 1967; Egbert, 1974, 123). What had emerged was the idea of programme sponsors coupled with local projects which would work with the sponsors. This 'planned variation' experiment was, in the words of one of the sponsors, 'a major gamble. Everyone was betting that well-implemented educational models could produce large gains among children from poor families on tests of academic skills' (A: Hodges et al., 1980, 2). An experiment of this kind on this scale was indeed unique and reflected a familiar level of optimism, though in this case derived in large measure from the experience of the sponsors, the explicit intention to discover what did and did not work, and therefore a very substantial commitment to built-in national and local evaluation. There was, from the outset, a decision that local projects would have to secure 'the direct participation of the parents of Follow Through children in the development, conduct, and overall direction of the project', though not all model sponsors fully accepted the principle (A: FT, Manual, 1969, ii; Hodges et al., 1980, 8). There was an underlying message that existing school experience was inappropriate for Head Start children, given the rigidity of curricula and teaching methods, and as sponsors began to be involved in local projects in schools, and as parents were involved to the extent of hiring personnel, resistance began to grow from teachers and their unions (Green, interview).

School districts were nominated by their state agencies to take part in Follow Through, and in addition to the 40 pilot projects, 51 new ones (out of 225 nominated) were added in 1968, and more than 70 in the following two years. Fourteen sponsors were involved at the beginning, increased to 20 a year later – partly under pressure from block consultants to identify minority sponsors (A: Egbert, 1974, 124). Each Follow Through site (either a single school or group of schools) chose a model from the ones available, and the sponsor became involved in planning the programme, evolving materials, training staff, providing for monitoring and evaluation. As a large-scale, complex action research programme, and given uncertainties surrounding the purposes of Follow Through, it was bound to give rise to evaluation difficulties at both the site and national levels. There were, for example, to be problems relating to the ability of the various national evaluations that took place to evaluate not only outcomes, but also the degree to which models were actually implemented, in what circumstances, and with what levels of support and constraint (A: Hodges, 1981, 21–5; Hodges et al., 1980, passim). In 1971 the children being served were being described as 43 per cent 'black', 13 per cent 'Spanish-surnamed', 33 per cent 'anglo', and 6 per cent 'Indian' – with 80 per cent of the total as 'low income', and 48 per cent having had Head Start, and 17 per cent Title I or other preschool experience (A: US, HEW, 1971).

Some of the sponsors – of whom there were eventually twenty-four – shared the same theoretical underpinnings to their models, reflected in their approaches to child development, cognition, structures or informal pedagogies, but there were also considerable differences, and therefore confusions in the overall presentation of Follow Through's aim, and in approaches to implementation. The process of 'pairing' sites and sponsors began at a 'hectic' four-day meeting in Kansas City, Missouri (A: Elmore, 1975, 31), and there was clearly great merit in inviting sites to choose their sponsor, and then in the partnership. The planning for divergence did not, however, make for an easy overall sense of direction or, as was soon discovered, for an easy evaluation of 'what works' – given the varieties of programme, site, control, management, quality of staffing and support, and involvement by school district and state personnel. Some Follow Through projects differed from others in being sponsored by the local school district or by parents and not being linked to a programme model (this applied to the original pilot sites), but the majority fell into three groups, as defined by the first national evaluation of Follow Through in 1971. The 'Structured Academic' approach emphasized academic skills and concepts. It included Engelmann and Becker's (University of Oregon) 'Direct Instruction' model, 'carefully controlling the sequence of tasks presented toward the child's growing level of competence', and Bushell's (University of Kansas) 'Behavior Analysis' model, emphasizing the mastery of basic skills, using a system of positive reinforcement. The second group, using a 'Discovery' approach, aimed at children's autonomy and self-confidence in learning, rather than the transmission of specific knowledge and skills. It included the 'Open Education' programme of the Education Development Center, Newton, Massachusetts, aiming to create (explicitly along the lines of British primary schools) 'classroom environments which are stimulating and responsive to a child's individual needs', and to promote self-directed learning, and the Bank Street College of Education approach making the classroom a 'rational and democratic situation in which a child's positive image as a learner and a person can develop', with an emphasis on learning how to learn. The third, 'Cognitive Discovery' group was more disparate, including Weikart's High/Scope (Ypsilanti, Michigan) 'Cognitively Oriented Curriculum', based on an understanding of the 'processes underlying mental development', emphasizing the thinking and communication skills the child will need in school and adult life, and Ira Gordon's (Florida Educational Research Development Council) 'Parent Education' model, training parents to supervise children's learning in the home, designing school teaching to be easily adaptable to the home, and educating school personnel to support parents' contribution (A: Bissell, 1973, 89–93; Cherian, 1973, 11–55).

The Follow Through sites chose the programme sponsors deliberately and carefully, having in mind their own situations and confidence in what the approach could do to support their constituencies of disadvantaged children. The Atlanta school system, for example, with the involvement of some of the Head Start teachers chose a 'Matrix Games' programme (later renamed the 'Interdependent Learning' model) offered by Lassar Gotkin of the Institute for Developmental Studies in New York. The intention was to improve reading attainment and the model seemed appropriate. Gotkin ran a four-week summer workshop for local Follow Through teachers and aides in the first year, focusing among other things on classroom organization. He returned in September to check on such things as classroom layout, and it took months of effort to get it right. The problems of implementation proved considerable (Lewis interview). Attention continued to be devoted to parent involvement, support services (including nutrition, social, health and psychological services), and staff development (A: Atlanta FT,

1971). A consultant's report on progress from 1968–74 talked of significant impact in the kindergarten, first and second grades, found nothing but enthusiasm for the project, considered 'reasonable goals' were being reached, and put achievement down to institutional strategies, teacher effectiveness and the inputs of the model sponsor (A: Atlanta FT, 1974). The Individualized Early Learning Program sponsored by the Learning Research and Development Center at the University of Pittsburgh sought to adapt instruction to individual differences, believing that there were characteristics shared by all children 'regardless of socioeconomic or cultural differences' (and that the greatest differences were *within* groups) (A: Wang *et al.*, 1980, 1–4). Of the seven sites which chose the IELP model one was the Randolph County schools in West Virginia. The model was attractive because it combined a structured curriculum and behavioural objectives with the development of basic academic and social skills at a rate and in ways tailored to the needs of individual children. The emphasis was on early success, an open learning environment, and parent involvement. It was a mixture which suited the educational and economic conditions of this isolated rural Appalachian area (A: West Virginia FT, RCounty, n.d.). As a result of working with the Pittsburgh programme a report in 1974 believed there to have been 'educationally meaningful increases in achievement', with Follow Through students achieving at or above the national norm in the areas tested (A: West Virginia FT, RCounty, 1974, 23–4).

Across the Follow Through models and sites, therefore, there was common concern for educationally under-achieving children in economically disadvantaged conditions, and for the most appropriate approaches to classroom environments, curriculum openness or structure, teaching style, the acquisition of knowledge and skills, and learning to learn – with different combinations, emphases and strategies. From the outset there was awareness of many of the difficulties and shortcomings of the overall scheme, including, for example, a warning from the director that many of the original models did not 'address themselves to institutional change', and recommending the development of new models that would focus 'on change in roles of teachers and administrators within the context of the school system rather than exclusively on children' (A: FT memo, 1968). Other problems emerged, many of them due to the erosion of the funding as a result of inflation, others to implementation difficulties associated with ambiguous aims. The national administration forecast difficulties associated with child-centred programmes which under-estimated the importance of child–teacher–parent *relationships*, or which trivialized instructional approaches (A: FT, meeting, 1968). A discussion of the concept of planned variation in the mid-1970s concluded that there was some scepticism about the strategy, but that there was a consensus amongst those concerned that it should be continued, more carefully planned, overcoming some of the weaknesses resulting from its rushed introduction, lack of sufficient planning and resources, weak experimental design and insufficiently clear objectives (A: Rivlin and Timpane, 1975, 14–21). By the second half of the decade the basic problems of evaluation were prominent.

National evaluations of the effectiveness of Follow Through ran into the difficulties arising from tackling too many models and sites with all their varieties and complexities, or too few to produce a 'representative' judgment. The methodological obstacles were considerable, and the many evaluations led to vastly conflicting judgments, evaluations of evaluations, in all a considerable bulk of description and comment which produced a variety of conclusions. By the end of the decade Follow Through seemed to some to have been 'successful but outlived its usefulness', implementing the project had 'not been as easy as we thought' (Eichelberger, interview). The evaluations seemed as much concerned with the legitimation of evaluation as a profession as with anything else (Haney, interview). Federal education programmes in general and Follow Through in particular could not be judged to have been a success or a failure, as both 'seem equally unverifiable':

There is growing evidence that compensatory instruction increases disadvantaged students' achievement in basic skills, but the beneficiaries of federal programs have made up little, if any, of the ground between themselves and their higher-achieving peers. Special federally-funded services are part of a much broader set of influences on children's academic performance...the truth is hopelessly tangled up in the complex and shifting context in which the programs operate. (A: Hill, 1981, 12–13)

The model sponsors' own views at the end of the 1970s was that Follow Through had achieved: 'increased academic achievement and improvement in school and home environments for many children; advances in the development of comprehensive instructional approaches; creation of alternatives for training and support of school faculty and staffs: progress in involving parents in the educational and political processes of schooling; knowledge about the potential of model-sponsorship (third party) as a way of improving schooling; new information concerning evaluation methodology for large- and small-scale field studies' (A: Hodges *et al.*, 1980, viii). Controversy continued into the 1980s around site as well as national evaluations, the difficulty of making judgments when experimental groups were not hermetically isolated from control groups, when criteria for the allocation of children to Follow Through projects were not uniform, when children were 'successful' in different ways, for example, in mastering information or learning problem-solving techniques. Site variations as well as curriculum content and pedagogy determined 'success', as was pointed out in discussion around an evaluation which indicated that 'direct instruction' was the most effective approach (A: Tavris, 1976, 73; Gersten, 1984, 411–12). Intense controversy around the Follow Through evaluations in the late 1970s arose to a large degree out of its being 'borne out of ambiguity and raised under conflicting expectations' (A: Haney, 1977, 291). It had become a 'porcupine of issues' (A: House and Hutchins, 1979, 1). As with Head Start, however, site participants, local administrators and model sponsors remained confident at the end of the decade that they had, in spite of all the difficulties, extended the range of approaches available to support the education of disadvantaged children. With Follow Through as with other programmes the difficulty lay in demonstrating precisely which approaches, and precisely which of their elements, 'worked'.

By focusing sustained attention on alternative approaches to children's learning, classroom practices and organization, Follow Through contributed to a rapid development of interest after the 1966 Coleman report in whether schools did, in fact, 'make a difference'. Clearly some disadvantaged children achieved more than others, some teachers and programmes were more 'successful' than others, some schools did 'better' than others. Interest gathered momentum in the ingredients of 'effective' teaching, curricula and schools, and the mosaic of programmes and evaluations formed part of a research and policy emphasis in what was to become a national and international movement to investigate 'effective schools' and the contributory factors to their success or failure with these or other children. Follow Through therefore became a bridge between the uncertainties generated by the first negative evaluation of Head Start, concern about the traditional roles and capabilities of schools, and doubts about the possible effects of schooling on the one hand, and a rigorous analysis of the characteristics of schools on the other hand. In the 1970s it was Title I of ESEA that continued, however, to be the main standard bearer of federal attempts to raise the achievement levels of children from poor families. Amendments to the Act, changes in funding formulas, concerns in the early 1970s about Title I implementation, and Congressional and other scrutiny of its effectiveness, at no point undermined it as a central policy thrust of the educational war on poverty.

Between 1967 and 1974 Congress altered the funding formula,

introduced incentive grants to states which exceeded the national norms for efforts in elementary and secondary education, required the National Advisory Council on the Education of Disadvantaged Children to report on the most promising programmes, and then finally mandated the National Institute of Education to undertake a major evaluation of compensatory education, including those 'financed by States and those funded under authority of ESEA Title I'. It was to submit an interim report to Congress in 1977, and then a final report the following year. The NIE mandate of 1974 followed several years of criticism of various aspects of Title I implementation. There were major instances of obvious non-compliance with the terms of the Act, particularly the use of Title I funds to 'supplant' instead of 'supplement' their existing educational expenditures, and failure to target Title I funds on eligible children ((A: Washington Research Project, 1969; McClure, 1982, 445–6). Government and the courts took action to secure compliance in many instances, including a judge's order in 1973 that Title I funding was not to be approved for Philadelphia school district until it complied with various requirements (including non-supplanting) (A: *Inequality in Education*, 1973, 86). What was involved in these cases was either inadequate administration and a failure by the states to monitor implementation (A: Murphy, [1970]), or in some cases deliberate abuse and misallocation of funds. All of this was, however, a small part of the background to the 1974 mandate, as in the states generally the machinery of implementation and evaluation was becoming more experienced and accountable in the operation of Title I programmes.

By the mid-1970s the states and districts had devoted considerable energy to interpreting and applying eligibility criteria and evaluating outcomes. In the reports from the states it was constantly being emphasized that individual children were not to be declared eligible for Title I services on the grounds of poverty, whatever criteria were used for the identification of eligible schools. West Virginia's Title I Reading Improvement Program was announced in 1976 as 'for educationally disadvantaged students', though, as the St Louis public schools were told in 1970, poverty was an 'accepted predictor of learning disability' (A: West Virginia, 1976; Missouri, St Louis, 1970, iv). Identifying the 'neediest' children was therefore a process which was to end in a statement of 'educational disadvantage', but which had poverty criteria applied along the way. It was the starting point of Title I as a poverty-related programme that underlay Republican Albert Quie's battle in the House Education and Labor Committee and in the House to change the direction of Title I into an exclusive concern with 'educational disadvantage'. Although by 1974 he had failed in this attempt the 1974 mandate for an evaluation was to a large degree an attempt to use the evaluation instrument as a means of keeping Quie's idea alive, to 'buy Quie off' in the words of one person interviewed. The NIE was asked to investigate not only the purposes and effectiveness of compensatory education programmes, but also 'the ways of identifying children in greatest need of compensatory education'. The mandate arose out of concerns which included 'the effects of altering the definition of poverty used in the Title I allocation formula', and 'the feasibility of using measures of student achievement rather than numbers of low-income children in the formula' (A: NIE, 1977a, ix–x). The NIE study was also to go considerably beyond previous attempts to evaluate the effectiveness of Title I.

The NIE study produced reports on the administration of compensatory education, services, the allocation of funds, the effects of services, and other related concerns, including the current formula for Title I funds allocation, and *Using Achievement Test Scores to Allocate Title I Funds*. Among the findings of the study was the conclusion that 'program effectiveness' had not been judged in any real sense by previous evaluations because in the early years Title I programmes and services had often been distributed indiscriminately in districts, so that evaluations were unaware of which children eligible for programmes had or had not received them (A: NIE, 1974, 14). Running through the reports is the conclusion that Title I had made its impact through its use of well-qualified teachers and small classes, as a result of which children in the programme had made relatively important gains which they had been able to sustain, and that Title I was accomplishing its intended purposes (A: NIE, 1977b, vii; 1977d, v; 1978a, 3, 87). It acknowledged that measuring outcomes was difficult given the diversity of programme aims, but one important general outcome was the fact that states had been encouraged to commit their own resources (A: NIE, 1977b, xiv; 1978b, 13). It made recommendations for the future operation of programmes, including the need to review the 'pull-out' system by which Title I children were taught separately for part of the time (A: NIE, 1977d, vi). It also concluded that the present funding formula did not need any fundamental change, and that a move to allocate funding on the basis of a national testing programme would be impracticable on the basis of existing testing and resources. Such a testing system would cost $53 million and take three years to establish. A change from poverty to achievement eligibility would produce effects within states, but not across regions (A: NIE, 1977e, vi; 1977f, v–vii). Between 1965 and 1978 Title I had served over 45 million children, and the study had found its management to be sound and state variations to stem largely from an unclear legal framework and differences in the size of staff. There were weaknesses that were being addressed, but two of the senior researchers in the study were left with some ambivalence about the findings in terms of impact on attainment, particularly when also taking previous evaluations into account. On the one hand:

state and local administrators told us unanimously, Title I has been significant in reversing the neglect of the poor and educationally disadvantaged by our nation's schools...And yet, Title I is at a crossroad. Despite some recent evidence that some individual programs under certain conditions have been successful in producing significant gains in student achievement, the weight of evidence from past Title I evaluations has not been encouraging; we still feel a lingering concern over whether Title I is having a significant impact on the educational development of large numbers of individual children.

Their conclusion was that the processes of providing technical assistance to local districts needed to be improved (A: Burnes and Moss, 1978, 7–8).

In 1978 Congress amended ESEA Title I, extending it for a further five years, altering the arrangements for the allocation of funds within districts, and permitting school districts to rank schools by a combination of poverty and educational deprivation criteria (A: US Public Law 95–561, 2, 12–13; HEW, OE, 1979, 1–10). The findings of the NIE study had not been what Quie had expected, but it went some way towards redefining the criteria by making it possible to substitute in the new ranking procedure a school with greater educational deprivation for one with greater poverty but less educational deprivation. It is not often that policy and legislation can be seen to follow directly from research findings, and the NIE study of compensatory education is important for that if for no other reason.

In addition to the NIE study the Office of Education in Washington in 1975 set up a continuing ('multi-year') 'Study of the Sustaining Effects of Compensatory Education', conducted by the System Development Corporation, mainly to cover Title I but to take in other programmes too. The kinds of question to be explored over time included who received the programmes and how effective the services were. From 1977 and SES research began to show the percentage of targeted schools students benefiting from compensatory funds. 82 per cent of elementary schools were receiving some form of compensatory funds, 68 per cent under Title I, and 'almost all schools with moderate to high proportion of students from poverty backgrounds receive at least some compensatory funds'. In those elementary schools where more than half were both from poverty families and were reading one or more years below their grade level, 91 per cent were receiving Title I funds and almost 97 per cent some form of compensatory funds (A: US HEW, 1977, 1–5). A later SES report indicated that in the provision of compensatory education services not enough 'poor' and 'educationally needy' children were in fact receiving those services, and 'the intent of Congress regarding who should be served' still needed clarification. In reading, Title I students, it was estimated, developed in the first three (but not later) grades of school at a faster rate than non-Title I 'needy students', and in mathematics they did so in grades 1–6 (A: Carter, 1980, 1–2, 119). The SES research not only kept in view trends in 'selection for compensatory education', but also tracked poor parents' estimation of Title I programmes (which was in the main very positive) and their expectations of children's attainment (which was generally low), and conducted studies of 'successful sites' (A: SDC, 1978; 1979, 10). Attainment by those receiving Title I services was higher than expected, though the reasons could not be precisely identified (A: US Department of Education, 1981, 16–17).

By the end of the 1970s there was, therefore, accumulating evidence that in some programmes, in some circumstances, Title I and other compensatory programmes at the school level could result in improvement in basic skills 'greater than expected'. The US Department of Education summarized the mixture of confidence and uncertainty at this stage:

A major accomplishment in... 1980 was the improvement in student achievement scores in several major cities. Detroit, Newark, New York City, Los Angeles, and Washington all reported gains in student achievement, as measured primarily by standardized tests in reading and mathematics. Although the Department has no specific evidence to suggest that these improvements were a direct result of federal compensatory education assistance, most education experts acknowledge that Title I and other compensatory education efforts have played a role in helping districts to improve the achievement of students. (A: US Department of Education, 1980, 22–3)

Nothing that the NIE, SES or other research could report ended controversy about either the ability of compensatory education programmes to reach an appropriately targeted population, or to demonstrate responsibility or otherwise for significant improvements in the education of disadvantaged children. Disputes continued into the 1980s about eligibility and the experience and effectiveness of Title I and other programmes (A: Colley, 1981; Dallam, 1981; Deimel, 1981).

The problems of evaluating the effectiveness of Title I were little different from those of other programmes and, in fact, mirror the development of evaluation as an integral part of educational and social policy from the mid-1960s. By the mid-1970s evaluation had become a 'professional' activity, operating on a scale and within organizational structures that made the first generation of evaluation reports in the late 1960s and early 1970s appear rudimentary, and these were increasingly regarded as useless. Reports from the states were treated by officials in Washington as 'garbage' (A: McLaughlin, 1975, 24). In the first seven years of its existence some $50 million dollars were spent on 'impact evaluations' of Title I (A: Kirst and Jung, 1980, 34), but enthusiasm for evaluation was not matched by a serious questioning of the methodologies and capabilities of evaluation until, for example, the later attempts to construct national evaluations of Follow Through, and the NIE evaluation of Title I. Central to the problems of Title I in this respect was its diversity, with what effectively constituted 15,000 different programmes, and aims that could be and were differently interpreted. Evaluations could ask to what extent Title I was succeeding in its task of appropriately distributing the nationally allocated resources, or what cognitive gains were being made by which children, in what conditions and with what long-term effects. One of the difficulties was to judge what impact the programmes and training activities had on teachers, and what impact teachers and their different characteristics had on Title I implementation. From 1973–4 the interest in 'implementation research' sharpened and some of those involved focused on the past failure to ask questions about what happened between inputs and outcomes – the nature of policy implementation. Evaluation was meaningless, it was argued, if it were demonstrated that policies had not in fact been implemented. McLaughlin indicated in 1976 that many educators believed Title I had 'failed' to have the required effect on target children, but judgments about the effectiveness of schooling as an anti-poverty strategy might be premature:

It is possible that Title I programs, as they have been evaluated, have never existed – that Title I has not yet been implemented as intended by reformers. Thus, the failure of Title I in this instance is not so much a failure of special programs, but a failure of a Federal policy to bring about these programs on the local level. The area between inputs and outputs – the implementation stage – is relatively unexplored in all social service areas, and is only recently beginning to receive attention in the area of education. But evidence exists that makes doubt about the implementation of Title I more than just an academic speculation...(A: McLaughlin, 1976, 278–80)

The continued evaluations, clarification of goals and revision of regulations indicate the extent to which, by the late 1970s, an underlying confidence remained that in terms of policy-making, implementation and evaluation the educational war on poverty had not been lost, and in some respects was still at an early stage.

What Title I had particularly done by this point was to underline the relationship between the structural and operational failures of the educational system and the poverty, inequality and injustice in the wider society, though there was little precise agreement about the nature of the relationship and the extent to which education could solve its problems. There was growing evidence that a significant proportion of those receiving Title I services made greater academic gains than those who did not, and ESEA in general had 'broken the logjam on federal aid to education' (A: Halperin and Wayson, 1975, 147). From a simple confidence in rapid results, however, Title I had moved into a situation by the beginning of the 1980s in which measures of cognitive gains were only one of the criteria by which it could be judged, and the effectiveness of federal aid needed to be interpreted by increasingly sensitive methods. Under a new Act, with a new name, and in different conditions, Title I was projected into the 1980s, against a backcloth of changing patterns of evaluation and judgment, but targeting the same populations. Its relationship with the educational effects of poverty remained essentially unchanged.

The growth of an evaluation industry in the United States was more than an attempt to produce an improved technology of analysis. It also became involved in controversy over the role of education in existing social structures. Asking about the effectiveness of programmes and schools was also asking about outcomes in terms of impact on employment, the 'cycle' of poverty, or the structure of power. Re-analyzing the Coleman and other data Christopher Jencks and his colleagues in *Inequality* emphasized the crucial role of family background in determining educational attainment: the egalitarian trend in education had not made the distribution of income or status appreciably more equal over the previous quarter of a century. The important focus was not on resources but on outcomes, and if the need was to achieve a more equal distribution of incomes something more direct than educational programmes was necessary. Americans had 'a recurrent fantasy that schools can solve their problems' and, having rediscovered poverty and inequality, they had turned to the schools for solutions, which did not materialize (A: Jencks, 1972, 37–41, 158–9, 261–3; Bane and Jencks, 1973, 79). The technology of evaluation, in this view, therefore had evaded the question of the limited effect of schooling on the outcomes programmes such as Head Start and Title I had been invented to influence. Critics suggested that, for example, the Jencks research was based on a narrow definition of cognitive ability, relied on data from standardized tests of quantifiable skills, trivialized the concept of equality, arrived at conclusions not derived from data, and ignored the realities of what schools could do in developing people (A: Longstreet, 1973, 3–9; Sexton, 1973, 53–61; Gordon, E.W., 1975, 15–16). As was to be seen from the late 1970s evaluators were also learning the virtues of attempting longer-term analyses than had been possible at an earlier stage, confronting the difficulties of the relationship between their research focus and the complex intentions and outcomes of educational programmes, and looking for ways of reconceptualizing their engagement with policy implementation and action on the ground. Determining what was meant by 'success' and 'failure' in such complex social processes had never been easy, and was not now. Whether 'compensatory education' was succeeding or failing, or was even being adequately tried, was a continuing question from the late 1960s and through the 1970s.

The concept of compensatory education survived the period, but it and its related vocabularies had been the object of research scrutiny, political attack, and doubts not only about whether it was successful, but whether it could in any serious way be known to be successful. In the closing years of the 1960s it was being described as 'band aid', surrounded by growing doubts about its credibility as a basis for policy-making, as setting goals that were so vague that measurement and evaluation were impossible, and as merely attempting to make more children as like the traditionally 'successful' as possible (A: Fantini, 1969, 237–8; McDill *et al.*, 1969, 46–7; Durham, 1969, 21). In the early 1970s it was being pilloried as a 'fraud', as having made little advance in defining its precise meaning, as 'progressive statusquoism', and as having no impact on the *system* of education (A: Winschel, 1970, 3; Frost and Rowland, 1971, 131; Farber and Lewis, 1972, 20; Clark, 1972, 9). Amidst the prolonged controversy around Jensen's views on heredity and environment was a particular debate about his view that compensatory education had failed. He argued that Coleman had demonstrated that the 'large educational differences between individuals, social classes, and social groups cannot be explained to any appreciable degree in terms of what goes on in the schools'. The explanation lay, in Jensen's view in the 'amalgam of innate abilities and dispositions, acquired habits, skills, and attitudes' and the experience of the home. The Banneker, Higher Horizons and other programmes had 'produced absolutely no significant improvement in the scholastic achievement' of these disadvantaged children. Compensatory education had been 'tried and it apparently has failed'. By 1969 it had 'been practiced on a massive scale for several years in many cities with unprecedented support and enthusiasm, but its goal of remedying the 'educational lag' of disadvantaged children and narrowing the achievement gap between 'minority' and 'majority' pupils had been 'utterly unrealized' in any of the programmes so far evaluated (A: Jensen, 1968,

29–31; 1969, 2–3). Jensen, interestingly, is here in the same position as radical critics of the 'racism' of the programmes in identifying compensatory education exclusively with provision for 'minorities'. It was not only the evaluators who pointed out that compensatory education may in fact not have been implemented in such a way by the early 1970s to enable judgments to be made. A Senate Select Committee on Educational Opportunity, chaired by Walter Mondale, reported in 1972 that so far

In a real sense, compensatory education has never had a chance – services have often been diluted to the point of meaningless [*sic*], and even extended to noneligible children. Funds have been expended on equipment which is never put to effective use. Most important, Title I-funded programs too often have lacked clear goals related to increasing academic achievement, as well as clearly defined strategies for reaching those goals (A: US Senate, 1972, 312).

Through the 1970s there were continuing attempts to counter all of these critiques, by tightening the allocation criteria and the monitoring procedures, looking for evaluative criteria that would take account of cultural differences, and defining how far programmes might be expected to go in producing specific kinds of outcome.

One criticism of compensatory education in 1970 continued a thread we have previously seen, and one that was to be present in increasing measure through the decade: it had been designed to make up for deficiencies in the home environment and had failed 'precisely because it concentrates on the student's failure to learn rather than the school's failure to instruct' (A: Gordon, S., 1970, 361). The focus of past discussion around these 1960s and 1970s themes has frequently been on the concepts of the deficits or differences of children and their home backgrounds, but the extent to which school failure underpinned all the programmes we have discussed and the critiques of those programmes cannot be underestimated. From the Ford projects onwards there had been bitter attacks on deplorable teaching methods and standards, particularly in relation to the needs of disadvantaged children. The traditional school was either 'obsolete' or had failed all children, who were therefore by definition all disadvantaged (A: Spaulding, [1971], ch. 1; Fantini and Weinstein, 1968). Many critics argued that the schools simply failed to understand and act on their weaknesses and responsibilities, that teachers rejected the children who did not fit into their middle-class mould, or that compensatory programmes aimed to 'ready' children for school norms, rather than tackle the problem of changing the schools (A: e.g. Hawkins, 1973, 497–8). A constant theme in the literature of disadvantage and education in the 1970s was – change the schools, not the children and their families.

In all of these developments of the 1970s the preoccupation was essentially one of locating policies and procedures to fit the American educational, social, budgetary and other structures. Many of the Follow Through sponsors, project leaders, policy-makers, evaluators and commentators of the 1970s had only limited interest in and contact with parallel activities in other countries relating to educational policies and practice regarding disadvantage. The problems of poverty, the cities, race, welfare seemed so massively American that other experience could be only marginal. American interest in British education focused mainly on Plowden and the primary school, and then to a limited extent in sharing the experience that flowed from Plowden's emphasis on educational priority areas and positive discrimination. Follow Through models, as we have seen, in some cases borrowed from the British 'open classroom', and the work of British sociologists of poverty that stemmed especially from Richard Titmuss played a part in some of the debates about the problems. The same was true of the work of Bernstein and his Sociological Research Unit at the Institute of Education in London, but apart from occasional references there is little evidence in the literature or the memories of participants of any international context to the American developments. In the case of Britain, the traffic in ideas about disadvantage was mainly in the opposite direction, initially, for the reasons we have discussed, in very limited ways, but in the 1970s with some acceleration.

13   Britain: units of concern

Following the Plowden report the British government made its short-term allocation for building purposes in priority areas, cautiously invited local authorities to recommend schools where teachers would be eligible for a special payment in recognition of exceptional difficulty and, under the Urban Programme introduced in 1968, included expenditure on education, notably nursery education. The concept of educational priority areas was widely accepted by the local authorities, and commitments to identifying and supporting schools were strong in many parts of the country. Situated amongst these developments was a national EPA 'programme' under which five 'projects' were located in England and Scotland, financed jointly by the Department of Education and Science and the Social Science Research Council. The programme was negotiated primarily by Michael Young, who had been on the Plowden Committee and was chairman of the SSRC, A.H. Halsey, Director of the Department of Social and Administrative Studies at the University of Oxford, and the Secretary of State for Education and Science, Anthony Crosland, to whom Halsey was at the time a part-time adviser. The EPA projects grew directly from Plowden, against an American background.

'We all began with a Plowden orientation', wrote Halsey in one place. The aims of the projects – to raise the educational performance of the children, to improve teacher morale, to increase the involvement of parents in their children's education, and to strengthen the role of schools in their communities – were, he wrote elsewhere, 'directly derived from Plowden' (B: Halsey, in Morrison *et al.*, 1974, ix; Halsey, 1972a, 57). George Smith, a student in Halsey's department, was recruited for the EPA scheme and once he had finished his course in June 1968 'started straight away on a study of American compensatory education' that was to lead him to American contacts and a visit to the United States with Alan Little from the Inner London Education Authority and their 1971 OECD publication *Strategies of Compensation*. Correspondence with Harry Passow and a conference at the Ford

Foundation pointed in directions concerned with education programmes and community action. In Halsey's words, they were exploring American experience in 1968–9, when 'morale among those concerned with the American poverty programmes probably reached its nadir'. With a slightly different emphasis Smith records that the EPA projects 'set out in 1968, at a time when optimism about education as an agent of social change was still high'. News of American disaster was beginning to filter through, but was too often greeted with an 'it couldn't happen here'. Pessimism was rapidly gaining ground as a result of 'the dismal series of reports on American compensatory education' and the Jencks evidence. Smith moved to the West Riding project, which 'took the American experience in compensatory education as its starting point in 1969, deliberately trying to avoid some of their mistakes' (Smith, interview; Halsey, 1972a, 20; Smith, G. 1975b, 246–8). Amongst the EPA activists familiarity with the relevant American literature was often a starting point, often a reinforcement. Charles Betty, director of the Deptford (London) project was loaned a copy of McVicker Hunt's *The Challenge of Incompetence and Poverty* by Lady Plowden, who had been given a copy by the author and who was a member of Betty's project steering committee. Betty found it 'very useful' (Betty, interview).

The arrangement, as it worked out, was for the scheme to receive funds from the DES (£100,000) and he SSRC (£75,000) in recognition of a central plank of the scheme – to make it an action–research project to test the effects of positive discrimination, in a sense with the DES supporting the action and the SSRC supporting the research (B: Halsey and Sylva, 1987, 6). Patrick Gordon Walker, who had taken over as Secretary of State from Crosland, wrote to Michael Young in October 1967 endorsing the idea of a pilot investigation of this kind: 'I know that you have made progress with your thinking about a poverty programme in your Council ... I shall be very glad to consider any proposal for action research' (B: EPA*, October 1967). When the proposal was introduced at the SSRC's Council meeting in April 1968 there were uncertainties about the costing and other matters, but these were overcome. Lord James 'thought that very rarely there came a time when in the interests of progress one had to walk into a void, not knowing whether one would step out successfully or not and that this was one of those times' (B: EPA, SSRC, 5.4.68). The application to the SSRC emphasized that it arose from the Plowden report, its picture of multiple deprivation, its recommendations for positive discrimination and research into developments in EPAs which could help long-term planning. A brief

* EPA as a reference indicates documentation of the central EPA project, in the possession of the Department of Social and Administrative Studies of the University of Oxford.

specification of the future programme had come out of discussion with some local education authorities, including the development of experimental preschool playgroups, the appointment of an educational social worker or workers to operate from designated schools, the creation of 'community schools', the establishment of in-service centres in conjunction with colleges of education, and efforts to involve parents more closely. The objectives of the project and the specification of aims amounted to roughly two short paragraphs of the application, and the outline of implementation procedures occupied more than six pages (B: EPA, SSRC, 1968). The project was to last three years, and it was to be directed by Halsey.

Although the EPA projects were launched in the autumn of 1968 with some of the hopes that underlay the earlier American projects, they were in the main more cautious in their optimism. The scheme was intended as a large-scale demonstration project but it was conducted in a different economic climate from that of the American programmes of only a few years earlier, and against the background of doubt about their effectiveness. Halsey was foreseeing a period when workers would become unemployable in the 1980s because they were unskilled, and therefore the intention was to tackle wastage 'at the bottom of education', mobilizing local initiative from a range of sources for action and research aimed at improving children's performance, encouraging teachers and involving parents (B: TES, 1968a). The objective of Michael Young, chairing the project steering committee, and Halsey was to bring in the five biggest cities – London, Birmingham, Liverpool, Manchester and Glasgow but, after prolonged negotiations, they failed to bring in both the last two and Sunderland, which was also considered. The West Riding of Yorkshire came into the scheme, and Dundee became the Scottish representative. Some aspects of the overall project were to be national decisions, but the five local projects were in fact relatively autonomous and loosely connected. The project directors were not in frequent contact with Oxford, and the projects – with the same recognizable aims – developed in quite different ways. The TES concluded that there was no coherent EPA policy (B: TES, 1970), and there was an HMI view that the scheme was 'very uneven' (B: Hopkinson, interview). It was in fact during the project itself that Halsey and others elaborated theories of poverty and disadvantage, addressed the limitations of educational strategies against poverty, and the problems of action research in the contexts in which they worked and the structures which they established.

The EPA programme became fully operational between September 1968 and January 1969. When a conference of the people so far involved was held in September 1968 the London and Liverpool teams were ready to start, West Riding and Birmingham were to start in the new year, Dundee was developing from an existing project (and at that stage the position of Sunderland was described as 'obscure'). An important discussion took place – and was to be continued at further meetings and within the local teams – regarding the relationship between research or evaluation and action, and the kind of research that was desirable and possible. A report of the two-day conference indicates that it concentrated on three separate but interlocking questions: '1. What should be the range of action? Should it embrace community action or limit itself to strictly educational objectives? 2. What kind of evaluation is required or possible? 3. What relevance has the American experience to the British programme?' Central to the discussion was clearly a potential conflict between 'measurable educational improvement' and 'wider community involvement':

Some speakers argued that action should take the form of controlled experimental research according to an overall programme and defined research as a set of properly conducted experiments which would provide a firm basis for specific action proposals. Others argued that the aim should rather be a community action type of programme, flexible enough to allow projects to be altered or dropped or new ones introduced as community pressures built up; research in the sense of controlled experiment would be precluded by the open-ended nature of the projects; a detailed account of what actually happened would be more appropriate.

A middle ground appears to have emerged: 'different levels of evaluation and different types of action could be envisaged within the same overall framework' (B: EPA, September 1968). The project teams included specifically 'action' people, including the directors, and 'research' people, who were not always able to find a middle ground, and the final reporting was to reflect precisely the dilemmas opened up at this first encounter. A proposed 'general research design' was discussed at a meeting in November, but tentative local plans were emerging and teams were in general anxious not to make hasty decisions about either action or research. A progress report for the November meeting described the functions of the people appointed. Dundee, for example, had a project director, a research officer and an action committee, and the West Riding, a project director, a research officer and an action assistant. Researchers from universities were also attached to the teams, including Professor W.A.C. Blyth, who was to play an active part in Liverpool, and Alan Little and the ILEA research and statistics unit of the Inner London Education Authority, which was to relate actively to the Deptford project. The local teams were meeting with designated schools, planning preschool activities, working on curriculum, in-service and community-related schemes, and defining their research intentions. The 'research group' met before the November conference and decided that an overall research design was likely to be too complex to implement, and Liverpool and London were already planning 'impressionistic material' to supplement any quantitative approaches adopted (B: EPA, November 1968).

At a conference of the EPA teams and members of the steering committee in January 1969 Halsey painted a clear picture of the context in which the programme was working. Following the Plowden report it quickly had to be assumed

that very little money would be forthcoming and that serious action to carry out the recommendations would probably have to wait until economic growth had permitted a very large increase in educational resources. Our research, then, has been framed in terms of political and administrative expectations. From Whitehall's point of view our aim is to discover how to improve education in schools in slum areas ... We ourselves should not be able to contribute very much that is new to this question.

Here and elsewhere, including in the final reports, Halsey emphasized the limits of education as a 'poverty programme'. The real aim of the programme, as he saw it, related to those 'educative forces in society which under the present dispensation are not in fact utilised for educational purposes'. Children performed badly in school because there was not 'the kind of partnership between parents and teachers in relation to children that there should be in an ideal community'. The aim was to find ways of releasing educational energies that would persist after the input was withdrawn. It meant a strong focus on community action, and he, and George Smith in a paper for the conference, emphasized that community-type projects should not be ruled out because they could not be adequately evaluated. The 'integrating focus' for the local projects should be the community school. As Eric Midwinter in Liverpool was by this time indicating, and as Halsey summarized it, the problem in these areas was:

not one of method but of getting something done. Liverpool want to concentrate on investigating ways of encouraging pre-schooling and argue that only when programmes are established is it worth worrying about what kind of pre-schooling is best.

Although this may have been, as Halsey admitted, an oversimplification of the Liverpool position, it again raised the dilemma of 'community aims as opposed to narrower aims' (B: EPA, January 1969).

By May, when Halsey wrote his next progress report, the programme was 'firmly established' with two aspects in common across the projects. There was general agreement that the local projects should be based on the idea of developing the community school, even though this might be defined and operated in different ways. Action in connection with preschool children was designed as a national project 'so that the experiments could be evaluated together as a nationally designed enquiry'. There were to be two kinds of evaluation – detailed descriptions to show changes during the project, particularly in teacher and parent attitudes, and the carefully planned, controlled preschool research project. In London and Liverpool the projects were emphasizing work on the curriculum, Dundee was focusing on courses in language for teachers, as a preliminary to curriculum development, the West Riding was developing a 'social education centre', with local authority and Rowntree Trust support, which could serve for preschool activities and for older children with learning difficulties, and promote community links. Liverpool was experimenting with adult education, and London was appointing a social worker to serve two of the EPA schools (B: EPA, May 1969). Reports from the individual projects were tracing their steps in more detail. In Birmingham, the project director, who had been in the post for four months, but whose research officer had only been in post for a few weeks, underscored the high percentage of immigrants in the area covered by the project, with schools having between 35 and 60 per cent of children from immigrant families, with 6 to 20 per cent unable to allow a normal school curriculum because of language difficulties. The area was one of 'slums, over-occupied houses, massive redevelopment and high-rise flats'. The problem of old school buildings was 'minimal' by comparison with the children's living conditions:

The project must be seen in its setting of a massive urban problem within which the statutory social agencies are overwhelmed by the sheer size of the problem.

Long-term promise was provided by two associations, including the Sparkbrook Association, with its purpose-built centre, which had been of interest to the Plowden committee. The main aims of the project were the establishment of preschool playgroups and community schools, and language development and curriculum enrichment in the primary school.

Liverpool was at the same time reporting more rapid, if careful, progress over a broad front, in its downtown but variegated area. There was a sense of adventure in the programme of action and the framework being established, one which resulted from a three-month 'renaissance' and the conclusion that this was a 'politico-administrative exercise, not merely an academic one':

It is an exercise in mobilising existing community resources and in establishing a fluent network of communication for channeling information to and from critical points in that community. Our hope is that the actual experience of attempting such a mobilisation will be in itself a help to others.

The project covered a comprehensive school, seven primary schools and a nursery school. All the primary schools were already engaged in a programme to 'enliven the climate and life of these schools', making them more relevant and satisfying to the urban child and heightening parental interest. All nine colleges of education in the Liverpool area had been 'attached' to specific schools. Plans for the project to tackle work linking the primary schools and the secondary schools were taking shape, including the modification of a double-decker bus by the secondary school's technical department to provide a mobile preschool unit. The local education authority was cooperating strongly and local Chief Inspector Tom McManners (whom Midwinter applauded at the time, and later described as a father figure and mentor to the project) played a significant part. Here, as perhaps only in the West Riding, action and research were seen as a conjoint activity: 'the project team find it difficult and undesirable to distinguish clearly between action and research, preferring to see action–research as a unified entity in its own right'. The project director and action-research officer resolved practical issues on a 'day-to-day basis', and did not see each other's role as constraining the other (B: EPA, June 1969; Midwinter, interview). Midwinter's report ended with a flourish that came from his background as a historian: the EPA problem 'has been two hundred years in the making, and the E.P.A. children have been dealt a crippling hand by social history'. They, their teachers and social workers, were nevertheless 'cheerfully valiant and resilient in unbelievable conditions', and the hope of the project was to make a small contribution towards a 'dynamic and healthy community life and education'. Most of this was a long way from 'controlled research'.

In London, where the project began by describing itself as a 'Plowden demonstration project', the ILEA was refining the area index that the Plowden committee had produced, and the director of the project, Charles Betty, was describing the 'pockets of social deprivation and human degradation that have to be seen to be believed'. The progress report emphasized the need over the three-year period to bring teachers, administrators, colleges and community together in a concerted effort to relieve some of the schools' problems. The curriculum innovation that was one of the project's objectives laid stress on environmental concerns, and this was soon to mean providing junior school children in particular with experience of Kent rural life. There was already 'fair provision' of nursery classes in the area, and the project directed its attention to the inter-connected roles of teacher, social worker and parents. The West Riding project, which covered a mining area that was not urban in the same way as the other four, was planning to use its Red House centre and some schools as bases for preschool groups, developing 'individual language programmes', and consulting with schools and others about the various uses to which Red House could be put. Dundee was also acquiring a settlement that it would use in part for a mothers' group and as a club for immigrant women, and was focusing on ways of developing nursery provision and strengthening community links and action. In 1967 the Scottish Education Department had initiated a project at Dundee College of Education which was concerned with developing young children's verbal skills, and resulted in the active involvement of college students in an enrichment programme with four-year-old children. Joyce Watt, a lecturer at the College, was also involved in this 'Project Four', which she later described as a 'very novel idea at the time', based on Head Start kind of thinking – naive in its approach to educational disadvantage in that it did not include the parents – and on a 'social educational rescue by professional people' (B: Watt, interview; Watt *et al.*, 1973). Watt became director of the Dundee EPA project, but by the time the project was well under way Project Four, which was in fact a pioneer programme in Britain, had almost run its course, but had contributed some energy and experience to the EPA development (B: EPA, June 1969; Morrison *et al.*, 1974, 3). Dundee was, however, to encounter more teacher resistance to the project than in the other areas (B: EPA, May 1970; Morrison *et al.*, 1974, 5).

Progress reports in 1969 and 1970 suggest, with different mixtures in different places, a combination of enthusiasm and caution. The Peabody Language Development Kit chosen for the controlled language experiment was American – there was no such British preschool programme available – and met with various degrees of suspicion and hostility. There was encouraging support from local authorities, though not uniformly so. A report to the SSRC at the end of the first year of operation again defined the limits of the EPA programme.

It is very clear, of course, that if our efforts succeed they would yet prove futile unless suitable jobs and social opportunities of all kinds are available for the children who have been educated for them and encouraged to expect them. But very little can be done directly within the E.P.A. programme to alter employment opportunities and social structure. (B: EPA, September 1969)

Other projects, notably in Swansea and Manchester, had emerged which ran in parallel and with some tenuous links to the national EPA project, and other developments in the late 1960s and early 1970s added to the momentum of interest in the disadvantaged child, and particularly in preschool opportunities. 'Priority area playgroups', for example, were being developed under the auspices of the Advisory Centre for Education, the Urban Programme and the Save the Children Fund. An

Association of Multi-Racial Playgroups could record by the end of the 1960s the kind of pioneering work done in this connection by the Sparkbrook Association in Birmingham and the Indian Workers' Association in Southall (B: Jackson, 1971; Jackson and Jones, 1971; Jackson and Rae, [1969–70]). How far the overall momentum reached can be seen from the establishment in 1971 of a joint working party of the Headmasters' Conference and the Head Masters' Association to 'look into the needs of disadvantaged children in normal secondary schools'. Predictably, many of the head teachers answering the questionnaire that was distributed, felt unable to comment:

I am returning your questionnaire as requested, but not completed. The crucial area is not applicable in any sense to this School, which is a Selective School...

We are still a Grammar School, and as such, have no serious problems on the disadvantaged, all our pupils are selected...

This is a Direct-Grant Grammar School and, in the context of your enquiry, all boys are advantaged...

The working party concluded that the process of selection for schools in operation at that time was 'as much a selection of social and physical advantage as it is of intellectual or cultural advantage', and underlined the interdependence of these factors. Members visited educational priority areas, and their report endorsed the EPA concept, called for the 'assault on deprivation' to be extended to a wider variety of districts, thought preschooling was vital, and agreed that the 'community school' in its 'educative community' (a phrase they borrowed from Eric Midwinter) needed to be strengthened. Its recommendations began with the proposal that 'disadvantage should be recognised as a basis for reframing the allocation of resources available to schools' (B: EPA, [1973]). Not everyone, of course, approved of the EPA idea and projects. When the DES funding was announced in 1968 the head of a Sheffield primary school wrote to *The Guardian* to protest that the money was needed for schools, not for projects to find out what everyone already knew, and 'to find research fellows something to do':

The only result of this extravagance will be a further imposition of the long haired on the long suffering, a report awaiting implementation, and a crop of higher degrees for redundant project directors. (B: *Guardian*, 1968).

A general report on the EPA projects edited by Halsey under the title *EPA Problems and Policies* was published in 1972. A volume of surveys and statistics appeared in 1974, and three area-specific reports on *Curriculum Innovation in London's EPA's*, *The West Riding Project* and *A Scottish Study* followed the next year. No report on Birmingham was published, and Midwinter – among a variety of publications – published separately *Priority Education: An Account of the Liverpool Project* in 1972. Halsey's famous Volume 1 was generally optimistic in tone. It traced the background in Plowden and the government's response to it, and in a chapter on 'Poverty and American compensatory education' considered both the American experience and theories of poverty, underlining the diversities concealed by the vocabularies of 'disadvantage' and 'poverty'. It discussed the evaluations of the American programmes, concluding that educational reforms may be most important in their 'impact on the political consciousness of the poor', which could be the most effective means of ensuring 'that the gross inequalities between social and ethnic groups are eradicated'. The report was fairly optimistic about the ability of socially handicapped children to make greater progress in language with a good preschool programme than such children who were at home. It outlined a number of lines of advance in the work on school and community, summarizing the principles on which the project had approached the relationship between preschool and primary school:

What essentially we have argued about the pre-school years is the need to develop educationally informed families. After that, and with increasing difficulty among the higher age groups, the problem is to create socially informed schools. But to put the matter in its broadest perspective the problem at all stages is to integrate school and life. That is the concept of the community school.

Halsey's report on the four English projects (given the somewhat different origins and funding of the Dundee project it was not included in the summary) offered a series of conclusions, not all of which were to be wholeheartedly endorsed by the later individual reports: the educational priority area was a viable way of applying the principle of positive discrimination; preschooling was 'the outstandingly economical and effective device' for raising educational standards in EPAs; the community school had 'more powerful implications for community regeneration' than even Plowden had recognized; there were practical ways of improving family–school partnerships, and of improving the quality of teaching in the schools; action–research was an effective method of policy formation and innovation, and EPAs could be 'no more than a part, though an important one, of a comprehensive social movement towards community development and community redevelopment in a modern urban industrial society'.

In some significant respects, therefore, the EPA programme had not confirmed the clouds of doubt visible in the United States at the end of the 1960s, and though Halsey stressed the 'limits of an educational approach to poverty', and the report signalled some 'gloomy findings' (including the failure of EPA increments to prevent the loss of teachers from the areas), the pointers were towards positive and generalizable outcomes of the main thrusts of the programme's work over the three years (B: Halsey, 1972a, particularly chs 2, 3, 7, 9, 12 and 14). The report suggested a range of urgent initiatives that could be undertaken to develop home–school liaison, build the community school, improve nursery provision, increase resources, change teaching attitudes and revise curricula. The steering committee and the project leadership had, however, had little success in persuading the SSRC to finance major follow-up studies, and although the local authorities concerned picked up some of the threads of the projects there was no great optimism that the programme of action that emerged would be substantially financed.

The fact that the local projects had considerable autonomy meant that they developed distinctive aims and methods even while respecting the national priorities. The West Riding project, for example, made both a major contribution to the preschool language study, identifying gains made by the pilot group by comparison with a control group – gains which were sustained in the reception year of primary school – and developed an important home visiting scheme. The latter, which explicitly drew on home visiting experiments by David Weikart and Susan Gray in the United States, was proposed by the West Riding team after the EPA project had been launched, given what they considered weaknesses in the conventional 'parent involvement' in school work. Such an approach laid too much emphasis on the importance of the school process and not enough on the 'educational climate of the home'. The proposal to set up a small-scale home visiting project was seen as an attempt to implement the objectives of parental involvement more effectively and with greater influence on the child's educational development. The SSRC made a grant for this experiment in August 1970, and the final report from the West Riding indicated that, though the number of families involved had been small, the findings, cautiously expressed, suggested that 'the programme had a positive effect on both the child's rate of development and certain features of the mother–child relationship' (B: EPA, 1970; Smith, G., 1975b, 162). When Halsey submitted a proposal to the SSRC for a follow-up evaluation of aspects of the EPA in Liverpool, Birmingham and the West Riding, only one-third of the amount requested was agreed, as the Educational Research Board of the SSRC felt that further research work was likely to be successful only in the West Riding area, and the money was to help with following through the preschool group and assessing the effect of the home visiting programme (B: EPA, 14 July 1971). The West Riding project also conducted what it called 'small but practical steps' to develop a form of 'community education' which rested on a commitment to community development:

...for an educational system to be effective even in its own terms, it has to be drawn into the wider questions of social and economic opportunities that amplify or undermine work in the schools. And even if education was effective on its own, the rate of change it could offer from generation to generation would be far too slow. A form of community education and community development is needed to supplement the existing system...Programmes of parental involvement and home visiting are a small step towards such a form of 'community education'.

The project had determined some of the limitations within which schools necessarily worked, but the report made a direct response to the feeling engendered in the United States by Jencks and others that educational and other factors were totally the 'prisoner' of economic factors. Educational levels could be changed by educational action 'up to a point': when such change 'begins to interact with family structures, school organisation, community relationships or job opportunities, we have to move to a broader programme covering these areas with complementary change' (B: Smith, G., 1975b, 253–4, 96, 247–8). The operations of the West Riding project were concentrated and sustained, with a precise blend of action and evaluation as it developed its own priorities and contributed to those developed nationally.

The Dundee project reported a range of activities not unlike the English ones in most respects, having grappled with the difficulties of an appropriate preschool approach, a primary school curriculum development programme, work with the secondary school and on the difficult links between social workers and schools. Though aware of the need for 'home support', there was no home visiting on the West Riding model. The project acquired a rural base and inaugurated outings, and parents were involved in limited ways with the life of the schools. In this and in other respects there were particular problems, with many teachers fearing their autonomy would be undermined:

Headteachers tell spine-chilling stories of how there have, somewhere, sometime, been cases of the parents taking over the school, and actually telling the teachers what to do. Consequently although very few teachers were not in favour of increasing parental contact, the vast majority wanted to do so in ways which would keep parents at a safe distance.

Although the report recorded important advances as a result of the project – including their emphasis not only on the expansion of preschool provision but also on the coordination of preschool and family services – it also indicated a number of constraints and difficulties specific to the area and to Scotland. There were doubts, for example, about the applicability of the area approach to a town the size of Dundee, and recommendations to move to a school-focused approach. The concept of the community school was challenged, in part because it was nebulous, in part because Dundee was not ready for such an approach, and in part because the broad version of it offered by Halsey was not seen as capable of effecting hoped-for changes:

We doubt the validity of the 'community school' idea for both theoretical and practical reasons...We simply do not see the school as the centre of the integrated programme of social development necessary for the radical improvement of disadvantaged areas...If equality is to be attained, the entire socio-politico-economic system would require radical alteration. Such change was quite beyond the scope and indeed the intentions of the Dundee E.P.A. authorities.

Action research as a strategy had, similarly, not demonstrated that it could have the intended impact, as Stephen Town, research fellow on the project, underlined in the report and elsewhere. The American experience of action–research had not, he suggested, been very successful, research in such conditions was submerged by the action, the practices were untestable and so what was the point? The process was, therefore, no guide to policy. Dundee, he thought, was like the other projects in experiencing internal conflicts and disharmony arising from action–research itself, and it was Halsey's national coordination that had countered 'the tendency for action and research to hold differing objectives'. The price paid for action–research included 'the neuroses which its ambiguities develop in the action and research personnel' (B: Morrison et al., 1974, 125, 64–72, 169; 182–5, 189, 213–14; Town, 1973, 574–95). The Dundee project had concluded that compensatory education was important but needed to be made more relevant, and that preschool programmes could be devised which 'effectively combined the kind of cognitive theory emerging from psychology with the accumulated pragmatic wisdom of the nursery school teacher'. If preschool gains were lost in the primary school this was beside the point, at least deterioration during primary school would not stem from 'a below average beginning' (B: Morrison et al., 1974, 195, 160–1). There is no doubt that the Dundee project had to take account of the realities of Scottish school traditions that were in many respects different from those in the four English areas, and needed to be less radical in the curricular and other steps taken. In this and other ways the Dundee project felt to some extent isolated from the English EPAs.

The Liverpool project gained much publicity through both its vigorous recruitment of community support for the schools and its emphasis on a 'community-oriented curriculum'. In a series of publications – as well as through media attention – the project, and particularly Midwinter himself, developed a theory of community education. The objective was not compensatory education but a curriculum and a set of community relationships which set the school squarely in its social environment (B: Midwinter, 1972b; 1972c). Midwinter made a prolonged attack on an established curriculum that he considered irrelevant to the needs of EPA children, and much of what he did and wrote at the time involved a search for relevance and its meanings. The project sought to capitalize on the richness of working-class life, and to relate education to the realities of the children's environment, including, but not exclusively, their local environment. The need was to build on the sympathy of school and parent for each other, and to harness community resources of all kinds in their efforts for children's education around an understood and accessible curriculum and around education strategies that reduced alienation:

So much school-work is second-hand, sterile academicism dolled up in escapist Edwardiana. Surely the only longterm hope for a 'deprived' area is that the next generation, through an acute appraisal of its social environment and a sturdy refusal to take it for granted, will rejuvenate the community, drawing on the rich veins of potential that already exist but which a uniform, national education system can do little to tap. (B: Midwinter, 1969, 9)

Exhibitions of children's work in shops and pubs, support from local firms, publications, and a variety of other immersions in the community established an identity for the project which was both one of considerable energy and one of reflection and principle. The first six months of reconnaissance and activity

enabled judgements to be made about the viability of hitherto theoretical ideas, the strengths and weaknesses of the outline schedule, the temper and character of the people and institutions under consideration...

Strong links were established with a Community Development Project in Coventry and the community school idea developed in Coventry 'in fuller flight' (B: Midwinter, 1972a, 79; Midwinter, interview). At the end of the first year Midwinter was also reflecting on the nature of action–research and deciding that it was not 'a coupling of a bit of objective research and a bit of subjective action'. It needed to have its own frame of reference, including a flexibility which allowed for 'the constant adaptation of action to situations'. Methodological and controlled evaluation in the accepted sense was therefore difficult and unnecessary: it was rather a 'day by day assessment of fluid situations' based on evidence which might be 'rigorously collated' or 'impressionistic'. Within the team, and with support from Alan Blyth at the university, the Liverpool project went beyond initial conflicts between the 'actionists and researchers as to which work should be uppermost', and produced its own blend of self-evaluating, reflective action (B: EPA, August 1969; Midwinter, 1972a, 46–7).

The Deptford project was the one where conflict between action and research ran deepest and was most sustained, where the outcomes are therefore least clear, and where only one of two overall perceptions of the project became publicly available. Although the published reports from Dundee and the West Riding were edited by researchers, the 'actionists' contributed. This was not so in London, where the project director was not invited to contribute, and where only the researchers' view was heard beyond the immediate reporting channels. The Deptford project was subject to more, and more 'objective', evaluation than the others, and the measured outcomes reported were mainly negative, and the project has considerable interest for judgments of community action of the kind undertaken at Deptford. As we have seen, the project was highly community-oriented and in many respects, developed along lines similar to those of Liverpool. The director, Charles Betty, as a former primary school head teacher, was intent on forms of action that would heighten children's awareness of their environment, involve families and the community and, more explicitly than in the other projects, raise teacher morale. The project engaged fourteen schools, mainly primary, and two colleges, focused on preschool as well as school issues, secured the release of two teachers for half a day a week to carry out school–home liaison activities, and had a social worker involved with the project. The aims were ambitious, and the work resulted in evening 'community school' activities, the day outings to rural Kent for junior school children, and supportive participation by most of the teachers concerned.

Betty's draft programme for the project was under four headings: children, parents, teacher support and general community links. The last three, with emphases on such things as encouraging parental interest, improving teacher morale and improving links with the social services and industry, were not easily amenable to evaluation, and the draft recognized this. Only aspects of children's ability and attainment could be approached quantitatively, and the proposal called for work on 'measuring the intangibles ... subjective reports ... intensive case studies ... assessment of improved teacher performance ... assessment of the factors which improve and enrich parental/school relations' (B: EPA, October 1968). Given this shape for what followed it is not surprising that the published report by the measurement-oriented evaluators was of a different order from the project director's own report to the steering committee and the ILEA, a report which was not published. The published report edited by Jack Barnes had, in Halsey's words, 'a relatively pessimistic and negative tone' by comparison with all the other EPA reports (B: Barnes, 1975, vi). The volume quarrelled with the concept of 'disadvantage' and the use of 'areas' as units for policy and action, resisted the idea of educational solutions to social problems, and defended a role for research in providing specific forms of feedback for action. The report included evaluations of ILEA-sponsored work in the field of language, and of a nursery school language programme which had substituted for the PLDK programme used in the other projects, and which the Deptford nursery school teachers had declined to operate. The results in this case were 'equivocal', with preschool experience seeming to be beneficial for disadvantaged children, but without a suitable control group of children not attending a preschool institution the effect had not really been demonstrated: no gains due to the programme had been evidenced. A junior school language project had begun before the EPA project and continued after it, and the report on it was of a trend 'towards no change'. The environmental studies scheme was described as 'an amalgam of relatively disparate ideas', and the predicament of evaluators seeking to implement strict research methods was clearly highlighted:

Two problems above all others made the evaluation a difficult and tortuous process...there was not one scheme but one for each class taking part...statements of intention were given more to formulations with which all the involved parties could agree than to objectives which could actually guide the behaviour of all.

The report quotes a letter by Betty to *The Times Educational Supplement* claiming success for the scheme in relation to seven stated objectives, all of which were of the 'intangible' kind, concerned with pupil and teacher motivation, parent involvement, a 'real' curriculum, the ability of children to work on their own initiative... Barnes underlined that 'there was only a limited concern for the cognitive skills of the subject children', and the basis of the scheme included what he called 'the pleasure principle'. His 'summary of the measured effects on the children' indicated that there was no effect by the environmental studies scheme either on English and mathematics performance, or on the children's attitudes or motivation. The innovation had been added to the existing curriculum, and 'at best there were no consistent observable effects on the measured behaviour of the children. At worst there were some signs that manipulations of the E.P.A. school curriculum of the sort described here have harmful effects on children's school performance' (*ibid.*, 3–24, 87, 127, 169–91).

Betty's 16-section, book-length report described the coverage and development of the project, including early agreement that it was not a 'package deal for prescribed action which had to be followed', and that 'as our courses of action were not definitive, alterations in method, ideas and implementation could be envisaged' (B: Betty, 1971c, Section 3, 21–4). Some intentions of the environmental studies scheme, which was eight months in the planning were 'incapable of being objectively evaluated in terms which a research worker would be prepared to accept'; their evaluation based on 'academic performance' needed to be supplemented with other evidence. Teachers, for example, reported improved attendance and motivation on the part of the children and a higher standard of creative English. Teacher motivation also improved, with a willingness to spend weekends organizing, and to engage in team teaching. The researchers were a minority reporting failure, while teachers and other observers reported success (ibid., Section 5, 8, 43–50). The community school activity (described as the most important feature of the project of the EPA programme nationally) had the essential aim of 'an informed local community', moving school into community and vice versa, and evaluation needed to take account of parent involvement, liaison with social services, and the development of a relevant curriculum (ibid., Section 7, 1, 40–4), and the role of the home–school liaison teachers in bringing parents in from the 'periphery' of the school's thinking (ibid., Section 8, 1). Strong school links with the borough, community relations officers and voluntary welfare organizations had been established (ibid., Section 11, 1–10). On action–research Betty considered collaboration difficult but possible, especially if researchers were sympathetic to action and primarily concerned with academic respectability (ibid., Section 13, 1–2). The conclusion was that many of the original aims had been achieved, including the raising of teacher morale and community and parent involvement, and a series of recommendations therefore followed (ibid., Section 16, 1, 6–14).

Betty pursued his optimistic view of action–research in other places (B: Betty, 1970, 1971a, 1975), including the virtues of the community school (B: Betty, 1969a, 1969b, 1971b, n.d.) and emphasized throughout the supportive and crucial cooperation of the ILEA and its inspectorate. The central EPA papers indicate some ambiguity of attitude towards Betty's work, at different times suggesting difficulties and vigorous approval (B: EPA, 27 May 1969, 31 June 1969). A lengthy joint report on the project by Her Majesty's and ILEA inspectors involved with the project made some critical comments – for example, about insufficient structure in the environmental studies scheme, and therefore limited impact on classroom activity – but pointed generally to important outcomes. The visits to Kent had in fact provided 'a structure to the work in the classroom for a major portion of the rest of the week'. For teachers:

One of the major contributions of the project was in helping to maintain the morale of the teachers ... By providing a framework in which the various aspects of the project could develop the work of the teachers has been recognised, their enthusiasm has been stimulated and their skills improved.

For Betty that alone vindicated the project and pointed towards the future (Betty, interview). In 1971 the ILEA agreed to continue the Deptford work after the project was concluded. It was already bearing some half of the cost of the project, and was implementing what became Betty's main recommendations. An ILEA press release on this decision commented that 'Mr Betty and his team have laid the foundations for what we hope will be real advances in helping the schools in all of the many deprived areas of inner London' (B: ILEA, April 1971). In June 1971 a member of the ILEA Education Committee asked the chairman of the Schools Sub-Committee '(i) in view of the success of the Deptford project is a similar scheme to be mounted elsewhere in the Inner London area? (ii) If so is a project director being appointed to be responsible for stimulating activities in the manner so outstandingly carried out by Mr Charles Betty?' The reply was that the new ideas and techniques developed in Deptford would be spread across the authority's schools under the guidance of the inspectorate and advisory teachers (B: ILEA, 30 June 1971). The steering committee expressed its 'very real appreciation' of the work of the project director and his team (B: ILEA, 2 October 1972, Appendix 1). The report of the social worker on the team, which had formed one of the sections of Betty's final report, was separately published in 1973 and strongly affirmed the value of the experience: a community-based, education-oriented social worker had a real contribution to make to EPA schools, and a development of social work in relation to schools would 'afford a real chance of preventative social work with the families of school children' (B: Lyons, 1973, 4).

There were, therefore, two utterly different perceptions of the project, its aims and methods and possibilities of evaluation. A report to the ILEA Education Committee from the Schools Sub-Committee attempted to combine the two views (B: ILEA, 25 October 1972), given the strength of support for Betty's conclusions, and the fact that the ILEA's own research and statistics unit had been involved in the research. In a sense the Deptford case throws into relief both the American and British difficulties in appraising strategies against poverty and disadvantage. What kind of action and what kind of measures of success or failure? What were the roles and perceptions of the various partners involved? What were the relationships between concepts such as 'area', 'disadvantage' and 'community', and short-term action and long-term policy? A member of the ILEA's Research Group, reviewing the two EPA volumes on the West Riding and London, talked of the London volume as 'largely a catalogue of failure', and questioned the quality of action at Deptford when it was out of the control of the evaluators. She pointed out that 'the negative results of objective testing' differed from the professional judgments of the director of the project and the teachers whose agreement he claimed. She deduced that it was 'fatuous to expect any educational improvement from ill-conceived, poorly executed programmes with multiple and often changing objectives':

... as Jack Barnes very clearly demonstrates, if objective tests conflict with professional assessment, then it is the latter which is more likely to carry weight with policy-makers – a salutory lesson for all of us who are in the research business. (B: Mabey, 1976, 93–4)

What the project suggests – and some policy analysts have later argued (A: Lindblom and Cohen, 1979) – is that research-based knowledge is important, but not all-important. The 'research business' is only one of the contributors to understanding and policy. Lindblom and Cohen argue the place of 'common sense' or 'ordinary' knowledge in the policy domain (*ibid.*, ch. 2), and the Deptford position, as in many other cases in Britain and the United States, does the same for what might be termed 'action knowledge' – the experience of what Betty termed at the beginning of the Deptford project the 'intangibles'. The EPA programme in general was to be a major contributor to a continuing debate about the nature of action research.

Halsey's first volume of the reports aroused considerable interest, less so the later volumes, though the whole output fed into continuing discussion through the 1970s. There was criticism in Britain as in the US that such educational strategies diverted attention from the 'harsh realities' and the need for wider policies (B: Hill, 1972, 2), but others thought the West Riding and other experience offered 'grounds for encouragement' after the disappointing messages from the United States (B: Spencer, 1973, 252). The EPA programme influenced at least the nursery content of the 1972 White Paper *Education : A Framework for Expansion*, but there was some cynicism on the political left, voiced strongly by the more radical participants at a conference on 'Social deprivation and change in education' held in York in 1972 (B: Ingram, 1972; Nuffield Teacher Enquiry, [1972]). Some critics thought that the report showed insufficient attention to social class (B: Byrne *et al.*, 1975). In general the prospects for developments from the research looked bleak in the economic conditions, and the DES itself showed a marked decline in interest in the scheme once Crosland had left the Department (B: Banting, 1979, 120).

The EPA projects were accompanied by a number of parallel or related developments which would have to be included in any fuller discussion of either action research or policies for urban decay or social disadvantage. From 1970 action research was the basis, for example, of a wide-ranging national Community Development Project, funded through the Home Office and also directed by Halsey. It drew directly on American experience of community action (B: Smith, 1982), had links with the EPA projects, and in Halsey's view such links were the way to carry forward the EPA work (B: Halsey, 1972, 198). The Urban Programme, triggered to a large extent in 1968 by the anti-immigration, racial stance of right-wing Enoch Powell, had particular importance for nursery education and related fields of health and welfare. A series of Inner Area Studies drew on EPA, CDP, Urban Programme and other predecessors, and the reports published mainly in 1977 broadly endorsed both the 'area' perspective and action research, the importance of preschool provision and coordinated early childhood services, links between school and community, and the position of education in a comprehensive urban policy (B: Department of the Environment, 1977–1978; Shankland et al., 1977).

Attempts to continue the EPA projects locally and nationally met with limited success, except where specific aspects of the project work were incorporated into local authority practices. Experiments with the community school developed, as we have seen, in Coventry but also in other parts of the country, though the concept was not one of the EPA emphases adopted by the ILEA. The West Riding follow-up study of the long-term effects of home visiting and support for early learning in the home indicated gains by the children visited and changes in mothers' attitudes and expectations, but pointed to the need for sustained support if early learning programmes were to work (B: Armstrong, 1973, 1975; Armstrong and Brown, 1979). Home visiting was to become an important development of the late 1970s. Midwinter and others continued to emphasize its importance in strengthening the work of the schools (B: Midwinter, 1975). The concept of 'educational visitors' or 'liaison teachers' took hold in many local authorities as a direct outcome of EPA experience. Among the local authorities making rapid strides in this direction was Nottinghamshire, which began to establish a pattern of home–school liaison teachers as early as 1970, with the aim of developing 'meaningful links' and breaking down barriers between school and community (B: Betty, 1978; Nottinghamshire County Council, n.d.). By 1975 the county had appointed 50 such 'community teachers', the number shortly to be increased to 70, and by 1983 the number was 110 (B: Nottinghamshire Education Committee, 1975, 131; Betty interview). Charles Betty moved from Deptford to Nottinghamshire to be District Inspector for Primary Disadvantage.

An attempt was also made to continue the EPA momentum through a national organization based on Midwinter in Liverpool, where the local education authority was also attempting to provide funding to continue some of the EPA work. *Priority* was to be a national centre for urban community education, and it began publishing *Priority News* in 1972. Neither this nor other formal continuations of the EPA projects lasted, but other developments emerged directly from the EPA programme. An Ealing Home/School Project in 1973 was EPA inspired, and one of the Scottish developments, the Govan Project – a 'Strathclyde Experiment in Education' – traced its ancestry to the EPA, Head Start and other American projects, CDP, Inner Area Studies and others (B: Fitzherbert, 1973, 3; Wilkinson *et al.*, 1977). Positive discrimination had been operationalized and sustained in sporadic but visible ways.

Alongside the EPA programme – by far Britain's largest and most widely discussed projects in the post-Plowden field – there were others, the most important of which was the Swansea-based compensatory education project that had taken shape before the Plowden and Gittins committees reported. Gittins, professor of education at University College Swansea, had given his inaugural lecture in 1957 on 'Educational opportunity', emphasizing the importance of the nursery school, the involvement of parents in the life of schools, and the school as a community (B: Gittins, 1980, 196–7). In the mid-1960s a group of ex-professional educational psychologists came together on the staff of his department and began to think of launching a project on reading, which turned into an interest in 'compensatory education'. Phillip Williams knew more about recent developments in the United States than the others, Alice Laing had a growing interest in Head Start and other American programmes, and in 1967–8 Maurice Chazan spent six weeks teaching in the United States and toured Head Start centres under Ford auspices. In April 1966 a proposal for a project had already been submitted to the Welsh Committee of the Schools Council (the Council was at that time willing to support fundamental research) (B: Chazan, Laing, interviews). The proposal for research into 'Reading development and compensatory education' was to identify children 'at risk' of reading retardation and to develop and evaluate forms of enrichment and compensatory intervention. Importantly, such research, it was suggested, could best be carried out in an establishment with 'interest and experience of research with handicapped children' (B:

University College, 1966), and the project – like others in the United States before it – was to adapt aspects of a mental handicap model, including sensory and other deprivation and special educational programmes and techniques, to the needs of socially disadvantaged children. The project was approved by the Schools Council in 1967, and the Swansea team embarked on a four-pronged study concerned with identification techniques, programme development, emotional development and response to schooling, and Welsh language (B: Schools Council [1968]; Chazan et al., 1976).

Crucial to the project and, as we have seen, a logical outcome of the Gittins committee's reservation about the educational priority area focus of the Plowden recommendations, was its conviction that 'area' solutions were too indeterminate, too 'global', an approach. The project was concerned with rural as well as urban disadvantage, and it was felt that a sharper focus on the children who were 'at risk' was needed. Although the context required a sociological analysis, what the project was anxious to achieve was a means of targeting psychological insights on children's responses to the demands of schooling. Chazan and colleagues summarized the project as being

concerned with the effects of material and cultural deprivation on children's educational progress and emotional development in the infant school years. It is also concerned with identifying these children as soon as possible after school entry and with suggesting programmes, materials and methods which might help such children to benefit more fully from present educational provision. (B: Chazan, Laing and Jackson, 1971, 5)

A system of early screening was therefore developed, involving the collection of data regarding home background and medical record and a series of assessments, and by the use of school schedules and psychometric criteria at age seven-plus groups of children were identified for attention. The identification of individual children therefore pointed towards implications for institutional change (B: Evans, R., 1972, 3–5; 1973, 82–3). Paradoxically, the Swansea project, explicitly rejecting the Plowden emphasis, was in this respect more child-centred than Plowden (B: Ferguson et al., 1971 (1973 edn), 224–30). Longitudinal studies confirmed the hypothesis that children from deprived backgrounds performed on a variety of scores worse than those from more advantaged backgrounds, that it was possible to identify the ones at risk, that helpful strategies could be devised, and that within socially and geographically delineated groups there was 'significant variation in the development and school progress of children'. The concept of the 'deprived area' was unsuitable as a basis for the most efficient use of resources (B: Chazan et al., 1977, 188, 195–6).

The Swansea project resulted in a considerable output of detailed reports on preschool and early years education, as well as discussions of its starting concept of 'compensatory education'. It was the most important British project to adopt the compensatory education vocabulary, and in doing so it explicitly and widely addressed the American experience. The project's first Occasional Publication in 1968, for example, contained a survey by Alice Laing of 'some current American programmes for culturally disadvantaged children', outlined the Weikart, Susan Gray, Bereiter and Engelmann and other programmes, and considered whether the implications were for children or for schools to change (B: Schools Council Research Project, 1968, 29–39), and Chazan and Williams and others used American projects constantly as touchstones for comparison. Although 'compensatory education' remained the overall title of the project and some of its major publications, the concept and related concepts of deprivation and disadvantage were not seen as homogeneous. Chazan produced a typology of compensatory education approaches, their strengths and weaknesses, and underlined that 'there is no clear-cut homogeneous category of children who can be labelled as "deprived" or "disadvantaged"' (B: Chazan et al., 1976, ch. 2; Chazan, 1973a, 14–22; Chazan and Williams, 1978, 3). Phillip Williams drew the general conclusion that 'the variation of children's characteristics within social classes is quite as important as the variation between social classes' (B: Chazan and Williams, 1978, 108).

The language of compensatory education also underlay an attempt to develop a major project at Didsbury College of Education, Manchester. The intention here, in parallel with the EPA initiative, was also to take up the Plowden recommendations and to learn from the American experience, and it produced an extensive annotated bibliography (B: Williams and Wein, 1970). There was to be research on the problems of teaching in EPAs, feeding an understanding of disadvantage into the training of teachers (B: Didsbury, n.d.). Ronald Goldman, the College Principal, who knew Americans like Deutsch and Passow, was the prime mover, and in order to develop a project he recruited two psychologists (one of whom Norman Wein, had worked with Deutsch), and a sociologist. There were some conceptual uncertainties in the group, with sociologist David Morton questioning the 'cultural deficit' assumption adopted for the project. Goldman had become a member of the SSRC's Education Research Board, and prospects looked promising for a successful application to the SSRC, given his status and the experience of the team. A site visit by the SSRC (including Basil Bernstein) recommended otherwise. Goldman had announced his departure to a post in Australia and, when asked, Wein said he could not commit himself to staying long in the UK. In Morton's words, the project 'fell apart' (B: Morton, interview). The ERB had asked the EPA national steering committee if a Didsbury project could be absorbed into it, but in March 1969 it simply offered liaison if the Didsbury project was funded by the SSRC. The ERB subsequently recommended the grant, subject to the site visit producing 'satisfactory evidence of the competence of the investigators to carry out the work'. The visitors had found the proposed investigators 'not sufficiently well-versed in research to enable the team to express any confidence or to recommend the grant' (B: EPA, 21 March 1969, 2 October 1969).

Although the incipient SSRC project 'fell apart' there were two outcomes. First, a number of publications emanated from the group's work, offering a critique of 'liberal' or 'individualistic' approaches and of Plowden-inspired concern with forms of 'positive discrimination' which sought to adjust children to the alien culture of the school, and discussing the failure of school–community strategies when there was weak community support (B: Morton, 1969, 1–3; Morton and Watson, 1971, 49–50; Wein, 1970a, 1970b). Compensatory education narrowly focused on the classroom could be ineffective or counter-productive:

...many social factors such as poverty, racism and discrimination, the support of parents and the conflicting values of home and school impinge upon a child's educational development and achievement and upon his life chances. In so far as any pre-school education or Compensatory Education programme ignores these factors and focuses upon improving the child in the classroom, such a programme may have a zero or negative influence upon his life chances and may obscure the need to reduce culture conflict and discrimination. It may reduce the pressure to eliminate economic and educational privileges as well as poverty, deprivation, prejudice and poor self-image... (B: Morton and Goldman, 1969, 24)

The second outcome was a Certificate in Compensatory Education in Primary Schools, and a Diploma in Compensatory Education, the latter of which, for example, entailed a three-paper written examination and a dissertation. The Diploma papers were in educational psychology, sociology of education with special reference to social disadvantage, and compensatory education. The third of these in 1970 included such questions as:

The creation of Educational Priority Areas was suggested by Plowden as part of a process of 'positive discrimination' for disadvantaged children. Consider the merits of this approach.

Outline the home and school factors associated with educational disadvantage and discuss briefly some of the ways suggested for dealing with them.

How would you define poverty? Examine the main causes of poverty in modern Britain.

How important to the teacher is a study of the cultures of immigrant children? Illustrate your answer by reference to a particular immigrant group. (B: University of Manchester, 1970)

The Didsbury case further illustrates the 'post-Plowden' climate, with its perceived opportunities, needs and conflicts, and increasing attempts to place education in the context of social strategies against poverty and disadvantage and – mainly from the early 1970s – growing attention to issues of poverty in a multi-racial society.

Other projects and activities in the 1970s pointed in the same directions. The National Foundation for Educational Research, for example, conducted a nursery education project in order to apply 'the philosophy and principles of compensatory education in a British context', from the starting point of growing evidence of 'inequalities in the educational attainment of children' and against the background of advocacy of positive discrimination. It treated compensatory education as a process of 'nipping educational failure in the bud', with a particular emphasis on language skills. It attempted to steer a course between the two extremes of informal nursery education and formal instruction, only to discover – as did the EPA projects – that a modified version of the American Peabody Language Development Kit depended for its success on teacher willingness and ability to adapt to an unfamiliar degree of programme structure, and the possible 'inappropriateness of the instruments for assessing learning which has taken place in the informal context' (B: Woodhead, 1976a, 9–14, 29–43, 114–15). Among 1970s Scottish projects was the Strathclyde Experiment in Education. The Govan Project, as it was commonly called, was another 'area' project, attempting 'to enhance the education of children from a poor area in the city of Glasgow using the theme of "Total Education"', and aiming to bring together the family, the community and the school around the education of children and thus 'strengthen the social fabric of a small inner-city area of Glasgow'. The approach adopted was to prove as politically sensitive as some of the American ones we have discussed: it made a case for

the devolution of power by blurring the responsibilities between home and school. This course of action required us to challenge, we hoped sensitively, the professional practices inherent in schooling and not simply to educate the parents to enhance the efficiency and effectiveness of the school.

Many teachers were uneasy about the redefinition of their roles, some parents reacted negatively to what they saw as the labelling involved in a family-based strategy, teachers were reluctant to visit children's homes, and there was little success in altering established views of teachers' professional responsibilities. The project was handed over, amidst some controversy, to a local committee of residents and teachers for its final phase, and this brought conflict with the local education authority. The evidence of improved children's reading scores proved to be 'encouraging but not outstanding' and, although the project generated a continuing Glasgow Home and School Programme, when it finished in 1979 a final report of the project was not published and in many respects those involved in conducting and evaluating it did not consider it to have been a great success (B: Wilkinson and Williamson, 1980, 1–6, 18–31).

In 1970 the Schools Council turned attention to social disadvantage in secondary schools with its publication 'Cross'd With Adversity'. Work on children's language continued unabated, for example developing and interpreting Bernstein's work with some optimism about programmes' ability to improve children's performance in such areas as verbal discrimination amongst objects and the organization of concepts. This was nevertheless in a context of explaining the language skills of working-class children and the family context of their development and perceptions of the school's culture (B: Gahagan, 1970, 104–6, 112–113; Creber, 1972, 19). The 'mainstream values' of the school were in fact under strong attack from critics who – albeit with differences – saw cultural or verbal deprivation, compensatory education and similar concepts as focusing blame on the child and family rather than the school and the system (B: Bernstein, 1970; Keddie, 1973, 7–8, 21–3). Increasing awareness of issues in the education of children of immigrant families had begun to stimulate language-focused research projects in the 1960s, including June Derrick's project to produce materials for non-English speaking immigrant children, and a project on teaching English to West Indian children. The latter project concluded that West Indian dialect did impede the learning of English in school, that West Indian children had some differences from English children in communication skills, but that there was no evidence of differences in concept formation and intellectual development (B: Schools Council, 1970, 7).

Amid the changing economic fortunes of the 1970s the researchers, funding bodies, local authorities and others struggled to develop such ideas, projects and activities to combat the persistent problems of poverty and disadvantage. The position was clearly delineated by an Under Secretary at the Scottish Education Department, opening a 'Seminar on educational disadvantage' in Edinburgh in 1975:

Educational disadvantage is not a new problem ... What is new ... is the increasing determination in our society, in local government, and in central government, to do more about it ... Our general aim is to move towards the formulation of a policy for tackling educational disadvantage ... We could hardly have chosen a less promising time to embark on a concentrated attack on educational deprivation. The restrictions on public expenditure are at their most severe ... (B: SED, [1975], 7)

Restrictions were to continue and to grow in the final years of the Labour government and the Conservative administration of the 1980s, but the momentum of the late 1960s was carried through the 1970s in these various ways, including the preschool playgroups sponsored under the Urban Programme and by the Save the Children Fund. Urban Aid itself sponsored nearly 4,000 local projects in the decade, many for nursery-age disadvantaged children not being reached by existing local authority provision. Under various, mainly local authority, auspices a particularly vigorous development of the 1970s was that of educational home visiting or other forms of the teacher–parent liaison that we have seen in the West Riding, Deptford and Nottinghamshire.

The home visiting 'movement' was given a major impetus both by the West Riding EPA project and follow-up and by interest in American schemes, notably that pioneered by Phyllis Levenstein – a relatively structured approach to assisting mothers with child development – and a particular inspiration for a Lothian Educational Home Visiting Project in Scotland (B: McCail, 1981, 2). Following the EPA project the West Riding authority appointed six 'educational visitors' in 1973, and *Priority News* published a 'Blueprint for educational visitors' in the same year, suggesting terms for their recruitment, training, salary and roles, including regular sessions with mothers of preschool children, using 'home study' kits and materials, providing advice and information on school methods and further and higher education (B: *Priority News*, 1973, 10). In some places the visiting was done by teachers, in others by specially recruited professionals, in others by volunteers. A scheme that was focused on Deptford began in 1974 and spread more widely, based at the Frobisher Adult Education Institute, and had as a prime interest to promote mothers' groups and parent-oriented activities, and therefore the relationship with adult education (Nicholls, Marsh, interviews; Jayne, 1976). Interest was at this point developing rapidly. Leicester began a Home Start scheme; the London borough of Newham appointed Pre-school Home Visiting Teachers following discussion of the Halsey report by local inspectors and heads of schools (B: Newham, [1978], 1); a Southampton 'Scope' scheme, supported by Hampshire County Council and Barclay's Bank Trust established fourteen groups of mothers to share anxieties, talk and action (B: Haigh, 1977, 16; Parker, 1982b, 17). The Southampton scheme involved organizers who had worked with the West Riding project. The momentum was national enough to mount a national conference in 1975 (hosted by the Frobisher Institute) and in 1978 schemes were being listed in Scotland, Birmingham, Liverpool, Coventry, Cheshire, Lincoln, several London boroughs, and other areas (B: Poulton, 1978, 42). In 1975 a Rochdale community primary school acquired two extra teachers, one to a nursery unit, 'to increase parents' awareness of the factors influencing their children's development', and the nursery class opened on Saturday mornings in conjunction with a junior youth club (B: Evans and Hannon, 1977, 17). Here, as in other schemes, home visiting involved toys, play, materials and an attempt to increase mothers' self-confidence. A report on *Disadvantaged Children and Playgroups* in 1977, from a study commissioned by the Department of Health and Social Service, concluded that 'it can now be said with some certainty that the pre-school problem, especially as it affects the disadvantaged child, can only be solved by treating mother-and-child as the unit of concern', and in the same year Midwinter said of schools in general that teachers needed to see the 'unit of treatment' as 'parents-and-child together' (B: Ferri and Niblett, 1977, 44–5; Midwinter, 1977, 17).

At the end of the decade the movement was widespread, but not without its critics. Some schemes ran into teacher opposition, most had to come to terms with the accusation of labelling or stigmatizing families. Some mothers were reported as gaining confidence, others as losing it in the face of middle-class professionalism (B: Newham, 1977; McCail, 1981, 88). Barbara Tizard discovered that teachers and parents often had quite different perceptions of the purposes of home visiting. She and Martin Hughes were also to claim in a research project report published in 1984 that the 1970s emphasis on poor mother–child communication in disadvantaged homes (including that of the Bullock report on *A Language for Life*, with its advocacy of home visiting) had been misguided. They suggested that a much higher level of communication took place than had been assumed, that play was different, but not lacking, that language deficit was a myth (B: Tizard, B., 1981, 8; Tizard and Hughes, 1984, 150–3, 159, 266–7).

One other initiative from 1975 indicates how far the poverty/disadvantage context of education was being followed through at an official or policy level in the mid-1970s. In that year a new national organization was set up in Manchester by the Labour government, a Centre for Information and Advice on Educational Disadvantage (CED). The main intention, following a Select Committee report and the work of an Education Disadvantage Unit within the DES, was to disseminate ideas and good practice in the education of ethnic minorities, but it also saw itself as helping in the struggle 'to get some continuity with the EPA work' (Roberts, interview) and to help with the development of what by now had been renamed 'social priority schools'. Colin Roberts, HMI, who had been attached to the EDU, became director of the Centre, and it established a range of work that included conferences (including an Anglo-European Conference on 'Disadvantage and the Education of Young Children' in 1977), lectures, meetings and publications of various kinds. Its newsletter, *Disadvantage in Education*, reported conferences and new courses relating to disadvantage and education for a multi-cultural society, and CED publications discussed such issues as 'vulnerable children' schemes, and *Are Educational Priority Areas Still Worthwhile?* Announcing the creation of the CED in parliament, Fred Mulley, the Secretary of State, offered the following terms of reference:

...to seek to promote good practice in the education of the disadvantaged at all stages of the system, taking into account the distinct needs of the ethnic minorities; to concern itself with the inter-action of educational establishments and the communities they serve; and with aspects of teacher education relevant to educational disadvantage. (B: CED, [1976], 1)

The Centre in fact interpreted its brief extremely widely, and concerned itself with the 'lower socio-economic group' as its main concern, ethnic minority groups and 'any sub-group with a distinctive culture such as gypsies or even some extreme religious groups', and all other groups 'who are not merely disadvantaged because, for example, they come from broken homes, but where this feature links with poverty, or lack of essential resource'. The needs of the mentally and physically handicapped were also its concern 'when their educational deficit becomes very marked'. In post-school education, illiteracy and educational backwardness were the criteria of need. Unemployment was 'mainly linked with major disadvantaged groups, and the Centre's priority must be with attempts to produce some satisfactory continuing provision for those who have earlier failed in or rejected their previous schooling' (B: Roberts, 1977, 4–5). A year before the Labour government went out of office a DES report on education declared that it was 'a central part of Government policy to combat disadvantage wherever it is found, but especially in inner city areas, where shortcomings in housing, employment opportunities, education and environmental conditions reinforce each other' (B: DES, 1978, 7). The CED had proved to be an important dissemination and networking agency, an assessment of its work had concluded that it was 'doing something useful', and its closure by the Conservative government in 1980 was 'political' (Roberts, interview). From the report of the Plowden committee in 1967 to the end of the Labour government in 1979 there had been a variety of strategies and attempts to use education as one of the points of leverage against the shortcomings which reinforced each other, and the CED was one of the last in the developments which included the EPAs, inner city, preschool and community school initiatives, and a range of broadly-based or narrowly targeted projects. One focus had been on poor areas, in order to bring complex and coordinated services to bear on multiply disadvantaged communities, families and schools. Another focus was on individual children at risk, in order to devote school resources and energies to anticipating and preventing failure. A third focus was on the parent-and-child as the 'unit of concern', particularly in the crucial preschool years. The school and the educational process were being perceived in relation to their community and to other institutions and agencies developed under an Urban Programme, a Community Development Project and other programmes, and often involving a reconsideration of traditional individual or institutional roles. Schools changed, cooperated or resisted, and their priorities and roles were in any case to be radically reviewed and revised in the late 1970s and 1980s.

Within all the 1970s projects and developments we have discussed there was persistent and increasingly detailed attention to the parallel 'follow through' work in the United States, with particular interest in the findings of and controversies surrounding the evaluation of major programmes. From Jack Tizard's visit to Susan Gray's project in 1967, through the contacts at the time of the EPA projects under the auspices of the Ford Foundation, the OECD or the Ditchley Foundation, the American connections of the Swansea and Didsbury projects and those of the home visiting schemes, there were increasing contacts between British and American researchers and activists. What had appeared to be essentially American problems and conditions in the 1960s became increasingly recognizable as British problems and conditions also in the 1970s. Questions of social class and structure had in many respects come closer to direct concern with the specific disadvantages and lack of resources and power of particular social groups. A publication such as Butler, Davie and Goldstein's *From Birth to Seven* reflects the convergence with its emphasis on social class differences in attainment and ability, parents' and children's development, and regional differences in the distribution of educational attainment (B: Silver, 1973, 324–52). The same may be said of some of the EPA work and the direction of interests of the CED. The struggle to maintain action-research and other research strategies that could influence policy directions was sustained with difficulty as resources became more constrained, and complaints about the limited amount of research taking place in Britain grew more frequent and sharp. Another focus that was to gather pace from the end of the 1970s in Britain, again taking some of its cues from the United States, was that of the school itself, its characteristics, its ability to serve the disadvantaged and other clienteles. At a conference convened by the Secretary of State prior to the establishment of the CED, under the title 'Educational disadvantage: perspectives and policies', the chairman, Sir Alec Clegg, who was also to become chairman of the CED itself, concluded that 'it would have a very valuable role by simply acting as a clearing house. There was much excellent work with the disadvantaged going on in schools up and down the country. "The difference between the really superb school and the really dreadful school", he said, "is enormous", and the role of the Centre should be to identify the schools where good work was taking place' (B: DES, 1975, 22). From the late 1970s, following on from the reactions to Coleman's 1966 report, the focus was to be not only on identifying such differences and examples of good practice, but also on how to account for them. In the 1970s, the search in Britain for educational strategies against poverty and disadvantage had brought all the institutions of education, all the participants in the educational process, all the relationships between the institutions and processes and related processes of society, politics and the economy under extensive and increasingly comprehensive scrutiny.

14   Directions

History does not move neatly by decades but the 1980s have an international identity, with profound economic and political changes taking place. The 1980s are in many respects a discontinuity, with major shifts of policy emphasis in Britain, the United States and other countries, from 'access' to 'excellence' in education, from equity to economic need. However, in the United States more than in Britain the continuities are of profound importance. In 1981 an Education Consolidation and Improvement Act – effective from October 1982 – did not, as originally intended when converting 'Title I' to 'Chapter I', subsume efforts for the disadvantaged in a block grant, but instead retained the principle of targeting. Parent Advisory Committees were no longer to be mandatory, but parents still had to be consulted. The fear that Chapter I would disappear into general aid accompanied by budget cuts proved unfounded. The evaluation of Chapter I services continued to show that students who received them registered larger achievement on test scores than those who did not, while not significantly reducing the gap with the advantaged (A: McClure, 1982, 450–3; McLaughlin *et al.*, 1985; Kennedy *et al.*, 1986, vii–viii; Birman *et al.*, 1987, 5–8). The Title I/Chapter I impetus not only survived the decade, it gained renewed vigour from the School Improvement Act of 1987. Chapter I funding had been increased by 12 per cent in 1986, and was further increased by 16 per cent under the Act. When the Act was debated in the House no member spoke against it and only one voted against. The policy was to double Chapter I funding in six years (A: Jennings, 1987, 108–9).

In terms of policy interests throughout the 1980s, however, there was a major shift in both countries away from priority attention for issues of poverty and disadvantage, except where these were synonymous with race and other issues therefore supervened. In Britain the EPA momentum all but disappeared, though individual local authorities – themselves struggling to preserve their financial base and powers against centralizing policy trends – sustained some of the activities generated in

318

the 1970s, including the widespread use of home–school liaison teachers. In Scotland, in 1984, pointing to sporadic legacies of the previous decade, two authors reviewing it traced the declining role assigned to schools in the range of efforts against disadvantage. In the early 1980s, they concluded, 'schools are no longer part of the action' (B: Nisbet and Watt, 1984, 5). The preoccupation in Britain in the mid-1980s was with unemployment, youth training, school curricula which could contribute to preparation for work, realigning emphasis towards basic skills, science, mathematics and technology. The 1988 Education Reform Act was the capstone of efforts to restructure the system – its management and ability for schools to 'opt out', and introducing a national curriculum under pressures that had been growing since the mid-1970s. Any explicit concern with the issues that flowed from the Plowden period had been distanced from educational policy-making. In this respect the position was similar in both countries, though with the important structural difference. Federal education strategies in the United States, as represented by ESEA, and other war on poverty and later programmes, had not fundamentally altered the fact that Washington could not determine the curriculum, funding and priorities of schools. In Britain, parliament and Whitehall could, and were increasingly doing so. The American 'reform' literature of the mid- and late-1980s consisted of appeals, rhetoric, argument and intention. Serious implementation depended on states, governors, pressure groups and school boards. 'Reform' in Britain was through nationally mandated change, and discontinuity was therefore easier to achieve.

An important element in later perceptions of the school in relation to disadvantage, particularly in the US case, was the evaluation of long-term outcomes of the 1960s preschool programmes. The results of such evaluations appeared in the late 1970s, after a fourteen-project Consortium for Longitudinal Studies had come into existence in 1975, when President Ford had threatened to phase out support for Head Start. Irving Lazar proposed that the original experimental and control group children should be traced and their subsequent school careers studied. Three quarters of them were in fact traced, and a number of 'lasting effects' were determined. A considerable body of literature describing these effects appeared, most influentially between 1978 and 1981. Early accounts by Lazar and colleagues of 'the persistence of school effects' from the preschool and infant experiments suggested that fewer children who had experienced Head Start and similar programmes had later been assigned to special education classes or been retained in grades, and had been better able to meet the minimum requirements of schools (A: Lazar et al., 1977; Lazar and Darlington, 1978). Accounts which followed emphasized these and other positive long-term effects, including a lower drop-out rate before high school graduation (A: Lazar, 1981, 304; Darlington, 1981). The analysis of the later school careers of these 3,000 children followed up in 1976–7 (from projects which included those of Deutsch, Gray, Weikart and Levenstein) did not find it possible to draw deductions about which projects were 'more effective' than others, but it did also suggest permanent effects on parent attitude. It also found that preschool programme children were less likely to have been in trouble for anti-social behaviour and to have been arrested, and were more likely to have found and held jobs. Fewer of the girls had teenage pregnancies and more of those who did went on to complete high school (A: *Phi Delta Kappan*, 1981, 463: Schweinhart and Weikart, 1986). Reports from specific projects, both inside and outside the Consortium, confirmed long-term gains on such criteria. The Perry Preschool Program at Ypsilanti was an important Consortium project which did so, as did a Title I Preschool and All-Day Kindergarten in Cincinnati, which conducted a longitudinal study of 551 children from 1970 to 1979 (A: Berrueta-Clemens, 1984; Nieman and Gastright, 1981). Susan Gray and colleagues reported on the 'enduring effects' as revealed by a study of the Early Training Project children, now 21 years old, in 1979 (A: Gray *et al.*, 1981; Gray, 1983). Some of the follow-up studies, particularly those of Head Start, reported on data concerning health, impact on families and communities, with a range of positive effects on these and other aspects of children's development (A: Takanishi, 1977; McKey *et al.*, 1985). Cognitive development was the most difficult to analyse with any certainty, and the reports consistently suggested no long-term effects other than those measured by the high incidence of successful progression through school without being held in grade, lower pre-graduation drop-out, and higher rate of college attendance – all widely reported in positive terms.

The war of evaluations had taken a decisively new turn. The messages were heard in Britain through now established networks, and Halsey wrote a *New Society* article entitled 'Education can compensate', summarizing the findings and stressing that it was still not clear what factors most made for success (B: Halsey, 1980, 172–3). By the new decade, however, the potential for influence of such findings was very different in the two countries.

Some features of the educational strategies we have discussed had similar origins and configurations in the late 1960s and 1970s, even though there were in the early years obstacles to recognizing common problems. Governments in the two countries, Martin Rein was able to suggest by 1970, wanted the same things, and were pursuing them under the same constraints (B: Rein, 1970, 8). In both countries compensatory education and positive discrimination represented forms of egalitarianism which targeted specific social groups and, in spite of early enthusiasms, it was rarely expected that schools alone could eliminate poverty. The vigour of support for the educational dimensions of the attack on poverty nevertheless effectively overrode radical and conservative doubts about the programmes. With slightly different time scales the United States experienced a 'liberal moment' and Britain a period of either social democracy or relatively consensual liberal politics. The post-war United States had not developed any kind of 'welfare state', and in the period we have discussed educational policies and programmes could be seen as reflecting a new liberalism, supportive of the liberal capitalist state or worse – part of a 'liberal' (used pejoratively) drive to serve profit and the political status quo by not questioning the basic structure of corporate capitalist society, property and power (A: Crittenden, 1970; Bowles and Gintis, 1976, 8–14). Radical critiques of the liberal position – including its educational components – focused on its inability to confront the realities of class and race, and its substitution of attempts to reduce inequality of opportunity for ones to reduce inequality itself. Amidst renewed optimism arising from the Consortium's evidence, and in reaction to the gathering power of neo-conservative policies, there were also radical educationists who saw strength in the liberal experience of the 1960s: 'liberal coalitions make it possible to propose radical visions, even though one of the chief aims of liberal reform is to defuse radical violence' (A: Featherstone, 1979, 49). The educational momentum we have described did in fact survive into the 1980s. Beginning a review of the post-war 'liberal era' of federal social policy, Haveman in 1981 considered it to have ended with the election of President Reagan in 1980: 'since 1981 there has been no War on Poverty – it is as if victory had been declared, when in fact there was no such conquest'. The war had begun in an 'intellectual void' with social scientists serving the newly proclaimed cause without knowing how to wage the war effectively (A: Haveman, 1987, 3–4). Some of those on whose doors the policy-makers knocked from 1964 realized, as we have seen, both the unique opportunity of the call, and the limitations of the exercise in which they were engaged. The same was true of Britain, where the exercise was not conducted in terms of a war, was funded at rudimentary levels, built on a different base, and its educational hopes lay in prospects of economic expansion which did not occur. The election of Margaret Thatcher as Prime Minister in 1979 was in fact a more decisive break with the 'liberal' policies of both Labour and Conservative administrations of the 1960s and 1970s. When

Haveman, in 1986 in the United States, looked back on his 1981 judgment he confessed to having been wrong: '1981 was not the end of an era, but only the beginning of moderate curtailment. Programmes to reduce poverty were scaled back and their objectives and rhetoric were modified. They were not, however, dismantled...Public concern with the problem of poverty has increased' (A: *ibid.*, 233). In educational terms the British hiatus was more complete and more sustained.

Given the continued levels of poverty in both countries the associated social and educational issues remained in some respects unchanged. There were still areas, groups and individuals in need of general or targeted support. Economic downturns left whole communities vulnerable and disrupted. Employment trends and large-scale unemployment raised basic questions about the structure and provision of education and training. Issues relating to poverty remained enmeshed with those relating to race and ethnicity. Policies directed towards the involvement of or support for the family could still be interpreted not as intervention but as interference. In fact, the target of any policy could be and often was seen as either beneficial to the constituency concerned, or yet another form of control or labelling, especially, for example, if a concentration of population in a poor area was also a minority population. Controversy continued around the characteristics and needs, or the reality and mythology of 'deprived areas'.

The most significant continuity over the decades covered by this discussion was that of poverty itself. 'Poverty', 'disadvantage' and 'deprivation' have continued to be no less common, if sometimes no less elusive, vocabularies, in spite of – or even because of – major political and economic changes, and in spite of major shifts in both countries towards the attenuated social policies of the 1980s. The bombardment of statistics in the United States in the 1980s was relentless. The new conservatives of the Reagan government claimed initially that poverty had been eradicated, but in late 1981 the National Advisory Council on Economic Opportunity considered that 25 million Americans were poor, and another 30 million, if they lost a job, fell ill or 'burned out', could be poor. Child poverty increased by more than 15 per cent from 1969 to 1979. In 1978, 40 per cent of black children were poor, and so were 25 per cent of Hispanic children (A: McCarthy, 1981). In 1982 *The New York Times* reported the latest Census bureau figures as showing the highest poverty rate since 1967, with 14 per cent of the population below the poverty threshold, an increase of 2.2 million on the previous decade (A: Herbers, 1982). By the end of the decade the poverty rate was being described variously as being between 12 and 25 per cent. Whatever the precise figure, that there had been an increase was not in doubt. A commission report on youth and young families reported in 1988 that the poverty rate had fallen from 18.5 per cent in 1959 to 8.8 per cent in 1973, and had risen to 12.3 per cent by 1983 (A: William T. Grant Foundation, 1988, 20). The mythology of the eradication of poverty was no more sustainable in Britain than it was in the United States.

It is unlikely that there were many in either society in the 1960s – even in the period of the most infectious Johnsonian rhetoric in the United States – who expected education to be the dominant force in *eliminating* poverty. The intention was to have impacts on precise targets – levels of unemployment, juvenile delinquency, school dropout – matters of political significance in Kennedy's or Johnson's visions of what the latter postulated as 'The Great Society'. Poverty was seen as a condition whose origins could be determined, for which apparently tangible solutions could be explored, and from at least the most pervasive aspects of which people could be helped to escape. It had both short-term and long-term implications for social action and policy. Resources could be concentrated on its solution, and education was a terrain on which the forces of advance could be mustered. In different ways in the two countries, therefore, poverty and its related terminologies interlocked or on occasion conflicted with other conceptual machineries, notably that of inequality. The inter-relationship between the two concepts as starting points for analysis and action has not disguised their distinctive implications. Both concepts are concerned with the distribution of resources and power, and for education have had meanings beyond merely the provision of access to existing structures. Inequality dominated much of the discussion in the 1960s and 1970s in Britain and the United States, focusing – with different combinations in the two countries – on social class, the reorganization of structures, inequalities based on race and ethnicity and, later, gender, together with changing assumptions about equality of opportunity, treatment and outcome. Different social theories and political policies were implied by these concepts and different versions of them. Poverty, either frankly so or euphemistically describing the condition of racial and ethnic minorities, was at the heart of American compensatory strategies developed in the 1960s. Though closely meshed in with issues of inequality it pointed towards educational and social policies less structurally oriented than those implied by inequality. Desegregation and integration were the salient policy outcomes of a concern with inequality in the United States, where the mesh between the concepts was strong and complex, whereas in British conditions it was weak. Inequality was the basis of British preoccupation mainly with secondary school structures, and poverty turned attention towards a different range of educational processes and issues, different forms of social action and strategies. The implications of the poverty starting point for educational analysis inhabit the middle ground of 'skeptical idealism between the unrealistic long-term and the pragmatic' which Miller and Rein felt to be lacking in the 1960s (A: Miller and Rein, 1965b, 273–4). These implications relate to questions such as those of language and learning, environmental handicap and the possibilities, in school, home and community, of compensating for it.

Criteria for defining poverty have been elusive and controversial throughout the period we have discussed. This was so at the time American policies were grounded in monetary definitions in the 1960s and in the poverty debates around absolute and relative deprivation in Britain at the same period. In Britain in the early 1980s Donnison was identifying a variety of meanings for poverty, including a standard of living so low as to exclude people from community (B: Donnison, 1982, 7), and later in the decade there were still attempts to redefine poverty in terms of 'an enforced lack of socially perceived necessities' and other criteria and measurements (B: Mack and Lansley, 1985; Piachaud, 1987).

We have seen some of the conceptual and operational difficulties attached to poverty-related analysis and policy-making. Means of targeting areas and individuals for support were one such controversial area. From the 1960s the concept of 'slums' disappeared from public debate, although at the beginning of the 1960s it was still prominent in both countries, as represented in the United States by Conant's *Slums and Suburbs* in 1961, and in Britain by the chapter in the Newsom report on 'Education in the slums' in 1963. The transition away from a vocabulary of 'slums' was from a concept that was mainly pejorative but occasionally romantic, towards attempts to explain the economic and social causes of poverty. Poverty was not just an individual or cumulative condition, it was also comparative, could be broken down into conditions with different causal explanations, and was the subject of a secular research tradition. The notion of an anti-poverty strategy was therefore – whatever the limitations of what actually took place – a dynamic concept, in which neither side of the poverty–strategy equation was fixed and homogeneous. Whether the intention was to reform the British welfare state or to extend the US federal commitment, the target was or seemed to be groups or categories or concentrations of people with identifiable and similar hardships or deprivations. The problem was to discover them, and to discover policies or action that could act as levers of substantial and permanent change.

Education, as a system, and as a process experienced by individuals, became a focal point in American thinking about these changing vocabularies and realities, as it had always done in the circumstances and crises of American society. Education for the disadvantaged, education as an instrument by which to change opportunities for population groups, education as a central policy for community development and cohesion, education as a policy against environmental deprivation in city ghettos, in poor rural areas, in the North or the South – all of these were features of the developments in the mid-1960s – as often for the same ends in different forms in the nineteenth and twentieth centuries. In Britain, in conditions of immigration, urban change, political readjustments of various kinds, similar roles for education were debated and tested, particularly from the late 1960s. The EPA focus on area projects and the Swansea focus on the disadvantaged child were parallel strands within the overall awareness of the relationship between educational 'failure' and disadvantage. Throughout the 1970s, however, social policy analysts, project evaluators and others argued over the legitimacy of one or the other kind of approach to intervention against poverty and disadvantage. It was commonly argued that many, perhaps even a majority, of those in 'disadvantaged areas' were not 'disadvantaged', and that the majority of the latter did not live in disadvantaged areas. It was also argued that *only* an area-based policy could harness enough resources and services to combat poverty (B: Donnison, 1974; interview). The American Sustaining Effects Study concluded that some 60 per cent of poor children in the 1970s were not being selected for Title I programmes, and that non-poor children exceeded poor children on many compensatory programmes (A: SDC, 1977–81, no. 2). In American and British projects across the 1960s and 1970s the difficulty within areas of identifying 'disadvantaged' children was seen as crucial, in order to avoid labelling, particularly in American classroom 'pull-out' situations. When the Deptford Educational Home Visiting Project began in 1974 'it was not thought advisable to screen for "disadvantage" or to attract only "priority" cases but rather to offer this service to all within a small geographic area, although the area itself is one of "disadvantage"' (B: Jayne, 1976, 3). In 1975 Halsey placed such difficulties in a context of the history of tension between social and individual approaches, which had been a constant and central theme in the social sciences and public policy – for example, with regard to the poor law, unemployment and suicide – and he offered an approach based on 'The juxtaposition of social and individual approaches in compensatory education projects' (B: Halsey, 1975b). The relationship between education and poverty has throughout this period emerged as at one level the difficult question of adequate and appropriate provision for the individual, socially handicapped child, and at another level the identification of broad conditions associated with poverty and its distribution, and the interconnection of these conditions with schools and other educational institutions and processes.

A number of core concepts have been prominent in the policies and activities we have discussed – disadvantage and deprivation, accompanied by various adjectival definitions, conceived of in 'cycles', directly or indirectly related to schooling or infant experience. Other vocabularies of social and particularly urban analysis appeared in the 1980s, including that of the 'underclass' (A: Wilson, W.J., 1987; B: Judd, 1988). None was more contested than the cluster of terminologies around the idea of compensation, and of deficit or difference. The twin concepts of 'positive discrimination' (mainly in Britain) and 'compensatory education' are historically recent innovations. They were shaped against earlier interpretations of environmental deficit, which often included the family as the main environmental agent, but also often looked at the wider environment. American environmental analysis of the 1960s included both an awareness of the oppressive squalor of urban poverty, and the limited stimulus provided by the poverty-stricken lives of Appalachian and other rural American areas in decline. If the environment was 'gray' and failed to stimulate, if resources for children's play were lacking, if social and family conditions reduced the amount of adult–child verbal interaction, if models of successful and satisfying learning were absent, if motivation to learn and succeed was lacking, and if the environment provided in general an inhibiting framework for childhood, then those children entered school 'deprived' of what children from other environments took for granted and carried into the educational process. Schools and preschool education therefore needed to 'compensate'. The enormous literature which appeared particularly in the United States in the mid- and late-1960s and early 1970s on disadvantage, teaching the disadvantaged, compensatory strategies, and so on, posed what seemed the obvious question: if children were environmentally, culturally and socially deprived, what could and should education do to compensate?

The concepts and the question implied a deficit, though it was never clear whose deficit it was. The initial American thrust was towards enrichment for children from 'culturally deprived' backgrounds, that is, bearing a deficit whose roots lay in the totality of the background, the family and the neighbourhood, the nature of the community, its economic and social structures, the learning situation on which severe constraints were imposed by the transmitted norms, the powerlessness, the discrimination. All of these were differently combined in different explanations, but they were all somewhere in the picture. Compensation might therefore take a one-directional form, from the school towards the child and home, suggesting a deficit model, the need to change the child and family. A rapidly developing critique of this model, in both countries, suggested that the strengths of the working-class family, and the experience of the working-class child, were being undervalued or ignored, that both the analysis and the policies reflected either middle-class values or the social-control strategies of a ruling class. In the continuing controversies the notion of cultural 'difference' emerged, the attempted neutrality of which suggested a commitment to pluralism. At the heart of the British controversy was the meaning and significance of Bernstein's work on language and cultural transmission, and into the debate was imported American – notably Labov's – affirmation of lower-class black speech as culturally different but in no way less expressive or less capable of carrying conceptual messages. The 'new sociology' of the early 1970s, most widely known through Michael F.D. Young's edited volume of 1971 on *Knowledge and Control*, was a British expression of the concern to replace existing models with one of knowledge as structured for purposes of power, and to define schooling more in terms of what it deprived the powerless of, not what it provided. All of the concepts, however interpreted, pointed a finger of 'blame'.

Some of the compensatory theory suggested that school failure was the fault or the weakness of the child, the family, the environment. One case for the defence of the disadvantaged child was built on an interpretation of education as an ideological process which served class interests and blamed the victim (A: Ryan, 1971, 8). What the critique underestimated, however, was the strength of the concurrent attack on the school within the policies and literature targeted on disadvantage and poverty. From the early days of the war on poverty, within the Title I and Follow Through justifications, there were sometimes cautious, sometimes powerful, criticisms levelled against teachers and teaching methods, the school and its purposes and practices, the educational system in general, as responsible for the failures of disadvantaged children, as inflexible, as unable or unwilling to adapt to the needs of children whose characteristics were different from those of middle-class children. In very many of the projects, British and American, that we have discussed a central aim was to change the teacher and the school, their relationships with families and the community, their curriculum and their roles in causing children to fail.

Of central importance in the literature of 'blame' was the increasingly explicit attack in the United States on the euphemistic analysis of poverty which in many instances was taken to mean race. Poverty and race did not form an equation, though some critics treated it as such in the 1970s. There is no doubt that some of the social-rescue element in public policy in the 1970s coincided strongly with anxieties about race. Many of the demonstration and research projects begun in the United States in the early and mid-1960s were, in their attention to the 'children of poverty', in fact concerned with black children. The educational concerns overlapped with widespread American debate about the culture of black and other minority Americans, triggered by a considerable literature, of which Moynihan's *The Negro Family* in 1965 provoked the most controversy. Although the compensatory education movement was never exclusively concerned with racial and ethnic minorities, the race issue was never far from the discussion. An important background was the *Brown* decision of 1954, the interpretative legal decisions which followed and the consequent struggle to desegregate the schools and public life. By the mid-1960s those diverse experiences, together with the civil rights campaigns, violence against civil rights activists – black and white – had produced not only new dimensions of black action, but also a heightened black consciousness of successes, opportunities and frustrations. The importance of that background for the new educational policies was twofold. First, it was a major part of the pressures for change, whether or not made explicit in the policy process. Francis Keppel, in 'Thank God for the civil rights movement' in 1964 talked of the 'chance which does not come often to the educational community'. The civil rights movement 'provides the very opportunity we have been looking for' (A: Keppel, 1964b, 9–10). Secondly, the civil rights movement pointed to specific questions about the relationship between minority cultures and the school, a question long present on the margins of American educational history but now assuming a different urgency and requiring different answers. Against that background, a problem for compensatory education was that it had been shown to have an unclear or unambiguous theoretical basis. It was liberating in that it dislodged notions of fixed, genetically dictated, inferior intelligence, and moved analysis firmly into the social, economic and behavioural sciences. It was suspect, however, in that in some of its forms (notably in the case of analyses based most directly on 'cultural deprivation') it suggested a new hierarchy in which black and minority cultures and experience appeared to be devalued. Amidst these social and political conflicts and debates the charge of racism came to be levelled against the research and intervention strategies of the 1960s. One of the most cited arguments was an article on 'Early childhood intervention: the social science base of institutional racism' (A: Baratz and Baratz, 1970), and although in both the United States and Britain there was some substance to criticism of the system as a whole on those grounds, the literature and practices of compensatory education and disadvantage in the late 1960s and 1970s does not substantiate a view of them as a unitary, ethnocentric approach to minorities based on a social pathology model. Much of the literature is explicitly concerned with research concerning all races subjected to the same conditions of poverty, much of it is aware of the cultural strengths of minority communities, much of it is concerned with the multi-racial inner city, and much of the initial and subsequent effort was directed explicitly at white – notably Appalachian – children. In 1964 Silberman was criticizing the schools for being 'not right for white any more than for black students' (B: Silberman, 1964, 251). The formulations of the leading researchers, of ephemeral project publications, research proposals, commission reports, statements of US Commissioners of Education and other research-based or policy-oriented material, do not uphold the view that there is an undeviating central thread of racism running through it all. Nor do these uphold the view that the developments were concerned with a basic model which laid exclusive blame for failure at the door of the poor, the working class, the black, the family, the environment. The director of the Follow Through programme described it as an 'assault on the *institutional* inadequacies that penalize children of poverty' (A: Egbert, 1974, 127). Riessman was arguing in 1963 against 'underestimating the underprivileged' and against imposing a middle-class model instead of genuine pluralism (A: Riessman, 1963b, 46–7). As early as 1962–3, articles in, for example, the *NEA Journal* and *Phi Delta Kappan* discussed how to direct programmes away from middle-class values and towards a recognition of cultural differences and the shortcomings of schools (A: Krugman, 1961; Kaplan, 1963; Shaw, 1963).

The theoretical and political problems involved in these debates continued into the 1980s and, in the United States at least, so did the vocabularies of disadvantage and compensatory education, as to a large degree did accompanying strategies. In 1987 California was spending $93 million dollars on its compensatory education programme (B: Kirp and Tuden, 1987, 18). The battle to persuade schools to involve low-income parents was continuing (A: McLaughlin and Shields, 1987). Chapter I, still the largest federal education programme, had a budget of $4.57 billion dollars in 1989, and it was being strongly argued that this was insufficient to reach all eligible students, 'despite their dire needs' (A: Shanker, 1990, 348). The movement to define and promote 'effective schools' was rooted in the apparent failure of schools to serve the poor, working-class and minority populations: the most influential article on the subject was entitled 'Effective schools for the urban poor'

(A: Edmonds, 1979). In Britain, the community school, school–parent links and the fight for increased nursery provision were all geared to a continued awareness of the problems of poverty. A Scottish project on the incidence of deprivation and its influence on educational attainment brought the neighbourhood into the diagram of explanations alongside the school and the home, all in answer to the question *Does Deprivation Damage?* (B: Garner, 1989). A Swansea follow-up study of 'culturally disadvantaged children' at the age of fifteen found that the attainment gap of the disadvantaged group when compared with the control group on several measures had widened from the age of eleven (B: Cox, 1988). These and other British examples were inevitably on a vastly smaller scale than the continuing American commitments, but they indicate a flickering activity intended to confront problems and realities which had not diminished in the changed political and economic circumstances.

In the late 1980s there were important American signs that poverty-related educational policies were in fact strengthening and, to some extent, 1960s wheels were being either reinvented or rediscovered. In 1985, at the height of the US flurry of concern about 'excellence' in education, the Committee for Economic Development published a statement entitled *Investing in our Children: Business and the Public Schools*. Prepared by a Research and Policy Committee consisting overwhelmingly of business executives, the statement was aware of the virtual unemployability of many high school graduates, the large proportion of whom never completed high school, the extent of functional illiteracy, and the higher levels of educational attainment of the main competitors, notably Japan. It was also aware of the demographic trend which would result in shortages of professional and skilled labour in the next century, and the rising proportion of minorities in the population – from whom the needed labour force would increasingly have to be recruited. For reasons which differed somewhat from those of the mid-1960s the CED therefore offered arguments and proposals not unlike those of a quarter of a century earlier:

...the earliest stages of educational development are where we will receive the best return on our investment in education. This means a stronger focus on the elementary schools and on well-designed preschool programs for children from disadvantaged backgrounds.

The CED had heard the messages from the Consortium for Longitudinal Studies (though without acknowledging it directly). There had been controversy about preschool programmes but 'despite early findings to the contrary, well-designed studies now make it clear that high-quality preschool programs lasting one year and targeted to four-year-olds from poor families can have enormous economic payoffs'. It commended the

Perry Preschool Program at Ypsilanti particularly, emphasized the need for school districts with support from their state governments to 'undertake a serious and systematic investment in enriched early childhood education for children from poor families', and suggested that 'early childhood education for high-risk children should exert a very strong claim on state and local budgets' (A: CED, 1985, 9, 43–6). The cumulative emphasis was very clear, including the need for an increased investment of public funds.

In 1986 a publication of the National Education Association was addressing the same 'emerging crisis' in *Educational Reform for Disadvantaged Students*. It was essentially an argument for 'remedial' and 'compensatory' education, 'preschool enrichment', 'home re-sources', 'parent involvement' and 'parent education', plus some of the newer teaching and learning strategies. Existing reform efforts by the states were not addressing 'the critical needs of educationally dis-advantaged students'. Disaster lay ahead unless 'the needs of the disadvantaged are addressed'. Disadvantaged students arrived in school 'with learning deficits...learning resources in their homes are inade-quate...most schools lack the programs and resources...The first part of any strategy...must be to address preschool needs'. Investment in the education of the disadvantaged 'should be viewed as a highly productive investment in the future of our society' (A: Levin, H.M., 1986, 21–5, 35). From very different political and educational directions the two analyses and conclusions were similar, and the resonance of the 1960s poverty programmes was distinct. In 1989 Democratic Representative George Miller edited a book entitled *Giving Children a Chance*, contributors to which argued for a higher proportion of eligible children to be reached by Head Start, for expanded early childhood programmes in association with policies for full employment, housing, health care and a decent standard of living. It underlined the known long-term positive effects of anti-poverty policies, particularly preschool pro-grammes, and contained two chapters with the titles 'Early intervention in cognitive development as a strategy for reducing poverty', and 'Equal opportunity for infants and young children: preventive services for children in a multi-risk environment'. What was being propounded, without mentioning the 1960s, was a set of aims almost identical to those that were shaped in the early war on poverty. Central to the whole book was an awareness that opinion had been moving in the late 1980s towards stronger commitment to addressing the problems of poverty, citing state governors' declarations, welfare efforts in Congress, editorial support in the media for early childhood programmes and anti-poverty policies, opinion poll support for increased attention to poverty-related issues, and the priority attached to them by leaders of the business community as exemplified in the Committee for Economic Development (A: Miller, G., 1989, 1–9, 23–36, 131–48). At this point in the 1980s in the United States, though with only the faintest echoes in Britain, attention was turning under a variety of auspices to disadvantaged or 'at risk' children and young people. A researcher at the federal Office of Educational Research and Improvement in 1989 shaped an article on 'Improving education for the disadvantaged' round growing public support for doing so. There were 'signs now pointing toward a willingness to provide new programs for young people identified as disadvantaged or "at risk" of school failure'; the 'warm glow of public support for Chapter 1' extended beyond political circles, and 'the momentum to improve education for disadvantaged children is gathering' (A: Ralph, 1989, 395–9). The period of 'moderate curtailment' appeared to be generating interest in enhancing old programmes to confront old problems with strategies and objectives modified only by demographic and economic change.

The Consortium and other evaluations of long-term effects were suggesting degrees of success when consensus was difficult to attain on what constituted success or failure, or what 'scale' of 'success' might be considered good news and justifying the effort and investment. This was particularly true of the educational programmes of the war on poverty that were concerned with preschool and the early years of schooling. Our major interest has been the processes which contributed to the emphasis on early childhood, the nature of disadvantage in relation to efforts to improve and sustain learning, the educational, community and caring processes which could improve the chances of success of disadvantaged children at early stages of their entry into informal and formal educational processes. Although Head Start, for example, was by 1967 'combining the newest findings in educational psychology with the then current community action philosophy of political liberals' (A: Steiner, 1974, 61), evaluating the implementation and outcomes of the ensuing structures and processes proved a tormented activity. One of the central features of the transatlantic relationship that developed was British perception of the American upsurge of interest in the preschool child as a catching up exercise with the British nursery and primary school. The Plowden committee and others hesitated over the American strategies and what one of the Plowden working parties described as American 'doubtful achievements' in the development of new classroom approaches. Given the possible range of identifiable weaknesses in the policies and practices, therefore, judging success and failure became increasingly difficult as the directions of attention became more diverse.

The educational war on poverty was in effect a combination of novelties. In Britain, in 1966, the Inner London Education Authority commented that with regard to education 'cultural and social handicap...[had] only recently received the attention they require' (B: ILEA, 1967, 89), and thereby summarized the position on both sides of the Atlantic.

Built into projects and programmes, and also following on their heels, were evaluation tensions, from the inexperienced local evaluation machinery of the late 1960s to nationally designed measures intending to illuminate policy and to address national audiences. Nothing in the evaluations of Title I written in the United States during the first decade of its existence is of any real value in making judgments, but as historical records of the enthusiasm, determination and intentions of the participants the earlier local or state-wide reports are extremely important. They are the records of the practitioners, the parents and the children, and the very unreliability of the accounts is important historical evidence. They, and many of the evaluations of other programmes in the late 1960s and 1970s, point up the sources of energy, the frustrations over past neglect, previously disappointed aspirations, new dimensions of political action, changed relationships between home and school, the optimism and ideals that could be captured by the activity. The action–research and evaluation we have discussed were therefore having to catch up with the pace of action dictated by a sense of opportunity. Neither American nor British policy-makers and politicians were able, in the conditions of the 1960s and 1970s to give primacy to the research they recruited, unless it could be rapidly related to the pace of action. After the first flourish of the war on poverty in the United States, in neither country could social scientists, educators, researchers, activists, rely on an expanding or even a sustained level of ideological or financial commitment to the efforts that had been encouraged. Considerations of success and failure rested on the insecure foundations of often contradictory and controversial evaluations. Long-term programme commitments to understand the conditions and components of success and failure stumbled on short-term judgments and new political agendas.

Although the Consortium messages have been important and influential, there are no conclusive answers from either programme evaluation or the sweeping analyses of large-scale social intervention. Judgments about positive discrimination and educational priority in the 1980s had to consider not only what had taken place, but also its limitations. The scale in Britain had been small and efforts *ad hoc*, resources had been severely limited, and teachers and schools had hardly been drawn into adopting new teaching approaches or deepening their understanding of children's differences and difficulties (B: Gray, 1980, 16–19). Educational priority approaches had not yet been tried 'with much vigour' (B: Brown and Madge, 1982, 316). Judgments of the success or failure of institutions, programmes or activities could be according to their own criteria, to those of national or other funding agencies, or to what one British reviewer of several American books on the war on poverty described as 'what might reasonably have been expected of them and what, given the constraints surrounding them, they could have achieved' (B: Higgins, 1977, 86). 'What might reasonably have been expected' is certainly a useful guide, but the diversity of expectations and the complexity of the constraints make judgment dependent on the difficulties of theoretical conflict and the wide-ranging nature of the constraints. Judgments of the war on poverty and its educational content, as of British policies and programmes from 1967, have to take account, for example, of policies relating to the economy and the distribution of resources, employment opportunities and welfare policies, and the whole pattern of political and social decision-making, as it was or could have been. Truth, in Paul Hill's words, is 'hopelessly tangled up in the complex and shifting context in which the programs operate', making success and failure 'unverifiable' (A: Hill, 1981, 12–13) As we have seen, some of those most involved with Head Start came to regret the obsession with measuring effects on the basis of intelligence rather than on a wider range of competences (A: Zigler and Seitz, 1980, 354–7). Judgments which have to take account of the validity of tests and the interests of parliaments, the attitudes of teachers and the reality of policy implementation, make 'reasonable' expectations difficult to determine.

Consensus may not be difficult around some judgments, particularly in the case of the American war on poverty programmes. In their beginnings they no doubt suffered from ambiguous principles, a variety of theories assembled into what one commentator called 'an eclectic mixture which determined major policy decisions' (A: de Wit, 1972, 384). Reasonable expectations were certainly distorted by the political rodomontade which concealed the caution of many of the researchers. At too late a stage the programme designers and activists considered the nature and resilience of institutions. The EPA focus on the community school, and in some cases the work of the project directors rather than of the researchers, did indeed point towards the need for institutional change, but in these cases as in many of the American ones the nature of the project, the required collaboration with schools and their authorities, precluded extensive efforts in that direction. More often than not national programmes and local projects left schools unchanged.

The difficulties of effecting widespread change through national political machinery, large-scale programmes or small demonstration projects, were insufficiently understood and addressed.

So far as a commitment to educational strategies against poverty and disadvantage was sustained in Britain in the 1980s, awareness of American developments remained keen. British journals such as *The Times Educational Supplement*, *New Society* and *New Scientist* took a particular interest in the more positive messages about long-term effects that came from the late 1970s. *New Scientist* was reporting in 1977 the outcome of the longitudinal studies of Head Start and other pro-grammes, and the following year, under the headline 'Headstart – alive, well and kicking back', the *TES* reported an American lecturer in Britain expressing astonishment at the view of Head Start still prevalent in Britain, stemming from the Westinghouse evaluation. Other evalu-ations had come up with more favourable results (B: Lewin, 1977; Makins, 1978). Halsey published his account of the new American material in his 'Education can compensate' in 1980, and the *TES* and others were further discussing the 'better news' in 1981 (B: Cookson, 1981). A National Children's Bureau publication in 1982 discussed the virtues of provision for under-fives from a restricted environment against the background of the rehearsal of early pessimism about the programmes in the United States (B: Grey, 1982). From 1982 the *TES* was consistently reporting the impact of David Weikart through a British movement to implement his Ypsilanti High/Scope preschool programme in a number of British locations (B: Parker, 1982a; Makins, 1984a, 1985, 1986, 1987). American educators' interest in Britain in the 1980s had little to do with disadvantage, and more to do with the direction of British policy-making for school curricula, management and other aspects of increasing central control of the operation of the system.

Basically we have discussed a momentum of effort begun in the United States and taken up in Britain. There were, of course, mainly in the 1970s, other countries which, in facing up to their poverty problems, also included education in their repertoire of attempted solutions. In the early 1970s in Australia, for example, a Commission of Inquiry into Poverty identified many of the same kinds of problems, and discussed the American and British experience. A Commission report on *Poverty and Education in Australia* in 1976 described one-sixth of Australian children as poor, and the poor as 'hidden people' in an affluent society (B: Australian Government Commission, 1976, 3–7). A Disadvantaged Schools Program was established in 1973, with a specific interest in rural areas, and a Language Program for Aboriginal children. The Dis-advantaged Schools Program began by focusing on the cities, with a scatter of a substantial number of projects – ninety-six in 1978–9. It broadened out into the sparse rural areas, and the Language Program for Aboriginal Children aimed at developing relevant materials, capitalizing on the children's own experience and increasing their self-esteem. By the time the programmes were designed and under way it was the American emphasis on equality of outcomes of schooling that had become important, and the language of 'positive discrimination' was part of the armoury (B: Schools Commission, 1978–9, 1979; Randell, 1980). Projects on American 'social action' models appeared in Canada, including summer projects. One, in Vancouver, began in 1971 with what it described as a number of 'givens': 'Two months' summer vacation; hundreds of school-aged children; an "inner city"; empty schools; seasonally "unemployed" school teachers, university and secondary school students; a proliferation of social agencies; a nucleus of concerned parents' (B: Morin and Martin, 1971, 1). One of the problems was lack of data on disadvantaged children in the Canadian provinces, and another was working against the knowledge that compensatory education was under attack in the United States and evaluations of Head Start were reaching negative conclusions. Canada did not have the same extremes of poverty as the United States, and a compensatory education project under the auspices of the University of Western Ontario had as its first step in 1973 to identify what precisely the needs were (A: Wright, 1983, xvi, 7–12).

Projects in similar moulds were mounted elsewhere. A Dublin preschool programme began in 1969 with some conflict over whether to adopt a community approach or focus on children's educational development. It adopted essentially cognitive objectives and built in a home visiting scheme, explicitly influenced by American home-based projects. There were other obvious American influences. Similar outcomes were registered to those in early Head Start evaluations, though it was important that on IQ measures scores were maintained where they might have been expected to fall. The involvement of parents and the active roles developed for and with them constituted what was considered one of the most positive outcomes of the project (B: Kellaghan, 1977; Holland, 1979). Other European projects were developed and the OECD took a direct interest both in considering the relevance of the US experience and in discussing the experience of Britain and Ireland which had come into the field in the late 1960s (B: CERI, 1978, 1982; Woodhead, 1979; Boudon and Lagneau, 1980). Socialist success in the French elections in 1981 was followed by the creation of a pattern of nearly 400 Zones d'Education Prioritaires. For a ZEP to be approved it was not sufficient for statistical criteria of 'défaveur sociale' to be met, there also had to be educational projects in the schools, coordinated as zone projects (B: CRESAS, 1985, 9, 29). There was no explicit reference to British EPAs in the creation of the ZEPs, but one of the researchers involved, Claude Chrétiennot, produced a study of EPAs and a bibliography of the British work from 1967 (B: *ibid.*, 195–208). She and other French researchers visited Britain in the 1980s and examined EPA and related experience in depth (B: Henriot and Plaisance, 1988). CRESAS, a centre for research into special education and 'adaptation scolaire', had a decade of research experience behind it, produced a ZEP index, and rapidly developed a wide programme of action–research (B: CRESAS, 1983). The different timings of these and other national projects would need the same kind of discussion as that of the relationship between Britain and the United States, combining an analysis of 'influence' or international transactions with specific social and economic histories. Broadly speaking, despite the 1980s developments in France, there is a relatively discrete period from the mid-1960s to the end of the 1970s in which most of these programmes were generated, in conditions which explain their shape, content and intentions.

The most important function of recent-historical analysis is probably to rescue complexity from the oversimplifications and amnesia which rapidly overcome events, especially when sharp changes of political direction are dismissive of policies being overturned. The meanings of vocabularies, the presence or absence of alternative theories of strategies, what was and what might have been 'reasonably expected', have all to be periodically rescued, before they are overwhelmed by myths created sometimes casually, sometimes by persistent dogma. Policy has to be rescued, not in its limited legislative or political decision-making forms, but in implementation, at the various levels of practice, in the interaction of those who carry policy messages and those who receive, interpret, resist or comply with them. Conceptual diversity and conflict have to be rescued. An important feature of the analysis of such diversities is its relationship to the historical search for motivation. 'Why did you...?' was a question constantly being asked in this study, and the answers are often difficult for the questioner and those questioned. 'Why did they...?' is the most difficult of all historical questions to answer. The language of decision and action is part of the evidence, and helps to interpret motive in relation to the actors' world view. The study of the mid-1960s American legislation or of the specific British or American projects involves an approach both to the short-term intentions and longer-term ideals held more or less explicitly, and often in uneasy harmony, by the collaborating participants. The literature of the war on poverty and the educational attacks on disadvantage in both countries, at the time and in retrospect, rightly insist that the targets were rarely clear. Was poverty to be abolished or mitigated, and with what implications? If education was one of a cluster of social action strategies, what were the others, and how did they relate? What were the political dimensions and aims of positive discrimination? What kind of society was postulated by the pronouncements of Johnson or Keppel, the Plowden working parties or the committee's final report, the EPA organizers and their reports, the Follow Through model sponsors? Was it, in fact, possible for the participants to answer in terms of postulates and ideals, or were they simply caught up in enthusiasms, critical moments, opportunisms and opportunities, in order to take next steps in vaguely conceived directions? Was being caught up a weakness, or a strength in attempting to 'capture' a policy process? How much more or less than they knew were participants aiming to achieve?

Questions of the ultimate acceptability or appropriateness of such policy directions and questions carry ideological and political implications. From the political right the questions often imply a misdirection of energies to inappropriate ends, inappropriate because education should point to other targets and values more central to the defence and development of British or American society and economy. From the left, the questions often imply a sense of fatality in present economic and social structures and processes, which it is at best romantic and utopian and at worst deliberately misleading to attempt to remedy by educational policies. From the liberal centre the questions often imply that policies and experiments have been inadequately resourced, have not had time to prove themselves, have been inconclusively or improperly evaluated, and have encountered obstacles which, given the will, could eventually be removed. These represent a range of approaches to questions which have often been submerged in the 1980s by a sense of a different world in which massive shifts in educational priorities have taken place. In it are different considerations of international economic competition and national survival, new technologies, new budgetary priorities, moves towards political and social values of a different order from those most salient in previous decades. The position of educational planning and experiment against poverty and disadvantage in the 1960s and 1970s was at least in part a function of economic growth – real or expected. Amidst economic reversal or uncertainty they then moved to the margin, and any return to the centre would have to be in new economic and political conditions.

Reinventing 1960s wheels without attention to the new conditions and changes within education itself is clearly not an option. Much of what has happened outside the immediate ambit of poverty- and dis-advantage-related programmes is germane. Weaknesses of programmes in intention and operation have been understood. The limitations and strengths of preschool and school have been strongly argued. Structures and contents have changed under the reform agendas of the 1980s. Notice has had to be taken of the characteristics of school cultures. The boundaries of vocational and liberal and general education, of school and preschool, have been redrawn. Gender has come more firmly into debate and action. Poverty and inequality have in the past often pointed to different policies and reflected different views of the politically possible and the ideologically attractive. The most radical objective in policies, coalitions and action is likely to be that which addresses the real issues of the world in which people live.

Interviews and consultation

Positions are those occupied at the time of the interviews (with indications in brackets, where appropriate, of former position of most importance to the project).

T – indicates a tape-recorded interview.

UNITED STATES

I INTERVIEWS

Anderson, Janice	Director, Elementary and Secondary Education Programs, Office of Program Evaluation, Department of Education, Washington DC (responsible for Sustaining Effects Study)		1 April 1981
Bailey, Stephen K.	Professor of Educational Policy and Administration, Graduate School of Education, Harvard University, Cambridge, Massachusetts	T	8 October 1981
Bickel, William	Learning Research and Development Center, University of Pittsburgh, Pennsylvania	T	5 October 1981
Burnes, Donald W.	Team Leader, Legal and Governmental Studies Team, National Institute of Education, Washington DC (formerly project member, NIE Compensatory Education Study)		30 March 1981
Bushner, Diane E.	Director, Title I, School Department, Cambridge, Massachusetts	T	29 December 1981
Cazden, Courtney B.	Professor of Education, Graduate School of Education, Harvard University, Cambridge, Massachusetts	T	13 July 1982
Cohen, David K.	Professor of Education, Graduate School of Education, Harvard University, Cambridge, Massachusetts		7 April 1981 31 December 1981
Cohen, Wilbur J.	Professor, Lyndon B. Johnson School of Public Affairs, University of Texas, Austin (formerly Secretary, Department of Health, Education and Welfare)		29 March 1983
⎧ Coughlin, Daniel S.	Director of Title I Programs, Public Schools Department, Boston, Massachusetts	T	28 December 1981
⎩ Mariani, Joseph	Assistant Director (Secondary)		

340

{ Whitaker, Grace	Associate Director (Secondary) (*group interview*)		
Deutsch, Martin	Director, Institute for Developmental Studies, New York University, New York City	T	19 July 1982
Eichelberger, Tony	Professor of Educational Research, University of Pittsburgh, Pennsylvania (formerly Follow Through project director, Learning Research and Development Center)	T	5 October 1981
Featherstone, Joseph	Professor of Education, Graduate School of Education, Harvard University, Cambridge, Massachusetts		7 April 1981
Foster, Carol	Professor, Department of Early Childhood Development, Georgia State University, Atlanta (formerly Training Director, Follow Through – Tucson Early Education model)	T	21 April 1981
Green, Susan	Education Program Specialist and Project Officer, Follow Through Office of Compensatory Education, Washington DC	T	1 April 1981
Haney, Walter	Huron Institute, Cambridge, Massachusetts (formerly Research Fellow, Follow Through evaluation)		7 April 1981
Hanson, Jack	Title I Administrator, Minnesota	T	6 July 1982
Hill, Paul	Head of Policy Research Center, Rand Corporation, Washington DC (formerly Director National Institute of Education Compensatory Education Study)	T	3 April 1981
Hodges, Walter	Professor, Department of Early Childhood Development, Georgia State University, Atlanta, Follow Through model sponsor	T T	14 April 1981 24 April 1981
Howe II, Harold	Professor of Education, Graduate School of Education, Harvard University, Cambridge, Massachusetts (formerly United States Commissioner of Education	T	13 July 1982
Johnson, Linden	(*see* Pinkerton)		
Keppel, Francis	Professor of Education, Graduate School of Education, Harvard University, Cambridge, Massachusetts (formerly United States Commissioner of Education)	T T T	9 October 1981 23 December 1981 4 January 1982 25 March 1983
Kravetz, Nathan	Professor of Education, California State College, San Bernardino (formerly New York Center for Urban Education)		17 June 1982
{ Lewis, Stella S.	Director, Follow Through, Atlanta Public Schools, Georgia	T	21 April 1981
Ross, Fay	Demonstration Training Specialist, Follow Through, Atlanta (*joint interview*)		

Longley, Dolores H.	Assistant Director, Desegregation Monitoring Office, St Louis, Missouri (formerly school principal, Banneker District, St Louis)	T	22 July 1982
Mariani, Joseph	(*see* Coughlin)		
Meade Jr., Edward J.	Program Officer, Ford Foundation, New York City	T	6 January 1982
Miller, S.M.	Professor of Sociology, Boston University, Massachusetts	T	14 July 1982
Moran, Edward	(*see* Purdy)		
Murphy, Jerome T.	Director, Institute for Policy Studies, Graduate School of Education, Harvard University, Cambridge, Massachusetts	T	8 October 1981
⎧ Pinkerton, Jean T.	Consultant-in-Charge, St Paul Public Schools Federal Programs, St Paul, Minnesota	T	6 July 1982
⎨ Johnson, Linden	Associate Consultant, Federal Programs, St Paul (*joint interview*)		
⎧ Purdy, David	Director of Compensatory Education, Bureau of Services and Federal Assistance, West Virginia Board o Education, Charleston	T	28 April 1981
⎨ Moran, Edward	Assistant Director of Compensatory Education and Supplementary Programs		
⎩ Taylor, Robert	Assistant Director of Compensatory Education (*group interview*)		
Quie, Albert H.	Governor, State of Minnesota, St Paul (formerly Republican Congressman)	T	9 July 1982
Reed, Hartwell, D.	General Counsel, House of Representatives Committee on Education and Labor, Washington DC		3 April 1981
Resnick, Lauren B.	Learning Research and Development Center, University of Pittsburgh, Pennsylvania (formerly Follow Through project director and model sponsor)	T	5 October 1981
Roberts, Beauton	Department of Federal and State Programs, St Louis Public Schools, Missouri		22 July 1982
Ross, Fay	(*see* Lewis)		
Taylor, Robert	(*see* Purdy)		
Wang, Margaret C.	Learning Research and Development Center, University of Pittsburgh, Pennsylvania (Follow Through project director and model sponsor)	T	5 October 1981
Weiss, Carol	Professor of Education, Graduate School of Education, Harvard University, Cambridge, Massachusetts		9 October 1981
Whitaker, Grace	(*see* Coughlin)		
Woock, Roger	Deputy Director, Melbourne State College, Australia (formerly project evaluator, Project Uplift, Harlem, New York City)	T	7 March 1982

| Yarmolinsky, Adam | Attorney, Washington DC (formerly Deputy Director, President's Anti-Poverty Task Force) | T   12 July 1982 |

II CONSULTATION (MAIN ONES ONLY)

Ballantine, Jean	Professor of Education, Wright State University, Dayton, Ohio
Berlak, Ann	Professor, Department of Sociology and Anthropology, Webster College, St Louis, Missouri
Berlak, Harold	Professor of Education, Graduate Institute of Education, Washington University, St Louis, Missouri
Dierenfield, Richard	Chairman, Education Department, Macalester College, St Paul, Minnesota
Freeman, M.N.	President, Concord College, Athens, West Virginia
Friedman, Laurence	Professor of Law, Stanford University, California
Gumbert, Edgar B.	Director, Center for Cross-Cultural Education, Georgia State University, Atlanta
Lazerson, Marvin	Professor of Education, University of British Columbia, Vancouver, Canada
Martin, Don	Professor of Education, University of Pittsburgh, Pennsylvania
Michael, Ed.	St Louis Public Schools department, Missouri
Newhall, Ann	Archivist, Ford Foundation, New York City
Ravitch, Diane	Professor of Education, Teachers College, Columbia University, New York City
Rothblatt, Sheldon	Professor of History and Education, University of California, Berkeley
Ruyle, Janet	Administrator, Center for Studies in Higher Education, University of California, Berkeley
Spring, Joel H.	Professor of Education, Case Western Reserve University, Cleveland, Ohio
Trow, Martin	Director, Center for Studies in Higher Education, University of California, Berkeley
Tyack, David	Professor of History and Education, Stanford University, California
Urban, Wayne	Chairman, Department of Educational Foundations, Georgia State University, Atlanta
Willis, Craig	Vice-President, Concord College, Athens, West Virginia

GREAT BRITAIN

I INTERVIEWS

Bernstein, Basil	Professor of Education, Institute of Education, University of London	T 21 July 1983
Betty, Charles	District Inspector, Nottinghamshire (formerly EPA project director, Deptford, London)	16 June 1983 T 8 September 1983
Blackie, John	Her Majesty's Inspector (retired) (formerly Assessor, Plowden committee)	T 5 November 1982
Burrows, John	Her Majesty's Inspector (retired) (formerly HMI for London Metropolitan District)	T 17 September 1982
Chazan, Maurice	Professor of Education, University College of Swansea (formerly Compensatory Education project co-Director)	T 17 September 1982

⎰ Laing, Alice	Senior Lecturer in Education (formerly Compensatory Education project assistant director) (*joint interview*)		
⎱ Cox, Theo	Lecturer in Education, University College of Swansea (formerly project senior research officer, Compensatory Education project)	T	17 September 1982
Davie, Ronald	Director, National Children's Bureau	T	6 September 1983
Donnison, David V.	Professor of Town and Regional Planning, University of Glasgow (formerly member of Plowden committee)	T	13 September 1983
Douglas, J.W.B.	Director, National Survey of Health and Development (retired)	T	7 June 1983
Duncan, Stella M.C.	Her Majesty's Inspector (retired) (formerly attached to the Plowden committee)	T	22 July 1983
Halsey, A.H.	Professor of Social and Administrative Studies, University of Oxford (formerly director, EPA programme)	T	27 October 1981
Hopkinson, David	Her Majesty's Inspector (retired) (formerly chairman HMI Research and Publication Committee)	T	2 July 1981
Kogan, Maurice	Professor of Government, Brunel University (formerly Secretary, Plowden Committee)	T	11 January 1983
Laing, Alice	(*see* Chazan)		
Lawton, Denis	Deputy Director, Institute of Education, University of London	T	20 January 1983
Marsh, Mary	Co-ordinator, South East London Educational Home Visiting Project		12 March 1981
Midwinter, Eric	Director, Centre for Policy on Ageing (formerly project director, Liverpool EPA project)	T	12 October 1983
Mittler, Peter	Director, Hester Adrian Research Centre, University of Manchester	T	11 June 1982
Morton, David	Lecturer, Faculty of Community Studies, Manchester Polytechnic	T	11 June 1982
Nicholls, Sally	Lecturer in Community Education, Frobisher Institute of Adult Education		12 March 1983
Plowden, Lady	(formerly Chairman, Central Advisory Council for Education (England))	T	28 March 1988
Roberts, Colin	Her Majesty's Inspector (formerly Director, Centre for Information and Advice on Educational Disadvantage, Manchester)		18 November 1982
Sheridan, Bill	Senior Lecturer in Education, University of Reading		25 January 1982
Smith, George	Department of Social and Administrative Studies, University of Oxford (Formerly research officer, West Riding EPA project)	T	26 October 1981
Watt, Joyce	Department of Education, University of Aberdeen (formerly project director, Dundee EPA project)		

Wedderburn, Dorothy	Principal, Bedford College, University of London	T	6 May 1982
Williams, Philip	Professor of Education, University College, Bangor (formerly co-director, Compensatory Education project)	T	30 November 1981
Wrigley, Jack	Professor of Education, University of Reading	T	21 October 1981

II   CONSULTATION (MAIN ONES ONLY)

Adelman, Clem	Research Co-ordinator, Bulmershe College of Higher Education, Reading
Blyth, W.A.L.	Professor of Education, University of Liverpool
Brunner, Jacqueline	Senior Lecturer in Primary Education, Bulmershe College of Higher Education, Reading
Gordon, Peter	Reader in Education, Institute of Education, University of London (formerly HMI)
Gray, John	Senior Lecturer in Education, University of Sheffield
Irving, Stanley	Principal Lecturer in Primary Education, Bulmershe College of Higher Education, Reading (formerly Adviser, Nottinghamshire)
Mabey, Christine	Inner London Education Authority, Research and Statistics
Nisbet, John	Professor of Education, University of Aberdeen
Pollock, Margaret	Reader in Developmental Paediatrics, King's College Medical School, London

Bibliography

Note: The bibliography is in two parts. The first part (A) contains references to works published in the United States (including those by British and other authors). The second part (B) contains those published in Britain and elsewhere. Place of publication is not given when this is obvious from the name of the publisher. Each author's entries are in date order.

A UNITED STATES SOURCES

Aaron, Henry J. (1978) *Politics and the Professors: the Great Society in perspective*, Washington, D.C., Brookings Institution.

Abelson, Willa D. (1974) 'Head Start graduates in school: studies in New Haven, Connecticut' in Sally Ryan (ed.), *A Report on Longitudinal Evaluations of Preschool Programs*, vol. 1: *Longitudinal Evaluations*, Washington, D.C.

Abelson, Willa D., Zigler, Edward and DeBlasi, Cheryl L. (1974) 'Effects of a four-year Follow Through program on economically disadvantaged children', *Journal of Educational Psychology*, 66 (5).

AFL–CIO (1965) 'Waging war on poverty' (1964) in Louis A. Ferman *et al.*, *Poverty in America*, Ann Arbor, University of Michigan Press.

Alden, Vernon R. (1965) 'Planning for education's forgotten men', *Saturday Review*, 48, 15 May.

Alinsky, Saul (1965) 'Behind the mask', *The American Child*, 47 (4).
    (1968) 'The War on Poverty – political pornography' in Chaim Isaac Waxman (ed.), *Poverty: power and politics*, New York, Grosset and Dunlap.

Allen, Vernon L. (ed.) (1970) *Psychological Factors in Poverty*, Chicago, Markham.

Almeida, Cynthia H. (1969) A Program to Strengthen Early Childhood Education in Poverty Area Schools, New York, Center for Urban Education, Educational Research Committee, mimeo.

Almy, Millie (1964) 'New views on intellectual development in early childhood education' in A. Harry Passow and Robert R. Leeper (eds.), *Intellectual Development: another look*, Washington, D.C., Association for Supervision and Curriculum Development.

Anderson, Marian P. (*see* California)

Anderson, Richard B. (1977) 'The effectiveness of Follow Through: evidence from the national analysis', *Curriculum Inquiry*, 7 (3).

Anderson, Richard B. *et al.* (1978) 'Pardon us, but what was the question again?

346

A response to the critique of the Follow Through evaluation', *Harvard Educational Review*, 48 (2).

Arnold, Robert (1964) 'Mobilization for Youth: patchwork or solution?', *Dissent*, 11 (3).

Asbell, Bernard (1966) 'Not like other children: the slum child is from another world', *Child and Family*, 5 (2).

Ashline, Nelson F. *et al.* (eds.) (1976) *Education, Inequality, and National Policy*, Lexington, D.C., Heath.

ATLANTA FOLLOW THROUGH PROGRAM

Cox, Frances M. (1970) The Interdependent Learning Model: Atlanta's approach to the implementation paper presented to the Southern Psychological Association, mimeo.

Follow Through program (1971) Revision of Proposal...1970, Atlanta Public Schools, 3 May, mimeo.

Educational Evaluation Services [1973] Annual Report: Follow Through program. Atlanta Public School System 1972–3, mimeo.

White, William (1974) Atlanta Follow Through Program. Technical report no. 3. Summative progress in school achievement, 1968–74, Atlanta Public Schools, mimeo.

Follow Through. Atlanta Public Schools (1978) Submission to Joint Dissemination Review Panel, 17 March, mimeo.

Follow Through, Interdependent Learning Model, Atlanta Public Schools (1979) *Games Children Play*.

Austin, Ernest H. Jr (1965) 'Cultural deprivation – a few questions', *Phi Delta Kappan*, 47 (2).

(1965) 'A parting shot from a still skeptical skeptic', *Phi Delta Kappan*, 47 (2).

Austin, Gilbert R. (1976) *Early Childhood Education: an international perspective*, New York, Academic Press.

Austin, Gilbert R. *et al.* (1977) 'Some perspectives on compensatory education and inequality', *Contemporary Educational Psychology*, 2 (3).

Ausubel, David P. (1963) 'A teaching strategy for culturally deprived pupils: cognitive and motivational considerations', *The School Review*, 71 (4).

(1964) 'How reversible are the cognitive and motivational effects of cultural deprivation? Implications for teaching the culturally deprived child', *Urban Education*, 1 (1).

(1966) 'The effects of cultural deprivation on learning patterns' in Staten W. Webster (ed.), *The Disadvantaged Learner: knowing, understanding, educating*, San Francisco, Chandler.

Bailey, Ann (1981) 'Parent involvement – is it too late?', *Title I Exchange: the newsletter of compensatory education* (Mass.), 5 (2).

Bailey, B.L. (1966) 'A crucial problem in language intervention as it relates to the disadvantaged', *Supplement to the IRCD Bulletin* (Information Retrieval Center on the Disadvantaged), 2 (3A).

Bailey, Stephen K. (1970) 'The Office of Education and the Education Act of 1965' in Michael W. Kirst (ed.) *The Politics of Education at the Local, State, and Federal Levels*, Berkeley, McCutchan.

(1981) 'Political coalitions for public education', *Daedalus*, 110 (3)

Bailey, Stephen K. and Mosher, Edith K. (1968) *ESEA : the Office of Education administers a law*, New York, Syracuse University Press.

Ball, Samuel and Bogatz, Gerry Ann (1973) 'Research on *Sesame Street*: some implications for compensatory education' in Julian C. Stanley (ed.), *Compensatory Education for Children Ages Two to Eight : recent studies of educational intervention*, Baltimore, Johns Hopkins Press.

Baltimore (*see* Ford Foundation)

Bamonte, Anthony (1978) 'Educational reform programs' in Herman Berliner (ed.), *Programs to Prevent or Alleviate Poverty : Hofstra University Yearbook of Business*, series 12, 2.

Bane, Mary Jo and Jencks, Christopher (1973) 'The schools and equal opportunity' in Erwin Flaxman (ed.), *Educating the Disadvantaged 1971–1972*, New York, AMS Press.

Baratz, Morton S. and Grigsby, William G. (1972) 'Thoughts on poverty and its elimination', *Journal of Social Policy*, 1(2).

Baratz, Stephen S. and Baratz, Joan C. (1970) 'Early childhood intervention: the social science base of institutional racism', *Harvard Educational Review*, 40 (1).

Bartlett, Lynn M. (1961) 'NDEA confirms school aid need', *The American Teacher Magazine*, 45 (4)

Bauman, John F. (1971) 'The scope of the poverty problem', *Current History*, 61 (363).

Baynham, Dorsey (1963) 'The Great Cities projects', *NEA Journal*, 52 (4).

Beck, John M. and Saxe, Richard W. (eds.) (1965) *Teaching the Culturally Disadvantaged Pupil*, Springfield, Ill., Charles C. Thomas.

Becker, Howard S. (ed.) (1966) *Social Problems : a modern approach*, New York, Wiley.

Begab, Michael J., Haywood, H. Carl and Garber, Howard L. (eds.) (1981), *Psychosocial Influences in Retarded Performance*, vol. 2, *Strategies for Improving Competence*, Baltimore, University Park Press.

Bell, Daniel (1973) *The Coming of Post-Industrial Society*, New York, Basic Books (edition of 1976).

Beller, E. Kuno [1973] 'Research on organized programs of early childhood' in Robert M.W. Travers (ed.), *Second Handbook of Research on Teaching*, Chicago, Rand McNally.

   (1974) 'Impact of early education on disadvantaged children' in Sally Ryan (ed.), *A Report on Longitudinal Evaluations of Preschool Programs*, vol. 1, Washington, D.C., HEW.

Bereiter, Carl (1965) 'Academic instruction and preschool children' in National Council of Teachers of English, Task Force on Teaching of English to the Disadvantaged, *Language Programs for the Disadvantaged*, Champaign, Ill., NCTE.

   (1967) 'Instructional planning in early compensatory education' in Jerome Hellmuth (ed.), *Disadvantaged Child*, vol. 1, New York, Brunner/Mazel.

   (1985) 'The changing face of educational disadvantagement', *Phi Delta Kappan*, 66 (8).

Bereiter, Carl and Engelmann, Siegfried (1966) *Teaching Disadvantaged Children in the Preschool*, Englewood Cliffs, N.J., Prentice-Hall.

Bereiter, Carl *et al.* (1966) 'An academically oriented pre-school for culturally deprived children' in Fred M. Hechinger (ed.), *Pre-School Education Today*, Garden City, N.Y., Doubleday.

Berg, Ivar (1970) *Education and Jobs: the great training robbery*, Baltimore, Penguin.

Bernstein, Basil (1961) 'Social class and linguistic development: a theory of social learning' in A.H. Halsey, Jean Floud and C. Arnold Anderson (eds.), *Education, Economy and Society: a reader in the sociology of education*, New York, Free Press of Glencoe.

(1964) 'Aspects of language and learning in the genesis of the social process' in Dell Hymes (ed.) *Language in Culture and Society: a reader in linguistics and anthropology*, New York, Harper & Row.

Berrueta-Clemens, John R. *et al.* (1984) *Changed Lives: the effects of the Perry Preschool program on youth through age 19*, Ypsilanti, Mich., High/Scope.

Biber, Barbara (1973) 'Goals and methods in a preschool program for disadvantaged children' in Bernard Spodek (ed.), *Early Childhood Education*, Englewood Cliffs, N.J., Prentice-Hall.

Bienenstock, Theodore and Sayres, William C. (1964) *Project ABLE: an appraisal*, New York, State Education Department, University of the State of New York.

Birman, Beatrice F. *et al.* (1987) *The Current Operation of the Chapter 1 Program*, Washington, D.C., Department of Education, Office of Educational Research and Improvement.

Bissell, Joan S. (1973) 'Planned variation in Head Start and Follow Through' in Julian C. Stanley (ed.), *Compensatory Education for Children Ages Two to Eight*, Baltimore, Johns Hopkins University Press.

(*see also* Follow Through)

Blake, Patricia (1964) 'A big break for poverty's children: New York gives 4-year-olds head start on school', *Life Magazine*, 3 April.

Blank, Marion (1970) 'Some philosophical influences underlying preschool intervention for disadvantaged children' in Frederick Williams (ed.), *Language and Poverty: perspectives on a theme*, Chicago, Markham.

(1982) 'Moving beyond the difference–deficit debate' in Lynne Feagans and Dale Clark Farran (eds.), *The Language of Children Reared in Poverty*, New York, Academic Press.

Bloom, Benjamin S. (ed.) [1964a], Research Problems of Education and Cultural Deprivation, Chicago, University of Chicago, mimeo.

(1964b) *Stability and Change in Human Characteristics*, New York, Wiley.

Bloom, Benjamin S., Davis, Allison and Hess, Robert (1965) *Compensatory Education for Cultural Deprivation...*, New York, Holt, Rinehart and Winston.

Blumenthal, Richard (1969) 'The bureaucracy: antipoverty and the Community Action program' in Allan P. Sindler (ed.), *American Political Institutions and Public Policy: five contemporary studies*, Boston, Little, Brown.

Bookbinder, Hyman (1966) 'Is America waking up?', *Childhood Education*, 42 (8).

BOSTON

Boston Community Schools (n.d.) *Boston Community Schools*, Boston, Mass.

Vreeland, Rebecca S. (1967) The effects of the Boston Educational Enrichment on children's attitudes, values, and creativity: report number 2, Cambridge, Mass., Harvard University, Center for Research and Development on Educational Differences, mimeo.

Heuristics, Inc. (1971) An Evaluation of the Individual Progress Program 1969–1970, Boston, Mass., Boston Public Schools, mimeo.

(1977) Evaluation of the Title I Program 1976–1977: Final Evaluation Report, Boston, Mass. Boston Public Schools, mimeo.

Boston Public Schools (1981) *Meeting the Needs – IX: a report of operations. Title I – ESEA, 1981*, Boston, Mass., Boston Public Schools.

Boston Public Schools (n.d.) *Title I Project Application 1980–1983*, Boston, Mass., Boston Public Schools, Department of Title I Programs.

Boswell, Anita Y. (1983) 'Some special programs of the Chicago Board of Education. Programs for disadvantaged children...' in US, DHEW, OE, *Programs for the Educationally Disadvantaged.*

Bowles, Frank (1969) 'Two school systems within one society' in C.E. Beeby (ed.), *Qualitative Aspects of Educational Planning*, Paris, UNESCO: International Institute for Educational Planning.

Bowles, Samuel and Gintis, Herbert (1976) *Schooling in Capitalist America*, New York, Basic Books, 1976.

Bowles, Samuel and Levin, Henry M. (1971) 'Critique of the Coleman Report' in Patricia Cayo Sexton (ed.) *School Policy and Issues in a Changing Society*, Boston, Allyn and Brown (reprint of 1968 article).

Brager, George A. and Purcell, Francis P. (eds.) (1967) *Community Action against Poverty: readings from the Mobilization experience*, New Haven, Conn., College and University Press.

Brazziel, William F. (1964) 'Higher Horizons in Southern elementary schools', *Journal of Negro Education*, 33 (4).

(1966–7) 'Head Start: assessment of two programs', *Integrated Education*, 4 (4).

(1968) 'Two years of Head Start' in Joe L. Frost (ed.) *Early Childhood Education Rediscovered*, New York, Holt, Rinehart and Winston (reprint of 1967 article).

Brecher, Charles (1973) *The Impact of Antipoverty Policies*, New York, Praeger.

Bremner, Robert H. (1956) *From the Depths: the discovery of poverty in the United States*, New York University Press.

Briggs, Paul W. (1969) 'Educational problems and the model cities program' in Roald F. Campbell (ed.), *Education and Urban Renaissance*, New York, Wiley.

Brittain, Clay V. (1966) 'Some early findings of research on...preschool programs for culturally deprived children', *Children*, 13 (4).

Broman, Betty L. (1966) 'Parents' reactions to Head Start Program', *Childhood Education*, 42 (8).

Bronfenbrenner, Urie (1974) 'Is early intervention effective?', *Teachers College Record*, 76 (2).

Brooks, Deton J. Jr. (1963) 'Helping Cook County's culturally deprived adults', *NEA Journal*, 52 (4).

Brotman, Sulvia (1961) 'Spirit of St. Louis: today's version', *NEA Journal*, 50 (2).

Brown, Bernard (ed.) (1978) *Found: Long-term Gains from Early Intervention*, Boulder, Col., Westview Press.

Bruner, Jerome (ed.) (1966) *Learning about Learning: a conference report*, Washington, D.C., DHEW, OE.

Brunner, Catherine (1964) 'Project Help: program for early school admission', *The Education Digest*, 29 (7) (reprint of 1963 article).

(1965) 'Deprivation – its effects, its remedies', *Educational Leadership*, 23 (2).

Burlage, Robb K. (1965) 'Appalachia: the heart of the matter' in Louis A. Ferman *et al.*, *Poverty in America*, Ann Arbor, University of Michigan Press (reprint of 1964 article).

Burnes, Donald W. and Moss, Richard L. (1978) 'From congressional intent to local program delivery: present reality in the administration of Title I, ESEA', IRCD Bulletin, 13 (1).

Burns, James MacGregor (ed.) (1968) *To Heal and to Build: the programs of President Lyndon B. Johnson*, New York, McGraw-Hill.

Buss, Dennis C. (1980) 'The Ford Foundation in public education: emergent patterns' in Robert F. Arnove (ed.), *Philanthropy and Cultural Imperialism: the foundations at home and broad*, Boston, G.K. Hall.

Butler, Annie L. (1968) 'From Head Start to Follow Through' *Bulletin of the School of Education, Indiana University*, 44 (4).

Caldwell, Bettye M. (1970) 'Introduction: period of consolidation' in Jerome Hellmuth (ed.), *Disadvantaged Child*, vol. 3, New York, Brunner/Mazel

Caldwell, Bettye M. and Richmond, Julius B. (1967) 'Social class level and stimulus potential of the home' in Jerome Hellmuth (ed.), *Exceptional Infant*, vol. 1: *The Normal Infant*, Seattle, Special Child Publications.

CALIFORNIA

Anderson, Marian (1965) Recent Legislation affecting the Education of Young Children in California, Santa Barbara, California Association for Nursery Education, mimeo.

Governor's Advisory Committee on Compensatory Education [1965] They Must Find Hope in their Schools: SB482 (McAteer), the Comprehensive Approach (leaflet)

Wilson, Alan B., Jensen, Arthur R. and Elliott, David L. (1966) Education of Disadvantaged Children in California: a report to the California State Committee on Public Education, University of California, Berkeley, mimeo.

State Department of Education, Office of Compensatory Education, Bureau of Evaluation and Research (1967) *Compensatory Education in California 1966–67* (annual evaluation report), Sacramento.

State Department of Education, Office of Compensatory Education (1967) *A Report on Research and Teacher Eduction Projects for Disadvantaged Children: description and special status 1965–1966*, Sacramento.

Sorensen, Philip and Thomas, C. (1967) *Summary Evaluation of the Compensatory Education Program of the San Francisco Unified School District 1966–1967*, Menlo Park, Stanford Research Institute.

State Department of Education, Bureau of Compensatory Education Program Evaluation (1968a) *Evaluation of ESEA Title I Projects of California Schools: annual report 1967–1968*, Sacremanto.

State Department of Education, Office of Compensatory Education and Bureau of Community Services and Migrant Education (1968b) *Handbook for California School District Advisory Committees: Elementary and Secondary Education Act of 1965, Title I*, Sacramento.

State Department of Education (1969) *California Laws and Policies Relating to Equal Opportunities in Education*, Sacramento.

CAMBRIDGE, MASS.

Essex County Education Evaluation Council (1971) *Evaluation of Cambridge Title I Project, Summer 1971*, Cambridge Public Schools.

Public Affairs Research Institute (1981) Evaluation of the Cambridge Title I Program 1980–1981, Selected Excerpts, Wellesley, Public Affairs Research Institute, mimeo.

Camp, Janet C. (1973) 'A skill development curriculum for 3-, 4-, and 5-year-old disadvantaged children: Demonstration and Research Center for Early Education, George Peabody College for Teachers', in Bernard Spodek (ed.), *Early Childhood Education*, Englewood Cliffs, N.J., Prentice-Hall.

Campbell, Roald F. *et al.* (eds) (1969) *Education and Urban Renaissance*, New York, Wiley.

Carl, David L. (1970) 'Project Mobilization: a suburban community's concern for its disadvantaged students', *The Clearing House*, 44 (9).

Carnoy, Martin (1974) *Education as Cultural Imperialism*, New York, David McKay.

(1976) 'Is compensatory education possible?' in Martin Carnoy and Henry M. Levin (eds.), *The Limits of Educational Reform*, New York, David McKay.

(1980) 'Segmented labour markets: a review of the theoretical and empirical literature and its implications for educational planning' in Martin Carnoy *et al.*, *Education, Work and Employment*, Paris, UNESCO: International Institute for Educational Planning, 1980.

Carter, Launor F. (1980) *The Sustaining Effects Study: an interim report*, Santa Monica, System Development Corporation.

Caruso, David R. and Detterman, Douglas K. (1981) 'Intelligence research and social policy', *Phi Delta Kappan*, 63 (3).

Cater, Douglas (1968) 'The politics of poverty' in Chaim Isaac Waxman (ed.), *Poverty: Power and Politics*, New York, Grosset and Dunlap.

Caudill, Harry M. (1962) *Night Comes to the Cumberlands: a biography of a depressed area*, Boston, Little, Brown (edition of 1963).

Cazden, Courtney B. (1968) 'Subcultural differences in child language: an interdisciplinary review' in Jerome Hellmuth (ed.), *Disadvantaged Child*, vol. 2 New York, Brunner/Mazel (reprint of 1966 article).

(1969) 'Sociolinguistic perspectives on speech' (review of Lawton, *Social Class, Language and Education*), *Contemporary Psychology*, 14 (8).

(1970) 'Language programs for young children: notes from England and Wales', *Early Childhood Education*.

(1970) 'The neglected situation in child language research and education' in Frederick Williams (ed.), *Language and Poverty*, Chicago, Markham.

Cazden, Courtney B. and Bartlett, Elsa J. (1973) (review of Gahagan and Gahagan, *Talk Reform*), *Language in Society*, 2.

Charms, Vernon, Butts, Bobbye and Mensel, Fr. Frank (1971) The Family Urban Project, Brooklyn, N.Y., State University of New York, Urban Center, mimeo.

Charters, W.W. Jr. *et al.* (*see* Missouri)

Cherian, Edward J. and Associates (1973) *A Guide to Follow Through*, Washington, D.C., DHEW, OE.

CHICAGO (*SEE* FORD FOUNDATION)

Chicago Public Schools (1964) Compensatory Education in the Chicago Public Schools: study report number four, 1964 series, Chicago Public Schools, mimeo.

Church, Alexandria and Eisman, Mary (1968) *Interim Progress Report* [*to the Ford Foundation*], *Part II: research and evaluation*, New York University, Institute for Developmental Studies.

Cicirelli, Victor G., Evans, John W. and Schiller, Jeffry S. (1970) 'The impact of Head Start: a reply to the report analysis', *Harvard Educational Review*, 40 (1).

Clark, David (1984) *Post-Industrial America: a geographical perspective*, New York, Methuen.

Clark, David L. and Astuto, Terry A. (1989) 'The disjunction of federal educational policy and national educational needs in the 1990s', *Journal of Education Policy*, 5(4).

Clark, John (*see* Follow Through)

Clark, Kenneth B. (1963) 'Educational stimulation of racially disadvantaged children' in A. Harry Passow (ed.), *Education in Depressed Areas*, New York, Teachers College Press.

(1965a) 'The cult of cultural deprivation: a complex social psychological phenomena' in Proceedings of the Fourth Annual Invitational Conference on Urban Education, New York, Yeshiva University, Ferkauf Graduate School of Education, mimeo.

(1965b) *Dark Ghetto: dilemmas of social power*, New York, Harper and Row.

(1968) 'Learning obstacles among children' in Arliss L. Roaden (ed.), *Problems of School Men in Depressed Urban Centers*, Columbus, Ohio State University.

(1969) 'Learning obstacles among children' in Arliss L. Roaden (ed.), *Problems of School Men in Depressed Urban Centers*, Columbus, Ohio State University.

Clark, Kenneth B. and Hopkins, Jeannette (eds.) (1968) *A Relevant War against Poverty: a study of community action programs and observable social change*, New York, Harper and Row.

Clark, Kenneth B. *et al.* (1972) *The Educationally Deprived Child : the potential for change*, New York, Metropolitan Applied Research Center.

Clark, Philip (1975) 'Compensatory education: the underlying stances and teachers' attitudes', *Urban Education*, 9 (4).

Clarke-Stewart, K. Alison (1981) 'Parent education in the 1970s', *Educational Evaluation and Policy Analysis*, 3 (6).

Clausen, John A. and Williams, Judith R. (1963) 'Sociological correlates of child behavior' in Harold W. Stevenson (ed.) *Child Psychology : the sixty-second yearbook of the National Society for the Study of Education*, Chicago, NSSE.

Cloward, Richard A. and Jones, James A. (1963) 'Social class: attitudes and perceptions' in A. Harry Passow (ed.), *Education in Depressed Areas*, New York, Teachers College Press.

Cloward, Richard A. and Ohlin, Lloyd E. (1960) *Delinquency and Opportunity : a theory of delinquent gangs*, New York, Free Press.

Cloward, Richard A., Piven, Frances Fox *et al.* (1975) *The Politics of Turmoil : essays on poverty, race and the urban crisis*, New York, Random House (reprints essays 1965–74).

Clowse, Barbara Barksdale (1981) *Brainpower for the Cold War : the sputnik crisis and the National Defense Education Act*, Westport, Conn., Greenwood Press.

Cohen, David K. (1968) 'Children and their Primary Schools: Volume II' (Plowden), *Harvard Educational Review*, 38 (2).

(1969) 'Policy for the public schools: compensation and integration' in *Harvard Educational Review, Equal Educational Opportunity* (reprinted from the 1968 *Review*).

(1970) 'Politics and research: evaluation of social action programs in education', *Review of Educational Research*, 40 (2).

(1975) 'The value of social experiments' in Alice M. Rivlin and P. Michael Timpane (eds.), *Planned Variation in Education*, Washington, D.C., Brookings Institution.

Cohen, David K. and Garet, Michael S. (1975) 'Reforming educational policy with applied social research', *Harvard Educational Review*, 45 (1).

Cohen, David K. and Van Geel, Tyll R. (1970) 'Public education' in Samuel H. Beer and Richard E. Barringer (eds.), *The State and the Poor*, Cambridge, Mass., Winthrop.

Cohen, Wilbur (1964) 'The administration's attack', *The American Child*, 46 (2).

(1973) 'Toward the elimination of poverty', *Current History*, June.

(1977) Discussion in Haveman, Robert H. (ed.) *A Decade of Federal Antipoverty Programs : achievements, failures and lessons*, New York, Academic Press.

Cohn, Werner (1966) 'On the language of lower-class children' in Staten W. Webster (ed.), *The Disadvantaged Learner*, San Francisco, Chandler.

Cole, Michael and Bruner, Jerome S. (1972) 'Preliminaries to a theory of cultural differences' in Ira Gordon (ed.), *Early Childhood Education*, Chicago, NSSE.

Coleman, James S. (1965) 'Equal schools or equal students?', *The Public Interest*, 1 (1).

(1969) 'The concept of equality of educational opportunity', *Harvard Educational Review, Equal Educational Opportunity* (reprinted from the 1968 *Review*).

Coleman, James S. *et al.* (1966) *Equality of Educational Opportunity*, Washington, D.C., DHEW.

Coles, Robert (1965) 'What migrant children learn', *Saturday Review*, 48, 15 May.

Coles, Robert and Piers, Maria (1969) *Wages of Neglect*, Chicago, Quadrangle Books.

Committee for Economic Development (1985) *Investing in Our Children: Business and the Public Schools*, New York, CED.

Committee for the White House Conference on Education (1956) *A Report to the President*, Washington, D.C., Government Printing Office.

Conant, James Bryant (1961) *Slums and Suburbs*, New York, McGraw-Hill.

(1964) *Shaping Educational Policy*, New York, McGraw-Hill.

Condry, Sandra McConnell and Lazar, Irving (1982) 'American values and social policy for children', *Annals of the American Academy of Political and Social Science*, 461.

Connecticut State Board of Education (1979) *A Plan for Promoting Equal Educational Opportunity in Education*, Hartford, Connecticut State Board of Education and Connecticut State Advisory Panel.

Cook County Department of Public Aid (1969) Project Breakthrough: a responsive environment field experiment with pre-school children from public assistance families, Cook County, Ill.

Cooley, William W. (1981) 'Effectiveness of compensatory education', *Educational Leadership*, 38 (4).

Cordasco, Francesco (ed.) (1974) *Toward Equal Opportunity: the report of the Select Committee on Equal Education Opportunity, United States Senate*, New York, AMS Press (reprint of 1972 edn, US Government Printing Office).

Corwin, Ronald G. (1973) *Reform and Organizational Survival: the Teacher Corps as an instrument of educational change*, New York, Wiley.

Cowles, Milly (ed.) *Perspectives in the Education of Disadvantaged Children: a multidisciplinary approach*, Cleveland, Ohio, World Publishing.

Cox, Frances M. (*see* Atlanta).

Crandall, Vaughn J. (1963) 'Achievement' in Harold W. Stevenson (ed.) *Child Psychology*, Chicago, NSSE.

Crittenden, Brian (1970) 'Equal opportunity: the importance of being in context', *Philosophy of Education 1970: proceedings of the Philosophy of Education Society*, Edwardsville, Ill.

Cronin, Thomas E. (1968), 'The President and education', *Phi Delta Kappan*, 49 (6).

Crow, Lester D., Murray, Walter I. and Smythe, Hugh H. (1966) *Educating the Culturally Disadvantaged Child: principles and programs*, New York, David McKay.

Cunningham, William J. (1962) 'Stirrings in the big cities: Boston', *NEA Journal*, 51 (10).

Curwood, Sarah T. *et al.* [1966] *Project Head Start in Action: a survey and evaluation of Head Start programs in the Commonwealth of Massachusetts*, Boston, Massachusetts Committee on Children and Youth.

Cutts, Warren G. (1963) 'Reading unreadiness in the underprivileged', *NEA Journal*, 52 (4).

Dale, Edwin L. Jr. (1965) 'The big gun on poverty', *The New Republic*, 7 August.

Dallam, William M. (1981) 'In defence of compensatory education', *Educational Leadership*, 38 (8).

Daly, Charles U. (ed.) (1968) *The Quality of Inequality: urban and suburban public schools*, University of Chicago Press.

Darlington, Richard B. (1981) 'The Consortium for Longitudinal Studies', *Educational Evaluation and Policy Analysis*, 3 (6).

Datta, Lois-Ellin (1971) 'A report on evaluation studies of Project Head Start, *International Journal of Early Childhood*, 3 (2).

(1975) 'Design of the Head Start planned variation experiment' in Alice M. Rivlin and P. Michael Timpane, *Planned Evaluation in Education*, Washington, D.C., Brookings Institution

(1983) 'A tale of two studies: the Westinghouse–Ohio evaluation of Project Head Start and the Consortium for Longitudinal Studies report', *Studies in Educational Evaluation*, 8.

Datta, Lois-Ellin *et al.* (n.d.) The Effects of the Head Start Classroom Experience on some Aspects of Child Development: a summary report of national evaluations 1966–1969, Washington, D.C., HEW, Office of Child Development, mimeo.

Davidson, Roger H. (1969) 'The War on Poverty: experiment in federalism' in Louis A. Ferman (ed.), *Evaluating the War on Poverty*, AAPSS.

Davignon, Charles P. (1966) 'Philosophy behind ESEA 1965', *The Catholic Educational Review*, 64 (1).

Davis, Allison (1948) *Social-Class Influences upon Learning*, Cambridge, Mass., Harvard University Press.

(1962) 'The future education of children from low socio-economic groups' in Stanley Elam (ed.), *New Dimensions for Educational Progress*, Bloomington, Ind., Phi Delta Kappa.

Davis, Richard H. 'The failures of compensatory education', *Education and Urban Society*, 4 (2).

Dawson, Helaine (1968) *On the Outskirts of Hope: educating youth from poverty areas*, New York, McGraw-Hill (1970 edition).

Day Care and Child Development Council of America (1970a) *Legislative Summary 1, Head Start Child Development Act of 1969*, Washington, D.C., DCCDCA.

(1970b) *Legislative Summary II: Comprehensive Preschool Education and Education and Child Day Care Act of 1969*, Washington, D.C., DCCDCA.

(1970c) *Legislative Summary V, Comprehensive Head Start Child Development Act of 1970*, Washington, D.C., DCCDCA.

(1970d) *Legislative Summary VIII, Comprehensive Child Development Act of 1970*, Washington, D.C., DCCDCA.

Deimel, Gilbert (1981) 'In defence of compensatory education', *Educational Leadership*, 38 (8).

de Lone, Richard H. (1979) *Small Futures: children, inequality, and the limits of Reform*, New York, Harcourt Brace Jovanovich.

Dentler, Robert A. (1969) 'Urban eyewash: a review of "Title I/Year II"', *Urban Review*, 3 (4).

Detroit (*see* Ford Foundation).

Deutsch, Cynthia (1965) 'Education for disadvantaged groups', *Review of Educational Research*, (35) 2.

Deutsch, Martin (1964a) 'Facilitating development in the pre-school child: social and psychological perspectives', *Merrill-Palmer Quarterly of Behavior and Development*, 10 (3).

(1964b) 'Papers from the Arden House Conference on Pre-school Enrichment: introductory comments', *Merrill-Palmer Quarterly of Behavior and Development*, 10 (3).

(1965a) 'The role of social class in language development and cognition', *American Journal of Orthopsychiatry*, 35 (1).

(1965b) 'Some psychological aspects of learning in the disadvantaged', *Integrated Education*, 3 (3).

(1971) 'Organizational and conceptual barriers to social change' in Allan C. Ornstein *et al*. (eds.), *Educating the Disadvantaged, School Year 1969–1970*, vol. 2, Part 2, New York, AMS Press (reprint of 1969 article).

(1971) 'Perspectives on the education of the urban child', in A. Harry Passow (ed.), *Urban Education in the 1970's*, New York, Teachers College Press.

(1972) 'Behavioral and environmental limits of change' in Kenneth B. Clark *et al*. (eds.), *The Educationally Deprived Child*, New York, Metropolitan Applied Research Center.

Deutsch, Martin and Associates (1967) *The Disadvantaged Child*, New York, Basic Books.

Deutsch, Martin, Katz, Irwin and Jensen, Arthur R. (eds.) (1967) *Social Class, Race, and Psychological Development*, New York, Holt, Rinehart and Winston.

de Wit, Jan (1972) 'Problems and issues in the study of deprivation and enrichment' in F.J. Mönks, William W. Hartup and Jan de Wit (eds.), *Determinants of Behavioral Development*, New York, Academic Press.

Dey, Charles F. and Jackson, Davis [1965] *A Better Chance: an educational program sponsored by Dartmouth College…in cooperation with the Independent Schools Talent Search Program* (no place, publisher).

Divine, Robert A. (ed.) (1981) *Exploring the Johnson Years*, Austin, University of Texas Press.

Dobbin, John E. (1966) 'Strategies and innovations demonstrated in Project Head Start', *Journal of School Psychology*, 4 (3).

Doll, Russell C. and Hawkins, Maxine (eds.) (1971) *Educating the Disadvantaged 1970–1971*, New York, AMS Press.

Donovan, John C. (1967) *The Politics of Poverty*, Western Publishing (edn of 1973, Indianapolis, Bobbs-Merrill).

Duncan, Otis Dudley (1968) 'Inheritance of poverty or inheritance of race?', in Daniel P. Moynihan (ed.), *On Understanding Poverty*, New York, Basic Books.

Durham (*see* Ford Foundation).

Durham, Joseph T. (1969) 'Who needs it? Compensatory education', *The Clearing House*, 44 (1).

Eckerson, Louise O. (1973) *Following through with Follow Through*, Washington, D.C., HEW, Education Division.

Edmonds, Ronald (1979) 'Effective schools for the urban poor', *Educational Leadership*, 37 (1).

Education U.S.A. (1967) *The New ESEA. Special Report: The 1967 Amendments to the Elementary and Secondary Education Act* (no place).

Educational Policies Commission (of the NEA and AASA) (1958) *The Contemporary Challenge to American Education*, Washington, D.C., NEA.
(1962) *Education and the Disadvantaged American*, Washington, D.C., NEA.
(1965) *American Education and the Search for Equal Opportunity*, Washington, D.C., NEA.

Educational Testing Service (1966) *Workshop on Evaluating Title I Programs*, Princeton, N.J., ETS.

Egbert, Robert L. (1968a) 'Follow Through: fulfilling the promise of Head Start' in Jerome Hellmuth (ed.), *Disadvantaged Child*, vol. 2, New York, Brunner/Mazel.
(1974) 'Planned variation in Follow Through' in HR, Committee on Education and Labor, Sub-committee on equal opportunities, *Extension of Certain Programs under the Economic Opportunity Act of 1964: hearings before the sub-committee*, Washington, D.C., Government Printing Office.
(1981) Some Thoughts about Follow Through Thirteen Years Later, paper prepared for the National Institute of Education, Washington, D.C., NIE, mimeo.
(*see also* Follow Through).

Egland, George O. (1966) 'Parents in Head Start programs', *Young Children*, 21 (5).

Eidenberg, Eugene and Morely, Roy D. (1969) *An Act of Congress: the legislative process and the making of education policy*, New York, W.W. Norton.

Eisenberg, Leon (1963–4) 'Strengths of the inner city child', *Baltimore Bulletin of Education*, 41 (2).

Eliot, Abigail Adam (1972) 'Nursery schools fifty years ago', *Young Children*, 27 (4).

Ellis, Richard R. (1967) 'Prekindergarten education for the disadvantaged child' in Jerome Hellmuth (ed.) *Disadvantaged Child*, vol. 1, New York, Brunner/Mazel.

Elmore, Richard F. (1975) 'Design of the Follow Through experiment' in Alice M. Rivlin and P. Michael Timpane (eds.), *Planned Variation in Education*, Washington, D.C., Brookings Institution.

Elsten, Marjorie G. and Klein, Jenni W. (1978) 'Early childhood education: issues and prospects' in Edith K. Mosher and Jennings L. Wagoner Jr. (eds.) *The Changing Politics of Education: prospects for the 1980's*, Berkeley, McCutchan.

Engelmann, Siegfried (1969) *Preventing Failure in the Primary Grades*, Chicago, Science Research Associates.

Epstein, Ann S. and Weikart, David P. (1979) *The Ypsilanti–Carnegie Infant*

Education Project: longitudinal follow-up, Ypsilanti, Mich., High/Scope Press.

Estes, Nolan (1967) 'Follow Through', *American Education*, 3 (8).

Evans, Ellis D. (1971) *Contemporary Influences in Early Childhood Education*, New York, Holt, Rinehart and Winston (edn of 1975).

Evans, John W. (1981) What Have We Learned from Follow Through? Implications for future R&D programs, paper prepared for the National Institute of Education, Washington, D.C. NIE, mimeo.

Exton, Elaine (1964) 'Education a weapon in the War on Poverty', *American School Board Journal*, 148 (5).

Fantini, Mario (1969) 'Intervention alternatives for urban education' in *Harvard Educational Review, Equal Educational Opportunity* (reprinted from 1968 *Review*).

Fantini, Mario and Weinstein, Gerald (1968) *The Disadvantaged: challenge to education*, New York, Harper & Row.

Farber, Bernard and Lewis, Michael (1972) 'Compensatory education and social justice', *Education Digest*, 37 (7).

Far West Laboratory for Educational Research and Development (1980) *Educational Programs that Work*, Washington, D.C., National Diffusion Network.

Fass, Paula S. (1986) 'Before legalism: the New Deal and American education' in David L. Kirp and Donald N. Jensen (eds.), *School Days, Rule Days: the legalization and regulation of education*, Philadelphia, Falmer.

Feagans, Lynne and Farran, Dale Clark (eds.) (1982) *The Language of Children Reared in Poverty: implications for evaluation and intervention*, New York, Academic Press.

Featherstone, Joseph (1979) 'Family matters', *Harvard Educational Review*, 49 (1).

Fein, Leonard J. (1971) *The Ecology of the Public Schools: an inquiry into community control*, New York, Pegasus.

Ferman, Louis A. (ed.) (1965) *Evaluating the War on Poverty: the annals of the American Academy of Political and Social Science*, vol. 385.

Ferman, Louis A., Kornbluh, Joyce L. and Haber, Alan (eds.) (1965) *Poverty in America*, Ann Arbor, University of Michigan Press.

Feshbach, Norma D. (1973) *Early Schooling in England and Israel*, New York, McGraw-Hill.

Fillerup, Joseph M. *et al. (see* Tucson).

Fischer, John H. (1969) 'Schools for equal opportunity' in Alvin Toffler (ed.), *The Schoolhouse in the City*, Voice of America Forum lectures.

Fishman, Leo (ed.) (1966) *Poverty and Affluence*, New Haven, Conn., Yale University Press.

Flanagan, John C. (1964) 'Early findings from Project Talent', *Education Digest*, 29 (8).

Flanders, Ricki (1981) 'Report card for Head Start', *Commonweal*, 108 (8).

Flaxman, Erwin (ed.) (1973) *Educating the Disadvantaged 1971–1972*, New York, AMS Press.

   (1976) *Educating the Disadvantaged 1972–1973*, New York, AMS Press.

Fleischmann, Manly *et al.* (1973) *The Fleischmann Report on the Quality, Cost, and Financing of the Elementary and Secondary Education in New York State*, vol. 1, New York, Viking Press.

FOLLOW THROUGH (RECORDS, WASHINGTON D.C.)

Memorandum of Understanding between the Office of Economic Opportunity and the Department of Health, Education, and Welfare relative to the Administration of the Follow Through Program under a Delegation of Authority [1967], mimeo.

Mueller, B. Jeanne, Consultation for Compensatory Education Programs (prepared for a conference of Follow Through consultants), New York, 26–9 October 1967, mimeo.

Follow Through Fact Sheet (joint statement by Sargent Shriver and Harold Howe II), 1967, mimeo.

Follow Through meeting with selected state representatives, US Office of Education, 1967 11–12 December, mimeo.

Clark, John, Memorandum enclosing draft OEO Instruction, Participation of the Poor in the Planning, Conduct, and Evaluation of Community Action Programs, 20 September 1968, mimeo.

Egbert, Robert, Memorandum to all Follow Through Staff Members, November 19, 1968 (attaching recommendations of consultants at a planning meeting, Harvard University, November 7–9), mimeo.

Follow Through Program, Staff Meeting – October 15, 1968: discussion of issues raised in Atlanta, mimeo.

Follow Through Program Manual (draft), 24 February 1969.

Profiles of Local Educational Agencies or Communities Nominated for Follow Through (selected grant application forms), 1969–70.

Bissell, Joan S., Review and Summary of the Stanford Research Institute Longitudinal Evaluation of Selected Features of the National Follow Through Program, 1971, mimeo.

Follow Through Program, Five Year Program Plan, [HEW OE] Division of Compensatory Education, 1971, mimeo.

Nero and Associates (1976) *Follow Through. A Story of Educational Change*, Portland, Oregon.

Commission of Education, memorandum (and enclosures): Regulations Action Memorandum: Notice of proposed rulemaking – Follow Through, 1980.

FORD FOUNDATION (NEW YORK)

Annual Reports, 1955–1962/3

Ford Foundation (1972) *A Foundation Goes to School: the Ford Foundation comprehensive school improvement program 1960–1970*, New York, Ford Foundation

Ford Foundation Oral History Project. Interview with Paul Ylvisaker, 9/27/73, transcript.

Records relating to individual city and organization projects, microfilm unless otherwise stated:

Baltimore

Kolodner, Mrs Fred (1961) The Unaccepted Baltimoreans: a report on the white Southern Rural Migrants. Sponsored by the Baltimore Section, National Council of Jewish Women, Baltimore, mimeo

[Baltimore City Public Schools] [1961] A Pre-School Admission Project Related to In-School Learning Activities and Experiences, mimeo.

Memorandum from Martin Deutsch to Henry Saltzman [December 1961].

Baltimore City Public Schools. Letter from George B. Brain, Superintendent, to Dr Henry Saltzman, 20 July 1962.

Memorandum from Henry Saltzman, 1 August 1962, to P. Ylvisaker, E. Meade, L. Nelson.

Baltimore City Public Schools, Project Help, An Early School Admission Project (1962) Research Design for the Project, mimeo.

Ford Foundation, Public Affairs Department. Gray Areas: Baltimore City Board of Education [1962] (recommendation for support).

Baltimore City Public Schools, letter from George B. Brain to Henry Saltzman, 8 December 1962.

Account by Mrs Elizabeth M. Phillips for fellow School Board members of a National School Board Association meeting, April 1963, with excerpts from a speech by Henry Saltzman.

Baltimore City Pubic Schools, An Early School Admissions project. Progress report 1962–1963, mimeo.

Stone, William S., Baltimore City's Early School Admissions project: a three year project related to in-school learning activities for culturally deprived children, 1964, mimeo.

Memorandum from Henry Saltzmann to Paul Ylvisaker, 8 March 1965. (*see also* Brunner, Catherine; Project Help)

Chicago

Great Cities School Improvement Program Chicago Proposal. A Re-designed, Non-graded Program of Education for School Children who are 15 years old or thereabouts and are still in Elementary School, 12/28/59, mimeo.

Detroit

Detroit Board of Education (1960) A Report of the Detroit Pilot Project of the Great Cities School Improvement Program 1959–60.

Mitchell, Charles (1962) The Culturally Deprived – a matter of concern, The Great Cities School Improvement Project.

Durham

Durham Education Improvement Program, letter from Duke University, 1 July 1964 enclosing proposal for a 'Center' in Durham to Improve Educational Opportunity for Underprivileged Youth.

Letter from Robert H. Connery to Frank Bowles (Director, Ford Foundation Education Division), 2 November 1964.

Memo from Ed. Meade, 3 December 1964.

A Proposal to the Ford Foundation for Support of an Education Improvement Project for Culturally Deprived Children in the Public Schools of Durham City and County, North Carolina, January 1965.

Mario Fantini, memo to Ed. Meade, 6 January 1965.

Memo from Brenda A. Cox, 6 December 1967.

Shenkman, Harriet (1968) A Language Program for Culturally Disadvantaged Children, Durham, N.C., Durham Education Improvement Program, mimeo.

Spaulding, Robert L. (n.d.) 'From the Director's desk' in *The Durham Education Improvement Program 1965–1966*.

[1972] Report of consultants, mimeo.

Milwaukee

Milwaukee Public Schools, Great Cities School Improvement Program (1960a) A Milwaukee Project Proposal: A Special Program for In-Migrant and Transient Children in Depressed Areas, January.

Acculturation Program Milwaukee, Wisconsin (grant application to Ford Foundation), n.d.

Orientation Classes for In-Migrant and Transient Children. A First Report, Part 1, 1960–1961

National Association of Independent Schools

Memorandum from Clarence Faust to Henry T. Heald, 14 February 1964.

National Association of Independent Schools Inc. Summer Program: Educational Enrichment for Students Handicapped by Educational and Cultural Deprivation (n.d.; proposal submitted 1963).

Yeomans, Edward, Conference on Summer Enrichment Programs, October 1965 (consultant's report).

Educational Enrichment Program, Inc., Annual Report, Boston, 1966.

Reports from Participating Schools, 1967.

Philadelphia

Philadelphia School District, Great Cities School Improvement Program, a Philadelphia Project Proposal: The School–Community Coordinating Team, mimeo.

Great Cities School Improvement Program, School–Community Coordinating Team. The Dunbar High Roads Project, September 1961.

Pittsburgh

Pittsburgh Public Schools, The Use of Teaching Teams to Improve the Education of In-Migrant Transient Pupils in Depressed Areas (approved by Ford, May 1960).

St Louis

(1960a) Ford Foundation, Great Cities Project. St Louis Meeting – 21 May 1960. Report.

(1960b) St Louis Public Schools, Great Cities School Improvement Studies, Education of Culturally Different Children: the School and Community Work-Related Education Program (approved by Ford, June 1960).

St Louis School District, Great Cities School Improvement Program: a Summer Remedial Reading Project (n.d.), mimeo.

St Louis Public Schools, Great Cities School Improvement Program. A Summer Remedial Reading Project 1961, mimeo.

Great Cities Improvement Program: The School and Community Work-Related Education Program. Progress Report 1962, mimeo.

Yale

Yale Summer High School, a Summer School for Able High School Students whose Environment Inhibits their Full Personal and Intellectual Development (proposal to Ford, December 1963).

Report of the Director, 1965 session.

(*see also* Magat; Meade; Woodring; Ylvisaker).

Forest, Ilse (1927) *Preschool Education : a historical and critical study*, New York, Macmillan.

Foster, Florence P. (1966) 'The impact of early intervention', *Young Children*, 21 (6).

Fowler, William [1967] *The Design of Early Developmental Learning Programs for Disadvantaged Young Children : supplement to the IRCD Bulletin*, 3 (1A).

Fraiberg, Selma H. (1959) *The Magic Years : understanding and handling the problems of early childhood*, New York, Scribner's (London, Methuen, edition of 1968).

Frazier, Alexander *et al.* (1968) *Educating the Children of the Poor*, Washington, D.C., Association for Supervision and Curriculum Development.

Frieden, Bernard J. and Kaplan, Marshall (1977) *The Politics of Neglect : urban aid from model cities to revenue sharing*, Cambridge, Mass., MIT Press.

Friedman, Lawrence M. (1977) 'The social and political context of the War on Poverty: an overview' in Robert H. Haveman (ed.), *A Decade of Federal Antipoverty Programs*, New York, Academic Press.

Friedman, Norman L. (1967) 'Cultural deprivation: a commentary in the sociology of knowledge', *Journal of Educational Thought*, 1 (2).

Friggens, Paul (1964) 'Sam Shepard's Faith', *The PTA Magazine*, 58 (7).

Frost, Joe L. (ed.) (1968) *Early Childhood Education Rediscovered*, New York, Holt, Rinehart and Winston.

Frost, Joe L. and Hawkes, Glenn R. (eds.) (1966) *The Disadvantaged Child : issues and innovations*, Boston, Houghton Mifflin.

Frost, Joe L. and Rowland, G. Thomas (1971) *Compensatory Programming : the acid test of American education*, Dubuque, Iowa, Wm. C. Brown.

Gaebler, Robert (1966) 'Head Start in Chicago: 1965', *Journal of School Psychology*, 4 (3).

Galbraith, John Kenneth (1958) *The Affluent Society*, Boston, Houghton Mifflin, (Penguin edition, 1970).

(1964) 'Let us Begin: an invitation to action on poverty', *Harper's Magazine*, March.

Gans, Herbert J. (1968) 'Culture and class in the study of poverty: an approach to anti-poverty research' in Daniel P. Moynihan (ed.), *On Understanding Poverty*, New York, Basic Books.

(1976) 'The role of education in the escape from poverty' in Nelson F. Ashline *et al.* (eds.), *Education, Inequality, and National Policy*, Lexington, D.C. Heath.

Garber, Howard L. and Heber, Rick (1981) 'The efficacy of early intervention with family rehabilitation' in Michael J. Begab *et al.* (eds.), *Psychosocial Influences in Retarded Performance*, Baltimore, University Park Press.

Gardner, John W. (1968) *No Easy Victories*, New York, Harper and Row.

Geismar, Ludwig and Krisberg, Jane (1967) *The Forgotten Neighbourhood: site of early skirmish in the war on poverty*, Metuchen, N.J., Scarecrow Press.

Gelfand, Mark I. (1981) 'The War on Poverty' in Robert A. Divine (ed.), *Exploring the Johnson Years*, Austin, University of Texas Press.

Gersten, Russell (1984) 'Follow Through Revisited: reflections on the site variability issue', *Educational Evaluation and Policy Analysis*, 6 (4).

Getzels, J.W. (1966) 'Preschool education', *Teachers College Record*, 68 (3).

Ginsburg, Herbert (1972) *The Myth of the Deprived Child: poor children's intellect and education*, Englewood Cliffs, N.J., Prentice-Hall.

Ginzberg, Eli and Solow, Robert M. (eds.) (1974) *The Great Society: lessons for the future*, New York, Basic Books.

Gladwin, Thomas (1967) *Poverty U.S.A.*, Boston, Little Brown.

Glazer, Nathan (1965a) 'Paradoxes of American poverty', *The Public Interest*, 1.

(1965b) 'A sociologist's view of poverty' in Margaret S. Gordon (ed.) *Poverty in America*, San Francisco, Chandler.

(1968) 'The grand design of the poverty program' in Chaim Isaac Waxman (ed.), *Poverty: power and politics*, New York, Grosset & Dunlap.

Goettel, Robert J. (1978) 'Federal assistance to national target groups: the ESEA Title I experience' in Michael Timpane (ed.), *The Federal Interest in Financing Schooling*, Cambridge, Mass., Ballinger.

Goff, Regina (1968) 'Title I promises fulfilled' in A. Harry Passow (ed.), *Developing Programs for the Educationally Disadvantaged*, New York, Teachers College Press.

Goldberg, Miriam L. (1963) 'Factors affecting educational attainment in depressed urban areas' in A. Harry Passow, *Education in Depressed Areas*, New York, Teachers College Press.

(1971) 'Socio-psychological issues in the education of the disadvantaged' in A. Harry Passow (ed.), *Urban Education in the 1970's*, New York, Teachers College Press.

Goodson, Barbara Dillon and Hess, Robert D. (1978) 'The effects of parent training programs on child performance and parent behavior' in Bernard Brown (ed.), *Found: Long-term gains from early intervention*, Boulder, Colo., Westview Press.

Gordon, Edmund W. (1965a) 'Editorial: help for the disadvantaged?', *American Journal of Orthopsychiatry*, 35 (3).

(1965b) 'A review of programs of compensatory eduction', *American Journal of Orthopsychiatry*, 35 (4).

(1967) 'Programs of compensatory education' in Martin Deutsch *et al.*, *Social*

Class, Race, and Psychological Develoment, New York, Holt, Rinehart & Winston.

(1968) 'Introduction' in Jerome Hellmuth (ed.), *Disadvantaged Child*, vol. 2, New York, Brunner/Mazel.

(1970) 'Compensatory education: evaluation in perspective', *IRCD Bulletin*, 6 (5).

(1970) 'Some theoretical and practical problems in compensatory education as an antidote to poverty' in Vernon L. Allen (ed.), *Psychological Factors in Poverty*, Chicago, Markham.

(1972) 'Toward defining equality of education opportunity' in Frederick Mosteller and Daniel P. Moynihan (eds.), *On Equality of Educational Opportunity*, New York, Random House.

(1975) 'New perspectives on old issues in education for the minority poor', *IRCD Bulletin*.

(1976) 'Education of the disadvantaged: a problem of human diversity' in Nelson F. Ashline *et al.* (eds.), *Education, Inequality, and National Policy*, Lexington, D.C., Heath.

Gordon, Edmund W. and Wilkerson, Doxey A. (1966) *Compensatory Education for the Disadvantaged. Programs and Practices: preschool through college*, New York, College Entrance Examination Board.

Gordon, Ira (ed.) (1972) *Early Childhood Education: the seventy-first yearbook of the National Society for the Study of Education*, Part 2, Chicago, NSSE.

Gordon, Margaret S. (ed.) (1965) *Poverty in America*, San Francisco, Chandler.

Gordon, Sol (1970) 'The bankruptcy of compensatory education', *Education and Urban Society*, 2 (4).

Gotkin, Lassar G., McSweeney, Joseph F. and Richardson, Ellis (1969) *The Development of a Beginning Reading Program*, New York, Institute for Developmental Studies, New York University.

Gotts, Edward Earl and Pierce-Jones, John (1968) 'Evaluating Head Start inputs and outcomes' in Joe L. Frost (ed.), *Early Childhood Education Rediscovered*, New York, Holt, Rinehart & Winston.

Gower, Calvin, W. (1967) 'The Civilian Conservation Corps and American Education: threat to local control?', *History of Education Quarterly*, 7 (1).

Graham, Hugh Davis (1981) 'The transforming of federal education policy' in Robert A. Divine (ed.), *Exploring the Johnson Years*, Austin, University of Texas Press.

(1984) *The Uncertain Triumph: federal education policy in the Kennedy and Johnson years*, Chapel Hill, University of North Carolina Press.

Graham, Patricia Albjerg (1980) 'Whither equality of educational opportunity?', *Daedalus*, 109 (3).

Grambs, Jean D. (1965) 'The culturally deprived child: achieving adequacy through education', *Child and Family*, 4 (2) (reprint of 1964 article).

Grant, Carl A. (1979) *Community Participation in Education*, Boston, Allyn and Bacon.

Gray, Susan W. (1966) Deprivation, Development and Diffusion (presidential address, Division of School Psychologists, American Psychological Association), Nashville, mimeo.

(1974) 'Children from three to ten: the Early Training Project' in Sally Ryan (ed.), *A Report on Longitudinal Evaluations of Preschool Programs*, Washington, D.C., HEW.

(1977) 'Home-based programs for mothers of young children' in Peter Mittler (ed.), *Research to Practice in Mental Retardation*, vol. 1: *Care and Intervention*, Baltimore, University Park Press.

(1983) 'Enduring effects of early intervention: perspectives and perplexities', *Peabody Journal of Education*, 60 (3).

Gray, Susan W. and Klaus, Rupert A. (1963) Early Training Project: interim report, Murfreesboro City Schools, Tennessee, mimeo.

(1965) 'An experimental preschool program for culturally deprived children', *Child Development*, 36 (4).

(1966) 'The Early Training Project: an intervention study and how it grew', *Journal of School Psychology*, 4 (3).

(1968) 'The Early Training Project and its general rationale' in Robert D. Hess and Roberta Meyer Bear (eds.), *Early Education: current theory, research and action*, Chicago, Aldine-Atherton.

(1970) 'The Early Training Project: a seventh-year report', *Child Development*, 41 (4).

Gray, Susan W., Klaus, Rupert A. and Ramsey, Barbara K. (1981) 'Participants in the Early Training Project: 1962–1977' in Michael J. Begab et al. (eds.), *Psychosocial Influences in Retarded Performance*, Baltimore, University Park Press.

Gray Susan W. et al. (1966) *Before First Grade: the Early Training Project for Culturally Disadvantaged Children*, New York, Teachers College Press.

(1967) Research, Change, and Social Responsibility: an illustrative model from early education, Nashville, Demonstration and Research Center for Early Education, mimeo.

(1981) *From 3 to 20: the Early Training Project*, Baltimore, University Park Press.

Greenberg, Polly (1967) 'CDGM... An experiment in preschool for the poor – by the poor', *Young Children*, 22 (5).

Greenleigh Associates (1969) Upward Bound: a study of impact on the secondary school and the community, New York, Greenleigh Associates, mimeo.

Gross, Beatrice and Gross, Ronald (1981) Planning for Follow Through Research and Development: a report of three conferences to develop guidelines for future funding, Washington, D.C., National Institute of Education, mimeo.

Grotberg, Edith H. (1969) Review of Research 1965 to 1969, Washington, D.C., Office of Economic Opportunity, Research and Evaluation Office, Project Head Start, mimeo.

(1972) 'Institutional responsibilities for early childhood education' in Ira Gordon (ed.), *Early Childhood Education*, Chicago, NSSE.

(1977) '"Formulating policies concerning effective early childhood education": education and development programs', *Journal of School Psychology*, 15 (2).

Grubb, W. Norton and Lazerson, Marvin (1980) 'Children, the state and the limits of reform' (review of de Lone, *Small Futures*), *Harvard Educational Review*, 50 (3).

(1982) *Broken Promises: how Americans fail their children*, New York, Basic Books.

Gussow, J. (1965) 'Language development in disadvantaged children', *IRCD Bulletin*, 1(5).

Guthrie, James W. (1968) 'A political case history; passage of the ESEA', *Phi Delta Kappan*, 49 (6).

Guthrie, James W. and Kelly, James A. (1965) 'Compensatory education – some answers for a skeptic', *Phi Delta Kappan*, 47 (2).

Guthrie, James W. *et al.* (1971) *Schools and Inequality*, Cambridge, Mass., MIT Press.

Haider, Donald H. (1971) 'Governors and mayors view the poverty program', *Current History*, 61 (363).

Halperin, Samuel and Wayson, William (1975) 'ESEA: decennial view of the revolution', *Phi Delta Kappan*, 57 (3).

Halsey, A.H., Floud, Jean and Anderson, C. Arnold (eds.) (1961) *Education, Economy, and Society: a reader in the sociology of education*, New York, Free Press of Glencoe.

Hamilton, Phyllis (1979) Vocational education for special-need students', in National Institute of Education, *The Planning Papers for the Vocational Education Study*, Washington, D.C., NIE.

Hamlin, Ruth, Mukerji, Rose and Yonemura, Margaret (1967) *Schools for Young Disadvantaged Children*, New York, Teachers College Press.

Haney, Walt (1977a) *The Follow Through Planned Variation Experiment*, vol. 5: *A Technical History of the National Follow Through Evaluation*, Cambridge, Mass., Huron Institute.

(1977b) 'The Follow Through experiment: summary of an analysis of major evaluation reports', *Curriculum Inquiry*, 7 (3).

Hanushek, Eric A. and Kain, John F. (1972) 'On the value of *Equality of Educational Opportunity* as a guide to public policy' in Frederick Mosteller and Daniel P. Moynihan (eds.), *On Equality of Educational Opportunity*, New York, Random House.

Harlem Youth Opportunities Unlimited (1964) Youth in the Ghetto: a study of the consequences of powerlessness and a blueprint for change, New York, HARYOU, mimeo.

Harmon, Carolyn and Zigler, Edward (1980) 'Parent education in the 1970s: policy, panacea, or pragmatism', *Merrill-Palmer Quarterly*, 26 (4).

Harrell, Adele (1983) *The Effect of the Head Start Program on Children's Cognitive Development: preliminary report*, Washington, D.C., CSR Inc.

Harrington, Michael (1962) *The Other America: poverty in the United States*, Baltimore, Penguin, edition of 1963.

(1965a) Introduction to Louis A. Ferman *et al.* (eds.), *Poverty in America*, Ann Arbor, University of Michigan Press.

(1965b) 'A social reformer's view of poverty' in Margaret S. Gordon (ed.) *Poverty in America: proceedings of a national conference...*, San Francisco, Chandler.

(1968) 'The politics of poverty' in Jeremy Larner and Irving Howe (eds.), *Poverty: views from the left*, New York, William Morrow.

(1980) *Decade of Decision : the crisis of the American system*, New York, Simon & Schuster.

Harvard University, Graduate School of Education (1950) *Dean's Report, 1950–51* and *1953–54*, Cambridge, Mass., Harvard University.

Hastings, Anne, H. (1982) 'More ways than one: federal strategies to equalize access in education and health care', *Peabody Journal of Education*, 60 (1).

Haubrich, Vernon (ed.) (1966) *Studies in Deprivation*, New York, AERA.

Haveman, Robert H. (ed.) (1977) *A Decade of Federal Antipoverty Programs : achievements, failures, and lessons*, New York, Academic Press.

(1987) *Poverty Policy and Policy Research : the Great Society and the social sciences*, Madison, University of Wisconsin Press.

Havighurst, Robert J. (1963) 'Urban development and the educational system' in A. Harry Passow (ed.), *Education in Depressed Areas*, New York, Teachers College Press.

(1965) 'Social class and education' in Stan Dropkin, Harold Full and Ernest Schwarcz (eds.) *Contemporary American Education*, New York, Macmillan.

(1966) 'Who are the socially disadvantaged?' in Staten W. Webster (ed.), *The Disadvantaged Learner*, San Francisco, Chandler.

(1971) 'Public education for disadvantaged urban minorities' in A. Harry Passow (ed.), *Urban Education in the 1970's*, New York, Teachers College Press.

(1974) 'Opportunity, equity, or equality' in Andrew Kopan and Herbert Walberg (eds.), *Rethinking Educational Equality*, Berkeley, McCutchan.

(1979) 'Local community participation in educational policy making and school administration' in Carl A. Grant (ed.), *Community Participation in Education*, Boston, Allyn & Bacon.

Havighurst, Robert J. and Moorefield, Thomas E. (1967) 'The disadvantaged in industrial cities' in Paul A. Witty (ed.), *The Educationally Retarded and Disadvantaged*, Chicago, NSSE.

Hawkins, David (1973) 'Liberal education: a modest polemic' in Carl Kaysen (ed.) *Content and Context : essays on college education*, New York, McGraw-Hill.

Hawkinson, Robert Eugene (1977) Presidential Program Formulation in Education: Lyndon Johnson and the 89th Congress, University of Chicago PhD dissertation.

Hawkridge, David G., Chalupsky, Albert B. and Roberts, A. Oscar (1968) *A Study of Selected Exemplary Programs for the Education of Disadvantaged Children*, Washington, D.C., HEW, Office of Program Planning and Evaluation.

Hawley, Willis, D. (1985) 'False premises, false promises: the mythical character of public discourse about education', *Phi Delta Kappan*, 67 (3).

Haywood, H. Carl (1982) 'Compensatory education', *Peabody Journal of Education*, 59 (4).

Hebb, D.O. (1949) *The Organization of Behavior : a neuropsychological theory*, New York, Wiley (reprint of 1964).

Hechinger, Fred M. (1964) 'Restless energy foretells a period of major change', *New York Times, Special Education Survey*, 16 January 1964.

(ed.) (1966) *Pre-School Education Today : new approaches to teaching three-, four-, and five-year-olds*, Garden City, N.Y., Doubleday.

Heffernan, Helen (1965) 'New opportunity for the preschool child', *Childhood Education*, 41 (5).

Hellmuth, Jerome (ed.) (1967) *Disadvantaged Child*, vol. 1, New York, Brunner/Mazel.

(1968) *Disadvantaged Child*, vol. 2: *Head Start and Early Intervention*, New York, Brunner/Mazel.

(1970) *Disadvantaged Child*, vol. 3: *Compensatory Education: a national debate*, New York, Brunner/Mazel.

Henry, Nelson B. (ed.) (1953) *National Society for the Study of Education. The Fifty-second yearbook*. part 2: *The Community School*, Chicago, NSSE.

Herbers, John (1982) 'Poverty rate, 14%, termed highest since '67', *New York Times*, 20 July.

Herman, Melvin (1965) 'Problems of evaluation', *The American Child*, 47 (2).

Hersey, John, (1964) 'Our romance with poverty', *The American Scholar*, 33, Autumn.

(1965) 'Education: an antidote to poverty', *Young Children*, 21 (2).

Herzog, Elizabeth, Newcomb, Carol H. and Cisin, Ira H. (1974) 'Double deprivation: the less they have, the less they learn' in Sally Ryan (ed.), *A Report on Longitudinal Evaluations of Preschool Programs*, Washington, D.C., HEW.

Hess, Robert D. and Shipman, Virginia (1966) 'Early blocks to children's learning' in Staten W. Webster (ed.), *The Disadvantaged Learner*, San Francisco, Chandler.

Hewett, Kathryn D. *et al.* (1977) *Partners with Parents: the Home Start experience with preschoolers and their families*, Washington, D.C., HEW.

Heyns, Barbara (1978) *Summer Learning and the Effects of Schooling*, New York, Academic Press.

High, Paul B. (1963) 'Educating the superior student', *The American Teacher Magazine*, 48 (2).

Hill, Charles H. (1972) 'Head Start: a problem of assumptions', *Education*, 92 (4).

Hill, Clifford, A. (1977) 'A review of the language deficit position: some sociolinguistic and psycholinguistic perspectives', *IRCD Bulletin*, 12 (4).

Hill, Paul T. (1978) *Evaluating Education Programs for Federal Policy Makers: lessons from the NIE Compensatory Education Study*, Santa Monica, Calif., Rand.

(1981) Follow Through and the Problem of Federal Educational Programs, paper prepared for the National Institute of Education, Washington, D.C., NIE, mimeo.

(1990) 'The federal role in education: a strategy for the 1990s', *Phi Delta Kappan*, 71 (5).

Hilliard III, Asa G. (1981) The Future of Follow Through, paper prepared for the National Institute of Education, Washington, D.C., NIE, mimeo.

Hodges, Walter L. (1973) 'The implications of design and model selection for the evaluation of programs for the disadvantaged child', *Merrill-Palmer Quarterly*, 19 (4).

(1978) 'The worth of Follow Through experience', *Harvard Educational Review*, 48 (2).

(1981) *Instructional Models, Model Sponsors, and Future Follow Through Research*, paper prepared for the National Institute of Education, Washington, D.C., NIE, mimeo.

Hodges, Walter L. and Cooper, Mark (1981) 'Head Start and Follow Through: influences on intellectual development', *Journal of Special Education*, 15 (2).

Hodges, Walter L. and Smith, Laurene (1980) *Modern Early Childhood Education: a review*, Atlanta, Georgia, Georgia State University, mimeo.

Hodges, Walter L. *et al.* (1971) *Diagnostic Teaching for Preschool Children*, Arlington, Virginia, Council for Exceptional Children.

(1980). *Follow Through: forces for change in the primary schools*, Ypsilanti, Mich., High/Scope.

Holtz, Barry W. (1981) 'Can schools make a difference?' (review of Rutter *et al.*, *Fifteen Thousand Hours*), *Teachers College Record*, 83 (2).

Horner, V. (1966) 'Misconceptions concerning language in the disadvantaged', *Supplement to the IRCD Bulletin* 2 (3A).

House, Ernest R. and Hutchins, Elizabeth J. (1979) 'Issues raised by the Follow Through evaluation' in Lilian G. Katz (ed.), *Current Topics in Early Childhood Education*, Norwood, N.J., Ablex, vol. 2.

House, Ernest R. *et al.* (1978) 'No simple answer: critique of Follow Through evaluation', *Harvard Educational Review*, 48 (2).

Howe, Irving (1966) *Steady Work: essays in the politics of democratic radicalism 1953–1966*, New York, Harcourt, Brace and World.

Hubbell, Ruth (1983) *A Review of Head Start Research since 1970*, Washington, D.C., Government Printing office.

Hubbell, Virginia Ruth (1978) 'The Developmental Continuity Consortium Study: secondary analysis of early intervention data' in Bernard Brown (ed.), *Found: Long-term Gains from Early Intervention*, Boulder, Colo, Westview Press.

Hughes, John F. and Hughes, Anne O. (1972) *Equal Education: a new national strategy*, Bloomington, Ind., Indiana University Press.

Hughes, Marie, Wetzel, Ralph J. and Henderson, Ronald W. (1973) 'The Tucson Early Education Model' in Bernard Spodek (ed.), *Early Childhood Education*, Englewood Cliffs, N.J., Prentice-Hall.

Humphrey, Hubert H. (1964). *War on Poverty*, New York, McGraw-Hill.

[1966] 'Education – the ideal and the reality' in National Conference on Education of the Disadvantaged, *Report*.

(1976) *The Education of a Public Man: my life in politics*, New York, Doubleday.

Hunnicutt, C.W. (1953) 'The community school as a social instrument' in Henry B. Nelson (ed.) *The Fifty-second Yearbook of the National Society for the Study of Education*, Part 2: *The Community School*, Chicago, NSSE.

Hunt, J. McVicker (1961) *Intelligence and Experience*, New York, Ronald Press.

(1964) 'The psychological basis for using pre-school enrichment as an antidote for cultural deprivation', *Merrill-Palmer Quarterly*, 10 (3).

(1967) 'Environment, development, and scholastic achievement' in Martin Deutsch *et al.* (eds) *Social Class, Race, and Psychological Development*, New York, Holt, Rinehart & Winston.

(1968) 'Revisiting Montessori' in Joe L. Frost (ed.), *Early Childhood Rediscovered*, New York, Holt, Rinehart & Winston.

(1969a) *The Challenge of Incompetence and Poverty : papers on the role of early education*, Urbana, Ill., University of Illinois Press.

(1969b) 'Has compensatory education failed? Has it been attempted?', *Harvard Educational Review*, 39 (2).

Hurley, Rodger, L. (1969) *Poverty and Mental Retardation : a causal relationship*, New York, Random House.

Husén, Torsten (1976) 'The equality–meritocracy dilemma in education' in Nelson F. Ashline *et al.* (eds.) *Education, Inequality, and National Policy*, Lexington, D.C. Heath.

Hyde, Floyd H. (1969) 'HUD builds partnership for participation', *Public Management*, July.

Hymes, Dell (1972) Introduction to Courtney B. Cazden, Vera P. John and Dell Hymes (eds.) *Functions of Language in the Classroom*, New York, Teachers College Press.

Inequality in Education (1973), 15

Iowa Child Welfare Research Station (1934) *Manual of Nursery School Practice*, Iowa City, University of Iowa.

IRCD Bulletin (Information Retrieval Center on the Disadvantaged) (1965), 1 (2).

Irvine, David J. *et al.* (1982) 'Evidence supporting comprehensive early childhood education for disadvantaged children', *Annals of the American Academy of Political and Social Science*, 461.

Isenberg, Robert M. (1963) 'The rural disadvantaged', *NEA Journal*, 52 (4).

Jablonsky, Adelaide (1968) 'Some trends in education for the disadvantaged', *IRCD Bulletin*, 4 (2).

(1971) 'Status report on compensatory education', *IRCD Bulletin*, 7 (1/2).

Jacobs, Paul (1965) 'Discussion' (of paper by Riessman) in Margaret S. Gordon (ed.) *Poverty in America*, San Francisco, Chandler.

(1968) 'America's schizophrenic view of the poor' in Jeremy Larner and Irving Howe (eds.) *Poverty : views from the left*, New York, William Morrow.

Jacobs, Paul *et al.* (1967) *Dialogue on Poverty*, Indianapolis, Bobbs-Merrill.

James, Dorothy Buckton (1972) *Poverty, Politics and Change*, Englewood Cliffs, N.J., Prentice-Hall.

Jeffrey, Julie Roy (1978) *Education for Children of the Poor : a study of the origins and implementation of the Elementary and Secondary Education Act of 1965*, Columbus, Ohio State University Press.

Jencks, Christopher (1969) 'A reappraisal of the most controversial educational document of our time', *New York Times Magazine*, 10 August.

Jencks, Christopher *et al.* (1972) *Inequality : a reassessment of the effect of family and schooling in America*, New York, Basic Books (Harper and Row edn of 1973).

Jennings, John F. (1987) 'The sputnik of the eighties', *Phi Delta Kappan*, 69 (2).

(1988) 'Working in mysterious ways: the federal government and education', *Phi Delta Kappan*, 70 (1)

Jensen, Arthur R. (1967) 'The culturally disadvantaged: psychological and educational aspects', *Education Research*, 10 (1).

(1968) 'The culturally disadvantaged and the heredity–environment uncertainty' in Jerome Hellmuth (ed.), *Disadvantaged Child*, vol. 2, New
York, Brunner/Mazel.

(1969) 'How much can we boost IQ and scholastic achievement?', *Harvard
Educational Review*, 39 (1).

(1985) 'Compensatory education and the theory of intelligence', *Phi Delta
Kappan*, 66 (9).

Jensen, Philip K. *et al.* (1972) 'Evaluating compensatory education: a case
study, *Education and Urban Society*, 4 (2).

John, Vera P. (1963) 'The intellectual development of slum children: some
preliminary findings', *American Journal of Orthopsychiatry*, 33 (5).

(1965) 'Research related to language development in disadvantaged children,
IRCD Bulletin, 1 (5).

John, Vera P. and Goldstein, Leo S. (1964) 'The social context of language
acquisition', *Merrill-Palmer Quarterly*, 10 (3).

John-Steiner, V. and Tatter, P. [1982] 'Language development of the
disadvantaged', University of New Mexico, mimeo.

Johnson, Lyndon B. (1965) 'President Johnson's message on poverty to the
Congress of the United States, 16 March 1964' in Louis A. Ferman *et al.*
(eds.), *Poverty in America*, Ann Arbor, University of Michigan Press.

[1966] 'Remarks' in National Conference on Education of the Disadvantaged,
Report.

(1972) *The Vantage Point: perspectives of the presidency 1963–1969*, New
York, Holt, Rinehart and Winston.

The Johnson Presidential Press Conferences (1978), London, Heyden, vol. 1.

Kagan, Sharon and Zigler, Edward F. (1987) *Early Schooling: the national
debate*, New Haven, Yale University Press.

Kamii, Constance 91973) 'A sketch of the Piaget-derived preschool curriculum
developed by the Ypsilanti Early Education Program' in Bernard Spodek
(ed.), *Early Childhood Education*, Englewood Cliffs, N.J., Prentice-Hall.

Kaplan, Bernard A. (1963) 'Issues in educating the culturally disadvantaged',
Phi Delta Kappan, 45 (2).

Kapp, Louise (1965) 'Will "success" spoil success?', *American Child*, 47 (2).

Karmin, Monroe W. (1965) 'U.S. program to help underprivileged pupils
begins amidst doubts', *Wall Street Journal*, 30 June.

Karnes, Merle B. (1973) 'Evaluation and implications of research with young
handicapped and low-income children' in Julian C. Stanley (ed.), *Compensatory Education for Children Ages Two to Eight*, Baltimore, Johns
Hopkins University Press.

Karnes, Merle B., Zehrbach, R. Reid and Teska, James A. (1974) 'The Karnes
preschool program: rationale, curricula offerings, and follow-up data' in
Sally Ryan (ed.), *A Report on Longitudinal Evaluations of Preschool
Programs*, Washington, D.C., HEW.

Karnes, Merle B. *et al.* (1968) 'An approach for working with mothers of
disadvantaged preschool children', *Merrill-Palmer Quarterly*, 14 (2).

(1970) 'Educational intervention at home by mothers of disadvantaged
infants', *Child Development*, 41 (4).

Katz, Lilian G. *et al.* (1979). *Current Topics in Early Childhood Education*,
Norwood, N.J., Ablex, vol. 2.

Keach, Everett T. Jr, Fulton, Robert and Gardner, William E. (eds.) (1967) *Education and Social Crisis: perspectives on teaching disadvantaged youth*, New York, Wiley.

Kearney, Charles Philip (1967) The 1964 Presidential Task Force on Education and the Elementary and Secondary Education Act of 1965, University of Chicago, PhD dissertation.

Kearns, Doris (1976) *Lyndon Johnson and the American Dream*, New York, Harper and Row.

Kelsall, R.K. and Kelsall Helen M. (1971) *Social Disadvantage and Educational Opportunity*, New York, Holt, Rinehart and Winston.

Kennedy, John F. (1963) 'A message on education' (to Congress, 29 January 1963), reprinted in *The Massachusetts Teacher*, 42 (6).

Kennedy, Mary M. (1977) 'The Follow Through Program', *Curriculum Inquiry*, 7 (3).

Kennedy, Mary M. *et al.* (1986) *The Effectiveness of Chapter 1 Services*, Washington, D.C., OE, Office of Educational Research and Improvement.

Kent, James K. (1969) 'The Coleman report: opening Pandora's box', *Phi Delta Kappan*, 49 (5).

Keppel, Francis (1963) 'Into the century of the educated man', *Saturday Review*, 21 December.

(1964a) 'The "pass along": a sign of change', *New York Times, Special Education Survey*, 16 January.

(1964b) 'Thank God for the civil rights movement', *Integrated Education*, 2 (2).

(1964c) recorded interview by Frank Sieverts, 18 September 1964, Boston, John F. Kennedy Library, Oral History Program, transcript.

(1964d) 'Poverty: target for education' in *Your AASA in Nineteen Sixty-Three-Sixty-Four*, Washington, D.C., American Association of School Administrators.

(1965a) 'Vocational education and poverty' in Margaret S. Gordon (ed.), *Poverty in America*, San Francisco, Chandler.

(1965b) 'Education and the states', *AAUW Journal* (American Association of University Women), 58 (3).

(1965c) '1965: education's year of promise', *Southern Regional Education Board*, 22 June.

(1965d) 'The emerging partnership of education and civil rights', *Journal of Negro Education*, 34 (3).

(1966) *The Necessary Revolution in American Education*, New York, Harper and Row.

(1987) 'The higher education acts contrasted 1965–1986: has federal policy come of age?', *Harvard Educational Review*, 57 (1).

Keppel, Francis, Gross, Calvin, E. and Shepard, Samuel Jr. (1965) *How Should We Educate the Deprived Child?*, Washington, D.C., Council for Basic Education.

(*see also* Lyndon B. Johnson Library).

Kershaw, Joseph A. (1970) *Government against Poverty*, Washington, D.C., Brookings Institution.

Kett, Joseph K. (1982) 'The adolescence of vocational education' in Harvey

Kantor and David B. Tyack (eds.), *Work, Youth and Schooling*, Stanford University Press.

Kiesling, Herbert J. (1968) 'Empirical evidence concerning the relative educational performance of children from disadvantaged backgrounds' in US Congress, Subcommittee on Economic Progress of the Joint Economic Committee, Federal Programs for the Development of Human Resources, vol. 1, Washington, D.C., Government Printing Office.

Kirp, David L. (1982) *Just Schools: the idea of racial equality in American education*, Berkeley, Calif., University of California Press.

Kirschner Associates (1970) A National Survey of the Impacts of Head Start Centers on Community Institutions, Washington, D.C., HEW, Office of Child Development, mimeo.

Kirst, Michael W. (1972) *Delivery Systems for Federal Aid to Disadvantaged Children: problems and prospects*, Stanford University, School of Education.

(1982) *Teaching Policy and Federal Categorical Programs*, Stanford University, Institute for Research on Educational Finance and Governance.

(1986) *The Federal Role and Chapter I: rethinking some basic assumptions*, Stanford University, Center for Educational Research.

Kirst, Michael W. and Jung, Richard (1980) *The Utility of a Longitudinal Approach in Assessing Implementation: a thirteen year view of Title I, ESEA*, Stanford University, School of Education.

Klaus, Rupert A. and Gray, Susan W. (1965) 'Murfreesboro Preschool Program for culturally deprived children', *Childhood Education*, 92 (5).

[1968] *The Early Training Project for Disadvantaged Children: a report after five years*, Nashville, George Peabody College for Teachers.

Koontz, John D. (1963) 'The Washington, D.C., Program' in HEW, *Programs for the Educationally Disadvantaged*.

Kraft, Ivor (1966) 'Head Start to What?', *The Nation*, 203 (6).

Kramer, Ralph M. (1969) *Participation of the Poor: comparative community case studies in the War on Poverty*, Englewood Cliffs, N.J., Prentice-Hall.

Kravitz, Sanford L. (1965) 'Community Action Programs: past, present, future', *The American Child*, 47 (4).

Kravitz, Sanford L. and Kolodner, Ferne K. (1969) 'Community action: where has it been? Where will it go?' in Louis A. Ferman (ed.), *Evaluating the War on Poverty*, *AAPSS*.

Krugman, Morris (1961) 'The culturally deprived child in school', *NEA Journal*, 50 (4).

Kuntz, Susan W. and Lyczak, Richard (1983) 'Sustained effects of Title I over the summer months', *Journal of Educational Research*, 76 (3).

Kvaraceus, Willia C., Gibson, John S. and Curtin, Thomas J. (1967) *Poverty, Education and Race Relations: studies and proposals*, Boston, Allyn and Bacon.

Lampman, Robert J. (1965), The Anti-Poverty Program in Historical Perspective, Los Angeles, University of California, Institute of Government and Public Affairs, mimeo.

(1974) 'What does it do for the poor? – a new test for national policy' in Eli Ginzberg and Robert M. Solow (eds.), *The Great Society*, New York, Basic Books.

Lander, Byron Gilbert (1967) The Emergence of Poverty as a Political Issue in 1964, Columbia, University of Missouri, PhD dissertation.

(1968) 'The role of major American institutions in poverty becoming a political issue in 1964' *International Review of History and Political Science*, 5 (4).

(1971) 'Group theory and individuals: the origin of poverty as a political issue in 1964', *Western Political Quarterly*, 24 (3).

Lane, Leonora (1965) 'A "Great Society's" children: historical antecedents of Project Head Start', *Journal of Human Relations*, 13 (4).

Lang, Arch D. and Smith, Robert R. (1955) 'The wider social context of education', *Review of Educational Research*, 25 (1).

Larner, Jeremy and Howe, Irving (eds.) (1966) *Poverty: views from the left*, New York, William Morrow.

Larson, Meredith A. and Dittmann, Freya E. (1975) *Compensatory Education and Early Adolescence: reviewing our national strategy*, Stanford University, Educational Policy Research Center, 1975.

Lasch, Christopher (1975) 'Inequality and education' in Donald M. Levine and Mary Jo Bane (eds), *The 'Inequality' Controversy*, New York, Basic Books.

Lazar, Irving (1970) 'Organizing Child Development Programs', *Appalachia*, 3 (4).

(1981) 'Early intervention is effective', *Educational Leadership*, 38 (4).

Lazar, Irving and Darlington, Richard (eds.) (1978) *Lasting Effects after Preschool: a report of the Consortium for Longitudinal Studies*, Washington, D.C., HEW, Office of Human Development Services.

Lazar, Irving *et al.* (1977) The Persistence of Preschool Effects: a long-term follow-up of fourteen infant and preschool experiments, Ithaca, NY, Cornell University, Consortium on Developmental Continuity, mimeo.

(1981) 'Policy implications of preschool intervention research' in Michael J. Begab, *et al.* *Psychosocial Influences in Retarded Performance*, vol. 2, *Strategies for Improving Competence*, Baltimore, University Park Press.

Lazarson, Marvin (1972) 'The historical antecedents of early childhood education' in Ira Gordon (ed.), *Early Childhood Education*, Chicago, NSSE.

Leacock, Eleanor Burke (ed.) (1971) *The Culture of Poverty: a critique*, New York, Simon and Schuster.

Leavitt, Florence E. (1967) 'The culturally disadvantaged', *Curriculum Bulletin* (School of Education, University of Oregon), 23 (282).

Lee, Ralph (1962) 'Stirrings in the big cities: Detroit', *NEA Journal*, 51 (5).

Lemann, Nicholas (1988–9), 'The unfinished war', *The Atlantic Monthly*, 2 parts, 262 (6) and 263 (1).

Levens, Dorothy (1966) 'A look at Project Head Start', *Childhood Education*, 42 (8).

Levin, Henry M. (1979) 'Education and earnings of blacks and the *Brown* decision' in M. Namorato (ed.), *Have We Overcome?*, Jackson, Miss., University Press of Mississippi.

(1979) 'A decade of policy developments in improving education and training for low-income populations' in Robert H. Haveman (ed.), *A Decade of Federal Antipoverty Programs*, New York, Academic Press.

(1986) *Education Reform for Disadvantaged Students: an emerging crisis*, National Education Association, West Haven, Conn.

Levin, Tom (1967a) 'The Child Development Group of Mississippi: a hot sector of the quiet front in the War on Poverty', *American Journal of Orthopsychiatry*, 37 (1).

(1967b) 'Preschool education and the communities of the poor', in Jerome Hellmuth (ed.), *Disadvantaged Child*, vol. 1, New York, Brunner/Mazel.

Levine, Donald M. and Bane, Mary Jo. (eds.) (1975) *The 'Inequality' Controversy: schooling and distributive justice*, New York, Basic Books.

Levine, Robert A. (1970) *The Poor Ye Need Not Have With You: lessons from the War on Poverty*, Cambridge, Mass., MIT Press.

Levitan, Sar A. (1969a) *The Great Society's Poor Law: a new approach to poverty*, Baltimore, Johns Hopkins University Press.

(1969b) *Programs in Aid of the Poor for the 1970s*, Baltimore, Johns Hopkins University Press.

(1973) *Programs in Aid of the Poor for the 1980s*, Baltimore, Johns Hopkins University Press.

Levitan, Sar A. and Johnston, Benjamin H. (1975) *The Job Corps: a social experiment that works*, Baltimore, Johns Hopkins University Press.

Levitan, Sar A. and Taggart, Robert (1976) *The Promise of Greatness*, Cambridge, Mass., Harvard University Press.

Levitan, Sar A., Mangum, Garth L. and Taggart III, Robert (1970) *Economic Opportunity in the Ghetto: the partnership of government and business*, Baltimore, Johns Hopkins University Press.

Lewis, Anne C. (1984) 'Washington Report', *Phi Delta Kappan*, 65 (6).

Lewis, Oscar (1968) 'The culture of poverty' in Daniel P. Moynihan (ed.), *On Understanding Poverty*, New York, Basic Books.

Liddle, Gordon P. (1963) 'Modifying the school experience of culturally handicapped children in the primary grades', *Illinois Journal of Education*, 54 (2).

Lindblom, Charles E. and Cohen, David K. (1979) *Usable Knowledge: social science and social problem solving*, New Haven, Yale University Press.

Littlewood, Tom (1966) 'David S. Seeley: an interview', *Integrated Education*, 3 (6).

Lohman, Joseph D. and Talagi, Paul T. (1967) Operation Fair Chance. Report on the first year operation, University of California, mimeo.

Longstreet, Wilma S. (1973) *Beyond Jencks: the myth of equal schooling*, Washington, D.C., Association for Supervision and Curriculum Development.

Loretan, Joseph O. and Umans, Shelley (1966) *Teaching the Disadvantaged: new curricular approaches*, New York, Teachers College Press.

LYNDON BAINES JOHNSON LIBRARY (AUSTIN, TEXAS)

Telegram, Editor, *The Baptist Standard*, Dallas, to the President, 1/24/64, WHCF, LE/FA2 Box 37.

Memorandum (unsigned) from White House aide to the President, 1964, WHCF LE/FA2 Box 37.

Letter to the Rev. Frank E. Dunn, 22 January 1964, from a White House Aide, EX ED 11/22/63–2/10/64.

Perry, Arthur C., letter to Dr John T. Dailey, Project Talent Office, University of Pittsburgh, 25 January 1964, EX ED 11/22/63–2/10/64.

Johnson, President Lyndon B., letter to Anthony J. Celebrezze, Secretary, HEW, 21 March 1964, EX ED 3/21/64–5/15/64.

Keppel, Francis, memorandum for Hon. Lee C. White, 12 June 1964, GEN ED 4/17/64–5/31/64.

President's Task Force on Education (John W. Gardner, chair), report 11/14/64, mimeo, Task Forces (outside, 1964) Box 1.

Johnson, President Lyndon B., press statement, 31 December 1964, W.H. Aides, Panzer, Box 492 (478), School Drop-Outs.

Memo [3/3/65] 'The American Jewish Community and the president's Elementary and Secondary Education Act of 1965', HEW Subject Files, Microfilm, Reel 47.

Johnson, President Lyndon B., Text of the Remarks by the President upon signing the Education Bill…11 April 1965, mimeo, EX LE/FA2, 10/14/64–4/11/65.

Cater, Doug memorandum to Bill Moyers, W.H. Aides, Cater, Douglass, Material on Education, Bill and Message Delivered, 19 January 1965.

Telegram from the AFT to the President, 1/5/65, WHCF, LE/FA2, Box 38.

Keppel, Francis, statement to General Subcommittee on Education of the Committee on Education and Labor, House of Representatives, 22 January 1965, mimeo, W.H. Aides, Duggan, Box 3.

Memorandum, O'Brien to the President, 3/8/65, WHCF, LE/FA2, Box 38.

Copy of statements in the Senate (Senator Mansfield…) WHCF, LE/FA2, Box 38.

Memorandum, Wilson to White, 3/11/65, WHCF, LE/FA2, Box 38.

A Response to the Chamber of Commerce's Commentary on Elementary and Secondary Education Legislation [1965], mimeo, W.H. Aides, Bill Moyers, file: Education, Box 1.

Riessman, Frank (1965) It's Time for a Moon-Shot in Education, New York, mimeo.

Moyers, Bill, Notebook on First 300 Days, White House Aides, files of Bill Moyers, Box 109.

President's Task Force on Early Childhood Development (J. McV. Hunt, chair), A Bill of Rights for Children, report, 14 January 1967, mimeo, Task Force Reports, Box 4.

President's Task Force on Education (William C. Friday, chair), report, 30 June 1967, mimeo, Task Force Reports, Box 4.

Peerboom, Pearl, Report on Summer 1967 Site Visits to Pre-Title I Compensatory Education Programs, mimeo, W.H. Aides, James Gaither, Box 187: file, 'Gaither: Task Force Child Devt 1967–68'.

Seeley, David, interview, Department of HEW, 7/25/68, transcript.

The Office of Economic Opportunity during the Administration of President Lyndon B. Johnson, November 1963–January 1969. Vol. 1 – Administrative History Part 1, mimeo [1969].

ORAL HISTORY INTERVIEWS:

Cater, Douglass (interviewer David G. McComb), 04/29/69 and 05/08/69
Celebrezze, Anthony (interviewer Page Mulhollan), 1/26/71.
Cohen, Wilbur (interviewer not known) 8/12/68.
Halperin, Samuel (interviewer David G. McComb) 2/24/69.
Halperin, Samuel (interviewer Steve Trachtenberg), Department of HEW interview, n.d.
Keppel, Francis (interviewer David G. McComb), General Services Administration, National Archives and Records Service, 4/21/69.
Keppel, Francis (interviewer John Singerhoff), Department of HEW interview, 7/18/68.
Muirhead, Peter P. (interviewer Herman R. Allen), Department of HEW interview, 7/23/68.
Perrin, C. Robert (interviewer not known), 1969.

FEDERAL RECORDS. DEPARTMENT OF HEALTH, EDUCATION, AND WELFARE, OFFICE OF EDUCATION, MICROFILM REEL 1, ADDRESSES BY FRANCIS KEPPEL COMMISSIONER OF EDUCATION:

'1964: Education's Time for Action', Regional meeting on New Educational Legislation, 16 January 1964.
'Slums, Schools and Social Welfare', Health and Welfare Council of the Baltimore Area, 9 March 1964.
'Research: education's neglected hope', Congress on Instruction of the National Educational Association, 30 April 1964.
'Civil Rights and Education Now', Convocation on Equal Justice under Law of the NAACP Legal and Educational Fund, 28 May 1964.
'Civil Rights: beyond the legislation', Session on De Facto Segregation of the Annual Convention of the NAACP, 26 June 1964.
Remarks at a dinner in honor of Governor Terry Sanford, 4 December 1964.
'Education: issues and trends in the federal role', Conference for Business Executives on Federal Government Operations, 18 February 1965.
'Poverty – the only war we seek', Union of American Hebrew Congregations Religious Action Centers, 3 March 1965.
'Education: turning point for the states', National Association of State Boards of Education, 2 April 1965.
'1965: education's moment', National Catholic Educational Association, 19 April 1965.

McAteer, J. Eugene (1963) 'A law for compensatory education', *Integrated Education*, 1 (1).
McCarren, Edgar P. (1965) 'What the informed public should know about ESA 1965', *Catholic Educational Review*, 63 (8).
McCarthy, Colman (1981) 'Reagan's turning away from the poor will be devastating', *Post-Gazette*, 30 October.
Maccoby, Eleanor E. and Zellner, Miriam (1970) *Experiments in Primary Education: aspects of Project Follow-Through*, New York, Harcourt Brace Jovanovich.

McClure, Phyllis (1982) 'Deregulation of Title I: a lesson to be learned from the past', *Education and Urban Society*, 14 (4).

McCreary, Eugene (1965) 'Teaching the culturally different', *Integrated Education*, 3 (1).

(1966) 'Some positive characteristics of disadvantaged learners and their implications for education' in Staten W. Webster (ed.), *The Disadvantaged Learner*, San Francisco, Chandler.

McDaniels, Garry L. (1975) 'Evaluation problems in Follow Through' in Alice M. Rivlin and P. Michael Timpane (eds.), *Planned Variation in Education*, Washington, D.C. Brookings Institution.

McDill, Edward L., McDill, Mary S. and Sprehe, J. Timothy (1969) *Strategies for Success in Compensatory Education: an appraisal of evaluation research*, Baltimore, Johns Hopkins University Press.

Macdonald, Dwight (1963) 'Our invisible poor', *New Yorker*, 19 January.

McGinness, Gael D. (1982) 'The language of the poverty child: implications from center-based intervention and evaluation programs' in Lynne Feagans and Dale Clark Farran (eds.), *The Language of Children Reared in Poverty*, New York, Academic Press.

McKay, Robert E. (1965) 'The President's program: "a new commitment to quality and equality in education"', *Phi Delta Kappan*, 46 (9).

McKey, Ruth Hubbell *et al.* (1985) *The Impact of Head Start on Children, Families and Communities. Executive summary*, Washington, D.C., CSR Inc.

Mackintosh, Helen K., Gore, Lillian and Lewis, Gertrude M. (1965) *Educating Disadvantaged Children Under Six*, Washington, D.C., HEW.

(1966) *Administration of Elementary School Programs for Disadvantaged Children*, Washington, D.C., HEW.

Mackler, Bernard and Giddings, Morsley, G. (1965) 'Cultural deprivation: a study in mythology', *Teachers College Record*, 66 (7).

McLaughlin, Milbrey Wallin (1975) *Evaluation and Reform: the Elementary and Secondary Education Act of 1965, Title I*, Cambridge, Mass., Ballinger.

(1976) 'Implementation of ESEA Title I: a problem of compliance' in Erwin Flaxman (ed.), *Educating the Disadvantaged*, New York. AMS Press.

(n.d.) Parent Involvement in Compensatory Education Programs, Cambridge, Mass., Harvard University Graduate School of Education, Center for Educational Policy Research, mimeo.

McLaughlin, Milbrey Wallin and Shields, Patrick M. (1987) 'Involving low-income parents in the schools: a role for policy?', *Phi Delta Kappan*, 69 92).

McLaughlin, Milbrey Wallin, Shields, Patrick M. and Rezabek, Dale J. (1985) *State and Local Response to Chapter 1 of the Education Consolidation and Improvement Act, 1981*, Stanford University, Institute for Research on Educational Finance and Governance.

Magat, Richard (1979) *The Ford Foundation at Work: philanthropic choices, methods and styles*, New York, Plenum.

Maier, Henry W. (1965) *Three Theories of Child Development: the contributions of Erik H. Erikson, Jean Piaget and Robert R. Sears and their applications*, New York, Harper and Row.

Maleska, Eugene (1962) 'Stirrings in the big cities: New York', *NEA Journal*, 51 (5).

Mann, Ada J., Harrell, Adele V. and Hurt, Maure Jr. (1978) 'A review of Head Start research since 1969' in Bernard Brown (ed.), *Found: long-term gains from early intervention*, Boulder, Colo., Westview Press.

Mann, Arthur (1968) 'A historical overview: the *lumpenproletariat*, education, and compensatory action' in Charles U. Daly (ed.), *The Quality of Inequality*, University of Chicago Press.

Marans, Allen A. and Lourie, Reginald (1967) 'Hypotheses regarding the effects of child-rearing patterns on the disadvantaged child' in Jerome Hellmuth (ed.), *Disadvantaged Child*, vol. 1, New York, Brunner/Mazel.

Marburger, Carl L. (1963) 'Working towards more effective education: a report on the Detroit Great Cities Project – after one year' in US, HEW, OE, *Programs for the Educationally Disadvantaged*.

March, Michael S. (1968) 'Public programs for the poor: coverage, gaps, and future directions' in US Congress, Subcommittee on Economic Progress of the Joint Economic Committee, *Federal Programs for the Development of Human Resources*, vol. 1, Washington, D.C., Government Printing Office.

Martin, Ruby and McClure, Phyllis (*see* Washington Research Project)

Mayer, Martin (1961) *The Schools*, New York, Harper.

Meade, Edward Jr. [1979] *Philanthropy and Public Schools: one foundation's evolving perspective*, New York, Ford Foundation.

Medford Public Schools (1969) Evaluation Report for 'Operation RISE' in the City of Medford, Medford, Mass., Medford Public Schools, mimeo.

Meier, Deborah (1966) 'Head Start or dead end?' in Jeremy Larner and Irving Howe (eds.), *Poverty: views from the left*, New York, William Morrow.

Meissner, Hannah H. (ed.) *Poverty in the Affluent Society*, New York, Harper and Row.

Mendelsohn, Robert (1970) 'Is Head Start a success or failure?' in Jerome Hellmuth, *Disadvantaged Child*, vol. 3, New York, Brunner/Mazel.

Meranto, Philip (1967) *The Politics of Federal Aid to Education in 1965: a study in political innovation*, Syracuse University Press.

Metcalf, Lawrence E. (1965) 'Poverty, government, and the schools', *Educational Leadership*, 22 (8).

Miller, George (ed.) (1989) *Giving Children a Chance: the case for more effective national policies*, Washington, D.C., Center for National Policy Press.

Miller, Harry L. (ed.) (1967) *Education for the Disadvantaged: current issues and research*, New York, Free Press.

Miller, James O. (1969) *An Education Imperative and its Fallout Implications*, Urbana, Illinois, National Laboratory on Early Childhood Education.

Miller, S.M. (1964) 'The politics of poverty', *Dissent*, 11 (2).

(1968) 'Poverty, race, and politics' in Chaim Isaac Waxman (ed.), *Poverty: power and politics*, New York, Grosset & Dunlap.

(1976) 'Types of equality: sorting, rewarding, performing' in Nelson F. Ashline *et al.* (eds.), *Education, Inequality, and National Policy*, Lexington, D.C. Heath.

Miller, S.M. and Rein, Martin (1964) 'Poverty and social change', *The American Child*, 46 (2).

(1965a) 'Escalating the War on Poverty', *The American Child*, 47 (2).

(1965b) 'The War on Poverty: perspectives and prospects' in Ben B. Seligman (ed.), *Poverty as a Public Issue*, New York, Free Press.

(1966) 'Poverty, inequality, and policy' in Howard S. Becker (ed.), *Social Problems*, New York, Wiley.

(1973) 'Will the War on Poverty change America?' in Marc and Phyllis Pilisuk (eds.), *Have We Lost the War on Poverty?*, New York, Transaction.

Miller, S.M. and Riessman, Frank (1968) *Social Class and Social Policy*, New York, Basic Books.

(1968) 'Standards for an Affluent Society' in Sar A. Levitan *et al.* (eds.), *Towards Freedom from Want*, Madison, Industrial Relations Research Association.

Miller, S.M. and Roby, Pamela (1966) 'The War on Poverty reconsidered' in Jeremy Larner and Irving Howe (eds), *Poverty: views from the left*, New York, William Morrow.

(1970) *The Future of Inequality*, New York, Basic Books.

Miller, Walter (1968) 'The elimination of the American lower class as national policy: a critique of the ideology of the poverty movement of the 1960s' in Daniel P. Moynihan (ed.), *On Understanding Poverty*, New York, Basic Books.

Milwaukee (*see* Ford Foundation)

MINNESOTA

St Paul Public Schools (1968) Elementary and Secondary Education Act. Public Law 89–10. Title I. Summary Report 1966–7, St Paul Public Schools, mimeo.

Educational Management Services (n.d.) *External Evaluation Report of the 1972–73 School Year Title I Program. St Paul Public Schools*, Minneapolis, Educational Management Services.

Minnesota State Department of Education (1982) Title I of the Elementary and Secondary Education Act of 1965 as Amended – the education of disadvantaged children, memorandum from Assistant Commissioner Waddick and Title I Manager Hanson, St Paul, 26 May.

MISSOURI

Charters, W.W. Jr. *et al.* (1965) The Banneker Schools of St Louis: a report on the feasibility of an extended investigation. Submitted to the St Louis Human Development Corporation, St Louis, Washington University, Graduate School of Education, mimeo.

St Louis Public Schools, Division of Evaluation and Research (n.d.) *Evaluation Report ESEA Title I 1968–1969*, St Louis Public Schools.

St Louis Public Schools, Division of Evaluation and Research (1970) *Evaluation Report ESEA Title I 1969–70*, St Louis Public Schools.

St Louis Public Schools, Division of Evaluation and Research (n.d.) *Follow Through 1978–79*, St Louis Public Schools.

Missouri Department of Elementary and Secondary Education (1981) *Title I, ESEA Manual of Operational Guidelines*, Jefferson City, Department of ESE.

St Louis Public Schools, Title I Office, Division of State and Federal

Programs 1981 [a set of guidelines for kindergarten, math, after-school and reading programs], St Louis Public Schools.

Morris, John D. (1964) 'Johnson presses Congress on aid', *New York Times Special Education Survey*, 16 January.

Morse, H.T. (1963) 'White House meeting on schools', *Integrated Education*, 1 (5).

Morse, Wayne (1961) 'The basic American philosophy and practice of federal aid for education', *American Teachers Magazine*, 45 (4).

Mosher, Edith K., Hastings, Anne H. and Wagoner, Jennings, L. Jr. (1979) *Pursuing Equal Educational Opportunity : school politics and the new activists*, New York, ERIC/Clearinghouse on Urban Education, Urban Diversity Series, 64.

Mosteller, Frederick and Moynihan, Daniel P. (eds.) (1972) *On Equality of Educational Opportunity*, New York, Random House.

Moynihan, Daniel P. (1961a) 'Liberalism and knowledge' in *Coping : on the practice of government*, New York, Random House (edn of 1975, contains reprint of 1970 address).

(1961b) 'The education of the urban poor' in *Coping : on the practice of government*, New York, Random House (edn of 1975, contains reprint of 1967 paper).

(1964) 'A modest proposal', *The American Child*, 46 (4).

(1965) 'The professionalization of reform', *The Public Interest*, 1.

(ed.) (1968) *On Understanding Poverty : perspectives from the social sciences*, New York, Basic Books.

(1969) *Maximum Feasible Misunderstanding : community action in the War on Poverty*, New York, Free Press (edn of 1970).

(1971) 'Toward a national urban policy' in Allan C. Ornstein *et al.* (eds.), *Educating the Disadvantaged*, vol. 2, New York, AMS Press.

(1972) 'Equalizing education': in whose benefit?', *The Public Interest*, 29

(1980) 'State vs. Academe: nationalizing the universities', *Harper's*, 261 (1567).

Mueller, B. Jeanne (*see* Follow Through)

Murphy, Jerome T. [1970] 'Title I: bureaucratic politics and poverty politics', *Inequality in Education*, 6.

(1971) 'Title I of ESEA, the politics of implementing federal education reform', *Harvard Educational Review*, 41 (1).

(1973) 'The education bureaucracies implement novel policy: the politics of Title I of ESEA, 1965–72' in Allan P. Sindler (ed.), *Policy and Politics in America : six case studies*, Boston, Little, Brown.

Myrdal, Gunnar (1966) 'National planning for healthy cities: two challenges to affluence' in Sam Bass Warner Jr (ed.) *Planning for a nation of cities*, Cambridge, Mass., MIT Press.

National Advisory Commission on Civil Disorders (1968), *Report*, New York, Bantam Books.

National Advisory Council on the Education of Disadvantaged Children (1972) *Educating the Disadvantaged Child : where we stand*, Washington, D.C., NACEDC.

National Association of Independent Schools (*see* Ford Foundation)

National Conference on Education of the Disadvantaged [1966] *Report of a National Conference held in Washington, D.C., July 18–20, 1966*, Washington, D.C., HEW.

National Council of Teachers of English, Task Force on Teaching English to the Disadvantaged (1965) *Language Programs for the Disadvantaged*, NCTE, Champaign, Ill.

National Education Association (1968) *Head Start Programs Operated by Public School Systems*, Washington, D.C., NEA.

National Institute of Education (1974) *Research Plan: Compensatory Education Study*, Washington, D.C., NIE.

(1976a) *Education, Social Science and the Judicial Process?: an international sympsoium*, Washington, D.C., HEW.

(1976b) *Evaluating Compensatory Education: an interim report on the NIE Compensatory Education Study*, Washington, D.C., HEW.

(1977a) *Administration of Compensatory Education*, Washington, D.C., HEW.

(1977b) *Compensatory Education Services*, Washington, D.C., HEW.

(1977c) *Demonstration Studies of Funds Allocation within Districts*, Washington, D.C., HEW.

(1977d) *The Effects of Services on Student Development*, Washington, D.C., HEW.

(1977e) *Title I Funds Allocation: the current formula*, Washington, D.C., HEW

(1977f) *Using Achievement Test Scores to Allocate Title I Funds*, Washington, D.C., HEW.

(1978a) *Compensatory Education Study: final report to Congress from the National Institute of Education*, Washington, D.C., HEW.

(1978b) *The Compensatory Education Study: executive summary*, Washington, D.C., HEW.

(1978c) *The Compensatory Education Study: major research projects. A supplemental report...*, Washington, D.C., HEW.

(1978d) *Perspectives on the Instructional Dimensions Study*, Washington, D.C., NIE.

(1978e) *State Compensatory Education Programs: a supplemental report...*, Washington, D.C., HEW.

National Urban League, Education Division [1971] *Parent Power and Title 1 ESEA*, New York, NUL.

NEA Research Bulletin (1969) 'Who are the poor?', 47 (2).

Neale, Noah S. (1966) 'Implementation of Title I, Public Law 89–10', *Illinois Journal of Education*, 57 (1).

Nelson, F. Howard (1983) 'Are the poor concentrated in poor school districts?', *Educational Evaluation and Policy Analysis*, 5 (1).

The New Republic (1964) *America Tomorrow: Creating the Great Society*, New York, Signet.

Newsweek (1965) 'The gadfly of the poverty war', 13 September.

(1965) 'Shriver and the War on Poverty', 13 September.

The New York Times (1964) *Special Education Survey*, 16 January.

New York State, Bureau of Guidance [1964/5] *Helping Educationally Disadvantaged Children: the second year of project ABLE*, Albany, N.Y., State Education Department, mimeo.

Office of Coordinator, Title I, Elementary and Secondary Education Act of 1965, Identification of the Educationally Disadvantaged, Albany, N.Y., State Education Department, mimeo.

Office of Title I, ESEA [1966] 100 Selected Projects, Albany, N.Y., Office of Title I, mimeo.

Office of the Coordinator, Title I, ESEA (n.d.) Federally Funded Programs Providing Educational Experiences for Disadvantaged Children and Youth in New York State: E.S.E.A.Title I, 1966–7, Albany, N.Y., State Education Department, mimeo.

Education Department (1968) *Closing the Gap : a report of the first two years of experience with ESEA, Title I in New York State*, Albany, N.Y., State Education Department.

Division of Education for the Disadvantaged, Federally Funded Programs Providing Educational Experiences for Disadvantaged Children and Youth in New York State: ESEA, Title I, 1969–70, Albany, N.Y., State Education Department, mimeo.

Office of ESC Educational Opportunity Programs [1976] Educational Opportunity Programs for Progress, Albany, N.Y., State Education Department, mimeo.

Nieman, Ronald H. and Gastright, Joseph F. (1981) 'The long-term effects of Title I preschool and all-day kindergarten', *Phi Delta Kappan*, 63 (3).

Nimnicht, Glen (1973) 'Overview of responsive model programs' in Bernard Spodek (ed.), *Early Childhood Education*, Englewood Cliffs, Prentice-Hall.

Nimnicht, Glen et al. (1973) *Beyond 'Compensatory Education' : a new approach to educating children*, San Francisco, Far West Laboratory for Educational Research and Development.

Nisbet, John (1953) 'Family environment and intelligence', reprinted in A.H. Halsey, Jean Floud and C. Arnold Anderson (eds.), *Education, Economy, and Society*, New York, Free Press of Glencoe, 1961.

Nixon, Richard M. (1969) 'The President's message to Congress, with recommendations on the Office of Economic Opportunity and its programs, February 19, 1969' in Robert H. Bremner (ed.) (1974), *Children and Youth in America : a documentary history*, vol. 3, *1933–1973, Parts Five through Seven*, Cambridge, Mass., Harvard University Press.

Norton, John K. (1962) 'NEA Urban Project: the Association and its affiliates take a long stride forward', *NEA Journal*, 51 (5).

Ogbu, John U. (1982) 'Societal forces as a context of ghetto children's school failure' in Lynne Feagans and Dale Clark Farran (eds.), *The Language of Children Reared in Poverty*, New York, Academic Press.

O'Hara, James M. (1963) 'Disadvantaged newcomers to the city', *NEA Journal*, 52 (4).

Ohio Department of Education (1974) *Profiles of Ohio : ESEA Title III Projects. Status and progress report, September 1, 1974*, Columbus, Ohio Department of Education.

O'Keefe, Ruth Ann (1979) 'What Head Start means to families' in Lilian G. Katz et al., *Current Topics in Early Childhood Education*, Norwood, Ablex.

Olsen, James (1965) 'Challenge of the poor to the schools', *Phi Delta Kappan*, 47 (2).

Olson, James L. and Larson, Richard G. (1965) 'An experimental curriculum for culturally deprived kindergarten children', *Educational Leadership*, 22 (8).

Omwake, Eveline (1966) 'Has Head Start made a difference?', *Childhood Education*, 42 (8).

(1968) 'Head Start: measurable and immeasurable' in Jerome Hellmuth (eds.), *Disadvantaged Child*, vol. 2, New York, Brunner/Mazel.

Orem, R.C. (ed.) (1967) *Montessori for the Disadvantaged: an application of Montessori education principles to the War on Poverty*, New York, Putnam's.

Organisation for Economic Co-operation and Development (1980) *Educational Policy and Planning: compensatory education programmes in the United States*, Paris, OECD (prepared by the US Department of Education).

(1981) *United States: federal policies for education for the disadvantaged*, Paris, OECD.

Ornstein, Allan C. (1965) 'Effective Schools for "disadvantaged children"', *Journal of Secondary Education*, 40 (3).

(ed.) (1970) *Educating the Disadvantaged. School Year 1968–1969*, New York, AMS Press.

(1971a) 'Recent historical perspectives for educating the disadvantaged', *Urban Education*, 5 (4).

(1971b) 'Urban teachers and schools: fashionable targets', *Educational Forum*, 35 (3).

(1971c) 'Who are the disadvantaged?', *Young Children*, 26 (5).

(1972) 'Reaching the disadvantaged' in William W. Brickman and Stanley Lehrer (eds.), *Education and the Many Faces of the Disadvantaged: cultural and historical perspectives*, New York, Wiley.

(1974) 'An overview of the disadvantaged 1900–1970' in Andrew Kopan and Herbert Walberg (eds.), *Rethinking Educational Equality*, Berkeley, Calif., McCutchan.

(1977) 'Compensatory strategies for American schools', *Illinois Schools Journal*, 57 (3).

(1982) 'The education of the disadvantaged: a 20-year review', *Educational Research*, 24 (3).

(1983) 'Educating disadvantaged learners', *Educational Forum*, 47 (2).

Ornstein, Allan C. *et al.* (eds.) (1971) *Educating the Disadvantaged. School Year 1969/1970*, New York, AMS Press.

Osborn, Keith (1965) 'Project Head Start – an assessment', *Educational Leadership*, 23 (2).

Osborn, D. Keith (1975) *Early Childhood Education in Historical Perspective*, Athens, Georgia, Education Associates.

Palmer, Francis H. (1978) 'The effects of early childhood education' in Bernard Brown (ed.), *Found: long-term gains from early intervention*, Boulder, Colo, Westview Press.

Palmer, Francis H. and Andersen, Lucille Woolis (1981) 'Early intervention treatments that have been tried, documented, and assessed' in Michael J. Begab *et al.* (eds.), *Psychosocial Influences in Retarded Performance*, Baltimore, University Park Press.

Park, Jeanne S. (1967) '"Follow Through" to "Head Start"', *The American School Board Journal*, August.

(ed.) (1978) *Winners, All! 50 outstanding education projects that help disadvantaged children*, Washington, D.C., OE (revised edn of 1980).

Parmenter, Tom (n.d.) 'Power to the people through Title I? Maybe', *Inequality in Education*, 6.

Passow, Harry A. (ed.) (1963) *Education in Depressed Areas*, New York, Teachers College Press.

(1965) 'Diagnosis and prescription' (review of Bloom, Davis and Hess, *Compensatory Education for Cultural Deprivation*), *Saturday Review*, 15 May.

(1967a) 'Education of the culturally deprived child' in Jerome Hellmuth (ed.), *Disadvantaged Child*, vol. 1, New York, Brunner/Mazel.

(1967b) 'Early childhood and compensatory education' in Edgar L. Morphet and Charles O. Ryan (eds.), *Implications for Education of Prospective Changes in Society*, New York, Citation Press.

(ed.) (1968) *Developing Programs for the Educationally Disadvantaged*, New York, Teachers College Press.

(ed.) (1970) *Deprivation and Disadvantage: nature and manifestations*, Hamburg, UNESCO Institute for Education.

(ed.) (1971) *Urban Education in the 1970's: Reflections and a Look Ahead*, New York, Teachers College Press.

(ed.) (1972) *Opening Opportunities for Disadvantaged Learners*, New York, Teachers College Press.

(1982) 'Urban education for the 1980s: trends and issues', *Phi Delta Kappan*, 63 (8).

Passow, Harry A. and Elliott, David L. (1967) 'The disadvantaged in depressed areas' in Paul A. Witty (ed.), *The Educationally Retarded and Disadvantaged*, Chicago, NSSE.

Passow, Harry A., Goldberg, Miriam and Tannenbaum, Abraham (eds.) (1967) *Education of the Disadvantaged: a book of readings*, New York, Holt Rinehart and Winston.

Patterson, James T. (1981) *America's Struggle against Poverty 1900–1980*, Cambridge, Mass., Harvard University Press.

Payne, James S. *et al.* (1973) *Head Start: a tragicomedy with epilogue*, New York, Behavioral Publications.

Pearl, Arthur (1970) 'The poverty of psychology – an indictment' in Vernon L. Allen (ed.), *Psychological Factors in Poverty*, Chicago, Markham.

Pells, Richard H. (1985) *The Liberal Mind in a Conservative Age: American intellectuals in the 1940s and 1950s*, New York, Harper & Row.

Pemberton, S. Macpherson (1981) *The Federal Government and Equality of Educational Opportunity*, Washington, D.C., University Press of America.

Perrone, Vito (1976) 'Parents and schools' in Clara A. Pederson (ed.), *Parents and Schools*, Center for Teaching and Learning, Grand Forks, University of North Dakota.

Perry, Gail (1966) 'We had a head start on Head Start', *Young Children*, 21 (5).

Persell, Caroline Hodges (1977) *Education and Inequality: the roots and results of stratification in America's schools*, New York, Free Press.

Phi Delta Kappan (1965) 'Schools and the Economic Opportunity Act of 1964. Administrators: seize the initiative now!', 47 (2).

(1965) 'Is compensatory education only palliative?', 64 (2).
(1982) 'New York study finds preschool effects durable', 64 (2).

PHILADELPHIA

School District of Philadelphia (n.d.) *Action Program* (flyer).
[1978/9] *Motivation Program* (flyer).
(1979) *Principal's Guide for the Motivation Program*, reprint.
(n.d.) *Motivation Program*.
(*n.d.*) *Motivation Program. Organization Manual and Guide*.
(*see also* Ford Foundation)
Pilisuk, Marc and Pilisuk, Phyllis (eds.) (1973) *How We Lost the War on Poverty*, New Brunswick, N.J., Transaction Books.
Pines, Maya (1966) *Revolution in Learning: the years from birth to five*, New York, Harper and Row (London, Allen Lane edn of 1969).
Pinkney, Alphonso and Woock, Roger R. (1965) *Poverty and Politics in Harlem: report on Project Uplift 1965*, New Haven, Conn., College and University Press.
Pious, Richard M. (1971) 'The phony War on Poverty in the Great Society', *Current History*, 61 (363).
Pitcher, Evelyn G. (1968) 'An evaluation of the Montessori method in schools for young children' in Joe L. Frost (ed.), *Early Childhood Education Rediscovered*, New York, Holt, Rinehart and Winston.

PITTSBURGH

Learning Research and Development Center [1976] The Individualized Early Learning Program, University of Pittsburgh, LRDC, mimeo.
Wang, Margaret C., Leinhardt, Gaea and Boston, M. Elizabeth (1980) *Individualized Early Learning Program*, University of Pittsburgh, LRDC.
Leinhardt, Gaea, Pallay, Allan and Bickel, William (1981), Unlabeled but still entitled: toward more effective remediation, University of Pittsburgh, LRDC, mimeo.
(*See also* Ford Foundation)
Piven, Frances (1967) 'The demonstration project; a federal strategy for local change' in George A. Brager and Francis P. Purcell (eds.), *Community Action against Poverty*, New Haven, College and University Press.
Piven, Frances and Cloward, Richard A. (1971) *Regulating the Poor: the functions of public welfare*, New York, Random House.
Platt, Anthony M. (1969) *The Child Savers: the invention of delinquency*, University of Chicago Press.
Plotnick, Robert D. and Skidmore, Felicity (1975) *Progress against Poverty: a review of the 1964–1974 decade*, New York, Academic Press.
Plunkett, Virginia R.L. (1985) 'From Title I to Chapter 1: the evolution of compensatory education', *Phi Delta Kappan*, 66 (8).
Powell, Arthur G. (1980) *The Uncertain Profession: Harvard and the search for educational authority*, Cambridge, Mass., Harvard University Press.
Powell, Douglas R. (1982) 'From child to parent: changing conceptions of early childhood intervention', *Annals of the American Academy of Political and Social Science*, 461.

Powledge, Fred. (1967) *To Change a Child: a report of the Institute for Developmental Studies*, Chicago, Quadrangle Books.

Practical Applications of Research (1981) 'Parent involvement in education: a powerful partnership', 4 (2).

President's Commission on Higher Education (1947) *Higher Education for American Democracy*, vol. 1: *Establishing the Goals*; vol. 2: *Equalizing and Expanding Individual Opportunity*, Washington, D.C., Government Printing Office.

Project Beacon (1965) summary in Proceedings of the Fourth Annual Invitational Conference on Urban Education (Environmental Deprivation and Enrichment), New York, Yeshiva University, mimeo.

Project SEED (Special Elementary Education for the Disadvantaged) (n.d.), summary account, mimeo.

Raab, Earl (1968) 'What war and which poverty?' in Chaim Isaac Waxman (ed.), *Poverty: power and politics*, New York, Grosset and Dunlap.

Ralph, John (1989) 'Inproving education for the disadvantaged: do we know whom to help?', *Phi Delta Kappan*, 70 (5).

Ramey, Craig T. and Haskins, Ron (1981) 'The causes and treatment of school failure: insights from the Carolina Abecedarian Project', in Michael J. Begab *et al.* (eds.), *Psychosocial Influences in Retarded Performance*, Baltimore, University Park Press.

Ratchik, Irving (1972) 'Trends and developments in state programs for the disadvantaged' in Harry A. Passow (ed.), *Opening Opportunities for Disadvantaged Learners*, New York, Teachers College Press.

Ravitz, Mel (1963) 'The role of the school in the urban setting' in Harry A. Passow (ed.), *Education in Depressed Areas*, New York, Teachers College Press.

Rees, Helen E. (1968) *Deprivation and Compensatory Education*, Boston, Houghton Mifflin.

Rein, Martin (1966) 'Poverty, policy, and purpose: the dilemmas of choice' in Leonard H. Goodman (ed.), *Economic Progress and Social Welfare*, New York, Columbia University Press.

Report on Education of the Disadvantaged (1971) 'Bereiter punctures preschool illusions', 4 (4).

Rescorla, Leslie A. and Zigler, Edward (1981) 'The Yale Child Welfare Research Program: implications for social policy', *Educational Evaluation and Policy Analysis*, 3 (6).

The Research Council of the Great Cities Program for School Improvement (1964) *Promising Practices from the Projects for the Culturally Deprived*, Chicago, The Research Council.

Rhine, W.H. (ed.) (1981) *Making Schools More Effective. New Directions from Follow Through*, New York, Academic Press.

Ribich, Thomas L. (1968) *Education and Poverty*, Washington, D.C., Brookings Institution.

Ricciuti, Henry N. (1981) 'Early intervention studies: problems of linking research and policy objectives' in Michael J. Begab (ed.), *Psychosocial Influences in Retarded Performance*, Baltimore, University Park Press.

Riessman, Frank (1962) *The Culturally Deprived Child*, New York, Harper and Row.

(1963a) 'The culturally deprived child: a new view' in US, HEW, OE, *Programs for the Educationally Disadvantaged.*

(1963b) 'Higher Horizons: a critique', *Integrated Education*, 1 (1).

(1965a) 'Anti-poverty programs and the role of the poor' in Margaret Gordon (ed.), *Poverty in America*, Berkeley, Calif., Chandler.

(1965b) 'A comparison of two Social Action approaches: Saul Alinsky and the new Student Left', September, mimeo.

(1966) 'The new anti-poverty ideology', *Teachers College Record*, 68 (2).

(1973) 'Self-help among the poor: new styles of social action' in Marc and Phyllis Pilisuk (eds.), *How We Lost the War on Poverty*, New Brunswick, Transaction.

(1978) 'The service society and the crisis in education' in Edith K. Mosher and Jennings L. Wagoner Jr (eds.), *The Changing Politics of Education: prospects for the 1980's*, Berkeley, Calif., McCutchan.

Riessman, Frank and Rein, Martin (1965) 'The third force: an anti-poverty ideology', *The American Child*, 47 (4).

(*see also* Lyndon Baines Johnson Library)

Rietz, Don and Rosetta (1967) 'Montessori classes for culturally deprived children' in R.C. Orem (ed.), *Montessori for the Disadvantaged*, New York, Putnam's.

Rioux, J. William (1967) 'The disadvantaged child in school' in Jerome Hellmuth (ed.), *Disadvantaged Child*, vol. 1, New York, Brunner/Mazel.

Rivlin, Alice M. and Timpane, P. Michael (eds.) (1975) *Planned Variation in Education: should we give up or try harder?*, Washington, D.C., Brookings Institution.

Roaden, Arliss L. (ed.) (1969) *Problems of School Men in Depressed Urban Centers*, Columbus, Ohio State University.

Robison, Helen F. (1972) 'Early childhood education for the disadvantaged: what research says' in Harry A. Passow (ed.), *Opening Opportunities for Disadvantaged Learners*, New York, Teachers College Press.

Rogin, Lawrence (1965) 'Education: a way out of poverty', *American Federationist* (AFL–CIO), 72.

Rose, Stephen M. (1972) *The Betrayal of the Poor: the transformation of community action*, Cambridge, Mass., Schenkman.

Rosenberg, Sidney and Adkins, Winthrop, R. (1967) A Design for Action Research at Project TRY, final report, New York, Training Resources for Youth, mimeo.

Rosenthal, Robert and Jacobson, Lenore F. (1968) 'Teacher expectations for the disadvantaged', *Scientific American*, 218 (4).

Rubin, Lillian B. (1969) 'Maximum feasible participation: the origins implications, and present status' in Louis A. Ferman (ed.), *Evaluating the War on Poverty*, AAPSS.

Rutherford, William L. and Hoffman, James V. (1981) 'Toward implementation of the ESEA Title I evaluation and reporting system: a concerns analysis', *Educational Evaluation and Policy Analysis*, 3 (4).

Ryan, Sally (ed.) (1974) *A Report on Longitudinal Evaluations of Preschool Programs*, vol. 1: *Longitudinal evaluations*, Washington, D.C., HEW.

Ryan, William (1971) *Blaming the Victim*, New York, Random House.

Safran, Daniel (1979) 'Preparing teachers for parent involvement' in Carl A. Grant (ed.), *Community Participation in Education*, Boston, Allyn and Bacon.

St Louis (*see* Missouri and Ford Foundation)

St Paul (*see* Minnesota)

Saltzman, Henry (1963) 'The community school in the urban setting' in A. Harry Passow (ed.), *Education in Depressed Areas*, New York, Teachers College Press.

Sanford, Terry (1966) *But What about the People?*, New York, Harper and Row.

Schlossman, Steven (1978) 'The parent education game: the politics of child psychology in the 1970s', *Teachers College Record*, 79 (4).

Schorr, Alvin L. (1964) 'The nonculture of poverty', *American Journal of Orthopsychiatry*, 34 (5).

Schottland, Charles I. (1963) review of Riessman, *The Culturally Deprived Child*, *Harvard Educational Review*, 33 (3).

Schrag, Peter (1965) 'The schools of Appalachia', *Saturday Review*, 48.

Schreiber, Daniel (1961) The Higher Horizons Program: first annual progress report 1959–1960, New York, Board of Education of the City of New York, mimeo.

Schweinhart, Lawrence J. (1981) 'Comment on "Intelligence research and social policy"', *Phi Delta Kappan*, 63 (3).

Schweinhart, Lawrence J. and Weikart, David P. (1981) 'Perry preschool effects nine years later: what do they mean?, in Michael J. Begab *et al.* (eds.), *Psychosocial Influences in Retarded Performance*, Baltimore, University Park Press.

(1985) 'Evidence that good early childhood programs work', *Phi Delta Kappan*, 66 (8).

Schweinhart, Lawrence J. *et al.* (1985) 'The promise of early childhood education', *Phi Delta Kappan*, 66 (8).

Scott, C. Winfield and Hill, Clyde M. (eds.) (1954) *Public Education under Criticism*, New York, Prentice-Hall.

Sears, Robert R., Maccoby, Eleanor E. and Levin, Harry (1957) *Patterns of Child Rearing*, Evanston, Ill., Row, Peterson.

Seay, Maurice F. (1953) 'The community school: new meaning for an old term' in Henry B. Nelson (ed.), *The Community School*, Chicago, NSSE.

Seidel, H.E., Barkley, Mary Jo and Stith, Doris (1967) 'Evaluation of a program for Project Head Start', *Journal of Genetic Psychology*, 110 (second half).

Seitz, Victoria, Apfel, Nancy H. and Rosenbaum, Laurie K. (1981) '"Projects Head Start and Follow Through": a longitudinal evaluation of adolescents' in Michael J. Begab (ed.), *Psychosocial Influences in Retarded Performance*, Baltimore, University Park Press.

Seligman, Ben. B. (ed.) (1965) *Poverty as a Public Issue*, New York, Free Press.

(ed.) (1968) *Aspects of Poverty*, New York, Thomas Y. Cromwell.

(1968) *Permanent Poverty: an American syndrome*, Chicago, Quadrangle Books.

Sexton, Patricia Cayo (1961) *Education and Income: inequalities of opportunity in our public schools*, New York, Viking Press (edn of 1964).

(1965) 'City schools' in Louis A. Ferman *et al.* (eds.), Poverty in America, Ann Arbor, University of Michigan Press.

(1973) 'The *Inequality* affair: a critique of Jencks', *Social Policy*, 4 (2).

Shaffer, Helen B. (1968) 'Education of slum children' in *Editorial Research Reports on Education in America*, Washington, D.C., Congressional Quarterly.

Shanker, Albert (1990) 'The end of the traditional model of schooling – and a proposal for using incentives to restructure our public schools', *Phi Delta Kappan*, 71 (5).

Shapiro, Bernard J. (1969) An Evaluation of the 1969 Summer Elementary Remediation and Enrichment Laboratories (SEREL), Boston Public Schools, Department of Title I Programs, Office of Research and Evaluation, mimeo.

Shapiro, Michael Steven (1983) *Child's Garden : the kindergarten movement from Froebel to Dewey*, University Park, Pennsylvania State University Press.

Shaplin, Judson T. (1966) 'Urban education in long-term crisis' in Sam Bass Warner Jr (ed.) *Planning for a Nation of Cities*, Cambridge, Mass., MIT Press.

Shaw, Frederick (1963) 'Educating culturally deprived youth in urban centers', *Phi Delta Kappan*, 45 (2).

Shelton, Willard (1961) 'Kennedy drives for federal aid for education', *The American Teacher Magazine*, 45 (4).

Shepard, Samuel Jr (1963) 'A program to raise the standard of school achievement' in US, HEW, OE, *Programs for the Educationally Disadvantaged*.

   (1964) Contribution to Francis Keppel *et al.*, *How Should We Educate the Deprived Child?*

   (1969) 'The disadvantaged child' in Alvin Toffler (ed.), *The Schoolhouse in the City*, Voice of America Forum Lectures.

   (1969) 'The responsible educational leader' in Arliss L. Roaden (ed.), *Problems of School Men in Depressed Urban Centers*, Columbus, Ohio State University.

Shipman, Virginia (1973) 'Disadvantaged children and their first school experiences, ETS–Head Start Longitudinal Study' in Julian C. Stanley (ed.), *Compensatory Education for Children Ages Two to Eight*, Baltimore, Johns Hopkins University Press.

Shostak, Arthur B. and Gomberg, William (eds.) (1965) *New Perspectives on Poverty*, Englewood Cliffs, N.J., Prentice-Hall.

Shriver, Sargent (1968) 'The long view' in Jerome Hellmuth (ed.), *Disadvantaged Child*, vol. 2, New York, Brunner/Mazel.

Siebert, Edna M. (1962) 'Stirrings in the big cities: Chicago', *NEA Journal*, 51 (1).

Silberman, Charles E. (1964) *Crisis in Black and White*, New York, Random House.

   (1970) *Crisis in the Classroom : the remaking of American education*, New York, Random House.

Siller, Jerome (1957) 'Socioeconomic status and conceptual thinking', *Journal of Abnormal and Social Psychology*, 55 (3).

Silverstein, Robert (1979) *A Policy Maker's Guide to Title 1 of the Elementary and Secondary Education Act and its Relationship to State and Local Special Programs*, Denver, Colo., Education Commission of the States.

Sizer, Theodore R. (1970) 'Low-income families and the schools for their children', *Public Administration Review*, 30 (4).

Skerry, Peter (1983) 'The charmed life of Head Start', *The Public Interest*, 73.

Slaughter, Diana T. (1982) 'What is the Future of Head Start?', *Young Children*, 37 (3).

  (1983) *Early Intervention and its Effects on Maternal and Child Development*, University of Chicago Press.

Slavin, Robert E. (1987) 'Making Chapter 1 make a difference', *Phi Delta Kappan*, 69 (2).

Smiley, Marjorie B. (1967) 'Objectives of educational programmes for the educationally retarded and disadvantaged' in Paul A. Witty (ed.), *The Educationally Retarded and Disadvantaged*, Chicago, NSSE.

Smith, Jr, Council L. (1977) A Study of Community Participation in the St Louis Model City Community School Project: a perspective from a community of poverty, Washington University, St Louis, PhD dissertation.

Smith, Marshall S. (1972) '*Equality of Educational Opportunity: the basic findings reconsidered*' in Frederick Mosteller and Daniel P. Moynihan (eds.), *On Equality of Opportunity*, New York, Random House.

  (1975) 'Evaluating findings in Head Start planned variation' in Alice M. Rivlin and P. Michael Timpane (eds.), *Planned Variation in Education*, Washington, D.C., Brookings Institution.

  (1976) 'Equal opportunity – some promise and a lack of vision' in Nelson F. Ashline *et al.* (eds.), *Education, Inequality, and National Policy*, Lexington, D.C. Heath.

  (1986) *Selecting Students and Services for Chapter I*, Stanford University, Center for Educational Research.

Smith, Marshall S. and Bissell, Joan S. (1970) 'Report analysis: the impact of Head Start', *Harvard Educational Review*, 40 (1).

Smith, Mortimer (ed.) [1966] *A Decade of Comment on Education, 1956–1966. Selections from the* Bulletin *of the Council for Basic Education*, Washington, D.C., CBE.

Smith, T. Lynn (1974) *Studies of the Great Rural Tap Roots of Urban Poverty in the United States*, New York, Carlton.

Sorensen, Philip and Thomas, Thomas C. (*see* California)

Sorensen, Theodore C. (1965) *Kennedy*, New York, Harper and Row.

  (1969) *The Kennedy Legacy*, New York, Macmillan.

Spaulding, Robert L. [1971] *Durham Education Improvement Program, Final Report*. Vol. 1: *Educational Intervention in Early Childhood*; vol. 2: *Appendices*, North Carolina, Duke University.

Spock, Benjamin and Hathaway, Mildred (1968) 'Montessori and traditional American nursery schools – how are they different, how are they alike?' in Joe L. Frost (ed.), *Early Childhood Education Rediscovered*, New York, Holt, Rinehart and Winston.

Spodek, Bernard (ed.) (1973) *Early Childhood Education*, Englewood Cliffs, N.J., Prentice-Hall.

(1979) 'Early childhood education' in Herbert J. Walberg (ed.) *American Education, Diversity and Research*, Washington, D.C., Voice of America.

Sprigle, Herbert A. (1971) 'Can poverty children live on "Sesame Street?"', *Young Children*, 26 (4).

(1974) 'Learning to learn program' in Sally Ryan (ed.), *A Report on Longitudinal Evaluations of Preschool Programs*, Washington, D.C., HEW.

Spring, Joel (1976) *The Sorting Machine : national educational policy since 1945*, New York, David McKay.

Stanley, Julian C. (ed.) (1972) *Preschool Programs for the Disadvantaged : five experimental approaches to early childhood education*, Baltimore, Johns Hopkins University Press.

(1973) *Compensatory Education for Children Ages Two to Eight : recent studies of educational intervention*, Baltimore, Johns Hopkins University Press.

Stearns, Marian S. (1971) Report on Preschool Programs: the effects of preschool programs on disadvantaged children and their families, Washington, D.C., HEW, mimeo.

Stephen, Mae (1973) *Policy Issues in Early Childhood Education*, Menlo Park, Calif., Stanford Research Institute.

Steiner, Gilbert Y. (1974) 'Reform follows reality: the growth of welfare' in Eli Ginzberg and Robert M. Solow (eds.), *The Great Society*, New York, Basic Books.

Steinfels, Margaret O'Brien (1973) *Who's Minding the Children? The history and politics of day care in America*, New York, Simon and Schuster.

Stendler-Lavatelli, Celia B. (1967) 'Environmental intervention in infancy and early childhood' in Martin Deutsch, *et al.* (eds.), *Social Class, Race, and Psychological Development*, New York, Holt, Rinehart and Winston.

Stevens, George L. (1967) 'Implications of Montessori for the War on Poverty' in R.C. Orem (ed.), *Montessori for the Disadvantaged*, New York, Putnam's.

Stickney, Benjamin D. and Marcus, Laurence, R. (1984) *The Great Education Debate : Washington and the Schools*, Springfield, Ill., Charles C. Thomas.

(1985) 'Education and the disadvantaged 20 years later', *Phi Delta Kappan*, 66 (8).

Stickney, Benjamin D. and Plunkett, Virginia R.L. (1983) 'Closing the gap: a historical perspective on the effectiveness of compensatory education', *Phi Delta Kappan*, 65 (4).

Stine, Ray M. (1964) Pre-school Environmental Enrichment Demonstration, Harrisburg, PA, Bureau of General and Academic Education, Department of Public Instruction, mimeo.

Stodolsky, Susan S. (1973) 'Defining treatment and outcomes in early childhood education', *Education at Chicago*, Spring.

Stone, James C. (1969) *Teachers for the Disadvantaged*, San Francisco, Jossey-Bass.

Stone, James C. and Hempstead, R. Ross (1968) *California Education Today*, New York, Thomas Y. Crowell (edition of 1970).

Strother, Deborah Burnett (1987) 'Preschool children in the public schools: good investment? Or bad?', *Phi Delta Kappan*, 69 (4).

Sufrin, Sidney S. (1962) *Issues in Federal Aid to Education*, Syracuse, N.Y., Syracuse University Press.

Summerfield, Harry L. (1974) *Power and Process: the formulation and limits of federal educational policy*, Berkeley, Calif., McCutchan.

The Sunday Oregonian (1980) 'Study supports preschool education', 14 December.

Sundquist, James L. (1968) *Politics and Policy, the Eisenhower, Kennedy and Johnson Years*, Washington, D.C., Brookings Institution.

(ed.) (1969) *On Fighting Poverty: perspectives from experience*, New York, Basic Books.

(1969) 'Origins of the War on Poverty' in Sundquist, *On Fighting Poverty*, New York, Basic Books.

Sussman, Leila (1971) *Innovation in Education – United States*, Paris, Organisation for Economic Co-operation and Development.

System Development Corporation (1977–81) Study of the Sustaining Effects of Compensatory Education on Basic Skills (overview of technical reports 1–11, a series of pamphlets by various authors), Santa Monica, SDS.

Taba, Hilda (1964) 'Cultural deprivation as a factor in school learning', *Merrill-Palmer Quarterly*, 10 (2).

Takanishi, Ruby (1977) 'The legacy of Headstart: our continuing struggle for children's rights', *International Journal of Early Childhood*, 9 (2).

Tannenbaum, Abraham J. (1967) 'Social and psychological considerations in the study of the socially disadvantaged' in Paul A. Witty, (ed.), *The Educationally Retarded and Disadvantaged*, Chicago, NSSE.

(1968) 'Mobilization for Youth in New York City' in A. Harry Passow (ed.) *Developing Programs for the Educationally Disadvantaged*, New York, Teachers College Press.

Tavris, Carol (1976) 'Compensatory education: the glass is half full', *Psychology Today*, 10 (4).

Tax Foundation (1968) *Antipoverty Programs under the Economic Opportunity Act*, New York, Tax Foundation.

Taylor, H. Ralph (1969) 'The educational dimensions of the Model Cities Program' in Roald F. Campbell *et al.* (eds.), *Education and Urban Renaissance*, New York, Wiley.

Tead, Ordway (1947) *Equalizing Educational Opportunities beyond the Secondary School*, Cambridge, Mass., Harvard University Press.

Templin, Mildred C. (1957) *Certain Language Skills in Children: their development and interrelationships*, Minneapolis, University of Minnesota Press (Greenwood Press edn of 1975).

Terbel, John (1965) 'Teacher of the unteachable', *Saturday Review*, 15 May.

Terte, Robert H. (1964) 'Pre-school plan for slums tried', *New York Times Special Education Survey*, 16 January.

Thomas, Norman C. (1975) *Education in National Politics*, New York, David McKay.

Timpane, Michael (1978) *The Federal Interest in Financing Schooling*, Cambridge, Mass., Ballinger.

Title I Exchange. The Newsletter of Compensatory Education (Mass.), 5 (2).

Title I Policy Manual – Evaluation, draft version, 5 September 1980, Mountain View, California, RMC Research Corporation, mimeo.

Titmuss, Richard (1965) 'Poverty vs. inequality: diagnosis', *The Nation*, 8 February.

Toffler, Alvin (ed.) (1969) *The Schoolhouse in the City*, Voice of America Forum Lectures.

Tolo, Kenneth W. (ed.) (1973) *Educating a Nation: the changing American commitment*, University of Texas at Austin.

Tough, Joan (1982) 'Language, poverty, and disadvantage in school' in Lynne Feagans and Dale Clark Farran (eds.), *The Language of Children Reared in Poverty: implications for evaluation and intervention*, New York, Academic Press.

Trombley, William (1981) 'Preschool gets an "A"', *San Francisco Chronicle*, 11 January.

Trow, Martin (1966) 'Two problems in American public education' in Howard S. Becker (ed.), *Social Problems*, New York, Wiley.

TUCSON EARLY EDUCATION MODEL (TEEM)

Statement of agreement (draft) (n.d.), mimeo.

TEEM, Tucson, Arizona Center for Educational Research and Development, revised, November 1975.

Arizona Center for Educational Research and Development (1976), *Implementing Teem's Goals: roles and responsibilities*, Tucson, CERD.

Fullerup, Joseph M., Paul, Alice S. and Butts, Louise P. (eds.) (1975) *Concepts and Strategies for Implementing TEEM, Instructor's Manuals*, Tucson, CERD.

(1976) *Concepts and Strategies for Implementing TEEM, Participant's Manual*, Tucson, CERD, and vol. 2 (1978).

Early Childhood Materials, Tucson, CERD, edition of 1980.

Tulkin, Steven R. (1972) 'An analysis of the concept of cultural deprivation', *Developmental Psychology*, 6 (2).

Tyack, David, Kirst, Michael and Hansot, Elisabeth (1979) *Educational Reform: retrospect and prospect*, Stanford University, Institute for Research on Educational Finance and Governance.

Tyack, David, Lowe, Robert and Hansot, Elisabeth (1984) *Public Schools in Hard Times: the Great Depression and recent years*, Cambridge, Mass., Harvard University Press.

Tyler, Ralph W. (1974) 'The federal role in education' in Eli Ginzberg and Robert M. Solow (eds.) *The Great Society*, New York, Basic Books.

UNITED STATES (ALL PUBLISHED BY GOVERNMENT PRINTING OFFICE UNLESS OTHERWISE STATED; ALL PUBLISHED WASHINGTON, D.C.)

Commission on Civil Rights (1967) *Racial Isolation in the Public Schools*, vol. 1: *Report*; vol. 2: *Appendices*.

Congress, House of Representatives

Subcommittee of the Committee on Appropriations, May 8, 1961 (contains McMurrin, 'Comments on the Present Condition of American Education').

National Education Improvement Act. Hearings before the Committee on Education and Labour...February...1963.

Economic Opportunity Act of 1964. Hearings before the Committee on the War on Poverty. Program of the Committee on Education and Labor...Part 1...March...April...1964; Part 2...April...1964: Part 3...April...1964.

Economic Opportunity Act of 1964. Report No. 1458 (from the Committee on Education and Labor), *June 3, 1964.*

Committee on Education and Labor. Poverty in the United States, 1964.

Aid to Elementary and Secondary Education: hearings before the General Subcommittee on Education of the Committee on Education and Labor. Hearings held...January 22, 23, 25, 26, and 27, 1965. Part I. Hearings held...January 28, 29, 30; February 1, 2, 1965, Part 2.

Elementary and Secondary Education Act of 1965. Report No. 143 from the Committee on Education and Labor, March 8, 1965.

Committee on Education and Labor. Education Goals for 1965, 1965.

Hearings before the Select Committee on Education of the Committee on Education and Labor...November...December...1969; February...March... 1970.

Report on the Activities of the Committee on Education and Labor during the 95th Congress, 1978.

Opportunities for Success: cost-effective programs for children. A staff report of the Select Committee on Children, Youth, and Families, 1985.

Senate

Elementary and Secondary Education Act of 1965. Report No. 146, from the Committee on Labor and Public Welfare, April 6, 1965.

Toward Economic Security for the Poor: a report together with minority views prepared by the Subcommittee on Employment, Manpower, and Poverty of the Subcommittee on Labor and Public Welfare, 1968.

Head Start Child Development Act. Hearings before the subcommittee on Employment, Manpower, and Poverty of the Committee on Labor and Public Welfare. Part I, August...1969.

Comprehensive Child Development Act of 1971. Joint Hearings before the Subcommittee on Employment, Manpower, and Poverty and the Subcommittee on Children and Youth of the Committee on Labor and Public Welfare, Part I, May...1971; Part 2, May...1971.

Equal Educational Opportunity in 1971. Hearings before the Select Committee on Equal Educational Opportunity, Part 12, July...August...1971.

Select Committee on Equal Educational Opportunity, Toward Equal Educational Opportunity, 1972.

Public Laws

88–204, Higher Education Facilities Act of 1963.

88–210, Vocational Education Act of 1963.

88–452, An Act to Mobilize the Human and Financial Resources of the Nation to Combat Poverty in the United States, 20 August 1964.

89–329, Higher Education Act of 1965.

95–561, Title I – Amendment to Title I of the Elementary and Secondary Education Act of 1965, 1978.
100–297, An Act to Improve Elementary and Secondary Education and for Other Purposes (Hawkins–Stafford).
Congressional Record. Proceedings and Debates of the 89th Congress, House of Representatives, 24 March 1965; Senate, 7–9 April 1965.

Department of Education

1980 Annual Report, Department of Education.
Federal Register. Part II. Vol. 46. No. 12. Financial Assistance to Local and State Agencies to Meet Special Educational Needs ... Rules and Regulations, Department of Education, Office of Elementary and Secondary Education, 1981.
Office of Planning, Budget, and Evaluation, *Executive Summary. Study of the Sustaining Effects of Compensatory Education. Interim report*, Department of Education, 1981.
Office of Planning, Budget, and Evaluation, Planning and Evaluation Service, *An Evaluation of ESEA Title I: Program Operations and Educational Effects. A report to Congress*, Department of Education, 1982.

Department of Health, Education, and Welfare

Annual Report, 1962.
Annual Report, 1963.
Annual Report, Title I, Elementary and Secondary Education Act of 1965, HEW.
Title I, Year II: the second annual report of Title I of the Elementary and Secondary Education Act of 1965, school year 1966–67, HEW.
Futures in Education: Teacher Corps, HEW, n.d.
Trio: Talent Search, Upward Bound, Special Services, HEW, n.d.
The Effectiveness of Compensatory Education: summary and review of the evidence, HEW, Office of Planning and Evaluation [1972], mimeo.
The Measure of Poverty: a report to Congress as mandated by the Education Amendment of 1974, HEW, 1976.
Department of Compensatory Education, *The Follow Through Program: five year program plan, 1971*.
Office of Child Development, Project Head Start 1968: the development of a program, HEW, 1970, mimeo.

Department of Health, Education, and Welfare, Office of Education

Programs for the Educationally Disadvantaged: a report of a conference on teaching children and youth who are educationally disadvantaged. May 21–23, 1962, HEW, 1963.
Summer Education for Children of Poverty: report of the National Advisory Council on the Education of Disadvantaged Children, HEW.
Profiles in Quality Education: 150 outstanding Title 1, ESEA, projects, HEW.
Project Head Start: a research summary. Reprinted from Senate Committee on Labor and Public Welfare hearings in integrated education, vol. 6 (5).

Education of the Disadvantaged: An evaluative report on Title I, Elementary and Secondary Education Act of 1965, fiscal year 1968, HEW.

History of Title I ESEA, HEW, 1969 (revised edn of 1972).

Upward Bound: a program to help youth from low-income families achieve a college education. 1970–71 guidelines: an Office of Education Program Administration Manual, HEW, 1969.

Appalachian Regional Commission, HEW, 1970.

It Works, HEW, 1969, mimeo.

Meeting Parents Halfway: a guide for schools, HEW, 1970 (edn of 1972).

Memorandum to Follow Through Program Sponsors, 18 October 1971 ('Program reviews of Follow Through projects').

Title I ESEA: selecting target areas. Handbook for local Title I officials, HEW [1971].

Compensatory Education. Model Programs: Higher Horizons 100, Hartford, Connecticut, HEW, 1972.

Compensatory Education. Model Programs: Learning to Learn Program, Jacksonville, Florida, HEW, 1972

Compensatory Education. Model Programs. More Effective Schools Program, New York, HEW, 1972.

Parental Involvement in Title I ESEA, Why? What? How? HEW, 1972.

Title I ESEA, Questions and Answers, HEW, 1979.

Division of Education for the Disadvantaged, *Title 1, ESEA, Working with Schools: a parents' handbook*, 1980.

Office of Planning, Budgeting and Evaluation, *Elementary Schools and the Receipt of Compensatory Funds. Evaluation study, executive summary*, HEW, 1977.

Office of Economic Opportunity

The Quiet Revolution. Second annual report, OEO, 1967.

Vista Fact Book, OEO, 1967.

OEO Instruction: Participation of the poor in the planning, conduct, and evaluation of community action programs, 20 September 1968, mimeo.

Miscellaneous

Office of Education and Office of Economic Opportunity, *An Answer to Poverty: programs which may be eligible for federal aid*, 1966.

Congress, Subcommittee on Economic Progress of the Joint Economic Committees, *Federal Programs for the Development of Human Resources*, vol. 1, 1968.

Council of Economic Advisors, *The Problem of Poverty in America* (reprint of ch. 2 of Annual Economic Report), in House of Representatives, *Economic Opportunity Act. Hearings before the Committee on the War on Poverty Program of the Committee on Education and Labor...Part I*, 1964.

Comptroller General, *Report to the Congress: Follow Through: lessons learned from its evaluation and need to improve its administration*, General Accounting Office, 1975.

The Urban Child Center (1965) Inventory of Compensatory Education Projects 1965, University of Chicago, School of Education, Urban Child Center, mimeo.

Utter, Lawrence W. (1963) 'Helping our culturally impoverished children', *NEA Journal*, 52 (11).

Van Doren, Ron (1967) 'Missionaries in the classroom', *American Education*, 3 (1).

Vanecko, James J., Ames, Nancy L. and Archambault, Francis X. Jr [1980] *Who Benefits from Federal Education Dollars? The development of ESEA Title I allocation policy*, Cambridge, Mass., Abt Books.

Villaume, John and Haney, Walt (1977) *The Follow Through Planned Variation Experiment*, vol. 5. *Appendix : Analysis of interim Follow Through evaluation reports*, Cambridge, Mass., Huron Institute.

Vreeland, Rebecca S. (*see* Boston)

Wang, Margaret *et al.* (*see* Pittsburgh)

Warden, Sandra A. (1968) *The Leftouts : disadvantaged children in heterogeneous schools*, New York, Holt, Rinehart and Winston.

Washington Post (1985) 'Helping poor children' (editorial), 19 August.

Washington Research Project and NAACP Legal Defense and Educational Fund [1967] *Title 1 of ESEA : is it helping poor children?*, Washington, D.C., Washington Research project (edn of 1969).

Watt, Lois B., Thomas, Myra H. and Horner, Harriet L. (1966) *The Education of Disadvantaged Children : a bibliography*, Washington, D.C., HEW, OE.

Watters, Pat (1966) Mississippi: children and politics' in Jeremy Larner and Irving Howe (eds.), *Poverty : views from the left*, New York, William Morrow.

Wayson, William (*see* Halperin)

Waxman, Chaim Isaac (ed.) (1968) *Poverty : power and politics*, New York, Grosset and Dunlap.

Weaver, W. Timothy (1982) *The Contest for Educational Resources*, Lexington, Mass., D.C. Heath.

Weber, Evelyn (1969) *The Kindergarten : its encounter with educational thought in America*, New York, Teachers College Press.

Weber, Lillian (1971) *The English Infant School and Informal Education*, Englewood Cliffs, N.J., Prentice-Hall.

Webster, Staten W. (ed.) *The Disadvantaged Learner : knowing, understanding, educating*, San Francisco, Chandler.

Weikart, David P. (1967) 'Preschool programs: preliminary findings', *Journal of Special Education*, 11 (2).

   (1972) 'Relationship of curriculum, teaching, and learning in preschool education' in Julian C. Stanley (ed.), *Preschool Programs for the Disadvantaged*, Baltimore, Johns Hopkins University Press.

   (1981) 'Effects of different curricula in early childhood intervention', *Educational Evaluation and Policy Analysis*, 5 (6).

Weikart, David P. and Lambie, Dolores Z. (1968) 'Preschool intervention through a home teaching program' in Jerome Hellmuth (ed.), *Disadvantaged Child*, vol. 2, New York, Brunner/Mazel.

Weikart, David P., Deloria, Dennis J. and Lawsor, Sarah (1974) 'Results of a preschool intervention project' in Sally Ryan (ed.), *A Report on Longitudinal Evaluations of Preschool Programs*, Washington, D.C., HEW.

Weinstock, Ruth (1984) 'A Title I Tale: high reading/math gains at low cost in Kansas City, Kansas', *Phi Delta Kappan*, 65 (9).

Westergaard, John and Resler, Henrietta (1975) *Class in a Capitalist Society: a study of contemporary Britain*, New York, Basic Books

Westinghouse Learning Corporation and Ohio University (1969) *The Impact of Head Start: an evaluation of the effects of Head Start on children's cognitive and affective develoment*. Vol. I: *Text and Appendices A–E. Presented to the Office of Economic Opportunity*... Washington Learning Corporation and Ohio University.

WEST VIRGINIA

Randolph County Schools, Follow Through Program: early childhood education (grades 1–3), Elkins, Randolph County Schools, n.d., mimeo.

Randolph County Schools, Follow Through End of Year Sponsor Report, Elkins, Randolph County Schools, 1974.

ESEA Title I Handbook for Local Education Agencies, Board of Education, Charleston, Bureau of Services and Federal Programs, 1975.

Secondary Reading Lab, ESEA Title I, Parkensburg, Wood County Schools, 1976.

Department of Education, *How to make Your ESEA Title One Parent Advisory Council More Effective*, Charleston, Department of Education, [1979].

Summary of ESEA Title 1 in West Virgina: program elements and approved expenditures, regular term fiscal year 1980, Charleston, Department of Education, Bureau of Services and Federal Assistance, 1980.

Department of Education, *Follow Through: a quiet reflection*, Charleston, Department of Education, n.d.

Elementary and Secondary Education Act Title 1 Evaluation Handbook, Charleston, Department of Education, revised edition of 1981.

White, Sheldon H. *et al.* (1973) *Federal Programs for Young Children: review and recommendations*. Vol. 1: *Goals and Standards of Public Programs for Children*, Washington, D.C., Government Printing Office.

White, William (*see* Atlanta)

Whiteman, Martin and Deutsch, Martin (1967) 'Social disadvantage as related to intellectual and language development' in Martin Deutsch *et al.* (eds.), *The Disadvantaged Child*, New York, Basic Books.

Wildavsky, Aaron (1980) *The Art and Craft of Policy Analysis*, London, Macmillan.

Wilkerson, Doxey A. (1965) 'Programs and practices in compensatory education for disadvantaged children', *Review of Educational Research*, 35 (5).

(1970) 'Compensatory Education: defining the issues' in Jerome Hellmuth (ed.), *Disadvantaged Child*, vol. 3, New York, Brunner/Mazel.

Wilkinson, J. Harvie III (1979) *From Brown to Bakke. The Supreme Court and School Integration, 1954–1978*, New York, Oxford University Press.

William Jewitt Tucker Foundation (n.d.) *A Better Chance*, Hanover, New Hampshire, Dartmouth College.

William T. Grant Foundation Commission on Work, Family and Citizenship (1988) *The Forgotten Half: pathways to success for America's youth and young families*, Washington, D.C., William T. Grant Foundation.

Williams, Frederick (ed.) (1970) *Language and Poverty: perspectives on a theme*, Chicago, Markham.

Williams, Walter and Evans, John W. (1969) 'The politics of evaluation: the case of Head Start' in Louis A. Ferman (ed.), *Evaluating the War on Poverty*, AAPSS.

Wilson, Alan B. (*see* California)

Wilson, William Julius. (1987) *The Truly Disadvantaged: the inner city, the underclass and public policy*, University of Chicago Press.

Winschel, James F. (1970) 'In the dark...reflections on compensatory education 1960–1970' in Jerome Hellmuth (ed.), *Disadvantaged Child*, vol. 3, New York, Brunner/Mazel.

Wirth, Arthur D. (1986) 'Contemporary work and the quality of life', draft of ch. 5 in Kenneth Benne and Steven Tozer (eds.), *Society as Educator*, National Society for the Study of Education, Chicago, mimeo.

Wise, Arthur E. and Weinstein, Shelly (1976) 'The politics of inequality: a case study', *Phi Delta Kappan*, 58 (2).

Wisler, Carl E, Burns, Gerald P. Jr and Iwamoto, David (1978) 'Follow Through redux: a response to the critique by House, Glass, McLean and Walker', *Harvard Educational Review*, 48 (2).

Witmer, Helen Leland and Kotinsky, Ruth (eds.) (1952) *Personality in the Makina. The fact-finding report of the midcentury White House conference on children and youth*, New York, Harper and Bros.

Witty, Paul A. (ed.) (1967) *The Educationally Retarded and Disadvantaged: the sixty-sixth yearbook of the National Society for the Study of Education*, Part 1, Chicago, NSSE.

Wolfbein, Seymour L. (1967) *Education and Training for Full Employment*, New York, Columbia University Press.

Wolff, Max and Stein, Annie (1966) *Six Months Later: a comparison of children who had Head Start, Summer 1965, with their classmates in kindergarten*, Washington, D.C. Office of Economic Opportunity.

(1967) 'Head Start Six Months Later', *Phi Delta Kappan*, 48 (7).

Woock, Roger (1967) 'Project Uplift – reflections on a quiet summer', *Urban Education*, 3 (1).

Woodring, Paul (1970) *Investment in Innovation: an historical appraisal of the Fund for the Advancement of Education*, Boston, Little, Brown.

Wright, Mary J. (1983) *A Canadian Approach: compensatory education in the preschool. The University of Western Ontario Preschool Project*, Ypsilanti, Michigan, High/Scope Press.

Wrightstone, J. Wayne (1960) 'Demonstration Guidance Project in New York City', *Harvard Educational Review*, 30 (3).

(1969) Contribution to symposium on 'Evaluating educational programs', *Urban Review*, 3 (4).

Wrightstone, J. Wayne *et al.* (1964) *Evaluation of the Higher Horizons Program for Underprivileged Children*, New York, Board of Education of the City of New York, Bureau of Educational Research.

Yale (*see* Ford Foundation)

Yarmolinsky, Adam (1969) 'The beginnings of OEO' in James L. Sundquist (ed.), *On Fighting Poverty*, New York, Basic Books.

Yinger, J. Milton *et al.* (1977) *Middle Start: an experiment in the enrichment of young adolescents*, New York, Cambridge University Press.

Ylvisaker, Paul N. [1963] *Community Action: a response to some unfinished business*, New York, Ford Foundation.

Zigler, Edward (1971) 'Contemporary concerns in early childhood education', *Young Children*, 26 (3).

(1973) 'Project Head Start: success or failure?', *Children Today*, 2 (6).

Zigler, Edward and Berman, Winnie (1983) 'Discerning the future of early childhood intervention', *American Psychologist*, 38 (8).

Zigler, Edward and Seitz, Victoria (1980) 'Early childhood intervention programs: a reanalysis', *School Psychology Review*, 9.

(1982) 'Head Start as a national laboratory', *Annals of the American Academy of Political and Social Science*, 461.

Zigler, Edward and Trickett, P. (1978) 'IQ, social competence, and evaluation of early childhood intervention programs', *American Psychologist*, 33 (9).

Zigler, Edward and Valentine, Jeanette (eds.) (1979) *Project Head Start: A Legacy of the War on Poverty*, New York, Free Press.

Zigler, Edward *et al.* (1982) 'Is an intervention program necessary in order to improve economically disadvantaged children's IQ scores?', *Child Development*, 53 (2).

B   UNITED KINGDOM SOURCES

Abel-Smith, Brian and Townsend, Peter (1965) *The Poor and the Poorest*, London, Bell.

Abrams, Philip (1963) 'Notes on the uses of ignorance', *20th Century*, 172 (1019)

Acland, Henry (1971a) 'What is a 'bad' school?', *New Society*, 9 September.

(1971b) 'Does parent involvement matter?', *New Society*, 16 September.

(1973) Social Determinants of Educational Achievement: an evaluation and criticism of research, University of Oxford, DPhil thesis.

(1980) 'Research as stage management: the case of the Plowden committee' in Martin Bulmer (ed.), *Social Research and Royal Commissions*, London, Allen & Unwin.

Adam, Ruth (1969) '*Project Head Start: LBJ's one success?*', *New Society*, 30 October.

Adams, F. J. (1973) 'An example of compensatory education', *Education News*, 14 (2).

Ainsworth, Marjorie E. and Batten, Eric J. (1974) *The Effects of Environmental Factors on Secondary Educational Attainment in Manchester: a Plowden follow-up*, London, Macmillan.

Anderson, Hugh, Hipkin, John and Plaskow, Maurice (eds.) (1970) *Education for the Seventies*: *transcriptions of the Cambridge Union teach-in*, London, Heinemann Educational.

Angus, Anne (1964) 'America's war on poverty', *New Society*, 16 July.

Annan, Noel (1964) 'Bitter priorities', *Encounter*, 23 (6).

Armstrong, Gina (1973) 'The preschool needs of EPA children', *London Educational Review*, 2 (1).

(1975) 'An experiment in early learning', *Concern*, 18.

Armstrong, Gina and Brown, Felicity (1979) Five Years On: a follow-up study of the long-term effects on parents and children of an early learning programme in the home. The West Riding EPA home visiting scheme, University of Oxford, Department of Social and Administrative Studies, Social Evaluation Unit, mimeo.

Atkinson, Paul (1985) *Language, Structure and Reproduction: an introduction to the sociology of Basil Bernstein*, London, Methuen.

Australian Government Commission of Inquiry into Poverty (1976) *Fifth Main Report. Poverty and Education in Australia*, Canberra, Australian Government Publishing Service.

Ball, David (1971) 'Urban Programme: imaginative investments', *New Society*, 21 January.

Banks, Olive (1968) *The Sociology of Education*, London, Batsford.

Banting, Keith G. (1979) *Poverty, Politics and Policy: Britain in the 1960s*, London, Macmillan.

Bantock, G.H. (1965) *Education and Values: essays in the theory of education*, London, Faber & Faber.

(1965) Letter to *TES* on comprehensive schools, 15 January.

(1971) 'Towards a theory of popular education' in Richard Hooper (ed.) *The Curriculum: context, design and development*, Edinburgh, Oliver & Boyd.

(1975) 'Equality and education' in Bryan Wilson (ed.), *Education, Equality and Society*, London, Allen & Unwin.

(1977) 'An alternative curriculum' in C.B. Cox and Rhodes Boyson (eds.), *Black Paper 1977*, London, Temple Smith.

Barnes, Jack (ed.) (1975) *Educational Priority*. Vol. 3: *Curriculum Innovation in London's E.P.A.s*, London, HMSO.

(n.d.) Interview for Open University Course DE 304 on tape 'Policy and action'.

Barnes J.H. and Lucas, H. (1974) 'Positive discrimination in education: individuals, groups and institutions' in Timothy Legatt (ed.), *Sociological Theory and Survey Research: institutional change and social policy in Great Britain*, London, Sage.

Barr, F. (1959) 'Urban and rural differences in ability and attainment', *Educational Research*, 1 (2).

Barratt, David John (1974) 'An Analysis of the Use made of the Work of Basil Bernstein in Studies on the Language of Culturally Deprived Children', University of Liverpool, MEd dissertation.

Batley, Richard (1978) 'From poor law to positive discrimination', *Journal of Social Policy*, 7 (3).

Batley, Richard and Edwards, John (1975) 'CDP and the urban programme' in Ray Lees and George Smith (eds.), *Action–Research in Community Development*, London, Routledge & Kegan Paul.

Batten, E. (1975) 'Attainment, environment and education' in James Rushton and John D. Turner (eds), *Education and Deprivation*, Manchester University Press.

Baum, Eugene L. (1966) 'The Banneker Elementary District in St. Louis, Missouri: a war on poverty educational effort', *New Era*, 47 (8).

Beichman, Arnold (1964) 'The other America', *The Spectator*, 31 January.

Benyon, Lois Mary (1973) 'An Analysis of Some of the Literature Relating to the Education of Children under Social Handicap', University of Liverpool, MEd dissertation.

Bereiter, Carl and Engelmann, Siegfried (1968) 'An academically oriented preschool for disadvantaged children: results from the initial experimental group' in David W. Brison and Jane Hill (eds.) *Psychology and Early Childhood Education*, Toronto, Ontario Institute for Studies in Education.

Bernstein, Basil (1961) 'Social structure, language, and learning' in Maurice Craft *et al.*, (eds.), *Linking Home and School*, London, Longmans.

(1963) 'Research for the 'sixties'', *20th Century*, 172 (1019).

(1970) 'Education cannot compensate for society', *New Society*, 26 February.

(1971) *Class, Codes and Control*. Vol. 1: *Theoretical studies towards a sociology of language*, London, Routledge & Kegan Paul.

(1973) *Class, Codes and Control*. Vol. 2: *Applied studies towards a sociology of language*, London, Routledge & Kegan Paul.

(1975) *Class, Codes and Control*. Vol. 3: *Towards a theory of educational transmissions*, London, Routledge & Kegan Paul (revised edn, 1977).

Bernstein, Basil and Davies, Brian (1969) 'Some sociological comments on Plowden' in Richard Peters (ed.), *Perspectives on Plowden*, London, Routledge & Kegan Paul.

Bessell, Arthur (1979) 'Helping the disadvantaged', *Disadvantage in Education*, 2 (1).

Betty, Charles (1969a) 'A community primary school', *Forum*, 11 (2).

(1969b) 'Race, community and schools', *Race Today*, 1 (2).

(1970) 'Deptford spearheads fight for viable policy', *Education*, 136 (21).

(1971a) 'EPA action research in educational priority areas: England and Scotland', *Urban Education*, 6 (2/3).

(1971b) *Focus on the Community School*, London, Copyprints.

(1971c) Deptford Educational Priority Area Action Research Project. Final report to the Social Science Research Council and the Inner London Education Authority, London, December, mimeo.

(1971d) The Community School, mimeo.

(1974) Home–School Liaison Scheme in Nottinghamshire: synopsis of reports received from home–school liaison teachers, 29 March, mimeo.

(1975) 'How the other half worked', *TES*, 9 May.

(1978) 'Meeting the challenge of educational disadvantage: a case-study', *Education 3–13*, 6 (2).

(n.d.) The Action/Research Dilemma, mimeo.

(n.d.) A Concept of a Community School, mimeo.

(n.d.) Handout on parent–school relationships, mimeo.

Bevan, Aneurin (n.d.) 'Plan for work' in G.D.H. Cole *et al.*, *Plan for Britain*, London, Labour Book Service.

Beveridge, William (1942) *Social Insurance and Allied Services*, London, HMSO.

(1944) *Full Employment in a Free Society*, London, Allen & Unwin.

Birchall, Dorothy (1982) *Home Based Services for the Under Fives : a review of research (Highlight 54)*, London, National Children's Bureau.

Birley, Derek and Dufton, Anne (1971) *An Equal Chance : equalities and inequalities of educational opportunity*, London, Routledge & Kegan Paul.

Blackstone, Tessa (1967) 'The Plowden report', *The British Journal of Sociology*, 18.

(1971) *A Fair Start : the provision of pre-school education*, London, Allen Lane.

(1973a) *Education and Day Care for Young Children in Need : the American experience*, London, Centre for Studies in Social Policy.

(1973b) 'Educational Priority in Britain' (review of Halsey, *Educational Priority*, vol. 1), *Journal of Social Policy*, 2 (3).

Blank, Marion (1971) 'Implicit assumptions underlying preschool intervention programs' in Stella Chess and Alexander Thomas (eds.), *Annual Progress in Child Psychiatry and Child Development*, London, Butterworths.

Bloom, Leonard (1968) review of Passow, *Education of the Disadvantaged*, *British Journal of Educational Psychology*, 38 (Part 2).

Blyth, W.A.C. (1965) *English Primary Education : a sociological description.* Vol. 1 : *Schools.* Vol. 2 : *Background*, London, Routledge & Kegan Paul.

Board of Education (1931) *Report of the Consultative Committee on the Primary School* (Hadow), London, HMSO.

(1933) *Report of the Consultative Committee on Infant and Nursery Schools* (Hadow), London, HMSO.

(1937 edn) *Handbook of Suggestions*, London, HMSO.

(1938) *Report of the Consultative Committee on Secondary Education* (Hadow), London, HMSO.

(1943) *Curriculum and Examinations in Secondary Schools: Report of the Committee of the Secondary School Examinations Council* (Norwood), London, HMSO.

Boudon, Raymond and Lagneau, Janina (1980) 'Inequality of educational opportunity in Western Europe', *Prospects*, 10 (2).

Bourne, Jenny (1972) 'Urban aid and catch-22', *Race Today*, 4 (7).

Bourne, Richard (1972) 'Explosion in the bottom class', *The Guardian*, 11 August.

Bovaird, A.G. (ed.) (1978) *Research and Intelligence for Deprivation*, University of Birmingham

Bowlby, John (1953) *Child Care and the Growth of Love*, Harmondsworth, Penguin.

(1954) 'The rediscovery of the family' in John Bowlby et al., *Rediscovery of the Family and Other Lectures* (Sister Marie Hilda Memorial Lectures 1954–1973), 1981, Aberdeen University Press.

Boyd, John (1977) *Community Education and the Urban Schools*, London, Longman.

Boyle, Edward (1963) 'School integration in England', *Integrated Education*, 2 (3).

Bradley, Martin Harry (1979) 'Coordination and Competition: the administration of services for children under five in a metropolitan district council, with special reference to voluntary preschool groups', University of Keele, PhD thesis.

(M.H.) (1982) 'The assessment of deprivation', *Journal of Educational Administration and History*, 14 (2).

Brian, Mike (1978) 'Research and intelligence for deprivation: a Nottinghamshire case study' in A.G. Bovaird (ed.), *Research and Intelligence for Deprivation*, University of Birmingham.

Brighouse, T.R.P. (1986) 'Home/school partnership', *Journal of Applied Educational Studies*, 15 (2).

Brimer, M.A. (1971) *Evaluation Research and Action Programmes amongst the Educationally and Socially Disadvantaged*, Paris, OECD.

Brison, David W. and Hill, Jane (eds.) (1968), *Psychology and Early Childhood Education*, Toronto, Ontario Institute for Studies in Education.

Brown, Muriel and Madge, Nicola (1982) *Despite the Welfare State. A report on the SSRC/DHSS programme of research into transmitted deprivation*, London, Heinemann.

Bruner, Jerome (1980a) 'The role of the researcher as an adviser to the educational policy maker' in W.B. Dockerell and David Hamilton, Rethinking Educational Research, London, Hodder & Stoughton.

(1980b) *Under Five in Britain*, London, Grant McIntyre.

Brunner, Jacqueline (1978) 'The History of the Curriculum of English Nursery Education from 1905–1973', London University Institute of Education, MA dissertation.

Burrows, John (1968) The Education of Disadvantaged Children: compensatory education in the United States (report of a visit in May 1968), mimeo.

(1969) 'The disadvantaged child – a report from the U.S.A.' *Trends in Education*, 14

Burt, Cyril (1937) *The Backward Child*, London, University of London Press.

(1964) 'Critical notice of J.W.B. Douglas, *The Home and the School*, British *Journal of Educational Psychology*, 35.

Butler, Lord (1968) 'The 1944 Act in the next decade' in Peter Bander (ed.), *Looking Forward to the Seventies*, Gerrards Cross, Colin Smythe.

Bynner, J.M. (1972) *Parents' Attitudes to Education*, London, HMSO.

(1975) 'Parents' attitudes to education and their consequences for working-class children' in James Rushton and John D. Turner (eds.), *Education and Deprivation*, Manchester University Press.

Byrne, D.S. and Williamson, W. (n.d.) *The Myth of the Restricted Code (Working Papers in Sociology* 1), University of Durham, Department of Sociology and Social Administration.

Byrne, D.S., Williamson, Bill and Fletcher, Barbara (1975) *The Poverty of Education : a study in the politics of opportunity*, London, Martin Robertson.

Canadian Teachers Federation (1972) *The Poor at School in Canada : observational studies of Canadian schools, classrooms and pupils*, Ottawa, CTF.

Carew, Jean V. (1977) 'Social class, experience and intelligence in young children' in Harry McGurk (ed.), *Ecological Factors in Human Development*, Amsterdam, North-Holland Publishing Co.

Carney, John G and Taylor, Clive (1974) 'Community development projects: review and comment', *Area*, 6 (3).

Carnine, Douglas (1979) 'Direct instruction; a successful system for educationally high-risk children', *Journal of Curriculum Studies*, 11 (1).

Carswell, John (1985) *Government and the Universities in Britain: programme and performance 1960–1980*, Cambridge University Press.

Central Advisory Council (*see* Department of Education and Science)

Central Advisory Council (Plowden Committee members) (1969) 1967–9: Two Years in Primary Education (Follow up statement on Plowden), 10 January, mimeo.

Centre de recherche de l'éducation spécialisée et de l'adaptation scolaire (CRESAS) (1983) *Écoles en transformation: Zones prioritaires et autres quartiers*, Paris, L'Harmattan and INRP.

(1985) *Depuis 1981, l'école pur tous? Zones d'éducation prioritaires*, Paris, L'Harmattan and INRP.

Centre for Educational Research and Innovation (1978) *Pre-School Education: report from five research projects*, Paris, OECD

(1982) *Caring for Young Children; an analysis of educational and social services*, Paris, OECD.

Centre for Information and Advice on Educational Disadvantage [1976], First Report, Manchester, CED, mimeo.

(1977a) *Are Educational Priority Areas still Worthwhile?*, Manchester CED.

(1977b) *The Bicester Vulnerable Child Scheme*, Manchester, CED.

[1977c] *Disadvantage and the Education of Young Children (report of a conference held at Saffron Walden College)*, Manchester, CED.

(1977d) The Work of the Centre on Educational Disadvantage, mimeo.

(1980) *Educational Disadvantage in Rural Areas: with special reference to pre-school and primary school provision*, Manchester, CED.

Chazan, Maurice (1968) 'Compensatory education; defining the problem' in Schools Council Research Project in Compensatory Education, London, Schools Council.

(1970) 'Compensatory programmes and early childhood education in the U.S.A.' in T. Cox and C.A. Waite (eds.) *Teaching Disadvantaged Children in the Infant School*, Swansea, Schools Council Research and Development Project in Compensatory Education.

(ed.) (1972a) *Aspects of Primary Education*, Cardiff, University of Wales Press.

(ed.) (1973a) *Compensatory Education*, London, Butterworths.

(1973b) 'Disadvantage and nursery schooling', *Special Education*, 62 (3).

(1975) 'Evaluation of pre-school education: research in the United Kingdom' in Council of Europe, *Problems in the Evaluation of Pre-School Education*, Strasbourg, Documentation Centre for Education in Europe.

(1979) 'Towards a comprehensive strategy for disadvantaged pre-school children?', *Early Child Development and Care*, 6 (1/2).

[1979/80] Disadvantage and Early Childhood Education, Swansea, mimeo.

(1982) 'Language and learning: intervention and the child at home' in Alan Davies (ed.), *Language and Learning in Home and School*, London, Heinemann Educational.

Chazan, Maurice and Laing, Alice (n.d.) Twenty Years of Research in Special and Compensatory Education at Swansea (1962–1981), University College of Swansea, mimeo.

Chazan, Maurice and Williams, Phillip (eds) (1978) *Deprivation and the Infant School: a report of the work of the Schools Council Research and Development Project in Compensatory Education*, Oxford, Blackwell.

Chazan, Maurice, Laing, Alice and Jackson, Susan (1971) *Just Before School*, Oxford, Blackwell.

Chazan, Maurice *et al.* (1976) *Deprivation and School Progress*, Oxford, Blackwell.

Chazan, Maurice *et al.* (1977) *Deprivation and Development*, Oxford, Blackwell.

Choat, Ernest and De'eath, Stephen, 'EPA – SPA – ?', *Dudley Educational Journal*, 2 (1).

Clark, Margaret M. and Cheyne, William M. (eds.) (1979) *Studies in Pre-School Education: empirical studies in pre-school units in Scotland and their implications for educational practice*, Edinburgh, Scottish Council for Research in Education.

Clarke, Ann M. and Clarke, A.D.B. (eds.) (1976) *Early Experience: myth and evidence*, London, Open Books.

Clegg, A.B. (ed.) (1972) *The Changing Primary School: its problems and priorities. A statement by teachers*, London, Chatto & Windus.

Clough, J.R. (1972) 'Compensatory education programmes: a review of research', *Australian Journal of Education*, 16 (2).

Coates, Ken and Silburn, Richard (1967) *Poverty, Deprivation and Morale in a Nottingham Community: St. Ann's*, Nottingham University, Department of Adult Education.

(1970) *Poverty: the forgotten Englishman*, Harmondsworth, Penguin.

Coffield, Frank, Robinson, Philip, and Sarsby, Jacquie (1980) *A Cycle of Deprivation? A case study of four families*, London, Heinemann Educational.

Collis, Arthur T. (1965) Primary Schools and the Welfare Services: report of a survey of Birmingham, University of Birmingham, mimeo.

Committee on Higher Education (Robbins) (1963) *Higher Education: Report* (and appendices), London, HMSO.

Committee on Local Authority and Allied Personal Social Services (Seebohm) (1968), *Report*, London, HMSO.

Community Development Project (1975) *The National Community Development Project Forward Plan 1975–76*, London, CDP Information and Intelligence Unit.

(1977) *Gilding the Ghetto: the state and the poverty experiments*, London, CDP Inter-Project Editorial Team.

Confederation for the Advancement of State Education (1967) *Dear Lady Plowden*, London, CASE.

Cookson, Clive (1981) 'Safe future for Head Start', *TES*, 13 February.

(1981) 'Reagan swings "brutal" axe', *TES*, 27 February.

(1981) 'Young disadvantaged better at reading', *TES*, 8 May.

Corbett, Anne (1968) 'Priority schools', *New Society*, 30 May.

(1969) 'Are educational priority areas working?', *New Society*, 13 November.

(1974) 'Top priority' (3 articles), 12, 19, 26 July.

Coss, David (1968) 'Liverpool project could mean changes in the classroom', *Liverpool Daily Post*, 9 September.

Council for Educational Advance (1965) *Obstacles to opportunity*, London, CEA.

(1969) *Plowden Two Years On*, London, CEA.

Cox, Theo (1979) 'A follow-up study of reading attainment in a sample of eleven-year-old disadvantaged children', *Educational Studies*, 5 (1).

(1982) 'Disadvantaged fifteen-year-olds: initial findings from a longitudinal study', *Educational Studies*, 8 (1).

(1988) Culturally disadvantaged Children: a second follow-up study, University College of Swansea, Department of Education, mimeo.

Craft, Maurice, Raynor, John and Cohen, Louis (eds.), *Linking Home and School*, London, Longmans, edns of 1967, 1972; London, Harper & Row, edn of 1980.

Creber, J.W. Patrick (1972) *Lost for Words: language and educational failure*, Harmondsworth, Penguin.

Cripps, Stafford (1943) *Shall the Spell be Broken?*, London, Hodder & Stoughton.

Crosland, C.A.R. (1956) *The Future of Socialism*, London, Cape.

(1962) *The Conservative Enemy: a programme of radical reform for the 1960s*, London, Cape.

(1967) Speech, Plowden debate, House of Commons, 16 March, mimeo.

(1974) *Socialism Now and Other Essays*, London, Cape.

Curtis, Audrey and Blatchford, Peter (1981a) 'Meeting the needs of socially handicapped children', *Educational Research*, 24 (1).

(1981b) *Meeting the Needs of Socially Handicapped Children: the background to* My World, Windsor, NFER–Nelson.

Cyster, R. Clift and Battle, S. (1979) *Parental Involvement in Primary Schools*, Windsor, NFER.

The Daily Telegraph (1967) 'Plowden priority areas seen as threat: councils fear delays', 16 May.

Davie, Ronald, Butler, Neville, and Goldstein, Harvey (1972) *From Birth to Seven: the second report of the National Child Development Study*, London, Longman.

Davies, Alan (ed.) (1977) *Language and Learning in Early Childhood*, London, Heinemann Educational.

(1982) *Language and Learning in Home and School*, London, Heinemann Educational.

Dean, D.W. (1968) 'The political parties and the development of their attitude to educational problems from 1918 to 1942', London University, MPhil thesis.

de Lissa, Lillian (1939) *Life in the Nursery School*, London, Longmans, Green, edn of 1942.

Demaine, Jack (1980) 'Compensatory education and social policy' in Maurice Craft *et al.* (eds.) *Linking Home and School*, London, Harper & Row.

Denby, Maeve (1973) *Preschool – the cycle of opportunity?*, London, National Elfrida Rathbone Society.

Dent, H.C. (1949) *Secondary Education for All*, London, Routledge & Kegan Paul.

Department of Education and Science (1964–5) *Education Under Social Handicap* (3 parts, *Reports on Education*, 17, 20, 22), London.

(1967) *Children and their Primary Schools: a report of the Central Advisory*

Council for Education (England) (Plowden), vol. 1: *The Report*; vol. 2: *Research and Surveys*, London, HMSO. Evidence to the Council, various dates 1964 and 1965, by London County Council and the Inner London Education Authority, Association of Educational Psychologists, Association of Teachers in Colleges and Departments of Education, Preston Education Committee, Standing Conference of Organisations of Social Workers, Nursery School Association of Great Britain and Northern Ireland (evidence to the Council was not published with the report).

(1967) *Primary Education in Wales: a report of the Central Advisory Council for Education (Wales)* (Gittins), London, HMSO.

(1968a) *Parent/Teacher Relations in Primary Schools* (Education Survey 5), London, HMSO.

(1968b) *Urban Programme* (joint circular with Home Office and Ministry of Health), London, 4 October.

(1970) *Urban Programme Circular No. 3* (joint circular with Home Office and Department of Health and Social Security), London, 12 June.

(1973a) *Adult Education: a plan for development* (Russell), London, HMSO.

(1973b) *Nursery Education* (Circular 2/73), London.

(1975a) *Educational Disadvantage: perspectives and policies. The report of a conference convened by the Secretary of State for Education and Science*, London, DES.

(1975b) *A Language for Life: report of the Committee of Inquiry appointed by the Secretary of State for Education and Science* (Bullock), London, HMSO.

(1978) *Progress in Education: a report on recent initiatives*, London, HMSO.

Department of the Environment (1977a) *Change or Decay: final report of the Liverpool Inner Area Study*, London, HMSO.

(1977c) *Inner Area Studies: Liverpool, Birmingham and Lambeth: summaries of consultants' final reports*, London, HMSO.

(1977d) *Policy for the Inner Cities*, London, HMSO.

(1977–8) *Inner Area Study for Birmingham: educational action projects*, 3 vols. (report by consultants), London, DoE.

Derrick, June (1976) *The Child's Acquisition of Language*, Windsor, NFER.

Didsbury College of Education, Compensatory Education Project (n.d.), *Studies in Urban Education*, Manchester.

Disadvantage in Education (1977), 1 (4).

The Ditchley Foundation (1970) *Education for the Less Privileged. Report of a conference at Ditchley Park*, Enstone, Oxon, The Ditchley Foundation. (*see also* Maclure and Makins)

Dodds, D.H. (1975) 'The Origins of the E.P.A. at Denaby. The anatomy of a decision', University of Leeds, MA dissertation.

Donachy, W. (1976) 'Parent participation in pre-school education', *British Journal of Educational Psychology*, 46 (part 1).

Donnison, David (1967) Educational Priority Areas: the genesis of the Plowden Commitee's proposals, London School of Economics, 1967, mimeo.

(1972) *A Pattern of Disadvantage: a commentary on From Birth to Seven*, Slough, NFER.

(1974) 'Policies for priority areas', *Journal of Social Policy*, 3 (part 2).

(1982) *The Politics of Poverty*, Oxford, Martin Robertson.

Donnison, David and Soto, Paul (1980) *The Good City: a study of urban development and policy in Britain*, London, Heinemann.

Douglas, J.W.B. (1964) *The Home and the School: a study of ability and attainment in the primary school*, London, MacGibbon & Kee

Douglas, J.W.B. and Blomfield, J.M. (1958) *Children Under Five*, London, Allen & Unwin.

Douglas, J.W.B. and Ross, J.M. (1964) 'The later educational progress and emotional adjustment of children who went to nursery schools or classes', *Educational Research*, 7 (1).

Douglas, J.W.B., Ross, J.M. and Simpson, H.R. (1968) *All Our Future: a longitudinal study of secondary education*, London, Peter Davies.

Dove, N. F. (1972) 'Cultural Deprivation and Compensatory Education: a critical overview', University of Reading, MEd thesis.

Duncan, Stella and Young, Michael (1976) 'Education on the defensive' in Peter Willmott (ed.) *Sharing Inflation? (Poverty Report 1976)*, London, Temple Smith.

Duncan, Stella, Young, Michael and Kirkwood, Marion (1974) 'Education' in Michael Young (ed.), *Poverty Report 1974*, London, Temple Smith.

Education (1967) news of 'Plowden follow-up' activities, 27 January.

    (1979) 'Inner cities programme: a progress report on education in the inner cities partnership areas', 27 July.

EPA (EDUCATIONAL PRIORITY AREAS)

(NB: The EPA material held at the Department of Social Administration, University of Oxford, is a collection of correspondence, applications, reports, drafts, minutes, local and national material, and at the time of the research was not filed in any systematic way. Although the highly selected list of material below is sub-divided, this does not necessarily indicate archive location. Only the material cited in the text or of immediate relevance to the analysis is listed. All are mimeo.)

Correspondence

Michael Young to C.A.R. Crosland, 30 August 1967.
Patrick Gordon Walker to Michael Young, October 1967

Social Science Research Council.

SSRC Educational Research Board, Educational Priority Areas: a note by Dr M. Young, 23 October 1967.

SSRC, Action Research on Educational Priority Areas (note on consultations), 2 February 1968.

SSRC, Extract from the Minutes of the Council held on 5 April 1968.

SSRC, Application for a research grant from A.H. Halsey, for an 'Educational Priority Area Action Research Programme' [1968].

SSRC, EPA Action Research Programme, National Steering Committee, Minutes of first five meetings, held on 20 November 1968, 10 January, 21 March, 2 October 1969, and 12 May 1970.
SSRC, Memo on Needs of National Steering Committee [1968].

Meetings and progress reports

EPAs. Action–Research. Report of the Conference held in Nuffield College, Oxford on 1 and 14 September 1968 (written by Teresa Smith).
EPA Conference 2–4 January 1969 (summary by A.H. Halsey).
Notes on the EPA Research Workers Meeting, Department of Education, University of Birmingham, 1 November 1968.
Educational Priority Areas. Action Research Programme. Progress reports, November 1968, May 1969, September 1968–69.
Reports from individual projects, 5 June 1969.

Birmingham

Birmingham Project on Educational Priority Areas. Synopsis of the Interim Report of September 1970 presented to the Social Science Research Council, up-dated to December 1970.
Paul Widlake, Educational Priority Areas: Action/ Research (paper prepared for the British Psychological Society), April 1970, University of Birmingham.

Liverpool

Liverpool Educational Priority Area Project: Progress Report ii, August 1969.
Proposed Follow-up of Liverpool EPA Project. Extension Programme, October 1970.

London

The Inner London Educational Priority Area Project explanatory leaflet, n.d.
Smith, Pamela (ILEA Research and Statistics), Positive Discrimination in Practice: a survey of a sample of EPA primary schools, 16 March 1990.
Inner London Educational Priority Area Project. Project Director's Progress Report to the Local Steering Committee, 2 February 1971.
Inner London Education Authority. Notes of a Meeting of the Steering Committee of the Inner London Educational Area (Project), 31 January 1972.
Inner London Educational Priority Area Project. Report of Steering Committee (with appendices) [1972].
Inner London Education Authority. Education Officer's Report to Education Committee, Staff and General Sub-Committee (Research Advisory Section), on 'Research Lessons from the National E.P.A. Demonstration Project', 31 May 1972.

West Riding

Proposal for a Home Visiting Programme in the West Riding EPA [1970]
G.A.N. Smith, Draft Proposal (for research into the effects of small group work with primary school children from an Educational Priority Area), 23 July 1972.

Didsbury

The Compensatory Education Project Didsbury College of Education, 29 August 1968 (sent by Goldman to Halsey).
Compensatory Education. Statement requested by the Academic Board, 2 October 1968 (Goldman)
SSRC, Application for a research grant from R.J. Goldman, G.W. Williams and N. Wein, for 'An experimental enrichment and structured nursery/infant school program' 1969.

Miscellaneous

Alec Clegg, The 'Welfare' Needs of Schools, 26 May 1967.
George Smith, A Report on the Demonstration and Research Center in Early Childhood (DARCEE) at Nashville, Tennessee, 18 February 1969.
George Smith and Jack Barnes, Some Implications of Action Research Projects for Research (paper prepared for the 7th World Congress of Sociology, Varna, Bulgaria, 1970).
Headmasters Conference and Head Masters Association, 'When will we ever learn': Thoughts on the needs of disadvantaged children in secondary schools, n.d.
(for the EPA project reports see Halsey (vol. 1), Payne (vol. 2), Barnes (vol. 3), Smith (vol. 4), and Morrison (vol. 5). See also Lyons, Betty and Midwinter for other reports.)

Edwards, John (1975) 'Social indicators, urban deprivation and positive discrimination', *Journal of Social Policy*, 4 (Part 3).
Edwards, John and Batley, Richard (1978) *The Politics of Positive Discrimination: an evaluation of the urban programme 1967–77*, London, Tavistock.
Elvin, H.L. (1967) 'A revolution in progress', *TES*, 6 October.
Ellison, Thomas (1973) 'Compensatory education in comprehensive schools', *Secondary Education*, 4 (1).
Engelmann, Siegfried (1968) 'Priority in preschool education' in David W. Brison and Jane Hill (eds.), *Psychology and Early Childhood Education*, Toronto, Ontario Institute for Studies in Education.
Entwistle, Harold (1978) *Class, Culture and Education*, London, Methuen.
Essen, Juliet and Wedge, Peter (1982) *Continuities in Childhood Disadvantage*, London, Heinemann Educational.
Evans, Barbara and Hannon, Peter (1977) 'Catching them early', *TES*, 27 May.
Evans, Keith (1971) 'A role for television in compensatory education' in M.

Chazan and G. Downes, *Compensatory Education and the New Media*, Swansea, Schools Council Research Project in Compensatory Education.

Evans, Roy (1972) Identification of Children in Need, Nuffield Teacher Enquiry, Conference on 'Social deprivation and change in education', mimeo.

(1973) 'The identification of children "at risk" of educational handicap', *Urban Education*, 8 (1).

A Fabian group (1964) *New Patterns for Primary Schools*, London, Fabian Society.

Fabian Society (1970) *Planning for Education in 1980* (Fabian Research Series 282), London, Fabian Society.

Featherstone, Joseph (1971) *British Primary Schools Today: an introduction*, London, Macmillan.

Feeley, Gill *et al.* (1980) *Education Visiting*, Coventry Education Committee, Community Education Project.

Feldmann, Shirley (1964) 'A preschool enrichment program for disadvantaged children', *New Era*, 45 (3).

Ferguson, Neil and Williams, Phillip (1969) 'The identification of children needing compensatory education' in Schools Council Research Project in Compensatory Education, *Children at Risk*, Swansea, Schools Council Project.

Ferguson, Neil *et al.* (1971) 'The Plowden report's recommendations for identifying children in need of extra help' reprinted in John Raynor and Jane Harden (eds.) *Cities, Communities and the Young*, London, Routledge & Kegan Paul, 1973.

Ferri, Elsa and Niblett, Rosalind (1977 *Disadvantaged Families and Playgroups*, Windsor, NFER.

Field, Frank (ed.) *Education and the Urban Crisis*, London, Routledge & Kegan Paul.

Fine, Benjamin (1956), *1,000,000 Delinquents*, London, Gollancz.

Fisher, Ian (1968) 'Operation Head Start', *The Teacher*, 23 February.

Fitzherbert, Katrin (1973) 'Limitations of an EPA project team', *TES*, 24 February.

Floud, Jean (1961a) 'Reserves of ability', *Forum*, 3 (2).

(1961b) '*Social class factors in educational achievement*' in A.H. Halsey (ed.), *Ability and Educational Opportunity*, Paris, OECD.

(1962) 'The sociology of education' in A.T. Welford *et al.* (eds.), *Society: problems and methods of study*, London, Routledge & Kegan Paul.

Floud, Jean and Halsey, A.H. (1958) 'The sociology of education (with special reference to the development of research in Western Europe and the United States of America)', *Current Sociology*, 7 (3).

(1961) 'Homes and schools: social determinants of educability', *Educational Research*, 2 (2).

Floud, Jean, Halsey, A.H. and Martin, F.M. (1956) *Social Class and Educational Opportunity*, London, Heinemann.

Flude, Michael, 'Sociological accounts of differential educational attainment' in Michael Flude and John Ahier (eds.), *Educability, Schools and Ideology*, London, Croom Helm.

Forum Editorial Board (1964) 'Evidence submitted to the Plowden Committee', *Forum*, 7 (1).

Forum (1967) 'Plowden perspectives', 9 (3).

(1969) 'Two years after Plowden', 11 (2).

Fraser, Elizabeth (1959) *Home Environment and the School*, London, University of London Press.

Freeland, George (1962) 'The impact of comprehensive education on the primary school', *Forum*, 5 (1).

Freeland, George, Harvey, Edward and Morris, Norman T. (1964) 'From *Forum* to Plowden', *Forum*, 6 (2).

Fuller, Roger and Stevenson, Olive (1983) *Policies, Programmes and Disadvantage: a review of the literature*, London, Heinemann.

Fulton, Edmund (1968) 'Teaching disadvantaged children in the preschool', *New Era*, 49.

Gahagan, D. M. and G.A. (1970) *Talk Reform: explorations in language for infant school children*, London, Routledge & Kegan Paul.

Gardner, D.E.M. (1949) *Education Under Eight*, London, Longmans.

(1956) *The Education of Young Children*, London, Methuen.

Gardner, D.E.M. and Cass, Joan E. (1965) *The Role of the Teacher in the Infant and Nursery School*, Oxford, Pergamon.

Garner, Catherine L. (1989) *Does Deprivation Damage? A study of the incidence of deprivation in Lothian and of its influence on young people's educational attainment*, University of Edinburgh, Centre for Educational Sociology.

Gittins, C.E. (1957) 'Educational Opportunity' reprinted in Peter Gordon (ed.) *The Study of Education: a collection of inaugural lectures*, London, Woburn Press, 1980.

Glass, D.V. (ed.) (1954) *Social Mobility in Britain*, London, Routledge & Kegan Paul.

Glazer, Nathan (1966) 'The war on poverty: what went wrong?', *New Society*, 3 March.

Glennester, Howard (1969) 'The Plowden research', *Journal of the Royal Statistical Society*, Series A, 132 (Part 2).

(1972) 'Education and inequality' in Peter Townsend and Nicholas Bosanquet (eds.) *Labour and Inequality*, London, Fabian Society.

Glennester, Howard and Hatch, Stephen (1974) *Positive Discrimination and Inequality* (Fabian Research Series 314), London, Fabian Society.

Glennester, Howard and Hoyle, Eric (1972) 'Educational research and education policy', *Journal of Social Policy*, 1 (3).

Goldman, Ronald J. and Poole, Millicent E. (1974) 'Structured or general enrichment programmes for preschool children?', *Australian Journal of Social Issues*, 9 (2).

Goldman, Ronald J. and Taylor, Francine M. (1966) 'Coloured immigrant children: a survey of research, studies and literature on their educational problems and potential – in the U.S.A.', *Educational Research*, 9 (1).

Goldman, R. Ronald (1969) 'Reactions to Plowden's educational priority areas', *Education and Social Science*, 1 (1).

Gonick, C.W. (1970) 'Poverty and capitalism' in W.E. Mann (ed.) *Poverty and Social Policy in Canada*, Vancouver, Copp Clark.

Goodacre, Elizabeth J. (1961) 'Teachers and the socio-economic factor', *Educational Research*, 4 (1).

(1970) *School and Home: a review of developments in school and home relationships*, Slough, NFER.

Gray, J.L. (1936) *The Nation's Intelligence*, London, Watts.

Gray, J.L. and Moshinsky, Pearl (1938) 'Ability and opportunity in English education' in Lancelot Hogben (ed.) *Political Arithmetic*, London, Allen & Unwin.

Gray, John (1975) 'Positive discrimination in education: a review of the British experience', *Policy and Politics*, 4 (2).

(1980) 'Positive discrimination: the rise of an idea and the fall of a commitment' in Open University, *Education and the Urban Environment* (E361, Supplementary Material), Milton Keynes.

Gray, J., McPherson, A.F., and Raffe, D. (1983) *Reconstructions of Secondary Education: theory, myth and practice since the war*, London, Routledge & Kegan Paul.

Grey, Eleanor (1982) *Why Provide for Under-Fives?: a review of research* (*Highlight* 52), London, National Children's Bureau.

The Guardian (1968) letter from Jack Holmes, 3 June.

Gulliford, R. (1971) *Special Educational Needs*, London, Routledge & Kegan Paul.

Gulliford, R. and Widlake, Paul (1975) *Teaching Materials for Disadvantaged Children*, London, Evans/Methuen Educational.

Haigh, Gerald (1977) 'Where there's Scope there's hope', *TES*, 27 May.

Hake, Barry J. (1974) 'Some problems of educational and social equality strategies', *Paedagogica Europaea*, 9 (2) (issue on *Compensatory Education*).

Halliday, M.A.K. (1973) Foreword to Basil Bernstein (ed.) *Class, Codes and Control*, London, Routledge & Kegan Paul.

Halsey, A.H. (ed.) (1961) *Ability and Educational Opportunity*, Paris, OECD.

(1963) 'Expansion and equality' (review of Pedley, *The Comprehensive School*), *The Guardian*, 25 April.

(1964) 'Education and mobility' in T.R. Fyvel (ed.), *The Frontiers of Sociology*, London, Cohen & West.

(1969) 'The dilemma of priority areas', *Encounter*, 32 (5).

(1970) 'Attacking social deprivation: the educational priority area' in Brian MacArthur (ed.), *New Horizons for Education*, London, Council for Educational Advance.

(ed.) (1972a) *Educational Priority*, vol. 1: *E.P.A. Problems and Policies*.

(1972b) 'New socialist philosophy in the making', *TES*, 22 December.

(1973) 'Education and social class in 1972' in Kathleen Jones (ed.), *The Year Book of Social Policy in Britain 1972*, London, Routledge & Kegan Paul.

(1974a) 'Government against poverty in school and community' in Dorothy Wedderburn (ed.), *Poverty, Inequality and Class Structure*, London, Cambridge University Press.

(1974b) 'Pre-school research: directions and organization' in Barbara Tizard (ed.) *Early Childhood Education: a review and discussion of current research in Britain*, London, SSRC.

(1975a) 'Educational Priority Areas' in James Rushton and John D. Turner (eds.) *Education and Deprivation*, Manchester University Press.

(1975b) The Juxtaposition of Social and Individual Approaches in Compensatory Education Projects, Strasbourg, Council of Europe, Compensatory Education Workshop, mimeo.

(1975c) 'Towards a more noble alternative', *The Guardian*, 27 May.

(1975d) 'Would chance still be a fine thing?', *The Guardian*, 11 February.

(1977a) 'The birth of educational priority areas' in Frank Field (ed.) *Education and the Urban Crisis*, London, Routledge & Kegan Paul.

(1977b) 'The governmental response to EPAs' in Frank Field (ed.) *Education and the Urban Crisis*, London, Routledge & Kegan Paul.

(1977c) 'Whatever happened to positive discrimination?', *TES*, 21 January.

(1980) 'Education can compensate', *New Society*, January 24.

Halsey, A.H., Heath, A.F. and Ridge, J.M. (1980) *Origins and Destinations: family, class, and education in modern Britain*, Oxford, Clarendon Press.

Halsey, A.H. and Sylva, Kathy (1987) 'Plowden: history and prospect', *Oxford Review of Education*, 13 (1).

Hamilton, Dorothy (1988) 'Paging parents', *The Guardian*, 5 May.

Hannam, Charles, Smyth, Pat and Stephenson, Norman (1978) 'Serving out their time', *TES*, 20 October.

Hargreaves, David (1974) review of Chazan, *Compensatory Education*, *British Journal of Criminology*, 14 (2).

Harrison, Paul (1975) 'Urban aid', *New Society*, 30 January.

Harvey, Audrey (1960) *Casualties of the Welfare State* (Fabian Tract 321), London, Fabian Society.

(1962) 'Medical rehousing', *New Left Review*, 13/14.

Harwood, Jonathan (1982) 'American academic opinion and social change: recent developments in the nature–nurture controversy', *Oxford Review of Education*, 8 (1).

Hatch, Stephen and Sherrott, Roger (1973) 'Positive discrimination and the distribution of deprivations', *Policy and Politics*, 1 (3).

Hawkins, Eric (1968) 'From "Hadow" to "Plowden". Selection or positive enrichment?', *Aspects of Education*, 8.

Henriot, Agnès and Plaisance, Eric (1988) La politique des aires d'éducation prioritaires en Grande-Bretagne, Paris, CNRS–Sociologie de l'éducation, mimeo.

Herbert, G.W. and Wilson, Harriett (1977) 'Socially handicapped children', *Child: Care, Health and Development*, 3 (1).

Her Majesty's Inspectorate [1990] *Aspects of Education in the US: teaching and learning in New York City Schools*, London, HMSO.

Higgin, Davida (1968) 'Contrast: EPAs in USA', *CASE News*, 2 (5).

Higgins, Joan (1974) 'A project that got lost', *New Society* 6 June.

(1977) Review of Ginzberg and Solow, *The Great Society*, Plotnick and Skidmore, *Progress against Poverty*, and Graham, *Toward a Planned Society*, *Journal of Social Policy*, 6 (1).

(1978) *The Poverty Business: Britain and America*, Oxford, Blackwell.

Higgins, Joan et al. (1983) *Government and Urban Poverty: inside the policy-making business*, Oxford Blackwell.

Hill, Barry (1972) 'Priorities and politics', *TES*, 21 April.

Hindley, C.B. (1962) 'Social class influences on the development of ability in the first five years' in Ase Gruda Skard and Torsten Husén, *Child and Education*, Copenhagen, Munksgaard.

Hodgson, Godfrey (1973) 'Inequality: do schools make a difference?', *TES*, 11 May.

Hofkins, Diane (1990) 'Shared concern on inner-city failure', *TES*, 19 March.

Holland, Séamas (1979) *Rutland Street*, Oxford, Pergamon.

Holman, Robert (1969) 'The wrong poverty programme', *New Society*, 20 March.

(ed.) (1970) *Socially Deprived Families in Britain*, London, Bedford Square Press.

(1971) 'The urban programme appraised', *Race Today*, 3 (7).

(1974) 'The American poverty programme 1969–71', *Journal of Social Policy* 3 (part 1).

(1978) *Poverty : explanations of social deprivation*, London, Martin Robertson.

Holman, Robert and Hamilton, Lynda (1973) 'The British urban programme', *Policy and Politics*, 2 (2).

Home Office (1964) *Second Report by Commonwealth Immigrants Advisory Council*, London, HMSO.

(1968) *Circular 225/68*, October 4.

House of Commons (1946) *Parliamentary Debates* (Hansard), vol. 418, 1–7, 2 February.

(1968) *Parliamentary Debates* (Hansard), Fifth Series, vol. 769, Session 1967–8, 22 July.

Select Committee on Education, Science and the Arts (1989) *Under 5s*, London, HMSO.

Select Committee on Race Relations and Immigration (1973), *Education*, vol. 1, London, HMSO.

House of Lords (1967) *Parliamentary Debates* (Hansard), Fifth Series, Session 1966–7, 14 and 16 March.

Houston, Susan H. (1971) 'A reexamination of some assumptions about the language of the disadvantaged child' in Stella Chess and Alexander Thomas (eds.), *Annual Progress in Child Psychiatry and Child Development*, London, Butterworths.

Howe, Elspeth (1966) *Under 5: a report on nursery education*, London, Conservative Political Centre.

Hubbard, Douglas and Salt, John (1973) 'Parenthood – too serious to be left to novices', *TES*, 16 February.

Hughes, Meredydd, G. (1967) 'The American scene', *Teacher in Wales*, 21 April.

Hunt, F.J. (1970) 'Some social bases of inequality' in Peter J. Fensham (ed.), *Rights and Inequality in Australian Education*, Melbourne, F.W. Cheshire.

Husén, Torsten (1972) *Social Background and Educational Career*, Paris, OECD.

(1975) *Social Influences on Educational Attainment : research perspectives on educational equality*, Paris, OECD.

Ibbotson, Peter (1958) 'Labour's educational policy', *The New Reasoner*, 6.

[1964/5] 'School for immigrants', *Socialism and Education*, 7.

Ilett, H.A. (1967) 'A school in the East End', *Special Education*, 16 (11).

Ingram, Philippa (1972) 'Halsey looks to community schools to pull down class barriers', *TES*, 6 October.

Inner Area Study (*see* Department of the Environment, and Shankland).

INNER LONDON EDUCATION AUTHORITY

The EPA project

ILEA (1968) Educational Priority Area Action Research Project. Draft Programme 1968–71, mimeo.

ILEA (1969) Proposed Fourth Year Junior Environmental Project, 4 July, mimeo.

Inner London Educational Priority Area Project [1969] Spring Report (Charles Betty), mimeo.

Deptford E.P.A. Project (1970) Interim Report to National Steering Committee, September, mimeo.

ILEA (1971a) Press Notice: ILEA to carry on Deptford EPA project, 13 April, mimeo.

ILEA (1971b) Letter from the Education Officer to C. Betty, 29 April.

Inner London EPA Project (1971) Summary of Teachers' Comments, December, mimeo.

Inner London Educational Priority Area Project [1972] Report of the Steering Committee, mimeo.

ILEA (1972a) *Extract from the Agenda Paper for the Education Committee meeting on…2 February. Report (No. 2) of the Schools Sub-Committee, 'Children with Special Difficulties'*.

ILEA (1972b) Education Committee – Schools Sub-Committee. Report by Education Officer. Deptford Educational Priority Area Action Research Project, 2 October, mimeo.

ILEA (1972c) *Education Committee: report of the Schools Sub-Committee*, 12 October.

Other

ILEA (1967a) *London Comprehensive Schools 1966*.

(1967b) *Education Committee Minutes*, 1 February.

(1967c) Schools Sub-Committee Minutes, 29 June, mimeo.

(1967d) *Education – Schools Sub-Committee. Children and their Primary Schools: the Plowden report. Report by the Education Officer*, June.

(1967e) *Education Committee Minutes. Report of the Schools Sub-Committee: Children and their Primary Schools – the Plowden report*, 12 July.

(1968) *Home and School: suggestions for the development of right relationships at the primary stage*.

Education Committee Minutes, 1 July 1969, 16 July 1969, 3 February 1971, 30 June 1971, 17 May 1972, 8 November 1972, 22 January 1974.

(1972) *Evidence … to the Committee of Enquiry into the Teaching of Reading and the Use of the English Language*.

(1976) 'Children with special difficulties: an ILEA action research project', *Educational Research*, 19 (1).

(1982a) *Education Committee, Schools sub-committee. Report by Education Officer: Education Priority Index – revision of criteria.*

(1982b) Research and Statistics, *Educational Priority Indices – a new perspective.*

Jackson, Brian (1961) 'Notes from two primary schools', *New Left Review*, 11.

(1964) *Streaming: an education system in miniature*, London, Routledge & Kegan Paul.

(1968) 'The Association of Multi-Racial Playgroups', *Where*, 38.

(1971) '*What did Lord Butler say in 1944? A discussion paper on a national pre-school policy*, Cambridge, Priority Area Children.

(1973) 'How the poorest live: education', *New Society*, 1 February.

Jackson, Brian and Jones, Joan (1971) *One Thousand Children*, Cambridge, Advisory Centre for Education.

Jackson, Brian and Marsden, Dennis (1962) *Education and the Working Class*, London, Routledge & Kegan Paul.

Jackson, Brian and Rae, Ruby [1969/70] *Priority: How we can help young children in educational priority areas*, Cambridge, Association of Multi-Racial Playgroups.

James, Terry (1975) West Riding Follow Up Studies. Red House Early Education Programmes, Part A: The impact of preschool. A review of American experience and an account of the local setting. Oxford University Department of Social and Administrative Studies, mimeo.

Jayne, Edith (1976) *ILEA Educational Home Visiting Project, Deptford: research report*, London, ILEA, Research and Statistics Group.

Jensen, Arthur, R. (1967) 'The culturally disadvantaged: psychological and educational aspects', *Educational Research*, 10 (1).

(1972) *Genetics and Education*, London, Methuen.

(1973a) *Educability and Group Differences*, London, Methuen.

(1973b) *Educational Differences*, London, Methuen.

Johnston, G. (1970) 'Equality of educational opportunity: a right variously defined' in Peter J. Fensham (ed.) *Rights and Inequality in Australian Education*, Melbourne, F.W. Cheshire.

Jones, Esmor (1970) 'The language of failure: retrospect', *English in Education*, 4 (3).

Jones, H.A. (1977) *Education and Disadvantage*, University of Leicester, Department of Adult Education (Vaughan Paper 22).

Jones, V. Creech (1967) 'The Plowden report: with reference to day nurseries and nursery education', *The Nursery Journal*, 57 (Part 549).

Joseph, Anne and Parfit, Jessie (1972) *Playgroups in an Area of Social Need*, Windsor, NFER.

Jowett, Sandra and Sylva, Kathy (1986) 'Does kind of pre-school matter?', *Educational Research*, 28 (1).

Judd, Judith (1988) 'Britain's educational under-class', *The Observer*, 10 April.

Kaim-Caudle, P.R. (1975) 'Poverty in Australia', *Journal of Social Policy*, 5 (4).

Kandel, I.L. (1933) *The Outlook in Education*, London, Oxford University Press.

Keddie, Nell (ed.) (1973) *Tinker, Tailor... The myth of cultural deprivation*, Harmondsworth, Penguin.

Kellaghan, Thomas (1977) *The Evaluation of an Intervention Programme for Disadvantaged Children*, Windsor, NFER.

Kempton, Murray (1964) 'The will to compassion', *The Spectator*, 212 (7084).

Kenn, A.J. (1966a) 'Can American teachers teach us anything?', *The Teacher*, 7 (11).

(1966b) 'A way to stop waste of talent', *The Teacher*, 7 (12).

King, Ronald (1969) *Education*, London, Longman.

Kirp, David and Tuden, Daniel (1987) 'Learn now or pay later?', *TES*, 26 June.

Kogan, Maurice (1968) 'The Welsh Plowden', *New Society*, 25 January.

(1971) *The Politics of Education: Edward Boyle and Anthony Crosland in conversation with Maurice Kogan*, Harmondsworth, Penguin.

(1973a) 'Education and Disadvantage: what the local community and social services can do', paper to a Council for Educational Advance conference, 31 March.

(1973b) 'The Plowden committee on primary education' in Richard A. Chapman (ed.), *The role of Commissions in Policy-Making*, London, Allen & Unwin.

(1978) *The Politics of Educational Change*, Glasgow, Fontana.

(1987) 'The Plowden report twenty years on', *Oxford Review of Education*, 13 (1).

(n.d.) Interview for Open University course DE304 on tape, 'Research and policy'.

Kogan, Maurice and Packword, Tim (1974) *Advisory Councils and Committees on Education*, London, Routledge & Kegan Paul.

Kraushaar, Robert and Loney, Martin (1980) 'Requiem for planned innovation: the case of the Community Development Project' in Muriel Brown and Sally Baldwin (eds.) *The Year Book of Social Policy in Britain 1978*, London, Routledge & Kegan Paul.

The Labour Party (1959) *Britain Belongs to You*, London, Labour Party.

(1961) *Signposts for the Sixties: a statement of Labour's home policy*, London, Labour Party.

(1973) *The Deprived Child: a discussion document on policies for socially deprived children*, London, Labour Party.

Laing, Alice (1968) 'Compensatory education for young children' in Schools Council Research Project in Compensatory Education, *Compensatory Education: an introduction*, Swansea, Schools Council project.

Laishley, Jennie and Coleman, John (1978) 'Intervention for disadvantaged pre-school children: an action research programme to extend the skills of day nursery staff', *Educational Research*, 20 (3).

Lapping, Anne (1969) 'Social action', *New Society*, 2 January.

Laski, Harold J. (n.d.) 'Choosing the planners' in G.D.H. Cole *et al.*, *Plan for Britain*, London, Labour Book Service.

Lawless, Paul (1979) *Urban Deprivation and Government Initiative*, London, Faber & Faber.

Lawton, Denis (1968) *Social Class, Language and Education*, London, Routledge & Kegan Paul.

Lees, Ray (1973) 'Action–research in community development', *Journal of Social Policy*, 2 (3).

(1975) 'The action–research relationship' in Ray Lees and George Smith (eds.) *Action–Research in Community Development*, London, Routledge & Kegan Paul.

Leissner, Aryeh (1972) 'Parents and children in high-need areas' in National Children's Bureau, *The Parental Role*, London, NCB.

Lewin, Roger (1977) '"Head Start" pays off', *New Scientist*, 73 (1041).

Leybourne, Grace G. and White, Kenneth (1940) *Education and the Birth-Rate: a social dilemma*, London, Cape.

Leyden, Gervase (1972) 'The psychological implications of cultural disadvantage', *Edge Hill Forum on Teacher Education*, 1 (1).

Lindsay, Kenneth (1926) *Social Progress and Educational Waste*, London, George Routledge.

Lines, G.W.R. (1968) E.P.A. Action Research. Educational Priority Areas and the Impact of Immigrants, mimeo.

Little, Alan (1974) 'Compensatory education and race relations: what lessons for Europe?' in Richard Rose (ed.), *Lessons from America: an explanation*, London, Macmillan.

(1975) 'Where are the priorities now?', *TES*, 21 February.

Little, Alan and Mabey, Christine (1972) 'An index for designation of educational priority areas' in Andrew Shonfield and Stella Shaw (eds.), *Social Indicators and Social Policy*, London, Heinemann Educational.

(1973) 'Reading attainment and social and ethnic mix of London primary schools' in David Donnison and David Eversley (eds.), *London: urban patterns, problems and policies*, London, Heinemann.

Little, Alan and Smith, George (1971) *Strategies of Compensation: a review of educational projects for the disadvantaged in the United States*, Paris, OECD.

Little, Alan and Westergaard, John (1964) 'the trend of social class differentials in educational opportunity in England and Wales', *British Journal of Sociology*, 15.

Liverpool Education Committee, *Report to City Council 1965–68*.

Lloyd George, David (1912) *The People's Insurance*, London, Hodder & Stoughton.

London County Council (1947) *London School Plan*, London, LCC.

Lovett, Tom (1975) *Adult Education, Community Development and the Working Class*, London, Ward Lock Educational.

Lunn, Joan C. (1970) *Streaming in the Primary School*, Slough, NFER.

Lynch, James and Pimlott, John (1980) 'Parents and teachers: an action–research project' in Maurice Craft *et al.* (eds.), *Linking Home and School*, London, Harper & Row (3rd edn).

Lynes, Tony (1979) 'Do it yourself', a review of Piven, Fox and Cloward, *Poor People's Movements*, *New Society*, 3 May.

Lynn, R. (1959) 'Environmental conditions affecting intelligence', *Educational Research*, 1 (3).

Lyons, K.H. (1973) *Social Work and the School: a study of some aspects of the role of an education social worker*, London, HMSO.

Mabey, Christine (1976) review of *Educational Priority* vols. 3 and 4, *Journal of Social Policy*, 5 (1).

MacBeath, John (1974) 'Breaking up the egg crates', *TES*, 11 January.

McCail, Gail (1981) *Mother Start: an account of an educational home visiting scheme for pre-school children*, Edinburgh, Scottish Council for Research in Education.

McCann, Phillip and Young, Francis A. (1982) *Samuel Wilderspin and the Infant School Movement*, London, Croom Helm.

MacDonald, Barry (1982) Introduction to Barry MacDonald and Saville Kushner (eds.), *Bread and Dreams: a case study of bilingual schooling in the U.S.A.*, Norwich, Centre for Applied Research in Education.

McDougall, E. (1967) Operation Head-Start (report of a visit in May 1967), London, DES, mimeo.

McGeeney, Patrick (1969) *Parents Are Welcome*, London, Longman, 1969
   (1970) 'Bernstein on compensatory education', *English in Education*, 4 (3).

McGovern, James J. (1976) 'Project Head Start', University of Dundee, MEd thesis.

MacGregor, Susanne (1981) *The Politics of Poverty*, London, Longman.

McKechin, W.J. (1976) *Plus or Minus: problems affecting implementation of 'positive discrimination' within schools in Strathclyde*, Paisley College of Technology, Local Government Unit.

Mack, Joanna and Lansley, Stewart (1985) *Poor Britain*, London, Allen & Unwin.

Maclure, Stuart (1975) 'High Jencks at OECD', *TES*, 17 January.

Maclure, Stuart and Makins, Virginia (1973) 'Is there an urban crisis? What might be done about it? What part do schools play?', *TES*, 16 February.

McMillan, Margaret (1919) *The Nursery School*, London, J.M. Dent.

McNally, J. (1968) 'Social deprivation and educational compensation: the problem in the educational field', *AEP Journal* 1 (10).

Makins, Virginia (1977) 'Mountains of know-how on nurseries', *TES*, 11 March.
   (1978) 'Headstart – alive, well and kicking back', *TES*, 17 March.
   (1984a) 'American way to give the young a head start', *TES*, 5 October.
   (1984b) 'Stories rather more than social class' (conversation with Gordon Wells), *TES*, 16 November.
   (1985) 'High Scope. The pre-school curriculum', *TES*, 5 July.
   (1986) 'Good work, bad behaviour', *TES*, 25 April.
   (1987) 'Curriculum cure-all?', TES, 2 October.

Mannheim, Karl and Stewart, W.A.C. (1962) *An Introduction to the Sociology of Education*, London, Routledge & Kegan Paul.

Marland, Michael (ed.) (1980) *Education for the Inner City*, London, Heinemann Educational.

Marmor, Theodore R. and Marmor, Jan S. (1990), *The Politics of Medicare*, London, Routledge & Kegan Paul.

Marris, Peter (1969) 'Against poverty', review of Moynihan, *Maximum Feasible Misunderstanding*, *New Society*, 3 *July*.

Marris, Peter and Rein, Martin (1967) *Dilemmas of Social Reform: poverty and community action in the United States*, London, Routledge & Kegan Paul (2nd edn 1972).

Marsden, Dennis (1964), 'The poisoned apple', review of Douglas, *The Home and the School*, *New Left Review*, 26.

Marshall, T.H. (1963) *Sociology at the Crossroads and other Essays*, London, Heinemann.

(1965) *Social Policy in the Twentieth Century*, London, Huthinson (revised edn 1970).

Mason, Mary (1986) 'The deficit hypothesis revisited (or, Basil Bernstein, you were right the first time!)', *Educational Studies*, 12 (3).

Mayo, Marjorie (1975) 'The history and early development of CDP' in Ray Lees and George Smith (eds.), *Action–Research in Community Development*, London, Routledge & Kegan Paul.

Mays, John Barron (1962a) *Education and the Urban Child*, Liverpool University Press.

(1962b) 'Social disadvantage and education', *Educational Research*, 5 (1).

(1964) *Growing up in the City: a study of juvenile delinquency in an urban neighbourhood*, Liverpool University Press.

(1967) *The School in its Social Setting*, London, Longman.

(1968) *The Introspective Society*, London, Sheed & Ward.

(1969) Letter to *New Society*, 27 November.

Midwinter, Eric (1969) 'The parents' case', *TES*, 25 July.

(1970) 'Students at the battle front', *TES*, 13 March.

(1971a) 'The Liverpool story', *Where*, 54.

(1971b) 'Stick with the system', *TES*, 19 November.

(1972a) 'Breaking the vicious circle: the lessons of the educational priority area projects', *London Educational Review*, 1 (1).

(1972b) 'The irony of schooling', review of Halsey, *Educational Priority*, *The Observer*, 8 October.

(1972c) *Priority Education: an account of the Liverpool Project*, Harmondsworth, Penguin.

(ed.) (1972d) *Projections: an educational priority area at work*, London, Ward Lock Educational.

(1972e) *Social Environment and the Urban School*, London, Ward Lock Educational.

(1972f) 'Where are the EPA project teams now?', *Where*, 66.

(1972g) (untitled) contribution to Barry Turner (ed.) *Education and the Urban Crisis*, London, Encyclopaedia Britannica International.

(1973) 'The strategy of the EPA movement' in Kathleen Jones (ed.) *The Year Book of Social Policy in Britain 1972*, London, Routledge & Kegan Paul.

(1975) 'Towards a solution of the EPA problem: the community school' in James Rushton and John D. Turner (eds.) *Education and Deprivation*, Manchester University Press.

(1977) 'The missing ingredient', *TES*, 20 May.

(n.d.) *Education: a priority area*, London, National Union of Teachers.

(n.d.) interview for Open University course DE304 on tape 'Policy and action'.

Mikardo, Ian (1948) *The Second Five Years: a Labour programme for 1950* (Fabian Research Series 124), London, Fabian Publications.

Miller, F.J.W. *et al.* (1960) *Growing Up in Newcastle upon Tyne: a continuing study of health and illness in young children within their families*, London, Oxford University Press.

(1974) *The School Years in Newcastle upon Tyne 1952–62*, London, Oxford University Press.

Miller, Gordon W. (1971) *Educational Opportunity and the Home*, London, Longman.

Miller, S.M. and Roby, Pamela (1970) 'Poverty: changing social stratification' in Peter Townsend (ed.) *The Concept of Poverty*, London, Heinemann.

Ministry of Education (1959) *15 to 18: Report of the Central Advisory Council for Education (England)* (Crowther), vol. 1: *Report*, London, HMSO.

(1959) *Primary Education: suggestions for the consideration of teachers and others concerned with the work of primary schools*, London, HMSO.

(1963) *Half Our Future: a report of the Central Advisory Council for Education (England)* (Newsom), London, HMSO.

Morin, Lloyd H. and Martin, Stewart U. (1971) A Development Area Project – a summer enrichment program – report submitted to Educational Research Institute of British Columbia, mimeo.

Morris, Ben (1957) 'Research for education. III. An example: social class and educational opportunity', *The Journal of Education*, 89 (1051).

Morris, Max (1953) *Your Children's Future*, London, Lawrence & Wishart.

Morrison, Charles, M., Watt, Joyce S. and Lee, Terence R. (eds) (1974) *Educational Priority. Vol 5: E.P.A. – A Scottish Study*, Edinburgh, HMSO.

Mortimore, Jo and Blackstone Tessa (1982) *Disadvantage and Education*, London, Heinemann Educational.

Morton, David (1969) Pre-School Education in Manchester (Didsbury College of Education Compensatory Education project, Occasional Paper 2), Manchester, Didsbury College of Education, mimeo.

(1973) review of Kelsall and Kelsall, *Social Disadvantage and Educational Opportunity*, Urban Education, 8 (1).

Morton, David and Goldman, Ronald (1969) *The Formal Institutions of Pre-School Education in Britain and the Sociological Context of their Emergence* (Didsbury College of Education Compensatory Education Project, Occasional Paper 1), Manchester, Didsbury College of Education.

Morton, David and Watson, D.R. (1971) 'Compensatory education and contemporary liberalism in the U.S.: a sociological view' reprinted in John Raynor and Jane Harden (eds.), *Equality and City Schools. Readings in Urban Education*, vol. 2, London, Routledge & Kegan Paul, 1973.

Mosher, Marcella (1965) 'U.S. report: helping poor children catch up', *New Society*, 2 September.

National Children's Bureau (1974) Programmes of Early Intervention: an abstract of some American research (Highlight 12), London, NCB, mimeo.

(1976) Nursery Education: an abstract of research findings (Highlight 21), London, NCB, mimeo.

(1977) *Educational Home Visiting (Highlight 29)*, London, NCB.

National Community Development Project: *Inter-Project Report 1973*, London, CDP Information and Intelligence Unit.

National Educational Research and Development Trust, Childminding Research and Development Unit (1976), *Childminding: action register three*, Cambridge, NERDT.

National Health Service Act (1946).

National Insurance Act (1946).

National Union of Teachers (n.d.) *Plowden : the Union's comments on some of the major issues of the Plowden report*, London, NUT.

Newham, London Borough of [1978] *Pre-school Home-visiting Teachers : report on experimental work in Newham September 1975 to December 1977*, London, Borough of Newham.

New Society (1966a) 'Poverty and politics' (report of lecture by S.M. Miller), 10 February.

(1966b) 'Findings: how to help deprived children', 31 March.

(1967) 'ILEA on Plowden', 6 July.

(1969) 'Britain's poverty programme', 16 January.

Newson, John and Elizabeth (1963) *Infant Care in an Urban Community*, London, Allen & Unwin.

(1968) *Four Years Old in an Urban Community*, London, Allen & Unwin.

Nicholls, Sally (1980) Educational Home Visiting: a paper presented to the Adult Education Seminar of the University of London Extra Mural Department. February, mimeo.

Nisbet, John (1970) 'Deprivation and disadvantage: Scotland' in A. Harry Passow (ed.) *Deprivation and Disadvantage: nature and manifestations*, Hamburg, Unesco Institute for Education.

Nisbet, John and Watt, Joyce (1984) *Educational Disadvantage : ten years on*, Edinburgh, HMSO.

North-Eastern Junior Schools Association (1949) *Basic Requirements of the Junior School*, University of London Press (edn of 1960).

Northern Economic Planning Council (1970) *Report on Education*. Part 1: *Education up to 18 years-of-age (excluding further and higher education)*, NEPC.

Nottinghamshire County Council Education Committee (n.d.) *Home School Liaison Teacher (particulars of post)*

(n.d.) *The Role of the Community Teacher* (leaflet).

[1972] The Education of the Disadvantaged Child, mimeo.

(1972) *School Questionnaire* (on social deprivation) from the Director of Education to head teachers, 18 May.

(1972) *Socially Disadvantaged Children in Primary Schools* (report by the Director of Education to the Schools Sub-Committee), 8 November.

(1975) *Home/School Co-operation* (Bulletin), March/April

Nuffield Teacher Enquiry [1972], Report of the conference on 'Social deprivation and change in education ', University of York, April.

Nursery School Association of Great Britain and Northern Ireland [1954] *The Needs of Young Children in Present Day Society*, London, NSA.

O'Bryan, K.G. (1975) 'Orientations in compensatory education' in K. Wedell (ed.) *Orientations in Special Education*, London, John Wiley.

Ogletree, Earl (1967) 'Follow-up to Head Start', *TES*, 22 September.

O'Neill, Josephine M. (1977) Patterns of Intervention in Educational Provision for Disadvantaged Pre-School Children, University of Liverpool, MEd dissertation.

O'Neill, Judith (1978) *Poverty and Education : a discussion paper prepared for the Disadvantaged Schools Program*, Canberra, Schools Commission.

Ottaway, A.K.C. (1953) *Education and Society : an introduction to the sociology of education*, London, Routledge & Kegan Paul (1968 edn).

Parker, Sara (1982a) 'Rewards of early investment: American educationist stresses value of pre-school programme', *TES*, 15 October.

(1982b) 'Scope for improvement', *TES*, 3 December.

Parry, Marianne and Archer, Hilda (1974) *Pre-School Education: the report of the Schools Council project on pre-school education* 1969–71, London, Macmillan.

Payne, Joan (1974) *Educational Priority*. Vol. 2: *E.P.A. Surveys and Statistics*, London, HMSO.

Payne, Joan and Smith, Teresa (1973) 'Pre-school programmes in the educational priority areas project', *Journal of Applied Educational Studies*, 2 (2).

Peaker, G.F. (1971) *The Plowden Children Four Years Later*, Slough, NFER.

Pedley, Robin (1963) *The Comprehensive School*, Harmondsworth, Penguin.

Pedley, Robin *et al.* [1954] *Comprehensive Schools To-day*, London, Councils and Education Press.

Piachaud, David (1987) 'Problems in the definition and measurement of poverty', *Journal of Social Policy*, 16 (2).

Planning (1952) *Poverty: ten years after Beveridge*, 19 (344).

Plowden, Lady (1967) Speech to a meeting of the Richmond-upon-Thames Association for the Advancement of State Education, in Confederation for the Advancement of State Education, *Dear Lady Plowden*, CASE.

(1970) 'Compensatory education and the infant school' in T. Cox and C.A. Waite (eds.) *Teaching Disadvantaged Children in the Infant School*, Swansea, Schools Council Research and Development Project in Compensatory Education.

(1972) '"Peril in our school failures" warning by Lady Plowden', speech to North of England Education Conference, reported in *The Guardian*, 5 January.

(1977) 'A decade of Plowden', *TES*, 14 January.

(1987) '"Plowden" twenty years on', *Oxford Review of Education*, 13 (1).

Pollack, Margaret (1972) *Today's Three-Year-Olds in London*, London, Heinemann Medical Books.

(1973) 'Parenthood – too serious to be left to novices', *TES*, 16 February.

Pollard, Michael (1967) 'Project Head Start', *Where*, 30.

Poulton, Geoffrey Arnold (1975) 'Educational-Visiting in England 1973–1974', University of Southampton, MA dissertation.

(1978) 'Educational home visiting' in National Association for Maternal and Child Welfare, *Off to a Good Start. Sixty-Fifth Annual Conference Report*, NAMCW.

(1980) 'The educational home visitor' in Maurice Craft *et al.* (eds.), *Linking Home and School* (3rd edn).

Poulton, G. A. and James, Terry (1975) *Pre-Schooling in the Community*, Routledge & Kegan Paul.

Preston, Peter (1968) 'Immigrant children in school', *Where*, 36.

Pringle, M.L. Kellmer (1965a) 'The challenge of prevention. I – Positive child care and constructive education' in M.L. Kellmer Pringle (ed.) *Investment in Children: a symposium on positive child care and constructive education*, London, Longman.

(1965b) *Deprivation and Education*, London, Longmans.

(ed.) (1965c) *Investment in Children*, London, Longmans.

Pringle, M.L. Kellmer, Butler, N.R. and Davie, R. (1966) *11,000 Seven-Year-Olds: First report of the national child development study*, London, Longmans.

Priority [1972] '*A New Landmark*': *The Halsey programme for educational priority areas*, Liverpool.

Priority News (1973) 'A blueprint for educational visitors', 5.

Projectile (1969) 'A project's progress', 1, Liverpool.

(1970) 'Stop press: EPA students conference', 3, Liverpool.

Quick, E.J. (ed.) [1965] *New Opportunities for the Culturally Disadvantaged*, Toronto, Canadian Education Association.

Raffe, David (1983) 'Education and class inequality in Scotland' in Gordon Brown and Rob Cook (eds.), *Scotland: the real divide. Poverty and deprivation in Scotland*, Edinburgh, Mainstream.

(1983) Review of Mortimore and Blackstone, *Disadvantage and Education*, and Essen and Wedge, *Continuities in Childhood Disadvantage*, *British Journal of Sociology of Education*, 4 (2).

Raggatt, Peter C.M. (1973) review of Halsey, *Educational Priority*, *Urban Education*, 8 (1).

Raison, Timothy (1967) 'The Plowden report: equality plus quality', *New Society*, 12 January.

Randell, Shirley K. (1980) The Disadvantaged Country Areas Program: a program designed to increase social and educational equity for rural children (paper to the 21st annual conference of the Australian College of Education, Brisbane), mimeo.

Raven, John (1980) *Parents, Teachers and Children: a study of an educational home visiting scheme*, Edinburgh, Scottish Council for Research in Education.

(1982) 'Language in its social context and the role of educational home visitors' in Alan Davies (ed.) *Language and Learning in Home and School*, London, Heinemann Educational.

Raynor, R. (1967) 'Pointers for Britain in America's Headstart', *TES*, 14 April.

Rein, Martin (1970) 'Community action in America' in Anne Lapping (ed.), *Community Action*, London, Fabian Society.

Richards, Martin (1968) 'Head Start in Mississippi' in Sonia Abrams (ed.) 'How much do we know about education in America?', *Where Supplement*, 14.

Roberts, Colin (1976) 'Educational disadvantage', *Disadvantage in Education*, 1 (1).

(1977) Deprivation and Disadvantage in Education: who are the educationally disadvantaged?, Manchester, Centre for Information and Advice on Educational Disadvantage, mimeo.

Robinson, Philip (1976) *Education and Poverty*, Methuen.

(1982) 'Where stands educational policy towards the poor?', *Educational Review*, 34 (1).

Rose, E.J.B. *et al.* (1969) *Colour and Citizenship: a report on British Race Relations*, Oxford University Press.

Rose, Gordon (1974) Review of Wedderburn, *Poverty, Inequality and Class Structure, Journal of Social Policy*, 4 (2).

Rose, Richard (ed.) *Lessons from America*, London, Macmillan.

Rosen, Connie and Harold (1973) *The Language of Primary School Children*: *Schools Council Project on language development in the primary school*, Harmondsworth, Penguin.

Rosen, Harold (1972) *Language and Class*: *a critical look at the theories of Basil Bernstein*, Bristol, Falling Wall Press.

Rowntree, B. Seebohm and Lavers, G.R. (1951) *Poverty and the Welfare State*, London, Longmans, Green.

Rubinstein, David (ed.) (1979) *Education and Equality*, Harmondsworth, Penguin.

Runciman, W.G. (1966) *Relative Deprivation and Social Justice: a study of attitudes to social inequality in twentieth-century England*, London, Routledge & Kegan Paul.

Rutter, Michael and Madge, Nicola (1976) *Cycles of Disadvantage : a review of research*, London, Heinemann.

Sammons, Pamela, Kysel, Florisse and Mortimore Peter (1983) 'Educational priority indices: a new perspective', *British Educational Research Journal*, 9 (1).

Schofield, Jack (1964) 'The Labour Movement and Educational Policy 1900–1931', Manchester University MEd thesis.

Schools Commission (1978–9) *Disadvantaged Schools Program. Doing Something about it*, 2 vols., Canberra, Schools Commission.

(1979) *Learning to Share*. Vol. 2 : *A report on the Disadvantaged Country Areas Program for 1978*, Canberra, Schools Commission.

Schools Council [1968] *Project in Compensatory Education : field report no. 6*, London, Schools Council.

(1968) Research Project in Compensatory Education *Compensatory Education*: *an introduction* (Occasional Publication 1), Swansea, Schools Council Research and Development Project.

(1970a) *Teaching English to West Indian Children : the research stage of the project*, London, Evans/Methuen Educational.

(1970b) '*Cross'd with Adversity*': *The education of socially disadvantaged children in secondary schools*, London, Evans/Methuen Educational.

Scottish Education Department (1965) *Primary Education in Scotland*, Edinburgh, HMSO.

(1975) *Seminar on Educational Disadvantage*, Edinburgh, SED.

(1976) *Circular 965 : Seminar on Disadvantage*, Edinburgh, SED.

Secretary of State for Education and Science (1972) *Education: a framework for expansion*, London, HMSO.

(1974) *Educational Disadvantage and the Educational Needs of Immigrants*: *observations on the report on education of the Select Committee on Race Relations and Immigration*, London, HMSO.

Selleck, R.J.W. (1972) *English Primary Education and the Progressives, 1914–1939*, London, Routledge & Kegan Paul.

Shankland, Graeme, Willmott, Peter and Jordan, David (1977) *Inner London*: *policies for dispersal and balance. Final report of the Lambeth Inner Area Study*, London, HMSO.

Shapiro, Michael Steven (1983) *Child's Garden*, University Park, Pennsylvania State University Press.

Sharrock, Anne (1968) 'Relations between home and school', *Educational Research*, 10 (Part 3).

Shinman, Sheila M. (1981) *A Chance for Every Child? Access and response to preschool provision*, London, Tavistock.

Shipman, Marten, (1971) 'Curriculum for inequality' in Richard Hooper (ed.), *The Curriculum: context, design and development*, Edinburgh, Oliver & Boyd.

(1980) 'The limits of positive discrimination' in Michael Marland (ed.), *Education for the Inner City*, London, Heinemann Educational.

Short, Edward (1972) 'In loco parentis' in National Children's Bureau, *The Parental Role*, London, NCB.

Silver, Harold (1965) *The Concept of Popular Education*, London, MacGibbon & Kee.

(ed.) (1973) *Equal Opportunity in Education: a reader in social class and educational opportunity*, London, Methuen.

(1980) *Education and the Social Condition*, London, Methuen.

(1983) *Education as History: interpreting nineteenth- and twentieth-century education*, London, Methuen.

Simon, Brian (1980) 'The primary school revolution: myth or reality?' in Edward Fearn and Brian Simon (eds.), *Education in the Nineteen Sixties*, Leicester, History of Education Society.

Simon of Wythenshawe, Lady (1948) *Three Schools or One?*, London, Muller.

(1962) 'London comprehensive schools', *Forum*, 4 (2).

Sinfield, Adrian (1968) 'Poverty rediscovered', reprinted in J.B. Cullingworth (ed.) *Problems of an Urban Society*. Vol. 3: *Planning for Change*, London, Allen & Unwin.

Smilansky, Moshe and Nevo, David (1979) *The Gifted Disadvantaged: a ten year longitudinal study of compensatory education in Israel*, London, Gordon and Breach.

Smith, George (1974) 'Community development rat-catchers or theorists?', *New Society*, 14 February.

(1975a) 'Action–research: experimental social administration' in Ray Lees and George Smith (eds.) *Action–Research in Community Development*, London, Routledge & Kegan Paul.

(ed.) (1975b) *Educational Priority*. Vol. 4: *The West Riding project*, London, HMSO.

(1977) 'Positive discrimination by area in education: the EPA idea re-examined', *Oxford Review of Education*, 3 (3).

(1982) 'Action research 1968–81: method of research or method of innovation?', *Community Education*, 1 (1).

(1987) 'Whatever happened to educational priority areas?', *Oxford Review of Education*, 13 (1).

Smith, George and James, Terry (1975) 'The effects of preschool education: some American and British evidence', *Oxford Review of Education*, 1 (3).

Smith, Teresa (1980) *Parents and Preschool*, London, Grant McIntyre.

Smith, Teresa and Smith, George (1971) 'Urban first aid', *New Society*, 30 December.

(1975) 'Educational priority areas: options in a no or low growth economy', *Education 3–13*, 3 (2).

Spaulding, Robert L. (1968) 'The Durham Education Improvement Program' in David W. Brison and Jane Hill (eds.), *Psychology and Early Childhood Education*, Toronto, Ontario Institute for Studies in Education.

Sparkbrook Association [1964] Memorandum and Annual Report, Birmingham, mimeo.

Spence, James *et al.* (1954) *A Thousand Families in Newcastle upon Tyne: an approach to the study of health and illness in children*, London, Oxford University Press.

Spencer, John (1973) 'Educational priority in Britain' (review of Halsey, *Educational Priority*), *Journal of Social Policy*, 2 (3).

Spinley, B.M. (1953) *The Deprived and the Privileged: personality development in English society*, London, Routledge & Kegan Paul.

Spolton, Lewis (1972) 'A comparative approach to changes in the primary school' in Maurice Chazan (ed.) *Aspects of Primary Education*, Cardiff, University of Wales.

Standish, E.J. (1959) 'Readiness to read', *Educational Research*, 2 (1).

Strathclyde Experiment in Education: Govan project (1979) Constitution of Moorpark Residents Education Committee, March 21, mimeo.

(1979) Some Preliminary Data on Achievement Levels, September, mimeo.

Stukat, K.-G. (1974) 'Some issues in compensatory education research', *London Educational Review*, 3 (3).

Swift, D.F. (1965) 'Educational psychology, sociology and the environment: a controversy on cross-purposes', reprinted in D.F. Swift (ed.) *Basic Readings in the Sociology of Education*, London, Routledge & Kegan Paul, 1970.

(1965/6a) 'Meritocratic and social class selection at age eleven', *Educational Research*, 8.

(1965/6b) 'Social class and achievement motivation', *Educational Research*, 8.

(1967) 'Social class, mobility-ideology and 11+ success', *British Journal of Sociology*, 18.

(1968) 'Social class and educational adaptation' in H.J. Butcher (ed.), *Educational Research in Britain*, London, University of London Press.

(1969) *The Sociology of Education: introductory analytical perspectives*, London, Routledge & Kegan Paul.

Tawney, R.H. (1922) *Secondary Education for All: A policy for Labour*, London, Allen & Unwin.

(1931) *Equality*, London, Allen & Unwin, 1952 edn.

Taylor, Francine (1974) *Race, School and Community*, Windsor, NFER.

Taylor, George and Ayres, N. (1969) *Born and Bred Unequal*, London, Longman.

Taylor, William (1966) 'The sociology of education' in J.W. Tibble (ed.), *The Study of Education*, London, Routledge & Kegan Paul.

Times Educational Supplement (1961) 'A survey of bilateral schools', 9 June.

(1964a) 'Sparkbrook lightens its darkness', 10 April.

(1964b) 'Liverpool: scheme for comprehensive education adopted', 23 October.

(1965) 'Great society', 15 January.

(1967) 'Antidotes to poverty', 3 November.

(1968a) 'Oxford leads research into priority areas', 31 May.

(1968b) 'Follow Head/Start', 5 July.

(1970) 'Coloured babies and priority areas', 13 March.

(1975) 'Data – How to pick out the ones who need help – No compensation for class', 19 September.

Titmuss, Richard (1958) *Essays on 'the Welfare State'*, London, Allen & Unwin.

(1960) *The Irresponsible Society* (Fabian Tract 323), London Fabian Society.

(1962) *Income Distribution and Social Change: a study in criticism*, London, Allen & Unwin.

(1964) 'The limits of the welfare state', *New Left Review*, 27.

(1967) *Choice and 'The Welfare State'* (Fabian Tract 370), London, Fabian Society.

(1968) *Commitment to Welfare*, London, Allen & Unwin.

Tizard, Barbara (1974) *Early Childhood Education: a review and discussion of current research in Britain*, London, SSRC, 1975 edn, Windsor, NFER.

(1977) 'No common ground?', *TES*, 27 May.

(1981) 'Parent participation in nursery and infant education' in Leslie A. Smith (ed.), *Parents and Education*, London, Goldsmiths' College.

Tizard, Barbara and Hughes, Martin (1984) *Young Children Learning: talking and thinking at home and school*, London, Fontana.

Tizard, Barbara, Mortimore, Jo and Burchell, Bebb (1981) *Involving Parents in Nursery and Infant Schools: a source book for teachers*, London, Grant McIntyre.

Tizard, Barbara et al. (1988) *Young Children at School in the Inner City*, Hove, Lawrence Erlbaum.

Tizard, Jack (1975) Issues in Early Childhood Education: the Dorothy Gardner lecture, University of London, Institute of Education, 3 May, mimeo.

Tizard, Jack, Moss, Peter and Perry, Jane (1976) *All Our Children: pre-school services in a changing society*, London, Temple Smith.

Topping, Phil and Smith, George (1977) *Government against Poverty? Liverpool Community Development Project 1970–75*, Oxford, Social Evaluation Unit.

Totten, Eileen (1972) 'All together now...', *The Guardian*, 16 May.

Tough, Joan (1976) *Listening to Children Talking: a guide to the appraisal of children's use of language*, London, Ward Lock Educational.

(1977a) *The Development of Meaning: a study of children's use of language*, London, Allen & Unwin.

(1977b) *Talking and Learning: a guide to fostering communication skills in nursery and infant schools*, London, Ward Lock Educational.

Town, Stephen W. (1973) 'Action research and social policy: some recent British experience', *Sociological Review*, 21 (4).

Townsend, H.E.R. (1971) *Immigrant Pupils in England: the L.E.A response*, Slough, NFER.

Townsend, Peter (1966) 'Two million children in poverty', *Where*, 25.

(1967) *Poverty, Socialism and Labour in Power* (Fabian Tract 371) London, Fabian Society.

(ed.) (1970) *The Concept of Poverty*, London, Heinemann.

(1974) 'Poverty as relative deprivation: resources and styles of living' in Dorothy Wedderburn (ed.), *Poverty, Inequality and Class Structure*, Cambridge University Press.

(1976) 'Area deprivation policies', *New Statesman*, 6 August.

(1982) 'An alternative anti-poverty programme', *New Society*, 7 October.

Trauttmansdorff, Antonia (1969) 'Compensatory bug hits Britain', *TES*, 6 June.

Trends in Education (1966) 'Schools and social welfare', 3.

Trethaway, A.R. (1970) 'Towards a policy of reduced inequalities' in Peter Fensham (ed.) *Rights and Inequality in Australian Education*, Melbourne, F.W. Cheshire.

Tyler, William (1977) *The Sociology of Educational Inequality*, London, Methuen.

University College of Swansea, Department of Education (1966) An application for financial support for a programme of research into reading development and compensatory education, submitted to the Welsh Committee of the Schools Council, April.

University of Manchester (1970) Calendars, prospectuses and examination papers, (including Diploma in Compensatory Education, Didsbury College).

Vaizey, John (1962) *Education for Tomorrow*, Harmondsworth, Penguin.

(1967) 'The Plowden report: school and society', *New Society*, 12 January.

(ed.) (1975) *Whatever Happened to Equality?*, London, BBC.

van der Eyken, William (1967) *The Pre-School Years*, Harmondsworth, Penguin.

(1978) 'Services or support?', *Concern*, 27.

(1982) *Home-Start: a four-year evaluation*, Leicester, Home-Start Consultancy.

Vereker, Charles and Mays, John Barron (1961) *Urban Redevelopment and Social Change: a study of social conditions in central Liverpool 1955–56*, Liverpool University Press.

Wall, W.D. (1958) 'The wish to learn', *Educational Research*, 1 (1).

(1959) *Child of Our Time: cultural change and the challenge to healthy mental growth*, London, National Children's Home.

(1965) 'The role of education. I – theory and policy' in M.L. Kellmer Pringle (ed.) *Investment in Children*, London, Longmans.

Wallace, R.G. (1965) 'Comprehensive schools and society', *Socialism and Education*, 9.

Warner, W. Lloyd, Havighurst, Robert J., and Loeb, Martin B. (1946), *Who Shall be Educated? The challenge of unequal opportunities*, London, Kegan Paul, Trench, Trubner.

Warnock, Mary (1977) *Schools of Thought*, London, Faber & Faber.

Watkins, K.W. (1967) 'Plowden – is it enough?', *Political Quarterly*, 38 (2).

Watkins, Roger and Derrick, Deborah (eds.) *Co-operative Care: practice and information profiles*, Manchester, Centre for Information and Advice on Educational Disadvantage.

Watt, Joyce (1984) 'And battles long ago?' in W.B. Dockrell (ed.) *An Attitude of Mind: twenty-five years of educational research in Scotland*, Edinburgh, Scottish Council for Research in Education.

Watt, Joyce *et al.* (1973) *Project Four*, Dundee College of Education.

Webb, Lesley (1974) *Purpose and Practice in Nursery Education*, Oxford, Blackwell.

Webster, Barbara (1978) 'Recent developments in research into deprivation' in A.G. Bovaird (ed.) *Research and Intelligence for Deprivation*, University of Birmingham.

Wedderburn, Dorothy Cole (1962) 'Poverty in Britain today – the evidence', *Sociological Review*, 10.

(1974) *Poverty, Inequality and Class Structure*, Cambridge University Press.

Wedge, Peter and Essen, Juliet (1982) *Children in Adversity*, London, Pan Books.

Wedge, Peter and Prosser, Hilary (1973) *Born to Fail?*, London, Arrow Books.

Weightman, Gavin (1974) 'Urban policy', *New Society*, 1 August.

(1976) 'The CDP file', *New Society*, 18 March.

Wein, Norman (1970a) 'Compensatory education', *Race Today*, 2 (3).

(1970b) *Compensatory Education : education in a multi-racial society* (Didsbury College of Education Compensatory Education Project. Occasional Paper 4), Manchester, Didsbury College of Education.

(1970c) 'The education of disadvantaged children: an international comparison', *Educational Research*, 13 (1).

Wells, Gordon (1982) 'Influences of the home on language development' in Alan Davies (ed.) *Language and Learning in Home and School*, London, Heinemann Educational.

Where (1977) 'Home link: the parents' home-visiting project', 124.

Whitaker, Ben (1968) *Participation and Poverty* (Fabian Research Series 272), London, Fabian Society.

White, F.M. (1967) 'Three years hard labour – or life on the Plowden committee', *Preparatory Schools Review*, 19.

Widlake, Paul (1971) 'The Effects of Two Intervention Programmes on the Language of Pre-School Children in an Educational Priority Area', University of Birmingham, MEd thesis.

(1973) 'Some effects of pre-school education', *Educational Review*, 25 (2).

Wilkerson, Doxey A. (1968) 'Helping poor children' in Sonia Abrams (ed.), *How much do we Know about Education in America? Where Supplement 14.*

Wilkinson, J. Eric and Williamson, David J. (1980) Education and the Community. A policy for school–community relations: the Govan Project, Manchester, Centre for Information and Advice on Education Disadvantage, mimeo.

Wilkinson, J. Eric, Grant, Doreen and Williamson, David J. (1977) Strathclyde Experiment in Education (Govan Project). An interim report, University of Glasgow, Department of Education, mimeo.

Williams, Gerald (1970) 'Compensatory education' in H.J. Butcher and H.B. Pont (eds.) *Educational Research in Britain 2*, University of London Press.

Williams, Gerald and Wein, Norman (1970) Education and the Disadvantaged Child (Didsbury College of Education Compensatory Education Project, Occasional Paper 3), Manchester, Didsbury College of Education.

Willis, Paul E. (1977) *Learning to Labour : how working class kids get working class jobs*, London, Saxon House.

Wilson, Harold (1959) 'The war on poverty', *New Statesman*, 3 October.

(1971) *The Labour Government 1964–1970: a personal record*, London, Weidenfeld and Nicolson and Michael Joseph.

Wilson, Harriett (1966) 'The pre-school training of culturally deprived children', *Howard Journal of Penology and Crime Prevention*, 12 (1).

Wilson, Harriett and Herbert, Geoffrey (1972) 'Hazards of environment', *New Society*, 8 June.

Wilson, J.A. and Trew, Karen J. (1975) 'The educational priority school', *British Journal of Educational Psychology*, 45.

Winkley, David (1987) 'From condescension to complexity: post-Plowden schooling in the inner city', *Oxford Review of Education*, 13 (1).

Winnicott, D.W. (1964) *The Child, the Family, and the Outside World*, Harmondsworth, Penguin.

Wiseman, Stephen (1964) *Education and Environment*, Manchester University Press.

(1965) Plowden Committee – the Manchester Experiment. Interim report: October 1965, Manchester, 1965, mimeo.

(1968) 'Educational deprivation and disadvantage' in H.J. Butcher and H.B. Pont (eds.), *Educational Research in Britain*, University of London Press.

Wiseman, Stephen and Goldman, Ronald (1970) 'Deprivation and Disadvantage: England and Wales' in A. Harry Passow (ed.) *Deprivation and Disadvantage*, Hamburg, Unesco Institute for Education.

Woddis, Margaret (1967) 'Some problems of poverty in Britain today', *Marxism Today*, 11.

Wolf, Alison (1972) 'Head Start growing still in spite of disappointments', *TES*, 27 October.

Woodhead, Martin (ed.) (1976a) *An Experiment in Nursery Education: report of the NFER Pre-School Project*, Windsor, NFER.

(1976b) *Intervening in Disadvantage: a challenge for nursery education (a review of British research into pre-school education for disadvantaged children)*, Windsor, NFER.

(1979) *Pre-School Education in Western Europe: issues, policies and trends. A report of the Council of Europe's project on pre-school education*, London, Longman.

(1985a) 'Pre-school education has long-term effects: but can they be generalised?', *Oxford Review of Education*, 11 (2).

(1985b) 'Pre-school promise', *TES*, 11 January.

Woodhouse, Jane (1981) 'The Origins of Compensatory Education in England – an historical analysis', University of Birmingham, MEd dissertation.

Wootton, Barbara (1976) *In Pursuit of Equality*, London, Fabian Society.

Worsthorne, Peregrine (1956) 'The new inequality: more dangerous than the old?', *Encounter*, 7 (5).

Young, Michael (1964) 'How can parent and teacher work together?', *New Society*, 24 September.

(1965) *Innovation and Research in Education*, London, Routledge & Kegan Paul.

(1967) 'Getting parents into school', *The Observer*, 29 October.

Young, Michael and McGeeney, Patrick (1968a) *Learning begins at Home; a study of a junior school and its parents*, London, Routledge & Kegan Paul.

(1968b) 'Parent power: 1. Ideas for England', *New Society*, 4 July.

Young, Michael and Willmott, Peter (1957) *Family and Kinship in East London*, London, Routledge & Kegan Paul, Penguin 1962 edn.

Young, Michael F.D. (ed.) (1971) *Knowledge and Control : new directions for the sociology of education*, London, Collier Macmillan.

Young, Roland (1976) 'The all-embracing problem of multiple deprivation', *Social Work Today*, 8 (9).

Yudkin, Simon (1967) *0–5. A report on the care of pre-school children*, London National Society of Children's Nurseries, 1968 edn.

Index